Private Security Today

Carter F. Smith
Frank Schmalleger
Larry J. Siegel

Boston   Columbus   Indianapolis   New York   San Francisco   Hoboken
Amsterdam   Cape Town   Dubai   London   Madrid   Milan   Munich   Paris   Montreal   Toronto
Delhi   Mexico City   Sao Paulo   Sydney   Hong Kong   Seoul   Singapore   Taipei   Tokyo

Editorial Director: Andrew Gilfillan
Senior Acquisitions Editor: Gary Bauer
Editorial Assistant: Lynda Cramer
Director of Marketing: David Gesell
Marketing Manager: Thomas Hayward
Product Marketing Manager: Kaylee Carlson
Marketing Assistant: Les Roberts
Program Manager: Tara Horton
Project Manager Team Lead: Bryan Pirrmann
Project Manager: Susan Hannahs
Operations Specialist: Deidra Smith
Creative Director: Andrea Nix
Art Director: Diane Six

Manager, Product Strategy: Sara Eilert
Product Strategy Manager: Anne Rynearson
Team Lead, Media Development & Production: Rachel Collett
Media Project Manager: Maura Barclay
Cover Designer: Melissa Welch, Studio Montage
Cover Image: Peter Kim, ra2studio, Jirsak, 24Novembers/ Shutterstock; ©68/Colin Anderson/Ocean/Corbis
Full-Service Project Management: Shylaja Gattupalli/SPi Global
Composition: SPi Global
Text Printer/Bindery: RR Donnelley/Kendallville
Cover Printer: Lehigh-Phoenix/Color
Text Font: ITC Century Std Light, 9.5/12

Credits and acknowledgments borrowed from other sources and reproduced, with permission, in this textbook appear on the appropriate page within the text.

Acknowledgements of third party content appear on page with the borrowed material, which constitutes an extension of this copyright page.

Unless otherwise indicated herein, any third-party trademarks that may appear in this work are the property of their respective owners and any references to third-party trademarks, logos or other trade dress are for demonstrative or descriptive purposes only. Such references are not intended to imply any sponsorship, endorsement, authorization, or promotion of Pearson's products by the owners of such marks, or any relationship between the owner and Pearson Education, Inc. or its affiliates, authors, licensees or distributors.

Many of the designations by manufacturers and sellers to distinguish their products are claimed as trademarks. Where those designations appear in this book, and the publisher was aware of a trademark claim, the designations have been printed in initial caps or all caps.

Library of Congress Cataloging-in-Publication Data
Names: Smith, Carter F., author. | Schmalleger, Frank, author. | Siegel, Larry J.,
Title: Private security today / Carter F. Smith, Frank Schmalleger, Larry J. Siegel.
Description: First Edition. | Hoboken : Pearson Education,
Identifiers: LCCN 2016002740 | ISBN-13: 978-0-133-37715-6 | ISBN-10: 0-133-37715-6
Subjects: LCSH: Private security services.
Classification: LCC HV8290 .S65 2016 | DDC 363.28/9--dc23
 LC record available at http://lccn.loc.gov/2016002740

10 9 8 7 6 5 4 3 2 1

PEARSON

ISBN 10: 0-13-337715-6
ISBN 13: 978-0-13-337715-6

Brief Contents

Contents

CHAPTER 3 Security Administration and Management 42

CHAPTER 9 **Retail Security and Loss Prevention** 180

At a recent symposium, FBI director James B. Comey noted the special importance of critical infrastructure in maintaining the American lifestyle. Comey said:

> Today, critical infrastructure is all encompassing. It is everything to our country and our world—our dams, our bridges, our highways, our networks. These are the things that keep our water flowing, keep our houses lit, keep our cars fueled, our goods manufactured, and connect us all over the world. The threats we face . . . to those interconnected systems—bioterrorism, agroterrorism, and sabotage, are as diverse as the infrastructure itself . . . .
>
> We have seen those threats manifest themselves in just the last few years. We've seen armed men shoot up a power station in Northern California. We've seen gunmen ravage the beautiful city of Mumbai. We've seen terrorists open fire in a mall in Kenya . . . We know those threats are real. We know that what they're aimed at is vital to our existence. So we must together figure out ways to protect our infrastructure. We must work together to strengthen our response to a terrorist attack, a tragic accident, or a natural disaster.[1]

Director Comey stressed the important role that private security plays in protecting important national assets, especially those involving critical infrastructure. "In addition to strengthening our partnerships at the government-to-government level, critical to our response to all the threats we face is working with the private sector. I knew this from my time in government ten years ago and before, when I got to the private sector and oversaw security at two different leading private entities, I saw it even more powerfully."

As the words of the FBI director indicated, we live in a dangerous world where private security is playing an increasingly important role. Consequently, it's not surprising that the security field has recently received increased media attention, making citizens much more aware of the profession and its activities. Today, the money spent on private security for personal and property protection far outweighs budgetary allotments for public policing. More than 1 million people are employed in security and the field is growing rapidly. That growth is expected to continue well into the foreseeable future—not just in the United States, but also around the world.

Since the mid-1900s, members of ASIS International and other professional security organizations have collaborated with university faculty groups and security directors to identify the education needs of the security profession. Building on such collaborations, we have written *Private Security Today* to help today's students—whether they come from the criminal justice discipline, business, or any number of other study areas—to get a broad understanding of the different topics and issues that confront the field of security. The text provides insight on staple security topics such as loss prevention, physical security, risk, and investigations. The text addresses also such current issues as computer and information security, including security of the Internet of Things (IoT), and critical infrastructure security. These topics have received increasing attention in the security field and media, but have little up-to-date coverage in current textbooks. The text also includes coverage of workplace violence, terrorist threats, and employee theft, topics that continue to be significant issues in the security profession.

The content and structure of *Private Security Today* is the result of current research supplemented with continuous communication and interviews with students and professors

---

[1]FBI press release, "Remarks of James B. Comey, Director, Federal Bureau of Investigation, "FBI WMD Directorate/Interpol International Law Enforcement Critical Infrastructure Symposium," Miami, FL, July 7, 2014.

in the discipline and professionals in the field. We designed *Private Security Today* with the assistance of many security scholars (both students and professors) to determine the right amount of coverage for each of the topics and subtopics. We then asked dozens of security professionals for must-have topics to ensure relevance. Finally, we followed the suggestions of our reviewers, including the recommendation that we organize the text based on the concept used by many security, intelligence, and emergency organizations, the All-Hazards Approach. Using what we learned, we worked toward these goals as we wrote:

1. To cover the most important issues in the security field.
2. To provide an objective review of security issues and topics.
3. To provide the most current information possible.
4. To present that information in a readable and interesting form that encourages students to continue their study of security.

The study of security encompasses two trends: one that includes a blended multidisciplinary analysis, often combining the disciplines of criminal justice, public administration, law, business management, sociology, disaster preparedness, computer technology, psychology, physical security, human resources, and contingency planning; and a second trend that highlights its international components. This text reflects both of these trends.

Organization of the Text

The authors of this text have collective experience working in the field, teaching in the discipline, and designing courses (both in-class and online), and are involved in the review of contemporary security issues with active professionals. We wrote this text to provide a fresh perspective of the security industry in the United States and globally. There is a focus on topical coverage that includes current and diverse issues in the security field from the evolution of security through the present security posture to the technology-laden future of security. Coverage of security-related theory (explanations of crime) was divided into analysis of why people commit crime, the protection of people and places from criminal activity, and how theory shapes the way we stop crime. Theories not often included in typical security textbooks were identified and explained. The book includes international focus with several security-related scenarios, solutions, and professional profiles from outside the United States. Pedagogical inserts include reflection, focused examination, identification of specific security professionals, and practical concept application.

Features

Private Security Today focuses on the role of private security professionals in industry and in the community. Colorful photographs, charts, graphs, and other visual aids help keep student attention and add variety to the text. "Think About It!" and "Security in Practice" boxes within the chapters combine with follow-up practical application sections at the end of each chapter to bring a critical thinking dimension to the text, and to provide prompts for in-class and self-study reflection and analysis. Our "Careers in Security" features introduce students to security professionals who are working in the security field. Each feature adds to the topical studies by providing access to personal insight from a current security professional.

Our social media component, the "Security Today—Cooperative Learning Platform" group on LinkedIn, provides a global platform on which students and professors can directly communicate with security professionals of all types, at all levels, around the globe. The group was intended to be a place where security experts, professors, and scholars meet, share insight and ideas, and contribute firsthand to the knowledge base in the learning environment. The authors are also active on the LinkedIn platform and are available for collaboration in a variety of ways. We hope to use this extension of the learning environment to help learners immerse themselves in the security community mind-set, not unlike a job shadowing or internship. By contributing to the ongoing discussions, learners can catalyze their exposure to the security profession. A secondary goal was to provide security professionals with a direct connection to the academic study of security, so they can ensure relevance in the research endeavors of the academic discipline.

This forum provides opportunities to discuss current, real-world issues, share lessons learned, and engage in insightful discussion with an extended community of practice. Students can also prepare and enhance their professional online presence and reputation and build a foundation for a successful career in security or a related field. All interested readers can access the group by **http://linkedin.com**, Search *Private Security Today* (choose Groups), or go to **http://group.securitytoday.co** (not .com).

Instructor Supplements

Instructor's Manual with Test Bank. Includes content outlines for classroom discussion, teaching suggestions, and answers to selected end-of-chapter questions from the text. This also contains a Word document version of the test bank.

TestGen. This computerized test generation system gives you maximum flexibility in creating and administering tests on paper, electronically, or online. It provides state-of-the-art features for viewing and editing test bank questions, dragging a selected question into a test you are creating, and printing sleek, formatted tests in a variety of layouts. Select test items from test banks included with TestGen for quick test creation, or write your own questions from scratch. TestGen's random generator provides the option to display different text or calculated number values each time questions are used.

PowerPoint Presentations. Our presentations offer clear, straightforward outlines and notes to use for class lectures or study materials. Photos, illustrations, charts, and tables from the book are included in the presentations when applicable.

To access supplementary materials online, instructors need to request an instructor access code. Go to **www.pearsonhighered.com/irc**, where you can register for an instructor access code. Within forty-eight hours after registering, you will receive a confirming email, including an instructor access code. Once you have received your code, go to the site and log on for full instructions to download the materials you wish to use.

Alternate Versions

eBooks. This text is also available in multiple eBook formats. These are an exciting new choice for students looking to save money. As an alternative to purchasing the printed textbook, students can purchase an electronic version of the same content. With an eTextbook, students can search the text, make notes online, print out reading assignments that incorporate lecture notes, and bookmark important passages for later review. For more information, visit your favorite online eBook reseller or visit **www.mypearsonstore.com.**

Acknowledgments

No worthy project can be accomplished without the assistance of a number of individuals, for whom we have the utmost appreciation, including:

- Our spouses Sharmyn, Ellen, and Terri (respectively).
- The many security professionals who assisted with insight and information, as well as accompanying us through the maze of private and government policy updates and changes, including Ahmed Salem, Alfred Birdsong, Anton Cooper, Antonio A. Rucci, Bernard Wilson, Calvin Rose, Charles Robinson, Dave Hawtin, David Jolley, Doug Riggins, Frank Taylor, Gene Smith, Herman Statum, Hunter Glass, Jason Klinger, Jeff Lockwood, Jerold Unruh, John Groseclose, Michael Knight, Michael Sampson, Mike Thornhill, Mike True, Patrick Coffey, Richard Novia, Rick McCann, Sandi Davies, and many others.
- Our academic advisory panel and reviewers, who provided extremely valuable insight and observations, and for whom we are most appreciative: John W. Bolinger, MacMurray College; Peter Curcio, Briarcliffe College; John L. Padgett, Capella University; Todd Scott, Schoolcraft College; Stephen Wofsey, Northern Virginia Community College.
- The editorial, production, and marketing staff, including Gary Bauer, Elisa Rogers, Thomas Hayward and Kaylee Carlson.
- And the students (and their professors) who are using this text to expand their understanding of the security profession.

We hope that you will learn from this book and enjoy reading it. As the security field continues to grow and expand we wish you success in your studies and encourage you to consider a career in security. If you identify areas in need of more coverage or would like to otherwise contribute to the knowledge base, feel free to connect with us on LinkedIn.

About the Authors

Carter F. Smith, JD, PhD, teaches security and criminal justice courses in the Department of Criminal Justice Administration at Middle Tennessee State University in Murfreesboro, Tennessee. He has also taught at Austin Peay State University, in Clarksville, Tennessee, where he helped launch the Homeland Security program, and the Florida Institute of Technology. Dr. Smith received a PhD in Business Administration from Northcentral University, a Juris Doctorate from Southern Illinois University, and a Bachelor of Science Degree from Austin Peay State University. He has taught security and security administration courses since 2005. Smith has taught classes for many Gang Investigators Associations, the Academy of Criminal Justice Sciences, the National Crime Prevention Council, the Regional Organized Crime Information Center, the National Gang Crime Research Center, the Southern Criminal Justice Association, the U.S. Department of Justice, and the U.S. Army. Smith is a retired U.S. Army Criminal Investigations Division (CID) Command Special Agent. He provided and directed the security of several U.S. Army bases, supervised multinational fraud and theft investigations, and conducted various criminal and cybercrime investigations in Germany, Korea, Panama, and the United States. He has been interviewed by several national, regional, and local television, print, Internet, and radio news sources, and has appeared twice in the History Channel's *Gangland* series. He is a member of the graduate faculty at MTSU, the Academy of Criminal Justice Sciences (ACJS), the American Society of Criminology, the Southern Criminal Justice Association, the American Criminal Justice Association, the Fraternal Order of Police, InfraGard, and ASIS International.

Frank Schmalleger, PhD, is Professor Emeritus at the University of North Carolina at Pembroke, where he also was recognized as Distinguished Professor. Dr. Schmalleger holds degrees from the University of Notre Dame and The Ohio State University; he earned both a master's and a doctorate in sociology, with a special emphasis in criminology, from Ohio State. From 1976 to 1994, he taught criminal justice courses at the University of North Carolina at Pembroke, and for the last sixteen of those years, he chaired the university's Department of Sociology, Social Work, and Criminal Justice. As an adjunct professor with Webster University in St. Louis, Missouri, Schmalleger helped develop the university's graduate program in security administration and loss prevention and taught courses in that curriculum for more than a decade. Schmalleger has also taught in the New School for Social Research's online graduate program, helping build the world's first electronic classrooms in support of distance learning through computer telecommunications. Schmalleger is the author of numerous articles as well as many books: *Criminal Justice Today: An Introductory Text for the 21st Century* (Pearson, 2017), now in its fourteenth edition; *Juvenile Delinquency*, second edition, with Clemmens Bartollas (Pearson, 2016); *Criminal Justice: A Brief Introduction*, eleventh edition (Pearson, 2016); *Criminal Law Today*, sixth edition (Pearson, 2017); *Corrections in the Twenty-First Century* with John Smykla (McGraw-Hill, 2017); and many other titles. He is also founding editor of the *Journal of Criminal Justice Studies* (formerly *The Justice Professional*).

Larry J. Siegel, PhD, a graduate of Christopher Columbus High School in the Bronx, received his BA at the City College of New York, and his MA and PhD in Criminal Justice at the State University of New York at Albany. Dr. Siegel began his teaching career at Northeastern University where he was a faculty member for nine years. He also held teaching positions at the University of Nebraska-Omaha and Saint Anselm College in New Hampshire before joining the faculty of the Department of Criminal Justice and Criminology at the University of Massachusetts-Lowell, where he has taught for the past twenty-six years. He is now a professor emeritus and adjunct professor in the graduate program in the School of Criminology and Justice Studies. Dr. Siegel has also written extensively in the area of crime and justice, including books on juvenile law, delinquency, criminology, corrections, courts, and criminal procedure. He is a court-certified expert on police conduct and has testified in numerous legal cases.

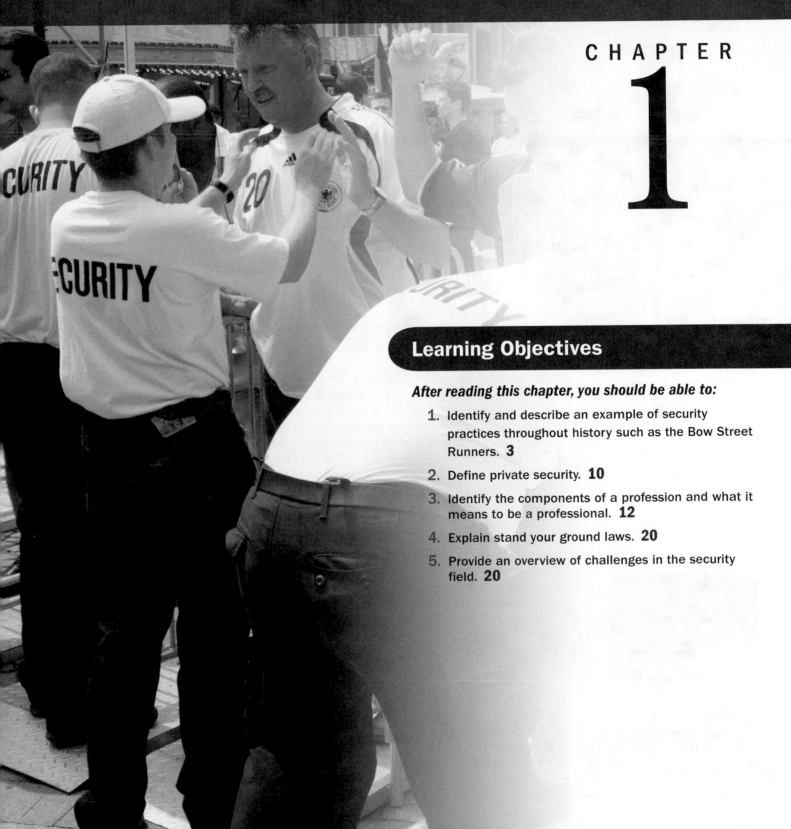

Origins and Foundations of Security

Learning Objectives

After reading this chapter, you should be able to:

1. Identify and describe an example of security practices throughout history such as the Bow Street Runners. **3**

2. Define private security. **10**

3. Identify the components of a profession and what it means to be a professional. **12**

4. Explain stand your ground laws. **20**

5. Provide an overview of challenges in the security field. **20**

Introduction

In 2012 G4S, one of the world's largest private security companies with operations in more than 125 countries,[1] signed a $443 million[2] contract with the organizers of the London Olympics[3] to provide 10,000 security personnel to protect tens of thousands of athletes, team officials, and visitors who gathered in London for the summer games.[4] More than 100 dignitaries were also in attendance at the event—including Queen Elizabeth II, U.S. first lady Michelle Obama, and various heads of state. The huge private security undertaking was coordinated with the efforts of almost 13,000 police officers and more than 18,200 British troops who were deployed to guard Olympic venues, airports, hotels, and public spaces. Additionally hundreds of British Telephone employees secured the Olympics' information technology (IT) infrastructure, working to make it impervious to electronic attacks while allowing 25,000 journalists and millions of members of the public instant access to Olympic websites. The cost of security operations during the six-week event totaled more than $897 million.[5]

G4S, with more than 620,000 employees worldwide (59,000 in the United States and Canada alone) is but one of the many private security companies that operate in the Americas. G4S provides services ranging from facility and computer security to operating juvenile justice facilities across the United States.[6]

The U.S. Bureau of Labor Statistics reported substantial and continued growth in employment in the security profession, projected to continue unabated in coming years.[7] The qualifications for many security positions often differ from traditional law enforcement jobs such as the necessary qualifications, security clearance, and required level of education. Because of the demand for security, many security positions are often more plentiful and attainable. Some career private security professionals find, in fact, that they prefer the businesslike aspects of security, the opportunity for job advancement, and the availability of financial reward when compared to jobs in public law enforcement.

▲ Securing the 2012 Olympics. Total costs for all security services at the event were estimated to be in excess of $897 million. What will the need for security services be like in the future?

Source: Daily Mail/Rex/Alamy

This book is about the provision of private security services, although the interface between public and private security is important to personal and public safety. Hence, our primary discussion will focus on private security agencies whose services are available for hire, but we will not ignore public operations focused primarily on security, like those undertaken by the Department of Homeland Security. Excluded from any detailed discussion, however, will be public law enforcement agencies whose role it is to enforce a broader mandate—which includes the enforcement of all criminal laws and judicial orders within the jurisdiction they operate; and the military whose defense function extends beyond the parameters of this text. Law enforcement agencies and their effective coordination with private security operations are crucial to a comprehensive security plan—whether for local venues or for the nation as a whole, and the laws and court precedents that govern their operations are often of relevance to security personnel and the agencies by whom they are employed.

This chapter will briefly examine the history of security, from ancient times to the present, in order to provide a better context for today's practice of security. We will then examine the many definitions of security to better understand the concept. Next, we will evaluate the requirements for classifying a career path or industry as a profession to determine whether the security field meets the criteria. We will conclude with an analysis of the current role of security, and the expanding interface between public and private security and spaces.

THINK ABOUT IT

Who needs private security services? Why will private security employment grow in the future?

The History of Security

Much of the history of contemporary security operations is intertwined with the history of law enforcement and policing.[8] Both follow the shift of legal foundations, taking the primary responsibility for protection and prevention of criminal activities from the private individual to the government.[9] The history of private security springs from a recurring inability of government to provide the level of security required by individuals and organizations.

The need for security can be traced back to the ancient world and actually predates by centuries the development of state-sponsored law enforcement agencies. Humans have always felt the need for security for both themselves and their possessions. The use of guards became popular at an early point in history, and they were used to protect persons and assets. In early civilizations, domesticated animals were protected from both human and animal predators by a shepherd who prevented them from wandering, or a herdsman who provided security for the flock or herd. Among the earliest examples of personal security professionals were those created in the 13th century BC when Egyptian Pharaoh Ramses II hired Nubians, Libyans, Syrians, and others to complement Egypt's military and native security forces. This practice continued in ancient Rome where wealthy citizens often hired security professionals to protect their families and property. The Praetorian Guard initially served as bodyguards for Roman generals, and later became the security force for much of the city, acquiring political power along the way. By AD 400, a trend had emerged, with the emperors hiring mostly foreign security professionals for personal security. Eunuchs, men who had been castrated at an early age, were employed as security forces in many cultures. Perhaps they were considered more trustworthy, as their loyalty would not be challenged or tempted by a woman to whom they might have otherwise have been attracted.[10]

Another practice of the ancient world was to provide security barriers. To enhance security, fires could be lighted at the entrances of caves, or large rocks could be moved to make the caves less accessible.[11] Walls and barriers protected people and property by surrounding many cities in Europe and Asia, such as Rome, Troy, and Constantinople. Perhaps the greatest example of a security barrier was the Great Wall of China, built along the northern borders of China to protect the Chinese Empire against attacks by various nomadic groups. Begun in the 7th century BC, the Great Wall of China stands today as a symbol of the efforts made by the ancients to establish security and protection.

The practice of security has continued throughout history, and many of the developments of the past are seen in today's security practices. Past goals were much the same as those involved in the contemporary practice of security: to keep others from accessing certain property while providing individual security.

Security in European History

In the Middle Ages (from the 5th to the 15th century), security involved wealthy citizens building moats to protect their property from potential intruders. In England, the citizens provided security in the community. The system of **Tens and Hundreds** represented a community organization strategy that used an early form of what we now know as neighborhood watch for security. The citizens lived in communities known as tuns, similar to contemporary towns. The tuns were divided into groups of ten families, and each was called a tithing. The tithings were also arranged in groups of tens, so each group of 100 families elected their own chief to oversee their security.[12]

When King William I (known as William, the Conqueror) invaded and conquered England in 1066, he divided the country into shires, an area similar to the counties in the United States today, and order was administered by an appointed official known as the shire reeve, a term that has morphed into the modern term *sheriff* as it is known today.[13] It was the responsibility of the shire reeves to maintain law and order.[14] They also administered justice in the county courts, and the King sent trusted noblemen in his own court to conduct important trials. In larger towns, constables were appointed to maintain the peace. King William is also remembered for changing the concept of crime from being that of an offense against the individual to an offense against the state or government.[15]

---

1 Identify and describe an example of security practices throughout history such as the Bow Street Runners.

tens and hundreds
Groups of citizens in early English society that maintained the right of self-protection. Citizens lived in communities known as tuns, similar to contemporary towns divided into groups of ten families, called a tithing, that were pledged to defend one another from danger. Ten tithings were known as hundreds that elected their own chief to oversee their security.

shire
A geopolitical division of a larger state or country. When King William I (William, the Conqueror) invaded and conquered England in 1066, he divided the country into shires, counties ruled and administered by a local nobleman, an earl, viscount, or baron.

shire reeve
An appointed official that administered order in shires, and also administered justice in the county courts. The term morphed into the modern term *sheriff*, or chief law enforcement officer in a county.

In the late 10th century (the 1200s) in England, ordinary citizens were still depended on for community safety. Legislation requiring this established a night patrol and guard force, provided by the men in town, to support the local constable's efforts to provide security. This was called the Watch and Ward. The wealthy and business owners were not always pleased with the level of security provided by this mandatory force, and many of those required to patrol the streets at night shared in this displeasure.

By the mid-1600s, policelike forces were set up to operate much like the military. Their duty was to capture and punish criminals. These **thief takers** acted as a private police force, and they were paid by the king for every criminal arrested, although they had no official status. Their main role was to make sure that travelers stayed safe, and after the governments accepted their activity, they were paid for the conviction of criminals and rewarded for their efforts with the bounty of weapons, money, and property seized from the criminals they caught.

By the mid-1700s, the concept of crime prevention had been implemented. Innovations in the responses to crime created many changes in the way communities implemented their security efforts. In London, groups of residents in the neighborhoods worked together to prevent crime by arming themselves and patrolling the streets, ensuring that homes in the community were physically protected. These individuals chased down criminals through back alleys, and became known as runners. This volunteer force evolved into the first detective agency in England, known as the **Bow Street Runners**. Henry Fielding, who lived on Bow Street, created the group by paying constables and ex-constables to locate and arrest serious offenders. Although their motivation was similar to the thief takers, with Fielding's oversight the group was more organized and professional.

By the mid-1800s, both crime and the enforcement of laws had evolved significantly. Many organizations were enforcing laws in the same jurisdictions, and there was much confusion. Sir Robert Peel, in England, pushed to organize the many efforts, and encouraged a consolidation of duties and organizations. Because of his efforts, Peel was seen as the catalyst for the modern police model.

Security in North America

The colonists in the New World lived in dangerous times and self-protection proved insufficient to defend settlers from harm. Prior to the colonists' decision to fight for their independence, protection of the colonists and their property was the responsibility of town constables and sheriffs, supplemented by watchmen who would patrol the streets at night. Most local governments used the **watch system** as the primary means of security until the development of full-time law enforcement agencies in the mid-1800s.[16] This system required each adult male to serve the community at a scheduled time between about 9 o'clock in the evening and sunrise the following day. Watchmen often encountered a variety of different security threats, including fires, wild animals, runaway slaves, thieves, and grave robbers.[17] They were expected to handle those incidents and maintain order by making arrests and enforcing the curfew. Most watchmen hired others to perform their duties and satisfy their community responsibilities. Although protecting their communities was difficult and demanding, watchmen were not treated well by their fellow colonists.[18] Many variations of these patrols developed and evolved.

During the **Industrial Revolution**, from 1760 to about 1870, manufacturing moved from hand production methods to machines.[19] The transition began in England, and within a few decades it had spread to the rest of Western Europe and the United States. Most aspects of daily life were influenced, in some way, by the Industrial Revolution, which transitioned many countries from a primarily rural to a primarily urban society. The new jobs for the working class were in the cities. People who had been raised on farms saw better opportunities in the cities and moved there. Providing housing was a problem, and many new residents lived in deteriorated conditions.[20] Western expansion was also underway, creating a significant population shift.[21]

As security challenges kept pace with the rapid growth of the country, citizens put pressure on community leaders demanding that they provide more protection. In response, some communities added daytime security to supplement the night watchmen, but the

---

thief takers
Private citizens who earned a living by capturing wanted criminals. They were paid first for every criminal arrested, and later for the successful conviction of criminals.

bow street runners
A group formed by magistrate Sir Henry Fielding in London in the mid-1700s who traveled around England to serve court-ordered writs and arrest offenders on the authority of magistrates.

watch system
Authorized by legislation in the late 1200s in England, requiring ordinary citizens to provide community safety with a night patrol and guard force, in support of the local constable's efforts to provide security. Watchmen often encountered a variety of different security threats, including fires, wild animals, runaway slaves, thieves, and grave robbers. Some watchmen hired others to perform their duties and satisfy their community responsibilities. The system was adapted in the American colonies in the 17th century.

Industrial Revolution
A time from 1760 to about 1870 in which manufacturing moved from hand production methods to machines. The transition began in England, and within a few decades it had spread to the rest of Western Europe and the United States. The Industrial Revolution transformed many areas in Europe and the United States from rural to urban societies centered in metropolitan areas.

Spotlight
Allan Pinkerton

Allan Pinkerton was the son of a police sergeant. Born in 1819 in Glasgow, Scotland, he emigrated to the United States when he was 23. He became a deputy sheriff in Illinois and later joined Chicago's new police force.

In 1850, he left the police force as a detective and started his own company, the Pinkerton National Detective Agency. His code called for his agents to have no "addiction to drink, smoking, card playing, low dives or . . . slang." Detectives at the Pinkerton Company specialized in tracking and capturing the gangs that robbed railroads. Through his work, Pinkerton met George B. McClellan, president of the Rock Island and Illinois Central Railroad, and the railroad's attorney, Abraham Lincoln. Those connections earned Pinkerton security contracts during the Civil War. Pinkerton was credited with foiling a plot to kill Lincoln just before his inauguration.

During the war, Pinkerton's detectives supported the Union by providing intelligence, and Pinkerton served as the head of the Union Intelligence Service, which was the forerunner of the U.S. Secret Service. After the war, Pinkerton returned to Chicago and led the agency that pursued notorious criminals such as the James brothers and Butch Cassidy and the Sundance Kid. Pinkerton also worked for the executives of companies battling the effects of rail workers and coal miner union strikes (organized work stoppages).

After Pinkerton died in 1884, the Pinkerton National Detective Agency continued as a family enterprise through four generations. Later outsiders bought it but kept the Pinkerton name. In 1999, Securitas, an international security firm, acquired the Pinkerton Company.

Source: Central Intelligence Agency website, "Intelligence in the Civil War," https://www.cia.gov/library/publications/intelligence-history/civil-war (accessed 2016).

watch system was no longer considered either adequate or efficient. This led to the creation of public police departments with full-time police forces in cities such as New York, Boston, Chicago, and others.[22]

By 1856, police departments had also been established in St. Louis, Detroit, Cincinnati, Chicago, San Francisco, Los Angeles, Philadelphia, and Dallas. However, these proved inadequate to meet all private security needs and business interests. Consequently, railroads, mining companies, and factories turned to the developing private security industry to protect their property.[23] During the U.S. Civil War (1861–1865), private security agencies provided intelligence in support of the war. The Pinkerton National Detective Agency, started in 1850, supported the Union by providing intelligence. The company's founder, former Chicago police detective Allan Pinkerton, served as the head of the Union Intelligence Service, now known as the U.S. Secret Service.[24]

As the United States expanded westward, railroad lines in the new territories received little coverage from public law enforcement. In many remote locations, railway police provided the only security.[25] Because of their remote location and limited protection, local outlaws robbed passengers, stole cargo, dynamited tracks, and disrupted communications. Various state legislatures passed railway police acts that enabled private railroads to establish their own security forces in response to demands for adequate protection of goods and passengers.[26] The St. Louis and San Francisco Railroads, as well as the Illinois Central, were the earliest to have their own police forces. Railway police had full police powers to protect the railroad company's assets. By 1914, there were over 14,000 railway police in the United States.[27] As railroads continued their growth, they employed more and more private security professionals, as did many steamship lines, banks, and factories, along with mines and retail establishments.

In the mid-1800s, no federal authorities were authorized to pursue criminals across state and territorial jurisdictional lines. The U.S. Marshals Service, formed in 1789, had the duty of protecting and enforcing the federal judicial process; in addition to their law enforcement duties they conducted the federal census, carried out death sentences, and pursued counterfeiters.[28] It was not until 1828 that the first federal investigations unit was formed within the Post Office. The Treasury Department started the second such unit in 1864.[29] Local law enforcement was unable to chase fleeing criminals very far, so crime victims often took up the task.[30] Many victims hired security professionals, who acted as their agents to do the job of modern-day bounty hunters. In addition to tracking down and apprehending criminals, security professionals of that time performed such services as guarding railroad (and stagecoach) shipments, investigating crimes, and providing security advice to businesses.[31] By the early 1900s, much of this work decreased after federal and local agencies improved their law enforcement capabilities and assumed more of those duties. By that time, the security industry had grown considerably, with large numbers of people working as private guards and detectives and in other security-related positions.[32]

The 20th century (the 1900s) brought an increase in labor unions that used strikes (work stoppages) to gain concessions from management.[33] With industrial expansion to the Midwest and Western United States, security organizations were employed by owners and managers to thwart the actions of labor unions.[34] Because many factories were located in areas that had no effective public police forces, these security agencies were called in to control strikers and to protect owners' lives and property.[35]

The Pinkerton Agency again made headlines in July 1892 at the Homestead Works of the Carnegie Steel Company near Pittsburgh, Pennsylvania. In the seventy-third time that Pinkerton agents were hired in such a situation, the local sheriff was persuaded that a posse was needed to preserve law and order, and Pinkerton employees were appointed to fill the role. The Pinkerton group was met with unexpected violence, supported by counterintelligence, and several on both sides were killed. The situation ended when the plant was occupied by troops who had been called out by the governor.[36]

In the early 1900s, especially during World War I, the use of security increased not only because of urbanization and industrial growth but also to protect government assets against sabotage and espionage by politically active nationalists. After the war, there was less of a focus on or perceived need for security. As a result, the use of security professionals declined during the Great Depression.[37]

During the 1940s, the increase in manufacturing during World War II caused another increase in the use of security professionals, as the U.S. government required many of their contractors to demonstrate that they were using strong measures that would protect classified material and information from sabotage and espionage before they were awarded contracts.[38] Additionally, more than 200,000 plant watchmen were given special auxiliary military police status.[39] Their duties included protecting products, supplies, equipment, and personnel. Because of these wartime requirements, manufacturers became more aware of the need for security. After the war, the use of private security services expanded from the limited use by defense contractors to all segments of both the private and public sectors.[40]

Through World War II, private security was seen as a somewhat unsavory occupation. Private security professionals were often seen as ill-trained thugs hired to break strikes, suppress labor, and spy on each other. Law enforcement often viewed private security companies as a dangerous and illegitimate intrusion into the government role of law enforcement and policing. Following World War II, a more tolerant attitude developed toward private security professionals, allowing them to be regarded as a necessary supplement to the overburdened public police.[41] By the mid-1900s, many private security companies had joined the ranks. Notable among the new arrivals was the William J. Burns Detective Agency, which represented the American Banking Association and the American Hotel Association.[42] George Wackenhut and three other former FBI agents formed a private investigative and contract security firm known as the Wackenhut Corporation.[43]

A 1957 New York State legislative report found the typical private security guard to be characterized by the following:[44]

- Was male, with minimal employment ability and stability.
- Was between 40 and 55 years of age, with little education beyond the ninth grade.
- Had little experience in private security.
- Earned between $1.60 and $2.75 per hour, often working a 48- to 56-hour week (annual salary with lowest-highest figures ranged from $3,900 to $8,000).

Some guards had retired from low-level civil service or military careers. Part-timers accounted for 20–50% of the guards at some larger contract firms, and the younger part-timers were often students, teachers, and military personnel. Annual turnover rates ranged from less than 10% for some organizations with in-house security to over 200% in some contract agencies.[45] The typical private investigator was a somewhat younger, white male 36 to 47 years of age, had completed high school, and had several years of experience in private security, earning between $6,000 and $9,000 annually.[46]

During the 1960s, the number of public law enforcement personnel at all levels of government grew 42%, while the U.S. population grew 12%.[47] The overall increase of in house private security guards (i.e., those directly employed by the company to whom they provided services) and investigators was only 7% (guard employment grew 6%, while investigative employment grew 19%). Meanwhile, the contract security segment (security officers employed by a security company whose services were contracted out to other companies) grew rapidly, almost doubling during that time. The explanations for such growth imbalance included that contract security services offered:[48]

- lower cost.
- administrative unburdening.
- flexibility in scheduling of relief manpower.
- less involvement between security and regular employees.

Security managers found new challenges and responsibilities with the social unrest and the changes in the social climate in the United States in the late 1960s.[49] To a significant extent, this occurred because public law enforcement was simultaneously being required to provide more protection while reducing expenses. The private sector had inherited the responsibility for a significant amount of the security and protective services mission, which was traditionally provided by local, state, and federal law enforcement.[50] Increases in security needs again dictated increases in the hiring of security professionals. By the end of the 1960s, there were more than 500,000 people working in the security profession (about 1% of the civilian labor force at the time). About 36% of all security professionals were employed in the private sector and about 64% were in the public sector.[51]

By the mid-1970s, crime rates had risen in every part of the United States. Cities, neighborhoods, transportation and recreational areas, schools and libraries, residential and commercial establishments all seemed to be under siege. It was estimated that before the end of 1976 one of every four Americans would be a victim of crime. Statistics by the U.S. Department of Justice showed that Americans paid more for private security services than federal, state, and local governments paid for the criminal justice system.[52] Foot patrol was the activity performed most often by contract security guards and involved little more than looking for potential security problems and checking for unlocked doors, open fences, and fire hazards.[53]

In the early 1990s, the average annual rate of growth in private security was 8%, double the growth in public law enforcement.[54] As public law enforcement were beginning to find the need to develop new priorities while at the same time receiving lower budget allotments, organizations of all sizes found it necessary to consider alternatives to protect the people and property in their organizations.[55]

Security Today

- Three men entered a jewelry store in the middle of the afternoon. One of them smashed a display case with a sledgehammer, according to the *Chicago Sun-Times*. An armed security guard shot the man with the sledgehammer as his two accomplices ran out of the store. About ten customers and six employees were in the store, but none were injured.[56]

- Pirates hijacked a fuel tanker and kidnapped both Nigerian and Pakistani sailors off the coast of Nigeria. Fox News reported the ship was one of several allowed to bring subsidized gasoline into the country. Oil tanker hijackings have become increasingly more common, with pirates stealing the fuel onboard and sometimes kidnapping sailors for ransom. Pirates are able to make as much as a $2 million profit for the standard load of 3,000 tons of fuel.[57]

- *The Wall Street Journal* reported that hackers disabled South and North Korean government websites in what was called *cyberspace guerilla activity*. Websites for South Korea's presidential office, other government agencies, and some broadcasters were inaccessible for several hours, and the North Korean state-controlled Korean Central News Agency website appeared to be offline, as well. There was no indication of attacks on military sites, sensitive data leaks, or economic damage. The South Korean government believed that at least some North Korean hackers were based in China. North Korea denied involvement in cyberattacks on the South. The international hacking group Anonymous claimed responsibility for attacks on North Korean websites but denied hacking the South Korean sites. North Korea's media accused Anonymous of being controlled by the United States and South Korea.[58]

- In 2014, hackers infiltrated the computer system at Sony Pictures Entertainment's headquarters in California and sent a threatening message that "This is just the beginning, we've obtained all your internal data," and warned that if Sony didn't "obey" their demands, they would release the company's top secrets. Among the damage they caused was releasing five Sony films, including some that had not yet been distributed, onto online file-sharing hubs where they could be downloaded for free. The cyberattackers also copied and released embarrassing emails issued by company executives. According to initial reports by the FBI, the suspected perpetrators were North Korean agents, upset that Sony was releasing a film, entitled *The Interview*, that spoofed Korean leader Kim Jong-un and depicted his assassination.[59]

These events provide examples of why security is needed in contemporary society and the varied and complex roles security agents are required to carry out on a daily basis. Today, private security is the primary resource for individual and property protection. Private security professionals far outnumber those employed in public law enforcement, with over 1 million people employed in private security, according to the U.S. Bureau of Labor Statistics.[60] The private security field is expected to continue this growth for many years.[61] Although entry-level officers are often required to have only a high school diploma and are paid commensurate with their experience and education, as the growth in the field increases, so will the ranks of supervisors, also receiving pay commensurate with their experience and education. Higher education for supervisors is a necessity for advancement with the improvements in security technology, and leadership demands facing today's security professionals.

The foundation of contemporary security exists as an adaptation of many improvements to the process of providing security. The history of the security profession is long and varied, roughly parallel to the history of policing and law enforcement. Security has a substantively different focus, however, with a default prevention mode instead of the enforcement mode of public law enforcement. Security engages in a more proactive approach, while law enforcement's focus is on reacting to reported violations.

Historically, security was often the primary responsibility of the citizens. Bayley and Shearing suggested that security is a responsibility shared between government and the citizens.[62] Although not to the extent that the watch system or runners of earlier times contributed to community security, private security professionals appear to have replaced law enforcement officers as the primary crime-deterrent presence in contemporary society.

The security field includes many subfields, with functions such as the following:

- Private investigation
- Asset protection
- Physical security
- Institutional security
- Executive protection
- Industrial security
- Disaster recovery

- Maritime security
- Private policing
- Homeland security
- Retail security
- Loss prevention
- Workplace security
- Information security
- Communications security
- Computer security

Each of these roles is important in contemporary society. Take, for instance, the role of the private investigator. Unlike what is often portrayed in the media, the typical private investigator spends more time in front of a computer screen compiling data than walking the streets looking for suspects or clues.[63] Private investigators today conduct background checks, search records, and locate and interview witnesses for criminal and civil cases. These investigators work closely with attorneys and others in the legal system. Private investigators work on a number of different cases including criminal murder and complex civil litigation. These investigators often serve as "evidence collectors" for the attorney or law firm on the case.[64]

Disaster recovery and maritime security are two subfields that have recently received increased attention. Disaster recovery includes actions preparing for and engaging in recovery or continuation of vital organizational activities after a natural or human-induced disaster.[65] Security professionals who engage in the support of such activity have to focus on the potential for inventory theft, or looting, by both employees and local residents, and weather-related damage of assets. Maritime security is the prevention of intentional damage through sabotage, subversion, or terrorism. It primarily encompasses the three roles of port security, vessel security, and facility security.[66] Security professionals' roles include deterring piracy and terrorist attacks as well as logistics diversion and theft. In the United States, the Coast Guard has primary responsibility for maritime security.

◀ Coast Guard crewmembers and emergency medical personnel help four boaters rescued from their sunken boat near Catalina Island. All boaters were safely recovered. What is disaster recovery?

Source: U.S. Department of Homeland Security. http://www.dhs.gov/photo/air-crew-rescues-boaters-sunken-ship-uscg.

Additionally, scholars have identified thirteen security knowledge categories in the academic security realm, including.[67]

- Criminology
- Business continuity management
- Facility management
- Fire and life safety
- Industrial security
- Information and computer security
- Investigations
- Physical security
- Security principles
- Security risk management
- Security law
- Security management
- Security technology

The inclusion of criminology as a security knowledge category demonstrates the need for an understanding of relevant criminological theory. Theories are designed to help us understand the intricacies of individual and group dynamics, with the premise that knowing what causes crime can help security professionals design ways to deter it. By using criminological theories, and the theories from other academic disciplines, security professionals will be equipped with the tools necessary to show value to their employers, peers, and other stakeholders in the organization. Physical security describes the actual (physical) steps taken to safeguard people and property. Security principles refers to the activities and steps followed during daily operations that support the organizational strategy. These principles come from the business sector, as well as the military, especially with respect to physical security. Each of these, as well as the remaining security knowledge categories are addressed throughout this text. The academic study of security includes a blended analysis of many academic disciplines, such as criminal justice, public administration, law, business management, sociology, disaster preparedness, computer technology, psychology, physical security, human resources, and contingency planning.[68]

Defining Security

2   Define private security.

Security today is a complex endeavor making it difficult to define. The word *security* originated from the Latin word *securus*, meaning without care or concern. Security is often defined as freedom from risk, danger, doubt, anxiety, or fear. For many, security results from the establishment and maintenance of protective measures that ensure freedom from destruction, violence, infringement, or desecration from hostile acts or influences by adversaries.

Post and Kingsbury explained that the act of providing security was the provision of two fundamental services: (1) protection against threats and hazards that are human-made, natural, or environmental; and (2) the prevention of unlawful events.[69] The provision of security can be seen in measures adopted by an organization, including corporations and governments, to prevent espionage, sabotage, or attack. Additionally, security is included in the measures taken to prevent a crime such as burglary or assault by a business owner or homeowner. Security is also the goal for corrections or other detention facilities when they implement measures to prevent escape.[70]

In developing a definition, there are two levels of security to be considered: governmental and proprietary.[71] Government security is composed of international security, national security, and state security. Government security comprises the problems and issues protecting the interests of the government and interactions with other nations. Proprietary security includes the actions of individuals and organizations to protect their private property and interests.

Development of a working definition of security is important in order to establish parameters on which to base the use and understanding of the term and its many components.[72]

The concept of security is quite diverse and wide-ranging, from a *philosophical security* (i.e., freedom from worry of danger) to *operational security* (i.e., physical, personnel, and national security).[73]

The term *private security* is traditionally used to describe individual and organizational measures and efforts that provide protection for persons and property. It also describes business enterprises that provide services and products to achieve this protection.[74] The 1976 Private Security Task Force formulated the following definition of private security:[75]

> [T]hose self-employed individuals and privately funded business entities and organizations providing security-related services to specific clientele for a fee, for the individual or entity that retains or employs them, or for themselves, in order to protect their persons, private property, or interests from varied hazards.

ASIS International (formerly known as the American Society for Industrial Security) has defined private security as:[76]

> the nongovernmental, private-sector practice of protecting people, property, and information, conducting investigations, and otherwise safeguarding an organization's assets, which may be performed for an organization by an internal department (usually called proprietary security) or by an external, hired firm (usually called contract security).

A more general definition of security by Post and Kingsbury utilizes a broad framework:

> *(Security means using both active or passive efforts)* . . . which serve to protect and preserve an environment which allows for the conduct of activities within the organization or society without disruption.[77]

The common characteristics for the definitions most relevant to our study include *private* (nongovernmental) *individuals and organizations providing* some type of *security*-related *services* designed for *protecting* persons, private property, or interests *from* varied *hazards* and *adversaries*. If we comprehensively synthesize these definitions, we see that **private security** can be defined as:

> The private sector-practice, by individuals and organizations, of providing security-related means or services, to protect and preserve persons, property, interests, information, and environments in order to allow for the continued conduct of needed activities within the organization or society, without disruption from varied adversaries or hazards, for compensation.

It is this definition that we will use throughout the remainder of this text.

private security
The private-sector practice, by individuals and organizations, of providing security-related means or services, to protect and preserve persons, property, interests, information, and environments to allow for the continued conduct of needed activities within the organization or society, without disruption from varied adversaries or hazards, for compensation.

THINK ABOUT IT
How does this text define private security? Why does it say that it is a *practice*?

The Need for Security

The security of individuals, families, communities, and nations appears to be connected to one overriding and basic human need: survival. Famed psychologist Abraham Maslow's research is considered to be the historical foundation of what security truly means.[78] In his well-known hierarchy of human needs, Maslow classified security as part of his second-tier need, safety, which was positioned just above (immediately following) the need for food, clothing, and shelter.[79] Security, in this context, is the feeling that people get when their fears and anxieties are low. Safety, on the other hand, is the feeling that people get when they are confident that no harm will come to them physically, mentally, or emotionally.

It appears that Maslow, in examining what motivated people, was identifying the basic human need for personal, physical security, although that individual need can easily be expanded to a group such as the family, community, and nation in which an individual lives. Given the importance of security in our lives, it is understandable that people have developed various mechanisms to obtain a sense of security. Although the lower levels of Maslow's hierarchy help to explain basic human needs, most security professionals will benefit from a focus at the top of the hierarchy, where *self-actualization* (our need to be and do that which we were "born to do") and *self-transcendence* (the need to further a cause and be part of something bigger than ourselves) depict the pinnacle of human needs.[80]

The term *security* represents a wide range of roles for individuals and organizations. These roles include professionals providing corporate security, security guard companies, armored car businesses, investigative services, and many others. The goals connected to providing security include the protection of materials, equipment, information, personnel, physical facilities, and preventing undesirable influences that are unauthorized or detrimental to the goals of the organization.[81] Security organizations provide various services that include crime control, the protection of both lives and property, and order maintenance.[82] They engage in such tasks as physical, personnel, and information systems security. They also conduct investigations to limit merchandise being illegally taken (loss prevention) and help manage crisis and reduce risks.[83] Some recent tasks including counterterrorism, competitive intelligence, and crime prevention through environmental design (CPTED), warrant further explanation.

Counterterrorism is the process of identifying and disrupting potential terrorist plots, sharing terrorist-related information, and providing strategic and operational threat analysis. Competitive intelligence is the continuous process of learning about one's industry, competitors, and perceptions of one's organization by customers, clients, competitors, and stakeholders. CPTED refers to the principle of design and use of the environment used in the practice of physical security to reduce opportunities of fear and incidence of crime, and improve the quality of life. Although these elements do not hold the same relative weight in every situation, they do represent the variety of services offered by contemporary security professionals.

Security Professionals

As observed by Post and Kingsbury, a **profession** is a vocation or occupation that requires advanced training, and usually involves mental rather than manual work. Teaching, engineering, writing, medicine, and law are examples of professions. The requirements for considering and identifying a career field include:

3   Identify the components of a profession and what it means to be a professional.

profession
A career field, vocation, or occupation requiring advanced training, and usually stressing mental or intellectual efforts rather than manual work. Teaching, engineering, writing, medicine, and law are examples of professions.

- Skills coming from and supported by a base of knowledge organized into an internally consistent system called a *body of theory*.
- Members possess a common *body of knowledge*, which is freely communicated among them.
- Members offer a *unique service* based on learned techniques.
- Standards for entry require an *extensive training* period, minimum qualifications, and licensing or certification by a regulatory body.
- Standards of conduct embodied in a *code of ethics*, which guides client relations and contact with one another and society.
- Heavy emphasis on *service to humankind* rather than individual gain for those performing the service.
- Existence of a *professional organization*, which establishes policy, regulates some actions, and exercises responsibility in keeping members current on technical research concerning their fields of interest.[84]

To determine whether security has in fact achieved societal acceptance as a profession, four criteria must be met, according to Axt:

Qualification criteria.   The security field must establish, promote, and enforce unambiguous qualification criteria. The voluntary criteria for certifications provided by professional organizations such as ASIS International can help meet these criteria.

Academic studies.   Security must achieve widespread academic acceptance and promotion of advanced security-related studies. A growing number of universities offer courses and degrees in security management. The extent to which security becomes an academic discipline may depend on this growth.

Business skills.   Security managers must develop business-related skills so that they can earn respect within the corporation. A recent survey of security professionals showed that most security managers have a background in the military and law enforcement.[85] With only government or public sector experience, many security professionals have not been exposed to the process of developing business plans, calculating a return on investment, or other critical business-related skills.

Corporate recognition.   Security managers must develop an understanding and appreciation of security by their organization's leadership. Security managers must also be able to speak the coWrporate language to convey their message. This is critical to senior management's understanding and appreciation of security and its value.[86]

Ultimately, the public's perception is what matters, both the attitude of society as a whole and the general opinion of security held by corporate leadership. Said another way, it is not for security professionals to decide, it is the responsibility of the consumers of their services who will decide when security has become a profession in the truest sense of the word.[87] Despite the relative similarities to public law enforcement, private security has been lacking in perceived professional status in the past, by both the general public and by law enforcement agencies. Those negative attitudes appear to have been replaced by a more positive and cooperative perspective recently, for two primary reasons. The first reason is that a number of professionally oriented agencies are consciously implementing policies to dispel the adverse image of private investigators and security personnel and improve the relationships they have with public law enforcement officials. The second reason for a change in perception is the large and increasing number of law enforcement officers working part time for private security organizations.[88] Scott and McPherson found that many former and retired law enforcement officers have become private security professionals, starting private security agencies, working full time for an established agency, or by joining the security division of a business or corporation. Their former careers bring them the credibility, credentials, and often network of contacts that can limit any perceived bias they might otherwise face.[89] However, one of the issues associated with experienced law enforcement officers is a lack of business experience.

Academic Recognition

Nalla found that progress in achieving widespread academic acceptance for the security profession has occurred due to the involvement in and encouragement of the academic discipline by professional organizations.[90] Since the mid-1900s, members of ASIS International have collaborated with university faculty groups and security directors to identify common security educational needs. Kooi and Hinduja found that although many criminal justice departments have added security courses and many schools have their own security departments, there has yet to be much of a corresponding substantive response from business schools to incorporate a security curriculum.[91] Although they found that security continues to be an important part of the business discipline, its similarity to law enforcement and related functions allows for its incorporation into most criminal justice programs if it does not enjoy its own department.[92]

It is critical that all members of the security profession contribute to its advancement and regard in the community. In fact, it has been said that a genuine desire to serve is the only true hallmark of a profession.[93]

THINK ABOUT IT

Why is effective communication between private security agencies and public law enforcement agencies crucial to public safety?

Security Careers

Private security as a career field offers a variety of alternatives. Just as differences exist between state and local law enforcement, the various sizes and missions of security organizations ensure that the functions security professionals perform differ considerably. An International Association of Chiefs of Police (IACP) report noted that "[a] security practitioner could be an experienced director of security at a major multinational corporation, a manager of contract security officers at a client site, a skilled computer crime investigator, an armed protector at a nuclear power plant, or an entry-level guard at a retail store."[94] The U.S. Department of Justice advised that for local police chiefs and sheriffs, some or all of the functions of private security might be appropriate to incorporate into their homeland security strategies, depending on the characteristics of their jurisdictions.[95]

Despite its growth, expansion into new areas, and increasingly sophisticated tools, private security continues to provide many of the services from which it originated in the 1850s:

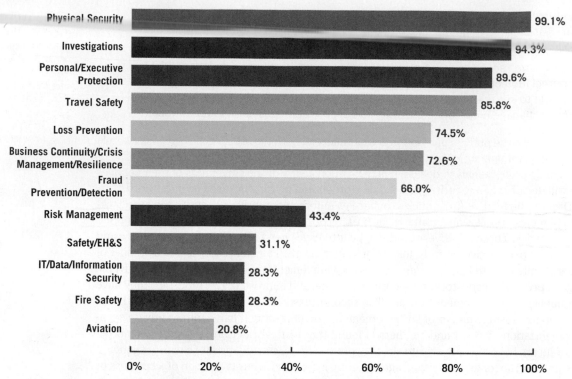

FIGURE 1–1
Security Functions
Source: Used with permission of ASIS International Alexandria, Virginia. (2012). "CSO Roundtable Survey: Security Department Organizational Structure," https://www.asisonline.org/Documents/CSOOrgSurvey.pdf

guards, investigators, and armored car and courier services.[96] Much of what security professionals do today can be classified as surveillance, normally a very mundane activity made up of many functions. But surveillance is not the only activity of security professionals. Security professionals fill many roles, including guard services, alarm monitoring, and investigations.[97]

Security professionals engage in a variety of tasks, from physical security to investigations to Risk Management and Fire Safety, as shown in Figure 1–1.

The Role of Security

The role of private security is generally characterized as a preventative approach to the protection of assets and the maximization of profits.[98] Any attempt to consistently classify the role of security is further complicated by the organizational hierarchy in which the security function is found in any given company. In a recent survey of Fortune 1000 executives, the corporate departments that security reported to were diverse and showed little organizational consistency. The largest groups (16%) reported to the Facilities area or Administration. Operations (13%), CEO/President (12%), Human Resources (11%), Environmental/Health/Safety (11%), Legal (9%), and Risk Management (7%) were the next most frequently identified areas.[99]

Security professionals can be armed or unarmed, employed in-house or as contract employees, and they can have many different responsibilities depending on their employer and their job description. As we saw earlier, private security services fall into two categories: proprietary corporate security and contract or private security firms. Corporate security generally refers to the security departments in large businesses or corporations. Contract security firms, by contrast, sell their services to the public, including businesses, homeowners, and banks.[100]

Security professionals report to a variety of administrative officers, depending on the size and function of the organization. Some examples include the chief operating officer (COO), the legal department, human relations, the compliance officer, and the like, as depicted in Figure 1–2.

The security profession is often distinguished based on the nature of the security department (proprietary or contractual), type of security provided (physical, information, or employment-related), services provided (e.g., guarding, armored transport), and target

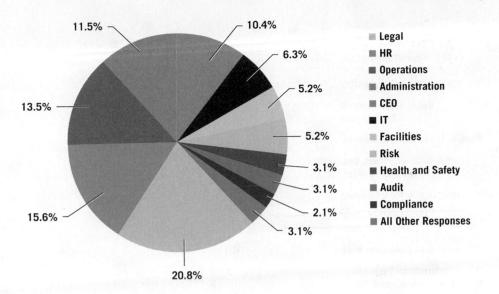

Legend:
- Legal
- HR
- Operations
- Administration
- CEO
- IT
- Facilities
- Risk
- Health and Safety
- Audit
- Compliance
- All Other Responses

FIGURE 1–2
Organizational Areas to Which the Top Security Person in the Organization Reports
Source: Used with permission of ASIS International Alexandria, Virginia. (2012). "CSO Roundtable Survey: Security Department Organizational Structure," https://www.asisonline.org/Documents/CSOOrgSurvey.pdf

market (e.g., critical infrastructure, commercial venues).[101] Security is an integral part of the organization, which it serves.[102] Private security organizations exist primarily to serve the interests of those who employ them.

Various organizations employ private security professionals in diverse roles, as we will see throughout the textbook. These include critical infrastructure, commercial, institutional, and residential. Figure 1–3 shows the distribution of proprietary security officer employment by industry.[103] This figure gives an indication of which industries are most

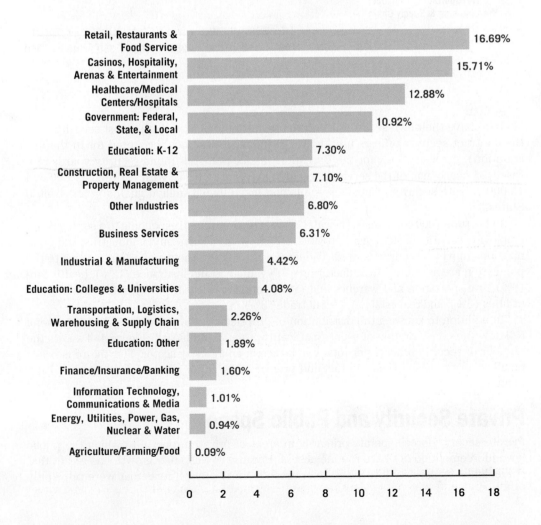

FIGURE 1–3
Number of Proprietary Security Officers per Employee by Industry Sector
Source: Occupational Employment Statistics (OES) Survey (BLS, 2010c).

FIGURE 1–4
Number of Employees per Security Officer by Industry Sector

Source: Security magazine (McCourt, 2009); via Strom, K., Berzofsky, Shook-Sa, Barrick, Daye, Horstmann, and Kinsey (2010). The Private Security Industry: A Review of the Definitions, Available Data Sources, and Paths Moving Forward. Literature Review and Secondary Data Analysis, Bureau of Justice Statistics.

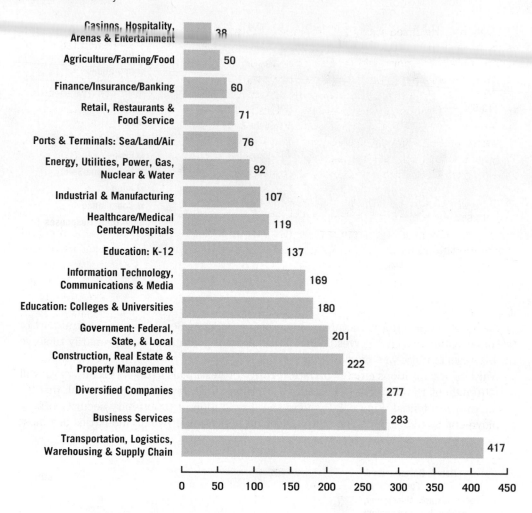

likely to have their own security departments, but not necessarily the most security (i.e., the contract security officers used by these industries are not accounted for in the distribution). A recent study for the Bureau of Justice Statistics found security guards represented nearly half of the services provided by security firms; with between 11,000 and 15,000 private security companies employing more than 1 million guards in the United States.[104]

In Fortune 1000 companies, the categories of organizations responding to a survey about employing security professionals provided a glimpse of the diversity of industries and organizations in which security is used. The largest groups and their proportion relative to the population are as follows: manufacturing (30%), finance and insurance (12%), health care (8%), transportation and warehousing (8%), rental and leasing (8%), information (5%), utilities (5%), and real estate and retail trade (3%).[105]

In addition to knowing the distribution of proprietary security officers, it is also useful to know the concentration of security officers within an industry.[106] Figure 1–4 shows the number of security officers per total employees in an industry sector. This figure is based on all security officers (i.e., contract and proprietary security officers) used by companies in an industry.[107]

Private Security and Public Space

Private security forces operate primarily in areas of private property to which the public law enforcement do not have routine access. Because of this, their growth has meant that surveillance by security forces has been extended into private areas that were previously immune from organized scrutiny.[108] These sections of private property have come to include areas, which can only be regarded as public places, as they are routinely frequented by the general public with permission of and invited by their private owners.

The line between public and private property and who is responsible for law enforcement in public and private space is becoming blurred. More and more venues and locations are considered "mass private property."[109] This term describes specific areas within shopping malls, college campuses, and public housing developments, as an example.[110]

These often include large tracts of privately owned space that are publicly accessible. They have traditionally not been patrolled or secured by public law enforcement. They often include facilities that are owned privately but offer regular public access.

Private Security and Law Enforcement

Private security cannot operate independent of public law enforcement. Interaction and cooperation between law enforcement and security professionals is required, as private security professionals are often unarmed and need law enforcement backup when arrests need to be made.[111] Cooperation between law enforcement and private security professionals takes place on a daily basis, most often when security professionals are responding to incidents and alarms.[112] With continued cooperation between public policing and private security companies, the use of private security will serve to increase security for all sections of society.

During the last decade of the 20th century, law enforcement has increasingly questioned their role in the security of the community. This was attributable to growing doubts about the effectiveness of traditional strategies in safeguarding the public from crime.[113] The central question underlying law enforcement deployment strategy was then and is now whether they can become more effective in actually preventing crime.[114] During this same time, private security continued to grow, and has become both an alternative and complement to traditional policing.

Agency Cooperation

Public law enforcement and private security agencies often establish cooperative relationships.[115] This type of cooperation often blurs the lines between the public and private sectors. A U.S. Department of Justice study found that law enforcement officers and private security professionals might share information about events in a particular area or about wanted persons who frequent such premises.[116]

The world is not divided between privately owned space used solely by its owners and public streets and property used by the general public any more. By blurring the distinction between the public and the private, mass private property limits government responsibility for security. It constricts government efforts at preventive policing to clearly public venues. Bayley and Shearing observed that preventive security in mass private property has become the responsibility of private security professionals.[117]

Despite the differences between private security and public law enforcement, their missions are often complementary and closely related. What appears to legally distinguish private security professionals from public law enforcement is the purposes for which they (private security professionals) are licensed and their method of compensation.[118] In addition, security professionals must be proactive in order to do their jobs, while the process of citizen complaint and police dispatch notification depicts the reactive role of most law enforcement.

That is not surprising, as security expert E. J. Criscuoli found: the security professional's goal is crime prevention, whereas law enforcement focuses primarily on investigating crimes and arresting criminals.[119] In most instances, security is not a legislative requirement. Safety is regulated, but not security. Trucks with millions of dollars in cargo are not required by the government to be locked. The decision to lock and secure the property is a business decision, made by the leadership of the organization, and a certain level of risk is acceptable. Most law enforcement officers consider this to be counterintuitive.

▲ A FEMA official surveys flooding damage in Minot, North Dakota. What is the role of FEMA?

Source: U.S. Federal Emergency Management Agency (FEMA), http://www.dhs.gov/photo/ surveying-flooding-damage-minot-fema

Overcoming Obstacles to Cooperation

The relationship between private security professionals and public law enforcement has been strained because private security professionals often fail to report crimes that happen in their organization or on the organization's private property. Some criminal activities, especially those involving minor crimes committed by an employee or customer, may not be reported to law enforcement by security professionals.[120] The reasons are numerous and include a desire to keep such activity private or a decision to avoid the cost of a proceeding through the criminal justice system. Many businesses consider termination of an employee or a reimbursement from a customer as the completion of what amounts to a private justice system. Policies like this often limit the amount of information available to law enforcement officers, and a high number of crimes and criminals could go unreported. In the private sector, relatively few rules and regulations guide one's conduct, whereas in public law enforcement, most actions are taken as a result of laws, codes of conduct, and regulations. In that sense, law enforcement can be considered more strictly regulated than private security can.[121]

As it stands, the public–private security relationship is self-regulated. First, there are no official laws or policies defining their relationships with each other. Second, there is a considerable range of attitudes on the part of individuals, particularly among public law enforcement officers, regarding private security professionals.[122] Some law enforcement officers tend to look at private security professionals as unqualified persons who could be mistaken for law enforcement officers.[123] Building a solid relationship with law enforcement officers is critical for the security professional. Security professionals must demonstrate professional competence and communicate an accurate picture of the security profession to overcome long-standing negative stereotypes.[124]

The Effect of Homeland Security and Emergency Management

The terrorist attacks of 9/11, along with recent natural disasters like hurricanes and tornadoes have further highlighted the need for professionals to coordinate more effectively across the private and public security sectors. This is especially important because private industry controls and protects most of the nation's critical infrastructure, which we will examine in more depth later.[125] Public law enforcement has made a lot of progress in obtaining terror-related information, but they have been reluctant to share this information with private industry for a number of reasons. The primary focus of law enforcement is on building a legal case related to a crime. Evidence is handled in a prescribed manner, and procedures must be followed precisely to ensure the case will be prosecutable. Because of their mission focus, intelligence agencies often collect information without concern for arrest and prosecution, and the evidence they collect is often not admissible in a U.S. court. As a result, law enforcement professionals have been reluctant to use intelligence information because of the potential of it being challenged in court and thereby jeopardizing a case.[126] Law enforcement may be reluctant to share information with security professionals for similar reasons. The danger of information being inadvertently released is a valid concern, as is the possibility that the control over such intelligence may not be as stringent after it is disseminated to additional security organizations. Private corporations have complained that law enforcement does not provide timely threat information, and some fear that information they give to law enforcement may end up being freely disseminated to the public.[127] The Department of Homeland Security (DHS) has recommended that public law enforcement and private security establish and maintain cooperative agreements to address homeland security needs.[128]

professional

THINK ABOUT IT

Why is professionalism important in the provision of security services?

The U.S. Bureau of Justice Assistance reported that in recent years, both police departments and private security have paid greater attention to the need for collaboration, information sharing, and partnership. The legal powers and training of law enforcement officers combined with the size, resources, and technical expertise of private security can create a successful relationship for the Federal Emergency Management Agency (FEMA) and other emergency response efforts.[129] In 2000, the Department of Justice reported that more than 60 private security–policing partnership programs were in operation. In the 2009 Operation Partnership report, the Law Enforcement–Private Security Consortium reported that there were more than 450 established private security–law enforcement partnerships. The consortium suggests that the success of these partnerships hinges on several key factors, including:[130]

- A compelling mission to keep members interested and attract new members.
- External support of models for formation.
- Strong, active founders, leaders, and facilitators.
- Regular communication (meetings, trainings, newsletters, email, websites, etc.).
- Established methods to sustain structure and sufficient resources.

Additionally, these partnerships must be nurtured. They cannot simply be started and expected to continue and grow under their own power. The common reasons for failure are:[131]

- Joint problems that do not get addressed or solved.
- Supporting leaders lose interest.
- The founders or coordinators are reassigned or retire.
- Personalities clash or egos get too big.
- Funding is inadequate.
- The partnership lacks support staff to carry out or communicate its activities.
- Meetings bore participants by failing to bring in interesting speakers or conduct meaningful activities.

Volunteers in Security

The security industry has also expanded as communities have tested a model that provides security using volunteered resources and people. Today community crime prevention efforts are seen everywhere, with citizen patrols, neighborhood watches, crime-prevention associations, and advisory councils. Like private security, the public acceptability of volunteer security has been changed.[132] While once it was thought of as vigilantism, security using volunteered resources and people is often popular with the public and actively encouraged by the police.[133] Students can participate in these activities on a regular or temporary committed basis. Scheduled times to accompany volunteers can be chosen, like a ride-along with the local police department, or perhaps even an internship, depending on the size of the organization. Students can also volunteer to be a member of the organization without a direct academic tie or benefit.

Neighborhood Watch

Neither public law enforcement nor private security is able to detect all crimes at all times. One of the solutions to this is the **neighborhood watch** program, where citizen volunteers actively identify and report signs of criminal activity to make their neighborhoods safer and improve the quality of life. According to USAonWatch.org, neighborhood watch is a crime prevention program that teaches citizens how to help themselves by identifying and reporting suspicious activity in their neighborhoods. Not only does neighborhood watch allow citizens to help in the fight against crime, it is also an opportunity for community members to get to know each other better while they are serving the community, as they assist their neighbors.[134]

neighborhood watch
An effort by citizen volunteers to actively identify and report signs of criminal activity to make their neighborhoods safer and to improve their quality of life.

The focus of the program is on observation and awareness as a means of preventing crime, and placing visible signs of the program on street signs, in window decals, and at community block parties and service projects.[135]

Stand Your Ground

4   Explain stand your ground laws.

In a number of jurisdictions, private citizens are empowered in their decision to use force by so-called <u>stand your ground</u> laws. Based on what is known as the castle doctrine, that is, every man's home is his castle, which he has a right to defend, the law generally designates a person's home, business, workplace, car, or another place they legally occupy as a place in which that person has certain protections and immunities. According to Post and Kingsbury, those protections permit a person to defend those areas with deadly force without fear of prosecution.[136] The U.S. version of this doctrine comes from English Common Law, which provided an unlicensed privilege of bearing arms for self-protection, not unlike the Second Amendment to the U.S. Constitution. Many U.S. states have such a law, as do several countries, including England, Israel, Italy, and Australia.[137] Some stand your ground laws require law enforcement to show specific evidence to refute a self-defense claim so they can arrest someone claiming self-defense.

Stand your ground laws became more familiar to people after a neighborhood watch volunteer George Zimmerman encountered a young man named Trayvon Martin, whom he shot dead during an altercation and later claimed self-defense.[138] This case is discussed in the accompanying Spotlight box.

stand your ground
Laws that grant people the right to defend themselves with reasonable or even deadly force if they are threatened, without making any attempt to flee or call for help. They are based on what is known as the castle doctrine, that is, every man's home is his castle—a principle of common law that allowed residents to defend themselves with deadly force if an intruder entered their home without invitation. Stand your ground laws typically extend the castle doctrine beyond the home or residence.

Spotlight
Trayvon Martin and George Zimmerman

Trayvon Martin was shot on February 26, 2012, as he returned home one evening from a 7-Eleven, walking in a gated community in Sanford, Florida, where he and his father were guests. George Zimmerman, the founder of the local neighborhood watch, called 911 and reported that Martin looked like "a real suspicious guy." The local police and prosecutors did not immediately arrest and charge Zimmerman, saying that Florida's self-defense law could make it difficult to prove a criminal case against him, according to the *New York Times*.[1]

Based upon the undisputed evidence, Martin was unarmed, carrying Skittles and an iced tea. Zimmerman called the local police and indicated that the individual was "just walking around looking about" and "looks like he's up to no good or he's on drugs or something." Zimmerman then reported that Martin was staring and coming toward him, then running "down toward the other entrance of the neighborhood." The dispatcher asked Zimmerman if he was in pursuit and Zimmerman responded that he was. The dispatcher replied, "We don't need you to do that," to which Zimmerman answered, "OK." Four minutes after Zimmerman ended his conversation with the police dispatcher, Martin was dead and Zimmerman admitted to killing him.[2] Zimmerman said he shot Martin in self-defense after Martin knocked him to the ground, punched him, and slammed his head repeatedly against the sidewalk.[3]

In the weeks after George Zimmerman killed Martin, amidst a growing public outcry across the nation, the Department of Justice opened an investigation into the killing; the Sanford police chief temporarily stepped down; the state attorney recused himself; and the governor appointed a special prosecutor. The national attention even prompted President Barack Obama to comment, calling the incident a "tragedy" and stating, now notoriously, "If I had a son, he'd look like Trayvon."[4] Zimmerman was found not guilty of second-degree murder and manslaughter by a jury, which deliberated 16 hours and 20 minutes over two days.[5]

---

[1] L. Alvarez and M. Cooper, "Prosecutor Files Charge of 2nd-Degree Murder in Shooting of Martin," The New York Times, April 11, 2012, http://www.nytimes.com/2012/04/12/us/zimmerman-to-be-charged-in-trayvon-martin-shooting.html

[2] L. S. Richardson and P. A. Goff, "Self-defense and the Suspicion Heuristic," *Iowa Law Review* Vol. 98, No. 1 (November 2012), p. 293.

[3] L. Alvarez and C. Buckley, "Zimmerman Is Acquitted in Trayvon Martin Killing," *The New York Times*, July 13, 2013, http://www.nytimes.com/2013/07/14/us/george-zimmerman-verdict-trayvon-martin.html?pagewanted=all&_r=0

[4] H. C. Aizenman, "Pretrial Publicity in a Post-Trayvon Martin World," *Criminal Justice*, Vol. 27, No. 3 (Fall 2012), p. 12.

[5] L. Alvarez and C. Buckley, "Zimmerman Is Acquitted."

Challenges in the Security Field

5   Provide an overview of challenges in the security field.

In the past few years, governments have gone beyond passive acceptance to active encouragement of commercial private security. There seems to be a general recognition that crime and the threat to public safety are too complex to be dealt with solely by public law enforcement agencies, and that the profit motive guiding private security should not be seen as a negative feature.[139]

According to Bayley and Shearing, since the early 1960s, when the contemporary rebirth of private security began, the private security sector has been growing faster than the public sector. Businesses and commercial firms are not the only customers for private security, and private security professionals are often used to guard government buildings, including some police stations.[140]

One of the most recent challenges across the security industry focuses on crisis and emergency management (EM). This focus includes preparation for and response to catastrophic events, whether from forces of nature or human action or inaction.[141] These events include droughts, famines, floods, fires, explosions, pandemics, volcanic eruptions, earthquakes, tsunamis, and other disasters. When a disaster or other emergency occurs, many decisions must be made while the event is still unfolding. Although it is impossible to predict or prevent all possible events, having a strategy to do so makes organizations more likely to survive the results. This function is increasingly becoming the responsibility of the security professional, and requires coordination with a different set of outside agencies and providers. But crisis management is not at the top of the list of contemporary security challenges.

Recent surveys showed that the threat of cyber and communications security was the greatest security concern now facing Fortune 1000 companies. This was followed by workplace violence; business continuity planning, including organizational resilience, were also critical issues (see Figure 1–5).[142]

Unethical business conduct, business espionage/theft of trade secrets, and global supply-chain security are among the areas that may be considered least familiar to the security student. Unethical business conduct can negatively impact an organization by damaging credibility, brand, and reputation, as well as potentially causing significant loss of customers and business failure. Unethical business conduct can be found in financial misconduct, including bribery, fraud, tax evasion, and price fixing; mistreating employees, including the use of child labor, sweat shops, and illegal practices; and misrepresentation—to include false marketing, falsified data on corporate reports, conflicts of interest, and lying for financial gain.[143]

1. Cyber/communications security
2. Workplace violence prevention/response
3. Business continuity planning/organizational resilience
4. Employee selection/screening
5. Property crime
6. General employee theft
7. Crisis management and response
8. Unethical business conduct
9. Litigation: inadequate security
10. Identity theft
11. Intellectual property/brand protection/product counterfeiting
12. Fraud/white-collar crime
13. Workplace substance abuse
14. Environmental/social: robberies
15. Crisis management and response: terrorism
16. Business espionage/theft of trade secrets
17. Litigation: negligent hiring/supervision
18. Executive protection
19. Bombings/bomb threats
20. Global supply chain security
21. Insurance/workers' compensation fraud
22. Environmental/social: pandemic
23. Labor unrest
24. Crisis management and response: kidnapping/extortion

FIGURE 1–5
Top Security Concerns for Fortune 1000 Executives
Source: D. Walker, L. Glovka, B. Greenawalt, and J. McNulty, eds. (2014). *"Top Security Threats and Management Issues Facing Corporate America: 2012 Survey of Fortune 1000 Companies,"* Securitas Security Services USA, Inc.

Business espionage and the theft of trade secrets is predominantly conducted from cyberspace. The main objective with business-related cyber penetrations is the desire to get sensitive business information. Business espionage is one of the most underreported security threats, and it is one of the least understood. Business espionage is closely linked to the cyber security threat, especially in terms of the potential consequences and risk to the business enterprise.[144]

According to the ASIS Foundation, the global supply chain is a worldwide network of transportation, postal, and shipping pathways, assets, and infrastructures used to move goods from the point of manufacture to the end consumer. The supporting communications infrastructure and systems are included in the global supply chain. Securing the global supply chain is vital to a country's national security and economic prosperity.[145] Many of these areas are included in the analysis for this textbook, and are similar to the priorities identified in the past by security professionals.[146]

Professional Organizations

As we addressed earlier, a *profession* requires advanced training, qualification criteria, and widespread academic acceptance; members of the profession with business-related skills should have the ability to communicate their message in executive boardrooms. Some of these skills can be learned on the job, but most can be honed only by participating in professional organizations. As with other professions, the security field has many such professional organizations, including those that follow.

ASIS International began in 1955 as the American Society for Industrial Security. The organization's name was changed in 2002 to ASIS International to reflect their international focus, with members in more than 125 countries. ASIS began work on a professional certification program in the early 1970s.[147] To provide a professional framework for security education, ASIS offers three certification programs:[148]

1. Certified Protection Professional (In the United Kingdom, CPP is part of the path for attainment of the Chartered Security Professional).
2. Professional Certified Investigator (PCI) designation
3. Physical Security Professional (PSP) designation

The *Association of Certified Background Investigators (ACBI)* includes contract background investigators who conduct national security background investigations for agencies of the U.S. government. ACBI members gain access to contract opportunities, can receive formal and informal training and education programs, and have a forum for information sharing.[149]

The *Association of Certified Fraud Specialists (ACFS)* is an educational organization providing learning and networking opportunities to law enforcement, attorneys, public- and private-sector investigators, auditors, and other risk management professionals. The ACFS administers the Certified Fraud Specialist (CFS) designation.[150]

The *Associated Locksmiths of America (ALOA)* offers services, programs, products and money-saving opportunities to help grow and develop business. The organization offers free listings at findalocksmith.com to qualified industry professionals, and assigns the Proficiency Program (PRP) designation, an international certification in premises security.[151]

The *Electronic Security Association (ESA)* is the largest U.S. professional trade association, representing the electronic life safety, security, and integrated systems industry. ESA provides government advocacy and delivers timely information and professional development. The association supports new technology and applications and proactively promotes the industry through consumer awareness activities. Member companies specialize in a wide variety of services to both commercial and residential consumers in five industry components: sales, manufacturing, installation, service, and monitoring.[152]

The *Institute for Professional Certification & Accreditation (IPCA)* is a societal membership organization dedicated to the assurance of quality certification and education in Loss Prevention/Asset Protection, Retail Security and Security Services. IPCA auditors evaluate both professional and program certifications and assure that they meet standards in partnership with professional associations and industry.[153]

The *International Anti-Counterfeiting Coalition Inc. (IACC)* combats product counterfeiting and piracy. The organization is made up of members from a cross section of business and industry. The IACC provides training for domestic and foreign law enforcement officials, provides input on intellectual property enforcement laws and regulations in the United States and abroad, and participates in regional and international programs to improve intellectual property enforcement standards. They promote laws, regulations, and directives to combat counterfeiting and piracy.[154]

The *International Association for Healthcare Security and Safety (IAHSS)* is dedicated to professionals that manage and direct security and safety programs in health care institutions. IAHSS members come from the security, law enforcement, and safety professions. The organization combines public safety officer training with staff training, policies, and technology to achieve the most secure hospital environments possible. They also partner with government agencies and other organizations representing risk managers, emergency managers, engineers, architects, nurses, doctors, and other health care stakeholders to further patient security and safety.[155]

The *International Association of Professional Security Consultants, Inc. (IAPSC)* serves to establish and maintain the highest industry standards for professionalism and ethical conduct. Each IAPSC security consultant is a professional with a specific area of expertise. IAPSC provides member security association consultants and prospective clients with information to find a security consultant.[156]

The *International Foundation for Protection Officers (IFPO)* is dedicated to providing meaningful, cost effective education for security professionals and students. They believe that education is an essential part of professional development for those charged with protecting others. The Foundation serves individuals, security service firms, and organizations that have their own security professionals. Members and students benefit from the recognition and professional standing that IFPO certification conveys. The IFPO awards certificates for[157]

- CPO—Certified Protection Officers
- CSSM—Certified Security Supervision and Management
- CPOI—Certified Protection Officer Instructors

The *International Professional Security Association (IPSA)* was formed to ensure professionalism in the management of security operations. IPSA is an organization established for individuals and companies working in security and associated roles.[158]

The *Loss Prevention Foundation (LPF)* is a not-for-profit, world leader in educating and certifying retail loss prevention and asset protection professionals. LPF's mission is to advance the retail loss prevention and asset protection profession by providing relevant, convenient and challenging educational resources.[159]

The *National Association of School Safety and Law Enforcement Officers (NASSLEO)* provides professional information, training, and other resources to school districts, charter schools, private educational institutions, and law enforcement agencies. NASSLEO works to make schools safe for students and staff. The organization's membership comprises educators, law enforcement and security directors and officers, as well as other professionals with an interest in protecting students, staff, and physical assets.[160]

The *National Association of Security Companies (NASCO)* promotes standards and professionalism for private security officers and professionals working within the contract security industry. The organization advocates raising standards at all levels for the licensing of private security firms and the registration, screening, and training of security officers. NASCO tries to increase public awareness of the important role and function of private security as a vital complement to public law enforcement, and publicize the valuable services.[161]

The *Operations Security Professional's Association (OSPA)* is dedicated to improving awareness of operations security procedures and building cohesion among the operations security (OPSEC) community. OSPA members work together toward creating and sharing information on subjects, such as information security, OPSEC briefings, security briefings, and OPSEC program management. OSPA also offers the OPSEC Academy, which provides public OPSEC courses, courses for members, and custom coursework.[162]

The *Security Industry Association (SIA)* advocates pro-industry policies and legislation, produces global market research, creates open-industry standards that enable integration, advances industry professionalism through education and training, and works to open global market opportunities. The SIA works in emerging markets, such as Brazil, Russia, India, and China, and is the sole sponsor of the International Security Conference (ISC) Expos, the world's largest security trade shows and conferences.[163]

The *U.S. Association of Private Investigators (USAPI)* offers membership to all "professional investigators." Any individual who is employed in the capacity of a professional investigator can join, though non sworn employees must have been employed for at least one year and be 21 years old. USAPI has a student category for students interested in learning more about the investigative profession.[164]

Summary

- **Identify and describe an example of security practices throughout history such as the Bow Street Runners.**
  - The Bow Street Runners were groups of residents who prevented crime by patrolling the streets and chasing down criminals, evolving into the first detective agency in England.
  - Tens and Hundreds represented an early form of what we now know as neighborhood watch. Each community (tun) was divided into groups of ten families, each called a tithing. The tithings were also arranged in groups of tens, so each group of 100 families elected their own chief.
  - Thief takers were policelike forces that operated much like the military. Their duty was to capture and punish criminals, and the king paid them for every criminal arrested.
  - Watch and Ward was a legislated program in which individual citizens were required to contribute to community safety by conducting night patrol to support the local constable's efforts to provide security.
- **Identify the components of a profession and what it means to be a professional.**
  - A profession is a vocation or occupation requiring advanced training and usually involves mental rather than manual work. A security professional is one who holds himself or herself and his or her role in security in high regard.
- **Define private security.**
  - Security is the private-sector practice, by individuals and organizations, of providing security-related means or services, to protect and preserve persons, property, interests, information, and environments to allow for the continued conduct of needed activities within the organization or society, without disruption from varied adversaries or hazards, for compensation.
- **Explain stand your ground laws.**
  - Stand your ground, also referred to as the castle doctrine, generally designates a person's home, business, workplace, car, or another place they legally occupy as a place in which that person has certain protections and immunities. People are allowed to defend themselves with force if they feel threatened to defend against an intruder without legal responsibility or threat of prosecution for the consequences of the force used.

- **Provide an overview of challenges in the security field.**
  - Contemporary challenges in the security field include the relatively recent focus on crisis and emergency management. The threat of cyber and communications security was the greatest security concern for Fortune 1000 companies followed by workplace violence, and business continuity planning. Unethical business conduct, business espionage/theft of trade secrets, and global supply chain security are other areas of concern for security professionals.

KEY TERMS

bow street runners **4**	profession **12**	tens and hundreds **3**
industrial revolution **4**	shire **3**	thief takers **4**
neighborhood watch **19**	shire reeve **3**	watch system **4**
private security **11**	stand your ground **20**	

REVIEW QUESTIONS

1. Which of the historical security practices is most like the practice of security with which you are familiar?
2. Explain the criteria for determining whether security is a profession. Where is the security field in that process?
3. What is your current personal definition of security?
4. How do the stand your ground laws relate to your own definition of security?
5. Which of the challenges in the security field are the most troublesome for you?

PRACTICAL APPLICATION

1. Examine the various criteria you see as important and devise your own definition of security. Take a moment now to write down what you consider to be the working definition for security. As you continue through the text, see how your definition changes.
2. Create a timeline depicting the major developments in the history of security. In addition to the events covered in the textbook, try to identify how the security-related developments related to other events in history.
3. Choose the top twenty historical events that shaped the security profession of today. Research both the Internet and an online research database to see what more you can learn about the events.
4. Research the early historical figures in the security industry. Identify someone in the history of security and create a profile of that person from available biographical data. Imagine you were in a business partnership with that person, and list the changes your skills, insight, or vision would allow you to make in the security field because of your partnership. Feel free to exaggerate.
5. In addition to the professional security associations listed in the chapter, search for others in your country and local area. If you qualify, consider joining, or at least reaching out to a member to learn more about the security profession. Consider volunteering to work with the organization.
6. Examine the impact of conflict on the security profession. Wars and related events with global impact have an effect on the security industry. After the impact of September 11, 2001, there was increased interest in protecting industrial and manufacturing facilities, both in Canada and the United States. Examine the text and your resources and create a list of ten changes in the security field that have happened as a result of such conflicts, and ten additional things that could change given the right circumstances.

Theoretical Foundations of Security

CHAPTER

2

Learning Objectives

After reading this chapter, you should be able to:

1. Define theories of crime for the purposes used by security professionals. **28**

2. Examine and differentiate between general and specific deterrence. **34**

3. Distinguish diffusion of benefits and displacement. **37**

Introduction

Robbers held the wife and children of a diamond company sales manager hostage at his home in Antwerp, Belgium, and ordered him to empty the diamond safe at his office and deliver the gems to a drop-off point. In a related crime, masked robbers sprayed automatic gunfire at a Brink's armored truck as it transported diamonds along the highway. Elsewhere in Antwerp, gunmen disguised as police or security guards held hostage the family of a partner at a diamond firm, and forced him to hand over diamonds from the vault in his office. No arrests have been made in at least six such well-organized attacks on Antwerp's diamond district in a five-year period.[1] This lack of arrests can be blamed on many things, including the possible failure of police to understand the motivation of the people who commit crime, the inability of those tasked with security to protect the people involved and the places where the crimes were committed, or missed opportunities to prevent or deter the crimes.

If you are a fan of police and detective television shows, you have observed fictional cops searching for criminal *motivation*, asking why the particular crime was committed at that precise moment. The idea of criminal motivation applies only to specific instances of law violations (i.e., he did it because he or she needed money to pay off a debt). In contrast, **theories** of crime are *explanations of causation* that apply to all people and all crimes. In so doing, criminological theories offer perspectives on why some people turn to crime while others, given the same set of circumstances, remain law abiding. For example, a theory might suggest that people commit crime because they lack self-control. Given the opportunity to commit crime, a person lacking in self-control will engage in an illegal act while another, who can better manage his or her behavior, will hold back. This theory would then apply to such varied behaviors as a teenage boy who decides to join a gang as well as a stock broker who engages in securities fraud, and a middle-class woman who shoplifts: they all lack self-control.

Theories are designed to explain a significant association between an underlying cause and a predicted effect. For example, one criminological theory suggests that people commit crime because they are economically disadvantaged (i.e., without financial resources, or poor) and are forced to live in disorganized, crime-ridden neighborhoods. We know that not everyone who is poor steals or commits crime and that some wealthy people, even celebrities, steal when they can clearly afford to purchase the goods legitimately. A list of celebrity shoplifters includes Lindsay Lohan, Winona Ryder, and Britney Spears, as well as Florida State quarterback and Heisman Trophy winner Jameis Winston, who was cited for stealing crab legs from a local supermarket.[2,3] However, the theory is not invalid just because some poor people are honest and some wealthy ones offend. A theory suggesting that poverty is a cause of crime would be considered valid if significantly more indigent folks are involved in crime, per capita, than their more well-off peers. Theories do not have to be absolute, but they must be significant. Put it this way: Not all smokers get cancer, and not all nonsmokers remain cancer free. However, we can say that the theory that smoking causes cancer is valid if a significantly greater proportion of smokers than nonsmokers become cancer stricken.

theories

Designed to explain a significant association between an underlying cause and a predicted effect. Theories do not have to be absolute, but they must be significant.

▲ Actress Lindsay Lohan. In 2011, Lohan pled no contest to a misdemeanor shoplifting charge and was ordered to serve 120 days in jail. Why do wealthy celebrities steal when they can afford to buy anything they desire? Does this indicate that crime has a psychological component?

Source: Pool, Supplied by PacificCoastNe/Newscom

THINK ABOUT IT

What is the value of theoretical understandings of human behavior? How do such understandings apply to the study of security?

Theory also guides practice. If we know why people commit crime then it would be possible to devise strategies that prevent it from occurring. For example, if people commit crime because they are psychologically damaged, then ordering counseling and treatment might be helpful. But it would be futile to create a jobs program for offenders if the motivation for their crimes was psychological.

These theories are offered to provide a platform on which to examine the actions, motivations, and inspirations for security professionals and their adversaries. The theories serve to provide a foundation with which to understand the actions and intentions of adversaries from many perspectives, and explain the troubles associated with the social integration of some adversaries into a law-abiding society. Some of the theories may make sense to the reader, and some may not. The theories presented here are by no means all inclusive. Additionally, they are not classified as they are in many security and criminal justice or criminology textbooks. They are simply presented for consideration by the reader in an attempt to expose present and future security professionals to a variety of theories. As a result, many traditional theories have been omitted, especially those related to life events that security professionals cannot affect. The absence of these theories was in no way intended to be dismissive of their validity or application in other contexts.

We have divided this chapter into three sections. The first will focus on why people commit crime in the first place. The second will examine how the different visions of crime causation guide the protection of people and places. In the third section we will discuss how theory shapes the way we stop crime, by either preventing its occurrence or deterring wrongdoers from committing crimes in the first place. We will also consider crime prevention through environmental design (CPTED) and other theories related to places.

Why Do People Commit Crime?

1 Define theories of crime for the purposes used by security professionals.

Most criminological theories focus on what makes people "criminal." So, we might ask, why do some people become security risks? And why are others law abiding? Suspected causes include improper child-rearing, genetic makeup, and psychological or social processes.[4] We further divide these into explanations of crime that focus on the individual, such as psychological makeup, and those that focus on society, such as living in a poverty-ridden area.

Focus on the Individual

One view of why people commit crime focuses on the individual. We know that there are people who are different from the rest of us. Some are greedy and willing to cut corners to get ahead, others are damaged biologically and psychologically. What are some of the most important individual views of crime?

It's a Rational Choice

rational choice
A view of crime causation based on the notion that law violators are reasoning people who make decisions by weighing the costs and the benefits of crime before they decide whether to violate the law. Potential criminals try to maximize the positive outcomes (gains) and minimize the negative outcomes (losses). People may choose to commit crime if they believe the risk of getting caught is low, the threat of being punished minimal, and that they can beat the legal system with a good lawyer.

Let's face it, not all of us are kind, considerate, and caring. There are people out there who are greedy and mean. If they want something they will steal it, if they are angry with you they will beat you up. If they commit crime it's because they want to; they are making a rational choice to commit crime.

According to this <u>rational choice</u> view of crime, law violators are reasoning people who make decisions by weighing the costs and the benefits of crime before they decide whether to violate the law; they make a rational choice. Potential criminals try to maximize the positive outcomes (gains) and minimize the negative outcomes (losses).[5] People may choose to commit crime if they believe the risk of getting caught is low, the threat of being punished is minimal, and that they can beat the legal system with a good lawyer.[6] Even supposedly honest people may risk crime on occasion if they believe they can get away with it and if caught they do not fear the consequences.

The standard decision-making process involves examining the perceived alternatives before deciding on what is the best option: Should you exceed the speed limit because you are late for work or school? What do you consider: the risk is being ticketed for speeding; the reward is making up for lost time by not being late? What goes into the decision making: observing the behavior of drivers in front of us (who are likely to encounter a speed trap before we do), or utilizing a smart radar detector, which uses GPS systems to relay information about police cars hidden by the roadside? Sometimes, however, choices are not fully thought out and/or are based on imperfect information or perceptions.[7] So while the cars ahead may escape detection, you get stopped because the police can catch only one speeder at a time and you lag behind the rest of the pack.

THINK ABOUT IT

According to the Cumulative Prospect Theory (CPT) a person's perception of risk depends on his or her frame of reference.[8] Similarly, overestimating risk (risk-avoidance) or underestimating risk (risk-seeking) depend on an individual's perception. Thus, a poor person is motivated to buy health insurance more than a wealthy person, simply because of his or her respective frames of reference. Similarly, a person "with nothing to lose" is more likely to underestimate the risk of being caught than someone with "a lot to lose." How can such a realization help security professionals perform their jobs?

It's in Your Makeup

Some criminologists believe that people who commit crime are not simply rational decision makers who consider the benefits and consequences before committing crime. Although people who engage in a million-dollar drug deal seem "rational," how do you explain the behavior of a young man who enters a school with a high-powered weapon and begins to shoot children? Can he truly be rational? Some criminologists believe that the key to understanding most criminal behaviors can be found in the offenders' abnormal biological makeup, which makes them aggressive and crime prone.

One suspected biological trait connected to crime is a person's biochemical makeup, ranging from food allergies to hormonal imbalance. People who engage in crime may have improper diets that are heavy in sugar and carbohydrates and deficient in protein and vegetables. Thomas O'Connor, for example, observed that vitamin deficiencies and/or dependencies (as well as food allergies, eating disorders, and cholesterol levels) have been implicated in crime.[9] Vitamin B3 and especially B6 deficiencies and/or dependencies have been found in 70% of criminals as well as in alcoholics and the mentally ill. People exposed to environmental contaminants, such as lead and pollutants, have higher crime rates than the nonexposed. Finally, people with excessive amounts (or deficient amounts) of hormones such as testosterone are believed to be more violent and aggressive than those with normal amounts of these hormones. Testosterone influences both males and females and affects the neocortex area of the brain, increasing arousal level.

Another suspected biological problem that may lead to crime commission is brain damage. Children who suffer minimal brain damage before, during, and after birth are more likely to engage in violence than those with normal brain functioning. There is also some evidence that aggression and violence has a genetic basis and may be inherited. Children whose parents are deviant and criminal are more likely to exhibit those traits themselves than those whose parents are crime free. Of course, this association may be a matter of learning and exposure rather than genetics: so, children growing up with criminal parents may learn a criminal way of life. To test whether there is actually a genetic effect, criminologists have conducted experiments comparing the behavior of identical twins separated at birth and found that if one twin is a criminal, so is the other, a finding that supports a genetic link rather than a learning one.

It's in Your Mind

In addition to biological views, psychological abnormality has been linked to antisocial behaviors. Like biological theory, there are a number of competing psychological views on why people commit crime. According to psychodynamic theory, criminal tendencies are a function of disturbances in early development that lead to mental instability and mood disorders, such as conduct, anxiety, and bipolar (also known as manic-depression) disorder. In extreme cases, psychosis may develop, including schizophrenia, paranoia, or clinical depression. People with these conditions suffer from disturbances of

- Content of thought: delusions, paranoia, being controlled by another
- Perception: hallucinations, especially auditory
- Bizarre behavior

psychodynamic theory
Provides explanations for development, human behavior, and psychopathology. It identifies methods to make predictions about treatment outcome. It emphasizes unconscious motives and desires, and highlights the importance of childhood experiences in shaping personality. Psychodynamic theory suggests that criminal tendencies are a function of disturbances in early human development that lead to mental instability and mood disorders, such as conduct, anxiety and bipolar (also known as manic-depression) disorder.

- Form of thought: loose associations and fragmented thoughts
- Incoherence
- Illogicality
- Affect: flat, blunted, or inappropriate speech
- Impaired emotional responses or detachment
- Apathy

Psychotics are more likely to engage in the most serious forms of violence.

Another psychological view, behaviorism, assumes that people copy behavior that is rewarded and avoid that which is punished. Behaviorists are concerned that children who watch violent TV shows and films and play violent video games may adopt the responses they see rewarded in the media. It was demonstrated that children model the behaviors demonstrated by their parents, older children, celebrities, and others they see as idols.

According to the cognitive approach, some people have problems with learning, perception, and maturity. They misperceive the world and have difficulty processing information. So when a date says "no, don't touch me," they interpret that as meaning "she is playing hard to get" and pursue her more forcefully leading to a sexual assault.

Some psychologists believe that personality development is the key to understanding the criminal mind. They have identified the sociopath-psychopath-antisocial personality. These people lack empathy, are risk takers, egocentric, and lack affect. They need excitement to feel good, are deceitful, and lack remorse. Some have been abused as children, while others are just wired incorrectly. They engage in serious violence throughout their lives.

It's a Lack of Self-Control

One element of the personality that has gotten a lot of recent attention is *impulsivity.* According to the self-control approach, criminal action is the result of a decision or action carried out by *impulsive people who lack self-control.* Those who lack self-control are shortsighted risk takers, selfish in regard to other people's feelings. They have a here-and-now orientation and refuse to work for distant goals because that takes too much effort. Their self-centered behavior leads to unstable marriages and poor employment histories.[10] Not surprisingly, they are also more likely to engage in dangerous behaviors such as drinking, smoking, and reckless driving.[11] Because they like to take risks and have a short-term horizon, these are the people who will enjoy risky, exciting, or thrilling behaviors such as shoplifting, vandalizing property, and engaging in violent acts.

Social Influences

Another view is that criminals are a product of their social world. Their environment, their family life, and their friends influence them. After all, most crime takes places in disorganized, lower-class neighborhoods and not wealthy suburbs.[12] The association cannot be a coincidence. What are some of the social views on crime causation?

It's the Environment

America is a stratified society containing the very rich and very poor with lots of people in between. Wealthy folks live in big houses, in gated communities that supply security personnel to protect the residents. The poorest in the community live in deteriorated, disorganized communities whose main public and private institutions—the family, school, police, social service agencies—have become broken and are unable to exercise social control over residents, both young and old. Because families are under stress, jobs are nonexistent, and social institutions handicapped and ineffective in these communities; disorganized communities become breeding grounds for crime. Police can do little to exert control because gangs and criminal groups often outnumber them. In such an environment children may be more easily lured into a life of crime. After all, the only successful people in the neighborhood appear to be drug dealers, pimps, and thieves.

More than seventy years ago Clifford Shaw and Henry McKay observed that in many communities, the traditions of crime and delinquency have been passed on through the generations in the same way language, roles, and attitudes were transmitted. This is referred to as cultural transmission.[13] In this vacuum, gangs can form and take over the community.

People who live in these deteriorated areas may have big dreams and goals, but do not have the qualifications or connections necessary to attain those goals. This results in what is referred to as *anomie*—a condition that is formed when there is a disjunction between social goals and the legitimate means people have to attain those goals. In an anomic state, people become angry and frustrated and feel strain: they have no hope of achieving what they want through legitimate means.[14] While all desire a nice home, fast car, and bling, not all of the people can achieve those goals through legitimate means.[15]

Because the keys to success—education, jobs, and wealth—are not distributed equally in society, those who find themselves at the bottom may feel that they cannot achieve their dreams through legitimate means. They therefore have a choice: remain conformists and live a life of poverty and deprivation or use innovative means to get ahead, such as burglary, car theft, and drug dealing. Not all people who are disadvantaged become criminals. Some, like retired U.S. Army General Colin Powell or U.S. Supreme Court Justice Sonia Sotomayor, are able to overcome adversity and become examples of success for others. Some drop out of school and live quiet yet unfulfilled lives. Others may turn to drugs or alcohol or become homeless and live on the streets. Others may even join radical groups and plot to destroy their nation or its infrastructure. So according to this vision of crime causation, it's the social forces in poverty-stricken areas that cause some people to turn to a life of crime and not personal choice or biological abnormality.

The environmental view reflects the inability of local government to solve problems and understand the needs of the community. This perspective may find application in civic engagement programs run by industry and organizations, which suggest community empowerment as a solution to a gang problem. By getting involved in the community, organizations can determine, first hand, where assistance is needed, especially regarding areas affecting the organization.

It is How You Are Raised

Though poverty is related to crime, and people growing up in disorganized areas may be lured into gangs and groups, not all residents become criminal. Many do not and instead go to school, get good jobs, and raise families.

So how do people growing up in the most deteriorated areas of the city remain law-abiding citizens? Children growing up in the worst neighborhoods may avoid a life of crime if they are given a proper upbringing and are positively socialized by caring parents, concerned teachers, and loyal friends. According to this view, it's not where you live but how you are raised that shapes your behavioral choices. There are actually two versions of socialization theory: learning view and control view.

Learning View

One prominent version of socialization theory holds that people are either taught to be good citizens or conversely learn to be criminals. Children who are taught that crime pays are the ones most likely to engage in illegal behavior themselves. Criminal behavior is learned in communication with others within intimate personal groups: friends, family, neighbors. The process of learning criminal behavior involves all the mechanisms involved in any other learning process.[16] So when parents tell children to be tough and to fight back, they should not be surprised when children use violence to solve problems.

People also learn **neutralization techniques** that allow them to justify their criminal behavior. Individuals who learn to neutralize the shame of committing crime feel free to engage in their criminal activities without damaging their conscience. Techniques associated with neutralization include a denial of responsibility, a denial of injury, a denial of the victim, condemnation of those condemning the perpetrator, and an appeal to higher loyalties. For example, "I didn't want to do it, but I had to stick by my friends."[17] This theory may find application in the understanding of employee theft, fraud, or sexual harassment.

neutralization techniques
Allow people to justify their criminal behavior. Individuals who learn to neutralize the shame of committing crime feel free to engage in their criminal activities without damaging their conscience. Techniques associated with neutralization include a denial of responsibility, a denial of injury, a denial of the victim, condemnation of those condemning the perpetrator, and an appeal to higher loyalties.

TABLE 2–1
Theories of Crime and Their Control

Focus on Individual	Major Premise	Crime Prevention Techniques	Crimes Best Explained
Rational choice theory	Crime occurs when an individual believes they will benefit from an illegal act and do not fear apprehension and punishment	Increase surveillance, improve security, target hardening, increase punishment, increase likelihood of apprehension	Predatory theft crimes, shoplifting, vandalism
Biological theory	An individual's biochemical, hormonal, and genetic makeup control their behaviors	Improve diet and use medications to control behavior	Irrational violent behavioral outbursts not designed for profit
Psychological theory	An individual's psychological makeup and/or mental abnormality determine his or her behavior choices	Personality testing of employees, individual counseling and group techniques, mood-altering medications	Workplace violence, serial murder and rape, child and domestic abuse, substance abuse
Self-control theory	People who are impulsive and lack self-control are crime prone	Teach proper parenting techniques; counseling programs	Impulsive acts ranging from violent responses to provocation to spontaneous thefts
Focus on Social Causes			
Social disorganization theory	Social control efforts break down in lower class, disorganized areas	Provide economic opportunities, encourage community organizations, fund schools	Gang crimes, drug dealing and trafficking, crimes against local business such as larceny and shoplifting
Social learning theory	Children learn to commit crime and hold deviant values in interaction with parents and peers	Teach proper behavior and values, educational and parenting programs	Crimes that involve learning criminal techniques such as car theft
Social control theory	Children who are not controlled by their ties to society are free to commit crime	Programs that involve children in conventional activities, sports, after-school programs	Youthful misbehavior, cutting school, theft

Control View

control view
Suggests that deviant, criminal, and illegal behavior can be fun, profitable, and beneficial and therefore adolescents must develop the ability to control their behavior lest they get involved in a delinquent way of life. Those who are attached to others, committed to their future, involved in conventional behaviors, and hold positive values and beliefs are the ones most likely to be able to maintain control.

According to the control view, children must be taught to control their behavior. Crime is often pleasant and brings quick rewards. Why wait to get a car when you can just steal the one you want? For most people, buying a car means getting a job, saving money, working long hours, and sacrificing other purchases. A criminal can obtain what he wants in a few minutes without much labor. So why don't we all commit crimes to get what we want? Most of us have been taught to control our behavior. We have developed a bond to society that would be broken if we became criminals. Our parents would be upset and our friends would avoid contact with us. Those of us who have strong attachments to others, who care about our future, and are involved in conventional activities such as work and school, either don't have the time for crime or are too afraid to take the risk.[18]

The various theories of crime, their main premise, suggested control techniques and typical crimes they explain are set out in Table 2–1.

Multiple Causes/Multiple Crimes

These different theories of crime tell us there is no single view that can explain all forms of criminal activity. People may commit crime for a variety of reasons. The reason why someone engages in stock fraud may be quite different from why someone joins a gang or vandalizes a store. There are many different types of crime so it should come as no surprise that it might have multiple causes. While it is convenient to believe that stock frauds, shoplifters, and serial killers all share similar motives, such as financial gain, a more analytical approach would consider the notion that there are alternative causes to criminal behavior (such as the ones mentioned earlier).

routine activity theory
Suggests that crime has been part of the human experience for quite some time. Crimes are events that people will engage in for a variety of reasons: some people are impulsive, some are driven by need, others are psychologically disturbed while still others choose to victimize others because they are selfish and greedy.

Considering the multiple sources of criminal motivation, it may be realistic to view crime as a routine activity, part of the human experience for quite some time.[19] Crime has been with us since the beginning of time, and it is unlikely to stop anytime soon. According to routine activity, crimes are events that people will engage in for a variety of reasons: they may be impulsive, driven by need, or psychologically disturbed, while others choose to victimize simply out of greed and selfishness. There are many different motivations for crime. As such, because people commit crime for lots of different reasons, a criminal event is said to occur when:[20]

- A motivated offender
- Spots a tempting target
- And there are no guardians present to prevent the offender from taking advantage of the situation.

According to this routine activity view, if a motivated offender (e.g., a drug-addicted gang member) sees someone with a valuable object (e.g., iPad, iPhone, Rolex watch), and there is no guardian around (e.g., police, security personnel), the offender will be highly likely to commit a crime. If, on the other hand, security guards are present and electronic tagging protects the merchandise, even the most motivated offender will forego committing the crime, no matter how valuable the target. Crime will occur when these factors intersect and the conditions are right.

The Crime Triangle

The crime triangle is a way of conceptualizing routine activities. It assumes the presence of a likely offender, makes no distinction between a human victim and an inanimate target, and defines a capable guardian as either a human actor or a security device. The Center for Problem-Oriented Policing advised that the use of this formulation led to the original problem analysis triangle with the three sides representing the offender, the target, and the location or place, found in the inner triangle (Figure 2–1).[21]

The outer triangle identifies controllers for each of the elements in the inner triangle. For the *target* (or victim), this is the capable guardian of routine activity theory, whether it is people protecting themselves and their property, or the public police or private security. The *offender* is controlled by a handler, who knows the offender well and is in a position to exert some control over his or her actions, possibly a parent, other close family member, teachers, friends, spouses, or probation or parole officer. For the *place*, the manager is in control. This position is held by the owner or designee, with responsibility for controlling behavior in the specific location. That could be a bus driver or teacher in a school, bar owners in drinking establishments, landlords in rental housing, or flight attendants on commercial airliners.

When crime occurs, all inner elements of the triangle are present and all outer elements are weak or absent. If potential offenders are constantly present, for example, but crimes occur only when guardians are absent, then rescheduling the guardians might be a useful solution.[22] An example is the approach to crime suppression that involves *hot spots*, where police focus on specific areas, times, or other indicators that crime is likely to occur, to increase the chances of thwarting crime.

THINK ABOUT IT

What is the crime triangle? How can it be used in creating loss prevention strategies?

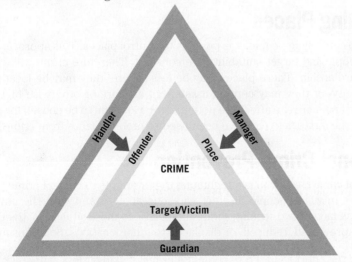

FIGURE 2–1
The Crime Triangle
Source: "The Crime Triangle", Center for Problem Oriented Policing, http://www.popcenter.org/learning/60steps/index.cfm?stepnum=8

Controlling People

If crime is a routine activity and suitable targets are present (there will always be targets worth taking) it stands to reason that crime can be controlled by either reducing the number of motivated offenders or increasing the guardianship of places. One approach to crime control then is reducing the number of potential offenders by reducing criminal motivation. A number of strategies have been devised to meet this goal.

General Deterrence

general deterrence theory
States that it is possible to create an environment in which criminal acts are absent because of the fear of punishment. If human beings are rational enough to consider the consequences of their actions and to be influenced by those consequences, then the threat or application of punishment should convince them that crime does not pay and that it would be foolish to attempt a criminal act.

According to the **general deterrence theory**, it is possible to create an environment in which criminal acts are absent because of the fear of punishment. If human beings are rational enough to consider the consequences of their actions and to be influenced and recognize that they are influenced by those consequences, then the threat or application of punishment should convince them that crime does not pay, and it would be foolish to attempt a criminal act. The probability that punishment will effectively deter crime is based on perceptions of certainty (how likely it is that detection and punishment will occur), swiftness (the speed with which the punishment follows the crime), and severity (how harsh or painful the punishment is).[23] The presence of security professionals in retail or storage facilities or the use of signage to publicly announce alarm and video systems are examples of general deterrence.

General deterrence may be achieved by the swift and effective capture of law violators, their prosecution and conviction, and the application of harsh punishment. It may also be seen when an employee is terminated or otherwise punished for policy violations (and crimes). If motivated offenders believe that they are certain to be captured and punished, it is likely that their enthusiasm for crime will quickly wane.

Specific Deterrence

2   Examine and differentiate between general and specific deterrence.

Specific deterrence assumes that once a person is severely punished, he or she will not chance future criminal involvement. The more severe the punishment, the less likely an offender will be to recidivate.

Of course, some experts believe that treating offenders with leniency rather than severity will produce better results. They reason that if people are punished, it will lock them into a life of crime. If someone was motivated to commit crime before he or she went to prison, it is unlikely that being locked behind bars will help the person become rehabilitated. Instead, it might be best for offenders to be treated rather than punished. Diversion programs, especially those used for juveniles and first-time offenders, reduce stigma and help people go "straight." Those programs are designed to punish a single offender by holding them accountable and requiring them to fulfill their obligations to the community.[24]

specific deterrence
Assumes that once having experienced punishment, a person will not chance future criminal involvement. The more severe the punishment, the less likely an offender will be to recidivate.

Controlling Places

In addition to controlling people, it is possible to control places. This approach assumes that motivated people and target suitability are constant. Therefore crime will occur in places that lack guardianship. These places may be less secure; they may be located in different parts of the city; or they may contain assets that are rare or otherwise highly valued. All these reasons and more can affect the potential for a location to be chosen for criminal activity. What are the strategies that have been used to protect places from crime?

Situational Crime Prevention

situational crime prevention
A method of crime control that relies on altering the circumstances in which people interact with one another and with the environment. By identifying risk factors for crime, and seeking solutions specific to those situations, the thought is that crime can be prevented, reduced, or displaced to other locations.

Situational crime prevention is a technique that attempts to control crime by altering the circumstances in which people interact with one another and with the environment. By identifying risk factors and seeking solutions specific to those situations, the thought is that crime can be prevented, reduced, or displaced to other locations. Solutions may include

- Increasing the effort required to commit a crime, making it less attractive.
- Increasing the risk of being caught.

- Reducing the potential rewards of crime.
- Reducing provocations and temptations.
- Removing excuses for committing crime.[25]

When using this design, some strategies for crime prevention might include the following:

1. **Increase effort.** This may be achieved by means of securing or blocking off access to a target (and ways out) through electronic surveillance. Other approaches involve increased guardianship through reception desks. Target hardening techniques such as better locks, secure doors, security grilles on windows, and alarm systems also increase the effort required for crime and therefore minimize the risk.

2. **Increase likelihood of getting caught.** By increasing employee surveillance and demanding greater vigilance by employees working in public places (e.g., bus conductors, parking lot attendants, groundskeepers, shop owners, caretakers) crime can be prevented.

3. **Reduce rewards.** Target reduction strategies can be designed to reduce the value of crime to the potential criminal by making goods less attractive These include making car radios removable so they can be kept in the home at night, and marking property so that it is more difficult to sell when stolen.

4. **Increase shame.** Prostitution can be reduced if the names of customers who get caught are published in the newspapers. Signs can be posted reminding people that littering is a crime or that taking forbidden photos is an offense.[26]

Security in Practice
Communities Feel Safer with Private Security

While official statistics have shown declining rates of crime for the past ten years, not everyone feels safe. A growing divide between rich and poor in American society has led to a deepening fear of personal crime among wealthy and upper-middle-class Americans, and an interest in protecting possessions has seen a significant rise in recent years.

For those with the most to lose, public policing, because its resources are often spread thin across communities, may not assuage feelings of vulnerability. Those feelings have given rise to a burgeoning private security presence in gated and well-heeled communities across the country. Two years ago, for example, the residents of Oak Forest, Texas—a small community northwest of Houston—joined together to collect a quarter of a million dollars to fund neighborhood patrols by uniformed private security personnel. The company that was hired, S.E.A.L.S., a local firm, already was providing security services for forty-five other local communities. An annual fee of $250 per homeowner provides extra benefits, including vacation check-ups and safety escorts.

Recent reports show that at least twenty Atlanta neighborhoods and four Detroit communities have hired private guards to supplement police patrols. Citizen groups in Chicago, Boston, Oakland, and elsewhere have taken similar actions.

Tracy Brandon, an Oak Forest resident who lost $20,000 in personal property to thieves before S.E.A.L.S. came on the job, says that she feels the additional protection provided by the company is well worth the cost. "I called 911 twice; it took about 45 minutes for Houston Police Department officers to get here," she said.

QUESTIONS

1. *Do you think that the movement toward supplementing public policing services with those of private security will continue to grow, or is it merely a passing fad?*

2. *What value can private security services bring to those living in private or close-knit communities?*

References: Tyler Rudick, "Guns for Hire: Oak Forest Residents Raise More Than $200,000 for Private Security Force," CultureMap.com, October 16, 2013, http://houston.culturemap.com/news/city-life/10-16-13-guns-for-hire-oak-forest-residents-raise-more-than-200000-for-their-own-private-security-force/slideshow; "As Police Budgets Dwindle, More U.S. Residents, Cities Hiring Private Security," Tribune News Service, August 9, 2012, http://www.governing.com/news/local/mct-more-residents-cities-hiring-private-security.html; Richard Gonzales, "With Robberies Up, Oakland Residents Turn to Private Cops," National Public Radio, November 13, 2013, http://www.npr.org/2013/11/15/245213687/with-robberies-up-oakland-residents-turn-to-private-cops

---

Defensible Space

Have you ever been in a crowd or a room full of people and observed a crime or other deviant act being committed and wondered why no one was doing anything about it? The theory of **defensible space** explains that a person's demonstrated claim to a defined and shared residential territory diminishes with an increase in the number of people who share that claim. We will examine these concepts in more depth in the section on *Physical Security*, and

defensible space
A residential environment whose physical characteristics allow inhabitants to be part of ensuring their own security. Four primary factors create defensible space territoriality, natural surveillance, image, and surroundings. The theory of defensible space explains that a person's demonstrated claim to a defined and shared residential territory diminishes with an increase in the number of people who share that claim.

are including them here to present the theoretical foundations. Oscar Newman's study of public housing and crime in New York City established a definite relationship between urban design and crime rates.[27] Newman found that high-rise buildings with lobbies, elevators, fire escapes, roofs, and corridors isolated from public view had much higher crime rates than low-rise buildings. He suggested that apartment blocks should be redesigned so that areas in public use would be under public surveillance at all times.[28] Newman came up with four crucial factors—territoriality, natural surveillance, image, and surroundings—that helped determine whether crime would occur in a particular place:

- *Territoriality,* which exemplifies the notion that a person's home is his or her castle.
- *Natural surveillance,* which is the ability of residents to be able to see what's going on in their neighborhood.
- *Image,* which describes the physical attributes of a residential development that make it defendable.
- *Surroundings,* which include making the most of a development's location relative to places that will help to prevent crime.

Newman learned that people need to mark out and defend their territory. A good design would encourage people to express these territorial urges; they would defend their territory from outsiders. A well-designed housing project would contain different spaces, some completely private, others shared with permission from the owner, and still others would be public.[29] An important aspect of this is household allocation, which requires management to assign groups in a housing project to environments they can best use and control, taking into consideration ages, lifestyles, backgrounds, incomes, and family structures.[30] Also needed was natural surveillance in which residents casually observe and monitor public and semipublic spaces in their environment and intercept those who do not belong. Residents would only do this if they had developed a territorial instinct about their housing project and felt responsible for its safety. Practically, people must be able to see all the nonprivate parts of the housing development if they are to help deter crime. Newman believed defensible space design could counteract the negative effects on residents of the bad image that housing projects often have in the community. The notion of image, or "milieu" addressed the need for harmony between housing and the immediate neighborhood and other factors such as proximity to a police precinct or a busy commercial area.

Crime Prevention through Environmental Design

Crime Prevention through Environmental Design (CPTED, pronounced "sep-ted") describes the concept of design and the use of the environment to reduce opportunities of fear and crime, and improve the quality of life.[31] CPTED, which is discussed in greater detail in Chapter 6, is the design or redesign of a building or area to reduce the opportunities for crime and the fear of crime through natural, mechanical, and procedural means.[32] CPTED includes concepts that are applicable for planned developments, private residences, and organizations of all types and sizes. CPTED works for two primary reasons:

1. Residents are affected by the things in their environment (e.g., noise, pollution, trash on the streets).
2. Certain social characteristics are keys to criminal behavior (e.g., alienation, loneliness, anxiety, dehumanization).

The practice of CPTED related to security can be seen in these examples of the core principles:

- *Natural surveillance.*   An example of natural surveillance is a parking garage with large panoramic windows designed to allow pedestrians and motorists to see into the parking area and detect criminal activity. This prevents crime because criminals will not usually commit crimes in areas where they feel exposed to observers.

- *Territorial reinforcement.*   The use of signs, pavement, and fences to demonstrate property ownership or to mark the transition from public space to private space is an example. This works because it suggests that the owner cares enough for the property to distinguish it from others, and is likely to protect it in other ways, too.
- *Access control.*   The physical guidance of people by the placement of entrances, exits, fencing, landscaping, locks, and other barriers are examples. This works because it creates a barrier against improper pedestrian or vehicle movement into the area, and makes inappropriate behavior clear to citizens passing by so they can notify police.[33]

Displacement and Diffusion

If you have ever used a broom to sweep the floor, you have experienced a concept related to crime prevention called **displacement.** You likely noticed that using a broom simply relocates the dirt from one place to the next. Until the dirt is swept into a dustpan, or otherwise picked up and discarded, it has simply been moved. One of the key concepts of CPTED, *displacement* maintains that, if we stop crime in one area, the criminals may simply move to areas with less-protected targets. Just like sweeping with a broom, displacement means that even if crime control efforts look like they are reducing crime, they merely may be pushing it to another community, store, or home.[34]

While displacement means that crime has not been effectively controlled but merely deflected, it may not always be a security failure.[35] Some criminals may become discouraged after they are displaced and decide to give up crime and get involved in legitimate pursuits.[36] Less committed criminals are the ones most likely to become discouraged.[37]

Displacement or deflection may advantage one company while disadvantaging another if the criminal activity moves to victimize a neighbor or corporate competitor.[38] This theory should be considered when applying physical security strategies in an industrial area. Coordinated efforts across organizations should be considered to ensure activities do more than simply cause the problem to relocate.

Diffusion

Have you ever experienced a time when you changed a process or action in order to specifically affect one thing, and another (or more) thing was also affected? **Diffusion of benefits** refers to the spread of beneficial crime reduction strategies beyond the places directly targeted, the individuals who were the subject of control, the crimes that were the focus of intervention, or the time periods in which an intervention was brought.[39] These reductions may take the form of crime not directly addressed by the measures, may occur at times when they were not in force, or may involve targets and places not protected (Table 2–2). This diffusion of the benefits is the opposite of displacement, as it is the prevention measure that is displaced rather than the crime.[40]

Diffusion focuses on the processes that spread the crime reduction benefits beyond those targets, and is also seen in the domino-effect context, although it is usually cast in a

> **3**   Distinguish diffusion of benefits and displacement.

displacement (or deflection)
A principle of crime prevention that maintains that, if crime is stopped in one area, law violators may simply move to other areas with less-protected targets.

diffusion of benefits
Refers to the spread of beneficial crime reduction strategies beyond the places, which were directly targeted, the individuals who were the subject of control, the crimes that were the focus of intervention, and the time periods in which an intervention was brought.

TABLE 2–2
Displacement and Diffusion of Benefits for Burglary of Apartments

Type	Definition	Displacement	Diffusion
Geographical	Geographic change	Switch to another building	Reduce burglaries in targeted building and in nearby buildings
Temporal	Time switch	Switch from day to evening	Reduce burglaries during day and evening
Target	Switching object of offending	Switch from apartments to houses	Reduce burglaries in apartments and houses
Tactical	Change in method of offending	Switch from unlocked doors to picking locks	Reduction in attacks on locked and unlocked doors
Crime Type	Switching crimes	Switch from burglary to theft	Reduction in burglary and theft

Source: Center for Problem-Oriented Policing. (n.d.). "Environmental Criminology. Expect Diffusion of Benefits," http://www.popcenter.org/learning/60steps/index.cfm?stepNum=13

more beneficial light than displacement. An example of diffusion strategy is the implementation of effective crime prevention measures by organizations in a close geographical area causing other organizations in that area to benefit because the initial measures cause adversaries to avoid the entire area as they are uncertain which areas are more secure.

Broken Windows Theory

According to the broken windows theory, maintaining urban environments in a well-ordered condition may stop further vandalism and the escalation of more serious crime. The theory posits that the police ought to protect communities as well as individuals.[41] Broken windows theory holds that the control of incivilities and nuisance behavior in urban areas may prevent the emergence of more serious crime patterns. The term came from this example, given by its creators James Q. Wilson and George Kelling:

> Consider a building with a few broken windows. If the windows are not repaired, the tendency is for vandals to break a few more windows. Eventually, they may even break into the building, and if it's unoccupied, perhaps become squatters or light fires inside.[42]

Property that is not maintained becomes fair game for people to steal, damage, or destroy just for fun or pleasure: dilapidated buildings and littered streets send the message that this is a community in which crime is tolerated and the police can do little to stop it from occurring. Wilson and Kelling found that communal barriers, the sense of mutual regard and obligations of civility, are lowered when action (or inaction) seems to signal that no one cares.[43] To change the social climate that promotes crime, police can help by changing their standard practices and operations: instead of waiting to respond reactively to criminal acts, they can take deliberate preemptive action to stop trouble before it starts.[44] Security agencies taking a broken windows approach to corporate maintenance must also be able identify the environmental factors that promote crimes such as shoplifting and vandalism and then create aggressive tactics to inhibit them before they take place, rather than investigate after the crime has occurred.

Game Theory

Another theoretical application, **game theory** is well suited to help us in understanding the adversarial reasoning process for security resource allocation and scheduling. Private security organizations have limited security resources and must deploy those resources intelligently, based on various priorities.[45] Game theory is the study of strategic decision making in the context of conflict and cooperation provides a trusted mathematical approach to consider when deploying limited security resources for maximum effectiveness.

Each actor in "the game" tries to maximize gains or minimize losses under conditions of uncertainty and incomplete information, which requires each actor to rank order preferences, estimate probabilities, and try to discern what the other actor is going to do.[46] For example, in a two-person *zero-sum* game, what one actor wins the other actor loses; in other words, if actor *A* wins, 5, actor *B* loses 5, and the sum is zero. According to Viotti and Kauppi, another variation is the two-person *nonzero* or *variable sum* game. Here, gains and losses are not necessarily equal, and it is possible that both sides may gain, sometimes referred to as a *positive-sum* game. In some games, both parties can lose, and lose by different amounts or to a different degree. So-called *n-person* games include more than two actors or sides.[47]

Game theory has contributed a new perspective to the development of models of deterrence, and although it may not be well known or understood by many security professionals, it can and should be used to increase the effectiveness and efficiency of security programs. The central problem is that the rational decision for a player may be to "defect" and go it alone as opposed to taking a chance on collaboration with another player.[48] Dealing with this problem is a central concern for those who use game theory for security purposes at many levels.

Researchers of game theory have developed algorithms for efficiently providing randomized patrolling and inspection strategies.[49] This work has led to much improved scheduling

broken windows theory
Suggests that (a) maintaining urban environments in a well-ordered condition and (b) controlling incivilities and nuisance behavior will prevent the emergence of serious crime patterns.

game theory
The study of strategic decision making in the context of conflict and cooperation, and provides a trusted mathematical approach to consider when deploying limited security resources for maximum effectiveness.

and resource allocation, by addressing key weaknesses regarding the predictability of human schedulers. According to Tambe and An, the algorithms are now used in multiple applications, such as the following:

- Assistant for Randomized Monitoring Over Routes (ARMOR) at the Los Angeles International Airport (LAX) to randomize checkpoints on the roadways entering the airport and canine patrol routes within the airport terminals.
- Intelligent Randomization In Scheduling (IRIS) for randomized deployment of the U.S. Federal Air Marshals (FAMS).
- Port Resilience Operational/ Tactical Enforcement to Combat Terrorism (PROTECT) in the ports of Boston and New York for randomizing U.S. Coast Guard patrolling.
- Game-theoretic Unpredictable and Randomly Deployed Security (GUARDS) is under evaluation for deployment by the U.S. Transportation Security Administration (TSA).
- Tactical Randomization for Security in Transit Systems (TRUSTS) is being tested by the Los Angeles Sheriff's Department (LASD) to schedule randomized patrols for fare inspection in the LA Metro system.[50]

These successes precede many large-scale applications in security. Security is a worldwide challenge and the use of game theory is an increasingly important contribution to strategy development for security resource allocation.

▲ The Coast Guard's new PROTECT system. The PROTECT system uses game theory to schedule the operations of Coast Guard response vessels like this one in a way that makes it impossible for observers to predict their activities, while still maintaining high levels of effective surveillance. What other applications could game theory have in the security profession?

Source: Stocktrek Images/Getty images *University of Southern California, http://viterbi.usc.edu/ news/news/2011/protect-system-now .htm*

Summary

- **Define theories of crime for the purposes used by security professionals.**
    - Theories of crime are explanations of causation that apply to all people and all crimes. These theories offer perspectives on why some people turn to crime while others, given the same set of circumstances, remain law abiding. Theories are designed to explain a significant association between a cause and effect. If security professionals know why people commit crime then it would be possible to devise strategies to prevent it from occurring.

- **Examine and differentiate between general and specific deterrence.**
    - General deterrence maintains that the faster, more sure, and more severe the punishment the less likely people will engage in crime. Rational criminals fear being apprehended and punished.

○ Specific deterrence is complementary to, not necessarily opposite from general deterrence, and focuses on punishments that address the actions of the individual, and are not meant to affect or deter members of the public. The intent is to hold the accused accountable and require them to fulfill their obligations to the community.

- **Distinguish diffusion of benefits and displacement.**
  ○ Diffusion of benefits refers to the spread of a beneficial reduction in the effect of crime beyond the places, which were directly targeted, the individuals who were the subject of control, the crimes, which were the focus of intervention, or the time periods in which an intervention was brought.
  ○ Displacement maintains that, if we stop crime in one area, the criminals may simply move to areas with less-protected targets.

KEY TERMS

broken windows
   theory **38**

control view **32**

defensible space **35**

diffusion of benefits **37**

displacement
   (or deflection) **37**

game theory **38**

general deterrence
   theory **34**

neutralization
   techniques **31**

psychodynamic
   theory **29**

rational choice **28**

routine activity theory **32**

situational crime
   prevention **34**

specific deterrence **34**

theories 27

REVIEW QUESTIONS

1. What can be accomplished in the security profession by using theories?
2. If your neighbor increased the security of their residence in some way and that affected the security of your residence, how would you determine whether it was more like diffusion or displacement?
3. If a mid-level supervisor in your manufacturing company regularly punished the employees who created security problems (that benefited criminals) like leaving locked doors ajar or not counting inventory, would that be more like general or specific deterrence?

PRACTICAL APPLICATION

1. Choose one theory from each section and write a paragraph for each theory detailing a real-world situation in which the actions of a person demonstrated some part of the theory as you understand it. If you are able to identify a historical fact or news item, reference the activity so others may delve into it.
2. If your neighbor increased the security of their residence in some way and that affected the security of your residence, how would you determine whether it was more like diffusion or displacement?
3. Research and study the terms *theoretical competition* (the process of direct and systematic comparison or two or more theories to rank-order them based on their strength and scope or coverage), *theoretical elaboration* (the expansion of a current theory with the end goal of building a more comprehensive and well-developed theoretical model), and *theoretical integration* (when more specific theoretical concepts are merged and regrouped into a larger concept). Explore the use of these concepts with some of the theories addressed in this section.

4. Police and detective television shows address the *theory of the crime* without taking the time to explain what it is. The theory of the crime is developed much like scientific and academic theory by focusing on the likely sequence of events and the locations and positions of everyone present during the crime. Initial hypotheses are developed and frequently adjusted when there are changes in the evidence showing the places or people involved or identified to help verify or disprove the many possible relationships. Good detectives continually test the theory against the evidence and avoid making assumptions, no matter how logical they may seem. Prepare a comparison chart summarizing the similarities between the treatment of academic theory and theory in practice.

5. As we will do many times in this textbook, we encourage you to use as much of your imagination as you can muster. By doing so, you will be more able to understand the daily challenges faced by security professionals on many levels. You are also encouraged to make contact with these professionals, so you can hear directly from them. This can be accomplished in a number of ways, from simply looking in the Yellow Pages, local chamber of commerce listings, or an open-access online social networking group. Many students find it is beneficial to spend time with security professionals at work. This can happen in many forms, the most frequent being volunteer work or internships. It is likely that you can arrange for either by contacting the security organization directly, although, if you are currently enrolled in a degree or certificate program, you may be able to receive college and university credit for doing such work. Make sure you check completely with both the university and the security organization to see what their policies are.

Security Administration and Management

CHAPTER

3

Learning Objectives

After reading this chapter, you should be able to:

1. Define ethics. **45**

2. Understand the role of ethics in the security profession. **49**

3. Identify and explain the differences between administrators and managers in organizations. **50**

4. Distinguish the importance of ethics to individuals and organization. **50**

5. Identify and explain Security Management Issues. **54**

Introduction

Security measures for sporting events with international interest require the coordination of thousands of security and police professionals. For the 2015 Super Bowl in Phoenix, Arizona, for example, the list of U.S. federal agencies supporting the efforts of local law enforcement and private security included the Domestic Nuclear Detection Office, Federal Air Marshals, Federal Emergency Management Agency, Secret Service, Transportation Safety Administration, National Cybersecurity and Communications Integration Center, and the U.S. Customs and Border Protection and Immigration and Customs Enforcement.[1] In addition to the personnel challenges, truck-sized X-ray devices were used to augment the event's security. In an abundance of caution, even the property of half-time performer Katy Perry and the on-site portable toilets were scanned for safety purposes.

Security administrators and managers must understand both traditional and contemporary business principles, as well as have a grasp on their organization's vision and mission. **Managers** who do so are best able to ensure that their organizational components remain valuable corporate resources that support organizational success. In contrast, security managers who fail to understand business principles are likely to focus on security as an end in itself, failing to understand how it serves the wider goals of the company that employs them. Such a narrow approach fails to take into account the overall mission of the business and lacks the balance needed between factors such as security and customer access. If security managers fail to retain a view of security balanced by the needs of the businesses they serve, security operations can impede the progress and profitability of those companies.

managers
Responsible for the smooth and effective operation of the specific system in which the administrator operates.

According to ASIS International the most effective security managers are recognized within their organizations as business partners.[2] They can use their expertise and business insight to effectively bring people together to achieve desired goals.[3] Seen this way, private security leadership must learn to adapt to challenges, be responsive to the needs of their customers (including fellow employees and organizational leadership), and be able to identify and implement innovative and effective solutions.

Take, for example, the adoption of an advanced video surveillance system by the director of security for Frenchman's Creek, the largest private residential community in Florida.[4] Those in charge of security at that facility needed a solution that would identify trespassers who accessed the property by vaulting the eight-foot-tall chain-link fences encompassing the four-square-mile community. They wanted to avoid the numerous false alarms that often keep security professionals tied up while limiting the amount of time spent watching video surveillance feeds—a task that usually produces few actionable results.[5] The solution began with installation of a second line of fencing, creating a "no-man's zone" that was watched by a network of trainable thermal cameras, capable of detecting human movement through dense foliage from up to 2,000 feet away. After about a month of programming and training the camera system to recognize the difference between humans and animals, the solution exceeded expectations.[6] The flexibility of deployment provided by this kind of innovative solution allows security managers to have many more choices when deciding the best way to protect their community.[7]

The Business of Security

Both security administrators and managers must be able to manage the expectations of the organization while maneuvering through the business culture. Although public law enforcement leadership encounters many of the same issues and challenges, private security leadership has a different primary focus. Public law enforcement works for the community and is paid with recurring financial support in the form of taxes and similar revenue-generating activity. Private security organizations are paid with funds from the company and must consistently demonstrate their contribution to the organization's overall mission, which always includes a focus on profit generation. Failure to focus on profit can lead to contract termination and replacement with a rival organization.

Security departments do not function on their own but instead support a company's broader mission. In many companies, security is seen as filling both obvious (overt) and unobtrusive (covert) roles. Ideally, it is a service, provided by dedicated individuals who display integrity, honesty, professionalism, and commitment. It is not surprising, then, that the practice of networking, which Smith defined in 2014 as intentionally acquainting oneself with a diverse group of professionals and using those acquaintances for the benefit of all, is critical for success in the security profession.[8]

Security Programs: Proprietary versus Contractual

Some organizations outsource physical security tasks, contracting with a security company in lieu of creating, staffing, and training their own security force. This may be the case when there are seasonal requirements, or when the cost of hiring and maintaining security outweighs the benefit. Most guard services are contracted, as shown in Figure 3–1.

A decision to contract out or outsource is typically made based on at least one of three existing criteria:

1. If the company cannot perform security services because they lack expertise, the logistics of such an endeavor exceed their abilities, the cost is deemed excessive, or there are legal restrictions.

2. If the need for security is temporary (like a university hosting a national championship or political conference) or unusual in nature.

3. If the cost for security personnel (wages, benefits, insurance, and other costs) make the service too expensive.[9]

There are advantages and disadvantages when outsourcing security is considered. A few of the advantages for contract security include the following:

- Lower cost if billing a flat rate.
- Manpower needs more easily filled for temporary increases in need.
- Simplicity of termination with undesirable individuals.
- Separation from labor issues and organized employee groups.
- Reduction of liability.[10]

The disadvantages include the following:

- Lower-quality personnel making lower wages.
- Limited loyalty from security personnel.
- Limited control of security personnel.
- Relationship with local law enforcement not as likely.[11]

FIGURE 3–1
Are guard services proprietary or contract?
Source: Used with permission of ASIS International Alexandria, Virginia. CSO Roundtable Survey: Security Department Organizational Structure. ASIS International, 2012. https://www.asisonline.org/Documents/CSOOrgSurvey.pdf

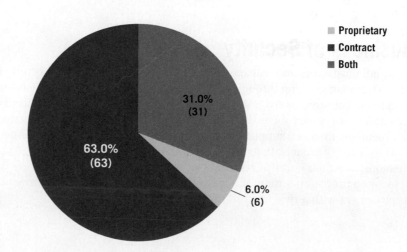

With so many things to consider, it is important for the company leadership to attempt to keep the security force (at least the contracting company) informed on a daily basis of changing priorities and conditions, and at the same time, for the security professional to remain very flexible in their approach to decision making.

Spotlight
What Security Executives Should Know about Ethics

Unethical behavior by employees can cause a profound loss of trust in any organization. Investors, employees, and even clients or customers may feel betrayed. These events may affect the security of the organization. Security professionals may need to conduct sensitive investigations into losses of physical property, personal safety, and physical assets. They also need to be concerned about risks to the organization's reputation. Examples of ethical issues today's security professionals are likely to encounter include these:

- *Workplace violence.* Given new levels of stress, incidents of violence may occur.
- *Physical safety.* Workplace accidents and outbreaks of e-coli in the food source demonstrate concerns for employee, citizen, and customer safety.

- *Employee screening.* Since 9/11, the need for employee screening and background checks have been given new importance by corporations and governments.
- *Employee negligence or abuse of data, including information regarding corporations, clients, and employees.* Confidential data can be stolen whether the computer or mobile device is present with the thief or not.
- *Doing business overseas.* The payment of bribes, or other fees, while prohibited by the Foreign Corrupt Practices Act, is an accepted (often expected) business practice in some countries.

Source: M. Moussa, "What Security Executives Should Know about Ethics," January 8, 2007, http://www.securityinfowatch.com/article/10546226/what-security-executives-should-know-about-ethics

---

Business Principles

There are business principles applicable to private security that includes a focus on budget management, policy development, and strategic communication, according to ASIS International.[12] They include recognition of the following:

- Clients' interests are a priority and the company's owners, investors, and shareholders deserve superior returns.
- Creativity, imagination, and teamwork are vitally important. Integrity and honesty are critical components in business.[13]
- A commitment to human rights, free market competition, product safety, and environmental protection, combined with a commitment toward customers, shareholders, employees, suppliers, and business partners is of great significance.[14]
- Aspiring to be the best, to execute tasks superbly, and to build a great and winning corporate culture are essential to the success of the company, and to the security personnel who serve it.[15]
- Long-term profitability is vital to achieving business goals and continued growth.
- The well-being of the communities served by and surrounding the client company must be taken into consideration when implementing security plans.[16]

Readers should review each of these points to get a sense of the corporate perspective required of private security professionals.

Ethics

1   Define ethics.

Ethics refers to the general principles a person uses to decide whether an action is good or bad. Ethics involves the critical and structured examination of how we should behave in a given situation. It exists in all facets, interactions, and locations of an organization. Johnson noted that each individual has his or her own set of ethical principles, and within an organization every leader assumes the ethical responsibilities that accompany that role.[17] Leaders have legitimacy and credibility because their roles give them authority, power, and status.

ethics
The general principles a person uses to decide whether an action is good or bad, and involves the critical and structured examination of how we should behave in a given situation.

Ethical leaders increase their legitimacy and enhance their credibility by living up to their individual values, demonstrating the shared values of the organization, and by being open and honest, with high moral standards.[18]

Ethics are the general moral principles a person uses to decide whether an action is good or bad. Some prefer to separate discussion about ethics from morals, but for simplicity's sake in this chapter we will combine and synthesize analysis of both concepts. Ethical practice must involve the whole organization. Each individual in an organization has his or her own set of ethical principles, and their collective interpretation guides the ethical practice of the organization. Many leaders will implement strategies to guide the decisions and actions of employees, but unless there is a commitment to a collective ethical standard, individual standards are likely to influence the ethical practice of the organization.

Explaining Ethics

Ethics generally guide the way an individual acts in response to events in the context of a group, community, or society. In fact, our discussion of ethics is grounded in a consideration of how individual actions affect others. As mentioned, each individual has his or her own set of ethical principles and his or her own set of ethical challenges. Whether one wants to admit it or not, the average person lies twice a day.[19] Responses to this in a personal relationship can range from disconcerting to extremely troubling. In business relationships, the cumulative nature of such individual actions can negatively impact the organization.

When we study the various theories and systems of ethics, we begin to understand why we think and act the way we do. This helps in many facets of the organization and is especially helpful for security professionals. If we are able to understand what influences us as individuals, we can then begin to understand what influences the behavior of others. According to Souryal, ethical theories and principles represent the viewpoints from which guidance can be obtained along the pathway to a decision.

The origins of ethics that apply to security professionals are seen in

- Natural law
- Ethical theory
- Religious principles
- Legal requirements
- Codes of ethics[20]

Natural Law

According to the concept of natural law, rules of conduct should be based on equity, fairness, and reason. Natural law argues that the entire universe is governed by unchanging rules on which human conduct should be based. The rules and concepts that come from them can be deduced through reasoning and the moral sense of what is right or wrong. Human-made laws must conform to these inherent unchanging views that are derived from nature. Because humans have the ability to reason, they can understand and adapt to the laws of nature. Therefore, people are morally obliged to use their reasoning to discern what the laws are and to act accordingly. Thus, activities in conformity with natural law—helping others to survive, not destroying the environment, not taking the possessions of another— are seen as morally good. Activities that work against our natural instincts are morally wrong.

Ethical Theory

Theories are abstract concepts that attempt to describe and explain certain phenomena. Ethical theories are generally applied to the individual's interaction or potential interaction with a group. Each theory emphasizes somewhat different points to allow us to reach an ethically appropriate decision. According to Rainbow, in order for an ethical theory to be useful, it must point us toward a common set of goals or principles. These goals include

- Beneficence (do what is good).
- Least harm (choose to do the least harm possible and do harm to the fewest people).
- Respect for autonomy (people should have control over their lives as much as possible).
- Justice (equity and fairness are governing principles).[21]

Religious Principles

There are many organized religions today. The more traditional or familiar include Christianity, Judaism, Islam, Hinduism, and Buddhism. Many of the individuals who follow the teachings of these religions hold deep religious convictions that influence their actions and perceptions.[22] According to Christian doctrine, for example, natural law is given by God and is therefore authoritative over all human beings.

Religion has a significant role in individual development and the stability of society. Some see religious values as matters of faith that require accepting certain assumptions without question.[23] Religious beliefs are deeply intertwined with one's ethical behavior, and affect one's desire to succeed, cooperation with coworkers, compassion for others, and respect for authority.[24] Religious customs, for example, may sometimes conflict with a security professional's work schedule, the policy on searching individuals, or interactions in the workplace. On the other hand, religious values may contribute to a firm work ethic, honesty in interpersonal dealings, and fairness in dealings with other people.

Legal Requirements

Legal requirements are laws that impose sanctions considered necessary for the continued existence of society. Laws are formal ordinances of reason directed toward a common goal.[25] Compliance with laws and regulations is an essential element of doing business.[26] From an ethical perspective, a law that does not serve as an instrument of reason or one that is not conducive to the common good should be removed, changed, or ignored.[27]

Codes of Ethics

Codes of ethics provide moral guidelines and define expected professional behavior.[28] They assist members in understanding what is right and wrong, and many organizations share their ethical expectations by creating, adopting, and sharing a code of ethics or code of conduct. Although the existence of such a code is not a guarantee that the organization or its members place a high value on ethics, it is a good indicator. Most codes address these issues:

- *Conflicts of interest*. These can be real or perceived. It is critical to avoid both the appearance of a conflict, as well as an actual conflict.
- *Records, funds, and assets.* It is essential that every organization keep records and safeguard its funds and other assets.
- *Information.* All for-profit organizations possess confidential knowledge that provides them with a competitive advantage in the marketplace.
- *Outside relationships.* The information shared in relationships with people outside the organization can be very sensitive and subject to both laws and ethics.
- *Employment practices.* These include everything from workplace harassment to volunteer activities.
- *Other practices.* This covers policies related to the environment, employee health and safety, and political activities.[29]

Codes of ethics are institutional guidelines used to reinforce general ethical conduct and expected professional behavior. They are not designed to mandate specific behavior.[30] Ethical codes are designed to motivate individuals to abide by the rules of the collective organizational

FIGURE 3–2
Security Professional Code of Ethics
Source: Used with permission of Alexandria, Virginia. ASIS International Alexandria, Virginia. "Code of Ethics," 2014, https://www.asisonline.org/About-ASIS/Pages/Code-of-Ethics.aspx

ARTICLE I
A member shall perform professional duties in accordance with the law and the highest moral principles.

ARTICLE II
A member shall observe the precepts of truthfulness, honesty, and integrity.

ARTICLE III
A member shall be faithful and diligent in discharging professional responsibilities.

ARTICLE IV
A member shall be competent in discharging professional responsibilities.

ARTICLE V
A member shall safeguard confidential information and exercise due care to prevent its improper disclosure.

ARTICLE VI
A member shall not maliciously injure the professional reputation or practice of colleagues, clients, or employers.

culture. Codes of ethics or conduct do not cover every situation. Police officers, attorneys, and corrections professionals all have codes of ethics, as do many other professions.

Understanding codes of ethics can help security professionals gauge how effective they are at maintaining ethical conduct in an organization. When creating a code of ethics, organizational leaders should consider these basic principles:

- For codes of ethics to be meaningful, they must be taken seriously by members of the organization.
- For codes of ethics to be successful, their importance must be acknowledged by the organizational leadership.
- For codes of ethics to be effective, the organizational environment must be healthy.[31]

Security organizations can demonstrate their adherence to high ethical standards by adopting and displaying a code of ethics similar to the one used by ASIS International, in Figure 3–2.

The basis of all professional ethical codes holds that to be a good professional, you must be a good person.[32]

Ethical Practice

While efforts need to be taken to protect an organization, its people and property, security professionals cannot violate ethical standards of conduct; it is important to encourage and expect ethical behavior.[33] As compliance officers, security professionals sometimes investigate calls placed to helplines, where charges of wrongdoing are sometimes being made against people in their own organization.[34]

Given their responsibilities, the personal standards of security professionals must be beyond reproach. Additionally, with the possibility that a privately investigated action may end up in a public trial, the ethical behavior of all security professionals must be able to withstand legal scrutiny.

How should security professionals approach ethical standards of behavior? *Ethics* is the term used to define the general principles a person uses to decide whether an action is good or bad. Ethics exist in all facets, interactions, and locations of an organization. When an organization is formed there must be a basis of principles to inform and guide the actions of individuals. Security professionals cannot ignore the ethical foundations upon which an organization rests. To do so defeats the purpose of its protection.

Ethical Systems

Ethical systems provide the framework in which decisions are made. Some people may examine ethical systems in a formal manner, whereas others feel drawn to one or two particular systems based on how they make them feel or how they have been taught. The major ethical systems include the following:

- *Ethical formalism.* Suggests that good is what conforms to the categorical imperative, a specifically required conduct.
- *Utilitarianism.* Tells us that what is good is that which results in the greatest utility for the greatest number.
- *Religion.* States that good is that which is in God's will.
- *Natural law.* Tells us that what is good is what is natural.
- *Ethics of virtue.* Proposes that what is good is that which conforms to the golden mean (the desirable middle between the extreme of excess and deficiency).
- *Ethics of care.* States that what is good is what meets the needs of those concerned.
- *Egoism.* Based on the notion that what is good is what benefits me.[35]

Ethical systems are

- The source of moral beliefs.
- The underlying premises from which judgments are made.
- Beyond argument.[36]

Ethics and Security

Security professionals conduct sensitive investigations that require rigorous attention to ethical issues.[37] Responses to a suggestion that ethics are critically important to security professionals may range from an assumption that all who work in the security field are naturally inclined to exhibit ethical behavior to a suspicion that all who are in the field should be watched and not trusted.

2 Understand the role of ethics in the security profession.

While conducting investigations, security professionals must use care to ensure that they don't give the appearance of inappropriate behavior. Moussa suggested that the organizations' leadership should not assume that their employees know and remember what is expected of them from an ethical perspective. Without clear, published, ethical standards, the expectations that security professionals will be able to protect intellectual property, confidential information, and corporate assets are significantly more challenging.[38]

Contemporary ethical challenges for security professionals include

- Workplace violence
- Physical safety
- Employee screening
- Employee negligence or abuse of data
- Doing business abroad[39]

Workplace violence is any act or threat of physical violence, harassment, intimidation, or other threatening disruptive behavior that occurs at the work site.[40] Given new levels of stress and increasing concerns about employee, citizen, and customer safety, Moussa found that more employees have reported incidents of violence.[41] The physical safety of employees may be threatened by any number of adversaries or events.

Employee screening, ranging from simple reference verification to criminal record checks is conducted for most employees of contemporary companies and should be done for all security professionals. Background checks, training, culture, and credit checks all factor into creating a strong ethical culture through effective screening of candidates. Employee negligence or abuse of data causes liabilities for employers and dangerous workplace situations for all employees. Doing business abroad often requires adding an entirely new set of policies and procedures to the company culture, and may involve ensuring that foreign employees are aware of and abide by the policies unique to the location.

THINK ABOUT IT

Are security professionals required to follow ethical principles or codes that were created by someone else? What if they conflict with the officer's personal ethical values?

Security in Practice
Insider Threats

In 2015, Yehuda Katz, a New York City Police Department (NYPD) auxiliary deputy inspector assigned to the 70th Precinct in Brooklyn, was arrested and charged with executing a scheme to hack into a restricted NYPD computer and other sensitive law enforcement databases.

According to the criminal complaint filed against him, Katz secretly installed multiple electronic devices in the Traffic Safety Office of the NYPD's 70th Precinct that allowed him to remotely access restricted NYPD computers and law enforcement databases, including one maintained by the FBI. One of the electronic devices contained a hidden camera that captured a live image of the traffic safety office and was capable of live-streaming that image over the Internet. The second electronic device was connected to one of the computers in the traffic safety office and allowed the computer to be accessed and controlled remotely.

Investigators with the NYPD's Internal Affairs Bureau and the FBI determined that the devices had been used to allow the defendant to remotely log onto NYPD computers with user names and passwords belonging to NYPD uniformed officers. After logging in as a legitimate user, Katz allegedly ran thousands of queries in various databases, including a restricted law enforcement database maintained by the FBI. In doing so, he obtained information, including the personal identifying information of victims, related to traffic accidents in the greater New York City area.

All told, according to prosecutors, during a four-month period in 2014, the defendant ran more than 6,400 queries in sensitive law enforcement databases that he accessed remotely via the compromised NYPD computer for information related to traffic accidents.

According to Loretta E. Lynch, U.S. Attorney for the Eastern District of New York, Katz "used his position as an auxiliary officer to hack into restricted computers and networks in order to obtain the personal information of thousands of citizens in a scheme to enrich himself through fraud." Part of the fraud involved contacting people who had been injured in automobile accidents while pretending to be an attorney. The scheme apparently involved payments to Katz for legal representation when, in fact, he was incapable of providing such representation. The charges against Katz support the observation made by security professionals that an organization's insiders are the most significant threat facing today's computer networks.

QUESTIONS

1. *How significant are insider threats to the security of private computer networks?*

2. *How can the threats represented by insiders be addressed?*

References: Some of the wording in this box is adapted from FBI Press Release, "New York City Police Department Auxiliary Officer Charged with Hacking into NYPD Computer and FBI Database," http://www.fbi.gov/newyork/press-releases/2015/new-york-city-police-department-auxiliary-officer-charged-with-hacking-into-nypd-computer-and-fbi-database?utm_campaign=email-Immediate&utm_medium=email&utm_source=fbi-in-the-news&utm_content=413753 (accessed March 17, 2015).

Administrator or Manager

3 Identify and explain the differences between administrators and managers in organizations.

Although the terms *administrator* and *manager* are often used interchangeably, they have slightly different meanings in application: An **administrator** oversees the performance of an organization's operations. Administrators guide and direct the activities of employees and other resources toward organizational goals and objectives.

Murray observed that managers are responsible for the effective operation of their systems.[42] Murray, like many scholars today, considered Peter Drucker, former General Motors Corporation executive and professor of management, to be the father of modern management. Drucker defined the work of managers to include the following:

administrators
Oversee the performance of an organization's operations and guide and direct the activities of employees and other resources toward organizational goals and objectives.

objectives
The strategies or steps used to achieve identified goals. Objectives are specific, measurable, and have an expected completion date.

goals
The general guidelines that explain expected achievements. They are usually long-term and often broad in scope.

1. *Set objectives*. This includes establishing **goals** and identifying the tasks required to meet those goals.

2. *Organize*. Effective managers must identify the people to do the work. They must often define specific and attainable activities that others can complete.

3. *Motivate and communicate*. Managers make personnel decisions and must be master communicators, providing a solid foundation for their teams.

4. *Measure*. Managers must ensure that measurements are appropriate and accurate, so the extent of employee productivity can be evaluated.

5. *Develop people, including oneself*. People are a company's most valuable asset. Managers must focus on ensuring the appreciation and improvement of those assets.[43]

Ethics of the Employees

4 Distinguish the importance of ethics to individuals and organization.

The ethical behavior of an organization's employees will affect the activities of the security professionals in the organization. Ethical standards may vary by region and or culture. Among the most common types of unethical behaviors are lying, safety violations, misreporting of time worked, and stealing.[44] Individual ethics is about choice, and people express their choices through actions, as well as their inactions.[45] When confronted with an ethical dilemma, Pollock advised that employees could take a series of steps before considering potential ethical resolutions:

- Identify the facts.
- Identify relevant values and concepts.
- Identify possible choices.
- Analyze the choices under an ethical system.[46]

  Then when deciding on ethical behavior, individuals should

- Examine all possible solutions.
- Determine whether any of the solutions would be considered unacceptable.
- Reconcile decision with personal values and ethical systems.[47]

Sometimes unethical behavior is not intentional. They may result from a lack of or misunderstanding of information, perceived management indifference, or pressures from unethical customers or competitors.[48] Organizational leadership and security professionals must ensure that all employees are aware of organizational policies. If able, security professionals should develop professional relationships with organizational employees so they can be aware of the ethical climate of the organization before behavior becomes a problem.

A recent survey of workplace ethics indicated that although some organizations may be significantly challenged by unethical conduct, many employees detect and are likely to report unethical behavior. During difficult financial times, employees perceive a heightened commitment to ethics and typically adopt a higher standard of behavior. When the economy is weak and job security is low, employees tend to be more careful to avoid making mistakes.[49] The economy has always affected workplace misbehavior.

Only 45% of individuals surveyed at the workplace reported witnessing employee misconduct. The five most frequently observed misconduct events were misuse of company time, abusive behavior, company resource abuse, lying to employees, and violating Internet use policies.[50] Keith Darcy, former executive director of the Ethics and Compliance Officer Association, said that unethical behavior can threaten the security of an organization[51] because, ultimately, the ethical practices of the employees influence the ethical practice of the organization.[52]

Ethics of Leadership

Leaders have legitimacy and credibility because their roles give them authority, power, and status. Johnson suggested that ethical leaders increase their legitimacy and enhance their credibility by living up to their individual values, demonstrating the shared values of the organization, and by being open and honest, with high moral standards.[53] Every leader in the organization assumes the ethical responsibilities that accompany that role.[54] Additionally, less than two-thirds of employees surveyed expressed confidence in the ethics of organizational leaders. The proportion of employees who believed their supervisors acted as ethical leaders fell from 76% in 2009 to 66% in the 2011 study.

Competitive Advantages

Encouraging ethical behavior is good for the organization in many ways. In addition to the likely avoidance of government investigations into legal and regulatory violations, ethical practice makes good business sense. Ethical organizations attract high-quality employees. Individuals will only choose to work for organizations with an unethical reputation if the compensation for doing so is significantly higher than for ethical organizations. Collins found that customers typically prefer ethical organizations as well.[55]

Spotlight
ACTION: Decision-Making Model—Raytheon

- *Act Responsibly*
  - Has someone taken responsibility?
  - Do you have all the information you need?
  - Has the information been clarified?

- *Consider our Ethical Principles*
  - Does the action foster respect and trust?
  - Does it reflect integrity? Promote teamwork?
  - Does it demonstrate quality, innovation, and citizenship?

- *Trust your Judgment*
  - Is the action fair?
  - Does it feel comfortable?
  - Is it the "right" thing to do?
  - Could it be shared publicly?

- *Identify Impact on Stakeholders*
  - Does the action positively impact the employee? Team?
  - Supplier? Customer? Company? Shareholders? Public?

- *Obey the Rules*
  - Does the action comply with
  - The law?
  - Company policy?
  - Regulatory agency requirements?
  - Customer requirements?

- *Notify Appropriate Persons*
  - Has communication been open and honest?
  - Have potential problems been disclosed?

Source: Raytheon Corporation, http://www.raytheon.com/ourcompany/ourculture/ethics/ethics_answers/index.html

Ethical Decision Making

Raytheon Corporation provides its employees with an Ethics Quick Test and Decision Making Model. When employees are confronted with an ethical dilemma, they are encouraged to follow the acronym ACTION. This decision-making model can help them assess whether or not a particular action is "the right thing to do." They are reminded that not taking action is itself an action that can have serious consequences.

Ethics and the Use of Force

Security officers often find themselves in stressful and dangerous situations. What are the ethical responsibilities when confronting a use of force situation? Both legally and morally it is important to have organizational policy and standards that limit the use of force to the most extreme conditions, when no other means of control are possible. Security personnel must use the minimum amount of force needed to protect themselves and others—and should use no more than they are facing. It would be unethical to escalate violence and it would also lead to serious legal consequences. Consequently, controlling force has both ethical and practical consequences.

Standards for arrest are different from standards for use of force. Burns observed that any force used by a security officer, except in direct defense of themselves and others, can be claimed to be excessive because there is no authority for private security officers to arrest or detain.[56] The legal authority for arrest and use of force varies widely by jurisdiction. Security professionals should consult both their organization's policy and local laws for assurance regarding their authority to use force. Where circumstances permit the use of force, arms, and firearms, security personnel must act proportionally to the level of the severity of the threat facing them.[57]

Ethical Hiring Practices

Ethics play a very important role during the recruiting process. While there are laws controlling discrimination in hiring, organizations, through policy and practice, should maintain ethical standards in these important areas. It is critical that the work environment be open and transparent, without the use of misleading advertisements or the misrepresentation of job requirements. Equally critical is *not* hiring people on the basis of who they know, but rather for what they know.

The Security Profession

A **profession** is a career field, vocation, or occupation requiring advanced training, and usually stressing mental or intellectual efforts rather than manual work. Teaching, engineering, writing, medicine, and law are examples of professions. According to Post and Kingsbury, the requirements for conferring professional status on a career field, vocation, or occupation include these:[58]

- Skills of individuals working in the field flow from and are supported by a fund of knowledge organized into an internally consistent system called a *body of theory*.
- Members of the profession possess a common *body of knowledge* that is freely communicated among them.
- Members offer a *unique service* based on learned techniques.
- Standards for entry into the profession require an *extensive training* period, minimum qualifications, and licensing or certification by a regulatory body.
- Standards of conduct are embodied in a well-established *code of ethics* which guides client relations and contact with one another and society.[59]
- The profession places heavy emphasis on *service to mankind* rather than on individual gain for those performing the service.
- Existence of a *professional organization,* which establishes policy, regulates some actions, and exercises responsibility in keeping members current on technical research concerning their fields of interest.

profession
A career field, vocation, or occupation requiring advanced training, and usually stressing mental or intellectual efforts rather than manual work. Teaching, engineering, writing, medicine, and law are examples of professions.

Security Professionalism

A **security professional** is one who holds oneself and his or her role in security in high regard, and who is well qualified to perform the duties expected of someone in his or her position. In today's world, security managers supervise personnel as well as prepare budgets and oversee operations. Consequently, formal education or training is being increasingly required for such positions.[60] Lack of adequate training can negatively impact the perception of private security as a profession in the eyes of the public; and ultimately it is the public's perception of professionalism that matters most. Said another way, it is not for private security personnel to decide whether theirs is a profession; rather it is the impression that consumers of their services have of the group as a whole that determines its status.[61]

security professional
One who holds oneself and his or her role in security in high regard, and who is well qualified to perform the duties expected of someone in his or her position.

Security Leadership

Security leaders are expected to adapt to changes and challenges as diverse as global company growth, swift changes in strategies employed by adversaries, and even the threat created by an active shooter situation in or near the property. Leaders also have to require a commitment to excellence from their employees. Contemporary security professionals are expected to learn fast, communicate well, have a good business sense, and engage adversaries in a variety of ways. A recent survey of security leaders found that security knowledge alone is not enough to meet all of these challenges. Instead, the development of certain habits was found to be critical, including the following:

- *Skill at communications.* Interpersonal communication is important because it helps security professionals get the best assignments and promotions.
- *Business acumen.* Knowing the business for which you are providing security and how to wrangle through political challenges in an organization is as important as the technical facets. It is very important for security professionals to be able to persuade business leaders to obtain the security resources needed.
- *Creativity.* Security professionals need the same skills that their adversaries have to prevent loss. Creativity also helps solve many other problems, including those that would benefit the business although they may not be directly related to the security field.

- *Problem-solving skills.* Analysis and problem-solving skills are necessary because new challenges are bound to arise, and it is impossible to train for the unknown.

- *Proficient consumer of knowledge.* The constant desire to learn new things, including the habit of keeping on top of news and changing developments in the field, is the mark of an effective professional.

- *Actively engage with business stakeholders.* Looking for ways to engage with business stakeholders, whether it is with company leadership or members of other work teams, builds the feeling of ownership a person has in both projects and the overall operation. This mind-set gives all parties a better understanding of the business objectives and many reasons why choices are made.

- *Being a student of offense and defense.* For security professionals, a good offense is based on an effective defense. Looking at the organization like your adversaries do with an understanding of their techniques for exploiting weaknesses will help you know how to thwart or limit their threat.[62]

These skills form the foundation for success as a security professional.

Security Management Issues

5 Identify and explain Security Management Issues.

management
A set of planning, organizing, training, commanding, and coordinating functions.

Security professionals who fill **management** roles in the organization must prioritize their response to security issues based on the goals and purpose of the organization. The top security-related issues are the following:

- Budgeting and maximizing return on investment.
- Promoting employee awareness.
- Training effectiveness.
- Implementing best practices and key performance indicators.
- Threat assessments.
- Keeping up with technological advances.
- Adequate security staffing.
- Selection and hiring methods for security staffing.
- Strategic planning.
- Regulatory and compliance issues.[63]

Nonsecurity employee awareness of the security mission is essential for the success of security operations. Simply knowing the basics of the security mission allows nonsecurity employees to be an additional set of eyes and ears in the organization. This may allow for a faster notification of issues than the established security network would if it operated alone. Take, for instance, threat assessments that initially provide security managers a baseline against which to measure an organization's security posture. Threat assessments must be more than a check-the-blocks exercise. To be effective, the commitment of top management is critical, both for conducting the assessment and for implementing necessary corrections identified during the assessment.

Planning and Decision Making

Security managers and administrators should know that planning and decision making are processes that should not be undertaken in isolation. Planning is a critical part of organizational success, and security managers and administrators who take the time to plan and engage others in planning will enjoy fewer unforeseen challenges, accidents, and crises.

Each security professional is expected to make decisions, and those decisions carry greater weight as the level of responsibility increases. The process of decision making can be complex, but it doesn't need to be overwhelming, and leaders who are prepared and have done sufficient planning will best be able to make informed decisions. The ability to make effective decisions is based on a mix of knowledge, training, experiences, and perception of the current situation. Because of this combination of elements, it is important for security managers and administrators to anticipate possible challenges and identify select individuals who may have special knowledge and skills, and with whom they can discuss decisions before making them.

Labor Relations

Labor relations often become a challenge to the security of the organization, and security managers must be able to support organizational leadership. Organizational leadership has many strategies for dealing with employees and employee issues, especially when an employee union is involved. Security professionals must be acquainted with the appropriate and necessary tactical options, as labor issues may occur spontaneously and progress swiftly. This is important whether labor is organized in a union or not, and requires a level of effort and attention that exceeds simply creating policy. Regular evaluation of employee morale and satisfaction along with coordination with all the key players in the organization will provide security professionals with advance notice of potential issues. As an example of the need for coordination with key players, overtime monitoring can be a large part of a security professional's job. Overtime is often unexpected, and when a security section or department has its own budget, these costs are unexpected as well.

A key labor-related security issue is the use of noncompete agreements. Executives in the organization are in a position of trust and confidence. Confidential information includes proprietary information and trade secrets including information and materials related to inventions, computer software and hardware, business procedures and plans, customer lists, and pricing information. Company executives who have access to these corporate secrets in the performance of their job may be required to promise to preserve the confidentiality of the information once they leave the organization. This obliges them to not knowingly use or disclose any proprietary information or trade secrets should they move to another company.[64] Security professionals may be asked to assist with investigating or enforcing violations of these agreements.

Financial Management

Depending on the size of the organization, security managers and administrators are likely to have their own budget. Although for some this may be an indicator of advanced responsibility and autonomy, for others it is a source of time-consuming frustration. The ability to capably manage a budget may mean the difference between success and failure of the security operation. Moran reported that with the median annual compensation for security managers exceeding $100,000, security administrators would find much of their budget is devoted to personnel.[65]

Change Management

Change management is another critical skill for security managers. Changes are not always made for logical and easily understood reasons. Sometimes political or personal decisions are the driving forces for change. In any event, the ability to manage the combination of emotions, opinions, and impressions as they affect the culture and climate of the organization will both test and demonstrate the capabilities of the security manager and administrator.

Security Programs in the Organization

Security professionals can be armed or unarmed, employed in-house or as contract employees, and they can have many different responsibilities depending on their employer and their job description. Private security services fall into two categories: proprietary corporate security and contract or private security firms. The U.S. Department of Justice found that **corporate security** generally refers to the security departments that exist within businesses or corporations. **Contract security firms** by contrast sell their services to the public, including businesses, homeowners, and banks.[66]

corporate security
The subdivision that exists within many organizations whose goal is to protect both physical and cyber elements of the corporate structure.

contract security firms
Sell their services to the public, including businesses, homeowners, and banks.

TABLE 3-1

Occupational Employment Statistics for Security Professionals

Occupation Title	Employment
Security guards	1,046,420
Miscellaneous protective service workers	324,650
Recreational protective service workers (lifeguards, ski patrol, etc.)	125,770
Protective service workers, all other	81,290
Crossing guards	70,390
Transportation security screeners	47,200
Private detectives and investigators	23,390
Gaming surveillance officers and gaming investigators	9,150

Source: Bureau of Labor Statistics (BLS), "Occupational Employment Statistics: May 2012 National Occupational Employment and Wage Estimates in the United States," 2013, http://www.bls.gov/oes/current/oes_nat.htm

A report for the U.S. Bureau of Justice Statistics suggested the security profession was often distinguished based on the nature of the security department (proprietary or contractual), type of security provided (physical, information, or employment-related), services provided (e.g., guarding, armored transport), and target market (e.g., critical infrastructure, commercial venues).[67] According to Post and Kingsbury, security is an integral part of the organization it serves.[68] Private security organizations exist primarily to serve the interests of those who employ them.

Various organizations employ private security professionals in diverse roles, including commercial, institutional, residential, and critical infrastructure. They work in manufacturing, finance and insurance, health care, transportation and warehousing, rental and leasing, information, utilities, real estate and retail trade, among other industries and professions.[69]

Table 3–1 shows the distribution of private security officer employment in a number of industries, as reported by the Bureau of Labor Statistics.[70] This may give an indication of which industries are most likely to have their own security departments, but not necessarily the most security. A recent study for the Bureau of Justice Statistics found security guards represented nearly half of the services provided by security firms, with between 11,000 and 15,000 private security companies employing more than 1 million guards in the United States.[71]

Motivation and Management Theories

Security administrators and managers are responsible for leading and motivating employees, both those in their direct line of supervision and those in other departments or areas of the organization. Security administrators and managers, such as those in other fields, may enjoy better results when they combine practical wisdom with a theoretical foundation. This section provides an overview of relevant theories of motivation and leadership. It was not designed to be cumulative, and you are encouraged to explore additional management and motivation theories to find those that fit your organization and specific situation.

scientific management approach

Analyzes and synthesizes workflows to improve economic efficiency in the form of productivity. It is one of the earliest attempts to apply science to management and is based on planning work to achieve efficiency, standardization, specialization, and simplification.

- The **scientific management approach** analyzed and synthesized workflows to improve economic efficiency in the form of productivity. It was one of the earliest attempts to apply science to *management*. It is based on planning work to achieve efficiency, standardization, specialization, and simplification. This increases productivity through mutual trust between management and workers.[72] This view states that maximum prosperity exists only when each worker turns out each day his or her largest possible day's work, that the great majority of workers are deliberately doing just the opposite, and that even when workers have the best of intentions their work is, in most cases, far from efficient.[73] Scientific management, it was said, involves knowledge so collected, analyzed, grouped, and classified into laws and rules that it constitutes a science. These are accompanied by a complete change in the mental attitude of workers and management, toward each other, and toward their respective duties and responsibilities.[74]

- The **bureaucratic approach** considers the security organization as a part of broader society. Famed sociologist Max Weber advised that the approach is rigid, impersonal, self-perpetuating, and empire building. Organizations are based on the principles of structure, specialization, predictability and stability, rationality, and democracy.[75]

- **Administrative theory** is based on several principles of management. Fayol saw management as a set of planning, organizing, training, commanding, and coordinating functions.[76]

- The **systems approach** considers individual organizations as systems composed of a set of interrelated and mutually dependent subsystems, according to Von Bertalanffy. Modern theories such as the systems approach are based on the concept that the organization is an adaptive system, which has to adjust to changes in its environment.[77]

- **Psychodynamic (personality) theory** is the systematized study and theory of the psychological forces that underlie human behavior. Psychodynamic theory provides explanations for development, human behavior, and psychopathology, and identifies methods to make predictions about treatment outcome. Psychodynamic theories emphasize unconscious motives and desires, and highlight the importance of childhood experiences in shaping personality. According to Ehrenreich, these theories come from a multidisciplinary foundation, including personality theory, which focuses on the study of individual differences: psychiatry, social work, a variety of psychology subdisciplines, and academic disciplines other than psychology (e.g., sociology, anthropology, political science, economics, and other social sciences).[78]

- **Total quality management** is a management system that involves all employees in continual improvement. Customer-focused, the approach uses strategy, data, and effective communications to instill a high level or quality and control into the culture and activities of the organization. All members of an organization are expected to participate in improving processes, products, services, and the culture in which they work.[79] *Total quality management* assumes that an organization's primary purpose is to stay in business, promoting a stable community, generate useful products and services, and provide satisfaction and growth opportunity for the organization's members. The focus is on the preservation and health of the organization, the organization's context (relationships with the community and customers), and the well-being of individual organization members. This theory may find application in the process used to reevaluate systems used for manufacturing. Quality focus is used to fine-tune the steps of any repeated process and can be easily applied to many facets of security.

- **Theory X and Theory Y** was a concept developed by Douglas McGregor in a 1960 book titled *The Human Side of Enterprise*.[80] The theory encapsulated a fundamental distinction between management styles. Theory X is an authoritarian management style that emphasizes productivity, the concept of a fair day's work, and the practice of rewarding performance.[81] It reflects an underlying belief that management must counteract an inherent tendency in employees to avoid work. Theory X predominated in business after the first few decades of the 20th century. Theory Y is a participative style of management, which assumes that people will achieve objectives to the degree that they are committed to those objectives. In this system, it is management's task to do what they can to maximize the commitment.[82] This theory may partially explain and evaluate the process used to motivate some employees or correct the periodic negative attitudes about middle management.

- **Theory Z** was developed by Ouchi, who focused on the Japanese practice of increasing employee loyalty by providing a job for life with a strong focus on the well-being of the employee, both on and off the job.[83] Theory Z management promotes stable employment, high productivity, and high employee morale and satisfaction.[84] Ironically, Theory Z was based on the foundational principles of quality management. This theory may find application in the working environment created by some companies with highly skilled, technical employees needing a creative or flexible work environment. These companies often focus on providing an enhanced quality of life in and beyond the workplace.

bureaucratic approach
Considers the security organization as a part of broader society and sees organizations based on the principles of structure, specialization, predictability and stability, rationality, and democracy.

administrative theory
Devoted to find an effective means to design, manage, and comprehend an organization as a whole.

systems approach
Considers individual organizations as systems composed of sets of interrelated and mutually dependent subsystems. Modern theories like the systems approach are based on the concept that the organization is an adaptive system, which has to adjust to changes in its environment.

psychodynamic (personality) theory
Provides explanations for development, human behavior, and psychopathology. It identifies methods to make predictions about treatment outcome. It emphasizes unconscious motives and desires, and highlights the importance of childhood experiences in shaping personality. Psychodynamic theory suggests that criminal tendencies are a function of disturbances in early human development that lead to mental instability and mood disorders, such as conduct, anxiety and bipolar (also known as manic-depression) disorder.

total quality management
A system that involves all employees in continual improvement. Customer-focused, the approach uses strategy, data, and effective communications to instill a high level or quality and control into the culture and activities of the organization. All members of an organization are expected to participate in improving processes, products, services, and the culture in which they work.

Theory X and Theory Y
Encapsulate a fundamental distinction between management styles. Theory X is an authoritarian management style that emphasizes productivity, the concept of a fair day's work, and the practice of rewarding performance. Theory Y is a participative style of management, which assumes that people will achieve objectives to the degree that they are committed to those objectives.

Theory Z
A management approach that promotes stable employment, high productivity, and high employee morale and satisfaction.

- *Needs Theory* identifies three needs important in the workplace. The first are power needs such as influencing others, defeating an opponent or competitor, winning an argument, or attaining a position of greater authority. The second are the achievement needs, satisfied when attaining challenging goals, setting new records, successful completion of difficult tasks, and doing something not done before. The third are the affiliation needs, which include establishing or restoring close and friendly relationships, joining organizations, participating in social activities, and enjoying shared activities with family or friends.[85]

- The **hierarchy of needs** proposes that human beings have certain needs, and these needs are arranged in a hierarchy. Maslow found that some needs (like safety) were more primitive or basic than others (like social needs).[86] The hierarchy is often presented as a five-level pyramid, with higher needs like esteem and self-actualization coming into focus only once lower, more basic physiological, safety, love, affection, and belongingness needs are met.[87] Beyond these needs are higher levels of needs such as understanding, esthetic appreciation, and needs that are purely spiritual. In the hierarchy of needs, we do not feel the second need until the demands of the first are satisfied, nor do we feel the third until the second has been satisfied, and so on.[88] Maslow classified safety and security as part of his second-tier need, which was positioned just above (immediately following) the need for food, clothing, and shelter. Maslow considered security as the feeling people get when their fears and anxieties are low, and explained that safety was the feeling people get when they know no harm will befall them, physically, mentally, or emotionally.[89] This theory may find general application in the process used to enlist neighboring citizens to address local causes of crime or to understand personnel issues in the organization.

- **Two-factor theory** states that some factors cause job satisfaction and other factors cause dissatisfaction. Satisfaction and dissatisfaction are not seen on a continuum with one increasing as the other diminishes, but are better considered independent phenomena. To ensure a satisfied and productive workforce, managers must give attention to both sets of job factors.[90]

Security Administration and Management Challenges

Security administration and management are facing many challenges. In the future, we can expect to see a blending of techniques and increasing partnering between the public and private sectors. Security professionals will be called on to engage adversaries on more fronts, and in more diverse situations, with an increasingly heterogeneous workforce. Going forward, security professionals will be working with and securing the workplace for a new generation of workers.

Demographics

Security professionals are aging, and there is currently a shortage of younger workers. The Bureau of Labor Statistics foresees a U.S. workforce in which more people work past their current retirement age; almost one-third of people ages 65 to 74 will still be working in 2022.[91] What this means for security administrators is that their overall workforce will likely age, possibly requiring adaptation on the part of current employees as seasoned and loyal workers delay their departure from the workforce. Younger administrators may feel frustrated when senior managers remain in the workforce longer than in the past, clogging the path to advancement for newer hires. There may also be an increased need for more proactive medical care to ensure current employers are able to meet the physical demands of the job.

The story is different for younger workers. The share of 20- to 24-year-olds in the workforce is expected to drop to 67% in 2022, which would be the lowest rate since 1969. A major reason for the decreasing labor force participation of younger workers is that they are now staying in school (specifically colleges and universities) longer.[92] That should be good news for the workforce in the future. On virtually every measure of economic well-being and career attainment, young college graduates outperform their less-educated peers. In fact the Pew Research Center found that college graduates ages 25 to 32 who worked full time earned

Generation	Born	Age in 2016
Millennials	After 1980	21 to 35*
Generation X	1965 to 1980	36 to 51
Baby Boomers	1946-1964	52 to 70
Silent Generation	1928 to 1945	71 to 88

FIGURE 3–3
The Generations
*The youngest Millennials are in their teens. No chronological end point has been set for this group.
Source: Pew Research Center, "The Rising Cost of Not Going to College," February 11, 2014, http://www.pewsocialtrends .org/2014/02/11/the-rising-cost-of-not-going-to-college

about $17,500 more annually than their high school–educated peers. Those who had college educations were also more likely to be employed full time than their less-educated counterparts (89% vs. 82%) and were significantly less likely to be unemployed (4% vs. 12%).[93]

These findings suggest that there will be many young adults looking for career opportunities in security who will have a college or university education, many preferring it to a career in the public sector. Examine Figure 3–3 for more information from the Pew Research Center on each generation.

Globalization

Globalization describes the development of an integrated global economy marked especially by free trade, a free flow of capital, and access to foreign labor markets. What that means for companies and their security professionals is that increased diversity acceptance and planning in the form of multiple-language workforces and cultural awareness will be required.

Growing companies may have multiple locations. Offices in one country can support sales teams in another country who sell products manufactured in a third country. The logistics and challenges involved in managing a multilocation workforce and working with the diverse groups in that workforce bring tasks that some might not expect, like difficulty with distance or in-person communication or customs that are incompatible with the current organizational culture.

International companies have a unique workforce profile. Figure 3–4 shows demographic trends in the kind of employees showing an interest in taking global assignments. Organizations with a global presence can expect that their foreign employees will come from a significantly different demographic than the local standard. This may bring an unusual modification to the cultural needs and requires security professionals to be aware of possible challenges, placing significant importance on their ability to adapt and provide solutions.

Because people don't always remain in their country of origin, international organizations will attract a diverse workforce. About 16% of the U.S. workforce is now foreign born, including about 38% from Mexico and countries in Central America; 28% were from Asia and the Middle East; the remainder of the foreign-born workers were from Europe and the Caribbean, about 10% each. Figure 3–5 shows the percentage of foreign-born U.S. workers, by region of origin.

hierarchy of needs
Proposes that human beings have certain needs, and that these needs are arranged in a hierarchy, with some needs (like safety) seen as more essential or basic than others (like social needs). The hierarchy is often presented as a five-level pyramid, with higher needs such as esteem and self-actualization coming into focus only once lower, more basic physiological, safety, love, affection, and belongingness needs are met.

two-factor theory
States that some factors in the workplace cause job satisfaction, while others cause dissatisfaction. Satisfaction and dissatisfaction are not seen on a continuum with one increasing as the other diminishes, but are better considered independent phenomena.

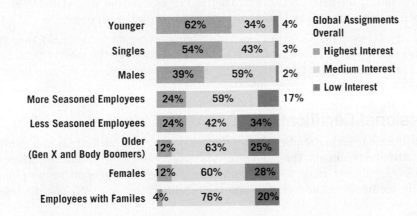

FIGURE 3–4
Demographic Trends in Kinds of Employees Interested in Global Assignments
Source: Based on data from *Mobility Issues* magazine, January 2014, http://mobility.worldwideerc.org/i/231351/57

FIGURE 3–5
Percentage of Foreign-Born U.S. Workers, by Region of Origin
Source: Bureau of Labor Statistics, "Spotlight on Statistics," 2013, http://www.bls.gov/spotlight/2013/foreign-born/home.htm

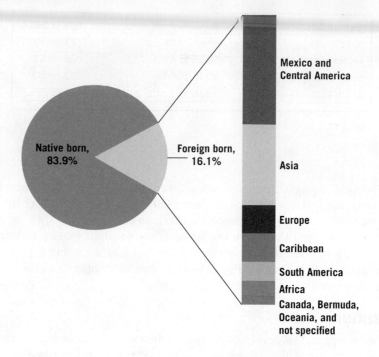

Such a diverse workforce will likely bring many experiential benefits but may also bring problems. Security professionals should be aware of the influence that an employee's language ability and culture have on work ethic and cooperation.

Cultural Awareness

Understanding the cultures of others in the organization will enhance communication, productivity, and unity in the workplace.[94] As organizations expand and move into new markets, interacting with people from other cultures becomes increasingly important.[95] Here are some cultural awareness techniques security professionals in managerial roles can use:

- *Cultural knowledge.* Research other ethnicities and in so doing increase your cultural knowledge. Becoming familiar with other cultural values will help you better understand not only those with whom you work, but also international clients, which will be good for interpersonal relations among employees, and good for business.

- *Put cultural knowledge to use.* Learning something about a coworker's culture can help. Ask about it or mention it in a relevant situation. Your colleague will appreciate the effort you took to understand his or her culture.

- *Listen up.* Listen actively to your coworkers, displaying positive body language and gestures during the listening process. They will recognize your willingness to listen and appreciate being asked to explain their different perspective on events.

- *Overcome stereotypes.* Once the onset of stereotypes begins to take hold, they are difficult to overcome. Those implanted in early childhood are the most difficult to eradicate. The knowledge you gain from taking the above steps will replace your negative stereotypes with positive knowledge.[96]

Professional Certification

We know from our earlier studies that considering security a profession as a career field requires advanced training. The existence of a *professional organization*, which establishes policy, regulates some actions, and exercises responsibility in keeping members current on technical research concerning their fields of interest also contributes to the

G4S Custom Protection Officer (CPO)

CPOs at G4S meet stringent experience requirements, and their training exceeds industry standards. CPOs must either hold a degree (Associates level or higher) from an accredited college or university with a concentration in criminal justice, police science, or security administration—or have been formally qualified in one of the following disciplines:

- Law enforcement
- Career military
- Military police
- Police academy graduate
- Corrections officer

- Federal agency officer
- Military elite forces

The CPO designation improves the way that security contractors provided service. It gives customers a higher quality officer based on education and experience.

Source: G4S website, "Custom Protection Officer," 2015, http://www.g4s.us/en-US/Careers/Security%20Officer%20Resources/Types%20of%20G4S%20Security%20Officers/; C. Sparkman, "6 Security Guard Company Innovations That Rock," May 15, 2014, http://www.officerreports.com/blog/security-guard-co-innovation/

---

professional classification. With advancements in the profession, many catalyzed by technology, we can expect additional opportunities for specialization and certification for security professionals. According to ASIS International, the benefits of certification for security professionals include:

- Demonstrated commitment to professional development and lifelong learning.
- Enhanced employment opportunities.
- Expanded network of security peers.
- Increased credibility and confidence in professional knowledge.[97]

Future Security Firms

Entrepreneurs in many industries have found that following a blueprint beats reinventing the wheel. Franchising, for example, allows business owners to use a tried-and-true strategy while accessing business knowledge from others who have been where they are. Many industries have proven this model, and security is no exception. The small-business mindset often leads to innovation in the name of efficiency and effectiveness. Consider these innovative security offerings that are possible with current technology:

- Imagine a rural regional or city-sector security firm with camera feeds to multiple residential and commercial locations to which operators can dispatch security professionals to assist law enforcement with first response verification.
- An automated security system with cameras everywhere, as depicted on the television shows *Person of Interest* and *NCIS: Los Angeles,* is just around the corner. Already, consumer products such as DropCam and GoPro are available for stationary and active digital video recording. Combine this with available patrols, either with a physical human presence or the virtual presence provided by driverless vehicles or unmanned aircraft (drones).
- Crowd sourcing observations can be mixed with other technologies for viewing a neighborhood, and provide a validation system before notifying law enforcement. This could be considered *just-in-time security* or *security when you need it.* Just like many manufacturing processes have limited storage space requirements by ordering parts only as they need them, this method could provide security only when it has been determined (when a sensor is triggered) to be necessary.
- Imagine that a security firm can collect and record events that threaten security. They are tied in to traffic cameras, bank and business cameras, and (by opt-in choice only) the surveillance cameras at private residences (which the security firm may sell, offering a discount for access permission). Because they are not a public institution, they are not required to report certain incidents, but if asked, they would provide reliable

Spotlight
Security Franchising

Many law enforcement agencies are suffering from budget cuts. That leaves individuals, businesses, and homes unprotected. Signal 88, guardNOW, and Arrow Security are examples of companies that innovate while offering a tested method for security professionals to run their own security business. Each has many franchises and opportunities. Visit their websites at http://www.signal88.com/, http://www.guardnow.com/, and http://www.arrowsecurity.net for more information.

information or evidence regarding a specific person, organization, or activity. What would this business model look like? What would limit the company's data collection potential? This is not a revisiting of George Orwell's classic book *1984*, where Big Brother Is Watching You. This is a picture of a corporation that has access to daily activity patterns because it is so embedded in our lives. Imagine that company had satellite imagery, driverless vehicles, access to public and private camera feeds, and wearable wireless technology and had the lion's share of the search engine market so they would know what topics people were interested in and would have an advantage in the marketplace.

Summary

- **Define ethics.**
  - Ethics is the term used to define the general principles a person uses to decide whether an action is good or bad.
- **Understand the role of ethics in the security profession.**
  - Ethics are critically important to security professionals, who must use care to ensure that they don't give the appearance of inappropriate behavior. Expectations are that security professionals will be able to protect intellectual property, confidential information, and corporate assets. Contemporary ethical challenges for security professionals include incidents of workplace violence, physical safety, employee screening, employee negligence or abuse of data, and doing business abroad.
- **Identify and explain the differences between administrators and managers in organizations.**
  - Administrators oversee the performance of an organization's operations, guiding and directing the activities of employees and other organizational resources toward organizational goals and objectives. Managers are responsible for the smooth and effective operation of the specific system in which the administrator operates.
- **Distinguish the importance of ethics to individuals and organization.**
  - The ethical behavior of an organization's employees will affect the activities of the security professionals in the organization. Individual ethics is about choice, and people express their choices through actions, as well as their inactions. Ethical leaders increase their legitimacy and enhance their credibility by living up to their individual values, demonstrating the shared values of the organization, and by being open and honest, with high moral standards. Every leader in the organization assumes the ethical responsibilities that accompany that role.
- **Identify and explain Security Management Issues.**
  - Security Management Issues include maximizing return on investment, training effectiveness, threat assessments, and keeping up with technological advances, among others. Threat assessments, as an example, must be more than a check-the-blocks exercise. To be effective, the commitment of top management is critical, both for conducting the assessment and for implementing necessary corrections identified during the assessment.

KEY TERMS

REVIEW QUESTIONS

1. How have ethics impacted your life personally and professionally? How is that likely to change in the next five years?

2. Describe a workplace violence incident in which the security professional responsible for investigating the initial report is unethical.

3. Is administration or management more responsible for the daily activities in an organization?

4. If you were in charge of a large company and had to choose, would you rather have a group of unethical employees or an organization with mostly ethical employees that did not have a solid ethical culture?

5. Imagine you were in charge of security when a labor relations dispute started. The CEO told you they were bringing in new hires while the workers were striking. A friend of yours is among the union representatives and advises you they do not plan to allow new hires to cross the perimeter they have set up in from of the plant. What is your next step?

PRACTICAL APPLICATION

1. Imagine you are a leader in a private security company. What is your ethical code? How would you go about creating an ethical code?

2. Identify a security management challenge from the text, news, or other source. Identify or imagine a theory that explains it.

Legal Aspects, Liability, and Regulation

CHAPTER

4

Learning Objectives

After reading this chapter, you should be able to:

1. Summarize the privacy rights in the context of search and seizure law. **71**

2. Define criminal law and explain why security professionals should be familiar with it. **72**

3. Distinguish between administrative law and employment law. **73**

4. Identify the basic requirements of contract law. **77**

Introduction

Legal issues can occur frequently and without warning in the security business, and companies and organizations that have not prepared for them can quickly find themselves in trouble. Actions by managers that affect an organization's employees must not only be in accordance with policy and procedure, but also within the law. The security professionals in an organization are likely to be consulted to create company policy and to prepare for and respond to threats. The variety and unpredictability of events that can occur require those engaged in security to be familiar with applicable law and court precedent prior to taking action.

Legal issues can vary widely. In South Africa, for example, security guards were accused of shooting several mineworkers following a clash between rival union factions fighting for occupancy of the union offices. Previous clashes between the labor unions resulted in the death of at least two miners. South Africa's mining sector employs around 500,000 people and accounts for nearly one-fifth of the country's gross domestic product.[1]

▲ Tear gas used to disperse rioting miners at Lonmin's Marikana mine in South Africa's North West Province. Security professionals have a variety of methods available to them when dealing with potential violence. How can security professionals ensure they are not liable for improper actions when responding to events?
Source: Cagdas Erdogan/AP Images

In Poland, two employees waiting for their shift to start engaged in a heated discussion in the factory changing room. Physical violence ensued, and one of the workers suffered a broken nose. A discussion followed over whether the injury counted as an "accident at work," which would mean that the injured employee was entitled to full sick-leave benefits. The country's courts decided that there was a sufficient relationship between the workplace and the accident, observing the link was even stronger as the employees were arguing about work.[2]

Events such as these represent potential legal problems for security professionals. In this chapter we will examine some of the legal aspects of security, including sources of law, contemporary law, issues of liability, and many of the regulations that govern the security industry and profession. We provide an overview of the many aspects of law relative to the security profession. As the security field evolves, the complexity of the laws and guidelines will grow. Security professionals will increasingly be called on to assist policymakers in the organization, and to ensure the safety and security of employees in time of crisis. By establishing a foundational knowledge of the legal requirements of an organization's security posture, security professionals will be well-positioned in supporting roles. Although likely to be called on to provide solutions that appear to be outside of their responsibility, security professionals should seek out opportunities to get involved in a variety of projects, thus ensuring their familiarity with the many facets of the organization. From that position, the liabilities and security issues will be more visible, and the organization's employees will have opportunities to gain comfort in the presence and involvement of the security professionals.

THINK ABOUT IT

Why is the study of law a necessary aspect to the study of security?

Security Exercise

If you are not currently working in the security field, it may help you to try to imagine doing so to conceptualize some of the legal issues we will cover in this chapter. Take some time before continuing to identify or imagine a security company and imagine you are working with the general counsel (legal advisor) for that company. Doing this can help you to envision why certain laws and regulations were created and to realize some of the difficulties of enforcement. Take notes while reading and imagine you were asked to explain why certain laws were created. Write down a brief summary for each.

Licensing and Professional Standards

Professional standards are based more on accounting from within an individual or professional organization. Licensing is provided by an external organization, often the government. Establishing standards and goals is an important step toward improving quality and effectiveness in the private security industry.[3] The security industry itself has indicated a strong desire to establish standards to upgrade its operations. One survey of security professionals found that 87% of the respondents expressed a need for the development of a set of standards.[4]

It is difficult to generalize licensing requirements because the licensing regulations vary from country to country and state to state. Most U.S. states have requirements that either private security companies or private security officers be licensed in some manner. Some states require all security officers to be licensed while others require only contract security officers or only those carrying firearms on the job to have licenses.[5] Firms in the U.S. that directly employ private security officers but do not offer security as a primary service do not have licensing or registration requirements except in Illinois, South Carolina, Tennessee, Montana, Oregon, and Georgia. The most likely reason for this is that it is easier to regulate all companies in a single industry, such as the contract security industry, than all industries where companies may or may not employ security officers.[6]

Table 4–1 provides the licensing requirements for officers in the ten most populous states. Seven of the states require all contract officers to be licensed or registered, two states require only armed contract officers to be licensed, and one state requires contract firms only to submit a list of employees on a quarterly basis. Only two states require all proprietary officers to be licensed. Five states require proprietary officers to be licensed if they are armed officers.

TABLE 4–1
State Licensing Requirements for Private Security Officers in the Ten Most Populous States, 2010

State	Licensing/ Registration Required (Contract)	License/ Registration Required (Proprietary)	License/ Permit for Being Armed	Time License/ Registration Valid (Years)	Time Firearms Permit/ License Valid (Years)	Initial Required Training (Hours)	Firearms Training (Hours)	Minimum Age	Criminal Background Check Required
California	X	X	X	2	2	40	14	18	X
Texas	X		X	2	2	30	10–15	18	X
New York	X	X	X	2	2	24	47	18	X
Florida	X	if armed	X	2	7	40	28	18	X
Illinois	X	if armed	X	3	1	20	40	18 (unarmed) 21 (armed)	X
Pennsylvania	if armed	if armed	X		5		40	18	X
Ohio	X		X	1	1		20		X
Michigan	Contract firms must submit quarterly rosters								
Georgia	if armed, but min. training requirement for unarmed (no registration)	if armed, but min. training requirement for unarmed (no registration)	X		2	24	15	18 (unarmed) 21 (armed)	X
North Carolina	X	if armed	X	1	1	16	20	18 (unarmed) 21 (armed)	X

Source: Kevin Strom, Marcus Berzofsky, Bonnie Shook-Sa, Kelle Barrick, Crystal Daye, Nicole Horstmann, and Susan Kinsey, "The Private Security Industry: A Review of the Definitions, Available Data Sources, and Paths Moving Forward," *Report to the U.S. Department of Justice* (Research Triangle Park, NC: RTI International, December 2010).

Spotlight
Private Officer International Helps Craft Security Laws

Private Officer International (POI) has worked with city and state officials to require training, background checks, and a standard of operations for security personnel. POI has successfully worked to change the laws in four cities and seven states during the past four years. POI representatives authored dozens of security-related legislative and regulatory pieces and assisted the states of Illinois, Virginia, Connecticut, Kentucky, Alabama, Michigan, and Hawaii as well as the cities of Montgomery and Birmingham, Alabama; Flint, Michigan; and New Orleans, Louisiana to increase training and to make assaulting a security officer a felony charge. POI's security officer training program is used for all security officer certifications.

POI was established as an international security–law enforcement organization in 2004, and employs a full-time staff, collecting and sharing data and content with numerous state and federal agencies including the Occupational Safety and Health Administration (OSHA), the U.S. Department of Labor, and the U.S. Department of Justice.

Source: R. McCann, "Partners in Professionalism-Education-Business," personal communication, Private Officer International, 2014.

Legal Foundations of Security Law

Studying the law is often seen as a difficult challenge. The legal foundation of law in the United States (as well as in other countries) has many contributors, and it is important to have a basic understanding of how each affects the workplace. The evolution of the law often depends on its history, including various political (and sometimes religious) influences. Legal sources are seen as either primary or secondary. A primary legal source comes directly from the state or country's statutes or prior court cases. Secondary sources are not as authoritative, and include cases and statutes from another state or jurisdiction, which a judge may use in deciding a case. Primary sources are considered the strongest sources of information available to help interpret the law of a particular jurisdiction.[7]

Though it may seem logical to use them, often because the circumstances are very similar, secondary sources are less influential and authoritative when making a legal argument or proposition. Legal decision makers including magistrates, judges, and justices fiercely protect their individuality and often refuse to be limited by decisions from another jurisdiction. Security professionals may find it helpful to familiarize themselves with relevant law reviews or bar association articles to acquire backgrounds on specific legal issues while formulating or examining policy. These articles, and those found in other scholarly journals, are secondary sources. Even so, they should always be included in a well-considered review of policies.[8]

The sources of U.S. law that are relevant to the study of security include:

- U.S. and state constitutional law
- Statutory criminal law
- Administrative law (rules and regulations of government agencies)
- Civil law

Each will be discussed in the sections below.

▼ The U.S. Constitution stands as a model of cooperative statesmanship and the art of compromise. Among the chief points addressed in the document are how much power to allow the central government, how many representatives in Congress to allow each state, and how these representatives should be elected—directly by the people or by state legislators. How does the Constitution affect the actions of security professionals?

Source: James Steidl/Fotolia

Constitutional Law

A Constitution is a collective system of fundamental laws and principles that explain the nature, functions, and limits of a government and its institutions. The Constitution of the United States was first written in 1787, ratified by the member-states in 1789, and has been amended from time to time since. For example, the Fourteenth Amendment, ratified in 1868 following the Civil War, states in part:

> *All persons born or naturalized in the United States, and subject to the jurisdiction thereof, are citizens of the United States and of the state wherein they reside. No state shall make or enforce any law which shall abridge the privileges or immunities of citizens of the United States; nor shall any state deprive any person of life, liberty, or property, without due process of law; nor deny to any person within its jurisdiction the equal protection of the laws.*

The Fourteenth Amendment addresses citizenship rights and equal protection of U.S. laws, designed to ensure that former slaves enjoyed the full rights and privileges of citizenship. Each constitutional amendment (unless revoked by a later amendment) has become a permanent change to the collective American legal system.

Bill of Rights

Bill of Rights
The first ten amendments to the U.S. Constitution, which guarantee such rights as the freedom of religion and press, freedom from search and seizure, confrontation of witnesses and counsel at trial. They are the cornerstone of procedural law in the United States.

▼ The first ten amendments to the Constitution of the United States are referred to as the Bill of Rights. Why is the Bill of Rights especially important to the practice of security?
Source: Timnewman/Getty Images

The first ten amendments to the U.S. Constitution are referred to as the **Bill of Rights**, and many of these amendments are especially relevant to the study of security.[9]

- The *First* Amendment provides for freedom of speech, religion, press, assembly, and to petition the government.
- The *Second* Amendment provides the right of citizens to keep arms (weapons).
- The *Fourth* Amendment prohibits unreasonable searches and seizures and requires that a warrant authorizing reasonable searches and seizures be supported by probable cause.
- The *Fifth* Amendment prohibits double jeopardy (being charged with the same crime twice), requiring someone to testify or be a witness against themselves, and government deprivation of life, liberty, or property without due process. The Fifth Amendment requires that a person be tried on felony charges only after a grand jury, a group of twenty or more citizens meeting behind closed doors, finds that the prosecution has presented sufficient evidence that there is probable cause that a crime has been committed and the accused is the one who has committed that crime.
- The *Sixth* Amendment requires that the accused be provided a speedy public trial, be informed of the charges against him, be able to confront witnesses against him, have compulsory process to obtain his witnesses, and have assistance of legal counsel for his defense.
- The *Seventh* Amendment provides the right to trial by jury.
- The *Eighth* Amendment prohibits excessive bail, excessive fines, and cruel and unusual punishment.

The first ten amendments to the U.S. Constitution were designed to protect citizens from adverse actions by representatives of the federal government. In the following 200 plus years, they have also been applied,

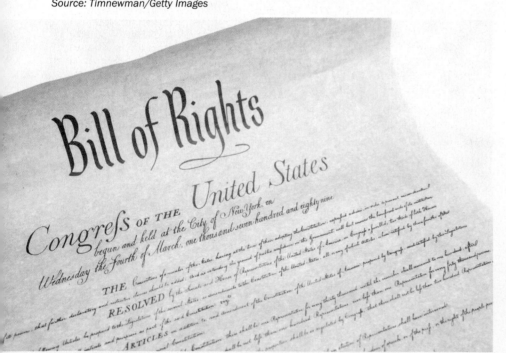

via Supreme Court decisions, to state and local jurisdictions as well. Constitutional law applies to the security field when security professionals are serving in a capacity that positions them as agents for police, in concert with the police, or when gathering evidence for use in a criminal prosecution. Some courts have shown a willingness to extend constitutional protections into the private sector, but in most instances, the restrictions on public security (police officers) generally do not apply to private security personnel. Nonetheless, security professionals might find it beneficial to operate within constitutional limitations to ensure employees and those with whom they engage sense that the company intends to provide fair treatment to all. Decisions regarding such policy should be made only after communicating with legal advisers.

Case Law (Judicial Decisions)

The Constitution is applied to everyday law enforcement through decisions made by the Supreme Court when they review a case. These decisions are considered precedent, or *stare decisis*, meaning they guide future lower court decisions. Precedent means that appellate **case law** should be considered as binding upon lower courts. For example, in 2011 the Supreme Court, in *J.D.B.* v. *North Carolina*, ruled that age does matter when interrogating juvenile offenders and that greater care must be taken by the police when questioning children in their custody.[10] J.D.B was a thirteen-year-old student when the police showed up at his school to question him about a string of burglaries in his neighborhood. He was escorted to a school conference room, where he was interrogated in the presence of school officials. His parents were not contacted, and he was not given any warnings about his right to remain silent or to have access to a lawyer.

J.D.B. confessed to the crimes but later sought to have his confession suppressed on the basis that he was never read his *Miranda* rights. The state countered that his confession should stand because he was not in police custody when he incriminated himself. The question for the Supreme Court to decide was whether a youth such as J.D.B. could fully comprehend whether he was in custody or was free to leave. Writing for the majority, Justice Sandra Sotomayor said, "It is beyond dispute that children will often feel bound to submit to police questioning when an adult in the same circumstances would feel free to leave. Seeing no reason for police officers or courts to blind themselves to that common-sense reality, we hold that a child's age properly informs the *Miranda* custody analysis."

As a result of this decision, law enforcement officers must consider a child's age when they question him or her without a lawyer being present, even if the child decides to speak to them voluntarily. If a similar issue comes before a lower court they must follow the judicial reasoning used by the Supreme Court in rendering its decision. If the court finds that the present dispute is fundamentally distinct from all previous cases, a different decision can be rendered.

In the sections below, the application of federal constitutional law, relevant to the security field that controls the actions and behavior of law enforcement are set out in detail.

Laws of Arrest

Although security professionals may not have arrest powers in some circumstances, it is beneficial to know what actions are required or authorized in the event they are given or deemed to have police powers depending on the situation they are in. The basic elements that determine whether an action can be considered an arrest are as follows:

- A purpose or intention to affect the arrest.
- An actual or constructive seizure or detention of the person to be arrested.

▲ *Roberts Court (2010–).* Chief Justice John G. Roberts, Jr., Associate Justices Antonin Scalia, Anthony M. Kennedy, Clarence Thomas, Ruth Bader Ginsburg, Stephen G. Breyer, Samuel A. Alito, Jr. The Supreme Court reviews many of the laws that govern security professionals. How can security professionals ensure they are acquainted with current law?
Source: S. Petteway, Collection of the Supreme Court of the United States, August 7, 2010; http://www.oyez.org/ courts/robt6

case law
Comprised of decisions made by the Supreme Court that are considered precedent, or *stare decisis*, meaning they guide future lower court decisions. Precedent means that appellate case law should be considered as binding upon lower courts.

THINK ABOUT IT
What federal laws and regulations are especially applicable to the practice of private security? How can a study of such laws benefit private security personnel?

- Communication from the arresting officer to the arrestee of an intention to place him under arrest.
- An understanding by the person to be arrested that he or she is being arrested.

Generally, a private citizen may arrest any person who has committed an offense, either in their presence or for a felony not committed in their presence when a warrant has been issued. When a private citizen acts in aiding a law enforcement officer, the citizen has the same rights and privileges as the officer and is protected from liability even if the officer was acting illegally. Simply saying to someone "you are under arrest" does not create the seizure or detention element of arrest.

The following topics related to the arrest and processing of suspects should be familiar to the security professional.

Confession/Admission

confession
A statement in which a person acknowledges guilt and may include a description of the details of a crime.

A **confession** is a statement in which a person acknowledges guilt. Confessions are usually in writing, and often include the details of the crime. An **admission** is a statement in which a person admits a fact or facts that would tend to prove him or her guilty of a crime, but which does not constitute a full acknowledgment of guilt of a crime.

admission
A statement in which a person admits a fact or facts that would tend to prove the person guilty of a crime, but which does not constitute a full acknowledgement of guilt.

Detention

detention
The process in which a government or citizen lawfully holds a person by removing their freedom of liberty, often due to pending criminal charges. A detention does not always result in being escorted to a particular area, either for interrogation or as punishment for a crime, but takes place when a suspect is placed in custody.

Detention is the process in which a government or citizen lawfully holds a person by removing his or her freedom of liberty, often due to pending criminal charges. A detention does not always result in being escorted to a particular area, either for interrogation or as punishment for a crime.

Interrogation

interrogation
(Sometimes called questioning) is interviewing with the goal of extracting a confession or obtaining information of a criminal enterprise. Interrogation may involve an array of techniques, ranging from developing rapport with the subject to outright torture.

Interrogation (sometimes called questioning) is interviewing with the goal of extracting a confession or obtaining information. Interrogation may involve an array of techniques, ranging from developing rapport with the subject to outright torture. Methods of interrogation often affect the usefulness of the information obtained, as in many jurisdictions the statement of a person who was interrogated must have been made willingly for it to be used against the person or others.

Rights of Accused Persons

For law enforcement professionals, the *Miranda* warning must be given before a custodial interrogation.[11] The suspect must be advised as follows:

1. You have the right to remain silent.
2. Anything you say can and will be used against you.
3. You have the right to contact and hire an attorney.
4. If you cannot afford an attorney, one will be provided at no expense to you.

Generally, these warnings need not be given by security professionals, as the typical security role is prevention, not apprehension, and if security professionals arrest someone, it is likely to be a *citizen's arrest:* an arrest that can be made by private citizens when they see a crime taking place.[12]

A private security officer, like a public law enforcement officer, *may* arrest someone for a felony based on *probable cause,* but there is no margin for error; otherwise, a suit for false arrest may be brought. Such an arrest is usually not advisable, and security professionals should only hold a suspect for as long as it takes to release him or her to the police.[13] In any event, as with many other activities in the life of a security professional, it is best to fully document all activities in which members of the organization interact with the public, and to contact supervisors and legal advisers when there are questions of propriety.

Security in Practice
Training Requirements in Private Security

South Carolina is home to 225 private security firms that employ around 15,000 personnel, of whom nearly 10,400 are armed. The state grants almost the same authority to security guards on private property as it does to deputy sheriffs—including the authority to carry weapons and to make arrests. Yet, state requirements mandate only four hours of training for unarmed guards and eight hours of training for armed guards before they can begin work.

Some people question the paucity of training required. Manicurists in the state, for example, must train for at least 300 hours before they can polish a set of nails, and South Carolina police officers must undergo a minimum of 531 hours of training. In one recent incident, an armed guard working in an Anderson County library fired his weapon at a library patron who triggered a door alarm and drove off with a stolen book. Thankfully, the guard was a bad shot and the woman, who apparently was unharmed, may not have even known she was being fired upon as she drove away.

Although a number of security agencies go well beyond the required state minimum training standards, a recent initiative in South Carolina has moved the State Law Enforcement Division (SLED) to assemble a panel of experts to discuss ways to improve state licensing standards. Randy Harrison, who runs a Greenville, South Carolina-based firm called American Security, notes "[t]here is an expectation of having qualified folks doing the work . . . and I think you will continue to see improvements coming to the business."

Training standards could be higher not only in South Carolina, but in many other places. A recent CNN investigation found that most states don't require mental health tests for armed security guards, and only a dozen states require security personnel to file a report when they have fired their weapons on duty. Worse still, fourteen states have no licensing procedures in place for security personnel, and nine states don't conduct a federal criminal background check on applicants for security jobs. Twenty-seven states do not require federal background checks to verify that an applicant is allowed to possess a gun. Prohibited possessors can include those who are under restraining orders, those with a history of mental health commitments, and former felons.

SLED officials in South Carolina report that about 40% of applicants for private security jobs have a criminal record, and more than half of those try to hide it when they apply for a security position. Training, firearm, and mental health requirements for security personnel for various states can be viewed at https://apps.cironline.org/hired-guns. Visitors to that site will see that New York requires 71 hours of training—the highest requirement of any populous state in the nation.

Harrison, who was mentioned earlier in this story, told reporters in December 2014 that not all security personnel need extensive training, but that some jobs require it. "I don't see us going from four hours to forty hours," he said, "but I do see us making incremental increases in training requirements. I know some folks would say four hours isn't a lot of training. And it isn't," he concluded.

QUESTIONS

1. *What would be a reasonable training requirement for private security personnel?*

2. *What subjects should training cover?*

3. *Should proficiency testing, background checks, mental health assessment, and such be required prior to employment?*

References: *Post and Courier* (South Carolina), "S.C. Security Guards Hold Same Powers as Deputy Sheriffs on Private Property with Fraction of Training," December 13, 2014, http://www.postandcourier.com/article/20141213/PC16/141219726ins (accessed December 27, 2014); Shoshana Walter and Ryan Gabrielson, "America's Gun-Toting Guards Armed with Poor Training, Little Oversight," The Center for Investigative Reporting, December 9, 2014, https://beta.cironline.org/reports/americas-gun-toting-security-guards-may-not-be-fit-for-duty (accessed December 27, 2014).

Search and Seizure

Search and seizure is a process in which police or other authorities, who suspect that a crime has been committed, search a person or his or her property and confiscate (seize) evidence thought to be relevant to the crime. Some countries have provisions in their constitutions that provide citizens and/or residents with the right to be free from what is called *unreasonable* search and seizure. This right is based on the premise that everyone is entitled to a reasonable expectation of privacy.

Generally, only searches by government representatives are subject to these provisions. If, however, security professionals are operating with some form of governmental authority (perhaps subcontracted or protecting government assets) it is possible that their actions may be guided by these requirements, but in many instances they will be working for a nongovernmental authority. It is important for private-sector security professionals to know the limitations of public-sector security (police officers), regardless of their role.

Constitutional law is developed through court decisions, or precedent, as opposed to legislation or regulations. Case law applies to the security field when security professionals are part of an investigation that results in a criminal trial. For example, if security professionals or an organization were appropriately tasked with assisting local, state, or federal law enforcement, they would be considered *agents* (legal representatives) of the government. In that position, they would need to precede some suspect interviews with an advisement of rights, specifically the right of the accused to have counsel and to be silent. Additionally, if they were assisting in a lawful search of an automobile or dwelling, they would need to be part of a lawful search preceded by a warrant and could search only for the items described in and authorized by the warrant.

1 Summarize the privacy rights in the context of search and seizure law.

search and seizure
A process in which police or other authorities, who suspect that a crime has been committed, search a person or his or her property and confiscate (seize) evidence thought to be relevant to the crime.

constitutional law
Developed through court decisions, or precedent, as opposed to legislation or regulations.

Statutory Criminal Law

| 2 | Define criminal law and explain why security professionals should be familiar with it. |

criminal law
Designed to regulate social behavior. Contemporary criminal law is concerned with actions that are regarded as harmful to society, or an omission to act when required by status or occupation, and provides for punishment of people who threaten, harm, or otherwise endanger the health, safety, and moral welfare of other people.

Statutory **criminal law** defines crime and sets out punishment. Criminal law is designed to regulate social behavior. It provides punishment for people who threaten, harm, or otherwise endanger the health, safety, and moral welfare of other people. A prosecutor (representing the government) enforces criminal law against an accused person. Unlike civil law, which controls disputes between individuals, criminal law involves conflicts between an individual and the state. For example, a criminal law may ban the possession and sale of marijuana, and someone arrested with marijuana in their possession may be subject to state sanctions; there is no easily identifiable individual "victim" in this crime. Because the criminal law is designed to protect society as a whole, actions that bring social harm are considered illegal. Consequently, the content of the criminal law is constantly changing to reflect social norms and contemporary values. What may have been a crime in the past may be legal today, and vice versa. The categories of crime most relevant to security and asset protection programs include crimes involving

- Unauthorized entry or presence.
- Theft or fraud.
- Force or threats of force against people.
- Damage or threats of damage against property.
- Computers.
- The environment.[14]

Theft and fraud are likely the most frequent and costly forms of dishonesty that security professionals will encounter. Theft and fraud by employees may be an organization's greatest threat, second only to competition from other organizations. The U.S. Chamber of Commerce estimated that 30% of business failures result from employee theft, with over one half of them failing in the first three years of their existence.[15] By suggesting or supporting policies aimed at reducing temptation and increasing the potential for detection, security professionals can help prevent much internal theft.[16] An important prevention strategy used to reduce employee theft, fraud, and embezzlement is a climate of trust, honesty, and cooperation.[17]

Some examples of crimes related to these categories that are relevant to the security industry are set out in Figure 4–1.

Additionally, federal criminal statutes considered relevant to the security profession include those in Figure 4–2.

FIGURE 4–1
Crimes Relevant to the Security Industry
Source: Lectric Law Library, http://www.lectlaw.com/

- Assault is an activity that causes another person to anticipate violence. *Assault* is distinguished from battery, which involves physical contact. The specific meaning of the term *assault* varies depending on the jurisdiction.
- *Battery* is unlawful physical contact with another. Battery in common law was defined as "any unlawful touching of the person of another by the aggressor himself, or by a substance put in motion by him."
- *Burglary* is the unlawful entering or remaining within the building with the intent to commit some crime therein.
- *Embezzlement* is the conversion of personal property by a person to whom the property was entrusted.
- *False pretenses* crimes involve obtaining the personal property of another, with the intent to deprive the owner of the use and benefit of it, by misrepresenting a past or present fact.
- *Larceny* (or *theft*) is unlawful taking of property from the possession of another with the intent of permanently depriving the owner of it.
- *Receiving stolen goods* involves receiving or concealing stolen property, while knowing the property to be stolen, with intent to obtain monetary gain or to prevent the rightful owner from the enjoyment of the property.
- *Robbery* is the unlawful taking of property from the immediate possession of another by force or the threat of force.
- *Trespass* is an unlawful violation of the person or property of another, and considered to be a tort as well as a crime.
- *Uttering* is drawing a check on a financial account in which there are insufficient funds to cover the check.
- *Vandalism* occurs when a person destroys or defaces someone else's property without permission.

- *Economic Espionage Act* (18 U.S.C. § 1831–1839) enacted to combat foreign economic espionage and provide criminal penalties for theft of trade secrets by a foreign power. The term **trade secret** applies to all forms and types of information, if the owner thereof has taken reasonable measures to keep such information secret and the information derives independent economic value, actual or potential, from not being generally known to, and not being readily ascertainable through proper means by, the public.[1]
- *Title III of the Omnibus Crime Control and Safe Streets Act* (18 U.S.C. § 2510 et seq.) authorizes law enforcement to use electronic surveillance, safeguards wire and oral communications, prohibits private-sector possession or use of electronic surveillance equipment, creates acceptable uniform circumstances for electronic surveillance, and sets constitutionally acceptable procedures for government surveillance.
- *Electronic Communications Privacy Act* (18 U.S.C. § 2510) extends Title III protection to cellular telephones, fiber-optic transmissions, teleconferencing, voice mail, electronic mail, encrypted transmissions, and most pagers, strengthens Title III criminal and civil penalties, and provides for court-ordered roving interceptions.
- *Mobile Tracking Devices* (18 U.S.C. § 3117) extends the validity of a court order for a tracking device to all jurisdictions. Expectations of privacy still apply where the warrant does not cover certain activities.
- *Pen Register and Trap and Trace Devices* (18 U.S.C. § 3121–3126) limits private use to communications providers and consensual situations. The devices addressed by this statute capture incoming electronic impulses, which identify the originating number and are reasonably likely to identify the source of the communication, but do not reveal the contents of communication. A pen register shows outgoing phone numbers (numbers a phone was used to call), while a trap and trace device shows incoming phone numbers (numbers that called the phone).
- *Foreign Intelligence Surveillance Act* (50 U.S.C. § 1801–1811) allows government surveillance for national security. FISA provides for use of electronic surveillance, physical searches, pen registers, and trap and trace devices, access to certain business records, and a reporting requirement.
- *Communications Assistance for Law Enforcement Act* (18 U.S.C. § 2522) requires a telecommunications company to assist a law enforcement agency in court-authorized interceptions of communications. The Act requires telecommunications companies to make it possible for law enforcement agencies to tap any phone conversations undetected (including those made on digital telephone networks), and to make call detail records available. Common telecommunications carriers, broadband Internet access providers, and providers of interconnected voice over Internet protocol (VoIP) service must comply with the Act. Eavesdropping is any unauthorized listening, regardless of the method used, though the term is often used to describe electronic surveillance. The prohibition applies to government monitoring of citizens. While laws addressing the activity specifically identify the conditions under which monitoring is allowed, few laws address the issue of citizens monitoring one another.
- *The Employee Polygraph Protection Act of 1988* (EPPA—29 U.S.C. § 2001 et seq.) prohibits any private employer engaged in, affecting, or producing goods for interstate commerce, from requiring or requesting any employee or prospective employee to take or submit to any lie detector test, or from using the results of any lie detector test.

FIGURE 4–2
Federal Laws Relevant to Security

Sources: ASIS International, "Protection of Assets (POA) Online [Legal Sources]," 2013; G. Stevens and C. Doyle, "Privacy: An Overview of Federal Statutes Governing Wiretapping and Electronic Eavesdropping," Congressional Research Service, 2012, http://www.fas.org/sgp/crs/intel/98-326.pdf

trade secrets
Processes, devices, or something else that is used continuously in the operation of the business. Trade secrets include processes, lists of customers, and discount codes. They may be forms and types of information, if the owner thereof has taken reasonable measures to keep such information secret and the information derives independent economic value, actual or potential, from not being generally known to, and not being readily ascertainable through proper means by the public. Salary information, profitability margins, unit costs, and personnel changes are not trade secrets.

Administrative Law

Administrative law is the application of statutory civil law to the activities of government agencies. Administrative law addresses the functions, powers, and procedures of the administrative agencies and departments of federal, state, and local government, and is relevant to the ways in which government agencies carry out the tasks assigned under statutes. Any agency or organization that has authority over actions affecting private rights; adjudicates cases; conducts investigations; issues, suspends, or revokes licenses; or institutes prosecutions is seen as having an administrative role.[18]

Government agencies have a high degree of autonomy and independence. The U.S. government currently has more than fifty major independent administrative agencies, many of which have little impact on the security field, but some of which play a major role in the provision of security. Administrative law agencies have authority to act in ways that affect private rights. These agencies have authority to promulgate rules and regulations, issue citations, hold administrative hearings, and assess penalties for violations. Administrative

3 Distinguish between administrative law and employment law.

administrative law
The application of statutory civil law to the activities of government agencies. Administrative law addresses the functions, powers, and procedures of the administrative agencies and departments of federal, state, and local government, and is relevant to the ways in which government agencies carry out the tasks assigned under statutes.

law concerns the power and procedures of administrative agencies, including the law governing judicial review of administrative action. Administrative law applies to the security field by setting governmental limitations on or guidelines governing the actions a security professional can engage in on behalf of their employer.

Agency Relationship

agency
A fiduciary relationship created by express or implied contract or by law, in which one party acts for another party and their words or actions bind or commit the other party.

The term **agency** describes a fiduciary relationship created by express or implied contract or by law, in which one party acts for another party and their words or actions bind or commit the other party. Examples of an agency relationship include the following:

- An express appointment (giving someone authorization to act on behalf of another).
- A ratification of actions taken (conduct implies an agency relationship).
- An apparent agency (established by law or actions that would reasonably lead a third party to conclude that an agency exists).

Employment Law

employment law
The laws, administrative rulings, and precedents, which cover the legal rights of, and restrictions on, working people and their organizations. Employment law guides the interactive relationship between trade unions, employers, and employees. Employment law is used to set the minimum socially acceptable conditions under which employees or contractors will work.

Employment law (also called labor law) describes the laws, administrative rulings, and precedents that cover the legal rights of, and restrictions on, working people and their organizations. Employment law guides the interactive relationship between trade unions, employers, and employees. Employment law is used to set the minimum socially acceptable conditions under which employees or contractors will work.[19] Employment law applies to the security field when security professionals are needed to ensure the safety of an organization's employees and security of its property.

As you may recall, situations involving labor issues, mostly because they represent one of the biggest challenges faced by organizations, are of special interest to security professionals. Though other issues may have more of an impact on present operations, labor issues go beyond just the employer–employee relationship. Their repercussions can extend to the host country, neighboring countries, and those that trade with the host country. Handled the wrong way, labor issues can be a significant problem for years to come.

Strikes

strikes or work stoppages
Any concerted stoppage, slowdown, or other interruption of work by employees. Economic strikes occur most frequently.

Strikes or work stoppages are the most common, and most problematic, of labor issues that security professionals are likely to encounter. A strike, according to the National Labor Relations Act (29 U.S.C. 142(2)), includes any concerted stoppage, slowdown, or other interruption of work by employees.[20] Economic strikes occur most frequently. They occur when there is a vote to stop work because a satisfactory employment agreement has not been negotiated. Economic strikes must be preceded by at least a 60-day notice that the union desires to modify the existing collective-bargaining agreement.

An Unfair Labor Practice Strike (ULPS) occurs when strikers employ work stoppages to force discontinuance of an alleged violation by an employer of the labor law. One difference between an economic strike and a ULPS is that the latter can occur suddenly and permit no effective real-time planning.[21] For that reason, it is critical to plan for such contingencies, because all striking employees who request to return to their jobs during such a strike must be allowed to do so.

Workers' Compensation

The Department of Labor's Office of Workers' Compensation Programs (OWCP) administers four major programs, which provide disability compensation to federal workers:

- Wage replacement benefits
- Medical treatment
- Vocational rehabilitation
- Other benefits

The OWCP helps ease the financial burden resulting from a workplace injury or contracting of an occupational disease.[22] The U.S. Department of Labor advised that workers' compensation laws are designed to ensure that employees who are injured or disabled on the job are provided with specific monetary awards, to eliminate the need for lawsuits. Dependents of those workers who are killed are also covered.

Hiring

The hiring process can be the most critical yet least engaged function for the security professional. In larger organizations, the process may be completely managed by another, unrelated department. It is imperative that security is included, with background checks or extended agency coordination at a minimum. Developing an effective background investigation and preemployment screening program requires much coordination and cooperation. Upper management must sanction and support the policy, and both security and human resources professionals should develop and implement the policy. Because of the many issues associated with collecting and using the applicant's personal infor- mation, legal advisers must also review and endorse the program.[23] A good preemployment screening policy should include well-written and defined job descriptions for all employment positions. Personal qualifications should include only those required for the employee to function in the position. Any prerequisites not seen as necessary for the prescribed duties can be expected to result in complaints to a regulatory authority or even civil action.[24]

These questions may be asked when determining the relevance of requirements:

- Will the employee have access to financial instruments or sensitive information?
- Is the employee likely to be working with or supervising others?
- Will the employee have regular or unsupervised contact with the public?
- Will the employee be given keys, alarm codes, and after-hours access to buildings?
- Does the position require the person to possess specific credentials, licenses, or professional standing?
- Does the position provide private access to the assets of the company or outsiders?
- Will the employee be required to handle a firearm?
- Will the employee have access to dangerous materials, such as explosives or certain chemicals?
- Will the employee be required to drive a motor vehicle?[25]

Different levels of screening may be used for different positions. It is important, though, to ensure the level of screening is appropriate and is administered consistently and fairly across the board. As an example, a credit check may be warranted for an accountant but may not be for a food service worker. If that is the policy, then all accountant applicants will be subjected to a credit check and all food service workers will not (unless, of course, they are handling cash at the register).[26] The process of hiring security professionals clearly qualifies as one where the requirements would be different from many other employees. The need for or depth of a background check generally depends on (1) the job being filled and (2) the potential risk for third parties (customers, clients, or coworkers) because of access allowed by the job.

Imagine if a security professional committed a crime against another person while on duty. This would be especially troublesome for the employer if the security professional only had contact with the person because of his or her job (in the role of customer, client, or coworker), but in any event there would be liability issues for the employer. Imagine how much worse it would be if it were learned that the security professional had committed a previous similar offense. The employer could be sued by the victim for *negligent hiring* or *negligent retention*, claiming the employer knew or should have known of the prior offense and should not have hired the security professional in the first place. By placing them in a position of trust, with access to a population of potential victims, the employer's liability and vulnerability to problems is greatly increased. Among the problems that a background check can reveal include substance-abuse problems, previous criminal convictions, poor driving habits, and bankruptcies (which might lead to financial risk).[27]

Unfortunately, when calling a previous employer, the person conducting the background check is only likely to be able to confirm that the applicant worked for that employer, and the dates of employment. Reasons for termination, the extent to which the person created a disruptive work environment, and other bits of information that a prospective employer would find useful are likely to be left out of the conversation by the past employer to limit the potential for retribution in the form of a defamation lawsuit. For organizations that incorporate some type of security clearance, the details that the former employer's representatives are not willing to openly disclose may be accessible in other ways. Accessing local police criminal intelligence reports (containing information on criminal activities not resulting in arrest or prosecution) or the use of inside, confidential sources of information may assist the security professional with acquiring relevant information. This will not be appropriate in all situations, and may not even be allowed by some companies. In all cases, the legal advisers for the organization should be involved in such policy creation.

Liability Insurance

Some jurisdictions require licensed private security companies to maintain a certificate of insurance (COI). In Washington State, for example, a licensed private security company must file a COI as evidence of general liability coverage of at least $25,000 for bodily or personal injury and $25,000 for property damage.[28]

The Central Insurance Agency (CIA) facilitates the obtaining of insurance and COIs for many security companies. The CIA has extensive experience, is nationally recognized, and is licensed in twenty-five states. CIA serves security professionals in thirty-seven U.S. states.[29]

Sexual Harassment

sexual harassment
All forms of gender-based harassment, including same-sex, opposite-sex, and harassment of transvestites and transgendered individuals. In the case of harassment by a supervisor of a subordinate where there is a tangible job action (like a demotion or undesirable reassignment), the employer's liability is absolute, and there is no defense.

Originally, the term **sexual harassment** was restricted to the harassment of a female by a male. Now the law applies to all forms of gender-based harassment, including same-sex, opposite-sex, and harassment of transvestites and transgendered individuals. In the case of harassment by a supervisor of a subordinate where there is a tangible job action (such as a demotion or undesirable reassignment), the employer's liability is absolute, and there is no defense.[30]

In the case of harassment that does not result in a tangible job action, employers are liable only if they knew or should have known of the harassment *and* failed to take prompt, effective remedial action.[31] Employers have an effective defense to a claim for unlawful harassment with no adverse job action if they can show that (1) they had in place an effective antiharassment policy that was communicated to the employees, and (2) the victim unreasonably failed to make use of the policy.

Employment decisions involve a variety of objective and subjective factors, and are often made by members of the same group the applicant is in or hopes to be joining. Under these circumstances, subjective judgments of interpersonal skills and collegiality are clearly vulnerable to stereotyping.[32] Employers need to be aware of the risks associated with bias in the workplace and take appropriate measures to remove or compensate for it. According to ASIS International, establishing policies that treat employees equally is often seen as the first step toward a solution.[33]

Figure 4–3 is a sampling of federal administrative legislation that security professionals are likely to encounter.

- *The Fair Labor Standards Act* (FLSA)[34] defines a normal workweek, sets minimum pay rates, established rules and standards for the payment of overtime, and created a national minimum wage.
- *The National Labor Relations Act* of 1935 prohibits management representatives from attending union meetings, and prohibits undercover operations where labor organizing efforts are occurring.[35]
- The *Labor Management Relations Act of 1947*[36] restricts the activities and power of labor unions, preventing union restraint or coercion of employees in the exercise of their rights, coercing employers to discriminate against employees, and striking to force an employer to bargain.[37]
- The *Labor Management Reporting and Disclosure Act of 1959* (LMRDA), known as the Landrum-Griffin Act, forbids unions from coercing an employer to pay for work not performed.[38]
- *The Equal Pay Act of 1963*[39] requires that employees receive equal pay for equal work, requiring equal skill, effort, and responsibility regardless of gender. The employer may not pay different rates at the same establishment, but may pay different rates at different establishments.
- *The Civil Rights Act (1964)*[40] prohibits employers with fifteen or more employees from engaging in discrimination, discharge, failure or refusal to hire, or limitation, and the classification or segregation of employees or applicants who are members of protected classes (i.e., race, color, religion, sex, or national origin).
- *The Age Discrimination in Employment Act of 1967* prohibits discrimination against applicants or employees over forty years of age in organizations with more than twenty employees.[41]
- *The Williams-Steiger Occupational Safety and Health Act* (OSHA) of 1970[42] provides for safe and healthy working conditions for all employees and makes every employee that affects commerce (except those in the mining industry) subject to its provisions.
- *The American with Disabilities Act of 1990* (ADA)[43] addresses many of the issues that citizens with disabilities face. Disabling conditions include blindness and deafness, as well as cerebral palsy, epilepsy, multiple sclerosis, and cancer, among others.[44]
- *The Fair Credit Reporting Act (FCRA)*[45] of 1970 promotes accuracy, fairness, and privacy of information, and establishes conditions for furnishing and using reports for employment purposes, insurance, licensing, and credit assessment.
- *The Family and Medical Leave Act* (1970)[46] provides employees with up to twelve weeks of unpaid leave in case of an emergency or situation such as childbirth, adoption, and serious health conditions of certain family members without fear of losing their job and group health insurance coverage.
- *The Patient Protection and Affordable Care Act*[47] makes it a requirement for all Americans to have insurance.

FIGURE 4–3
Federal Administrative Legislation

THINK ABOUT IT

How is the study of the law of arrest and the law of search and seizure relevant to private security operations?

Civil Law

Contemporary criminal law is concerned with actions that are regarded as harmful to society. In contrast, civil law is concerned mainly with disputes between private parties and with the duties private parties owe to one another. Private parties can include individual people as well as organizations. When an individual is held criminally liable, he or she may be punished by the state with sanctions ranging from fines to death. The civil law is designed to determine the parties' legal rights and then settle on appropriate remedies, such as monetary damages, in which the party considered in the wrong can be ordered to pay money to the other party. In another type of remedy, the court may order one party to perform certain acts or refrain from certain actions, known as injunctive relief.

The following are five important categories of civil law that are frequently resolved via civil litigation:

1. *Tort law.* Torts are civil wrongs recognized by law to be grounds for a lawsuit. Understood differently, tort law deals with conduct that leads to injuries not considered acceptable by societal standards. Nearly all personal injury claims stem from civil law. Medical malpractice lawsuits also fall in the tort category, as do many lawsuits against criminal justice officials.

4 Identify the basic requirements of contract law.

civil law
Controls disputes between individuals and with the duties private parties owe to one another, to be settled with appropriate remedies like monetary damages or injunctive relief.

monetary damages
Occur in civil cases when the party considered in the wrong is ordered to pay money to the other party.

injunctive relief
A civil court remedy in which the court orders one party to perform certain acts or refrain from certain actions.

contract law
Used to enforce agreements between two or more parties to perform an agreed-upon activity. Parties to the contract must be competent and must have the legal capacity to enter into a contract. The subject matter of the contract must be legal, meaning two parties can agree to illegal acts but the agreement cannot be considered a contract for enforcement or other legal purposes.

property law
Concerned with the acceptable uses of property, like those identified in zoning laws. Property law also governs property ownership, such as land but also personal property such as cash, conveyances, automobiles, and valuable items.

family law
Concerned with matters of marriage, divorce, child custody, and children's rights. Family law also spells out requirements as far as who can enter into marriage, what sort of testing (e.g., blood testing) is necessary, what license and fee requirements exist, what waiting periods are necessary, and so on.

2. *Contract law.* Contracts, generally, are an agreement between two or more parties to do a certain thing or perform an agreed-upon activity. For example, a person enters into a contract to have her house painted. The expectation is that the painter will perform the task in a satisfactory manner, finish in an agreed upon time, and perform all the tasks that were listed in the contract (e.g., paint the window sashes); in return, the client will pay for the services in a timely manner. The basic elements of a contract are an "offer" and an "acceptance" by "competent persons" with legal capacity, exchanging "consideration" to create "mutuality of obligation." Contract law varies from one jurisdiction to another. Parties to the contract must be competent and must have the legal capacity to enter into a contract. The subject matter of the contract must be legal, meaning two parties can agree to illegal acts, but the agreement cannot be considered a contract for enforcement or other legal purposes.[48] Security professionals should have a general understanding of contract law so they are able to engage in discussions related to enforcement of contracts, or if they themselves are contractually hired (an employee–employer relationship). When contracts are violated, lawsuits often are filed.

3. *Property law.* Property law is concerned with the acceptable uses of property, such as those identified in zoning laws. Property law also governs property ownership, such as land but also personal property including cash, conveyances, automobiles, and valuable items. Leases, such as apartment leases, fall under property law as well, and they are contractual.

4. *Law of succession.* The law of succession dictates how property is passed from one generation to the next through a will or other means.

5. *Family law.* The area of family law is concerned with matters of marriage, divorce, child custody, and children's rights. Family law also spells out requirements as far as who can enter into marriage, what sort of testing (e.g., blood testing) is necessary, what license and fee requirements exist, what waiting periods are necessary, and so on.

Of these, contract and tort law are the most relevant to the security industry. For example, the right to use force is the right to settle conflicts or prevent actions by using force to dissuade another from a specific course of action, or physically intervene to stop them from committing crime is a common element for security agents. If the use of force is applied inappropriately or excessively, security agents are liable to be sued civilly under tort law. Take, for example, this scenario:

> An attacker carrying explosives or weapons attempted to force his way into a church, mosque, or synagogue. A security professional acting to defend the people inside that building would be considered using appropriate force if, after evaluating the situation, he drew his weapon and attempted to stop the individual. This would be especially appropriate if there had been a prior threat or incident that he or she was aware of pertaining to the same location.

An example of an inappropriate use of force might be an aggressive response, like using pepper spray or physical force, to break up a group of protesters who were engaging in nonviolent demonstration with no prohibition against such assembly. Many police and security officers wrongly believe that every order they give must be followed instantly. With situations where no one's life is in danger, it is best to seek guidance from leadership and legal advisors. To be safe, security professionals should be aware that the use of force is usually authorized in a progressive series of actions. These are identified as the *use of force continuum* (Figure 4–4).[49]

The continuum progresses from verbal orders, through physical restraint, up to, in some cases, deadly force. Only the force necessary to gain compliance with the law may be used, and only that force which is reasonable and necessary given the circumstances.[50] When a level of force beyond verbal commands is used, the individual authorizing the force

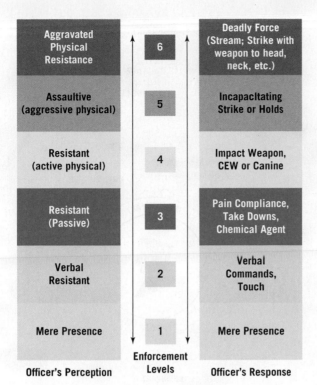

FIGURE 4–4
Use of Force Continuum
Source: Charlie Mesloh, Mark Heych, and Ross Wolf, "Less Lethal Weapon Effectiveness, Use of Force, and Suspect and Officer Injuries: A Five-Year Analysis," U.S. Department of Justice, 2008, p. 11, https://www.ncjrs.gov/pdffiles1/nij/grants/224081.pdf

is accountable for the degree of force applied. In the case of deadly force, other levels of force must have been attempted first unless deadly force is the only way to minimize loss of life.

Burns observed that some have suggested that the use of force continuum as a useful conceptual tool may be near the end of its life cycle.[51] Some organizations have had problems incorporating force-continuum policies into training, and others have had difficulty applying or understanding the policies. Also, because there is no legal standard of force, attorneys are able to manipulate them in litigation to benefit the plaintiff.

In Canada, the National Use of Force Framework (NUFF) is used to represent how a law enforcement officer should apply the use of force policy. The theory of the model is based on the principle of control, that law enforcement officers must use force that is proportionate to the perceived threat they are facing and employ the measure of force that will ensure they are able to obtain, and maintain, control. This model is similar to the use of force continuum, but visually different so it appears less likely that progression through the steps is necessary or expected.[52]

The use of force, regardless of which model is followed, requires a continuous state of assessing, planning, and acting, from the earliest stages of an incident until the situation is resolved. The process involves three closely related processes:

1. The situation itself.
2. The subjects observed or known behavior.
3. The officer's perception and tactical considerations.

As all of these factors are said to create a "totality of circumstances," and an appropriate response can be chosen and later be articulated to show others how the situation was perceived, assessed, and responded to. In either of the above examples, the critical part is following the incident, when the security professional will be asked to take a relatively lengthy period of time to explain the split-second decision he or she made in what may have seemed like an emergency.

FIGURE 4–5
Use of Force
Source: RCMP "Incident
Management Intervention
Model" (IMIM), p. 8. http://
www.cacole.ca/resource%20
library/conferences/2009%20
Conference/Chris%20Butler.pdf

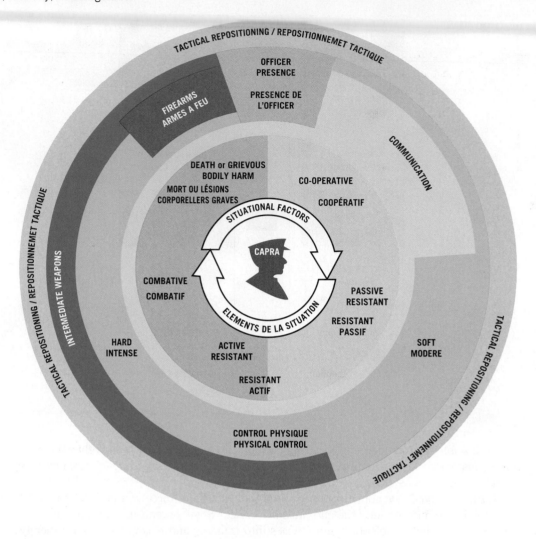

The use of force process typically occurs in seconds or fractions of seconds. The process of explaining the decision should be based on the circumstances, prior experiences, training, and organizational policy. Figure 4–5 shows another way to view the decision to use force. *Deadly force*, generally, should be used only by law enforcement officers, and only as a last resort, *only* when the life of the officer *or* another person is in danger.[53]

Contract law also applies to security professionals. For example, as we discussed in the section on Constitutional law, the concept of agency describes a fiduciary relationship created by express or implied contract or by law, in which one party acts for another party and binds that other party by words or actions.[54] This means that security professionals may be agents of their employers, or they may be agents of a government entity that is not employing them. It also means that another person could potentially be their agent. Agency can lead to liability, so it is necessary to have and apply policy in this area. Additionally, the security professional may injure a visitor or illegally arrest an adversary on company property while working as a contract provider. If a security officer is hired for contract work, his or her duties would be governed by that contract. Similarly, if a security company were contracted for such duties by another organization, those duties, according to the contract, might be different from what is the norm.

In addition to force, there are a number of other instances when the civil law is applied to the security industry. These are set out in Figure 4–6.

- Negligence
  - Negligence is conduct that fails to protect others from unreasonable risk of harm. A person has acted negligently if he or she does not conduct him or herself as a reasonably prudent person would, when acting under similar circumstances.
- Trespass
  - In modern application, the *trespass* describes the wrongful invasion of another's property such as an apartment building, home, or business property. An action for trespass can be maintained against anyone who interferes with the right of ownership or possession by the owner or someone who has a lawful right to occupy the property. The action can be maintained against anyone who interferes with the right of ownership or possession, whether the invasion is by a person or by something that a person has set in motion.
- Liability
  - Liability means legal responsibility for one's acts or omissions. Liability may arise from contracts, either express or implied, or in consequence of torts committed. Failure to meet that responsibility leaves a person open to a lawsuit for any resulting damages. Liability also applies to criminal acts. The defendant may be responsible for his or her acts when they constitute a crime.

FIGURE 4–6
Civil Law Applied to Security Law
Sources: "Liability," *Legal Dictionary: The Free Dictionary*, 2015, retrieved from http://legal-dictionary.thefree dictionary.com/liability "Negligence," *Legal Dictionary: The Free Dictionary*, 2015, retrieved from http://legal-dictionary.thefree dictionary.com/Negligence+(law) "Trespass," *Legal Dictionary: The Free Dictionary*, 2015, retrieved from http://legal-dictionary.thefree dictionary.com/trespass

Careers in Security

Name: Michael L Thornhill

Position: Director of Security

Year hired: 2002 and promoted to Director of Security 2011

City, state where you are based: Lebanon, Tennessee

College(s) attended (degree): Ashworth University online, took Criminal Justice courses.

Please give a brief description of your job. I am in charge of the security dept. for a private university with between 1300–1500 students. I am responsible for the safety of all visitors, facility, staff and property. I try to make sure everyone is up to date as far as Active Shooter training.

What qualities/characteristics are most helpful for this job? You need to have an eye for detail and I try to make sure all aspects are of my job are carried out to as near perfection as possible. I do not take the safety of my university lightly.

What is a typical starting salary? $10.00/hr.

What is the salary potential as you move up into higher-level jobs? You need to keep educating yourself so you can go for the higher-level jobs.

What advice would you give someone in college beginning studies in security? Learn all you can the different areas of security loss prevention, cyber security, private security, etc.

What appealed to you most about the position when you applied for it? The challenges that come with the job.

How would you describe the interview process? I will set up an appointment for a job interview and I will see if the applicant is early, on time, or late. I will see how the person is dressed and groomed. I see what kind of personality a person has friendly, outgoing, etc.

What is a typical day like? I normally arrive in the office 30 to 45 minutes early every morning so I can look over the security logs for the past 24 hrs. I then have a briefing with 3rd shift to see if there were problems I needed to be aware of either personal, safety, etc.

In a typical day, what do you like best/least about it? When the facility or staff does not take security seriously; for example, leaving doors opened or unlocked, leaving iPhones, iPads, or other valuables out where people can steal them.

How would you suggest interested applicants gain experience? By working the jobs; there is nothing better than hands-on experience.

Would you recommend military experience? Yes, hopefully if you have served in the military you have learned how to take orders or in the security field known as job duties and do them to the best of your ability.

Does holding a full-time job during college help applicants get hired afterward? Possibly if you are already working at a security company or a law enforcement agency, this may give you an upper hand for job advancement.

Summary

- **Summarize the privacy rights in the context of search and seizure law.**
  - Search and seizure is a procedural process in which police or other authorities, who suspect that a crime has been committed, search a person or his or her property and seize any evidence deemed relevant to a crime. Some countries, notably the United States, have

provisions in their constitutions that provide citizens and/or residents with the right to be free from unreasonable search and seizure. This right is generally based on the premise that everyone is entitled to what is referred to as a reasonable expectation of privacy. Generally, searches by security professionals are not subject to these provisions. If they are operating with some form of governmental authority (perhaps subcontracted or protecting government assets) it is possible that their actions may be guided by these requirements, but in many instances they will be working for a nongovernmental authority. It is important for private-sector security professionals to know the limitations of public-sector security (police officers) regardless of their role.

- **Define criminal law, and explain why security professionals should be familiar with it.**
  - Criminal law is the law that relates to crime. Criminal law is designed to regulate social behavior. It provides for punishment of people who threaten, harm, or otherwise endanger the health, safety, and moral welfare of other people. Criminal law is enforced by the government against the accused. If security professionals are operating with some form of governmental authority (subcontracted or protecting government assets) their actions may be guided by criminal law. Private security professionals need to know the limitations of public-sector security (police officers) regardless of their role. The emphasis with criminal law is on punishment.

- **Distinguish between administrative law and employment law.**
  - Administrative law refers to the rules and regulations of government administrative agencies, including the functions, powers, and procedures of the agencies and departments of federal, state, and local government. Administrative law concerns the power and procedures of administrative agencies, including the law governing judicial review of administrative action.
  - Employment law describes the laws, administrative rulings, and precedents that address the legal rights of, and restrictions on, working people and their organizations. Employment law guides the relationship between trade unions, employers and employees, and is used to set the minimum socially acceptable conditions under which employees or contractors will work.

- **Identify the basic requirements of contract law.**
  - Contract law varies greatly from one jurisdiction to another. Parties to the contract must be competent and must have the legal capacity to enter into a contract. The subject matter of the contract must be legal, meaning two parties can agree to illegal acts, but the agreement cannot be considered a contract for enforcement or other legal purposes.

KEY TERMS

administrative law 73	contract law 78	property law 78
admission 70	criminal law 72	search and seizure 71
agency 74	detention 70	sexual harassment 76
Bill of Rights 68	employment law 74	strikes or work
case law 69	family law 78	stoppages 74
civil law 77	injunctive relief 77	trade secrets 73
confession 70	interrogation 70	
constitutional law 71	monetary damages 77	

REVIEW QUESTIONS

1. What authorities should security professionals consult to determine the extent to which they need to respect employee privacy during searches for stolen company property?
2. Which criminal laws are most relevant for security professionals?
3. Identify situations in which a security professional is directly affected by employment law.
4. Would contract law govern an agreement between a manager and his friend in which the manager agreed to leave the door to the warehouse unlocked so the friend could steal company property?

PRACTICAL APPLICATION

1. The CEO of your new company has asked you to develop a security policy to ensure the company is in compliance with local, state, and federal laws and regulations. Identify the company you work for, the new position you are in, and the process you will use to create the policy.

2. In your new role as security manager, the human resources director asks you to review a new vendor's contract. The vendor is asking for unrestricted access to your company's telecommunications hardware. Who else should you consult in order to determine the risk and potential problems with such access?

3. Write a job description in the security field that closely fits your current education and experience, and then write a job description that far exceeds your current abilities. What steps would you need to take to apply for the second position?

4. Research the news for coverage of recent events such as those profiled at the beginning of the chapter. Choose a geographic area and time frame and compare and contrast the events within those parameters.

5. Contact representatives of three security organizations by any method (phone, email, face-to-face). Ask them what their top legal concerns on the job are.

6. Find five job postings in the security field. Determine to what extent the material in this chapter is referred to in those postings. Consider the logic of your findings (why so much or why so little?).

Understanding, Analyzing, and Managing Risk

CHAPTER
5

Learning Objectives

After reading this chapter, you should be able to:

1. Define and explain risk. **85**

2. Understand the basic steps inherent in a risk assessment. **85**

3. Examine and describe the risk management process. **92**

Introduction

In 2014 former Delta airline employee Mark Henry and current employee Eugene Harvey, a Delta luggage handler in Atlanta, were involved in a gun smuggling scheme. According to authorities, once Henry cleared security, he met up with Harvey inside the airport and the two allegedly exchanged guns for cash. From May to December 2014, Henry and Harvey smuggled guns, some loaded, and ammunition onto at least twenty flights from Atlanta to New York. More than 150 guns, including AK-47s, were recovered when they were sold to undercover officers.[1]

This breach of security was especially troubling because of the well-known level of safety precautions that travelers submit to in U.S. airports and the fact that all airline employees must submit to a background check designed to weed out potential troublemakers. Many governments and organizations play a part in airport security, and each organization conducts an ongoing joint risk and security assessment in support of the organization's goals and responsibility.

Once security goals and responsibilities have been defined, the ongoing task of security professionals is to identify potential areas of loss and to develop and install the appropriate security countermeasures. This process of identifying potential areas of loss is called *risk analysis*, and plays a significant part in security-related strategies. Risk assessment is a process that helps identify potential hazards and analyzes possible responses. A risk assessment is used to identify vulnerabilities or weaknesses that would make an asset more susceptible to damage.

Security and risk management professionals do not typically run organizations (other than their own). Instead they fill an advisory role for senior management in companies where they work.[2] Consequently, unless there is legislation or company policy that requires action, the results of many of the assessments that security professionals conduct may or may not be implemented by management.

▲ A transport security officer (TSO) from the Transportation Security Administration (TSA) checks a passenger's identification at a security checkpoint. TSOs ensure the security of many U.S. airports. What sort of activities do you think they need to perform?

Source: U.S. Transportation Safety Administration, http://www.dhs .gov/photo/tso-checks-passenger-identification

Risk

As with many other terms, the concept of **risk** is elusive and hard to define precisely. According to security expert M. L. Garcia, risk is "the measure of probability and severity of adverse effects."[3] The U.S. Department of Homeland Security (DHS) similarly defines risk as "the potential for an unwanted outcome resulting from an incident, event, or occurrence, as determined by its likelihood and the associated consequences."[4] In sum, risk characterizes the likelihood of an unfavorable outcome or event occurring.[5]

Risk can be understood and expressed as a function of the likelihood of damage and the expected consequences, as shown in Figure 5–1.[6] The likelihood of damage is represented along the horizontal axis, increasing from left to right. The likelihood of damage is a function of the hazard level and vulnerability. The consequences or losses are depicted on the vertical axis, increasing from bottom to top. Risk is shown as four distinct quadrants, each of which depicts the extent of risk.

Risk Assessment

A **risk assessment** is a process that helps identify potential hazards and analyze possible outcomes if a hazard occurs.[7] There are numerous hazards to consider and many possible scenarios for each hazard. When conducting a risk assessment, security professionals identify vulnerabilities or weaknesses that would make an asset more susceptible to

risk
The measure of probability or potential and severity of adverse effects. Risk characterizes the likelihood of an unfavorable outcome or event occurring.

1   Define and explain risk.

risk assessment
Helps identify potential hazards and analyze possible outcomes if a hazard occurs. When conducting a risk assessment, security professionals identify vulnerabilities or weaknesses that would make an asset more susceptible to damage, to determine the probability of security risks actually happening, determine the impact and consequences of such an occurrence, and prioritize the risk factors so they can be dealt with effectively.

2   Understand the basic steps inherent in a risk assessment.

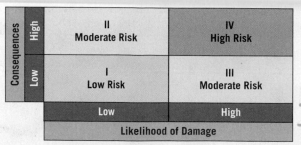

		Low	High
Consequences	**High**	II Moderate Risk	IV High Risk
	Low	I Low Risk	III Moderate Risk
		Low	High
		Likelihood of Damage	

Quadrant I, Low Risk: low likelihood of damage and low consequences.

Quadrant II, Moderate Risk: low likelihood of damage and high consequences.

Quadrant III, Moderate Risk: high likelihood of damage and low consequences.

Quadrant IV, High Risk: high likelihood of damage and high consequences.

FIGURE 5–1

Risk As a Function of Likelihood of Damage and Consequences

Source: Federal Emergency Management Agency (FEMA), *Primer for Design Professionals: Communicating with Owners and Managers of New Buildings on Earthquake Risk*, Risk Management Series, FEMA 389, 2004.

damage.[8] Vulnerabilities contribute to the severity of damage when an incident occurs. The impacts from hazards can be reduced by mitigation. If there is potential for significant impacts, then mitigation should be a high priority.[9]

A risk assessment attempts to answer three questions:

1. What can go wrong?
2. What is the likelihood that it would go wrong?
3. What are the consequences?[10]

The answers to these three questions help professionals assess risk by identifying, measuring, quantifying, and evaluating potential hazards.[11]

An effective assessment provides a way to identify which risks represent opportunities for corrective action and which represent potential pitfalls.[12] In this context, opportunities are events that benefit the organization by their presence or existence, and pitfalls are events that hurt the organization. PricewaterhouseCoopers advises that risk assessments provide management with a view of events that could impact the achievement of objectives.[13] They are designed to give organizations a clear view of internal or external variables to which they may be exposed. Risk assessment should be examined in the context of the organization's desired risk appetite and tolerance, and should provide a basis for determining risk responses.[14] A risk assessment of security (or crime) is conducted to determine the probability of a security incident actually happening, as well as to determine the impact and consequences of such an occurrence, and to prioritize the risk factors so they can be dealt with effectively.[15]

Determining Risk

A risk assessment often starts by determining the baseline for the organization's risk. First, a preliminary security survey—defined as a brief exploratory on-site investigation to identify vulnerable assets and security risks that confront the organization to establish the current state of on-site security measures—should be conducted.[16] Residents and small businesses can ask the local police for assistance or information to help them conduct a security survey. Security professionals should coordinate with the local police regardless of who conducts the survey.

More detailed security surveys can then follow. The U.S. Federal Emergency Management Agency (FEMA) provides the Threat and Hazard Identification and Risk Assessment (THIRA) protocol, which is a four-step common risk assessment process.[17] The THIRA protocol helps the whole community understand its risks and can be used to estimate capability requirements by matching risks to core capabilities. The process informs a variety of emergency management efforts, and helps communities answer the following questions:

- What do we need to prepare for?
- What shareable resources are required in order to be prepared?
- What actions could be employed to avoid, divert, lessen, or eliminate a threat or hazard?[18]

The THIRA process involves four basic steps:

1. *Identify threats and hazards of concern.* Based on a combination of experience, forecasting, subject matter expertise, and other available resources, identify a list of the threats and hazards of primary concern to the community. Examples of threats include an earthquake, train derailment, or sabotage of a highway overpass.

THINK ABOUT IT

In your average day, you assess risk in a variety of ways. Consider the last twenty-four hours. What type of security-related considerations did you make? What decisions were made based on your assessments of risk?

2. *Give the threats and hazards context.*   Describe the threats and hazards of concern, showing how they may affect the community. An example might be a natural disaster or terrorist attack with information on the threats.

3. *Establish capability targets.*   Assess each threat and hazard in context to develop a specific capability target for each core capability identified in the National Preparedness Goal. The capability target defines the measurement of success. In other words, what is the goal and how can it be measured? This might include returning to pre incident status, finding living arrangements for all displaced residents, or establishing a service or provision within a specified completion time.

4. *Apply the results.*   Estimate the community assets and mutual aid resources required to achieve the desired result, while considering preparedness activities and mitigation opportunities. Specific resource should be identified.[19]

Once the process is completed, results must be applied in a systematic fashion. For each core capability, resources required to achieve the capability targets must be estimated through the use of community assets and mutual aid, while also considering preparedness activities, including mitigation opportunities.[20]

Carry Out the Survey

1. Analyze the overall environment (neighborhood, block, and so forth).
2. Assess the general vulnerability of the premises.
3. Define the specific points of vulnerability.
4. Recommend specific security procedures.
5. Include specific remedial hardware recommendations.

Follow-Up Steps

6. Urge the implementation of the recommendations.
7. Conduct a follow-up to ensure that recommendations have been implemented.
8. Keep crime statistics to evaluate the survey's effect and the implementation of recommendations.
9. Conduct a second survey of the premise's statistical analysis to determine the alteration in criminal activity in the areas surveyed.

Security Exercise

Conduct an informal site survey and vulnerability assessment of your residence using the THIRA protocol. Compare it to and contrast it with another location (your workplace, someone else's residence, a public facility or private facility that you can access). Compile a list of problems and solutions for each and contrast the specific differences.

Security Surveys

Both for their own security assurance and to provide an example of the process, all security students (and professionals) should conduct a security survey of their home and office, as well as of any other location at which they regularly spend time. Residential security surveys are typically done informally and intuitively, and consist of checking to make sure doors and windows are locked and lighting is sufficient for normal visibility. Office or workplace security surveys may also be done informally and, unless assigned to security duties within the organization, are limited to a person's immediate area and responsibility.

A security survey is an in-depth, on-site examination of a physical facility and its surrounding property. They are typically conducted to determine the security status of an organization or residence, to identify deficiencies or security risks, to define the protection needed, and to make recommendations to minimize criminal opportunity.[21] It is the primary tool used in crime prevention to recognize, appraise, and anticipate potential loss in residential areas. As part of an ongoing process, a proper security survey provides a foundation for future action.[22]

The U.S. Department of Defense offers guidance on conducting a basic security survey. As a starting point, five steps must be used in carrying out the actual survey, while four additional steps must be attended to afterward.

Spotlight
Home Security Survey

The Tucson Police Department (TPD) provided a booklet for their citizens, outlining some physical security measures that can enhance the security of residences. Those recommendations include using or doing the following:

- Security strike plate for external door locks.
- Single- or double-cylinder deadbolts to secure external doors.
- 190-degree viewer for windowless doors to see visitors without unlocking the door,
- Secure window air-conditioning units from inside so they cannot be removed to allow access.
- Secure access to attic and basement.
- Block off or replace pet doors and secure skylights.
- Use a burglar alarm.
- Use a smoke and/or fire alarm.
- Engrave property so it can be identified if it is lost or stolen.

- Photograph valuables to help in identification.
- Update inventory regularly.
- Use a security cabinet or safe.
- Have a security closet.

For residential security enhancements that can be done outside, the TPD suggested

- Trimming shrubbery.
- Using additional lighting.
- Locking gates.

For Secure tools and other property so it cannot be stolen or used to gain access to your residence.

Source: Tucson, Arizona, Police Department, "Home Security Survey: Improve the Safety of Your Home," (n.d.), http://police.tucsonaz.gov/files/police/home_security_booklet.pdf

An Ongoing Process

Once the survey is completed, the job is still not finished. Professionals should realize that the security survey process is not a one-shot operation, and it is not to be looked on as a simple, straightforward task.[23] Take, for instance, residential security. As residences are diverse in type, size, and geographic placement, it is difficult to identify a standard form or template usable for all locations. A residential security survey is an examination of your residence to

- Determine the present security status.
- Identify any deficiencies or excesses in security.
- Determine what level of protection is needed.
- Make recommendations to improve the overall security.

According to the Tucson, Arizona, Police Department (PD), low- to medium-skilled burglars use rocks, screwdrivers, and pliers to gain entry to commit most burglaries there. Their targets are often selected at random, and they can gain entry to their targets in four to forty-five seconds.

To meet the challenges presented by diverse settings, a checklist can be a helpful tool. Take, for example, the risk-assessment checklist now being used for a school system in

Northern Ireland. The list is divided into three parts to give a picture of the risks a school faces and the security measures in existence:

- *Part 1.*   Incidence of crime (assess the type, scale, patterns, and trends of incidents in the last twelve months).
- *Part 2.*   Environment and buildings (assess the environmental and building factors which contribute to school security).
- *Part 3.*   Security measures (assess the degree and effectiveness of the security measures employed).[24]

Each element of the checklist is graded from 0 for low security risk to 5 for high security risk. Security survey checklists should be carefully tailored to the organization and security priorities. The effectiveness of the survey is found in the combination of the security survey and the experience and skill of the security professional(s) conducting the survey.[25]

Diagram the Location

It is helpful to have a sketch or diagram of each room, area, and building when conducting the survey so the results can be shared with others. Whether drawn by hand or on a computer, in great detail or mere outline, the diagrams should depict the general shape and layout, large objects contained within the space, and problem areas identified during the survey. For example, a diagram of a building could include only the basic shape of the rooms on the inside and the trees and structures on the outside, while separate diagrams of each of the rooms and outdoor structures would identify doors, windows, and furniture.

A legend should be used for each diagram to explain the annotations to readers. Photographs can be used to supplement the diagrams and narrative of the survey. As with the diagrams, they can include as much or as little as deemed necessary. Because it is not a good idea to rely solely on memory to interpret photographs, careful notes should be developed immediately to explain the images and their meaning for the security process.

Cost Effectiveness

Because they are critical to organizational security, failure to conduct an effective risk assessment, including the important step of cost–benefit analysis, may reduce an organization's level of security. Those security practitioners who do not perform risk assessments will deprive senior management of clear and present danger data, thereby compromising the organization's level of security effectiveness.

Once risks are identified, decisions should be made on the most cost-effective measures to implement to manage the risks. The relationship between risk factor and cost should be identified, as it will likely guide many of the risk management decisions. This decision is often made after calculating the savings that are likely to be gained by effective security measures. That calculation can be made by using a simple cost–benefit analysis: Benefits – Costs = Savings.

In this equation, benefits include the anticipated profits or advantages, both direct and indirect, expected to be realized with the implementation of a measure or change in procedure. Costs are the direct and indirect anticipated expenses, charges or fees that will most likely be incurred because of the action.[26]

Security measures should result in risk reduction that may arise from a combination of reduced likelihood of threat, vulnerability, or consequences. A security measure is cost effective when the benefit outweighs the cost of providing the security measure, that is, the benefit-to-cost ratio exceeds 1 using this equation: Benefit-to-cost ratio = Benefit / Cost = (Risk) × (Reduction in risk generated by the security measure) + (Co-benefits) / (Cost of security measure).

The benefit of a security measure is the sum of the losses averted due to the security measure and any expected co-benefit from the security measure not directly related to mitigating vulnerability or threat (e.g., reduction in crime, improved passenger experience, etc.). This benefit is then compared to the cost of the security measure, which should include opportunity costs. A security measure is cost effective if the benefit exceeds the cost.[27]

THINK ABOUT IT

In what ways do you conduct a cost–benefit analysis with your personal security? Are there steps that you do or don't take because of the cost, even though taking those steps might provide more security?

Spotlight
Security Vulnerability Self-Assessment

The State of Utah Department of Public Safety provided its residents with a Security Vulnerability Self-Assessment. The survey includes general questions designed to apply to all components of a facility (buildings, equipment, storage areas, and equipment storage sites). General questions for the facility include the following:

1. **Do you have a written emergency response plan (ERP)?**
   A plan is vital in case there is an incident that requires immediate response. Your plan should be reviewed at least annually (or more frequently if necessary) to ensure it is up-to-date and addresses security emergencies.

2. **Is access to the critical components of the facility (i.e., a part of the physical infrastructure of the facility that is essential for sensitive operations) restricted to authorized personnel only?**
   You should restrict or limit access to the critical components of your facility to authorized personnel only. This is the first step in security enhancement for your infrastructure.

3. **Are facilities fenced, including warehouses and equipment yards, and are gates locked where appropriate?**
   The fence perimeter should be walked periodically to check for breaches and maintenance needs. All gates should be locked with chains and a tamper-proof padlock that at a minimum protects the shank.

4. **Are your doors, windows, and other points of entry, such as roof hatches and vents, kept closed and locked?**
   Lock all building doors and windows, hatches and vents, gates, and other points of entry to prevent access by unauthorized personnel. Check locks regularly.

5. **Is there external lighting around the critical components of your facility?**
   Adequate lighting of the exterior of the facility's critical components is a good deterrent to unauthorized access and may result in the detection or deterrence of trespassers. Motion detectors that activate switches turning lights on or triggering alarms also enhance security.

6. **Are warning signs (no trespassing, no unauthorized access, etc.) posted on all critical components of your facility?**
   Warning signs are an effective means to deter unauthorized access.

7. **Do you patrol and inspect your buildings, equipment, equipment storage sites, and other critical components?**
   Frequent and random patrolling by your facilities staff may discourage potential tampering. It can also help identify problems that may have arisen since the previous patrol.

8. **Is the area around the critical components of your facility free of objects that may be used for breaking and entering?**
   When assessing the area around your facility's critical components, look for objects that could be used to gain entry (e.g., rocks, metal objects).

9. **Are the entry points to your facility easily seen?**
   You should clear fence lines of all vegetation. Overhanging or nearby trees can also provide easy unauthorized access. Avoid landscaping that will permit trespassers to hide or conduct unnoticed suspicious activities.

10. **Do you have an alarm system that will detect unauthorized entry or attempted entry at critical components?**
    Consider installing an alarm system that notifies the proper authorities or your facility's designated contact for emergencies when there has been a breach of security. Inexpensive systems are available and should be considered whenever possible for securing sensitive items.

11. **Do you have a key control and accountability policy?**
    Keep a record of locks and associated keys, and to whom the keys have been assigned. This record will facilitate lock replacement and key management (e.g., after employee turnover or loss of keys). Vehicle and building keys should be kept in a lockbox when not in use. Keep the key to the key box secure location not in the top drawer next to the key box.

12. **Are entry codes and keys limited to company personnel only?**
    Suppliers and personnel from colocated organizations (e.g., organizations using your facility for telecommunications) should be denied access to codes and/or keys.

13. **Do you have a neighborhood watch program for your facility?**
    Watchful neighbors can be very helpful to a security program. Make sure they know whom to call in the event of an emergency or suspicious activity.

Source: Utah Department of Public Safety, Division of Homeland Security Office of Emergency Services, "Security Vulnerability Self-Assessment Guide for Critical Infrastructure Protection," 2005.

The cost–benefit analysis process typically comprises eight major steps.

1. Define the problem or opportunity, including background and circumstances.
2. Define the scope and formulate facts and assumptions.
3. Define and document alternatives (including status quo if relevant).
4. Develop cost estimates for each alternative (including status quo if relevant).
5. Identify quantifiable and nonquantifiable benefits.
6. Define alternative selection criteria.
7. Compare alternatives.
8. Report results and recommendations.[28]

Cost–benefit analyses provide decision makers with facts and data required to make informed decisions. The primary objective of developing cost–benefit analyses is to identify and obtain approval of the optimum course of action to solve a specific problem or capitalize on a specific improvement opportunity. Development of a cost–benefit analysis should be done in a group or team, not by an individual. Team members should be chosen based on expertise in specific areas addressed by the cost–benefit analysis. Expertise could be needed in any number of areas, such as cost estimating, personnel, equipment, facilities, and logistics. The size of the group may be influenced by factors such as the scope, size, and complexity of the subject of the cost–benefit analysis.

The U.S. Army Cost–Benefit Analysis Guide observed that a cost–benefit analysis:

- Is a decision support tool that documents the predicted effect of actions under consideration to solve a problem or take advantage of an opportunity.
- Is a structured proposal that functions as a decision package for organizational decision makers.
- Defines a solution aimed at achieving specific organizational objectives by quantifying the potential financial impacts and other business benefits such as:
  - ○ Savings and/or cost avoidance.
  - ○ Revenue enhancements and/or cash-flow improvements.
  - ○ Performance improvements.
  - ○ Reduction or elimination of a capability gap.
- Considers all benefits to include nonfinancial or nonquantifiable benefits of a specific course of action (COA) or alternative.
- An analysis of needs and problems, their proposed alternative solutions, and a risk analysis to lead the analyst to a recommended choice before a significant amount of funds are invested by the bill payer.
- Must be tailored to fit the problem, because finding the optimal solution is the focus of the cost–benefit analysis.
- Supports the decision-making process, but will not make a final decision. That will be the responsibility of the decision maker/leadership.
- Is not a substitute for sound judgment, management, or control.
- Is a living document. It is important for the preparer to keep the cost–benefit analysis updated so that the decision maker can make an informed decision based on the best available information.[29]

Types of Risk

There are five different types of risk that security managers need to assess:

1. *Dynamic risks.*   These may change under certain conditions, including weather, time, or location.
2. *Static risks.*   These usually remain constant, regardless of their environment, such as laws, standards, and regulations.
3. *Inherent risks.*   These are associated with the particular product, location, or industry and cannot be avoided.
4. *Speculative risks.*   These affect the organization when new activities or programs are initiated.
5. *Pure risks.*   These include natural disasters and criminal or terrorist acts.

Sources of Risk

Risks come from a variety of sources, and each organization may be exposed to a unique combination of risk factors. In general, the following must be considered regardless of the organization or its location.

1. *Human factors.*   Both human error and failure.
2. *Mechanical factors.*   From machinery or equipment.

0. *Environment, crime risks, and civil disorders*

4. *Procedural factors.*   Some risk is caused by the use of specific procedures or routines.

The Process of Risk Management

3 Examine and describe the risk management process.

risk management
The process used to plan for continuing operations after a loss or other incident.

Risk management is the process used to make plans for continuing operations after a loss or other incident. According to Garcia, the risk management process answers the following questions:

1. What can be done?
2. What options are available?
3. What are the associated trade-offs in terms of costs, benefits, and risks?
4. What are the impacts of current management decisions on future options?[30]

To practice risk management, security professionals must serve as an integral part of the organization. The first step in the process of risk management is recognizing the threat or threats.[31] Security professionals must be aware that risks are inevitable and formidable and that security systems exist so that they can be reduced or at least managed.

The Department of Homeland Security (DHS) policy on risk management is based on the concept that security depends on connecting information about risks, activities, and capabilities. An understanding of that information should be used to guide prevention, protection, response, and recovery efforts. The establishment of sound risk management practices will help with avoiding or mitigating the effects of emerging or unknown risks. Risk management at the organizational level complements planning efforts, policy development, budget formulation, performance assessments, and reporting. Risk management will not keep events from occurring, but it enables security professionals to focus on and mitigate or prevent those things that are likely to bring the greatest harm.[32]

Security professionals in the past simply used their work experience and skills learned in previous positions to manage risk. This often resulted in a hodgepodge of industry and organizational policy, blending a variation of risk management from fields so diverse as military, law enforcement, finance, law, and occupational safety.[33] Security professionals today are more inclined to apply more uniform industry-accepted risk management principles. These principles are security specific, and provide the cost-effective solution needed in today's private- and public-sector climate. [34]

The Cycle of Risk Management

Risk management and assessment plays a significant part in security-related strategies. Not only is the size of the risks security professionals encounter getting larger, but the complications entailed in managing them are increasing as well.[35] Consequently, security professionals now view risk management as a continuous cycle containing a number of different elements (Figure 5–2):

- *Risk assessment.*   Assess the risks to the organization and assets in terms of likelihood and impact of envisioned threats.
- *Implementation.*   Identify and implement security measures to reduce the assessed risks to an acceptable level.
- *Evaluation.*   Assess the effectiveness of countermeasures and identify the corrective action necessary.

The DHS promotes a process that employs comparability and a shared understanding of information and analysis, and facilitates better structured and informed decision making (Figure 5–3). The process is comprised of:

- Defining and framing the context of decisions and related goals and objectives.
- Identifying the risks associated with the goals and objectives.

FIGURE 5–2
The Risk Management Cycle
Source: Center for the Protection of National Infrastructure (CPNI), "Personnel Security Risk Assessment: A Guide," 4th ed., 2013.

- Analyzing and assessing the identified risks.
- Developing alternative actions for managing the risks and creating opportunities, and analyzing the costs and benefits of those alternatives.
- Making a decision among alternatives and implementing that decision.
- Monitoring the implemented decision and comparing observed and expected effects to help influence subsequent risk management alternatives and decisions.[36]

When a critical incident occurs, it is usually because either there was a lack of knowledge that a risk existed, or the risk was known but decision makers failed to act. After news of such an incident becomes widely known, organization managers are often quite embarrassed with folks outside the organization and maybe even their stakeholders, wondering why the risks were not considered. Sometimes, a decision maker did not follow policy. In other instances, there was no policy in the first place.[37]

The biggest breakdown in risk management cycle can occur in the response stage, where specific risks should be identified and actively managed.[38] Although an organization's managers will invest effort in identifying and assessing the risks, they may fall prey to any of the four lures that keep them from following up, according to Kutsch and Browning:

1. *The lure of positivity.*   If they call attention to risks, managers may undermine stakeholders' confidence in their ability to deliver. The lure of positivity causes discussion of risk responses to become suppressed or deemphasized.
2. *The lure of noncommitment.*   Managers may tend to defer commitments as long as possible, in some cases deferring action until a risk actually materializes. They may act as if risk is fiction until it materializes.
3. *The deterrent of powerlessness.*   Managers may perceive that identifying risk gives the impression of having too little control. Managers tend to believe that they lack the resources necessary to respond to the risk.[39]
4. *The lure of the measurable.*   All too often, risk management depends on what can be counted and quantified, and doesn't consider qualitative measures such as a company's image.[40]

Addressing these lures may require altering the associations attached to the practice of risk management. Risks are normal and should be expected. Managers must be encouraged to respond proactively to risk before it materializes, and they must be provided the resources to do so.[41]

FIGURE 5–3
Risk Management Process
Source: Department of Homeland Security (DHS), "Homeland Security Risk Management Doctrine," *Risk Management Fundamentals*, 2011.

Risk Management Activities

Risk management activities are quite diverse. Some risk management activities address multiple aspects of risk, while others are more targeted to address specific aspects. Risk management activities can be categorized in the following ways:

- Identify, deter, detect, disrupt, and prepare for threats and hazards.
- Reduce vulnerabilities.
- Mitigate consequences.[42]

These activities are undertaken to support the overall achievement of security and resilience, at organizational, community, sector, and national levels.[43]

Risk Management Programs

A good risk management program involves four basic steps:

1. Identification of risks through the analysis of threats and vulnerabilities.
2. Analysis and study of risks, which includes the probability and severity of an event.
3. Optimization of risk management alternatives by use of risk avoidance, reduction, spreading, or transfer.
4. Ongoing study of security programs.

Risk Management Applications

Situations where risk management can be applied include:

- Strategic planning
- Capabilities-based planning
- Resource decisions
- Operational planning
- Exercise planning
- Real-world events
- Research and development[44]

Examples of these are found in the use of risk management by planners to prioritize which of the organization's capabilities could have the greatest return on investment in preparedness activities. Risk management is also used when requesting and allocating resources, including grant funding. With risk management strategies, organizations can better understand which scenarios are more likely to impact them, the likely consequences, and what resources are likely to be needed. Risk management can also be used to identify realistic scenarios for exercises, focusing on special threats and hazards.[45]

Risk Management Principles

The key principles for effective risk management include:

- Unity of effort
- Transparency
- Adaptability
- Practicality
- Customization[46]

Unity of effort is critical because risk management should be an enterprisewide process that promotes integration and synchronization across all entities that share responsibility for managing risks. The principle of transparency demonstrates the dependence on open and direct communications for effective risk management. The principle of practicality indicates that security risk management cannot eliminate all uncertainty nor can it identify all risks. This is especially true when facing threats from adaptive adversaries. Risk management programs should be customized to match the organization, while being balanced with the environment they support.[47]

Organizational Risk

Managing risk requires identifying the sources of risk and those facets of the organization affected by risk. We need to examine the types of risks faced by organizations, and identify some necessary practices for managing these risks. Organizational risks come from both internal and external sources.

Internal Risk

Internal risks that affect the individual include egotism, ambition, resistance to change, and pessimism. Bruch and Kreutzer found that the internal risks that affect organizations include lack of checks and balances, tunnel vision or short-term thinking. Internal risks could also be seen as management failure or mismanagement. Internal risks can include the following:

- Errors in strategic decision making (short-term thinking, selection of unsuitable advisers).
- Lack of leadership (technical incompetence, lack of credibility, negative role model behavior, lack of self-criticism).
- Lack of separation of powers (dependencies between supervisory board, management board and auditors).
- Corporate crime (corruption, embezzlement, personal gain, creative accounting, fraud).
- Lack of innovation allows competitors to gain market share and eventually put the organization's profitability and viability in jeopardy.[48]

Internal sources of risk include financial stewardship, personnel reliability, and systems reliability. Organizations of all types are subject to these types of internal risks. Risks from within can derail otherwise effective operations and negatively affect the organizational mission.[49]

External Risk

External risk is risk that an organization is exposed to as based on factors external to the organization. External organizational risks include trends on a global, political, or societal scale, the effects of extreme weather, acts of terrorism, cyberthreats, pandemics, and human-caused accidents or technical failures. It is important that the risks from external threats remain at the forefront of consideration, especially for organizations with critical infrastructure responsibilities.[50]

Threats, vulnerabilities, and consequences have all evolved dramatically in the Internet age. Critical infrastructure is increasingly exposed to cyber risks.[51] This stems from the increasing integration of information and communications technologies with critical infrastructure operations along with adversaries intent on exploiting cyber vulnerabilities. Figure 5–4 illustrates the evolving threats to critical infrastructure.

internal risks
Affect the individual and include egotism, ambition, resistance to change and pessimism, lack of checks and balances, tunnel vision, corporate crime, and lack of innovation or short-term thinking. Internal risks could also be seen as management failure or mismanagement.

TIIINK ABOUT IT

What are some of the external security risks that the average contemporary household faces? How much of a threat are they thought to be? How much of a threat should they be regarded?

external risk
Risk to an organization that is based on factors external to the organization. External organizational risks include trends on a global, political, or societal scale, the effects of extreme weather, acts of terrorism, cyberthreats, pandemics, and human-made accidents or technical failures.

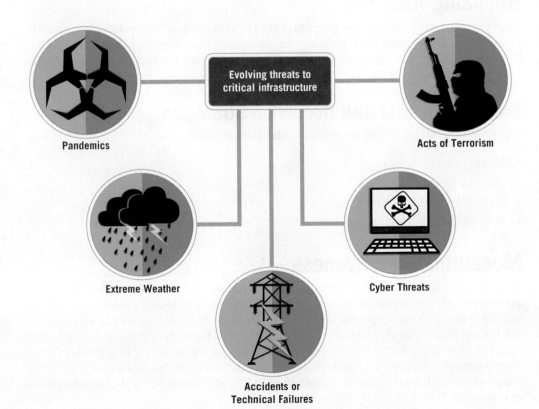

FIGURE 5–4
Evolving Threats to Critical Infrastructure
Source: Department of Homeland Security, National Infrastructure Protection Plan (NIPP), Partnering for Critical Infrastructure Security and Resilience, 2013.

TABLE 5–1
Categories of Organizational Risk

	Strategic Risks	Operational Risks	Institutional Risks
Definition	Risk that affects an organization's vital interests or execution of a chosen strategy, whether imposed by external threats or arising from flawed or poorly implemented strategy.	Risk that has the potential to impede the successful execution of operations with existmg resources, capabilities, and strategies.	Risk associated with an organization's ability to develop and maintain effective management practices, control systems, and flexibility and adaptability to meet organizational requirements.
Description	These risks threaten an organization's ability to achieve its strategy, as well as position itself to recognize, anticipate, and respond to future trends, conditions, and challenges. Strategic risks include those factors that may impact the organization's overall objectives and long-term goals.	Operational risks include those that impact personnel, time, materials, equipment, tactics, techniques, information, technology, and procedures that enable an organization to achieve its mission objectives.	These risks are less obvious and typically come from within an organization. Institutional risks include factors that can threaten an organization's ability to organize, recruit, train, support, and integrate the organization to meet all specified operational and administrative requirements.

Source: Department of Homeland Security (DHS), "Homeland Security Risk Management Doctrine," *Risk Management Fundamentals*, 2011.

Organizations should use a comprehensive risk management approach. This ensures that all internal and external risks are examined and responded to in a way that considers and benefits the whole organization. The underlying factors that directly impact organizational effectiveness and mission success must be considered. Organizations should use the comprehensive approach to risk management so they have a more complete perspective in order to manage risks and promote organizational effectiveness. Table 5–1 shows the categories of risks that face organizations.

Reducing Risk

Most organizations, whether government, private, industrial, or nonprofit, know that the practice of reducing risks when they are identified can reduce expected costs in the future. Experience shows that expenditures made to reduce risk can generate a positive return on investment by preventing future claims and reducing insurance premiums.

Steps to Optimal Risk Reduction Strategies

The FEMA identified several steps to optimal risk reduction strategies:

- Identify potential losses
- Quantify losses
- Identify risk reduction strategies
- Select and implement strategies[52]

Measuring Effectiveness

The use of performance metrics is important in the risk management process. It enables assessment of improvements in security and resilience, and shows progress in meeting priorities and goals and objectives.[53] For example, security professionals can rank the risk level in every country in which their company does business on a scale of 1 to 10. They can then determine the local effect on a global risk. If the economy in a given location were ranked and measured, risks regarding hiring or buying decisions could be determined as well. These calculations would need to be coordinated with other organizational departments.

Spotlight
Managing Risk on Campus

University campuses provide a unique example of the complex considerations needed for evaluating risk in an organization. They often consist of many different types and sizes of buildings, with many different functions. FEMA identified unique issues associated with higher education facilities that should be considered during the design and construction phase include:

- Protection of students, faculty, and staff is a very high priority.
- Higher education facilities have a high daytime occupancy and some evening use, with reduced use in the summer months.

- Ensuring the survival of records, whether in electronic or written form, is essential for continued operation.
- Protection of valuable contents such as library inventories, research equipment, and materials is a high priority.

Source: Federal Emergency Management Agency (FEMA), *Primer for Design Professionals: Communicating with Owners and Managers of New Buildings on Earthquake Risk*, Risk Management Series, FEMA 389, 2004.

Careers in Security

Name: Douglas S. Riggin

Position: Manager, Security

Year hired: 2009

City, state where you are based: Nashville, Tennessee

College(s) attended (degree): Newberry College – BA

Majors: Sociology/Criminal Justice

Please give a brief description of your job. Part of the Altria (a Fortune 500 company). Corporate Security team headquartered in Richmond, Virginia. Altria owns companies such as Philip Morris and US Smokeless Tobacco (USSTC) as well as premier wineries. My responsibilities include physical security for all the locations operated by USSTC to include a seed farm in Brazil. Protection of the company's personnel, products, and properties are the key priorities. I also participate in high-threat employee terminations, executive protection, the Threat Assessment Team, policy implementation, contractor management, and Corporate Security goals and objectives.

What qualities/characteristics are most helpful for this job? Communication, organization, and discipline are qualities managers should espouse and demand from their Security Departments. A disciplined approach to everyday activities allows smooth transitions between shifts and, in the event of an emergency, all security personnel know and have practiced their roles.

What is a typical starting salary? For a security manager the normal starting salary for a reputable company is in the $100,000 range plus bonus.

What is the salary potential as you move up into higher-level jobs? There is a wide range of salaries depending on the position, from a Vice President in charge of the Security Program making $500,000 to a Chief Security Officer at a Fortune 500 company making $300,000 plus stock options and bonus. A manager's compensation package may reach to the $200,000 range plus a company car.

What advice would you give someone beginning studies in security? The most important thing is to plan ahead. Understand that if you use illegal drugs, are arrested, or just act irresponsibly it will be difficult to pass a background investigation. Although a state has legalized marijuana employers may still refuse to hire an individual who has used marijuana. I recommend studies that include accounting, language, and engineering. A criminal justice degree doesn't lend itself to a private-sector job unless it has a Security or Law Enforcement focus. Plan on obtaining a Master's Degree in the future when you know what you are going to do.

What appealed to you most about the position when you applied for it? I enjoy the ability to have freedom to run my own program and participate in outside organizations to improve the Security industry while learning from other security practitioners.

How would you describe the interview process? Be prepared to discuss accomplishments and the ability to work within a corporate framework. In the Security industry, budgets for infrastructure are limited and often it is necessary to share resources. Interviewers want to know if you are a self-starter and able to work as part of a team to be successful.

What is a typical day like? There is not a typical day. If you are a manager you are on call 24 hours a day and must be able to respond immediately. Be prepared for any event and have an educated answer available for executive management should there be a critical event. Always add value and a return on the company's investment. Simple things like checking fire extinguishers for the Safety Department, monitoring weather activity, and disseminating bad-weather alerts or emailing traffic problems allow Security to be indispensable.

In a typical day, what do you like best/least about it? Communication with and assisting other employees and security officers are what I like best. Instructing employees regarding workplace violence and responding to their questions is enjoyable. Unfortunately, all companies find it necessary to reduce headcount or terminate employees for such things as absenteeism or nonperformance, which normally requires Security to escort the employee off the premises. That is never pleasant.

How would you suggest interested applicants gain experience? Start at the bottom. If their field is Security then work for a security contractor to determine if they want to pursue that career. Even if they go to the highest levels of Security they should know what the line employees do on a daily basis.

Would you recommend military experience? Yes, for work experience and life experience.

Does holding a full-time job during college help applicants get hired afterward? Not necessarily; however, if I am the employer I am very interested in an individual who was able to improve their position in life by concurrently obtaining an education and working full time. It is impressive if the candidate made good grades and acquired additional responsibilities at work.

Summary

- **Define and explain risk.**
  - Risk is the measure of probability and severity of adverse effects or unwanted outcome resulting from an incident, event, or occurrence, as determined by its likelihood and the associated consequences.

- **Understand the basic steps inherent in a risk assessment.**
  - The risk assessment process helps identify potential hazards, vulnerabilities, or weaknesses and analyze possibilities to reduce the effects by mitigation. A risk assessment attempts to answer three questions:
    1. What can go wrong?
    2. What is the likelihood that it will go wrong?
    3. What are the consequences?

- **Examine and describe the risk management process.**
  - The risk management process helps security professionals determine what options are available, and the associated trade-offs and impacts of those options. The risk management process answers the questions:
    1. What can be done?
    2. What options are available?
    3. What are the associated trade-offs in terms of costs, benefits, and risks?
    4. What are the impacts of current management decisions on future options?

KEY TERMS

external risk	95	risk	85	risk management	92
internal risks	95	risk assessment	85		

REVIEW QUESTIONS

1. How can *risk* be best understood by someone who is not familiar with the term?
2. Describe the basic steps of a risk assessment and explain why they are necessary.
3. In the risk management process, which process includes implementing corrective action?

PRACTICAL APPLICATION

1. Conduct a risk assessment of a "friend" of yours based on what you know and have open, unrestricted access to.
2. Conduct a risk assessment of a specific function of an organization with which you are familiar and to which you have some access.
3. You are the security director of your company. Your president calls you into a meeting of the top-level executives and asks what the leaders in each branch of the organization can do to assist you with your annual risk assessment. What is your response?

Physical Security

Learning Objectives

After reading this chapter, you should be able to:

Introduction

Two men in two vans parked in an alley behind a block of warehouses one night. Wearing bandanas, the men disabled security cameras and forced open a metal shutter at an auto repair shop and drove one of the vans inside. Almost four hours after the break-in, an alarm was triggered from inside an electronics company that was in the same building. A manager with the company checked the building with the police and found all the doors to be secured. They then left, with the thieves hiding inside. The next morning, electronic company employees discovered four pallets of flat-screen televisions worth more than $100,000 were gone, and there was a huge 4-foot-wide by 3-foot-high hole in the wall. According to the *Lauderdale Sun Sentinel*, the manager suspected the men carried the televisions through the hole and loaded them into the vans hidden next door in the auto repair shop. The auto repair shop did not have an alarm system although it did have security cameras.[1]

In another incident, two men entered a high-end wine retail and storage facility, spray-painted the lenses of surveillance cameras and placed plastic bags over motion sensors to disable them. They then stole more than 200 cases of wine and released gas into the building in an attempt to spark an explosion. The break-in was discovered when the building manager noticed the smell of gas and notified the authorities. A utility worker found two gas lines had been damaged and a gas-powered heater had been lit. It was later learned that the thieves took 13 hours to steal the wine valued at $648,000. They had overlooked one camera, which captured images that later led to the arrest of one of them.[2]

These crimes demonstrate the kinds of threats to physical security that retail and commercial enterprises must prepare for every day. In the security profession, the term *physical security* is used to describe the steps taken and the material employed to safeguard (ensure the *security* of) people and property. The U.S. Department of Defense defines physical security as "That part of security concerned with physical measures designed to safeguard personnel; to prevent unauthorized access to equipment, installations, material, and documents; and to safeguard them against espionage, sabotage, damage, and theft."[3,4] The two primary concerns of physical security are prevention and protection. Both serve the interests of people, equipment, and property.

Physical security is often a difficult concept to master, and it can be even more difficult in application. Security is often seen as effective at keeping honest people out of a building or area. Many security professionals will tell you that the perception of security (something that looks like it's locked or otherwise protected) is more important than the actual security itself. Perhaps the best advice is to do your best to secure the premises from threats, but be prepared to the point of expectation of a breach, and have a response plan in place. Said another way, ask yourself, "How can my best efforts be defeated?" and then take steps to guard against the best responses.

Guiding Principles

Security professionals in a company or organization are expected to safeguard property from such actions as loss, theft, destruction, and vandalism, and protecting people from injury, whether by physical accident or victimization by crime. Two principles guide the actions of security professionals. The first is the duty or legal obligation to protect an individual on company property or elsewhere while doing company business. This duty is often based on a relationship the company or organization (and its employees and representatives) has with individuals, whether clients, customers, or anyone else who is legally on company property. The second principle is foreseeability, or whether a risk can be seen and protected against given the company-related activity that is occurring.[5] The risk could be seen or anticipated in any number of ways including whether similar actions had previously occurred in similar situations in the past, whether employees had complained about the potential for such activities, or police or security reports warned about the security threat.

THINK ABOUT IT

One way of evaluating physical security is to envision a number of locations with which you are familiar—home, workplace, another building (school, mall, exercise facility, place of worship, etc.). Imagine you were involved in some of the situations that were described at the beginning of this chapter. Look at each of those situations from a security professional's perspective. Some security experts might suggest you examine buildings or facilities security while imagining yourself in the role of a criminal or terrorist. Imagine that you are trying to gain unauthorized access to the structure or facility to vandalize something on the outside, steal or destroy something on the inside, or in some way harm a person in either area. Vary these scenarios as you proceed through this chapter and see if the process helps you to focus on the material presented.

Physical Security

As mentioned, **physical security** describes the physical protection of an organization's resources, including people, data, facilities, equipment, and systems. Physical security is primarily concerned with the safety of personnel, which always takes precedence over other security concerns.[6] Physical security is generally focused on a design that ensures only authorized people gain physical access to a facility. A focus on physical security should also protect the facility from many other threats. According to security expert K. Wan, the major sources of physical security threats are:

- Weather (e.g., temperature, humidity, water, flood, wind, snow, lightning)
- Fire and chemical (e.g. explosion, smoke, toxic material, industrial pollution)
- Earth movement (e.g., earthquake, volcano, landslide)
- Object movement (e.g. building collapse, falling object, car, truck, plane, etc.)
- Energy (e.g. electricity, magnetism, radio wave)
- Equipment (e.g., mechanical or electronic component failure)
- Organism (e.g., virus, bacteria, animal, insect)
- Human (e.g., strike, war, sabotage)[7]

Additional threats include blackouts or power outages. A power outage can take down several security systems at once and an alert security officer would be required to notify the organization of an outage to reset computers and safeguard perishables such as food products and medicine.

The key distinction between threats to physical security is their cause. Different events create different situations for organizations, and they often require different responses. The Royal Canadian Mounted Police advised that in order to be effective, physical security strategies must incorporate each of the following elements:

- **Protection** is achieved through the use of physical, procedural, and psychological barriers to delay or deter unauthorized access.
- **Detection** involves the use of appropriate devices, systems, and procedures to signal that an attempted or actual unauthorized access has occurred.
- **Response** entails the implementation of measures to ensure that security incidents are reported to appropriate officials so that immediate and long-term corrective action can be taken.
- **Recovery** refers to the restoration of full levels of service delivery following an incident.[8]

Designing the Security System

The process used to design a security system involves many of the same considerations and steps regardless of the level of security. This applies to activities as diverse as high-security government facilities, fraud detection and espionage detection and prevention, and security barriers.[9] The first step in the process of designing a security system is to determine its objectives. To accomplish this step, the security professional must:

- Characterize (understand) the facility operations and conditions.
- Define the threat.
- Identify potential adversary targets.[10]

Characterization of the facility operations and conditions begins with developing a thorough description of the facility itself. The U.S. Department of Energy advises that this should include the site boundaries, building locations, interior floor plans, and access points.[11] A list of the processes carried out in each facility, with any existing physical security features

physical security
The physical protection of an organization's resources, including people, data, facilities, equipment, and systems. Physical security is primarily concerned with the safety of personnel.

protection
Involves actions used to deter threats, mitigate vulnerabilities, or minimize the consequences associated with an emergency or crisis incident. Protection can include a wide range of activities, such as improving physical security, building redundancy, incorporating resistance to hazards in facility design, initiating active or passive threat countermeasures, installing security systems, promoting workforce security, training and exercising, and implementing cybersecurity measures to delay or deter unauthorized access.

detection
The process of discovering, discerning, or ascertaining something, usually something not previously known or of which you are unaware. Detection involves the use of appropriate devices, systems, and procedures to signal that an attempted or actual unauthorized access has occurred.

response
The implementation of measures to ensure that security incidents are reported to appropriate officials so that immediate and long-term corrective action can be taken.

recovery
The restoration of full levels of service delivery following an incident.

activities, should also be completed. Finally, the security professional should tour the site and interview key personnel to understand the requirements for the facility and an appreciation for the constraints, which must be considered.[12] Compromises to accommodate individuals and entire departments will be necessary so physical security can be maintained during normal business operations. It is important for the security professional to be able to anticipate the need for and implement security alternatives.

Next, a threat definition for the facility must be made. To accomplish this, information must be collected to answer three questions about the adversary:

1. What kind of adversary is anticipated?
2. What is the range of the adversary's tactics?
3. What are the adversary's capabilities?[13]

An **adversary** is typically a person, group, or force that opposes, attacks, or plans to attack a target. In short, an adversary is an opponent or an enemy. Security professionals have widely adopted the U.S. Department of Energy's practice of separating human adversaries into three classes:

1. Insiders
2. Outsiders
3. Outsiders in collusion with insiders[14]

Insiders are those who have regular, authorized access to a company's location, its physical components, and its intellectual property. They potentially include all employees, subcontractors, and vendors—although each may have limited access to only certain company components. According to ASIS International, **outsiders** are those who do not have authorized access to a site.[15]

A specific facility may face several threats, and the security system should provide protection against all of the threats. For each type of adversary, the full range of tactics (deceit, force, stealth, or a combination) should be considered while defining the facility threat.

- Deceit is the attempted defeat of a security system with false authorization and identification.
- Force is the overt forcible attempt to overcome a security system.
- Stealth is the attempt to defeat the detection system and exit the facility covertly.[16]

According to B. J. Steele, important adversary capabilities to be considered in the last step of facility threat definition include:

- Knowledge of the physical security system.
- Level of motivation.
- Skills useful in an escape attempt.
- Speed with which the attack can be carried out.
- Ability to obtain, carry, and utilize tools and weapons.[17]

Since it is rarely possible to test and evaluate all of the possible adversarial capabilities, we must make assumptions based on the information available regarding human performance and the vulnerabilities of physical security elements.[18] Security professionals can use experience, both theirs and the experience of others, in strategizing against adversaries as they plan the physical security posture of their facilities. Adversaries may be motivated by ideological, financial, or personal reasons, so planning to defend against their capabilities should incorporate a variety of scenarios that take the adversary's motivation into account.[19] In these situations, a healthy imagination and the ability to brainstorm hypothetical scenarios are valuable assets for the security professional.

Finally, the identification of potential facility targets should be made, including targets like a defeated security system, breaching of structural features and barriers, use of force or

adversary

A person, group, or force that opposes, attacks, or plans to attack a target. Security professionals typically separate human adversaries into classes, identified as insiders and outsiders.

insiders

Those who have regular, authorized access to a company's location, its physical components, and its intellectual property. They potentially include all employees, subcontractors, and vendors—although each may have limited access to only certain company components.

outsiders

Those who do not have authorized access to a site.

stealth, or access by deceitful means such as forged gate passes.[20] As with the consideration for adversarial capabilities, security professionals should use experience in strategizing against adversaries as they plan the physical security posture of their facilities. A variety of possible escape scenarios should also be considered. Credibility of developed escape scenarios usually depend on the identification of key features or vulnerabilities in the security system. These vulnerabilities should become the focal points of the physical security system design.[21]

Labeling the Threat

The simplicity of the adversarial classes (insiders, outsiders and outsiders in collusion with insiders) may not appropriately identify the threat to all facilities. Security professionals need to defend against a variety of threats, and it may be more appropriate to use different categories or labels to describe the threat characteristics for various threats. Any method may be used to collect information, but the process must result in specific characterizations, not simply a general listing of threats. Many organizations have used labels such as vandals, disgruntled employees (insiders), criminals, and extremists to more thoroughly describe their threats.[22] Some of these types may have come to mind when you were reading the introduction to this chapter.

Vandals. Are individuals or groups who intend to cause relatively minor damage or disruption to an organizational system. They operate mostly at night and may be under the influence of drugs or alcohol. They can carry basic hand tools and cans of spray paint, paintball guns, or similar items. They usually do not have insider assistance, are not highly motivated, and will flee or surrender if they feel they are about to be caught.

Disgruntled employees. Are usually individuals, but could be a small group, who are typically under the influence of alcohol or drugs, and may be mentally unstable. The desire for this threat is usually to attack someone or cause damage to property at the site. If the intent is to attack a person, they may carry weapons. If property damage is the goal, the person will more likely use tools that are already on-site. These threats are highly motivated and do not expect to be caught due to their authorized access.

Criminals. This threat may comprise a small group of people whose goal is theft from the site; and financial gain from selling the stolen items. They may carry tools and will carefully plan their attack. They may carry small weapons but are unlikely to use them. They may have insider assistance and can be expected to break off the attack if detected.

Extremists. This threat consists of an organized group of people whose goal is to bring attention to a practice at the targeted site with which they disagree. The threat may be comprised of environmentalists, animal rights groups, anti- or pro-abortion demonstrators or shareholders, and they have an ideological motivation. This threat is typically nonviolent but may resist eviction from a site and will ignore verbal commands to leave.

Ranking the Threat

Another typology of threats can be found in a ranking system: "low," "medium," or "high" are labels that can be used to describe threats in place of the descriptive labels shown in the previous example. A ranking strategy is a flexible and scalable typology that assesses a security posture relative to a subjective standard. This method gives security professionals the ability to classify activities as diverse as vandalism, criminal activity, and terrorism, at any step in the analysis without the need to reexamine the type of adversary or threat once such a determination has been made. Simple labels such as insiders and outsiders, or a limited view of the threat, may not be sufficient when identifying vulnerabilities or estimating risk to determine the appropriate security measures to implement. The security measures required to stop vandals, for example, are quite different from those required for stopping criminals and terrorists.

THINK ABOUT IT
Consider the labels of adversaries identified in this chapter. How would you change the labels to make them more applicable to the threat to an organization with which you are familiar? Consider, for example, organizations connected with education, retail establishments, manufacturing facilities, restaurants, and houses of worship.

vandals
Individuals or groups who intend to cause relatively minor damage or disruption to an organizational system. They operate mostly at night, may be under the influence of drugs or alcohol, and may carry basic hand tools and cans of spray paint, paintball guns, or similar items.

disgruntled employees
Usually individuals, but could be a small group, who used to or currently work at a site and intend to attack a person or cause damage to property at the site. These threats are highly motivated and the people perpetrating them do not expect to be caught due to their authorized access.

criminals
In the context of physical security, people whose goal is theft from the site and financial gain from selling the stolen items.

extremists
People and groups with an ideological motivation, whose goal is to bring attention to a practice at the targeted site with which they disagree. Extremists range from religious fanatics to animal rights activists.

Protecting against the Threat

The strategies for protecting assets or property from threat are based on the threat's characteristics and the design of the physical security system. Physical security systems protect assets from threats by integrating physical protective measures and security procedures.[23] The foundational goals of these systems include deterrence, detection, defense, and defeat of the adversary or threat.

deterrence
The practice of using threats to convince another to refrain from some course of action. A potential adversary who perceives a risk of being caught may be deterred from attacking.

Deterrence, as you may recall (from Chapter 2), is defined as the practice of using threats to convince another to refrain from some course of action. A potential adversary who perceives a risk of being caught may be deterred from attacking.[24] Deterrence may serve as a first line of defense, but additional measures will often be needed.[25] The effectiveness of deterrence will vary with the adversary's sophistication and objective, and the asset's attractiveness. A threat is a deterrent only to the extent that it convinces the person not to carry out the intended action because of the costs or losses that person would incur.[26] Deterrence may be best accomplished by giving the target the impression they are constantly being watched and monitored. The perceived likelihood of detection combined with the expected severity of punishment are factors in deterrence, yet most adversaries feel they will never be caught, so deterrence cannot be the only strategy.

detection
The process of discovering, discerning, or ascertaining something, usually something not previously known or of which you are unaware. Detection involves the use of appropriate devices, systems, and procedures to signal that an attempted or actual unauthorized access has occurred.

Detection is the process of discovering, discerning, or ascertaining something, usually something not previously known or of which you are unaware. We will examine detection in more depth later in this chapter, especially with regard to detection systems. An effective detection strategy must provide three capabilities:[27]

1. Sense acts against a facility.
2. Assess the validity of the detection.
3. Provide a preprogrammed response.

Detection systems may detect an adversary's activity by any number of ways, usually by technology, human, or animal (canine) sensing. Examples of technology detection range from detecting hidden weapons with an X-ray machine to access-control devices that assess the validity of identification (ID) credentials to traditional security guards with canine support. Each method has positive and negative aspects and should be used based on the anticipated effect on the threat. After sensing an unauthorized action, each of these control elements may respond by admitting or denying access, or they may relay information to another entity for processing and action.[28]

defense
The act of making or keeping something or someone safe from danger, attack, or harm; warding off an attack from another; or guarding against assault, theft, damage, or injury. In the context of physical security, defense is provided by a response force located either on-site or off-site.

Defense is generally considered the act of making or keeping something or someone safe from danger, attack, or harm; warding off an attack from another; or guarding against assault, theft, damage, or injury. In the context of an organization's physical security, defense can be provided by a response force located either on-site or off-site. Defensive measures may be active or passive, and protect an asset from aggression by delaying or preventing an adversary from contact with the asset or by shielding the asset.

defeat
To thwart or prevent something from happening, to beat or overcome in a contest, or to prevail over.

Defeat means to thwart or prevent something from happening, to beat or overcome in a contest, or to prevail over. Most protective systems depend on response personnel, such as those used in defense, to defeat an adversary. Although defeat is not an objective of the design of the physical security system, systems must be designed to accommodate (or at least not interfere with) response activities.[29]

Perimeter Security

Perimeter security is a primary focus of physical security. Securing the boundaries of the company or organization's property may seem like a daunting task. A systematic approach will often provide the best solutions. Security professionals should examine the area to determine what they can block access to and what must remain accessible. That process allows a focus on security for fewer access points. The placement of barriers creates a psychological deterrent, the perception of security, for anyone thinking of unauthorized entry. The proper placement of barriers will often delay or prevent access.[30] Most barriers, like fences, locks, doors, and barred windows, can be used to delay forcible entry, although the delay may not last very long.[31] Ensuring that effective barriers are in place at all times may be difficult to accomplish without adversely affecting normal operations. The hardest part (and the first step for savvy security professionals) is often to ensure the organization's employees know why barriers and other security measures are critical, and how they will be protected because of these security measures.[32]

Access Barriers

Barriers that can be used to delay an adversary's access include passive barriers, security officers, and dispensable barriers. Passive barriers include structural barriers such as doors, walls, floors, locks, vents, ducts, and fences.[33] Security officers can be used to delay adversaries who are trying to breach the perimeter. Sometimes, security officers may not be able to stop adversaries who use force unless they are armed and in fixed, protected positions. Dispensable barriers, for example, chemical fog, smoke, foam, and irritants, can be deployed during an attack or similar emergency situation. Each type of barrier has advantages, and many physical security systems combine all three types.

The use of passive barriers provides a solution that is always in place and even if the barriers fail they will likely delay the adversary. The benefits of using security officers include their mobility (they can be moved around a site) and flexibility (shifts can be arranged to provide needed coverage). The use of passive barriers often limits the number of security officers needed and their frequency of use.[34] Dispensable barriers provide flexibility and support to the other barrier options, though their persistence is limited.

Structural Barriers

Structural barriers (barriers serving as part of a building or other structure) include walls, doors, windows, roofs, and floors. Most walls and locked doors can be breached or penetrated quickly, and windows and utility ducts often serve as nothing more than an additional route for entry or exit.[35]

Doors

Doors are vulnerable security points of any building. Doors should be installed so the hinges are inaccessible or on the inside of the structure. This prevents removal of the screws holding the hinges and the use of chisels or cutting devices.[36] The best door is of little value if there are exposed and removable hinge pins, breakable panels, or weak locks that would allow entry.[37]

Windows

Windows are also a vulnerable security point. They should be secured on the inside using some type of locking device, with the window frame securely fastened to the building so that it cannot be pried loose. As is the case with the glass panels of doors, window glass can be broken to allow an adversary access.[38] If installed, bars used to prevent access should be at least one-half inch in diameter, round, and spaced apart 6 inches to prevent an adversary from easily bending the bars or gaining access by slipping between them.[39]

Heating, Ventilation, and Air-Conditioning (HVAC) Systems

Ventilation shafts, vents, ducts, and openings in the building to accommodate heating, fans, or air-conditioning systems can be used by a criminal or terrorist to introduce a chemical, biological, and radiological agent into a facility. Outdoor air intakes at or below ground level are the most risky because they provide access to the building if not secured.[40]

Some access points can be equipped with sensors to sound an alarm when disturbed. Placing the sensor where it will be activated toward the beginning of the delay time can create an effective combination of detection and delay.[41]

Fences

Three types of fence are used for perimeter security of restricted areas: chain link, barbed wire, and barbed tape or concertina. The type used depends on the threat and the degree of permanence desired. A perimeter fence should be continuous, free of plant growth, and in good condition.[42]

Chain-Link Fences

These form a visible boundary around a facility. They do not pose much of an obstacle, however. A person can easily drive a vehicle through a fence, climb over it, crawl under it, or cut through it.[43] Chain-link fencing should be laid out in straight lines to permit uninterrupted observation.[44] According to ASIS International, adding barbed tape or concertina wire to the structure adds little delay value when the adversary is prepared.[45]

Barbed Wire

This is twisted, double-strand, number 12 gauge wire, with four-point barbs spaced 4 inches apart.[46]

Concertina Wire

This is a type of barbed or razor wire that is formed in large coils that can be expanded.[47]

Gates

closed-circuit television (CCTV)
A type of video surveillance system that is used to transmit a signal from cameras set up in a specific place to a limited set of monitors, so that areas that may need surveillance such as banks and convenience stores can be monitored.

digital imaging systems
A current type of video surveillance system, which will eventually replace CCTV.

Gates provide access through a controllable break in a fence or wall. Gates are secured using locks, guards, alarms, video surveillance systems such as **closed-circuit television (CCTV)** or **digital imaging systems (DIS)**, or a combination of these. The number of gates should be limited to those absolutely necessary, but sufficient to accommodate the peak flow of traffic through the perimeter break where the gate is located.[48] Gates should be locked when not used, when not being watched, and during hours when the facility is closed.[49]

Safes and Vaults

1   Identify differences between a safe and a vault.

Safes and vaults (and locked filing cabinets to an extent) protect high-value items and important records. A safe is a metal box with a high-security locking device. A vault is a completely enclosed and secured space, often a specially constructed room. Both safes and vaults provide a high degree of protection against forced entry by adversaries. Safes and vaults are often used to prevent removal of classified information and valuable materials.[50]

The degree of protection provided depends on the constructed purpose of the safe or vault and the lock's strength and resistance.[51] A safe or vault made for fire protection is not effective in preventing a forced entry. Materials used to protect a safe's contents from heat may do little to resist the blow of a hammer. A safe with thick, solid steel walls designed to protect valuables from theft, provides little protection against fire because steel will transfer heat rapidly to the interior.[52] When deciding which construction and design standards to follow (for fire or security), the characteristics of the asset being protected must be considered. Another consideration is the legal responsibility and liability of the organization to meet any special regulatory requirements or standards established by an insurance provider or regulatory guidelines.[53]

Locks

locks
Devices for securing a door, file cabinet, access, and also used to secure the movable portions of barriers and gates, typically consisting of a bolt or system of bolts propelled and withdrawn by a mechanism operated by a key or dial.

Locks are used to secure the movable portions of barriers. Although locks are the most widely used method of controlling physical access, they should not be the only means of physical protection, as they are no more than a delaying device. A lock can (and will) be defeated. Bumping, a recent burglar trend noted by the media, has demonstrated the need for residents to know how secure locking devices make their homes. All that is needed is a "bump key," a normal key that is specially altered and manipulated to pick the lock without other tools. There are many "how-to" videos online demonstrating how easy bumping is. There are no signs of a break-in when bumping is done, so insurance companies may refuse to replace stolen items. The National Crime Prevention Council recommends installing high-quality locks as a good defense against home burglaries.[54] Because an individual with enough skill and time can compromise them, locks should be used with complementary protection measures, such as periodic guard checks, video surveillance systems, and sensors.[55]

The National Crime Prevention Council suggests that good locks are the first line of defense. When using locks:

- Check for high-security locks or electronic-access control units on all doors, including closets that have private information or hazardous materials, outside doors, and basements.

- Verify that any electronic-access control unit in use has secure key bypass using patented control of duplication of keys. Any access control unit is only as good as its mechanical override devices.

- Make sure all doors are solid. Look for sheet steel on both sides of back and basement doors.

- Make sure doorframes and hinges are strong enough that they cannot be pried open.

- Lock steel bars or door barriers with high-security padlocks that have a hardened steel body and shackle to resist drills, hammers, blowtorches, and bolt cutters.

- Be certain all windows are secure.

- If doors only have a locking knob or lever, install or have installed a dead bolt for additional security.

- Have management change locks before you move into a new office unless they can account for all keys and provide assurance that keys have not been made without their knowledge.

- Don't assume someone else has reported a door, window, or lock that is broken or not working properly. Report these problems immediately.[56]

▲ Key-in knob lock. Key-in knob locks are very popular for residential construction. How could they be a problem for security professionals?
Source: Greg Russ/123RF

Locks generally use physical or digital keys, or require the user to input a combination. There are many types of key locks, including the following:

Cylindrical locksets.   These are often used to secure offices and storerooms. The locking cylinder is located in the center of the doorknob. Some cylindrical locksets have keyways in each side that will lock and unlock them. Others unlock with a key on the outside, but may be locked by pushing or rotating a button on the inside knob. These locks are useful for very low-security applications.

Dead-bolt locks.   Sometimes called tubular dead bolts, these are mounted on the door similar to cylindrical locksets. When the bolt is locked, the dead bolt extends into the doorframe at least 1 inch, and it cannot be unlocked by applying pressure to the bolt. The dead-bolt lock provides acceptable levels of protection for areas where more security is desired. In situations where there is a window in or near the door, a double-cylinder dead bolt (requiring a key to open either side) should be used.

Mortise locks.   Mortise locks are recessed into the edge of the door, often with a doorknob on either side of the door. Entrance doors often have an exterior thumb latch combined with a handle rather than a doorknob. The lock can be activated from inside with a thumb

▲ Dead-bolt lock. Dead-bolt locks provide an added measure of security. What could keep someone from wanting more security?
Source: Bigchen/Shutterstock

Mortise Lock
▶ Mortise locks can be activated with the push of a button from inside. What special precautions should security professionals take when these are used?
Source: User's Guide on Controlling Locks, Keys, and Access Cards, DoD Lock Program, Naval Facilities Engineering Service Center, UG-2040-SHR, Figure 4–8, pp. 4–10.

▲ Combination lock, backed up by a dead-bolt lock. Locks are often used in combination. Why would that be?
Source: Robert J. Beyers II/Shutterstock

turn or by pushing a button. These are considered low-security devices since they weaken the security of the door in the mortised area.

Drop-bolt locks.   These are used as auxiliary locks similar to dead bolts. The lock and the strike both have interlocking leaves, similar to a door hinge. When closed, locking pins in the lock body drop down into the holes provided in the strike and secure the lock, making the lock a single unit and extremely difficult to separate.

Rim-cylinder locks.   Rim-cylinder locks are mounted to the inside surface of the door and secured by screws in the door face. These locks are generally used with drop-bolt and other surface-mounted locks and latches. They consist of an outer barrel, a cylinder and ring, a tailpiece, a back-mounting plate, and two mounting screws.

Unit locks.   Ideal in heavily accessed facilities like hospitals, unit locks are a complete, one-piece unit that slides into a notch cut into the door's latch edge.

Combination locks.   These are mechanical, push-button digital (numbered 0 to 9) devices requiring specific number combinations to open. These locks are normally used for basic access control and should be backed up by additional locking devices when the facility is unoccupied.

Padlocks.   Padlocks are detachable locks that are typically used with a hasp. Low security padlocks are made with hardened steel shackles and provide only minimal resistance to force. High-security padlocks provide the maximum resistance to unauthorized entry when used with a high security hasp.[57]

Locks are generally classified as either mechanical or electrical.

Mechanical Locks

A mechanical lock uses an arrangement of physical parts to prevent the opening of a bolt or latch. According to ASIS International, in such a lock the functional assemblies or components are as follows:

- The bolt or latch that actually holds the movable part (door, window, etc.) to the immovable part (jamb, frame, etc.).

▲ Low-security padlocks provide a low level of security. Why would they be used?

Source: User's guide on controlling locks, keys, and access cards, DoD Lock Program, Naval Facilities Engineering Service Center, UG 2040-SIIR Figure 4–7, pp. 4–7.

▲ High-security padlock. These locks are designed to be more secure. In what applications would they be best used?

Source: User's guide on controlling locks, keys, and access cards, DoD Lock Program, Naval Facilities Engineering Service Center, UG-2040-SHR, Figure 5–3, pp. 5–7.

- The keeper or strike into which the bolt or latch fits. The keeper is not an integral part of the lock mechanism but provides a secure housing for the bolt when in a locked position.
- The tumbler array that constitutes the barrier or labyrinth that must be passed to move the bolt.
- The key or unlocking device, which is specifically designed to pass the barrier and operate the bolt.[58]

▲ Community mailboxes using Lever locks. Lever locks don't offer the same degree of protection as many of the other locks. Why would they still be used in certain situations?

Source: Morozova Tatiana/123RF

In most mechanical locks, the bolt and barrier are in the permanently installed hardware or lockset, while the key is separate. The primary types of mechanical locks are:

Warded lock. This was the first developed and longest in use, with an open, see-through keyway and a long, barrellike key, still found in older homes and buildings.

Lever lock. The tumblers in this lock are flat pieces of metal held to a common pivot and retained in place inside the lock case by a spring. This lock is used in desks, cabinets and lockers, safe deposit boxes, and mailboxes.[59]

Pin tumbler lock. The pin tumbler consists of the same basic elements as all mechanical locks: a bolt moving device, a maze or labyrinth, and a keyway. Conventional cylinders usually contain only five, six, or seven pins. High-security cylinders have the pins and driver interlocked so that random movement of the pins by lock picks or keys not specifically coded for the lock will not properly align the pins and drivers. The pin tumbler is probably the most widely used lock in the United States for exterior and interior building doors.[60]

Wafer tumbler lock. The wafer tumbler lock uses flat tumblers fashioned of metal or other material to bind the plug to the shell.

Combination locks. Combination locks are low-security padlocks that require the choice of specific and ordered number combinations to be opened. The gates on the lock's tumblers align to allow insertion of a fence in the bolt. The tumblers are fully circular and are interdependent, so moving one moves the others. This makes the order of movement for number choices important.

Mechanical locks will sometimes fail and keys may break off inside making the lock unusable. Lockouts like this may be accidents, but should have at least a cursory investigation to ensure the lockout did not result from tampering.[61] Lubrication is an important maintenance item to ensure the many small parts of the lock will continue to work properly.[62]

master keying
The practice of having several locks keyed alike, with one master key that will open them all, while each individual lock retains the ability to be opened by a separate subordinate key. In large organizations with security plans involving many individual locks, master keying is done for the convenience of persons with broad or variable access requirements to keep them from having to carry a separate key for each lock.

2   Explain the purpose of master keying.

▲ Keyed-alike systems provide one key for many locks. In what circumstances would that not be a good idea?

Source: User's guide on controlling locks, keys, and access cards, DoD Lock Program, Naval Facilities Engineering Service Center, UG-2040-SHR, Figure 3–1, pp. 3-6.

▲ Master-keyed systems keep users from having to carry around too many keys. What measures need to be taken to keep these systems secure?

Source: User's guide on controlling locks, keys, and access cards. DoD Lock Program, Naval Facilities Engineering Service Center, UG-2040-SHR, Figure 3–2, pp. 3–7.

Lock Picking

Mechanical locks are subject to a variety of attacks that can result in their failure or compromise. Lock picking is the process of unlocking a lock by manipulating the lock device without using the key. Although the practice of lock picking gets frequent exposure on crime-related television shows, it is a necessary skill for a locksmith. Lock picking is a complex solution for an often-simple problem. If access to a locked door or window is desired, most locks can be opened using a drill, bolt cutters, a bump key, or other devices. The door, hasp, or other fixture they are connected to can be cut, broken, or otherwise removed. The picking of a lock is done to avoid destroying the lock, either to save the replacement cost or to avoid detection.

Master Keying

In most common uses, locks are designed to be opened by only one key. In some situations, locks are keyed alike, and one master key will open them all, while each individual lock retains the ability to be opened by a separate subordinate key. In large organizations with security plans involving many individual locks, **master keying** is done for the convenience of persons with broad or variable access requirements to keep them from having to carry a separate key for each lock. Master keying represents the controlled loss of security.[63] Very effective accountability must be maintained of all master keys since the compromise of such a key exposes all the locks in that group.[64]

Electromagnetic Locks

The electromagnetic lock, also known simply as a magnetic lock, has an electromagnet and a metal strike plate. When energized, the magnet exerts an attractive force upon the plate and holds the door closed.[65] Electromagnetic locks require less maintenance than mechanical or electromechanical devices as they have no moving parts. The locks will operate as long as they are kept clean and there is electrical power. In high-security applications, backup power should be used, although electromagnetic locks are intrinsically fail-safe because of their design—removal of power releases the strike plate.[66]

Electrified Locking Mechanisms

Electrified locking mechanisms allow doors to be locked and unlocked remotely. The device may be a simple push button or a motion sensor, or may be sophisticated like a card reader or digital keypad. Electrified locking mechanisms include:

Electric dead bolt.   The electric dead bolt is the oldest and simplest of all electrical locking devices. With an electric dead bolt, a solenoid moves a dead bolt either into or out of a strike plate on a door. The electric dead bolt is not recommended for doors required to be unlocked automatically in response to a fire alarm.

Electric latches.   These are also solenoid activated, mount on the door frame, and use a strike plate in the door. Instead of a dead bolt, a beveled latch is used. Unlike a dead bolt, the latch does not need to be withdrawn for the door to close.

Electric strike.   Electric strike locks supplement any standard mechanical lock. Electrical energy opens or closes a mechanical latch keeper or strike plate. Such devices have been used for many years in apartment houses, business offices, and commercial installations to remotely control passage through a doorway in one or both directions.[67]

Electric locksets.   Electric locksets use a regular mortise lockset that has been electrified to turn the handle. This type of lock is becoming increasingly popular for automated access control applications in situations where the normally fixed, unsecure side handle of a storeroom can be controlled by an access control device while the handle on the secure side remains operational for unimpeded access.

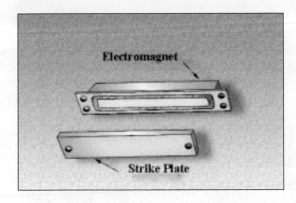

▲ Electromagnetic locks can be opened remotely. When might the use of these locks be most convenient?
Source: User's guide on controlling locks, keys, and access cards, DoD Lock Program, Naval Facilities Engineering Service Center, UG-2040-SHR, Figure D–11, p. D–16.

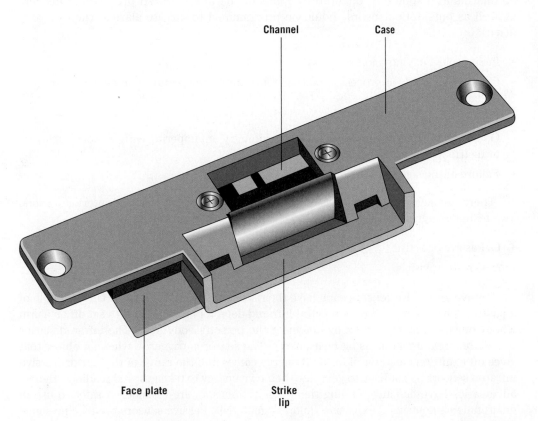

Channel   Case

Face plate   Strike lip

FIGURE 6–1
Electric Strike Locks Can Be Used to Supplement Any Other Mechanical Lock. In What Application Would you Recommend They Be Used?
Source: User's guide on controlling locks, keys, and access cards, DoD Lock Program, Naval Facilities Engineering Service Center, UG-2040-SHR, Figure D–8, p. D–15.

When an electronic access control component (credential reader, electric strike, or magnetic lock) fails, a credential denies access to someone, or when any forced entry or bypassing of the locking device is detected, further inquiry should be made.[68]

Motion Sensors

Sensors provide the detection function of a security system. Sensors detect and report intrusion and tamper attempts.[69] Intrusion detection is the process of identifying threats to physical systems by detecting a person or vehicle attempting to gain unauthorized entry into an area. Intrusion detection systems include exterior and interior intrusion sensors, video alarm assessment, entry control, and alarm communication systems working in combination.[70] Newer technologies ranging from fence-mounted sensors, rattler-vibration sensors, buried sensors (fiber optic, leaky coaxial, geophone), sound and video sensors are finding their place among the choices used by security professionals.[71]

The probability of intrusion detection depends primarily on these factors:[72]

- Activity of the target to be detected (walking/running/crawling, etc.)
- Sensor hardware design
- Installation conditions
- Sensitivity adjustment
- Weather conditions
- Equipment condition

If sensors are correctly placed, installed, maintained, and tested, they can generate alarms in response to unauthorized acts or the unauthorized presence of insiders as well as outsiders. Sensors should be programmed to initiate alarms when there is a(n):[73]

- Intrusion event (intrusion sensors).
- Change in a safety or process condition, for example, temperature or smoke (state sensors).
- Power loss (fault event sensors).
- Opening, shorting, or grounding of device circuitry or tampering with sensor's enclosure or distributed control panels (tamper sensors).
- Failure of the sensor itself.

There are several ways of classifying the many types of exterior and interior sensors. Two main distinguishers are:

1. Passive or active.
2. Covert or visible.

Passive and active sensors each have their strengths and weaknesses. One example of a passive sensor is an infrared detector. Infrared detectors can be used to set off an alarm when someone enters an area by detecting the person's body heat. The infrared sensor "sees" the area around it using heat energy. The sensor is triggered when an object that gives off a different amount of infrared energy comes into the range of the sensor. Passive infrared sensors do not have to generate their own energy to take infrared readings. Hence, adversaries have difficulty finding them. Passive sensors are considered safer to use in environments containing explosive vapors or materials. Passive sensors produce no signal from a transmitter and are simply receivers of energy in the proximity of the sensor. The presence or location of a passive sensor is more difficult to determine, putting the adversary at a disadvantage.[74]

Active sensors create fewer nuisance (false) alarms because of their stronger signals.[75] They transmit a signal from a transmitter and a receiver detects changes or reflections of that signal. Because active sensors generate a field of energy when the sensor is in operation, a sophisticated adversary could detect the presence of the sensor prior to entering the active sensing zone.[76]

Covert (or hidden) sensors present certain advantages. They are hidden from view, often located in walls or under the floor or ground. They are also more difficult for an adversary to identify, and they rarely negatively affect the appearance of the environment. By contrast, visible sensors may deter adversaries from acting because of their presence. They are also usually easier to install and access (to repair and maintain).[77] They are easy for an adversary to detect or locate, like sensors that are visibly attached to a door or mounted on the side of a building. Covert sensors are more difficult for an adversary to detect and locate, and thus they can be more effective; also, they do not disturb the appearance of the environment.

An intrusion detection system is vulnerable to attack by adversaries from both outside and inside the organization. Because insiders have authorized access to many areas or facilities, many perimeter sensors on the outside will not alert on their presence. Interior sensors can be useful for detecting insider theft or sabotage, along with any attacks by outsiders. Interior sensors are often placed in normal access mode during working hours, making them more susceptible to tampering by an insider.[78]

Access and Entry Control

Access control is the process of managing and using databases or other records to limit entry, such as whom or what will be granted access, when they may enter, and where access will occur. Entry control refers to the use of equipment to control, limit, or restrict the movement of people or material into an area. According to ASIS International, the terms are often used interchangeably in the security profession, although there are advantages to differentiating between them.

Access control usually requires that the system be able to identify and differentiate among users. Access controls prescribe not only who (user) or what (process) is to have access to a specific system or resource, but also the level of access that is permitted. Access control is based on least privilege, which describes the granting to users of the access minimally required to perform their duties.[79]

Entry control allows movement of authorized personnel and material into and out of facilities, while detecting and possibly delaying movement of unauthorized personnel and contraband. Entry control elements may be found at a facility perimeter, at vehicle gates, building entry points, or doors into rooms within a building.[80]

The objectives of an entry control system used for physical protection are:[81]

- To permit only authorized persons to enter and exit.
- To detect and prevent the entry or exit of contraband material (weapons, explosives, unauthorized tools, or critical assets).
- To provide information to security personnel to facilitate assessment and response.

Methods of verifying entry authorization include credentials, personal identification numbers, and automated personal identity verification. None of these systems should be considered the complete solution to security, as most credentials can be counterfeited and errors (false rejection and false acceptance) happen. Also, it is important to remember that it is the credential being verified more than the person presenting the credential.[82] Credential devices assume the person presenting the acceptable credential is authorized to enter. A credential identifies a legitimate authority to enter a controlled area.[83] A coded credential (such as a plastic card) contains a prerecorded code. When the code presented matches the code stored in the system, the device unlocks the door.[84]

Various technologies are used to store the code upon or within a card. The most commonly used cards are:

Magnetic-strip card. A strip of magnetic material located along one edge of the card is encoded with data, which is read by moving the card past a magnetic read head.

access control
Prescribes who or what is to have access to a specific system or resource, and the level of access that is permitted.

entry control
Allows movement of authorized personnel and material into and out of facilities, while detecting and possibly delaying movement of unauthorized personnel and contraband.

FIGURE 6–2
Typical Simple Access Control System
Source: User's guide on controlling locks, keys, and access cards, DoD Lock Program, Naval Facilities Engineering Service Center, UG-2040-SHR, Figure D–1, p. D–3.

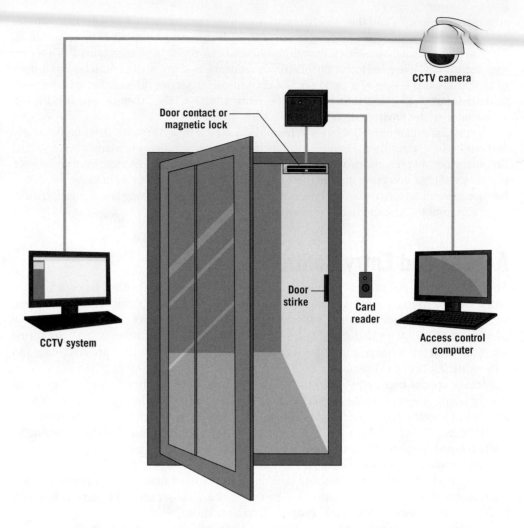

Wiegand-effect card.   A series of small-diameter, parallel wires about one-half inch long, are embedded in the bottom half of the card. The wires are made of ferromagnetic materials that produce a change in magnetic flux when exposed to a slowly changing magnetic field. The card reader contains a read head and a magnet to supply the applied magnetic field.

Proximity card.   The code on the card is read when it is brought within several inches of the reader, without being physically inserted. The reader contains a transmitter that sweeps through a specified range of frequencies and a receiver that senses the pattern of resonant frequencies contained in the card.

Laser card.   A laser card (also called an optical memory card) uses the same technology developed for recording video and audio disks. Data is recorded on the laser card by burning it into the film covering the card with a laser. Data is read by using a laser to sense the locations of the holes.

Smart card.   The card is embedded with a microprocessor, memory, communication circuitry, and a battery. Contacts on the edge of the card enable a reader to communicate with a microprocessor.

Bar code.   A bar code is an image of black bars of varying widths printed on white paper or tape that can be easily read with an optical scanner. Bar coding is not widely used, as it can be easily duplicated. It can provide a cost-effective solution for low-level security.[85]

▲ Magnetic Strip Card and Proximity card, with a Magnetic Strip Card Reader. Both of these cards can be used to control access. What do you see as the benefits of each?
Source: Author Smith.

Biometrics

Personnel identity verification systems (PIVS) work using one or more unique physical biometric characteristics of an individual. All PIVS consider the uniqueness of the feature used, the variability of the characteristic, and the difficulty of implementing the system that processes the characteristic.[86]

Biometric devices differentiate between verification and recognition, which have a different focus and can be used for different purposes. Biometrics identify one or more of a person's characteristics for personal verification. Use of biometric security such as a fingerprint, or face and voice recognition is in use in many locations. When in verification mode, a person presents the specific biometric feature for authorization, and the equipment then signifies agreement. In recognition mode, the biometric device attempts to identify the person, and if the biometric information from the person agrees with the database, entry is allowed.[87]

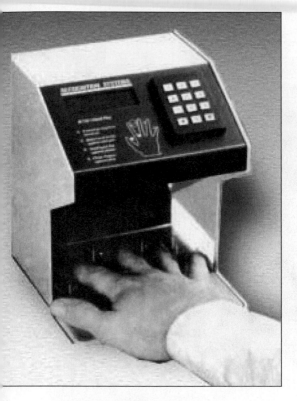

▲ Biometric identification system (hand geometry). Biometric identification identifies unique body features. Can security professionals use the data collected for access control for other purposes?

Source: User's guide on controlling locks, keys, and access cards, DoD Lock Program, Naval Facilities Engineering Service Center, UG-2040-SHR, Figure D–7, p. D–11.

The available physical biometric characteristics used by PIVS include.[88]

Hand/finger geometry.   This is based on the shape of the hand. It measures three-dimensional features of the hand, such as widths and lengths of fingers and the thickness of the hand.

Handwriting verification systems.   These systems use handwriting dynamics, such as displacement, velocity, and acceleration. An individual's signature technique is unique and reasonably consistent.

Eye pattern.   Eye pattern uses a video camera to image the iris (the colored part of the eye) for identification. No physical contact between the person's face and the scanner is required.

Voice systems.   These require the user to speak a specific, predetermined word or a series of words or numbers to verify access. The technology currently offers a low-security alternative with ease of deployment and general public acceptance.

Face verification systems.   Face verification systems use distinguishing characteristics of the face to verify identity. Most systems use a video camera, extracting distinguishing features from the image and comparing them with previously stored features.

Fingerprint verification systems.   These use minutiae points, the ridge endings, bifurcations, and other physical fingerprint identifiers, as the identifying features. Although some uses are averse to the identification connotations attached to them, fingerprint systems have a high resistance to counterfeiting.[89]

Palm print recognition systems.   These systems measure features of the palm or identify the pattern of blood vessels below the surface, or both. They are fairly easy to use and do not carry the emotional connotations of fingerprint ID systems. They are more cumbersome than fingerprint verification systems, however, and users need some practice before the process becomes natural.[90]

With technology innovations come new challenges for security professionals who will be required to learn new processes and procedures. Consider the introduction of biometric technologies as a standard feature in mobile phones and landline phone systems. People generally seem more willing to submit their biometric data to mobile devices such as phones and tablets.[91] Scanner technology has improved so rapidly that it's now possible to detect irises from 1,000 feet away.[92]

The size of the biometric market is difficult to measure, with estimates ranging from $3.6 billion to nearly $7 billion per annum. With a growth rate of approximately 12% per year, some experts claim that the biometric systems market will be worth $23.5 billion by 2020.[93] With such rapid growth come serious problems, such as what would happen if the stored biometric data were compromised? Security professionals will need to add these challenges to their risk assessments because biometric data is difficult (if not impossible) to revoke or replace.[94]

Recently, an artist named Selvaggio claimed that his invention *That's My Face*, which transforms 2D pictures into 3D sculptures, allows others to use Selvaggio's own face as a

▶ Privacy rights advocates find ways to defeat security. Should that concern security professionals?

Source: L. Selvaggio, URME Surveillance project, 2014, http://leoselvaggio.com/urmesurveillance/

decoy to create masks so that surveillance cameras are essentially tracking what they see as Selvaggio, not as the person wearing the mask. Because video systems with military-grade facial recognition software are in cities all over the world, Selvaggio devised a way to show the cameras a different, alternative identity.[95] According to Selvaggio, all products have been tested for facial recognition and each identifies the wearer as Selvaggio on Facebook.

Security Lighting

Security lighting can significantly improve visibility in areas or periods of low-light. Security professionals should use lighting to enhance their visibility while controlling entrance or detecting adversaries both outside and inside buildings and grounds. Security lighting should be positioned to illuminate shadowed areas and be directed at potential routes of access.[96] Security lighting serves as a safety-enhancement (when lighting pathways and parking lots), and to light areas for the use of video surveillance systems.[97] Security lighting can also be a deterrent.[98] It gives the *perception of security*, so an individual who might consider stealing, trespassing, or otherwise acting against the property may consider an unlit area over one with minimal lighting. Security lighting should not be limited to use as a psychological deterrent; however, it should also be used along perimeter fences, whether for continuous or periodic observation.[99]

Security lighting is also useful to light outside areas or structures that need to be observed. Such areas include piers, important buildings, storage areas, parking lots, communication hubs, and power- and water-distribution systems.[100] Roads, driveways, and sidewalks should also be lit for both safety and security reasons. Ground lighting focused upward into trees and shrubs is most effective for deterring their use by adversaries as hiding places.[101]

Adequate lighting inside of buildings facilitates the detection and deterrence of unauthorized persons, as well. Lighting is relatively inexpensive and may reduce the need for security forces or other more costly alternatives. It may also enhance personal protection for security forces by reducing the advantages of concealment and surprise for a determined adversary.[102]

ASIS International advised that the following areas require security lighting:[103]

Perimeter fencing.   Lighting acts as a deterrent to unauthorized intrusion while enhancing the physical barrier. Lighting also aids in the use of video security systems if perimeter intrusion detection systems are used, and helps the security response force target adversaries and delay or apprehend them.

Building facade.   The lighting of a building facade provides a high contrast to facilitate identification of shapes and movement of adversaries when individual exterior objects cannot be adequately lit. If the facade has good reflectance, there will also be horizontal light for a viewer (person or camera).

Parking structures.   These areas are difficult to light since there are few vertical elements to reflect light or provide contrast to moving objects. In some locations, a bright white horizontal stripe is painted on walls, at waist height, to improve contrast.

Open parking.   The height of lighting is often less restricted in open parking than in parking structures. Higher light sources provide better horizontal illumination.

Guard and gate positions: The area surrounding a guard or gate position or structure should be well lit on the exterior at night. Task lighting on the interior of structures should be high during daytime operations, but should be reduced at night to permit good visibility of the surroundings and approaching pedestrian and vehicular traffic.

The National Crime Prevention Council suggests that a good workplace lighting strategy includes:[104]

- Installing motion-sensitive and constant outside lights.
- Illuminating shadowed areas around the building by trimming shrubs, adding lighting, and so on.
- Leaving some interior lights on even when the business is closed.

Emergency Lighting

Emergency power for security lighting should always be considered, as both natural and intentional events can cause power to be lost, thereby limiting the security of an area. The emergency power lighting system may duplicate the other systems in whole or in part, and is normally limited to emergencies like periods of main power failure. Whereas regular security lighting should be connected to an uninterruptible power system in most instances, the U.S. Department of Transportation advised that emergency lighting should depend on a separate, alternate power source, such as portable generators or batteries.[105] These sources should be tested and maintained at regular intervals.

Security Forces

A security force is an effective and useful component of a facility's physical security program. Basic security measures such as alarms, physical barriers, and intrusion detectors are only effective if they alert a security force.[106] Often, the use of additional security forces is used to offset the security risks encountered during certain operations.[107] A well-trained and equipped security force provides a solid foundation on which to base an organization's physical security program. The security force significantly contributes to efforts at reducing risk through effective implementation of security policies and procedures.[108]

Depending on the organization and its requirements, security forces can include:

- Uniformed guards
- Fixed posts
- Random foot patrol
- Directed patrol
- Visibility posts
- Vehicle patrol
- Mounted patrol
- K-9 patrol
- Alternative vehicles (bicycle, scooter, electric cart)
- Emergency services
- Surveillance cameras/video monitoring[109]

The number of personnel in each of the duties will depend on many factors, including the size of the facility, the hours of operation, perceived risk factors, and management priorities. The standard rule of thumb is that the cost of security services should not exceed the value of the protected items.[110]

When making a decision about whether to use a security force, the organization's leaders should consider the duties that guards perform:

1. Entrance control
2. Roving patrol
3. Traffic control
4. Key control
5. Monitoring security and fire systems
6. Monitoring utility systems
7. Lost and found
8. Prepare reports and records
9. Respond to emergencies
10. Maintain law and order
11. Report hazardous conditions[111]

Security Personnel and the Use of Force

If security forces are armed for a deterrent effect, the organization's leaders must weigh that advantage against such disadvantages as the danger to innocent people if a firearm is used by security forces; the possibility of an accidental discharge; and the possibility, no matter how remote, of irrational behavior on the part of a guard in a weak moment or under pressure.[112]

Security forces must be trained and certified to limit liability. According to the U.S. Department of the Interior, maintaining the appropriate performance and conduct standards is critical for all security professionals, and especially those who are armed. Firearms should be used only in a defensive posture and only for the protection of life and property. When making a decision as to whether security forces should be armed, strong consideration should be given to the factors below to ensure properly selected and trained personnel:[113]

- Firearms training, including judgment shooting and firearms safety.
- Knowledge of criminal activities and proper law enforcement response procedures.
- Judgment and emotional stability.
- Experience and demonstrated ability to retain composure under pressure.
- A personal history free of arrests or other criminal activity.

Dogs in Support of Security

Dogs are trained in many skills that can contribute significantly to the success of an organization's physical security efforts.[114] Dogs have been used in military, law enforcement, and security applications with much success for many years. Security professionals should consider the unique capabilities of dogs as well as their limitations.[115]

The organized use of dogs for law enforcement dates back to at least 1899, when the town of Ghent, Belgium, established a law enforcement training program for dogs. The dogs accompanied police on night shifts and were kenneled during the day in comfortable boxes. The dogs were taught to seek, attack, seize, and hold (without hurting seriously) in a four-month training program.[116] The dogs were first trained by using dummies posed as concealed adversaries. Canine bite suits, which started out as thick clothing, soon became specialized training gear, as real persons were used to train the dogs after they worked with the dummies. The dogs were also taught to scale walls and to jump into water to save people from drowning.[117]

Around 1910, dogs began to be used by law enforcement agencies in England and Germany.[118] By 1956, the Baltimore Police Department pioneered the use of dogs by law enforcement in the United States. Dogs are now in regular use in law enforcement agencies around the world.[119]

Proper Use of Security Support Dogs

Security forces' patrol dogs should be employed in all areas, both day and night. Such public visibility increases the patrol dog team's ability to deter theft, burglary, and vandalism by adversaries.[120] ASIS International proposed that a dog selection and training program should include tasks such as:[121]

- Protection of an area with a handler.
- Protection or patrol of an area without a handler.
- Guarding or holding a person in a location.
- Aggressive attack.
- Tracking.
- Detection of drugs, explosives, accelerants, and other substances.

▲ A drug-detecting dog shown with bundles of marijuana found in a residence in Tucson, Arizona. Drug-detection dogs are used by security professionals in many areas. In what ways do you envision dogs being used best?

Source: U.S. Drug Enforcement Administration (DEA), DEA.gov—Year in Review, http://www.justice .gov/dea/pr/multimedia-library/ image-gallery/year_in_pictures_12/ images/2012/1212/09.jpg

A dog's superior detection ability is especially useful at night or when there is limited visibility. Dogs can detect a fleeing adversary that a human cannot and, if necessary, can pursue, attack, and hold the adversary when the handler believes that a serious offense has been committed. Except in unusual circumstances, dogs should not be used for apprehensions for minor offenses.[122]

Dogs can respond to certain sensory stimuli (sights, odors, or scents) and alert their handler when the stimuli are detected. ASIS International observed that humans and dogs have the same basic senses (smell, hearing, sight, touch), but some of the dog's senses (like smell and hearing) are much more acute and developed.[123] Most dogs are capable of receiving additional training in advanced skills such as explosive detection, narcotics detection, and ammunition and weapons detection.[124]

Additional roles found useful by the military include when a patrol dog is also trained in drug or explosives detection.[125] Because of the time and effort needed to keep skills at the optimal level, generally a security dog is trained for protection or detection, but not both, as detection dogs need constant retraining.[126] Dogs supporting security forces with and without handlers present a strong crime deterrent when conducting security checks.[127]

Dogs are conditioned to use the fastest and easiest means of satisfying their basic needs. As an example, if they are taught to search for a hidden adversary, they learn that by using their sense of smell rather than sight, they will more quickly complete the task and receive the desired reward.[128] That is not to suggest that all dogs can be trained as trackers. Tracking is a difficult skill for a dog to learn and not every dog is capable of such training.[129]

Use of Force with Security Support Dogs

Policies and procedures developed for security support dogs should acknowledge the potential danger of bodily injury to a suspect if a dog is released. Dogs should be used with caution in all situations, as their presence might aggravate a situation. The release of a patrol dog to apprehend a suspect represents a greater degree of force than the use of a club, but less than deadly force because a patrol dog is trained to terminate an attack on voice command of its handler.[130] A dog can be used to prevent the escape of a suspect but should not be released if a lesser degree of force would accomplish the apprehension.

Handlers should take special care to follow the organization's policies and procedures for use of force and should use the minimum force necessary to withdraw safely from a confrontational situation, then immediately report the incident.[131] Dogs should not be used for crowd control or direct confrontation with suspects unless it is absolutely necessary. When they are used for crowd control or in direct confrontation, dogs should be kept on a short leash, and dogs should not be released into a crowd.[132] This minimizes the danger to innocent people.

The use of dogs in security forces operations can result in significant criminal or civil liability for injuries. Criminal liability occurs when one party, without justification or excuse, directs or allows his or her dog to attack another person. In general, dogs are viewed as a weapon or an extension of the handler. It is the conscious use of the dog that establishes intent.[133] The extent of civil liability depends on a variety of conditions and circumstances. The relationships among the various parties and any special legal doctrines that produce unusual or extraordinary results are also factors.[134] Conditions and circumstances typically seen as instances of potential liability may include when the person injured is a trespasser, a licensee, or a business visitor.[135] Additional circumstances that may bring liability are when the person controlling the animal is the person whose property is being protected, such as a homeowner or proprietor, an employee of the property owner or person being protected, an independent contractor or the employee of an independent contractor property owner or person being protected.[136]

Video Surveillance Systems

3 Define and distinguish between CCTV and DIS.

Hit television shows with global popularity such as *Person of Interest*[137] and public discussions about local government use of red light cameras have ensured that most citizens possess a basic awareness of the capabilities of this technology. With the proliferation of CCTV and DIS in both the public and private sector, we can expect government policy and regulation to require video surveillance etiquette from organizations and private citizens. With security systems becoming cheaper, complaints about residential and personal privacy are more common.

In response, the British government introduced a "surveillance code of practice" to guide public video surveillance systems, especially those used by police forces and local governments. Regular reviews of all camera systems should be conducted to see whether they are still *necessary, proportionate, and effective*. If they do not meet those criteria, they should be removed. Dominiczak noted that various governmental departments are encouraged to publish the location of every video surveillance camera used by their organization on their websites.[138]

By deploying remote video surveillance systems, organizations are able to expand the areas monitored by their security forces. Video surveillance systems may include fixed cameras and pan/tilt/zoom cameras, and often include video-recording systems. The visible presence of video surveillance cameras serves as a deterrent to potential adversaries as well, according to the U.S. Department of Transportation.[139] Organizations contemplating video surveillance should be aware of the labor intensity of watching banks of monitors, and be cautious about relying on video surveillance beyond the ability to monitor activities. When combined with a recording system, a video surveillance system can provide vital information about security events. Security forces can use the information to identify and apprehend adversaries or to communicate descriptions of those adversaries to law enforcement agencies. Later, the video record can be used as evidence in a trial; it provides information about the causes of events and can improve the likelihood that an adversary is convicted.[140]

Organizations must follow the requirements of local and state governments for auditing, handling, storage, and retention of video recordings, as some jurisdictions require that it be possible to trace any recorded images to a specific date, time, recording device, and recording medium and operator. Failure to comply with data protection rules may affect the police's ability to use video surveillance images to investigate crime and may hamper the prosecution of adversaries.[141]

Video surveillance should be established at locations where visual monitoring from a remote location is advantageous, such as gates, doors, corridors, elevators, and areas where it is not practical or cost effective to post a guard. Security professionals can monitor several video surveillance cameras simultaneously. The signal can be recorded by a digital video recorder for later playback and analysis, and many devices have a time-lapse mode for quick playback of lengthy periods of tape coverage. Care should be taken when assigning security forces to monitor video surveillance cameras, as the attention span of persons monitoring the images is traditionally short, and there are often distractions at monitoring stations.[142]

There are only three reasons to have video surveillance cameras in security applications:

1. Obtain visual information about something that is happening.
2. Obtain visual information about something that has happened.
3. Deter undesirable activities.

A video surveillance system, whether analog or digital, consists of four main components:[143]

1. Camera (used to transform a reflected light image into an electronic signal).
2. Transmission cable or wireless transmission capability.
3. Monitor (TV, PC, or remote viewing device, such as a smartphone or tablet computer).
4. Video recorder, which retains the video information on a magnetic tape, CD, DVD, hard drive, or other medium.

▲ Video surveillance cameras with transmission cable. Cameras can augment the use of security professionals. What additional benefits do you imagine can be realized from the use of security cameras?
Source: Martin33/123RF

Legal Issues

Privacy is a primary concern when using video surveillance systems. If another nonadversarial person might consider a camera to be a violation of their privacy, serious consideration should be given to such placement. It is generally inappropriate to install cameras in locker rooms, bathrooms, and other places where people would have a reasonable expectation of privacy. Although the use of hidden cameras is legal in many circumstances, ASIS International advises it is acceptable practice to post signs at entry points informing people that an area is under video surveillance.[144] Additionally, to be certain that images recorded with video surveillance meet the legal requirements of the jurisdiction, consultation with both a legal adviser and law enforcement agency in the jurisdiction is recommended.[145]

The Future of Surveillance Systems

Imagine a select group of people in the private and public sector with access to a computer system that conducts mass surveillance by monitoring and analyzing data from surveillance cameras, electronic communications networks, and audio input throughout the world. The system is able to analyze the data and predict violent acts, notifying the group shortly before the acts are to occur so they can attempt to prevent the violence. Under control of the federal government, the system's stated purpose was to foresee terrorist attacks, allowing the government to thwart terrorist activity. However, the computer detects future violent acts of all kinds, not just terrorism, and the group has access to that information. This generally describes the television show *Person of Interest*, which was based on a screenplay and revolved around a former CIA agent recruited by an eccentric billionaire to prevent violent crimes in New York City. The show depicts the potential for access to a broad array of loosely connected video surveillance systems in use by government and quasi-government entities. After breaking U.S. viewing records for CBS Broadcasting, the show was picked up by dozens of networks for broadcast in many other countries.

In the future, with the decreasing cost and increasing quality of video surveillance hardware combined with any perception of increasing security needs by the public, we can expect an increase in private acquisition and implementation of such video surveillance systems. Laws governing private use are likely to be slow in coming, so it will be incumbent upon responsible organizations and individuals to self-regulate their conduct. Any anticipated use of subcontractors or freelance video surveillance specialists should be reviewed and critiqued beforehand by a variety of organizational representatives.

Imagine a time when, perhaps combined with other up-and-coming technology such as driverless cars and domestically targeted, privately owned unmanned aerial vehicles, security companies conduct business by approaching organizations and individuals with information regarding past security testing or breaches. This suggested practice may seem far-fetched, but at its core bears resemblance to the activity of freelance photographers and bloggers in the past. As has been suggested in other chapters, ongoing analysis of policy and procedures by the organization's legal advisers is critical.

The use of CCTV technology will soon be completely obsolete as it is fully replaced by DIS. The functions and features of video surveillance systems will continue to expand as the capabilities of the system continue to become more automated.[146] It will not be long before we see the availability of fully automated, intelligent digital systems. Those systems, once programmed, will not require manual monitoring of any sort. Such systems will include full facial recognition on an average system as well as point-to-point, system-to-system (city-wide) tracking of individuals or groups.[147]

Layered Security

The use of a **layered security** strategy provides security professionals with multiple opportunities for disrupting adversaries, whether criminal or terrorist. Layered security is a key aspect of an effective access management strategy.[148] Layered security is the practice of combining multiple security controls to protect resources and data. The U.S. National Security Agency considers the practice of layered security similar to **defense in depth**, a practice adopted from military strategy that involves multiple layers of defense that resist rapid penetration by an attacker.[149] That practice, as well as layered security, is regularly used by information technology professionals to protect against the adversaries in that realm. A minor stretch of the imagination allows traditional security professionals

THINK ABOUT IT

Security professionals need to be able to combine their training and experience with imagination. Although they may never have encountered a specific security challenge before, they need to assume control and begin making critical decisions immediately. Take a few minutes and see how you would do. Imagine being tasked to protect each of these from loss or theft and fire:

Residential Challenges

Neighborhoods, street design, urban planning
Private residences—house, apartment, mobile home, public housing, hotel
    New homes
    Old homes
Security systems
    DIY versus professional installation
    Include panic alarm, water freezing, etc.
Key locks
    Former residents
    Hide-a-key spare

Non-residential challenges

Hospitals and health care operations (labs)
Government buildings
    Office buildings
    Utilities
Educational facilities
    Colleges and universities
    Secondary schools
    Elementary (students feeling less autonomous)
Museums
Houses of worship/cemeteries
Mass-transportation facilities (not in-transit)
    Airports
    Bus/train station
    Port, depot (ships and trucks)
    Parking lots and garages
    Subways
Public access
    Amusement park
    Casino
    Beach
    Movie theater
    Sports park
Retail
    Stand alone
    Strip mall
    Shopping center
Postal and logistics hubs and satellite facilities
    USPS
    FEDEX
    UPS

to see the similarities between the two focuses, which both intend to thwart adversaries who are intent on breaching perimeters and taking, damaging, or destroying something inside.

The Canadian government has applied these principles by defining a hierarchy of zones, identified as the following:[150]

1. *Public zone*, where the public has unimpeded access and surrounds, or is part of, a government facility. Examples include the grounds of a building, public corridors, and elevator lobbies.

2. *Reception zone*, where there is a transition from a public zone to a restricted-access area. It is typically located at the entrance to the facility where initial contact with visitors is made and can include places where services are provided and information is exchanged.

3. *Operations zone*, where access is limited to personnel who work there and to properly escorted visitors. The areas include open office space or electrical rooms. There must be a recognizable and monitored perimeter.

4. *Security zone*, where area access is limited to authorized personnel and visitors who are both authorized and properly escorted, as indicated by a recognizable and monitored perimeter. This includes areas where secret information is processed or stored and are classified as a security zone.

5. *High-security zones* are areas with limited access. Only authorized, appropriately screened personnel and authorized and properly escorted visitors may enter these zones. There should be a perimeter barrier built and monitored continuously, and details of access should be recorded and audited. Areas where high-value assets are handled by selected personnel and are considered high-security zones.

Operations, security, and high-security zones are also referred to as restricted-access areas. According to the Royal Canadian Mounted Police, instituting a hierarchy of zones allows organizations to:[151]

- Store assets of different threat levels in the same facility.

- Implement varied levels of access control to protect various levels of assets.

- Process various levels of information and assets in the same facility.

Access to the zones should be based on specific access needs and restricting access should be implemented to protect employees and valuable assets.[152]

These measures, and others like them, are considered active defense measures. Highly visible security forces combined with security countermeasures should serve to convince adversaries they will be unsuccessful, and may reduce the likelihood of an attack. Use of these measures may also cause adversaries to change methods or switch to a less secure target, requiring security professionals to frequently reassess their target vulnerability.[153] The concept of layered security recommends placing the more critical or vulnerable assets toward the center of concentric levels with increasingly stringent security measures.[154] Security measures implemented at several different levels or layers provide a redundancy in security in case other measures fail.

Crime Prevention through Environmental Design

4   Describe the practice of CPTED.

crime prevention through environmental design
(CPTED, pronounced "sep-ted")   Describes the concept of design and use of the environment to reduce opportunities of fear and incidence of predatory crime, and improve the quality of life.

The name **Crime Prevention through Environmental Design** (CPTED, pronounced "septed") describes the concept of design and use of the environment to reduce opportunities of fear and incidence of predatory crime, and improve the quality of life.[155] CPTED has its roots in the practice of *defensible space*, which posits that a person's demonstrated claim to a defined and shared residential territory diminishes with an increase in the number of people who share that claim. As an example, it is easier for outsiders to access and linger in the common areas of a building shared by twenty-four to a hundred families than it is in a building shared by six to twelve families.[156] **Defensible space** is defined as a residential environment whose physical characteristics allow inhabitants to be part of ensuring their own security. Newman identified four primary factors that create defensible space:

1. Territoriality, which exemplifies the notion that a person's home is his castle.
2. **Natural surveillance**, which is the ability of residents to be able to see what's going on in their neighborhood.
3. Image, which describes the physical attributes of a residential development that make it defendable.
4. **Surroundings**, which include making the most of a development's location relative to places that will help to prevent crime.[157]

To provide maximum control, an environment should be divided into smaller, clearly defined areas or zones, which become the focal points for the application of the various CPTED elements. Gardner noted that *defensible space* describes an area that has been made a *zone of defense* by design.[158] The physical mechanisms that create safety and improve upkeep as part of the defensible space concept also influence the natural security inclinations of residents rather than forcing or requiring them to surrender their shared social responsibilities to any formal authority.[159] With defensible space, all areas are designated as public, semiprivate, or private. These designations define the acceptable use of each zone, much like the hierarchy of zones we looked at before, and identify who has a right to occupy it:[160]

- Public zones are the least secure of the three zones. They are generally open to anyone.
- Semi-private zones serve as a buffer between public and private zones. They are common-use spaces that are accessible to the public but set off from the public zone.
- Private zones are areas of restricted entry, such as a private residence, with controlled and limited access to specific individuals or groups.

In the early 1970s, several studies demonstrated that architectural design could be used to influence crime rates in public housing developments. These studies showed that a physical environment could be created that would discourage crime.[161] CPTED is best described as the design or redesign of a building or area to reduce crime opportunity and fear of crime through natural, mechanical, and procedural means.[162] CPTED includes concepts that are applicable for planned developments, private residences, and both public and private organizations of all types and sizes. CPTED was practiced well before it was named, as history documented many instances when caves, cliffs, and other natural barriers were used to enhance security. CPTED is grounded in environmental criminology, the proposition that places such as buildings, parks, parking lots, and other structures that are carefully designed, can deter crime, reduce the residents' fear of crime, and improve the quality of life of the residents.[163]

CPTED works for two primary reasons. First, residents are affected by the things in their environment such as noise, pollution, and trash on the streets. Second, certain social characteristics such as alienation, loneliness, anxiety, and dehumanization are keys to criminal behavior. When residential buildings are constructed, these environmental influences and characteristics are rarely considered, and the design of the buildings adds to the dangerousness of the community, with corridors and passageways hidden from public view.[164] In 2007, Zahm identified the problem-solving process used in CPTED as one that uses a series of steps designed to answer these four questions:[165]

1. What is the problem?
2. Why here?
3. What can be done to solve the problem?
4. How well are we doing?

To change environments that support criminal behavior, the reinforcement that sustains that behavior must be removed.[166] Such action changes the environment to which the individual responds. The goal of CPTED is the reduction of opportunities for crime to occur by using design features that discourage crime, while encouraging legitimate use of the environment.[167] CPTED is based on the application of common sense and awareness about how people use their space for both legitimate and criminal intentions.

defensible space
A residential environment whose physical characteristics allow inhabitants to be part of ensuring their own security. Four primary factors create defensible space: territoriality, natural surveillance, image, and surroundings. The theory of defensible space explains that a person's demonstrated claim to a defined and shared residential territory diminishes with an increase in the number of people who share that claim.

natural surveillance
The ability of residents to be able to see what's going on in their neighborhood.

surroundings
In the context of CPTED, describes location relative to places that will help to prevent crime.

► Multiple-unit building landscape designs using CPTED. Using CPTED principles in the design phase helps building security. What difficulties might there be with getting security professionals engaged in the design phase?

Source: Craig Cozart/Getty Images

For the security professional, CPTED is a set of tools designed to affect:[168]

- Places, like residential and office buildings, which can be designed to produce behavioral effects that reduce the opportunity for certain types of crime and the fear of those crimes.
- Behavior, by eliciting compliant and law-abiding conduct instead of criminal activity or unruly behavior.
- Design and use of space, to encourage desirable behavior and discourage crime and related conduct.

Security professionals should consider using a CPTED strategy that takes advantage of as many elements as possible, such as appropriate building layout and pedestrian flow, lighting, landscaping, and surveillance.[169] The use of such strategies may help reduce the need for guards and technology. Security professionals should have a thorough understanding of the CPTED concepts to be able to work effectively with local crime prevention officers, planners, designers, architects, landscapers, law enforcement, security professionals, and facility users (residents, employees, etc.) when designing new or renovating existing properties.[170] With CPTED, use of fortress-type or prisonlike construction is minimized, in a cost-effective building design strategy.[171] The goal of CPTED is to make unauthorized access difficult and time-consuming, not to prevent it. Careful design of public spaces and buildings using CPTED principles can help prevent crime and make us feel safer.

The following are examples of CPTED techniques that have proven effective in certain situations for the U.S. Army:[172]

- Widening major pathways and using colored decorative paving.
- Differentiating small private areas (front lawns) outside each dwelling unit from the public path with low, symbolic walls.
- Adding public-seating areas in the center of public paths far enough from private-dwelling units to eliminate conflicts of use but close enough to be under constant surveillance by residents.
- Designing play areas as an integral part of open space.
- Adding decorative lighting to highlight various paths and recreation areas at night to extend the residents' surveillance potential and feeling of security.
- Adding seats and path networks to recreational facilities where large, central court areas exist, to increase the interest and usability of the area.

- Redesigning parking and play areas around buildings to create the illusion that the buildings are grouped where natural opportunities exist.

- Modernizing building entrances to create breezeways into building courts and to accommodate a telephone intercom for opening entry doors to the lobby.

- Providing video surveillance of public grounds and central paths for security by public monitors.

- Installing audio surveillance capabilities in elevators and at the doors of residences.

The importance of CPTED in the design and planning process is based on the belief that preventing crime and loss is inherent in many human functions, behaviors, and activities, and is not just something that police or security professionals do. The best time to design architectural characteristics is prior to the building phase. Once a property is built, whether it is a planned development or a private residence, it is more difficult and expensive to make structural changes.[173] Planning public, semi-private, or private zones and implementing the CPTED principles is best done early in the design process.

Fire Safety

According to the Bureau of Labor Statistics, fires and explosions accounted for 3% of work-place fatalities in 2013.[174] Although the number of fire-related deaths is declining, fires can have a devastating impact on an organization of any size.[175] Fire safety may be considered part of the security professional's duties and responsibilities in some organizations and is often seen as a logical fit. The security professional's overall strategy need not apply simply to threats from human adversaries, and in many events more loss is incurred from fire- and weather-related damage. Property damage, injuries, and death are standard risks associated with fires. In addition to fire prevention training, Rudy suggested that every workplace fire safety checklist should include regular inspection and maintenance to help prevent and reduce the impact of fires.[176]

Fire safety is addressed in the workplace standards of the U.S. Occupational Safety and Health Administration (OSHA) for positions such as record keeping, general industry, ship-yard employment, marine terminals, longshoring, gear certification, and the construction industry.[177] Fire safety is everyone's job at a worksite. Employers should train all workers on fire hazards in the workplace and what to do in a fire emergency. According to OSHA, the organization's fire safety plan should outline the assignments of key personnel in the event of a fire and provide an evacuation plan for workers on the site.[178]

Rudy identified six critical components to a workplace fire safety program.

1. *Fire extinguishers.*   OSHA and the U.S. National Fire Protection Association (NFPA) require businesses to provide functioning, portable fire extinguishers. Organizations should inspect fire extinguishers once a month, and more often in higher-risk environments.

2. *Fire extinguisher training.*   A 2011 Harris Poll revealed that one in five Americans would be afraid to extinguish a fire using a portable fire extinguisher, but three of four reported they would be more comfortable if they received training.

3. *Exit signs and emergency lights.*   With illuminated exit signs, businesses provide occupants with a clear path to safety. All occupied buildings must have exit signs that are brightly lit and visible from all directions. In the event of a total power loss, emergency lighting effectively guides building occupants to the nearest exit.

4. *Alarm systems.*   An important step for fire safety involves early detection and a process that warns building occupants before the situation becomes critical. When smoke, heat, or fire is detected, alarm systems should notify a central dispatching station or nearby fire department to dispatch the first responders.

5. *Sprinkler systems.*   Automatic sprinkler systems can save lives during a fire. They can protect buildings on a 24-hour basis, reduce the spread of flames, and limit property damage, and they are often required by national and local fire codes.

6. *From protection to prevention.* Proactively preventing fires reduces the risk of injuries and structure damage. Organizations should encourage employees to read all hazardous chemical directions thoroughly because the chemicals could be flammable or could ignite when mixed. Organizations should maintain machinery to prevent overheating and report any visible electrical or mechanical hazards that might lead to a fire.[179]

National Fire Incident Reporting System (NFIRS)

NFIRS is the world's largest, national, annual database of fire incident information. The U.S. Fire Administration, part of the Federal Emergency Management Agency (FEMA), provides access to NFIRS for fire departments across the country. About 23,000 fire departments in all fifty states and the District of Columbia report NFIRS data each year.[180]

Fire Detectors

5 — Identify two types of detectors used for fire protection.

Automatic fire detection systems can significantly reduce property damage, personal injuries, and loss of life from fire in the workplace, according to OSHA. Their main function is to quickly identify a developing fire and alert building occupants and emergency response personnel before extensive damage occurs. They do this by using sensors to detect the smoke, heat, or flames from a fire to provide an early warning.[181] A residential fire alarm system, with which more people may be familiar, supervises doors, windows, and spaces within the home and may provide monitoring services to report a fire or intrusion to a contracted security office, where it will be reported to your local police or fire department.[182]

Fire detectors should be selected based on the burning characteristics of the materials present and the nature of the location they will be used to protect. Fire detectors work by sensing one or more products of fire. The three most common detectors are:

- Smoke detectors
- Heat detectors
- Flame detectors[183]

Smoke detectors detect the visible or invisible smoke particles from combustion. Smoke detectors are suitable for:

- Indoor areas with low ceilings such as offices, closets, and restrooms.
- Areas that are relatively clean with minimal amounts of dust and dirt.
- Areas that contain solid fuels such as wood, paper, fabric, and plastic materials.

Smoke detectors warn occupants of the presence of fire, and are thought to play a significant role in the decrease in reported fires and fire deaths. Their use began to increase in the mid-1970s and has continued to increase since then. Widespread public awareness programs that focus on the proper maintenance of alarms are needed. A number of initiatives are focused on this problem, to include nationally broadcast messages reminding the public to check and maintain their alarms when daylight savings time goes into effect.[184]

Some locations are unsuitable for smoke detectors because there is potential for unwanted alarms. Work areas with kitchens, stairs, shafts, high airflow locations, areas that are dusty or dirty, as well as outdoor areas may not be suited for smoke detector use. The two main types of smoke detectors OSHA identified are ionization detectors and photoelectric detectors.[185]

Ionization detectors contain a small radioactive source that charges the air inside a chamber. The charged air allows a small current to cross through and complete an electrical circuit. When smoke enters the chamber, it shields the radiation, which stops the current and triggers the alarm. These detectors respond quickly to very small smoke particles (even

fire detectors
Automatic fire detection systems designed to reduce property damage, personal injuries, and loss of life from fire in the workplace. Their main function is to quickly identify a developing fire and alert building occupants and emergency response personnel before extensive damage occurs through the use of sensors to detect the smoke, heat, or flames from a fire.

smoke detectors
Detect the visible or invisible smoke particles from combustion. Smoke detectors warn occupants of the presence of fire, and are thought to play a significant role in the decrease in reported fires and fire deaths.

those invisible to the naked eye) from flaming or very hot fires, but may respond very slowly to the dense smoke associated with smoldering or low-temperature fires.

Photoelectric detectors have a light source and sensor arranged so that the rays from the light source do not hit the sensor. When smoke particles enter the light path, some of the light is scattered and redirected onto the sensor, causing the detector to activate an alarm. These detectors react quickly to visible smoke particles from smoldering fires, but they are less sensitive to the smaller particles associated with flaming or very hot fires.

Heat detectors are normally used in dirty environments or where dense smoke is produced. Heat detectors may be less sensitive, but they are more appropriate than a smoke detector in these environments. The most common heat detectors either react to a broad temperature change or to a predetermined fixed temperature using resistors that decrease in resistance with an increase in temperature. These work because one resistor is protected while the other is exposed. A sharp increase in temperature reduces the resistance in the exposed resistor, and that activates the detector's alarm. According to OSHA, heat detectors are also suitable for:[186]

heat detectors
Normally used in dirty environments or where dense smoke is produced. The most common heat detectors either react to a broad temperature change or a predetermined fixed temperature, using resistors that decrease in resistance with an increase in temperature.

- Dirty, dusty, or smoky environments.
- Indoor areas without winds or drafts that can prevent heat from reaching the detector.
- Manufacturing areas where vapors, gases, or fumes may be present.
- Areas where particles of combustion are normally present, such as in kitchens, furnace rooms, utility rooms, and garages or where ovens, burners or vehicle exhaust gases are present.

Flame detectors are devices that look for specific types of light (infrared, visible, ultraviolet) emitted by flames. When the detector recognizes light from a fire, it signals an alarm. OSHA considers flame detectors best for protecting:[187]

flame detectors
Devices that look for specific types of light (infrared, visible, ultraviolet) emitted by flames. When the detector recognizes light from a fire, it signals an alarm.

- Areas with high ceilings and open spaces, such as warehouses and auditoriums.
- Outdoor or semi-enclosed areas, where winds can prevent smoke from reaching a heat or smoke detector.
- Areas where rapidly developing flaming fires can occur, such as petrochemical production, fuel storage areas, paint shops, and solvent areas.
- Environments unsuitable for other types of detectors.

Fire Extinguishers

Portable fire extinguishers are classified to indicate their ability to handle specific classes and sizes of fires. Labels on extinguishers indicate the class and relative size of fire that they can be expected to handle.[188]

- Class A extinguishers are used on fires involving ordinary combustibles, such as wood, cloth, and paper.
- Class B extinguishers are used on fires involving liquids, greases, and gases.
- Class C extinguishers are used on fires involving energized electrical equipment.
- Class D extinguishers are used on fires involving metals such as magnesium, titanium, zirconium, sodium, and potassium.

Automatic extinguishing systems include sprinkler, dry chemical, foam, halogen, and carbon dioxide systems. They have been reported to be present in only 18% of nonresidential building fires nationally and 17% of nonresidential building fires with dollar loss. In buildings, sprinklers are widely thought to be the most effective type of system, not only serving to alert occupants of the presence of fire, but also helping to extinguish it.[189]

Careers in Security

Name: Michael J. Finklestein

Position: Security Administrator

Year hired: 2013

City, state where you are based: Twinsburg, Ohio

College(s) attended (degree): Kent State University—Bachelor of Arts

Majors: Double major in Psychology and Justice Studies

Please give a brief description of your job: I am in charge of physical security of the production facility as well as maintaining compliance with all PCI-CP Physical Security Standards.

What qualities/characteristics are most helpful for this job? Attention to detail, follow-through on security deficiencies, the ability to work with other managers of varying backgrounds with competing interests, time management.

What is a typical starting salary? $50,000

What is the salary potential as you move up into higher-level jobs? $65,000–$80,000

What advice would you give someone in college beginning studies in security? Develop a wide-ranging skill set that includes an understanding of Physical Security, Data/IT Security, and some knowledge of budgeting and project management.

What appealed to you most about the position when you applied for it? Work in a stable industry and the ability to expand my knowledge base.

How would you describe the interview process? The interview process was typical for a professional setting. The first interview was a phone interview with HR, primarily to gauge my experience and fit for the job. The second interview was with the direct supervisor for the position. The final interview was with the vice president of security.

What is a typical day like? A typical day requires the ability to handle interruptions. I may be working on a long-term project (i.e., a major physical security expansion project or developing a companywide policy and training plan) and will be interrupted numerous times by calls from our contracted security staff, managers requesting particular access for an employee, etc. I have to field these calls and respond promptly and then be able to resume the work I was pulled away from. Time management is also a major necessity. I have to balance my time between these long-term projects, daily anticipated tasks (such as security and compliance checks throughout the facility), and the spur of the moment items that come up daily.

In a typical day, what do you like best/least about it? What I like best is that each day is a little different and broken up. I'm not chained to my desk. What I like least is that, as with most Security positions, it is often a struggle to implement the necessary changes. Other managers resist Security implementation if they feel it may impact the metrics they focus on (budget, production numbers, etc.)

How would you suggest interested applicants gain experience? Working for contract Security companies is always good exposure. It is very easy to stand out as a top performer in these positions if you are dedicated to the job. Civilian work in law enforcement is great experience as well (working in a jail, for example). This in particular helps to vet you as a reliable employee with integrity and a clean background, two things that are critical in the Security field.

Would you recommend military experience? Some companies value military experience, some do not. There are some very specific skills that can be gained in the military that can be useful in the Security field, but in my opinion, military experience does not give you an "edge" over the competition as it does in some law enforcement agencies.

Does holding a full-time job during college help applicants get hired afterward? I don't believe that the job has to be full-time. What I believe to be more important is steady work history as a young adult and developing reliable references. During college you do not want to overload yourself and allow coursework to suffer, but steady employment during college is definitely a plus.

Summary

- **Identify differences between a safe and a vault.**
  - A safe is a metal or high-strength box with a high-security lock and locking device. Safes come in many sizes and are often affixed to an immovable object.
  - A vault is a completely enclosed space, often a specially constructed room. Vaults do not typically move.
- **Explain the purpose of master keying.**
  - Master keys are a single key that will open many locks, although the locks are individually keyed differently. Master-keying is done for the convenience of persons with broad or variable access requirements to keep them from having to carry a separate key for each lock.

- **Define and distinguish between closed-circuit television and digital imaging systems.**
  - A closed-circuit television is a type of video surveillance system, often known by its acronym CCTV. Digital imaging systems (DIS) are the more current type of video surveillance system, eventually replacing CCTV.
- **Describe the practice of Crime Prevention through Environmental Design.**
  - Crime Prevention through Environmental Design (CPTED) is the purposeful design and use of the physical environment as a means to reduce fear of injury or victimization and to improve the quality of life.
- **Identify two types of detectors used for fire protection.**
  - Flame detectors are line-of-sight devices that look for specific types of light (infrared, visible, ultraviolet) emitted by flames during combustion.
  - Smoke detectors are devices that detect the visible or invisible smoke particles from combustion.

KEY TERMS

access control **113**

adversary **102**

closed-circuit television (CCTV) **106**

crime prevention through environmental design **124**

criminals **103**

defeat **104**

defense **104**

defense in depth **122**

defensible space **125**

detection **101**

deterrence **104**

digital imaging systems **106**

disgruntled employees **103**

entry control **113**

extremists **103**

fire detectors **128**

flame detectors **129**

heat detectors **129**

insiders **102**

layered security **122**

locks **106**

master keying **110**

natural surveillance **125**

outsiders **102**

physical security **101**

protection **101**

recovery **101**

response **101**

smoke detectors **128**

surroundings **125**

vandals **103**

REVIEW QUESTIONS

1. If you are asked to protect the valuable items of your employer, what questions should you ask to assist you in determining whether to use a safe or a vault?
2. Your company's CEO needs to have access to a total of 165 doors in 3 buildings. What keying solution should you offer him?
3. What choices need to be made when deciding the type of video surveillance system an organization will use?
4. Describe the main differences between defensible space and defense in depth.
5. You conduct a risk assessment and determine the need to protect a warehouse from both chemical fires and adversaries who use bottles filled with a flammable fluid and a makeshift wick (known often as Molotov cocktails). What type of fire detector(s) should be used?

PRACTICAL APPLICATION

- Imagine you work for a company that installs and repairs heating, ventilation, and air-conditioning units (HVAC) instead of a security company. Your new role involves preventing air from outside the building from entering without going through a filter. Analyze the requirements of your new job and compare it to the one you had as a security professional.

- Using your understanding of the CPTED principles, conduct a survey of a building or facility with which you are familiar and have authorized access.

- Using your understanding of physical security principles, complete a physical security plan for a building or facility with which you are familiar and have authorized access.

- Sketch the basic layout of one of the spaces suggested at the beginning of this chapter (home, work, third place). Identify the top five high-value areas in the space (darken the lines, highlight in a different color, or otherwise mark the areas).
  - List three ways the high-value locations could be accessed, in order of likelihood.
  - List three ways access to the high-value locations could be limited.
  - Identify three CPTED strategies that could be implemented to limit that access.

- Conduct a security survey of the place where you spend the most time. This can be a residence or another building where you spend a lot of time. Although you may use your memory (and a bit of your imagination), you will find it useful to physically walk around the buildings and examine what is missing or could be improved upon. Create a survey of at least two pages that has a checklist from the information in the chapter. Reflect on the survey and write out additional thoughts after using the checklist.

- Create a chart using the information from the adversaries and threat ranges. Along the left margin, create rows for the adversaries: insiders, outsiders, and outsiders in collusion with insiders. Along the top margin, create columns for the tactical range (deceit, force, stealth, and combination). Brainstorm with a classmate to complete the boxes using the information from adjoining adversaries and ranges. In each remaining box, write the type of threat that comes to your mind when you combine the two (i.e., an insider using deceit could change reports). Summarize the process in a paragraph.

- Review the section on threat labels. Conduct two searches each for keywords identifying vandals, disgruntled employees (insiders), criminals, and extremists. One search should be conducted in a public Internet-accessible database such as the website for the Federal Bureau of Investigations (FBI.gov) or a nonprofit organization such as the Southern Poverty Law Center (SPLC.org). Another search should be conducted in the library database for your school (which includes a variety of scholarly journal articles). Your academic librarian should be able to help you conduct both types of searches. Analyze the results of your searches for each keyword and hypothesize regarding the differences you find.

Institutional and Workplace Security

EMERGENCY

Main Entrance

Entrance A | B

Learning Objectives

After reading this chapter, you should be able to:

1. Identify indicators and types of workplace violence. **139**

2. Understand the recommended initial responses of active shooter situations. **140**

3. Identify employer responsibilities for preventing workplace violence. **143**

4. Identify employee responsibilities for preventing workplace violence. **146**

Introduction

From 2014 to 2015, instead of depending on contract positions, technology giants Google and Apple decided to hire full-time employees to handle their security. The decisions followed frequent high-profile discussions regarding the wages and diversity of the blue-collar workforce in the technology sector, including cooks, janitors, and security officers. These moves, according to the Rev. Jesse Jackson, suggest "a new climate for working people in Silicon Valley where they can negotiate for better wages, health care and fair working conditions."[1]

Institutional security describes the unique security requirements of specific organizations, foundations, and associations. An associated function, **workplace security** encompasses many practices to secure the workplace, such as risk management, physical security, cybersecurity, and loss prevention practices. Security professionals involved in institutional and workplace security find themselves performing guard services, alarm monitoring, investigation, armored transport, pre-employment screening, and information security, among other tasks.[2]

While each of these tasks are critical, in this chapter we focus on dealing with violence in the workplace that is a central concern of security professionals. **Workplace violence** is any act or threat of physical violence, harassment, intimidation, or other disruptive behavior, ranging from threats and verbal abuse to physical assaults and homicide that occurs at the workplace. Acts of violence at the workplace can range in seriousness from simply raised voices and profanity to violent crimes such as robbery or homicide.

Workplace violence frequently affects employees, clients, customers, and visitors to the workplace. Nearly 2 million Americans report being victims of workplace violence each year; although incidents have finally stabilized in the past few years as official rates of crime have declined.[3] A Bureau of Justice Statistics special report estimates that approximately 1.7 million incidents of workplace violence occur each year, with simple and aggravated assaults comprising the largest portion.[4] Recent reports show that 16% of workplace fatalities resulted from assaults and other violent acts, and that most workplace homicides happen during robberies or related crimes. It is estimated that these events cost approximately $36 billion dollars per year in the United States.[5]

Institutional security professionals have a unique challenge in the variety of possible security situations they could encounter. Adaptability and the ability to learn general procedures as well as specific solutions will serve the security professional well. Workplace security is a growing problem, and media attention has increased. Security professionals who have an established framework of information sharing both within and outside the organization will be best prepared and equipped to respond to the varied challenges facing them.

This chapter starts with an overview of incidents that have challenged security personnel. The security concerns of specific institutions are provided so that you can get a feel for the varied difficulties experienced by security professionals. Some of the difficulties are unique to particular industries, but many are not. With proper planning, a security professional can help an employer prepare the workplace for incidents of violence. We then turn to workplace security, including an examination of contemporary workplace violence issues such as domestic violence and active shooter situations.

Institutional and Facilities Security

Security professionals are employed in a diverse group of industries and must be prepared to act effectively in a variety of different settings. The scenarios set out below are designed to give you a feel for the circumstances, problems, and contingencies a security professional must deal with on a daily basis:

Airport Security

Paul Ciancia, 23, armed with an assault rifle and carrying materials expressing antigovernment sentiment, entered the secure area of the Los Angeles International (LAX) Airport on November 1, 2013, through a gateway normally used by travelers exiting the terminal. Ciancia pulled a semiautomatic .223-caliber rifle from his duffel bag and opened fire on the unarmed Transportation Safety Administration (TSA) officer Gerardo Hernandez before

institutional security
The unique security requirements of specific organizations, foundations, and associations.

workplace security
Encompasses many practices to secure the workplace, such as risk management, physical security, cybersecurity, and loss prevention practices.

workplace violence
Any act or threat of physical violence, harassment, intimidation, or other disruptive behavior, ranging from threats and verbal abuse to physical assaults and homicide that occurs at the workplace. Acts of violence at the workplace can range in seriousness from simply raised voices and profanity to violent crimes like robbery or homicide.

being chased down; Hernandez was the first TSA officer to be killed in the line of duty. Ciancia had prepared a note that made reference to LAX airport security. He was carrying antigovernment literature outlining a purported conspiracy to create a single global government, or New World Order.[6] The TSA is responsible for securing U.S. airports and screens all commercial airline passengers and baggage.[7]

Amusement Parks

In 2013, two people were hurt in a shooting at Fun Spot Park, in Orlando, Florida. Jamal LaFortune was accused of shooting inside the park, and police officers were called to arrest him after a brief foot pursuit. Fun Spot said its security team will now come in earlier and be stationed at both the north and south entrances, instead of scattered throughout the park, as they had been.[8]

▲ TSA agents provide security for all modes of transportation, whether air, rail, or vehicle. What types of transportation do you think would be the most difficult to secure?

Source: Bill Ingram/The Palm Beach Post/ZUMA Press, Inc/Alamy

Banking and Financial Institutions

Four people recently used stolen Social Security numbers to obtain credit for purchases, including for cars worth up to $60,000. Stores, financial institutions, and young people—some just 16 and 17 years old—were victimized. The suspects used forged documents to obtain new driver's licenses with false addresses, and the licenses were presented to financial institutions to qualify for loans. The suspects were charged with multiple crimes, including forgery, fraud, perjury, and theft.[9]

Chemical Security

A multinational plan for Syria to transport stockpiles of chemical substances and precursors to be destroyed required much planning. To avert punishment and retaliation from other countries, Syria agreed to reduce its stockpile. A key challenge was finding a country that was willing to accept the stockpiles and also had the capability to destroy them. Federal and international security professionals are responsible for securing these types of shipments.[10]

Convenience Stores

Suspects attempted to shoplift beer from a convenience store and were approached by a plain-clothed store security guard, who was assisted by a uniformed security guard. A struggle ensued, and the security guards used OC pepper spray to try to gain control of the suspect. At some point, the suspect produced a handgun and fired several rounds at the security guard, striking him several times in his bulletproof vest. The suspect then dropped his gun and produced a knife, cutting the guard. The suspect fled, but responding police officers were unable to locate the suspect in the area. The uniformed security guard sustained one nonlife-threatening gunshot wound and a knife wound. The plain-clothed security guard sustained minor injuries.[11]

Correctional Facilities (Private)

In 2012, one guard was killed and twenty people were injured in a riot at the privately run Adams County Correctional Facility in Mississippi, which holds immigrants who are convicted of crimes while they are illegally in the United States. Most of the injured inmates were convicted of returning to the United States after being deported. The facility was owned by Nashville, Tennessee-based Corrections Corporation of America, one of the nation's largest private prison companies, according to the Associated Press.[12] The proportion of privately operated prisons in the United States has increased since the mid-1980s, and today private prisons make up more than 10% of U.S. incarceration facilities. Private prison security professionals, with assistance from local and state law enforcement when needed, help maintain security at such facilities.

Food Service Organizations

Recently, thieves stole a ton of rib eye steaks, worth $19,500 wholesale from a local meat supplier. The steaks were in 6-pound pieces, with a total of 2,260 pounds being taken. The burglars broke a padlock on a gate and then forced their way into a storage building and loaded up the meat into their van.[13] Private security professionals and local police investigate these types of crimes.

Government Buildings

In 2013, a contract employee at the Naval Sea Systems Command shot and killed twelve people and injured three others in an office building of the Washington Navy Yard. A Navy review found that the company that employed him withdrew his access to secret-level data for two days after a previous incident. The company then reinstated his access without ever having informed the Navy. He was killed by police who responded to the shooting incident.[14] Private security along with local, federal, or military law enforcement agencies have primary responsibility for these types of incidents.

Health Care Industry

A man was charged recently with felony theft and criminal mischief after staff reported he had transported a woman to the hospital for treatment, and then was seen rummaging through cabinets and drawers in the emergency room. The *Sun Journal* reported that the man left the hospital with a bag containing bed pads, a diaper, buckets, booty socks, a magazine, and a box of rubber gloves.[15] Private security professionals, as well as local police, are responsible for investigating and prosecuting crimes such as this.

Hospitality and Lodging (Hotels and Motels)

A woman who pretended that she had been locked out of her room requested, and was given, a key from the front desk. Dressed only in a bathing suit and towel, she was calm while she stood with other guests while waiting to be helped. Using the key that she had fraudulently obtained she stole cash and a handgun from the room's occupants. As a result of the incident, hotel policy now limits the issuance of replacement keys to the person whose driver's license is on file.[16] Private security professionals and local law enforcement provide security in these locations.

Maritime/Port Security

An officer on an oil tanker opened his cabin door at five minutes before midnight to find two men pointing AK-47s at him. They pushed him into the cabin and told him to remain silent. They then took control of the ship and stole clothes, toiletries, electronics, and the ship's cargo—about 10,000 tons of fuel oil belonging to France's largest oil company. The fifteen pirates kept control of the tanker for a week while they siphoned off the fuel. Contemporary pirates were interested in taking over the ships, stealing the cargo, taking the crew's possessions, and leaving. Recently, pirates have begun taking hostages for ransom.[17] Private security, as well as local, federal, military, and international law enforcement are likely to engage with pirates, depending on location and jurisdiction.

Medical and Legal Marijuana Distributions

A recent addition to the growing list of workplaces needing security is the medical and legal marijuana industry. Companies vying for medical and legal marijuana business licenses, where the substance has been legalized, will bring new challenges to security professionals, including protecting growth, laboratory and storage facilities, and retail sales outlets.[18]

THINK ABOUT IT

Health care facilities are often busy, and the people who work there are focused on treating patents. How would a security professional go about trying to get the people who work there to be more focused on security?

Security teams are part of a rush of ancillary businesses expected to appear with the legalization of marijuana dispensaries. Cash-payment kiosks and other solutions could help eliminate questions of legality for banks.[19]

Movie Theaters

In 2012, James Holmes entered a multiplex theater in Aurora, Colorado, and then exited through a rear door, leaving the door propped open. He returned through the open door, throwing two tear gas canisters into the theater and then opened fire. Twelve people were killed and fifty-eight were wounded. He surrendered to police outside the theater. Holmes left his apartment booby-trapped, and police learned that he had fashioned a tripwire at the front door that would have triggered an explosion. Makeshift bombs in his apartment, including more than thirty homemade grenades and 10 gallons of gasoline, were disarmed by police.[20] Private security professionals and local police are responsible for securing public venues like cinemas.

Museums

In 2013, two men broke into the Portland (Maine) Head Light museum and looted an exhibit, causing about $3,000 worth of damage. The museum's alarm system alerted the security company, and the security company called the police department. Leaving the scene, the men crashed their getaway truck into a stone wall not far from the museum. The pair was charged with burglary, theft, aggravated criminal mischief, refusal to submit to arrest, failure to give correct names, and failure to notify police of their accident. Police found a copy of a lithograph from the museum depicting Portland's Central Wharf near the crashed vehicle.[21]

Retail Complex Security (Mall, Shopping Center, General Retail Security)

Two vehicles parked at the front entrance of a mall in Kenya one Saturday afternoon in 2013. About fifteen gunmen exited the vehicles and began throwing hand grenades at shoppers. Half of the gunmen ran into the main pedestrian entrance. The other half opened fire, ran to the side parking lot, and continued throwing hand grenades. The second group focused on killing people who were trying to flee.[22] Security in retail complexes is provided with a combination of security professionals and public law enforcement. There are many challenges in these environments, due to the fluid nature of the clientele and others moving throughout the complex and the variety of products and people in the area.

Schools and Campuses

A few years ago, a young man who was obsessed with mass murders and the 1999 Columbine High School shooting shot and killed twenty first-graders and six educators inside Sandy Hook Elementary School. He had also shot and killed his mother inside their home before he had driven to the school. He used a handgun to take his own life as police arrived.[23] Since that incident, school and campus security have become significant concerns, with some proposing that private security personnel or public police officers be hired to patrol school grounds.

Sporting Events and Arenas

Two bombs exploded near the finish line of the 2013 Boston Marathon, killing three people and injuring at least 264. The bombs contained pellets and nails, and one was contained in a pressure cooker, hidden inside a black backpack. The second bomb was also in a metal container. Two bombing suspects were identified: They were of Chechen origin and had legally immigrated to the United States, and were currently living in Cambridge, Massachusetts. One of the suspects was killed when police tried to arrest them.[24] Local, state, and federal law enforcement as well as private security professionals provide security for such events and investigate these types of incidents.

Many of these scenarios, although specific to the locations described here, could happen at any number of different organizations or locations. Security professionals must be prepared for events that are both unplanned and unexpected, and be adaptable to a variety of situations that threaten the workplace.

THINK ABOUT IT

Consider a workplace with which you are familiar. What unique features or characteristics are there that make it more or less safe if there was an incident of workplace violence? How could that be changed?

The Nature of Workplace Violence

As these scenarios suggest, violence in the workplace takes many different forms. Romano and others found that it occurs between employees, between an employee and someone otherwise unaffiliated with the organization, or between two people without any employment connection (like customers).[25] While more information on the causes of violence and how to handle it is becoming known, there is often no way to predict this conduct. Despite everything we know or do, violent situations will sometimes occur. The U.S. Department of Labor advised that no employer is immune from workplace violence.[26] No employer can totally prevent it, and the cost is significant. There is not only the immediate and profound loss of life or physical or psychological repercussions, there is also the effect on the victim's family, friends, and coworkers. In addition, the loss of productivity and morale that sweeps through an organization may continue long after the incident, as well as the public relations impact on an employer when news of the violence reaches the media.[27] Workplace violence can happen anywhere, regardless of job setting and occupational category.

Workplace violence costs organizations in the United States an estimated 3 to 7 million lost workdays per year at a cost estimated at more than $192 million. Additionally, Licu and Fisher found that violence in the workplace takes a toll on employees and employers in other ways, such as long-lasting negative physical and mental health effects.[28] We must also consider the toll that outbursts of school violence have on teachers. Victimized teachers may experience symptoms of posttraumatic stress disorder (PTSD), heightened levels of stress, and increased fear, according to Wilson, Douglas, and Lyon.[29] Additionally, as a result of workplace violence, teachers can exhibit avoidance behavior toward students and certain social situations, feel threatened, and have a sense of personal intrusion.[30] In addition to the personal consequences of workplace violence, there may also be consequences at the organizational level. Wilson's research determined that teachers who feel unsafe at school due to potential violence tend to be unmotivated and less committed to their job and can suffer both physically and psychologically following a violent incident.[31] There is also the potential for serious negative consequences for the educational system, like an increase in a teacher's absenteeism or a negative effect on teaching ability. They found that this could result in classroom instability and a lack of continuity for students. It may even have severe negative consequences for the quality of education.[32]

Types of Workplace Violence

Four types of workplace violence can be identified based on the relationship among victims, perpetrators, and the work setting, according to Romano, Levi-Minzi, Rugala, and Van Hasselt.

- Violent acts by criminals who have no other connection to the workplace, but enter it in order to commit robbery or another crime.
- Violence directed at employees by customers, clients, patients, students, inmates, or any others for whom an organization provides services.
- Violence against coworkers, supervisors, or managers by a present or former employee.
- Violence committed in the workplace by someone who doesn't work there, but has a personal relationship with an employee, like an abusive spouse or domestic partner.[33]

Workplace violence occurs in all types of workplaces and can occur at any time. The Federal Bureau of Investigation (FBI) reported that some organizations are more likely to experience these incidents, such as convenience stores and gas stations that remain open late at night.[34]

Violence in the workplace by otherwise unconnected people accounts for nearly 80% of workplace homicides. In workplace homicides, the motive is usually theft according to the FBI, and in a great many cases, the criminal is often carrying a gun or other weapon. That increases the likelihood that one or more victims will be killed or seriously wounded.[35] After a crime like this has occurred, security professionals will notify law enforcement officials for investigating, finding, and arresting the suspect, and collecting evidence for prosecution. Assaults are the typical crime when the incident involves an employee and someone receiving a service from the organization. These generally occur as workers are performing typical tasks. In some occupations, dealing with dangerous people is part of the job, especially for police officers, correctional officers, security guards, or mental health workers. For other occupations, violent reactions by customers or clients are unpredictable, and may be triggered by an argument, anger at the quality of or denial of service, delays, or some other precipitating event.[36] Industries considered high risk for homicide in the workplace include those with late-night operations, contact with the public, exchange of money, delivery (such as taxis and couriers), working with unstable people, guarding valuable property, and working in community-based treatment settings.[37] Employees experiencing the largest number of assaults are those in the health care occupations.[38]

▲ A smiling group of health care workers. Health care employees experience a large number of assaults. Why?
Source: New York City Health and Hospitals Corporation, http://www.nyc.gov/html/hhc/html/professionals/ForHCPros-JobOpportunities.shtml Monkey Business Images/ Shutterstock

Indicators of Potential for Workplace Violence

Organizational characteristics thought to contribute to opportunities for workplace violence include those with:

- Poor work organization
- Organizational restructuring
- Coercive leadership
- Aggressive cultures
- Poor accommodations for increases in activity[39]

1 Identify indicators and types of workplace violence.

Poor work organization may undermine the perception of fairness in the workplace and cause violent responses. Excessive delays may be a by-product of disorganization and add to the frustration in the workplace. Activities such as downsizing, outsourcing, and others aimed at organizational restructuring can cause tension in the workplace.[40] Organizations with coercive leadership may restrict communication and dialog, making it difficult for leaders to identify or anticipate volatile situations. Aggressive, violent, or oppressive workplace cultures create an environment that may either create or reward workplace violence. Workplaces that do poorly at accommodating increases in activity include places that get overcrowded and places with excessive noise.[41]

Domestic Violence in the Workplace

Domestic violence is often seen as patterns of abusive behavior used to gain or maintain power and control over others in a relationship. Domestic violence can be physical, sexual, emotional, economic, or psychological. Except when those involved in domestic violence are coworkers, most incidents are perpetrated outside the organization. Some early warning signs include the victim showing increased fear, emotional episodes, physical injury, or work performance deterioration. Early intervention is the key to prevention.[42] According to Romano et al., signs that may help determine if an employee is experiencing domestic violence include:

- Disruptive phone calls and emails.
- Poor concentration.
- Unexplained bruises or injuries.
- Frequent absences and tardiness.
- Use of unplanned personal time.
- Disruptive visits from current or former partners.[43]

Security professionals and supervisors must take care when dealing with these potentially highly charged situations. Security professionals may lack the training and experience to handle these incidents and may be better off consulting with experienced professionals.[44] Figure 7–1 lists suggested actions when employees are affected by domestic violence.

FIGURE 7–1
Things to Do When an Employee Is affected by Domestic Violence
Source: U.S. Department of Labor (DOL). (2013). DOL Workplace Violence Program.

- Talk with the employee about your concern of the possibility of the violence extending into the workplace.
- Recommend that the employee seek counseling assistance in dealing with the problem.
- Recommend that the employee call the National Domestic Violence Hotline for more information about domestic violence or to help find local resources.
- Contact Human Resources for more information and/or assistance, if needed.
- Recommend that a workplace safety plan be developed in case an incident occurs at the workplace.
- Don't be a hero if the perpetrator shows up. Follow your security plan and call for help.[45]

Security professionals should receive training on protective orders and other forms of legal recourse for domestic and intimate partner violence.[46] All employees should be made aware that security personnel can be approached if domestic violence is an issue, and a file on each reported incident should be maintained. Security professionals for multilocation companies or landlord companies may find it beneficial to share workplace violence policies with other locations and tenants.[47] Having an interlinked and complementary policy may provide additional security for adjacent organizations. As with other areas, security professionals will find it necessary to coordinate with local law enforcement and emergency responders prior to an actual emergency. Local public safety personnel may need special access to buildings, such as keycards with specific access or hard keys in case countermeasures are in place or to avoid the audible noise that keycards produce.[48] Floor plans, as well as an awareness of nuances within the building should also be shared.

Active Shooter Situations

2 Understand the recommended initial responses of active shooter situations.

An **active shooter**, as defined by the FBI, is an individual actively engaged in killing or attempting to kill people in a confined and populated area.[49] In most cases, there is no pattern or method to the selection of victims. The FBI has found a disturbing rise in the number of "active shooter" incidents across America.[50]

Active shooters target locations that are both large and small, with most incidents going largely unnoticed outside of the immediate community.[51] Most people who have been identified as active shooters were organization insiders or were otherwise known by their victims.

Active shooters are adversaries or assailants with an objective to kill as many people as possible at a target location. They often use violence against others because of a perception that they've lost control. Active shooting incidents are typically spontaneous, random, unplanned events and therefore do not include incidents such as bank robberies or drug deals that may turned lethal.[52]

Over a 10-year period beginning in 2002, there were 154 active shooter events. Most (96%) of the suspects were male, and 37% of the incidents happened in the workplace. Forty-three percent of the shooters ultimately committed suicide. Forty percent of the incidents, according to Hayes, had no clear motive, while 21% involved some type of workplace retaliation.[53]

The first needed response to an active shooter incident is to figure out what is occurring. Employees should be taught to rapidly assess the situation and evaluate the available options for survival. This may include evacuating the building, and this should be done as fast as possible. If escape is not possible, getting behind a locked door, or creating a barricade that would protect the employee from gunshots is the best alternative.[54] Sometimes hiding is the only option. In other instances, escape may be possible. Employees should be trained to continuously assess the situation and take the best action at the time. The process of assessing the situation and evaluating options should continue until the threat is over.[55] There is no need to seek approval from others or take the time to collect belongings. Once safe, each individual, both security personnel and regular employees, should immediately make contact with emergency personnel to report their safety.[56]

Finding a hiding place in active shooter situations can often mean the difference between life and death. If possible, employees can lock themselves in a room, barricade the door, and be very quiet so the perpetrator cannot hear them. Employees should move individually because spreading out will create confusion and provide fewer targets, resulting in fewer victims. If possible it is also important to establish and maintain ongoing communication with fellow employees. Keeping everyone informed of the situation and getting help for those who are injured are important steps for surviving an active shooter event.[57]

Security professionals, in all organizations, must plan for events like these and stay abreast of industry best practices, such as those outlined in Figure 7–2 and 7–3.

active shooter
An individual actively engaged in killing or attempting to kill people in a confined and populated area. Active shooters arrive on the scene with the specific intent to commit mass murder. Unlike other mass killings or mass shootings, active shooter situations do not include incidents such as bank robberies or drug deals that may turn lethal.

- Be aware of your environment and any possible dangers.
- Take note of the two nearest exits in any facility you visit.
- If you are in an office, stay there and secure the door.
- If you are in a hallway, get into a room and secure the door.
- As a last resort, attempt to take the active shooter down. When the shooter is at close range and you cannot flee, your chance of survival is much greater if you try to incapacitate him or her.
- CALL 911 WHEN IT IS SAFE TO DO SO!

FIGURE 7–2
Good Practices for Coping with an Active Shooter Situation
Source: Department of Homeland Security (DHS), *Active Shooter: How to Respond, 2008,* http://www.dhs.gov/xlibrary/assets/active_shooter_booklet.pdf

---

1. **Evacuate**
   Have an escape route and plan in mind.
   Leave your belongings behind.
   Keep your hands visible.
2. **Hide out**
   Hide in an area out of the shooter's view.
   Block entry to your hiding place and lock the doors.
   Silence your cell phone and/or pager.
3. **Take action**
   As a last resort and only when your life is in imminent danger.
   Attempt to incapacitate the shooter.
   Act with physical aggression and throw items at the active shooter.

FIGURE 7–3
Active Shooter – What to Do When an Active Shooter Is in Your Vicinity
Source: Department of Homeland Security, *Active Shooter: Pocket Card Information, 2014,* https://www.dhs.gov/xlibrary/assets/active_shooter_pocket_card.pdf

FIGURE 7–3
(continued)

What to do when law enforcement arrives.

- Remain calm and follow instructions.
- Put down any items in your hands (i.e., bags, jackets).
- Raise hands and spread fingers.
- Keep hands visible at all times.
- Avoid quick movements toward officers, such as holding onto them for safety.
- Avoid pointing, screaming, or yelling.
- Do not stop to ask officers for help or direction when evacuating.

Information you should provide to law enforcement or 911 operator.

- Location of the active shooter.
- Number of shooters.
- Physical description of shooter(s).
- Number and type of weapons held by shooter(s).
- Number of potential victims at the location.

The Workplace Violator

In addition to institutional characteristics that are conducive to violence, there are also personal qualities that define a typical workplace violator. Some of these are listed in Figure 7–4.

An employee with attendance problems may be taking excessive sick leave or have excessive incidents of tardiness. They may leave work early and have improbable excuses for their absences. Those with decreased productivity may also show poor judgment, have missed deadlines, and be wasting work time. Employees with safety issues may be more accident prone or may have disregard for their personal safety. Those showing evidence of serious stress may be overly emotional, make or receive excessive phone calls, or have been through a recent relationship separation, according to the U.S. Department of Labor.[58]

Romano's research found specific behaviors related to potential workplace violators include sadness, depression, threats, menacing or erratic behavior, aggressive outbursts, references to weapons, verbal abuse, an inability to handle criticism, hypersensitivity to perceived slights, and partaking in offensive commentary or jokes referring to violence.[59] These

FIGURE 7–4
Typical Characteristics of a Workplace Troublemaker
Sources: J. H. Lombardi, "Workplace Violence: Anticipation through Process, Not Prediction of Results, Revisited," in J. H. Fennelly, ed., Handbook of Loss Prevention and Crime Prevention, 4th ed.(Waltham, MA: Butterworth- Heinemann, 2004); U.S. Department of Labor (DOL), DOL Workplace Violence Program, 2013, http://www.dol.gov/oasam/hrc/policies/dol-workplace-violence-program.htm

- Disgruntled chronic complainer
- Caucasian
- Late 30s to early 40s
- Avoids responsibility
- Difficult to supervise
- Marginal performer
- Obsessed with weapons
- Defensive and suspicious
- Chronically angry
- Attendance problems
- Adverse impact on supervisor's time
- Decreased productivity
- Inconsistent work patterns
- Concentration problems
- Safety issues
- Poor health and hygiene
- Unusual/changed behavior
- Evidence of possible drug or alcohol use/abuse
- Evidence of serious stress in the employee's personal life
- Continual excuses/blame

may be warning signs of imminent workplace violence. According to the U.S. Department of Labor, although it is possible that only one of these indicators will be detected, it is more likely that a pattern will occur and represent a change from normal behavior.[60] Behavior can help workers recognize potential problems with fellow employees. If a coworker begins acting differently, determining the frequency, duration, and intensity of the new, and possibly troubling, behavior can be helpful, according to Romano.[61]

The presence of any of these behaviors does not mean a violent act will occur. They may simply be indicators of another type of problem.[62] No single behavior is more suggestive of violence than another. All actions should be evaluated in context to determine the person's potential for violence.[63]

Jobs with higher risk of workplace violence are workers who exchange money, delivery drivers, health care professionals, public service workers, customer service agents, law enforcement personnel, and those who work alone or in small groups.[64] When these crimes occur where we live, the police take the report and investigate the crime. When these crimes occur in the workplace, there may be more of a sharing of the investigative responsibilities by the police and security. The extent of this sharing of responsibilities will likely vary in different jurisdictions.

Controlling Workplace Violence

Many corporations and organizations have instituted programs to help prevent workplace violence. These programs can be used to mitigate the threat of such occurrences.[65] Workplace violence does not happen randomly, and the perpetrators usually display indicators prior to the act. Awareness of these indicators is an essential component of workplace violence prevention.[66]

3 Identify employer responsibilities for preventing workplace violence.

Many people think that most workplace violence incidents consist of a disgruntled employee committing a workplace homicide. More often, an incident of workplace violence is a robbery gone awry. With proper planning, employers can prepare their workplace and employees to survive incidents of violence. To assess a workplace's vulnerability to violence, the U.S. National Crime Prevention Council suggests we answer these questions from an employee's perspective:

- Does the organization have available an easy-to-use phone system with emergency buttons, sign-in policies for visitors, panic buttons, safe rooms, security guards, office access controls, good lighting, safety training?
- Does the employer take care in hiring and firing?
- Before hiring, are employment gaps, history, references, and criminal and educational records thoroughly examined?
- Are termination procedures defined clearly with attention to advance notice, severance pay, and placement services?
- Could you recognize potentially violent employees?
- Are you encouraged to report unusual or worrisome behavior?
- Is there a clear, written policy that spells out procedures in cases of violence and sanctions for violators?
- Do you know to whom you should report unusual behaviors?
- Do you work in a supportive, harmonious environment?
- Is there a culture of mutual respect?
- Does your employer provide an employee assistance program or counseling?[67]

Once an assessment of the workplace's vulnerability to violence is conducted, security professionals should take steps to implement a workplace violence prevention program.[68] For this program to work, it must be supported by all levels of employees. It addresses physical security, hiring and firing practices, and employee vulnerabilities.[69]

Employers must promote a work environment free from threats and violence. If they do not, the FBI advised that employers can face economic loss as the result of violence in the form of lost work time, damaged employee morale and productivity, increased workers' compensation payments, medical expenses, and possible lawsuits and liability costs.[70]

There are several steps that management can take to help prevent workplace violence. These include:

- Promoting sincere, open, and timely communication among managers, employees, and union representatives.
- Offering opportunities for professional development.
- Fostering a family-friendly work environment.
- Maintaining a process for complaints and concerns and allowing them to be expressed in a nonjudgmental forum that includes timely feedback to the initiator.
- Promoting "quality-of-life" issues such as up-to-date and welcoming facilities and job satisfaction.
- Maintaining impartial and consistent discipline for employees who exhibit improper conduct and poor performance.[71]

Increasingly, digital communication in the form of postings on social media (Twitter, Facebook, Instagram, and YouTube) has been identified and found to be related to acts of violence in the workplace. Employers should have a plan to identify and respond to potential threats before an event occurs. Employers should develop policies on workplace violence, including the organization's commitment to ensure the workplace remains free of violence, examples of activities that are considered workplace violence, and proper procedures for reporting workplace violence, both officially and anonymously.

Planning for Prevention

Violence in the workplace represents one of the most challenging security problems that organizations face. Two accredited standards developers, ASIS International and the Society for Human Resource Management (SHRM), created the American National Standard (ANS) for preventing violence in the workplace.[72]

The American National Standards Institute (ANSI) established policies, processes, and protocols that organizations can adopt to identify and prevent threatening behavior and violence affecting the workplace. ANSI also facilitates their ability to better address and resolve threats and violence that have occurred. The standard's recommendations are intentionally broad in order to provide organizations the flexibility they need to implement prevention and intervention strategies appropriate for their workplace.[73]

According to the FBI, prevention of workplace violence begins with planning. It is easier to persuade managers to focus on the problem after a violent act has taken place than it is to get them to act before anything has happened. If the decision to plan in advance is more difficult to make, however, it is also more logical.[74]

Any organization, large or small, will be far better able to spot potential dangers and defuse them before violence develops if it has a strategy to deal with it. In forming an effective workplace violence strategy, important principles include the following:

- There must be support from the top.
- There is no one-size-fits-all strategy.
- A plan should be proactive, not reactive.
- A plan should take into account the workplace culture.
- Planning for and responding to workplace violence requires varied expertise.
- Managers should take an active role in communicating the workplace violence policy.
- The plan should be practiced.
- Reevaluate, rethink, and revise.[75]

This organization does not tolerate workplace violence. We define workplace violence as actions or words that endanger or harm another employee or result in other employees having a reasonable belief that they are in danger. Such actions include:

- Verbal or physical harassment.
- Verbal or physical threats.
- Assaults or other violence.
- Any other behavior that causes others to feel unsafe (e.g., bullying, sexual harassment).

Company policy requires an immediate response to all reports of violence. All threatening incidents will be investigated and documented by the employee relations department. If appropriate, the company may provide counseling services or referrals for employees.

The following disciplinary actions may also be taken:

- Oral reprimand
- Written reprimand
- Suspension
- Termination

It is the responsibility of all employees to report all threatening behavior to management immediately. The goal of this policy is to promote the safety and well-being of all people in the workplace.

FIGURE 7–5
Sample Written Policy Statement
Sources: Federal Bureau of Investigation (FBI), *Workplace Violence: Issues in Response*, in E. A. Rugala and A. R. Isaacs, eds., Critical Incident Response Group, National Center for the Analysis of Violent Crime (Quantico, VA: FBI Academy, U.S. Department of Justice, 2002).

Support from the top is essential for any plan, and security professionals should ensure there is commitment at every level. If a company's senior executives are not truly committed to a workplace violence prevention program, it is unlikely to be effective. The workplace culture includes the atmosphere, relationships, traditional management styles, and other unique facets. If there are elements in the culture that appear to encourage or tolerate such behavior as bullying, intimidation, poor communication, inconsistent discipline, or erratic enforcement of company policies, these influences should be corrected. Varied expertise in planning ensures a team approach that includes multidisciplinary influences. Figure 7–5 provides a sample policy statement for organizations regarding domestic violence.

Prevention Strategies

A secure and physically safe workplace is the intended result of any good organizational workplace violence prevention strategy. Employers should use a variety of measures to help ensure workplace safety. The measures used depend on the resources available, which may include:

- Designated security personnel to respond to requests for assistance.
- Employee photo identification badges and coded keys for secure area access.
- On-site security guard services.
- Security assistance in registering, badging, and directing visitors in larger facilities.
- Other appropriate security measures (such as metal detectors).

Additional law enforcement assistance is available for emergency situations through local police departments. The U.S. Department of Labor advised that employees should notify the appropriate security office or designated police of suspicious or unauthorized individuals on the organization's property.[76]

The best protection employers can offer toward workplace violence is a zero-tolerance policy. Employers should establish a workplace violence prevention program and incorporate the information on their relevant policies in employee handbooks and in manuals of standard operating procedures.[77] All workers must know the policy and understand that all claims of workplace violence will be investigated and remedied promptly. Additionally, employers should develop additional methods to protect employees in high-risk industries.[78] The U.S. Department of Labor advised that this policy should cover all workers, patients, clients, visitors, contractors, and anyone else who may come in contact with an organization's personnel.[78] The program should support a work environment in which violent or potentially violent situations are effectively addressed. The expectation is that each employee will treat all others, whether employees, customers or clients, with dignity and respect.

Employee Responsibilities

Employees can also contribute to a reduction of incidents of workplace violence. Employees have the right to expect a work environment that is safe from violence, threats, and harassment. The FBI suggested that employees can actively contribute to preventing workplace violence by:

- Accepting and following an employer's preventive policies and practices.
- Being aware of and reporting violent or threatening behavior by coworkers.
- Following procedures outlined in the workplace violence prevention program.[80]

Additionally, the U.S. Department of Labor advised that employees are responsible for:

- Interacting responsibly with fellow employees, supervisors, and clients.
- Being familiar with the organization's policy regarding workplace violence.
- Promptly reporting actual or potential acts of violence.
- Cooperating fully in investigations of workplace violence.
- Being familiar with services provided for victims of workplace violence.
- Informing appropriate personnel about restraining or protective court orders related to domestic situations so that assistance can be offered at the work site.[81]

Managers and supervisors are additionally responsible for:

- Informing employees of policies and programs addressing workplace violence.
- Taking all reported incidents of workplace violence seriously.
- Timely investigation of all acts of violence, threat, and similar disruptive behavior and taking appropriate action.
- Providing feedback to employees regarding the outcome of their reports.
- Requesting, where appropriate, assistance from functional area expert(s).
- Being aware of situations that can provoke violent behavior and promptly addressing them.
- Encouraging employees who show signs of stress or domestic violence to seek assistance.
- Assuring, where needed, that employees have time and opportunity to attend training for topics such as conflict resolution and stress management.[82]

Also, security professionals are responsible for:

- Providing security and helping to defuse violent situations at the workplace.
- Providing technical advice and support regarding security matters.
- Maintaining an ongoing security awareness program.
- Assisting with or conducting investigations of threats or incidents of violence.
- Requesting, where appropriate, assistance from functional area expert(s).
- Providing liaison with local law enforcement.[83]

4 Identify employee responsibilities for preventing workplace violence.

Security in Practice
Securing the Olympics

▲ South Korean athletes prepare to welcome the 2018 Winter Olympics to Pyeongchang. Why is Olympic security of special concern?

Security preparations for the 2018 Winter Olympics began in earnest as soon as South Korea learned that the resort city of Pyeongchang had been chosen to host the games. Pyeongchang is not far from the heavily militarized North Korean border, a fact that raised special concerns among planners. Experts estimate that more than 24,000 personnel will work to secure the games, and security services are expected to cost around $33 million.

In 2014, the Olympic Winter Games were held in Sochi, Russia, a resort city on the Black Sea. They involved a massive security operation that saw authorities deploying more than 50,000 police and soldiers amid threats from Muslim insurgents. Prior to the opening of the Sochi event, President Vladimir Putin assured those planning to attend that he would "do whatever it takes" to protect them. Fifteen thousand Americans attended the games, including athletes, their families, sponsors, and enthusiasts. Putin was true to his promise, and the Russian venue was free of serious incidents.

QUESTIONS

1. *What special security concerns do the Olympics hold?*

2. *If you were in charge of security for the next Olympics, what threats would you consider?*

References: C. Clarey, "For 2018, a Different Plan Is in Place," *New York Times*, February 24, 2014, http://www.nytimes.com/2014/02/25/sports/olympics/south-korea-awaits-2018-games-with-a-different-plan.html (accessed May 20, 2015); Around the Rings, "2018 By the Book: Security," http://aroundtherings.com/site/A__37189/Title__2018-By-the-Book—Security/292/Articles (accessed May 20, 2015); http://www.nytimes.com/2014/01/20/world/europe/us-congressmen-raise-concerns-about-security-at-sochi-olympics.html?_r=0 Jo Yong-Hak/Reuters/Corbis

Emerging Forms of Institutional and Workplace Security

During the past decade, security professionals have been faced with a number of new challenges brought about by changing social norms and economic conditions. A number of these emerging problems for institutional and workplace security are set out below.

Petroleum Manufacturing and Distribution

Up to 150,000 barrels of crude oil are stolen in Nigeria and sold internationally every year. Illegal refineries tap into established oil pipelines and steal oil during the night. Unemployed welders, many who previously worked for the oil companies, typically do the work. Oil and gas experts believe oil theft is growing rapidly.[84] Private security professionals in the oil industry, as well as some local and federal law enforcement organizations, should be capable of investigating these crimes.

Pharmaceutical Manufacturing and Distribution

An increase in the manufacture, trade, and distribution of counterfeit, stolen, and illicit medicines and medical devices has been reported around the globe. In some areas of Asia, Africa, and Latin America counterfeit medical goods can form up to 30% of the market.[85] According to the International Criminal Police Organization (INTERPOL), pharmaceutical crime includes the manufacture, trade, and distribution of fake, stolen, or illicit medicines and medical devices. These crimes also include counterfeiting and falsification of medical products, packaging and associated documentation, in addition to theft, fraud, illicit diversion, smuggling, trafficking, the illegal trade of medical products, and the money laundering associated with it. Many organized crime networks are drawn to these crimes by the significant profit potential. They operate across national borders and the import, export,

manufacture, and distribution of counterfeit and illicit medicines. Coordinated and cross-sector action by INTERPOL and other law enforcement operating internationally is vital in order to identify, investigate, and prosecute these criminals.[86]

Cruise Ships

Cruise ships offer a unique set of security challenges. Cruise ship passengers experience a variety of crimes, including art sculpture taken from the ship's art gallery, stolen jewelry, and sexual assault. Many of the events that occur on ships are subject to international law or the laws of a country that may have little interest in investigation and prosecution. Often, jurisdictional issues prevent investigative organizations from conducting thorough investigations. Cruise lines employ their own security personnel and report criminal incidents

▲ Cruise ship passengers experience a variety of crimes. What special security challenges do you think cruise ships present?

Source: State of Washington, http://www.ecy.wa.gov/PROgrams/wq/wastewater/cruiseship.jpg
Olga Gavrilova/Shutterstock

to the FBI.[87] The U.S. Federal Maritime Commission (FMC) has some jurisdiction and responsibility over cruise lines that board passengers at U.S. ports for vessels with berth or stateroom accommodations for fifty or more passengers. The FMC has jurisdiction as a result of the authority to require cruise lines to maintain sufficient financial coverage to indemnify passengers in cases of nonperformance of the voyage, or for instances of injury or death on voyages. The FMC has no jurisdiction in cases where a passenger flies out of the United States and then boards a vessel at a foreign port, passenger line vessel operations, safety issues, amenities on board vessels, or fare levels.[88]

Energy Manufacturing and Distribution Sector

The energy sector in the United States experienced a significant number of malware attacks in the spring and summer of 2012. The attacks caused expensive outages at pipelines, oil refineries, and drilling platforms. Based on data from the U.S. Department of Homeland Security's (DHS) Industrial Control System-Cyber Emergency Response Team (ICS-CERT), many of the malware attack reports they received were for attacks made on the systems of energy companies, such as grid operators and natural gas pipeline companies.[89] Private security and federal law enforcement investigate these types of breaches in security, as they often involve multiple jurisdictions.

Careers in Security

Name: Stacy Lane Lavelle

Position: Safety and Security Officer

Year hired: May 2012

City, state where you are based: Nashville, Tennessee

College(s) attended (degree): Middle Tennessee State University, B.S.

Majors: Criminal Justice Administration

Minors: History

Please give a brief description of your job: Monitor the safety and security of the property and surrounding complex; assists guests with room and safe access; conduct routine inspections of the fire protection system; monitor CCTV, perimeter alarm system, duress alarms and fire life safety system; respond to accidents and medical conditions involving employees and guests, and contact EMS or administer first aid/CPR as needed; defuse guest/employee disturbances and escort any unwelcome persons from property without disrupting the flow of business operation; handle interruptions and complaints; train new officers on the operations, policies and procedures of the department;

and complete reports to document all Loss Prevention/Security related incidents.

What qualities/characteristics are most helpful for this job? To work as a Security Officer in the hospitality industry, one must be courteous, patient, professional, and understanding as most of the people that you will encounter are guests of the hotel attending conventions. These guests/groups spend a lot of money, so it's important to treat them as guests and not criminals.

What is a typical starting salary? A typical starting salary is approximately $10/hr depending on the industry and if you possess an armed or unarmed security license.

What is the salary potential as you move up into higher-level jobs? It depends on the industry.

What advice would you give someone in college beginning studies in security? Keep an open mind. There are a lot of preconceived notions and stereotypes regarding "security guards" but "security" isn't necessarily just about protecting someone or something; it also entails asset protection, loss prevention, and risk management.

What appealed to you most about the position when you applied for it? After graduation, I could not immediately find a job so I moved back home to Memphis where I found that there was little to no opportunity for me. I continued looking for a job in the Nashville area that would enable me to move back and search for a career related to my degree field. Safety and security seemed like good experience to have on my resume. The company I work for is very reputable and even paid for my security license and CPR/AED certification.

How would you describe the interview process? First, I had a phone screening with an HR recruiter to ensure I possessed the qualities desired to uphold the company's values. Then, I was scheduled for a group interview with seven others who were applying for the same position. Once the candidate pool was narrowed down to three, we each interviewed with the Operations Manager and Assistant Director of Security.

What is a typical day like? A typical day working as a Safety and Security Officer in the hospitality industry includes investigating and submitting reports involving guest and employee accidents, missing or damaged property, food-borne illness, and complaints about insects. It also includes responding to service calls including door unlocks, safe unlocks, noise complaints, wake-up calls, Lost and Found assists, wheelchair escorts, jump starts, way finding and responding to fire alarms, panic alarms, and/or security alarms. Safety and Security Officers are also responsible for conducting routine inspections of the fire protection system, which includes sprinkler control valves and fire extinguishers.

In a typical day, what do you like best/least about it? I dislike that most of the interaction I have with guests is the result of a mistake that another department has made or because the guest is having a bad experience in general. There's only so much I can do to make it right for them. I do like that I have the freedom to go anywhere in the hotel, which makes it easy to walk and talk with guests. They seem to enjoy that as much as I do.

How would you suggest interested applicants gain experience? Security is not the same in every industry, so I would recommend researching the industries that utilize security and choose the one you are most interested in before trying to gain experience.

Would you recommend military experience? I would recommend having military experience in some industries but hospitality isn't one of them.

Does holding a full-time job during college help applicants get hired afterward? It did not help me but my job during college was in retail.

Summary

- **Identify indicators and types of workplace violence.**
  - Four types of workplace violence can be identified based on the relationship among victims, perpetrators, and the work setting.
    - Violent acts by criminals who have no other connection with the workplace, but enter it in order to commit robbery or another crime.
    - Violence directed at employees by customers, clients, patients, students, inmates, or any others for whom an organization provides services.
    - Violence against coworkers, supervisors, or managers by a present or former employee.
    - Violence committed in the workplace by someone who doesn't work there, but has a personal relationship with an employee, such as an abusive spouse or domestic partner.

- **Understand the recommended initial responses of active shooter situations.**
  - ○ The first response to an active shooter incident is to figure out what is occurring. Escaping the building as fast as possible is the best option. But if escape is not possible, both advise getting behind a barricade. Sometimes the only alternative is concealment. Individuals should disperse because it is easier to inflict a greater number of casualties when shooting at a group or a cluster of people. Ongoing communication with fellow employees is critical.
- **Identify employer responsibilities for preventing workplace violence.**
  - ○ Employers should use a variety of measures to help ensure workplace safety. The measures used depend on the resources available, and may include:
    - Designated security personnel to respond to requests for assistance.
    - Employee photo identification badges and coded keys for secure area access.
    - On-site security guard services.
    - Security assistance in registering, badging, and directing visitors in larger facilities.
    - Other appropriate security measures (such as metal detectors).
- **Identify employee responsibilities for preventing workplace violence.**
  - ○ Employees are responsible for:
    - Their own behavior by interacting responsibility with fellow employees, supervisors, and clients.
    - Being familiar with organizational policy regarding workplace violence.
    - Promptly reporting actual and/or potential acts of violence to appropriate authorities.
    - Cooperating fully in investigations/assessments of allegations of workplace violence.
    - Being familiar with the service provided for victims of workplace violence.
    - Informing appropriate personnel about restraining or protective court orders related to domestic situations so that assistance can be offered at the work site.

KEY TERMS

active shooter **141**	institutional	workplace security **134**
domestic violence **140**	security **134**	workplace violence **134**

REVIEW QUESTIONS

1. What are some of the indicators that you may have identified as a workplace violator?
2. You are in the cafeteria at your workplace when you hear gunshots. What are the next steps you should take?
3. What responsibilities do employers have to prevent workplace violence?
4. What responsibilities do employees have to prevent workplace violence?

PRACTICAL APPLICATION

- List at least ten of the subfields of security from the text. Based solely on the terms used to describe the functions, attempt to define the roles of security professionals working in those areas. After you complete your list, use the library and public Internet to determine the accuracy of your definitions.

- Profile an industrial segment of the security field and a private company within that segment. Include the roles that security professionals fill in the industry and company you chose, and identify the many contributions they make in the way of security. Find out as much information as you can and provide it, in your own words and properly referenced and cited, as if you were researching the industry and company to determine whether you (or someone for whom you worked) were contemplating an investment in or purchase of the company.

- Choose an organization with which you are familiar. Determine if it has a policy for addressing workplace violence. If you are able to examine the policy, draft a summary of what is being done right and what could be done better, based on your personal opinion and what you have learned. If you are unable to view the policy, draft a policy that especially addresses the unique characteristics of the organization.

- Search the Internet for news in your area regarding workplace security issues and identify one incident. What was the biggest problem? How did it affect the workplace? Could the employer have prevented the incident?

- Research the Injuries, Illnesses, and Fatalities data maintained by the Bureau of Labor Statistics (BLS) for your state.[90] Compare it to neighboring states or other states with which you are familiar. What is different? What is similar? Research the factors that may affect these answers.

Security Investigations and Prosecution

Learning Objectives

After reading this chapter, you should be able to:

Introduction

M. J. Martinez, with Advantage Unlimited Investigations, was hired by a female client in Canada to find out about someone named Adrian Thomas—one of 70 million users on the Plenty of Fish website. The client told Martinez that this "Adrian" had sent her flowers, emailed love letters, and made romantic phone calls. Then one day Adrian contacted the client and said he desperately needed help: something happened with his credit card, just when his daughter, who was going to school in London, required immediate cash. He asked the client to send money via Western Union to a mail drop located inside a train station. The client became suspicious and hired Martinez to find out what was going on and whether Adrian was legit. Martinez soon discovered that Adrian Thomas was a fake name being used by someone who had obtained a counterfeit Florida driver's license with a made-up home address. Detective Martinez told the client that he suspected an international ring of cyber criminals was behind this attempted fraud.[1]

Within the scope of their employment, whether working with an individual client or large public institution, private security personnel may function as investigators engaged in a variety of tasks aimed at identifying culprits and bringing them to justice. Security professionals working as detectives or investigators assist individuals, businesses, and attorneys by finding and analyzing information regarding problematic or illegal behavior.[2] They collect and connect clues to uncover facts about legal, financial, or personal matters. Consequently, they must be prepared to identify and secure evidence and then testify in court hearings.[3]

Conducting private investigations involves many services, including those providing activities such as executive, corporate, and celebrity protection; preemployment verification; and individual background profiles.[4] Some security professionals specialize in cybercrimes or computer crimes, such as identity theft, finding the source of harassing emails, and identifying people who illegally downloaded copyrighted material. Investigators also provide assistance in criminal and civil liability cases, as well as insurance claims, fraud investigations, child custody and protection cases, missing persons cases, and premarital screening. Also, they sometimes investigate individuals to prove or disprove infidelity.[5] Within the context of these tasks, private detectives and investigators engage in

- Interviewing people to gather information.
- Searching records to uncover clues.
- Conducting surveillance.
- Collecting evidence, maintaining a chain of custody to present in court.
- Verifying employment, income, and other facts about a person.
- Investigating computer crimes and information theft.[6]

Contemporary security professionals, working with organizations with a global footprint, are today investigating cases with greater complexity than in the past. Advances in science, technology, legal theory, and international affairs affect investigations.[7] Belshaw found that today's typical private investigator spends more time in front of a computer screen compiling data than walking the streets looking for suspects or clues.[8]

Private investigators who conduct background checks, records searches, and witness locating and interviewing for criminal and civil cases often work closely with attorneys and others in the legal system. They may also work on a number of different cases, including criminal homicide and complex civil litigation. Such investigators often serve as "evidence collectors" for an attorney or law firm, according to Belshaw.[9]

Private versus Public Investigators

While their duties often overlap, there are some significant differences between investigators working in public law enforcement departments and those who are security professionals who take on investigations. Public enforcement investigators focus on criminal investigations that take place after a crime has already occurred. Their goal is to gather evidence to identify, prosecute, and convict a criminal defendant. An experienced investigator knows what happens in court, how to be prepared for cross-examination by hostile defense attorneys, and the level of evidence needed to gain a conviction.

In contrast, private-sector investigators serve primarily to protect the interests of their employer. They are more likely to be proactive than reactive. In other words, when hired to protect their clients' valued assets, whether they be personnel, material goods, or intellectual property, they will design security procedures to counteract crimes before they occur.

However, there is often an overlap between the two forms of investigation, creating opportunities for investigators in the public and private sector to work together. For example, identifying the perpetrator of a simple shoplifting offense detected by a private security professional working in a retail establishment may lead police to solve an interstate organized crime group. Similarly, law enforcement officers may arrest a subject in possession of company property or technology, and notify private security professionals of the theft. That may result in the breakup of an employee theft ring. As we see in critical infrastructure security, the need for a public–private partnership is demonstrated in many scenarios.

In the future, it is likely that the contribution of private security investigations to society will increase at a faster pace than those resulting from investigations conducted by public law enforcement officers. Recent surveys conducted to determine the greatest security concern facing Fortune 1000 companies showed employee selection/screening, property crime, and general employee theft were all in the top ten.[10] Each of these is an example of the type of threat that can be countered by proactive enforcement by private investigators. The U.S. Department of Labor projects the growth of careers such as private detectives and investigators to continue at over 10% per year for the coming decade.[11] For a field where a high school diploma is often the minimum education requirement, the average pay of $45,740 appears quite attractive.[12]

Qualifications of Private Investigators

Most states require private detectives and investigators to have a license, according to the U.S. Bureau of Labor Statistics.[13] Although requirements vary, the evaluation of an investigator should be based both on his or her professional qualifications and on personal traits. The degree of formal education the investigator has should be considered as well. ASIS International found the college experience exposes students to the concepts of culture and society in a way that other experiences do not.[14] Learning how to learn is often seen as the best product of a higher education experience. For investigators, learning is an everyday event.

THINK ABOUT IT

When public and private investigators work together, several agreements must be in place regarding who has primary control over the investigation. What sort of things should be agreed upon? How flexible should the agreement be?

Investigators with advanced training and certification should also be considered, as such accomplishments demonstrate their commitment to the field and their understanding that security professionals need to keep learning. Actual experience should also be considered, especially when it involves those jobs that provide exposure to a variety of investigative skills. Simple exposure, though, does not ensure mastery, and the level of exposure should be evaluated.

In most instances, security professionals can and will be required to summarize their activities in reports to others. This can be required orally or in writing, and must be done succinctly and professionally. Communication skills are critical for investigators as they must communicate with a diverse population and provide a convincing summary of their investigations and observations.[15]

The Investigation Process and the Investigative Mind-Set

1 Explain the investigative process.

Investigating is the process of examining, studying, or inquiring into the particulars of a specific subject in much detail. Investigators often need to learn the facts about something hidden, unique, or complex, especially when trying to find a motive, cause, or culprit.[16] Investigators typically find facts and analyze information about legal, financial, and personal matters. The profession includes many services, including verifying people's backgrounds, finding missing persons, and investigating breaches of databases and computer networks. Investigators work in many places, spending part of their time in offices and part of their time in the field conducting interviews and performing surveillance.

investigating
The process of examining, studying, or inquiring into the particulars of a specific subject in much detail.

To effectively conduct an investigation, security professionals must develop what is known by law enforcement professionals as the "investigative mind-set." The mind-set centers on a way of disciplined thinking supported by the principle that *from information comes evidence*.[17] The application of an investigative mind-set brings order to the way investigators make decisions. It involves applying a set of principles to the investigation process. The investigative mind-set contains five principles:

2 Identify the five qualities of effective and reliable investigation.

1. Understanding the source of material
2. Planning and preparation
3. Examination
4. Recording and collation
5. Evaluation[18]

Understanding the source of material enables investigators to identify characteristics that may determine the way the material should be examined. Planning is required to ensure that the examination reveals all the available material that the particular source can provide. Examination usually includes:

Account (an opportunity for interviewees to provide an account of their knowledge of, or involvement in, the incident)

Clarification (of any inconsistencies or ambiguities)

Challenge (both the meaning and the reliability of any material gathered)

The investigators most likely to be misled are those who have not paid attention to detail.[19]

Conducting Effective Investigations

An effective and reliable investigation has five qualities: Objectivity, thoroughness, relevance, accuracy, and timeliness.[20] *Objectivity* is difficult, as it requires us to avoid prejudging someone or something. It is especially difficult because the best way to successfully complete an investigation (solving the puzzle) is to maintain an updated working hypothesis

THINK ABOUT IT

Other than working in the security or law enforcement fields, how could a student develop and improve on the investigative mind-set?

regarding what occurred, based on the information we have gathered. Doing so, while remaining open to other possibilities, can be a challenge. The requirement for *relevance* means that the information gathered should relate to the subjects and have sufficient detail for the assignment.[21] The need for *accuracy* cannot be overstated. Many law enforcement and security professionals are of the impression that eyewitnesses give the best information. In fact, eyewitness accounts are the least accurate.[22]

▶ A private investigator mulls over information obtained for a client. What are the various sources of information that an investigator uses?

Source: Bureau of Labor Statistics (BLS), Occupational Outlook Handbook: Private Detectives and Investigators, 2015, http://www.bls.gov/ooh/protective-service/private-detectives-and-investigators.htm.

Criminal Investigations

Security professionals should be familiar with the requirements needed to successfully resolve criminal investigations. As the organization's leadership will likely want to stay abreast of the developments, it is important for security professionals to be familiar with good investigative practice. The security professional may be the first to detect or receive notification that a crime occurred, so there will be a need for them to stay in touch with law enforcement investigators. Security personnel should not interfere in any way with a law enforcement investigation. The more helpful security professionals are to law enforcement, the more responsive law enforcement is likely to be regarding requests for shared information and updates. A sampling of the criminal offenses likely to be initially investigated by or reported to security professionals include violent and property crimes, ranging from murder, rape, and sexual assault to white-collar and business enterprise crimes, including embezzlement and fraud. A few of the most important areas for investigation are discussed below.

White-Collar Crimes

white-collar crimes
Committed by a person of respectability and high social status in the course of the person's occupation. The term covers the full range of crimes committed by business and government professionals within the scope of their job or the jobs held by subordinates, including bribery, exploitation, fraud, chiseling, embezzlement, and other crimes involving business enterprise.

American criminologist, Edwin Sutherland, coined the term **white-collar crime** in a speech to the American Sociological Society in 1939. He defined it as crime committed by a person of respectability and high social status in the course of the person's occupation.[23] The term now covers the full range of frauds committed by business and government professionals within the scope of their job or the jobs held by subordinates, including bribery, exploitation, fraud, chiseling, embezzlement, and other crimes involving business enterprise.[24]

Spotlight
Sarbanes-Oxley Act

The **Sarbanes-Oxley Act** of 2002 (SOX) is the most important piece of legislation in the financial services industry since the 1934 formation of the Securities and Exchange Commission. The act was created to provide balance to the American financial system and help it recover from the criminal fraud scandals that crippled two of the Fortune top fifty companies, Enron and MCI WorldCom.

Named for its sponsors, U.S. Senator Paul Sarbanes and U.S. Representative Michael G. Oxley, SOX requires top management in large, publicly traded corporations to individually certify the accuracy of financial information. Penalties for fraudulent activity are increased under the act, as is the independence of outside auditors who review financial statements. The primary intent of the legislation was to improve corporate governance and restore the faith of investors. Many in the business world, however, saw it as politically motivated and feared that it would lead to a loss of risk-taking and competitiveness in American enterprise. The act also affected technology in business, as it required that all business records, including electronic records and electronic messages, must be retained for at least five years. The consequences for noncompliance are fines, imprisonment, or both.

Sarbanes-Oxley Act

Federal legislation created to provide balance to the American financial system and help it recover from the criminal fraud scandals. The act requires top management in large, publicly traded corporations to individually certify the accuracy of financial information. Penalties for fraudulent activity are increased under the act, as is the independence of outside auditors who review financial statements.

Source: J. Hanna, "The Costs and Benefits of Sarbanes-Oxley," *Forbes* [online edition], March 10, 2014, http://www.forbes.com/sites/hbsworkingknowledge/2014/03/10/the-costs-and-benefits-of-sarbanes-oxley/ and Sarbanes-Oxley Act (SOX). Topics " Enterprise data centers and virtualization "Enterprise data storage management " Sarbanes-Oxley Act (SOX), TechTarget, http://oooorohoio.techtarget.com/definition/Sarbanes-Oxley-Act

Fraud Investigations

Fraud is the intentional use of deception to cause an individual to give up property or some other lawful right.[25] It is different from theft as fraud uses deceit rather than stealth to obtain goods illegally. Fraud is committed in many ways, including identity theft, checks and credit card fraud, and forgery. A number of the most common fraud schemes are insurance fraud, medical and health care fraud, and workers' compensation fraud.

fraud
The intentional use of deception and deceit to obtain goods illegally. Fraud involves many individual acts, ranging from identity theft to forgery.

Insurance Fraud

Insurance fraud occurs when someone deceives an insurance company to try to obtain money to which he or she was not entitled. This can be when someone enters false information onto an insurance application and when false or misleading information is given or important information is left out of an insurance transaction or claim. According to the Utah Insurance Department, individuals from all walks of life commit insurance fraud.[26] Insurance fraud can be classified as hard or soft. Hard insurance fraud occurs when someone commits arson or deliberately fakes an accident, injury, theft, or other loss to collect money illegally from insurance companies. Soft insurance fraud occurs when normally honest people tell "little white lies" to their insurance company when filing a claim.[27]

Medical and Health Care Fraud

Health care fraud is the filing of dishonest health care claims for a profit. The Legal Information Institute advised that fraudulent health care perpetrated by providers can include obtaining subsidized or fully covered prescription medications that are not needed and selling them on the black market for a profit. It can also include billing for care that was not provided; filing duplicate claims for the same service; altering information submitted; modifying medical records; reporting incorrect diagnoses or procedures to maximize payment; accepting or giving kickbacks; waiving copays; and prescribing unnecessary treatment. Patients who commit health care fraud may do so by providing false information when applying for certain programs or services, forging prescriptions, selling their prescription drugs, using medical transportation benefits for nonmedical-related purposes, and using another's insurance card or loaning someone else their own card.[28]

▲ Signs warning of fraud in a doctor's office. How many different types of fraud can you identify?
Source: Carter Smith

Private security professionals would be likely to investigate these types of criminal activities as hospital security professionals, insurance investigators, or defense investigators. In the United States, the Federal Bureau of Investigation, the U.S. Postal Service, and the Office of the Inspector General are charged with investigating health care fraud. These agencies rarely have enough time to perform an adequate investigation before an insurer has to pay, however, because U.S. federal laws require that health care insurance pay what appears to be a legitimate claim within thirty days. Violators in the United States may be prosecuted under Title 18 U.S. Code Section 1347: Health Care Fraud.[29]

Workers' Compensation Fraud

There are two main types of workers' compensation fraud: premium fraud and claimant fraud. Both are criminal acts.[30] Premium fraud occurs when the policyholder business owner reports false information in his or her application and other papers. Sometimes, policyholders allege their agent told them to change the application or that the agent amended it. Law enforcement and the insurance carrier investigate those claims to see if there is a trend or pattern. Insurance premium fraud creates an unfair advantage in the marketplace for business policyholders who misrepresent their business to reduce workers' compensation costs. Fraud also artificially reduces the insurance premium paid to the carrier and trims the amount of sales commission paid to the agent.[31]

Claimant fraud occurs when an employee of the policyholder files a false claim. Claimant fraud can be totally fraudulent or partially fraudulent. Jones noted that when a policyholder suspects workers' compensation claimant fraud, they need to identify the witnesses, identify the misstatements, and gather as much information as they can and then get in touch with the insurance carrier.[32] Private security professionals will likely conduct the preliminary work in these types of cases.

FIGURE 8–1
The Warning Signs of Workers Compensation Fraud
Source: Employers Insurance Group, Inc. "How to Identify Workers' Compensation Fraud," 2006, http://www .employers.com/assets/How-to-Identify-Fraud-Flyer.pdf

These indicators may help employers identify instances of workers compensation fraud:

1. Injury Report Monday Morning. The reported injury occurred Monday morning or late Friday but was not reported until Monday.
2. Change of Employer. The reported event occurred immediately before or after a labor strike, termination of employment, layoff, or at the end of a big project or seasonal work.
3. Questionable Medical/Legal Providers. The medical or legal providers are those that typically handle suspicious claims, or are used by several claimants.
4. No Witness Injury. No one witnessed the incident or the employee's description of the incident does not logically support the reported injury.
5. Conflict in Description The employee's description of the event conflicts with the medical provider's observations or the filed injury report.
6. Repeated Claims. The employee has filed a number of suspicious claims.
7. Refused Treatment. The employee refuses a diagnostic procedure designed to confirm the injury or determine its extent.
8. Reporting Late. The employee delays reporting the incident without a reasonable explanation.
9. Claimant Unavailable. The employee claiming to be injured or disabled is difficult to reach at their listed telephone number or residence.
10. Frequent Changes. The employee has frequently changed doctors, addresses, or jobs.

Experience shows that when two or more of these factors are present in a workers' compensation claim, there is a chance the claim may be fraudulent. Remember though, that these are simply indicators. Many perfectly legitimate claims are filed on Mondays, and some accidents have no witnesses. Additionally, as weekends are often nonbusiness days, thefts or losses may not be realized until the next business day. Security professionals should look for trends and patterns but should not jump to conclusions simply because one of the observations on this list was made.

Product Counterfeiting

Product counterfeiting is the practice of manufacturing goods, often of inferior quality, and selling them under a brand name without the authorization of the brand owner. Counterfeit goods are usually sold with a trademark that appears identical to or very similar to the actual trademark.

Product counterfeiting is different from trademark infringement, which involves the use of confusingly similar trademarks or service marks with similar—as opposed to fake—products or services, according to the International Trademark Association.[33] The U.S. Secret Service investigates violations involving the counterfeiting of U.S. obligations and securities. Some of the activities investigated by the Secret Service include counterfeiting U.S. currency (to include coins), U.S. Treasury checks, Department of Agriculture food coupons (commonly known as food stamps) and U.S. postage stamps. The U.S. Food and Drug Administration (FDA) investigates reports of counterfeiting associated with FDA regulated products such as food, prescription drugs, medical devices, vaccines, cosmetics, and tobacco products. Private security professionals who work for manufacturers may receive reports of these crimes. Retail security professionals may serve as the point of contact when counterfeit money is used in a transaction. Security professionals who encounter counterfeits should make contact with the agency responsible for investigating such activities.

product counterfeiting
The practice of manufacturing goods, often with inferior quality, and selling them under a brand name without the authorization of the brand owner.

▲ Handbags and wallets are among the most counterfeited items. What threats do counterfeited items represent? To whom?

Source: USA Today, http://www.usatoday.com/story/money/business/2014/03/29/24-7-wall-st-counterfeited-products/7023233/ Cheong Kam Ka/Xinhua/Corbis

Noncriminal Investigations

It is especially important for security professionals to investigate incidents of workplace misconduct. Many of these will be troublesome for the employer, who may face legal action for such employee actions as discrimination, sexual harassment, defamation, and false arrest. Security professionals may be called on to conduct a number of investigations into noncriminal incidents. These would include specific incidents such as:

- Fires
- Personal injury
- Product liability
- Property damage
- Losses
- Medical malpractice
- Missing persons
- Sexual harassment
- Unethical conduct
- Wrongful death
- Conflicts of interest
- Employee theft
- Misuse of organizational resources
- Workplace violence
- Substance abuse[34]

THINK ABOUT IT

What kind of damage is done to a company when someone counterfeits their products? How is the consumer affected?

Examples of noncriminal incidents that security professionals may be asked to investigate include due diligence investigations, accidents, and theft of trade secrets and economic espionage.

Due Diligence Investigations

Security professionals with specific skills may be asked to conduct financial due diligence investigations on companies their employer is contemplating for acquisition, for investment, or for a business relationship. The term **due diligence** simply means doing one's homework on a particular subject. Due diligence is not measured by an absolute standard: It is seen as the level of activity expected from a reasonably prudent person, given the circumstances of a particular case, the goals of the investigation, and the available information.

According to ASIS International, due diligence investigations are valuable when one or more parties are deciding future actions or inactions based on correct conditions or on representations made by another party.[35] Explained another way, due diligence can be conducted if a person is trying to make a decision about whether to do something that depends on the actions of another. Real due diligence goes beyond simply verifying information. It includes an attempt to verify the information while covering additional information, raising questions, and looking into new areas for investigation.[36]

Accidents

An accident is an unplanned event that interrupts the completion of an activity, and may (or may not) include injury or property damage, according to the Canadian Centre for Occupational Health and Safety.[37] A distinguishing feature of most accidents is that they are caused by carelessness or ignorance, or by chance rather than design. Accidents are different from incidents, near misses, and dangerous occurrences. An incident is usually considered an unexpected event that did not cause injury or damage this time but had the potential to do so. Near misses or dangerous occurrences are events that could have caused harm but did not.[38]

Most accidents can be attributed to the failure of people, equipment, supplies, or surroundings to behave as expected. Accident investigations determine how and why these failures occur. By using the information gained through an investigation, a similar, or perhaps more disastrous, accident may be prevented in the future. It is important to conduct accident investigations with prevention in mind.[39] There are no specific standards in the United States for accident investigations.[40]

Health and safety investigations form an essential part of the accident investigation process that private security professionals may be required to conduct.[41] Incidents, including near misses, can tell the investigator a lot about things. Some tips, according to a health and safety executive, include

- Investigating accidents and reported cases of occupational ill health will help investigators uncover and correct any breaches in health and safety legal compliance.
- Thoroughly investigating an incident and taking remedial action to prevent further occurrences helps demonstrate that the organization has a positive attitude to health and safety.
- Investigation findings and results provide essential information for insurers in the event of a claim.[42]

Additionally, an investigation can help identify why risk control measures failed and what improvements or additional measures are needed. It can

- Provide a true snapshot of what really happens and how work is really done (workers may find shortcuts to make their work easier or quicker and may ignore rules).
- Improve the management of risk in the future.
- Help other parts of your organization learn.
- Demonstrate commitment to effective health and safety and improving employee morale and thinking towards health and safety.[43]

due diligence
Reasonable steps and investigations taken by a person in an investigation of a business or person prior to signing a contract, purchasing property, or engaging in a business venture. It is seen as the level of activity expected from a reasonably prudent person, given the circumstances of a particular case, the goals of the investigation, and the available information.

Ideally, someone experienced in accident investigations and fully knowledgeable of the work processes, procedures, persons, and environment of a particular situation should conduct an investigation.[44] Some jurisdictions require that investigations be conducted jointly, with both management and labor represented, or that investigators must be knowledgeable about the work processes.[45]

Theft of Trade Secrets and Economic Espionage

The theft of trade secrets occurs when someone steals or misappropriates formula, practice, process, design, instrument, pattern, commercial method, or compilation of information, which is not generally known or reasonably ascertainable by others, for the economic benefit of anyone other than the owner. According to the U.S. Federal Bureau of Investigations, economic espionage occurs when a trade secret is stolen for the benefit of a foreign government, instrumentality, or agent.[46] Both are federal crimes in the United States, investigated and prosecuted under the Economic Espionage Act of 1996, Title 18, Sections 1831 and 1832 of the U.S. Code.

Businesses, academic institutions, cleared defense contractors, and government agencies are increasingly targeted for economic espionage and theft of trade secrets, often with foreign state backing.[47] Foreign adversaries and competitors are determined to acquire, steal, or transfer a broad range of trade secrets. Protecting against their attack is vital to a country's economic and national security.

While fighting economic espionage and theft of trade secrets from U.S.-based companies is in the purview of the FBI's Counterintelligence Division, members of private organizations may detect theft or espionage. Economic espionage and the theft of trade secrets are increasingly linked to both insider threat and the growing impact of cyber-enabled trade secret theft.[48] In other words, an employee who poses an insider threat may be stealing information for personal gain or may be serving as a spy to benefit another organization or country. Foreign economic competitors steal trade secrets by aggressively targeting and recruiting company insiders; conducting economic intelligence through bribery, cyber intrusions, theft, and dumpster diving (in search of intellectual property or discarded prototypes); and establishing joint ventures with U.S. companies.[49]

Interviewing and Interrogating

The goal of any investigator should be to determine what happened, by discovering all of the facts relating to an event.[50] Part of this method of fact-finding often involves interviewing people to gather necessary information. These **interviews** may be with relatives of missing individuals, victims of crime, or someone who has witnessed a crime or has other relevant information. Through interviews and additional research, investigators gather evidence to solve a case or present court evidence.[51]

Interviewing skills are among the most basic and essential tools of a private investigator.[52] The success of an investigator is often measured by his or her ability to gather information during interviews and interrogations.[53] There is only one sure way to know what really happened: talk to someone who was at the scene and who can relate what really occurred.

One of the toughest types of evidence to obtain can be testimonial evidence. The key to obtaining testimonial evidence is the style of and the approaches used during questioning. Criminals are more likely to confess to someone they like, trust, and respect. Rapport-based interview techniques are often more effective in gaining cooperation and truth than other more confrontational styles.[54] Testimonial evidence from victims, witnesses, and the offender fully document and explain the events.

The first thing that must be addressed in determining whether to interview or interrogate a suspect is to recognize the difference between an interview and an interrogation. The main goal of an interview is to gather information that is relevant to the investigation. In their classic book on criminal interrogation, Inbau, Reid, Buckley, and Jayne advise us that this information includes (1) finding the who, what, when, where, how, and why events unfolded; and (2) assessing the credibility of the source of the information.[55] An interview is generally unstructured and takes place in a variety of locations, such as a residence,

interviews
Conducted to gather information that is relevant to the investigation, and include (a) finding who, what, when, where, how, and why things events unfolded; and (b) assessing the credibility of the source of the information.

Spotlight
Differences between Interviews and Interrogations

Some of the main differences between interviews and interrogations include the following:

- The presence or absence of an accusation during the interaction. An interview is intended to be nonaccusatory. An interrogation is accusatory.

- The goals are different. The primary goal of an interview is to gather information that is relevant to the investigation. The goal of an interrogation is to learn the truth about the details of the crime from someone who is suspected of committing the crime.

- Interviews tend to be flexible and free-flowing interactions, whereas interrogations are generally more tightly structured.

An interview is a dialogue, a question-and-answer session, between the investigator and the subject. An interrogation involves active persuasion on the part of the interrogator.

- An interview can be conducted at any point during an investigation, but an interrogation should be conducted only when the investigator is reasonably certain that the suspect is guilty.

Source: F. E. Inbau, J. E. Reid, J. P. Buckley, and B. P. Jayne, *Criminal Interrogations and Confessions* (Gaithersburg, MD: Aspen, 2001), as cited by J. P. Blair, "Interview or Interrogation?: A Comment on Kassin et al.," 2003, http://www.reid.com/pdfs/Blair2003Interview.pdf

interrogations
Conducted to learn the truth about the details of the crime from a suspect.

workplace, or police station.[56] It is conducted as a dialogue where investigators are seeking answers to typically open-ended questions, and the guilt or innocence of the person being interviewed is generally unknown by the interviewer.

An **interrogation** is usually more planned and structured than an interview. The main goal of an interrogation is to learn the truth about the details of the crime from someone suspected of committing it.[57] That person might not be forthcoming or volunteer the information. An interrogation is generally conducted in a controlled environment free from interruption or distraction and is monologue-based. An investigator should be reasonably certain of the suspect's guilt before initiating an interrogation.[58]

It is important not to overwhelm the interviewee by having more than one or two interviewers in the interview room. Although many investigators prefer to be alone with the interviewee, ASIS International suggests that having a second person in the room can ensure against false accusations and assist with memory and recollection.[59]

Interview Types

There are various types of interviews. The type used depends on the situation and the person to be interviewed. Interview types consist of canvass, victim, witness, and suspect.[60]

Canvass interviews are conducted in areas surrounding the location where criminal acts are committed. Canvass interviews are conducted when investigators physically walk through the immediate area where a crime was committed and talk to every individual they can locate. Canvass interviews can be conducted in a residential area, business district, or public gathering place.[61] They are designed to capture information or identify witnesses from individuals who possess material facts that can aid in the resolution of a criminal investigation. Many of the witnesses identified in a canvass interview may not be aware that a crime was committed.[62]

Victims (the people who suffer an injury or loss) should be interviewed as soon as possible. The victim may be able to describe items used in the commission of the offense that may not otherwise be identified.[63] The investigator must always be aware that the victim may be traumatized and emotionally affected, and interviews with victims can be delicate matters.

A witness is anyone having direct knowledge of criminal activities. Witnesses should always be interviewed individually and separately to obtain facts about the incident under investigation. Witnesses should not be allowed to discuss the case before being interviewed.[64] If witnesses are traumatized as a result of what they observed, they will often want to be with people with whom they feel comfortable, such as family or friends. Whether to allow this or not should be decided on a case-by-case basis, though it is usually not a good idea to add additional personnel to an interview setting, as the people requested may have also witnessed the incident or may want to control the flow of information.

Nonverbal Communication

Nonverbal communication includes signals such as facial expressions, voice tone and pitch, body language, and the distance maintained between people who are communicating. Nonverbal signals can give clues and additional information and meaning beyond what can be interpreted from spoken (verbal) communication. Nonverbal messages allow people to modify what they said in words, convey information about their emotional state, provide feedback to the other person, and regulate the flow of communication. Examples of nonverbal messages include nodding one's head, shrugging shoulders, looking away when talking about a certain topic, or simply focusing on the other person to signal that you are finished speaking and you are prepared to listen to them.[65] It's important to be aware of nonverbal indicators so that people cannot conceal them and mask their true intent. Nonverbal cues can be falsified, concealed, or misread, and should be considered along with other information acquired through the interview, but not something on which the interviewers' complete impression is based.

nonverbal communication
Includes signals such as facial expressions, voice tone and pitch, body language, and the distance maintained between people who are communicating. Nonverbal messages allow people to modify what they said in words, convey information about their emotional state, provide feedback to the other person, and regulate the flow of communication.

Listening Skills

Listening is the ability to accurately receive and interpret messages. Listening is critical to all effective communication. Without the ability to listen, what we say can be misunderstood. The skill of listening is considered so important that many top employers provide listening skills training for their employees. Good listening skills can lead to better customer satisfaction, greater productivity, fewer mistakes, increased sharing of information, and more creative and innovative work.[66]

Here are some tips that Schilling compiled to help interviewers develop effective listening skills.

listening
The ability to accurately receive and interpret messages.

- Maintain eye contact with and face the speaker. Eye contact is often considered critical in effective communication, especially in Western cultures. Interviewers should focus on the speaker and not their notes, phone, or other distractions.

- Be natural and attentive. Interviewers should not stare at the other person. They should appear normal and pay attention to the interviewee to encourage them to share.

- Be open-minded. Listen to the other person without mentally criticizing what they are saying or jumping to conclusions, and avoid being influenced by personal thoughts, feelings, or biases. Remember that the interviewee is sharing their thoughts and feelings.

- Visualize what is being said. Listen carefully and try to picture what the speaker is saying. Create a mental model of the information to help you remember what was said. When the interviewee talks without much of a pause, concentrate on key words and phrases that they use.

- Don't interrupt. We learned as children that it's rude to interrupt. That is good advice for interviewers, too. Many interviewees will answer your questions without being asked.

- Wait for the speaker to naturally pause before you ask a clarifying question. When something doesn't seem to make sense, ask the interviewee to explain it to you, but make it a natural part of the back and forth dialog of the conversation.

- Ask questions only for understanding. Avoid asking questions that sidetrack the conversation or that may seem abruptly off topic. Find other ways to bring the conversation where you want to take it for a more smooth transition.

- Try to understand what the speaker is feeling. If you find yourself feeling sad when the interviewee expresses sadness or joyful when the interviewee expresses joy, then you are an effective listener.

- Give feedback. Show that you understand and can relate to the interviewee by reflecting the speaker's feelings or paraphrasing what they are saying to ensure you

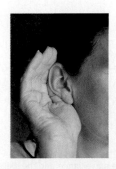

THINK ABOUT IT

Do you know or know of someone who has great listening skills? How do you think someone with those skills developed them? Do they help personally or professionally? How could others be helped to develop such skills?

understand them. Interviewers may also nod and show understanding with appropriate facial expressions and an occasional well-timed "hmmm" or "uh huh."

- Pay attention to what isn't said. We gather a great deal of information about others without words. This is called nonverbal communication, and can include voice inflection, face or hand gestures, or voice tones.[67]

Taking Notes

Note taking is done to assist with memory. Although most people are likely to remember the finer details of a significant event immediately after it has occurred, over time our memory lapses and fades. Security professionals should take notes on all facets of the investigation as soon as possible after they happen. This is especially true with interviews. If it seems appropriate, some note taking can be done in one-on-one interviews. This is often avoided, as it is likely to give the person being interviewed the impression that he or she does not have your attention. If written notes are taken during an interview, it is often best done by a second person, who may or may not be present in the room. Audio and video recordings can also be made and transcribed, depending on the local laws and policies of the organization.

For example, the U.S. federal law and most U.S. state laws require consent by both parties in order to record a conversation. The requirement holds true whether the conversation is face to face or long distance via a cell phone or the Internet. Some state laws limit approval requirements to only a single party, so that if two people have a conversation one can legally create a recording without the second partie's knowledge or agreement. Security professionals must be aware of both local and federal laws because violations can result in civil liability or criminal prosecution.

Investigators may want to take notes for another reason. According to John E. Reid and Associates, taking written notes slows down the pace of questioning.[68] Innocent subjects are usually comfortable with the silence that happens when an interviewer takes notes. Deceptive subjects, on the other hand, are often uncomfortable with this silence. Because deceptive subjects know their original response to the question was less than truthful, they may modify or qualify it during the time the investigator is writing a note. Taking notes also helps the investigator focus on key aspects of the subject's behavior during a response. The notes taken after a response should include not only the subject's answer but also the essence of the response along with any significant behavior symptoms. Finally, the process of taking written notes allows an investigator to review an interview days or weeks after it was conducted. This is especially beneficial when multiple suspects have been interviewed so the investigator can make comparisons to help identify who can, or cannot, be eliminated as a suspect.[69]

Consistency in note taking is critical. If written notes are taken, they need to be taken following every response. If sporadic notes are taken following only selected responses, the subject may become guarded and hesitant when offering further information, as she understands the apparent importance of a particular response.[70]

Surveillance

3 Describe surveillance and the skills needed to conduct surveillance effectively.

Surveillance is the covert observation of individuals, places, or objects for the purpose of gathering information or intelligence.[71] Surveillance techniques are used to identify criminal activity associated with terrorism, organized crime, drug and contraband trafficking, and serious crimes. Surveillance involves watching a person without being detected to see where he goes and what he does.[72] Although we identify a variety of observations and techniques regarding surveillance, mastering the ability to conduct surveillance is difficult and comes only with experience.

ASIS International observed that the primary purpose of surveillance is to obtain information about the subject or subjects under investigation.[73] Personnel selected for surveillance must have well-developed observation and description skills. They must have patience and be able and prepared to endure long tedious hours of observation.[74] Usually,

surveillance
The covert observation of individuals, places, or objects for the purpose of gathering information or intelligence. Surveillance techniques are used to identify criminal activity associated with terrorism, organized crime, drug and contraband trafficking, and serious crimes.

personnel who are selected are of average height and weight and do not have unique physical features, and are able to blend in with their surroundings. Sometimes surveillants are chosen for their appearance, ethnic background, or language qualifications. Both the type of surveillance and the area in which it will take place are important factors to consider when selecting a surveillance team.

Security professionals planning to conduct surveillance must dress and adopt the demeanor of local inhabitants to blend into the setting. Security professionals should carry items such as caps, jackets, and glasses to make quick changes in appearance.[75] They should carry sufficient money to pay for meals, transportation, or other expenses incurred during the surveillance, and should have a reserve fund for use in emergencies.

Surveillance Methods

The three basic surveillance methods are loose, close, and a combination of the two.[76] Security professionals can conduct a loose surveillance to periodically spot-check or compile long-term information on a subject. Loose surveillance should be terminated if it appears the suspect is aware of the surveillance. Close surveillance requires continued alertness on the part of the surveillance team. Usually, a combination of these two methods works best.[77] Surveillance teams may need to change between loose and close surveillance because of an act or contact made by the suspect.

An important aspect of surveillance is the observation of persons, places, events, and objects so that who or what was seen may later be identified. Making detailed descriptions helps an individual conducting surveillance relate what he saw to others. Accurate observations and descriptions add to the credibility of an investigator's identifications of persons, places, and objects. The ability to observe accurately is developed through practice and experience. Most people are not trained to remember and evaluate what they see, so the observations and descriptions they typically provide may not be as detailed or as objective as those of a trained observer. Observations can also be affected by lack of sleep, illness, perceptions, or other outside influences.[78]

Surveillance Types

There are two general types of surveillance: stationary and mobile.[79] Stationary surveillance is used when the suspect is stationary or when all of the important information can be learned at one place. A stationary surveillance is conducted to observe a home, building, or location to obtain evidence of criminal activity or to identify suspected offenders. Surveillance teams can use a vehicle such as a car, a van, or a truck with a camper shell, but the preferred method is to use a building that provides an unobstructed view of the area or person being observed. Unattended parked surveillance vehicles may create suspicion or become the target of criminal activity. In a mobile surveillance, the surveillants move from one vantage point to another for closer observation of the area or the suspect. A mobile surveillance can be conducted on foot, in a vehicle, or, depending on the suspect's movements, through a combination of the two. Although foot surveillance is used frequently, vehicle surveillance is used more often as a means of gathering general intelligence.[80] Vehicles are used in the surveillance of premises, but their primary use and value is the surveillance of other vehicles. Foot surveillance can go with the suspect only so far. When the suspect becomes mobile, as one often does, then the surveillant must depend on a vehicle to keep pace.

It is essential that security professionals take notes during surveillance. This may best be done when two people are paired, whether physically together or communicating in some way, often by telephone, radio, or other communication device. In this situation, one of the investigators should observe the actions of the subject, while carrying on a conversation with the other person. The conversation should be out of the earshot of others but allow the second person to take notes on the first person's observation, even if the second investigator's position did not allow her to personally view the activities.[81]

▲ A private detective conducting surveillance. Detectives generally try to blend in with the public to avoid being noticed. What methods could they use?

Source: Rasmus Rasmussen/ Getty Images

Spotlight
Ten Tips and Suggestions for Covert Operators

The Protection Circle Blog offers tips and suggestions for covert operators conducting surveillance. The tips apply to most types of covert operations and cover both the activity to look for in others and what you should avoid doing yourself. Training can certainly help here, but you also need a sincere willingness to step out of your familiar comfort zones, make a few mistakes, and never stop learning.

1. **Cover and cover story.**   Cover is the visual projection of what a covert operator wants people to see and think of him or her. A cover story is the verbal representation of your cover. The cover story has to fit, and even strengthen, the cover; otherwise it would be suspicious or curious if the person who looks homeless, for example, talks like a law enforcement officer.

2. **Posture and movement.**   In most cases, movement attracts more attention than nonmovement; standing attracts more attention than sitting. Most people who gravitate toward covert operations tend to have backgrounds in military, law enforcement, security or all of the above, and may already be aware of these principles.

3. **Sit down.**   Sitting down gives you a less noticeable appearance and the ability to see and notice more yourself. There are relatively few reasons for being in a fixed position without sitting down, and most of those reasons keep you from being as observant as you could otherwise be.

4. **No changing fixed positions.**   After you've assumed a vantage point you are likely to discern an even better vantage point. In the best-case scenario, changing position will make you more visible than before, and in the worst-case scenario, your movement will be detected by one of the people you are trying to observe. Once you have chosen a position, stay there.

5. **The bus stop.**   A bus stop seems to be perfectly positioned for surveillance. Bus stops do provide a logical justification for remaining in very central locations, but only if the bus stop is used to get on a bus. Using a bus stop for surveillance activity for more than twenty to thirty minutes is only a good idea if you actually board a bus.

6. **Cell phones.**   Playing with your phone during an important operation makes you appear distracted and unprofessional, which is a great idea if you are working covertly. If you use your phone to justify your presence or to justify a quick stop, don't just pretend to play with a blank screen. Staring into a blank cell phone screen can give away the fact that you're pretending. You should also silence your ringer. A ringing cell phone can draw attention to you, and if you're pretending to talk on the phone, you don't want your cell phone to actually start ringing while you hold it to your ear.

7. **Working with others.**   The typical covert operator is the lone male; so if that's you, consider getting a partner or two. Few things are more innocuous looking than a man and a woman sitting together in a coffee shop or walking down the street. Working together can provide easy cover. Two people can sit facing each other, pretending to have a casual conversation, as one is focusing on the target and describing what they see, and the other (the one who's facing away from the target) can be jotting down the information. Avoid changing the dynamic. If you come alone to the meeting, you should leave alone, and if you come together, you should leave together. People who split up are more noticeable than people who arrive together and leave together.

8. **Coffee shops.**   Coffee shops often provide some of the best vantage points. Unlike most other businesses, they will let you spend pretty much all day in them, without interrupting you. If you don't order and pay before receipt, make sure to pay for your order as soon as it arrives. You won't want to search for your server if you need to leave unexpectedly.

9. **Demographics.**   The typical covert surveillance operator is male, in his twenties to fifties, usually with a background in military, law enforcement, security or all of the above. Simply being a female gives an operative a natural advantage, as does being of a younger or more advanced age.

10. **Personality traits.**   One of the most important, yet difficult, factors for covert operators to deal with is their personality, and how it affects the way they appear when seen by others. Work on your attitude and how you respond to your environment by emulating the behavior of someone who clearly acts and thinks differently from you. The most common manifestation is the classic off-duty or low-profile officer or agent look. Many people fail to realize that there's a big difference between nonuniformed low-profile work and covert undercover operations. Try to wear something that doesn't represent who you are. Most people have some articles of clothing in their house that they don't like. You can wear these: The fact that these don't suit your taste will likely mean they will do such a good job of masking who you really are and what you're doing.

Source: A. Toben, "Tips and Suggestions for Covert Operators," Protection Circle Blog, May 23, 2014, www.protectioncircle.wordpress.com/2014/05/23/tips-suggestions-for-covert-operators

Undercover Operations

4 Identify the reasons for conducting an undercover operation.

Undercover investigations, taking on a covert role to gain needed information, is another technique used by corporate security professionals. Undercover investigations are meant to gather relevant information unavailable by other means according to ASIS International.[82] During an undercover operation the investigator conceals his or her true identity but not his or her presence. Security professionals in an undercover role do not attempt to operate unnoticed but rather give the impression they are ready to join in an illegal group or activity.[83] Undercover investigators use a variety of disguises, especially those that make them inconspicuous in the community or location in which they operate. Investigators may appear as a jogger in the park, as a technician with the local telecommunications company, or as a retail salesperson.

The undercover investigator, as described in military field manuals, associates with a person or becomes part of a group believed to have critical criminal information.[84] The investigator must gather and study supporting information and intelligence, such as reports, witness statements, and the results of surveillance prior to beginning such an undercover operation. The nature, habits, interests, and routines of a suspect should be studied. Undercover operations are a useful option to investigate crimes involving stolen property sales and frauds.

The general objectives of an **undercover operation** are to obtain information, observe criminal activity, and collect evidence.[85] Undercover operations, regardless of the time devoted to them are dangerous and should be used only when absolutely necessary and supported by a surveillance team.[86] The investigative team should complete a formal risk assessment and plan risk mitigation strategies. Leaders must continuously conduct the risk assessment process, as it assists in the identification of hazards or hotspots involved with any mission.

There are five phases of an undercover investigation identified by ASIS International:

1. Planning and preparation
2. Information gathering
3. Verification and analysis
4. Disciplinary and corrective action
5. Prevention and education[87]

Information and Intelligence

Information is knowledge in raw form, or raw data of any type. Security professionals will likely encounter many **sources of information** in their daily routine. Information can be provided by and gathered from other employees, law enforcement personnel, anonymous sources, and other means, according to the United Nations Office on Drugs and Crime. For investigators, information must be collected and processed before it becomes useful.[88]

Intelligence describes information that has been processed, evaluated, analyzed, or interpreted to give it meaning within a particular context. Intelligence is information that, because it has been processed, has added value. Unlike raw information, intelligence has been evaluated in context to its source and reliability.[89] The term *intelligence* also describes information that is acquired, exploited, and protected by the activities of law enforcement and security organizations to decide upon and support their investigations.

Whether it is intelligence collected for business, criminal, or national security purposes, intelligence helps support decision makers in a variety of ways.[90] Business leaders, law enforcement, and the military need to keep some information secret from others and, at the same time, have ways of obtaining information from those who wish to keep their knowledge confidential. This makes having intelligence services vital for all types of organizations.[91] The process and procedures of gathering intelligence are set out in Figure 8–2.

The intelligence cycle is the foundation of the intelligence analysis process, at both operational and strategic levels. The cycle is depicted in circular form, moving in a clockwise direction from tasking (direction) to collection, to evaluation and then collation, on to analysis and then inference development, and completing the circle/cycle with dissemination and reevaluation.

undercover operations
Describe the process of taking on a covert role to gain needed information unavailable by other means. During an undercover operation the investigator conceals his or her true identity but not his or her presence, giving the impression they are ready to join in an illegal group or activity.

information
Knowledge in raw form or raw data of any type. Security professionals will likely encounter many sources of information in their daily routine. Information can be provided by and gathered from other employees, law enforcement personnel, anonymous sources, and other means.

sources of information
Describe any person, document, or activity that provides information of an investigative nature is a source. Victims, witnesses, first responders, subject matter experts, and informants will provide some form of information that may assist in an investigation.

intelligence
Information that has been processed, evaluated, analyzed, or interpreted to give it meaning within a particular context. The term also describes information that is acquired, exploited, and protected by the activities of law enforcement and security organizations to decide upon and support their investigations.

The Intelligence Cycle
Source: United Nations Office on Drugs and Crime (UNODC). *Criminal Intelligence Manual for Analysts* (Vienna: UNODC, 2011), https://www.unodc.org/documents/organized-crime/Law-Enforcement/Criminal_Intelligence_for_Analysts.pdf

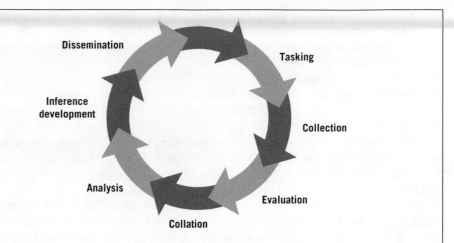

Direction. Intelligence analysis is often directed based on the needs and desires of the client.

Collection. One of the main problems with intelligence is the process of collecting and storing the intelligence data. An unmanageable amount of data, or data overload, is a problem, but so is collected data that is not examined and processed for dissemination.

Evaluation. Evaluation of intelligence data should be conducted when it is obtained or immediately thereafter. Evaluation requires assessing the reliability of both the source of information and the information itself, as well as assessing the validity and accuracy of the information.

Collation. Collation describes the process of transferring the intelligence into a storage system (files or a database) in a format that permits quick access and retrieval. During this process the data is assessed, and irrelevant, incorrect, and otherwise useless information is removed.

Analysis. The analysis stage is an in-depth examination of the information, specifically examining its meaning and features. Analysis of intelligence data highlights gaps, strengths, and weaknesses and helps the analyst suggest the next steps to take. Analysis should be a cyclical process.

Dissemination. Dissemination includes the organized release of information summaries using presentations, notes, briefings, and reports. The dissemination phase completes the initial cycle of the intelligence process.

Reevaluation. Reevaluation of the intelligence process involves a continuous review to identify ways to improve. Constant improvement can yield better processing of more quality information, serving all areas of the intelligence process.

Polygraph Examinations and Behavioral Analysis Interviews

polygraph machines
Measure the truthfulness of a person's statements by tracking bodily functions such as blood pressure, respiration, and perspiration.

Polygraph machines, perhaps better known as lie detectors, were routinely used on employees and job applicants in the past. The polygraph used to be considered the quickest and most effective method for verifying information provided by an applicant. Polygraphs are designed to measure the truthfulness of a person's statements by tracking bodily functions such as blood pressure, respiration, and perspiration.[92] Private employers can offer employees a polygraph examination in connection with an ongoing criminal investigation. If they have a reasonable suspicion of employee involvement in a variety of crimes, including embezzlement, theft, industrial espionage, or sabotage, the employer can administer the test.

Use of the polygraph is covered by the Employee Polygraph Protection Act (The Act) of 1988, which prohibited the standard use of a pre-employment polygraph examination.[93] The act allows polygraph examinations to be used in connection with jobs in security. A written notice must be sent at least forty-eight hours before the test, letting people know that they are a suspect. There must be a provable, reasonable suspicion that the employee was involved in the theft or other conduct triggering the investigation. The act does not apply to employees of federal, state, or local government, nor does it apply to certain jobs that handle sensitive work relating to national defense. Many states have statutes that apply to state and local government employees.[94] The laws in several states provide that an employee may volunteer to take a polygraph. These laws have safeguards, requiring that the tests be administered under approved and supervised conditions. Employees must be clearly informed about how and why test results may be used.

Today, interviewers must find other tools and techniques to verify the truths and identify the falsehoods told by interviewees, according to ASIS International.[95] One of those alternatives is the Behavioral Analysis Interview (BAI), a systemic evaluation of a subject's verbal and nonverbal behavior during a structured interview. Investigators using this technique are able to carefully observe both verbal and nonverbal responses from the subject of interest.[96]

Sources and Other Information Resources

Any person, document, or activity that provides information of an investigative nature is a source. ASIS International observed that sources of information and intelligence might include:

- Radio, newspaper, television, and Internet-based news outlets
- Non-news Internet sources
- Local court filings and records
- Files from criminal justice agencies
- Organizational files and records
- Regulatory and tax-related documents
- Motor vehicle records
- Financial records[97]

Victims, witnesses, first responders, subject matter experts, and informants will provide some form of information that may assist in an investigation. It is up to the investigator to determine the level of reliability of that information.[98]

Managing Human Sources

A human source may provide an investigator with specific information about a particular case or background information that is useful in a number of investigations. The most important consideration for selecting sources is reliability. The investigator must evaluate both the source and information provided by the source to arrive at the facts. Information received from human sources must be tested for consistency by checking it against data from other sources.[99]

Investigators should approach every individual they encounter as a potential source. In order to better protect the sources of their information, security professionals need to determine what laws, if any, provide for confidentiality in the jurisdiction where they operate. Unlike news reporters, who are protected by shield laws from identifying their sources in many places, and law enforcement officers, protected by privilege from publicly identifying their sources in court absent a judge's order, private security professionals generally don't have such a protection. This becomes less of a problem when dealing with information regarding an incident not treated as a crime or when issues regarding employment are being investigated.

Most nonlaw enforcement witnesses to crime are not obligated to proactively report crimes, although there may be a provision to report the truth and to answer police questions honestly. Consequently, unless there are laws requiring the reporting of specific crimes in certain jurisdictions, private investigators are primarily obligated to serve their employer or client when they detect a crime. When deemed necessary, it might benefit the private security professional to protect his or her source by reporting the incident to the police as a confidential source, then referring to the provider of relevant information in the report as a police source. Arrangements like this must be carefully coordinated with the responsible police supervisor and should be discussed to the extent necessary within the private organization.

Restricting the release of the source's identity, exercising appropriate security measures regarding communications between the source and the handler, and using caution in documenting the source's activities can provide a significant level of confidentiality. Additional measures that support confidentiality may include providing physical protection and transferring an individual to another location, although these are likely to be outside of the realm of routine operations for most security professionals.[100]

Report Writing

Generally, reports should be complete stand-alone documents and should not require reference to other reports.[101] Reports should include the name of the subject, the appropriate file number, the type of case investigated, the status of the case, the reporting investigator, and the date of the report. It will include a summary of information and a more detailed narrative. Exhibits or enclosures that assist in the description of the findings should be attached to the report.[102]

The five basic steps of report writing are gathering the facts, recording the facts, organizing the facts, writing the report, and evaluating and editing the report as necessary.[103] Depending on organizational policy, any number of reports can be generated by security professionals. Typically, though, there will be an initial report, progress reports if additional information is developed, special reports for actions not included in other reports, and a final report indicating that the investigation is complete.[104]

Case Management for the Investigator

Case management for private security professionals is necessary to integrate all aspects of the security task. Case management allows for the coordination of investigations, safety and compliance incidents, access control measures, risk analysis, and other processes so that management can determine which process is in what status at any given time. Case management is critical not only for current investigations but also for those processed for court and completed. The case management system may be manual or automated.[105] Management of cases includes the decisions necessary when initiating investigations, assigning investigators, prioritizing investigations, and conducting follow-up investigations. One important saying known to most investigators is *if it is not written down, it did not occur*. This attests to the significance of an investigator's notes and the thoroughness of the report. If details or descriptions of an event are not documented in the notes or report, the investigator will be challenged in court, often months or years after the event occurred.

Bringing the Case to Court

If an investigation proves fruitful the case may be brought to court for trial. If a crime has been committed, the suspect will be charged either with a felony (serious crimes) or misdemeanor (petty crime).[106] If after a criminal trial, the suspect is convicted, he or she will be sentenced either by being ordered to pay a fine and/or make restitution, supervised on probation in the community, sentenced to a term of incarceration, or some combination thereof.[107]

Suspects may also be tried civilly if the facts of the case do not support a criminal charge. Civil cases involve private disputes between persons or organizations.[108] A civil case begins when the plaintiff, a person or entity (such as an organization or the government), claims that another person or entity (the defendant) has failed to fulfill a legal duty owed to the plaintiff. The plaintiff may ask the court to require the defendant to fulfill the duty, make compensation for the harm done, or do both.

Civil suits can be brought in either state or federal courts. A civil case will be tried in a state court when a complaint is filed stating that the defendant harmed another state resident by the defendant's action or inaction. For example, a homeowner enters into a contract with a security company to set up and monitor a home alarm system. An alarm is triggered during a burglary and the security company fails to respond. As a consequence, the homeowner lost valuable goods. A lawsuit can be brought in state court charging failure to honor the contract and asking for compensation from the security company for losses.

An individual can also sue a government entity for failure to perform a duty or for violating his or her rights under the law. For example, an arrestee can sue a local police department if members of the department used excessive force while performing their duties.[109]

Individuals, corporations, and the federal government can also bring civil suits in federal court claiming violations of federal statutes or constitutional rights. For example, an individual or the federal government can sue a hospital for overbilling Medicare and Medicaid, a violation of a federal statute. In the sections below, the various stages and practices of the trial process and the investigator's role during the process are discussed in some detail.

Depositions

A **deposition** is a witness's sworn out-of-court testimony.[110] Depositions are used to gather information during the discovery process and they are rarely used at trial. Depositions usually do not directly involve the court. The deposition is initiated and supervised by the involved parties. Usually, the only persons present at a deposition are the deponent (the person being deposed), attorneys for all interested parties, and a person qualified to administer oaths. All parties may question the witness at the deposition. The testimony given during a deposition is usually considered hearsay and is thus inadmissible at trial. There are three exceptions to the hearsay rule.

- The first exception is when someone admits something in a deposition that is against his or her best interests.
- The second exception to the hearsay rule is when the witness's testimony at trial contradicts what he or she said when they were deposed.
- The third exception is when a witness is unavailable at trial, regardless of the reason (e.g. the person is dead, no longer remembers, or refuses to testify).[111]

Deposition rules vary by jurisdiction.[112] Guidance from Securityofficerhq.com suggests that security professionals prepare for depositions by reviewing the incident report and all subsequent documents that include testimony about the incident from the security officer.[113] Clear, concise, and honest testimony should be provided, without creating avenue for attack from the defense or opportunities to confuse the testimony. Lengthy responses that go beyond the question should be avoided.

In a deposition, the lawyer for one side asks questions of a witness on the opposing side to learn about the opponent's case.[114] Deponents may be required to bring documents to the deposition specifically requested in a subpoena. No other records or documents should be brought, nor any other material that was not requested.[115] After a question is asked, the security professional should pause before responding to allow his or her attorney time to interject. Often the same question will be asked in a number of different ways. Inconsistencies may be used to discredit a witness, so be careful about what you say.[116]

Survival tips for testifying in depositions from WORLDLawDirect include:

- Do not try to memorize answers.
- Admit that you consulted with a lawyer.
- Do not answer incomprehensible questions.
- Pause before answering.
- Be clear and concise.
- Do not over-answer.
- Do not speculate or guess.
- Use neutral language.
- Avoid speaking in absolutes.
- Do not tip off the opposing counsel.
- Listen for compound questions.
- Expect similar questions.
- Every question is important.

deposition
A witness's sworn out-of-court testimony, used by prosecutors, plaintiffs, and defense attorneys to gather information during the discovery process.

- Pay careful attention to summaries of your prior statements.
- Hide your anger.
- Stay calm and in control of your emotions.[117]

Discovery

discovery
The process in which prosecutors in criminal court must provide the defendant with copies of all the materials and evidence that the prosecution intends to use at trial. This process extends from the time the case begins to the time of trial. If the prosecutor does not provide the defendant with documents and other information, the prosecutor can be fined or sanctioned by the court.

Prosecutors in criminal court must provide the defendant (usually through his or her law-yer) with copies of all the materials and evidence that the prosecution intends to use at trial. This process is called **discovery**, and it extends from the time the case begins to the time of trial. If the prosecutor does not provide the defendant with documents and other information the prosecutor can be fined or sanctioned by the court. The prosecutor is also required to provide the defense with exculpatory evidence, which is evidence that may hurt the prosecutor's case or show the defendant's innocence. If the prosecution does not provide it to the defense, the court may require a new trial.[118]

Court Testimony

The final test of an investigator's efficiency is often as a witness in court. The effectiveness of the evidence can be affected by the impression the investigator makes as a witness.[119] Testimony in court is only effective when it is credible. Credibility is established when the investigator articulates his or her testimony with sincerity, knowledge of the facts, and a sense of impartiality. Although the substance of the testimony is of great importance, equal if not greater significance is attached to the investigator's conduct on the stand and to the manner in which he or she presents the facts discovered during the investigation.[120]

Direct Examination

The investigator must always prepare carefully for testimony and ensure that all known facts are in order. Whenever the investigator is preparing for trial, he or she should coordinate with trial counsel in advance to prevent misunderstandings and surprises.[121] A prosecuto-rial witness must be positive and firm in answering all questions. Investigators must learn to defend against a variety of tactics used by defense lawyers in the courtroom. Investigators must use intelligible and understandable language when talking to members of the court. They must give a good first impression and give solid concluding statements.[122] Effective testimony depends on delivery, and these tips should be followed:

- Speak slowly and deliberately, with expression, and loud enough to be heard.
- Do not use profanity or vulgarity unless asked to provide the exact words of the suspect, victim, or witness. If profanity or vulgarity is present in those words, forewarn the court.
- Pause briefly to form answers before answering each question.
- Only refer to notes for clarification of exact details; do not rely on them.
- Answer questions from either counsel in a polite, courteous manner.
- When a question is not understood, ask that it be repeated or clarified.
- If you do not know the answer to a question, respond with "I do not know."[123]

Cross-Examination

Cross-examination is usually the most difficult part of testifying. Some tactics used by the defense counsel include:

- Acting overly friendly or, in contrast, officious and brutal.
- Attacking the investigator's skills or knowledge of investigative procedure.
- Using rapid-fire questioning.
- Employing the silent treatment after the investigator's response.
- Demanding a simple answer to a complex question.
- Asking leading questions.
- Misquoting the investigator and declaring him incompetent or inconsistent.[124]

THINK ABOUT IT

Why might security personnel be called on to serve as witnesses in a criminal trial? If summoned, how should they prepare for their day in court?

If misquoted by the defense counsel, investigators should not become defensive but may simply restate their previous testimony in correcting the perception of inconsistency. The investigator should politely say, "As I previously stated," and repeat the earlier response.[125] Investigators must remain calm and respectful during cross-examination and avoid arguing with the defense counsel, who may use a variety of questioning techniques to establish possible inconsistencies or prejudice. Investigators should remember that the defense counsel is merely doing a job and the attacks are not personal, merely a tactic used to create doubt.

The Spotlight feature discusses a number of intricate steps and procedures involved in testifying in court.

Spotlight
Courtroom Testimony

Because of the incidents that they regularly encounter in their work, security professionals are often called to provide testimony. Security professionals may be required to testify in formal or informal regulatory hearings, be interviewed by government authorities, give formal depositions, appear before grand juries, or give testimony in civil or criminal courts. Security professionals may also need to assist the prosecutor and later the judge and/or jury with understanding the crime and the environment in which the crime was committed. In these instances, security professionals serve much like the police do, filling the role of a subject matter expert in the community.

The U.S. Department of Justice has compiled the following tips for testifying in court:

- Refresh your memory before you testify, to assist in recalling the facts more accurately when asked a question.
- Speak in your own words, and don't try to memorize what you are going to say.
- Appearance is important, and appearing overly casual or overly dressy will distract the jury so much that they may not listen attentively to your testimony.
- Speak clearly, slowly, and loud enough so that the juror sitting farthest away from you can easily hear and understand everything you say.
- Do not discuss the case with anyone outside of the courtroom, and avoid saying anything about the case until you are on the witness stand.
- When you are called to testify, stand up straight, pay attention to the clerk, and when sworn in, say "I do" clearly.
- Tell the truth, and answer the questions to the best of your memory.
- Do not exaggerate, and do not allow an attorney to put words in your mouth.
- When someone asks you a question, listen carefully to avoid confusion, and don't get mad if you feel you are being doubted during the cross-examination.
- Respond aloud to the questions; do not just nod your head for a "yes" or "no" answer.
- Think before you speak, and listen carefully to all the questions you are being asked.
- Explain your answer if necessary, especially if a question can't be truthfully answered with a "yes" or "no."
- Correct your mistakes immediately if your answer was not correct or was not clear. If you realize you have answered incorrectly, immediately say, "May I correct something I said earlier?"

- Do not volunteer information, give conclusions and opinions, or state what someone else told you, unless you are specifically asked. Answer only the questions asked of you.
- Don't set yourself up for error or contradiction by saying something like "nothing else happened." Instead say, "That's all I recall."
- Be positive and confident. Avoid saying, "I think," "I believe." or "in my opinion" if you can answer positively. If you do know, then say so. But do not make up an answer.

Regarding body language and answering strategy issues, witnesses should do the following:

- Look comfortable but do not slouch, rest head on hand, chew gum, play with earrings or mustache, or move around in the chair.
- Ask for a restroom break or drink of water if needed.
- Speak authoritatively but not arrogantly.
- Answer questions directly but volunteer nothing.
- Be aware of time and distance distortions, as few people estimate accurately.
- Admit to meeting with counsel.
- Admit discussing the case with others (if true), if the discussions are not privileged.
- Keep an even temper even if opposing counsel appears to lose his or her temper.
- Stick to an answer even if opposing counsel repeats the question numerous times with increasing incredulity.
- Make opposing counsel ask simple questions, not multiple questions within a question.

No matter what role they fill in the courtroom, witnesses should avoid being stiff, argumentative, arrogant, evasive, and uncaring, and should not take questions personally. They should strive to be personable, charming, professional, polite, earnest, and knowledgeable. Security professionals who are testifying must also emphasize self-confidence.

Sources: U.S. Attorney's Office, Middle District of Pennsylvania, n.d., http://www.justice.gov/usao/pam/Victim_Witness/testifying_tips.html; ASIS International, Protection of Assets (POA) Online [Legal Sources], 2013; M. J. Pitera, "Courtroom Attire: Ensuring Witness Attire Makes the Right Statement," *The Jury Expert: Litigation Insights,* July 31, 2012, www.thejuryexpert.com/2012/07/courtroom-attire-ensuring-witness-attire-makes-the-right-statement/

Expert Testimony

expert testimony
A form of testimony provided by an expert witness, a person who can provide insight as to the significance of the evidence collected in criminal and civil trials. Expert witnesses are generally qualified based on their qualifications or expertise, the acceptance of their theories or opinions, and the relevance of their theories or opinions to the case.

Many courts need and use subject matter experts to inform trials, especially if the average juror (or judge) does not have the necessary experience and knowledge regarding the areas involved in the facts or circumstances of the case. This is known as **expert testimony**. An expert witness is a person who can provide insight as to the significance of the evidence collected and what that evidence indicates with regard to guilt or innocence.[126] An expert witness, whose expertise is in the analysis of crime scenes, can interpret crime scene evidence, such as how the crime may have been committed. Expert witnesses are generally qualified based on their qualifications or expertise, the acceptance of their theories or opinions, and the relevance of their theories or opinions to the case.

The judge will decide whether the expert's qualifications relate to the subject matter and if the expert's knowledge can assist the jurors in deciding issues. The judge reviews the expert's rationale and the reasonableness of the process used to reach conclusions. The judge will also ensure that any and all testimony or evidence is relevant and reliable. There must be a sufficient "fit" between the testimony and the facts of the case so the testimony will assist the court in finding facts.[127]

Professional Certifications for Investigators

Certifications, while not necessarily required, are likely to add to a security professional's credibility. The National Association of Legal Investigators offers the Certified Legal Investigator Certification, while ASIS International offers a Professional Certified Investigator certification.[128]

The Association of Certified Fraud Examiners offers the Certified Fraud Examiner (CFE) credential. CFE denotes proven expertise in fraud prevention, detection, and deterrence. CFEs are trained to identify the warning signs and red flags that indicate evidence of fraud and fraud risk. CFEs combine knowledge of complex financial transactions with an understanding of methods, law, and how to resolve allegations of fraud.[129]

California-based security professionals can also receive certification from the California Association of Licensed Investigators. The designations Certified Professional Investigator (CPI) and Certified Security Professional (CSP) may be used by designees who are certified and remain current on their qualifications as a licensed Private Investigator (for the CPI designation) or licensed Private Patrol Operator (for CSP designation) for a minimum of three consecutive years.[130]

Spotlight
ASIS Professional Certified Investigator

The Professional Certified Investigator (PCI) credential ensures an individual's knowledge and experience in case management, evidence collection, and preparation of reports and testimony to substantiate findings. Those who earn the PCI are ASIS board-certified in investigations. PCI recipients must possess a high school diploma or equivalent and have five years of investigation experience with at least two years in case management. The PCI examination consists of questions that cover tasks, knowledge, and skills in three primary domains that have been identified by professional investigators as required areas of competency in the field.

The primary domains (topics) are Case Management, Investigative Techniques and Procedures, and Case Presentation. Case Management subtopics include the following:

- Ability to analyze a case for applicable ethical conflicts and demonstrate knowledge of:
  - Conflict resolution elements.

  - Nature/types/categories of ethical issues related to cases (fiduciary, conflict of interest, attorney-client).
  - Applicable aspects of laws, codes, and regulations.

- Analyze and assess case elements and strategies and demonstrate knowledge of:
  - Case categories (computer, white collar, financial, criminal, etc.).
  - Analytical methods to data.
  - Strategic/operational analysis.
  - Lethality of crime intelligence.

- Determine the need, develop a strategy by reviewing procedural options, and demonstrate knowledge of:
  - Case flow.
  - Negotiation process.
  - Investigative methods.

- o Cost–benefit analysis.
- o Applicable aspects of laws, codes, and regulations.
- Manage and implement investigative resources necessary to address case objectives and demonstrate knowledge of:
  - o Manpower and assignment.
  - o Time management.
  - o Quality assurance process.
  - o Review chain of custody procedures.
- Identify and evaluate investigative process improvement opportunities and demonstrate knowledge of:
  - o Management/legal review.
  - o Liaison resources.
  - o Internal and external analysis.
  - o Resolution.

Investigative Techniques and Procedures subtopics include

- Conduct surveillance by physical and electronic means in order to obtain relevant information and demonstrate knowledge of:
  - o Methods of surveillance.
  - o Types of surveillance.
  - o Types of surveillance equipment.
  - o Pre-surveillance routines.
  - o Applicable aspects of laws, codes, and regulations.
  - o Documentation of surveillance activities.
- Conduct interviews/interrogations of witnesses and subjects to obtain relevant information and demonstrate knowledge of:
  - o Interview and interrogation techniques (electronic, face-to-face, telephonic).
  - o Techniques for detecting deception (e.g., nonverbal communication).
  - o Methods and techniques of eliciting admission and/or confession.
  - o Documentation and completion of witness/subject statement.
  - o Applicable aspects of laws, codes, and regulations (e.g., individual rights, privacy, interrogation).
- Collect and preserve objects and data for assessment and analysis and demonstrate knowledge of:
  - o Requirements of chain of custody.
  - o Methods/procedures for seizure of various types of evidence.
  - o Methods/procedures for preserving various types of evidence.
  - o Forensic opportunities and resources.
  - o Applicable aspects of laws, codes, and regulations (e.g., rules of evidence and discovery).
- Conduct research by physical and electronic means and analyze data to obtain relevant information and demonstrate knowledge of:
  - o Methods of research using physical resources.
  - o Methods of research using electronic resources.

- o Methods of analysis of research results.
- o Documentation and reporting of analytical efforts.
- o Applicable aspects of laws, codes, and regulations.
- Collect and report relevant information and demonstrate knowledge of:
  - o Obtaining information from federal, state, and local agencies.
  - o Obtaining information from companies and private/public enterprises (e.g., mutual aid).
  - o Documentation and reporting of information.
  - o Applicable aspects of laws, codes, and regulations.
- Use computers/digital media to gather information/evidence and demonstrate knowledge of:
  - o Concepts and principles of computer operations and digital media.
  - o Concepts and principles of digital forensics.
  - o Computers to retrieve, store, and document digital information.
  - o Documentation and reporting of information.
  - o Applicable aspects of laws, codes, and regulations.
- Use special investigative techniques to gather critical information/evidence and demonstrate knowledge of:
  - o Concepts, principles, and methods of polygraph examinations.
  - o Concepts, principles, and methods of video/audio recordings.
  - o Concepts, principles, and methods of forensic analysis (e.g., writing, documents, fingerprints, DNA, biometrics, chemicals, fluids, etc.).
  - o Concepts, principles, and methods of undercover investigations.
  - o Documentation and reporting of information.
  - o Applicable aspects of laws, codes, and regulations.
  - o Development of confidential sources.

Case Presentation subtopics include

- Preparing reports to substantiate investigative findings and demonstrating knowledge of:
  - o Critical elements and format of an investigative report.
  - o Investigative terminology.
  - o Logical sequencing of information.
  - o Applicable aspects of laws, codes, and regulations.
- Preparing and presenting testimony by reviewing case files, meeting with counsel, and presenting relevant facts and demonstrating knowledge of:
  - o Witness preparation.
  - o Types of testimony.
  - o Applicable aspects of laws, codes, and regulations (e.g., applicable privileges, hearsay, rules of procedure).

Source: ASIS Online, ASIS Online Board Certifications, PCI, https://www.asisonline.org/Certification/Board-Certifications/PCI/Pages/default.aspx

Networking and Liaison

5 Distinguish between networking and liaison for investigators.

networking
Intentionally acquainting oneself with a diverse group of professionals and using those acquaintances to the benefit of all.

liaison
Communicating with other professionals for the purpose of establishing, maintaining, and improving mutual understanding and cooperation.

Networking is intentionally acquainting oneself with a diverse group of professionals and using those acquaintances to the benefit of all.[131] For security professionals, the art of networking can be critical to career success. For investigators, proactively cultivating and maintaining a personal network can be critical to the successful resolution of investigations. So much of the investigative process is built on trust, and trust is often developed by regular and predictable contact with individuals over time.

Liaison is communicating with other professionals for the purpose of establishing, maintaining, and improving mutual understanding and cooperation.[132] Liaison for security professionals means building strategic relationships with individuals and organizational representatives with whom you have a sufficiently similar industry presence to be mutually beneficial. Perhaps the best reason for actively engaging in liaison and networking activity is to demonstrate professionalism in your field.

Most security professionals are willing and eager to share their expertise and to learn from others. Security professionals can increase their professional relationships by asking their acquaintances for introductions and the contact information of people with whom they want to be acquainted, and other networking strategies. Joining professional or civic organizations is another good strategy for increasing the number of people to whom you are exposed. Volunteering for community activities, especially those related to the security profession like emergency planning exercises, also provides exposure to a variety of professionals in related fields.[133] Many organizations will allow you to conduct these activities during the course of a normal business day.[134]

Any security professional should consider joining a professional organization. Membership in the local Infragard chapter, for example, as well as other business-oriented organizations will also increase your exposure to professionals in other fields.[135] Additionally, online forums can be used to expand your list of contacts and acquaintances beyond those with whom you have had personal contact and geographic proximity.[136]

Many professionals have the mistaken opinion that the process of networking is simply making the acquaintance of a lot of professionals. Such activity is often seen as worthless if nothing beyond simply meeting others is done. Professional relationships require ongoing maintenance. It is advisable to establish a system that reminds you periodically to make contact with key individuals in your network. You can cultivate the relationship by proactively sharing information, periodically getting together with your acquaintances to see where business interests may intersect, introducing two unacquainted people whom you feel would work well together, and other strategies.[137]

Suggestions for maintaining strong and sustainable professional relationships include:

- Make sure each party derives some benefit from the relationship without taking undue advantage of the other.
- Understand and stay within legal and regulatory limits with respect to gifts or expenses meant to strengthen their relationship.
- Maintain the trust of professional acquaintances at all times. Violating the trust will generally terminate the relationship with that person and may taint the relationship with others.
- Maintain periodic contact, even when there is nothing specific to discuss. This demonstrates that you value the relationship and shows an intention to maintain familiarity with the individual, and perhaps their organization.[138]

Although it can be difficult and time-consuming, the security professional must establish, nurture, and appropriately maintain proper liaison relationships. This is often an accepted function of management, but the individual investigator should not shirk that responsibility completely. Critical liaison relationships include those that are internal and external to the organization, those that are both formal and informal, and those that include individuals and other organizations.[139]

When conducting security operations in a foreign country, it is often necessary to establish and conduct a liaison with local law enforcement, all local security, and local intelligence agencies. The security professional will benefit from periodically conducting discrete research and regarding the reputation and business practices of all with whom he or she engages.[140]

Careers in Security

Name: Anton L. Cooper

Position: Security Director

Year hired: 2015

City, State where you are based: Cleveland, Ohio

College(s) attended (degree): Cuyahoga Community College (CCC) and Cleveland State University (CSU)

Majors: Law Enforcement at CCC and Public Safety Management at CSU

Minors: None

Did you attend graduate school? Yes

College(s) attended (degree): Pennsylvania State University, Master in Homeland Security

Please give a brief description of your job: Responsible for continuous safety and security, emergency preparedness planning, performance management and disciplinary measures of subordinate personnel, physical protection and security of company property and assets by staying current with state-of-the-art security technologies, industry trends and best practices, and that all new initiatives are aligned with the organization's strategic plan.

What qualities/characteristics are most helpful for this job? Ability to first seek to understand then be understood, embrace conflict as an opportunity for problem solving, value-based leadership, strategic planning, lead change, external environment management, building trusting relationships, and empower others so that they can discover their potential.

What is a typical starting salary? $60K–$90K

What is the salary potential as you move up into higher-level jobs? $150,000+

What advice would you give someone in college beginning studies in security? Identify what area(s) of security they are most

passionate about that can inspire lifelong learning and then take ownership of their own personal development plan.

What appealed to you most about the position when you applied for it? The opportunity to make a tremendous difference by implementing value-based leadership, partnering with public and private sector, grow and develop new organization, and take on problems/challenges that stimulate further growth and development.

How would you describe the interview process? It was challenging to say the least since it took time to complete phone screens, 1-1 interviews, and Q&A from groups/panels.

What is a typical day like? You never know from one day to the next what will happen, and, therefore, it requires that I always remain vigilant and on top of my game.

In a typical day, what do you like best/least about it? The best part is that I love serving my team, stakeholders, and reflecting on the accomplishments of today with an eye on tomorrow. The least is having quality work/life balance.

How would you suggest interested applicants gain experience? Throughout the undergraduate/graduate experience, interested applicants should already be honing in on specialty areas of interest by understanding industry trends and best practices so that once they enter the job market prospective employers will be able to detect how their skill-sets translate into a position of interest. Also, it's paramount to seek out mentors who enjoy assisting others in their growth and development.

Would you recommend military experience? It depends on what the prospective applicant did in the military and how that experience can translate into a position of interest.

Does holding a full-time job during college help applicants get hired afterwards? It demonstrates applicants are high performers, can prioritize and multitask, and possess strong work ethics vital to success within the industry.

Summary

- **Explain the investigative process.**

  The investigative process consists of examining, studying, or inquiring into the particulars of a thing in detail. Investigations are often conducted to learn the facts about something hidden, unique, or complex, especially in an attempt to find a motive, cause, or culprit.

- **Identify the five qualities of effective and reliable investigation.**

  The five qualities of effective and reliable investigation are objectivity, thoroughness, relevance, accuracy, and timeliness.

• **Describe surveillance and the skills needed to be able to successfully accomplish it.**

Surveillance is the covert observation of individuals, places, or objects for the purpose of gathering information or intelligence. Private security professionals connect clues to uncover facts about legal, financial, or personal matters. Personnel selected for surveillance must have well-developed observation and description skills, patience, and the ability to endure long tedious hours of observation. Sometimes surveillants are chosen for their ethnicity or language qualifications.

• **Identify the reasons for conducting undercover operations.**

Undercover operations are considered when other efforts have failed or proved impractical. Undercover investigations gather relevant information unavailable by other means, and are a useful option to investigate crimes involving stolen property sales and frauds. The general objectives of an undercover operation are to obtain information, observe criminal activity, and collect evidence.

• **Distinguish Networking and Liaison for investigators.**

Networking is intentionally acquainting oneself with a diverse group of professionals and using those acquaintances to the benefit of all. Liaison is communicating for the purpose of establishing and maintaining mutual understanding and cooperation.

KEY TERMS

REVIEW QUESTIONS

1. Which of the listening techniques could you most improve?
2. Which of the five principles of investigation do you find easiest to understand?
3. What affects your observations? How can you improve your ability to observe things?
4. Examine the phases of an undercover investigation and identify and describe an exercise that exemplifies each.
5. How can security professionals increase their professional relationships?

PRACTICAL APPLICATION

1. You were recently hired as a private investigator. Describe your ideal average day.

2. You are the senior new hire for a private investigations department in your organization. Your department is expanding and needs to hire several new employees. Your manager asked you to prepare a checklist describing the qualities and qualifications sought in an investigator. Create this checklist.

3. Think of the people with whom you are acquainted, and select five of them to assist you on a surveillance of your choice. For each person chosen, list three qualities that this person demonstrates that will strengthen your surveillance team.

4. Imagine you have been assigned to a new location with your company. The job requires a lot of interaction with local police and other private- and public-sector personnel. Make a list of the first ten things you can accomplish to get to know those critical contacts.

Retail Security and Loss Prevention

CHAPTER

9

Learning Objectives

After reading this chapter, you should be able to:

1. Define and distinguish retail security and loss prevention. **181**

2. Identify indicators of shoplifting. **187**

3. Define organized retail crime. **189**

4. Identify ways an organization's leadership can discourage employee theft. **194**

Introduction

During a seven-month crime spree, John Patrick Weismiller repeatedly visited stores in Oregon such as Safeway, Target, and Best Buy and stole a variety of health and beauty products, over-the-counter pharmaceuticals, and other items, usually by hiding the items under his clothing. Weismiller then sold the stolen merchandise on the eBay website, often at half the retail price, but still netting $43,200, which represented more than $73,000 in retail losses. Weismiller's downfall started when Safeway's loss prevention team caught him stealing merchandise from its stores 105 times. Despite being stopped and forbidden to return, he was observed just two days later shoplifting at a different Safeway store. Prosecutors noted that the 41-year-old Weismiller listed 6,681 items for sale on eBay, including hundreds of packages of Crest Whitestrips. Safeway's loss prevention specialists collaborated with local and federal law enforcement agents to connect the stolen goods and online sales to Weismiller. He pled guilty to the thefts and was sentenced to a year and a day in prison, along with three years of supervised release. According to the U.S. Federal Bureau of Investigations (FBI), Weismiller was ordered to pay restitution of nearly $21,000.[1]

Weismiller supported himself, his wife, and his kids solely by shoplifting. His story illustrates the dangers faced by retail and commercial establishments that seek to protect their valuable goods from shoplifters. While presenting a collective economic threat to retailers, lone thieves like Weismiller may be a mere nuisance when compared to cyber phenomenon such as flash robbing where social media is used to bring groups of people together to engage in organized retail theft and assault.[2] Sometimes flash mobs are pulled together to harass customers and disrupt mall security. Youth gather together and jump up and down, and bang on the store windows. They climb in the windows and push through the doors while regular customers are trying to conduct business.[3] Such an event occurred in Brooklyn when a mob of hundreds of kids rioted in the Kings Plaza mall disrupting Christmas shoppers and causing damage to stores.[4]

Although these examples highlight mass thefts of merchandise and some variations of disturbing the peace, the activity involves much more than shoplifting and a brief disruption of business. The prevalence of similar events in the recent past indicates there may be a trend developing, indicating the need for increased attention to retail security and loss prevention. In this chapter we first define the concept of retail security and loss prevention, discuss the various forms of retail theft, and then review techniques to reduce or eliminate its occurrence. We will also examine ways to limit a typically less dangerous, although more prevalent method of inventory loss: employee retail theft.

Retail Security, Loss Prevention, and Asset Protection

1 Define and distinguish retail security and loss prevention.

The terms *retail security* and *loss prevention* are often used interchangeably to identify security efforts in support of retail organizations. According to Frost, the term **retail security** also refers to retail loss prevention and/or asset protection, and generally describes the process of reducing theft and shrinkage in a retail organization. It involves the process that securely sells goods to the public for both the consumer and store proprietor, preventing theft or harm.[5]

Loss prevention is broadly defined as any method used by individuals or organizations to increase the likelihood of preventing and controlling a loss of business or profits from an adverse event.[6] Loss prevention for retail purposes has been defined as the act of preventing harm to the organization's bottom line caused by lost money, goods, and the like in a business context.[7] Loss refers to the loss of people, money, productivity, or materials. The adverse occurrences might be incidents of crime, fire, accident, natural disaster, error, bad investment, or poor managerial decision. The various methods of loss prevention include the use of security officers, safety measures, and audits. The term also addresses the methods used to reduce shrinkage, or inventory shortage, in a retail organization. Those strategies

retail security
Retail loss prevention and/or asset protection, generally the process of reducing theft and shrinkage in a retail organization. It involves the process in which goods are securely sold to the public for both the consumer and store proprietor, preventing theft or harm.

loss prevention
Any method used by individuals or organizations to increase the likelihood of preventing and controlling a loss of business or profits from an adverse event.

are important to retail organizations, and they spend about 0.5% of their total sales income on loss prevention, according to Hayes.[8]

ASIS International, an association dedicated to developing the security profession, appears to favor **asset protection** as an overarching term for retail security that involves managing and protecting both physical property and information storage capacity.[9] Asset protection involves the following considerations:

asset protection
An aspect of retail security that involves managing and protecting both physical property and information storage capacity. Asset protection involves providing a safe and healthy environment and maintaining smooth business operations.

- Providing a safe and healthy environment is a central goal.
- Both the current and future risk environments must be considered.
- Liability reduction/management is an important component.
- Both tangible and intangible assets must be considered.
- A key objective is maintaining smooth business operations.
- Post-incident business or mission continuity is important.[10]

Goals of Retail Security and Loss Prevention Professionals

Historically, retail security departments have focused primarily on apprehending shoplifters and dishonest employees to deter further losses.[11] Although the focus on deterring and detecting theft was admirable, studies have not convincingly shown that there is any significant correlation between apprehension statistics and inventory losses. To effectively reduce shortages, the focus was adjusted to the concept of loss prevention. The term *loss prevention* in the context of retail security usually identifies the protection efforts devoted to inventory shortage reduction, which increases profitability.[12] Loss prevention professionals play a vital role in the profitability and financial success of retail organizations. They help protect the company's assets, minimize and prevent merchandise shrinkage, reduce fraud and prevent theft. Jared noted that loss prevention teams have access to powerful tools and technological advancements that equip them to anticipate and prevent loss.[13] Loss prevention security professionals work in both traditional, physical, retail locations, and the distribution centers that support online, e-commerce companies.

In the following sections we discuss some of the most significant challenges faced by loss prevention professionals. Security professionals with a loss prevention mission have a variety of areas of application, ranging from protecting the physical world to guarding cyber- and e-commerce from Internet-based criminals.

Shrinkage

Shrinkage is the term used to describe the losses that occur during the merchandise production-distribution-sales process.[14] **Retail shrinkage** is defined as a reduction in inventories not accounted for through sales or other legitimate activity.[15] Shrinkage represents the difference between the physical inventory that is *actually available for sale* and what the records say *should be available for sale*.

retail shrinkage
The losses that occur during the merchandise production-distribution-sales process. It is a reduction in inventories not accounted for through sales or other legitimate activity, and represents the difference between the physical inventory that is actually available for sale and what the records say should be available for sale.

Shrinkage occurs in one of two types of events: malicious and nonmalicious.[16] It is important to distinguish the two, as the type of event indicates the needed response. Malicious events are those that occur when someone intentionally divests an organization of goods, cash, or services without proper compensation. Nonmalicious events are those in which loss is unintentionally caused through routine businesses practices, design mistakes, and other systemic problems.[17]

Security professionals are most concerned with preventing or mitigating the effects of malicious events by identifying the causes or sources of losses due to those events. Hollinger found that employee (also known as internal) theft, shoplifting, organized retail crime, and administrative error are the main sources of loss affecting U.S. retailers.[18] Shrinkage accounts for a little more than 1% of total retail sales or roughly $54 billion annually in the

United Kingdom.[19] The Center for Retail Research found that shrinkage occurs in a variety of stores, including (though not limited to):

- Appliance stores
- Clothing stores
- Convenience stores
- Department stores
- Discount stores
- Drug stores
- Furniture stores
- Grocery stores
- Supermarkets

Shrinkage has a variety of sources, and the most common (44%) is attributed to employee theft; about 26% is due to shoplifting; 12% to organized retail crime; and 12% to administrative error.[20] These ratios may be culturally relative: North America and Latin America have a higher percentage of employee-caused shrinkage than that caused by shoplifters, suppliers, or internal error. The Asia Pacific region and Europe reported far higher rates of shoplifting than employee theft, as illustrated in Figure 9–1.[21]

According to the Center for Retail Research, India, Russia, Morocco, and South Africa top the list of countries with the highest reported shrinkage rates of approximately 1.75%. Brazil, Mexico, Thailand, and Turkey follow, with Malaysia and the United States finishing the top ten, all of which reported a shrinkage rate exceeding 1.5%. For another perspective, Figure 9–2 shows a comparison of shrinkage as a percentage of sales.

Because of its size, the United States has a very large shrinkage problem, costing retailers more than $40 billion per year. At a distant second place is Japan with losses of almost $10 billion, followed by the United Kingdom (about $8 billion), Germany ($7 billion), and France (almost $7 billion).[22] Top cities for retail loss in the United States include Atlanta, Baltimore, and Chicago.[23]

THINK ABOUT IT

What might explain the placement of the top countries on the list of those experiencing retail shrinkage? How can the development of such explanations help to lower losses through shrinkage losses?

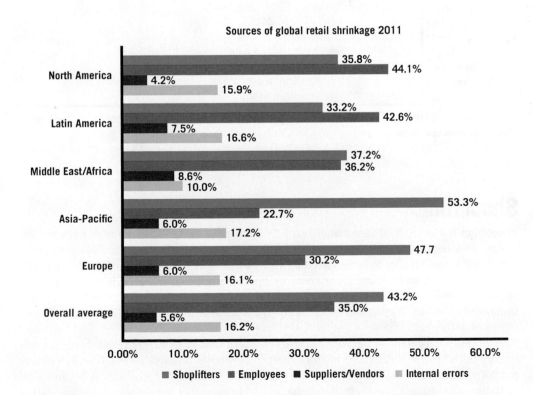

FIGURE 9–1
Sources of Retail Shrinkage Loss by Continent
Source: Prof J.A.N. Bamfield, Centre for Retail Research, Nottingham, http://www.retailresearch.org.

FIGURE 9 3
Retail Shrinkage by Country (percentage of sales)
Source: Prof J.A.N. Bamfield, Centre for Retail Research, Nottingham, http://www.retailresearch.org.

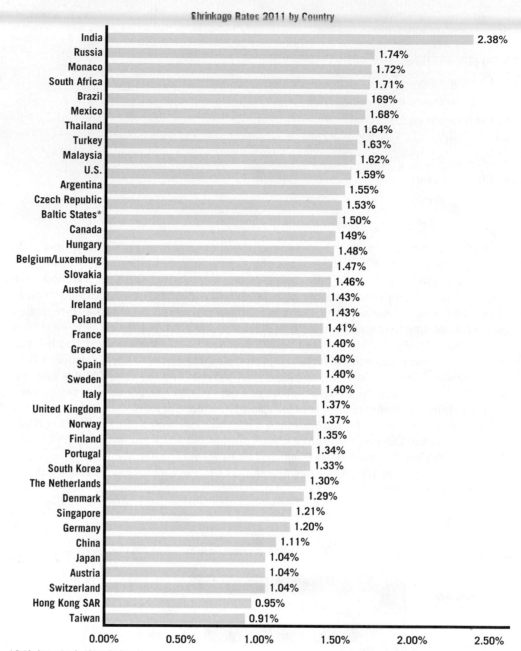

Shrinkage Rates 2011 by Country

India	2.38%
Russia	1.74%
Monaco	1.72%
South Africa	1.71%
Brazil	169%
Mexico	1.68%
Thailand	1.64%
Turkey	1.63%
Malaysia	1.62%
U.S.	1.59%
Argentina	1.55%
Czech Republic	1.53%
Baltic States*	1.50%
Canada	149%
Hungary	1.48%
Belgium/Luxemburg	1.47%
Slovakia	1.46%
Australia	1.43%
Ireland	1.43%
Poland	1.41%
France	1.40%
Greece	1.40%
Spain	1.40%
Sweden	1.40%
Italy	1.37%
United Kingdom	1.37%
Norway	1.35%
Finland	1.34%
Portugal	1.33%
South Korea	1.30%
The Netherlands	1.29%
Denmark	1.21%
Singapore	1.20%
Germany	1.11%
China	1.04%
Japan	1.04%
Austria	1.04%
Switzerland	0.95%
Hong Kong SAR	0.91%
Taiwan	

* Baltic States: Latvia, Lithuania, Estonia

Shoplifting

shoplifting
The theft of merchandise from commercial public display areas by a person posing as a legitimate customer.

Shoplifting is the theft of merchandise from commercial public display areas by a person posing as a legitimate customer.[24] Woolworth's department store may have been the first U.S. retail establishment to have a need for retail security in 1879, after the founder decided to increase sales and reduce labor costs by openly displaying merchandise.[25] Shoplifting appears to have occurred before then, as the term was placed in the Oxford English Dictionary in 1673 and mentioned by the British Parliament as early as 1673 (as an offense punishable by death).[26]

Contemporary retail organizations have estimated that 30 to 40% of retail shrinkage can be attributed to shoplifting and in-store theft.[27] This costs retailers as much as $15 billion annually. It has been estimated that retail organizations lose 1 to 2% of their sales and 25% of their profits to loss and theft of merchandise.[28] In response, retailers look for innovative solutions to tackle theft and protect their bottom line.[29] In the recent past, volume discount stores trying to gain and keep customers have experienced their own challenges. In addition to keeping prices low for customers, they have to keep profits up for shareholders while ensuring customers and employees are safe in the stores.[30]

The average shoplifter is caught with approximately $200.00 in stolen merchandise in his or her possession.[31] Research of convenience store crime found that many of the suspects were prolific offenders, in some cases committing crimes on a weekly or even daily basis. They had extensive criminal histories and were likely involved in other more serious types of crime.[32] It should be observed that figures regarding shoplifting can only be treated as informed estimates, as the majority of shoplifting reports to police end in neither a formal arrest record nor criminal prosecution.[33]

◄ Shoplifting from a grocery store. Shoplifters steal from merchants in all types of retail establishments. From candy bars to televisions, thefts affect the business's inventory and profit margin. What can be done to prevent such thefts?

Common shoplifting methods include:

- Hiding items under clothes or in carried containers (purses, bags, boxes).
- Lining a shopping bag with aluminum foil to thwart the exit sensor.
- Switching price tags.
- Using a bag or box with a false bottom or trap door.
- Wearing an item out of the store.

There are two primary categories of shoplifters—professionals and amateurs—each with different characteristics.[34] Effective methods to prevent theft vary for each group, and the identifiers of group members are often different.

Characteristics of professional shoplifters include the following:

- Highly skilled and difficult to identify.
- Focus on products that are sought after by consumers and easy to sell.
- Familiarize with the store in advance to facilitate the crime.[35]

Characteristics of amateur shoplifters include the following:

- May steal based on impulse, or be driven by an addiction.
- Are often clumsy or erratic in their behavior.
- May be easier to detect.

Examine the differences between amateur and professional shoplifters. If shoplifting were a sport, what sort of training could amateurs attend to become more professional? If shoplifting were a legitimate job, what skills would an employer (of shoplifters) look for in new employees?

- May steal simply for the thrill of it.
- Often expect store owners and courts to go easy on them.
- May enter stores in groups in an attempt to intimidate team members.[36]

Amateur shoplifters typically work alone, while professional shoplifters are more likely to work in teams. A recent study of retail store customers found that 75% of observed shoplifting involved a lone individual and 25% involved more than one person.[37] It is also probable that the potential diversion provided by one person helped conceal the behavior of the others.

Types of Products Targeted for Theft

Regardless of whether the shoplifter is an amateur or professional, their targets are often quite similar. Some commonly stolen items include mobile phones, jewelry, and other fashion accessories, electronic goods, personal care items, cash and food, according to the New South Wales Police Force.[38] It may seem counterintuitive that the item cost is relatively low for many of these items. The top five items stolen in Australia, for example, are lipstick, shaving products, fragrances, infant formula, and clothing.[39] These items have characteristics that can be remembered using the acronym CRAVED:

- *Concealable*—easy to hide and not easy to be identified.
- *Removable*—not connected to a large object or locked down.
- *Available*—widely used and easy to locate.
- *Valuable*—increases the social status of an individual.
- *Enjoyable*—pleasing, satisfying, or gratifying for personal use, profit, or psychological gain.
- *Disposable*—can be sold with little effort to a ready market.[40]

Preventing Shoplifting

Most of the strategies implemented by retailer security professionals involve simply discouraging or disrupting shoplifters.[41] Many organizations use signage and the presence of loss prevention professionals to discourage shoplifters. The job tasks and work situations of retail security professionals can be classified into five primary domains, sometimes called the five A's:

- *Apprehension* of shoplifters and dishonest employees.
- *Awareness* of nonsecurity employees through asset protection awareness training.
- *Auditing* as a protective measure.
- *Area* focus, including collecting data to focus protective efforts.
- *Additional* duties as assigned, such as safeguarding bank deposits en route, ensuring general safety, and assuming various roles during emergencies.[42]

According to Sennewald and Christman, four elements are necessary for a successful loss prevention plan: total support from top management, positive employee attitudes, maximum use of all available resources, and a system that establishes both responsibility and accountability for loss prevention through evaluations that are consistent and progressive.[43] Studies show that the most effective deterrent against all forms of external theft is excellent customer service. This is true both for amateur and professional thieves, as it is much more difficult to steal merchandise when you are being served well, and the person serving you is close to you. In fact, when shoplifters have been caught and questioned about their shoplifting, many admit that they actively seek out stores with poor service.[44]

Here are some strategies from the New South Wales police that retail security professionals can share with responsible employees to help deter shoplifters:

- *Staffing*: Schedule enough employees to work at the same time to support both retail and security operations.
- *Greeting*: Ensure employees greet every customer as they enter the store.
- *Be attentive*: Staff must be available to customers and aware of their needs.
- *Receipts*: Each purchase should be documented with a receipt, and receipts should be required for refunds.
- *Stay focused*: Employees must avoid distraction while another person is being served or observed.
- *Bag check*: Backpacks and bags brought in by customers should be checked if they are to be brought into the store.
- *Service calls*: Employees should alert other employees immediately when they notice suspicious activities.
- *Helping hand*: Customers who seem lost, unable to locate merchandise, or appear suspicious should be asked if they are finding everything they need.[45]

Honest people will be pleased with the service.

Spotlight
Probable Cause Steps

To establish a solid base for probable cause and prevent false arrest claims, a merchant should follow six universally accepted steps before detaining someone suspected of shoplifting:

1. You must see the shoplifter approach your merchandise.
2. You must see the shoplifter select your merchandise.
3. You must see the shoplifter conceal, carry away, or convert your merchandise.
4. You must maintain continuous observation of the shoplifter.
5. You must see the shoplifter fail to pay for the merchandise.
6. You must approach the shoplifter outside of the store.

Source: C. E. McGoey, "Shoplifting Probable Cause Steps," Crime Doctor: Your Prescription for Security and Safety, 2014, http://www.crimedoctor.com/shopliftingPC.htm

---

Shoplifter Identification: Profiling

The process of preventing shoplifting often involves the identification and surveillance of suspected shoplifters. Retail security professionals often employ the same methods that public law enforcement officers use to identify criminals and prevent crime—their experience combined with observations of suspicious activity. Some retail security professionals (such as some law enforcement officers) increase their chances of success by **offender profiling**, which involves an effort to narrow the field of potential suspects by focusing on those believed to present the greatest risk.[46] According to Dabney, Dugan, Topalli, and Hollinger, the technique uses what is known about crime and criminals to more efficiently and accurately differentiate potential thieves from the average shopper. Law enforcement and private security personnel have long relied on a host of behavioral and demographic data to aid them in identifying and apprehending criminals. To accomplish this task, police and other security officials draw on existing apprehension reports to identify common factors found in the offender pool.[47]

2 Identify indicators of shoplifting.

offender profiling
Focusing on those people believed to present the greatest risk of committing crime based on traits and characteristics of known criminals. The technique uses what is known about crime and criminals to more efficiently and accurately identify potential criminals.

Retail security professionals should be leery of shoppers who:

- Seem more attentive and focused on store employees than shopping.
- Wear coats or heavy clothing during warm weather or when otherwise unnecessary.
- Walk as if they are concealing stolen items.
- Leave the dressing room with (apparently) fewer items than they entered with.
- Appear nervous, perhaps picking up random items and feigning interest.
- Enter the store multiple times yet never make a purchase.[48]

A recent analysis of more than 1,200 shoppers provides some clarity about the usefulness of offender identification by retail security professionals. Trained observers saw 105 shoppers (8.5%) committing an act of merchandise theft and concealment.[49] Further analysis determined that adults between the ages of 35 to 54 had been much more likely to shoplift than the 35 and under shopper. Social class clearly affects a person's propensity to steal: lower- or working-class shoppers were more than twice as likely to take a "five finger discount," than middle- and upper-class shoppers.[50]

Profiling Problems

While shoplifting surveys show that focusing on people and groups who have a higher percentage of shoplifting can pay off, profiling also brings with it a slew of problems. Unfortunately, some retail security professionals (like some law enforcement officers) will misuse profiling techniques by identifying suspects based on their personal bias. Such actions are considered lazy and ineffective, amounting to no more than negative stereotyping; racial or ethnic profiling can lead to personal and organizational civil liabilities.

While any profiling based on race or ethnicity is troubling, there are in fact racial and ethnic patterns uncovered in shoplifting studies: a significantly larger proportion of shoplifters were found to be black and Hispanic males, between the ages of 35 and 54, coming from low or working classes.[51] Do these findings suggest that race and ethnicity should be used in creating shoplifting profiles? The answer is a resounding *no*!

First, such practices unfairly target millions of shoppers who have no intention of engaging in criminal activity. Second, they open retail establishments to civil lawsuits based on the claim that innocent people are being unfairly targeted. For example, in 2013 actor Rob Brown, an African American then in his late twenties, filed a lawsuit against the Macy's department store chain, alleging that he was "paraded" through the Herald Square location in handcuffs and placed in a holding cell after making a purchase—for no reason other than a store employee was skeptical his credit card was really his. Brown has starred in blockbusters such as *Finding Forrester* and *Coach Carter*; he had a role in *The Dark Knight Rises* and appeared in the HBO show *Treme*.[52] Third, using profiling based on demographic characteristics may have far less value than using behavioral characteristics.

According to Dabney, Dugan, Topalli, and Hollinger, for example, the odds of stealing for a person who exhibits one of the three cues of shoplifting (e.g., scanning the store, tampering with products, displaying an awareness of security countermeasures) are 6.25 times higher than for those who exhibit no such behavior; those who exit the store without having made a purchase are almost six times more likely to be carrying a stolen product than those who walked out of the store after buying something at the checkout.[53] Consequently, a shopper's behavior, not the shopper's race or gender, is by far the single strongest predictor of whether he or she is likely to steal.

Changing Behavior

Although behavior has been shown to be a better predictor of shoplifting potential, it appears it may be quite difficult to change the inherent bias in security professionals. Trained researchers recently identified this potential problem. Despite intensive training and specific instructions to ignore shopper demographic characteristics in selecting potential or probable offenders, the observers were unable to resist the power of implicit cultural stereotypes in shaping their selection of individuals.[54] Specifically, observers included disproportionate numbers of shoppers with demographic characteristics stereotypically attributed to shoplifters (non-white adolescent males) when selecting potential offenders for further analysis. This suggested that offender stereotypes translate into offender profiling behaviors by security professionals, even when training to the contrary is provided.[55]

Additionally, there is a possibility that years of racial profiling in the security profession have produced a change in the behavior patterns of the shoppers most commonly targeted by such efforts.[56] Young black males, for example, may repeatedly look over their shoulders when shopping to see if they are being watched. Ironically, Dabney, Dugan, Topalli, and Hollinger found this behavior even further attracts the attention of those focused on behavior-based profiles.[57] Recently, a coalition of major retailers produced a customer bill of rights that would ban racial profiling and unreasonable searches. The bill of rights was planned for posting in stores and on retailers' websites.[58]

Spotlight
Credentialing Loss Prevention Professionals

The Loss Prevention Foundation provides LPQualified (LPQ) and LPCertified (LPC) credentials that identify proficiencies and competencies that are critical for today's loss prevention professional. Designed and developed by in a collaborative effort led by business and loss prevention leaders, as well as educators, these web-accessible prep-courses are focused on advancing individual industry knowledge, growing careers, and elevating the profession.

The LPQ is designed for entry-level LP professionals with less than 3 years experience. It canvasses loss prevention practices, core competencies, foundational tools, business processes, and best practices. The LPC is an advanced certification for experienced professionals such as multi-unit, field and corporate LP management. The course further integrates the business of loss prevention into retail profit center practices and logistics.

Loss Prevention Magazine, "LPQ and LPC Certification Updates are Now in Progress," November 4, 2014, http://www.losspreventionfoundation.org/___pdfs/lpfpublished/20141104_LPQLPC_CertificationUpdates.pdf

Organized Retail Crime

In addition to the lone amateur or professional shoplifter, traveling groups of organized criminals and gangs who steal for their livelihood have been in operation for decades.[59] **Organized retail crime** (ORC) is defined as the activity of theft or fraud conducted with the intent to convert illegally obtained merchandise, cargo, cash, or a cash equivalent into financial gain (not personal use) where or when the following elements are present:

3 Define organized retail crime.

organized retail crime
The activity of theft or fraud conducted with the intent to convert illegally obtained merchandise, cargo, cash, or a cash equivalent into financial gain (not personal use). This includes theft or fraud and involves multiple items, over multiple occurrences, or in multiple stores, or in multiple jurisdictions, by two or more persons, or an individual acting in dual roles.

- Theft/fraud involves multiple items.
- Theft/fraud is conducted
  - over multiple occurrences,
  - and/or in multiple stores,
  - and/or in multiple jurisdictions,
  - by two or more persons, or by an individual acting in dual roles (booster and fence).[60]

North America leads in the percentages of retailers with increases in organized retail crime, as shown in Figure 9–3.

How common is organized retail crime? Of 125 retail companies surveyed in the 2013 Organized Retail Crime Survey, 93.5% of the retail organizations surveyed reported that they had been a victim of organized retail crime in the past year, although this figure was down slightly from 96% in 2012. According to Brown and Grannis, the 2013 ORC Survey marked the third year in a row that more than 90% of the surveyed retailers reported being victims of ORC.[61] Equally disturbing was the finding that eight in ten retailers believe that ORC activity in the United States had increased over the past three years.[62]

In addition to organized shoplifting, ORC groups affect the profits of retail organizations in other ways. They are diversified, innovative, and constantly evolving. They employ sophisticated credit card, gift card, and check schemes. They hijack and steal truck or rail cargo, and collude with dishonest employees to steal from manufacturers and distribution

FIGURE 9–3
Organized Retail Crime (2011)
Source: Prof J.A.N. Bamfield, Centre for Retail Research, Nottingham, http://www.retailresearch.org.

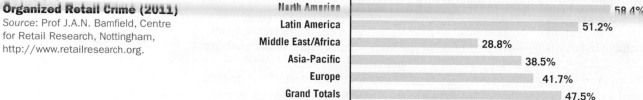

centers. ORC groups frequently travel across state and international borders to sell stolen, counterfeit, or diverted goods.[63] ORC group crimes can destroy retailer and brand credibility by contaminating or diluting medications and food, altering expiration dates and contents, and moving merchandise through unsanitary or infected areas.[64]

In an attempt to prevent theft, retail organizations increase the security of merchandise by making it less accessible to customers, often limiting sales in the process. Manufacturers, retailers, and consumers all lose when items that are routinely stolen are locked up for protection and cannot be readily purchased. Some stores have even been forced to close due to very high theft activity. This deprives local residents of safe, nearby shopping locations. ORC also funds other criminal activity, such as firearms trafficking, illegal immigration, and terrorism.[65]

What is taken? Where does it go? Items targeted by ORC groups include medical testing kits, baby formula, pain relievers, electronics, video games and music, power tools, and apparel. Certain stores, such as drug, food, and mass merchants, are heavily targeted for theft because they carry hot items and allow easy access by creating low-risk (of apprehension) environments.[66] As reported by Hayes and Cardone, this practice can be used in a variety of market strategies, from the local flea market to the truck stop to the Internet auction site.[67]

The ultimate status of goods stolen by ORC groups may be surprising. These groups operate across state and national borders, and they frequently outwit many security professional or law enforcement intelligence networks. They eventually sell their stolen wares to individual shoppers, overseas buyers, and sometimes back to large retailers. This can be accomplished without suspicion especially for items with no unique identifiers (like a serial or lot number), especially when stolen items are mixed with legitimately obtained goods.

Spotlight
Gate Cutters Organized Retail Crime Group

According to the FBI, an organized criminal ring dubbed the Gate Cutters Jewelry Crew has successfully burglarized more than fifty jewelry stores, stealing more than $5 million in jewelry. The organization burglarizes primarily national, mall-based stores and has victimized sixteen different companies in twelve East Coast states. To create a unified investigative strategy useful in capturing these elusive thieves, the FBI and other law enforcement agencies, along with representatives from the jewelry industry, formed the Gate Cutters Jewelry Task Force. The Task Force has pooled information and resources to streamline the coordinated multijurisdictional investigation.

Aspects of this criminal ring's modus operandi include:

• Jewelry stores are generally burglarized when lighting conditions in a mall or store are low.
• Jewelry stores are usually burglarized before or after normal store business hours.

• The subjects cut through roll-down security gates and pry open display cases and remove products that are not secured in a safe.
• In most cases, the subjects do not attempt to enter safes and are usually in the store for a very short period of time.
• The subjects typically wear hooded sweatshirts.
• The subjects generally target men's gold jewelry, such as chains, bracelets, and rings.

Despite all of these efforts the Gate Cutters have not yet been captured.

Source: U.S. Federal Bureau of Investigation (FBI), "Gate Cutters Jewelry Task Force Announced," http://www.fbi.gov/news/pressrel/press-releases/gate-cutters-jewelry-task-force-announced

Combating Organized Retail Crime

Because security professionals are more engaged with preventing loss and theft than the display of merchandise, it is critical that they collaborate with employees responsible for item placement and display. Goodchild suggested that security professionals should make retail employees aware of the following factors when anticipating the possibility of large groups, including ORC groups, in a retail setting:

- *Product placement*: Keep high-value items up high and in the back of the store, where they can't be reached easily and where thieves can't quickly grab them and run.

- *Cameras*: Have people on staff trained to use still cameras to supplement video surveillance systems.

Security in Practice
Mall Security

▲ Kings Plaza shopping center in Brooklyn, New York. Shortly after Christmas in 2013, hundreds of teenagers terrorized the mall, forcing it to close down. What steps can be taken to enhance security at the nation's shopping malls?

In 2015 Canadian police announced that they had foiled a plot by two people who had been planning to attack shoppers inside of a Nova Scotia mall. The alleged plotters, a 19-year-old Canadian man and a 23-year-old American woman, had written a number of tweets to be released after their deaths. According to the Nova Scotia Royal Canadian Mounted Police (RCMP), the two had become obsessed with death and killing. "Had they been able to carry out their intentions, the possibility for a large loss of life was definitely there," said RCMP commanding officer Brian Brennan.

Two years earlier, shoppers in Kenya weren't so lucky when the upscale Westgate shopping mall in Nairobi came under siege by Islamist radicals. The attack, which lasted four days, resulted in sixty-seven deaths, including those of four heavily armed attackers who perished when police blew up a wall to gain access to the building. Another 175 people were wounded in the attack. Afterward, Kenyan authorities arrested dozens of people suspected to have been linked to the attack, although only four were taken to court. Because the attackers may have blended in with fleeing shoppers it is uncertain whether some attackers survived the incident and escaped in the crowd.

Not long after the mall attack in Kenya, more than 400 teenagers descended on the Kings Plaza shopping center in Brooklyn, New York, beating up customers and security guards as they looted and vandalized stores. Officials said that the attack was gang-related and that it may have been sparked by a game of "knockout" that was organized through social media. The mall was forced to close during the crucial post-Christmas selling season, and later initiated a policy banning anyone under age eighteen unless accompanied by an adult.

Over the past few years, there have been other violent incidents in American shopping centers. In 2013, for example, a shooting at a mall in Paramus, New Jersey, left the gunman dead and terrified thousands of shoppers. A year earlier, another shooting at a mall near Portland, Oregon, left three people dead, including the gunman.

According to CoStar, a real estate information company, there are more than 115,600 retail centers in the United States—ranging from strip malls to large, enclosed shopping centers. The provision of mall security services, however, is complicated by the fact that shopkeepers and store owners want to make people feel safe, and are generally unwilling to implement intrusive security methods such as metal detectors and bag screenings because they don't want to discourage customers from visiting. Matthew W. Horace, chief security officer of FJC Security Services, noted that "There is that careful balance between making people feel safe and the infringement on civil liberties." Horace thinks that customers are likely to be wary of shopping centers secured by armed guards, especially those who display automatic weapons.

In an effort to enhance security, a number of shopping centers are installing shatterproof windows and bomb-resistant trashcans, enhancing video surveillance, and encouraging shoppers to report suspicious persons or circumstances. Store employees are routinely trained in disaster response and are shown how to help customers escape from dangerous situations. Even so, the desire to keep foot traffic flowing will continue to limit the types of security measures that can be employed.

QUESTIONS

1. *Most shopping centers are relatively "soft" targets, and mall security often focuses primarily on theft prevention. How can malls be made more secure?*

2. *How might mall-based business in the United States be impacted if mall violence were to become commonplace?*

References: Ronda Kaysen, "Malls Work on Their Security, But Keep It in the Background," *New York Times*, November 26, 2013, www.nytimes.com/2013/11/27/realestate/commercial/malls-work-on-their-security-but-keep-it-in-the-background.html (accessed May 20, 2015); "Suspect in Halifax Plot Confessed to Wanting to Attack Mall," Associated Press, February 14, 2015, http://www.foxnews.com/world/2015/02/14/apnewsbreak-suspect-in-halifax-plot-confessed-to-wanting-to-attack-mall/ (accessed May 20, 2015); "Westgate Mall Massacre Suspects: Four Somalis in Nairobi Court Charged with Aiding Islamist Attack," *World News*, November 12, 2013, http://wn.com/westgate_mall_massacre_suspects_four_somalis_in_nairobi_court_charged_with_aiding_islamist_attack (accessed May 20, 2015); Ryan Gorman, "Hundreds of Teens Terrorize Brooklyn Mall," *Daily Mail*, December 27, 2013, http://www.dailymail.co.uk/news/article-2530092/Horror-hundreds-teens-terrorize-Brooklyn-mall-attack-coordinated-social-media.html (accessed May 20, 2015).

- *Staff*: Have personnel stationed in key areas where more valuable items are located.
- *Safety*: Remind employees not to get involved physically with shoplifters and thieves.[68]

Additionally, retail security professionals can employ the following strategies to counter the problems associated with ORC:

- *Educate*: The act of shoplifting does not necessarily indicate ORC. If there is no proof of multiple offender involvement, then the offenders are shoplifters.
- *Document*: Show repeat offenses or evidence of conspiracy. Every major theft or attempted theft needs to be well documented.
- *Share information (internally)*: Sharing subject information on public ORC websites, at local meetings, and in regional alerts should *not* be done. The key to preventing loss is letting the bad guys know your organization makes felony arrests, and they should avoid your stores and target another company instead.
- *Prioritize*: Too many ORC teams spend time hunting suspects that don't shoplift in their own store, or working credit card fraud cases that don't affect the bottom line. Instead they should focus on watching high-theft items, deterrence, intelligence collection, and customer service.[69]

Another approach, adapted by the Target Corporation, uses a slightly different method in retail security to counter ORC:

- *Diverse hiring*: Target doesn't just hire employees with law enforcement experience, but it also hires people with experience in information systems, finance, and analytics to look for patterns that help predict where thieves might strike next.
- *Intergroup cooperation*: The retail chain collaborates with others using information-sharing networks between big retailers and law enforcement, as well as government and industry collaboration.
- *Technology*: Target employs IP-based camera systems that allow for remote surveillance of its stores.
- *Partnerships*: The chain employs information-sharing efforts and works to form alliances with law enforcement officials and with other retailers.[70]

Flash Mobs

In addition to ORC groups, a relatively new phenomenon, the criminal flash mob, is a product of the age of social media. Duran found that the typical flash mob was a group of people, usually previously unknown to each other, who assembled suddenly in a public place, perform some unusual or notable (though not always criminal) activity according to predetermined instructions, and then quickly disperse.[71] The National Retail Federation says the trend of flash mobbing, or using social networks such as Twitter and Facebook to organize en masse and get together in one place, has taken on a nefarious form called flash robbing.[72] **Criminal flash mobs** or flash robs, occur when a group of people coordinate to overwhelm a retail outlet and steal merchandise. These seemingly random acts of organized retail crime challenge security and law enforcement professionals with what has also been referred to as *flash-gangbanging*.[73] This synthesis or morphing of flash mobs and ganglike activity has produced a hybrid to which few security or law enforcement professionals are prepared to effectively respond. Smith observed that the spontaneity and secrecy of the flash mob combined with the targeted crime and/or violence of the ganglike activity produces a mix that would be hard to combat even with inside intelligence.[74]

Employee Theft/Theft from Within

Many companies have shifted their focus from an apprehension-driven external-theft (shoplifter prevention) mindset to one of operational knowledge and holistic vision. Custer observed that the current focus is more centered on the mitigation of sales reducing activities and their causes. Moving the focus away from external theft and more on reducing

THINK ABOUT IT

How could a retail establishment thwart the activity of a criminal flash mob? Could they be stopped before they act? Could they be stopped once they have started? How could they be identified for potential prosecution?

criminal flash mobs
When a group of people coordinate the arrival of a crowd to overwhelm a retail outlet and steal merchandise.

employee shrinkage can help improve gross margin, net profit, and stock value. Such a shift in focus can also reduce the pressures from management to apprehend shoplifters, and decrease the risk of injury, death, or litigation.[75]

Employee theft is the primary cause of inventory shrinkage. A recent U.S. survey found that the largest source of retail loss was from employees, accounting for 37% of all theft.[76] Some estimates indicate that employees steal more than $600 billion in merchandise, or roughly $4,500 per employee. According to the U.S. Department of Commerce, about a third of all business failures each year can be connected in some way to employee theft and other employee crime.[77]

Many organizations depend on trust in order to grow and thrive. That becomes difficult if the corporate culture provides employees with opportunities to steal without detection. Security professionals estimate that as many as 30% of company employees steal, and another 60% would steal if given a motive and opportunity.[78] As much as 80% of retail loss is due to internal theft or employee error.[79] Security procedures should be designed and implemented to limit such opportunities. Security professionals can protect the organization against loss by helping leadership become familiar with some of the typical ways employees steal.[80] The National Federation of Independent Business reported that the most common ways in which employees steal are through larceny, skimming, and fraud.

- **Larceny** is the theft of property or cash. Larceny is often the easiest to detect because adequate financial controls (like recording the cash property in the books) are in place.
- **Skimming** is the theft of cash before it is recorded on the company's books. Retail employees can skim cash when the customer pays them directly for products or services.
- **Fraudulent disbursements** may occur when salespersons charge a customer one amount, complete a transaction record for less, and pocket the difference. Fraudulent disbursement also include billing or payroll schemes, and fraudulent expense reports.[81]

A recent U.S. survey, the Retail Fraud Survey 2013, suggested that retail fraud was damaging retail in the United States by $54 billion per year.[82] Aronhalt and Grannis advise that retail companies expect to lose almost $9 billion per year to return fraud alone.[83]

Motivations

Employees who steal from their employers obviously have justified their actions to themselves, but what are they thinking? Few steal company property to ease economic pressures.[84] Apparently, most believe their actions are completely justified under the circumstances. There are many factors that enhance an employee's potential for criminal conduct, according to Bologna, especially internal theft, fraud, and embezzlement within the business entity, including:

- Inadequate pay, benefits, job security, and promotional opportunities
- Lack of recognition for good work, loyalty, longevity, and effort
- Lack of periodic audits and inspections
- Tolerance or indifference toward antisocial behavior
- Bias or unfairness in selection, promotion, compensation, or appraisal
- Failure to screen applicants thoroughly for sensitive positions before appointment
- General job-related stress or anxiety[85]

Conspiracies with Outsiders

In some instances, employees work with outsiders to defraud their employer. Some of the fraudulent techniques that are employed include:

- **Counterfeit coupons**: Fake coupons are a huge problem for grocery stores, where the profit margin is very small, between 1 and 2% each year.
- **Self-checkout fraud**: Some customers use self-checkout systems as an opportunity to steal. Often, employees who monitor the lines are so used to problems with

larceny
The unauthorized taking and carrying away of the personal property of another by an individual who intends to permanently deprive the owner of its possession.

skimming
The embezzlement of cash before it is recorded on the company's books, typically when the customer pays an employee in cash for goods or services.

fraudulent disbursements
Include billing schemes, payroll schemes, register disbursement schemes, expense reimbursement schemes and check tampering. Salespersons can charge a customer one amount, ringing up a receipt for less and pocketing the difference.

self-checkout fraud
Occurs when customers use self-checkout systems as an opportunity to steal.

self-checkout machines that they don't pay close attention to customers who use them. This works to a thief's advantage.

sweet-hearting

When a customer goes through the checkout line with an expensive item, and a confederate running the register runs through a bar code for a much less costly item they had obtained beforehand.

building a bank (in the register)

The unauthorized practice by a cashier of taking the money paid for an item(s) and voiding the order after the customer leaves. The cashier puts money in the drawer, keeps track of how much he or she is banking, and embezzles the money as the shift ends.

refund fraud

When a sales associate gets an item off the rack, processes the refund for the sale amount, and then puts the money on a gift card which is largely untraceable.

- **Sweet-hearting**: This occurs when a customer goes through the checkout line with an expensive item, and the person running the register (a friend) runs through a bar code for a much less costly item. An alternative occurs when they pass items around the scanner and give them to a friend or accomplice for free.

- **Building a bank (in the register)**: The cashier takes the money paid for an item(s), and voids the order after the customer leaves. The cashier puts money in the drawer, and then keeps track of how much they are banking. At the end of the shift, they pull out the stolen money.

- **Refund fraud**: A sales associate gets an item off the rack, processes the refund for the sale amount and then puts the money on a gift card. Because the refund is on a gift card, it is largely untraceable.[86]

The Retail Fraud Survey of 2013 suggests that the prevalence of refund fraud, by both customer and employees, comprises around 30% of all inventory shrinkage.[87] Regardless of their methods or motivation, employee theft harms business owners who lose profits and retail customers end up paying higher prices due to higher merchandise costs and insurance premiums.[88]

Preventing Employee Theft

4 | Identify ways an organization's leadership can discourage employee theft.

Although it appears many employees may be predisposed to theft, the majority possess a sense of morality that will not allow them to steal. How is it possible then to thwart those who would betray their employer's trust? Is there a system that makes detection likely and prevention a reality?[89] Retail security professionals should base their strategies on these premises:

- Employees who steal are frequently involved in other counterproductive workplace activities.
- The greater the opportunity for theft, the greater the chance that it will occur.
- Employees who are satisfied with their jobs are less likely to steal.
- The greater the chance of detection, the less likely the employee will steal.
- A strong management commitment to deter theft reduces losses by employing policies and procedures to reduce the organization's exposure to litigation and liability.
- Theft on the job is not necessarily correlated to external factors or influences.
- Peer pressure and attitude significantly affect individual employee attitudes toward theft.[90]

Organizational leadership has an important role in preventing employee theft, too. According to the New South Wales Police Force, among the many things that can be done to affect the organizational culture are the following:

- *Positive work environment*: Encourages employees to follow policies and procedures and support the organization.
- *Internal controls*: Ensures effective operations, legal and regulatory compliance, asset protection, and accurate reporting of finances.
- *Restrict personal belongings*: Restrict staff from taking personal items, such as bags, wallets, and money, into the retail or warehouse areas.
- *Background checks*: Preemployment background checks may help limit the hiring of potentially criminal employees.
- *Employee awareness*: Inform employees about policies and provide training on fraudulent and criminal behavior.
- *Focus your efforts*: Security measures should be focused on the most expensive and easily stolen items, including expensive merchandise and cash.

- *Anonymous reporting systems*: Provide an anonymous reporting system for employees, vendors, and customers for violations of policies or procedures.

- *Perform audits*: Conduct regular and random, unannounced audits and assessments.

- *Keep watch*: No prevention strategy is effective if it is not checked frequently and adjusted, as needed.

- *Investigate everything*: A thorough and prompt investigation of all incidents (policy and procedure violations, allegations of fraud, etc.) will provide the information needed to make informed decisions and reduce losses.

- *Sign-in procedure*: Ensure employees sign in and out to help identify who is in the building and when.

- *Set the example*: Senior leadership sets the example for the organization's employees. A relaxed approach to security by the leadership will be reflected in the attitude of employees.[91]

New Loss Prevention

Beck and Peacock suggest that most incidents of shoplifting are merely symptoms of deeper operational failures that must be identified and resolved. One approach is to identify how criminal opportunities are created by operational failures and how thieves exploit these security breaches. Developments such as situational crime prevention and crime prevention through environmental design (CPTED) have identified the way environmental conditions and cues can provide an opening that sophisticated offenders have the technical ability to exploit.[92] Crime becomes more difficult, less rewarding, or more risky as these breaches are closed. Even the most sophisticated criminal may then seek an alternative or desist from the behavior altogether. Operational failures do not necessarily create the opportunity, but provide the circumstances within which the opportunity presents.[93]

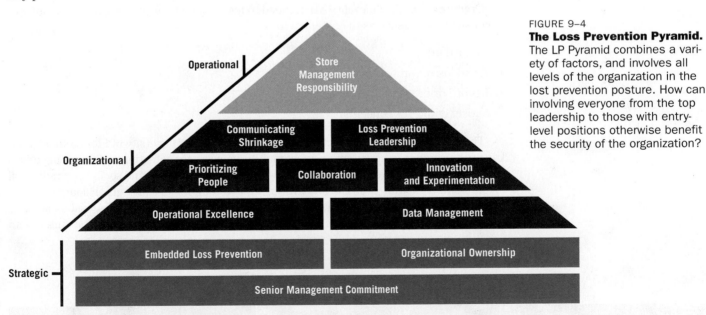

FIGURE 9–4
The Loss Prevention Pyramid.
The LP Pyramid combines a variety of factors, and involves all levels of the organization in the lost prevention posture. How can involving everyone from the top leadership to those with entry-level positions otherwise benefit the security of the organization?

Recognizing this threat, Beck and Peacock created the New Loss Prevention (NLP) approach, that brings together strategic, organizational and operational factors using what they call the Loss Prevention Pyramid. The NLP approach is purposefully conceived as a pyramid because all critical elements need to be in place for it to be sustainable.[94] Focused themes comprise each of the three levels, with commitment from senior management and empowered security professionals at the foundation, organizational communication and collaboration with a loss prevention focus throughout the organization in the middle, and store management responsibility for balancing sales and security at the top.

The foundation of the Loss Prevention Pyramid is the ability to create, sustain, and embed awareness of, and commitment to, correcting the problem of shrinkage throughout the organization. It is important to ensure that all members of the organization take ownership of the problem. Security professionals become the agents of change, implementing and overseeing a cross-company response to shrinkage. This commitment should be embedded within the business practices, policies, procedures, and strategic thinking of the organization.[95]

The factors in the core of the Loss Prevention Pyramid relate to the organizational framework. The loss prevention department can influence business functions by ensuring strong loss prevention leadership, using high-quality data and data management systems, and identifying and minimizing operational failures.[96] Wherever possible, the right people should be in the roles for which they are best suited, and innovation and experimentation should be prioritized, while ensuring that effective solutions to retail shrinkage are communicated to everyone in the organization.

Operationalizing retail shrinkage at the top of the pyramid is the responsibility of store management.[97] Managers must have access to the necessary resources and expertise to manage shrinkage effectively in a retail environment in which shopper satisfaction is paramount. With these strategies, organization employees will be more able to achieve an appropriate balance between selling and security.[98]

Technology

Many companies realize the need for security and have embraced an appreciation of, and commitment to, innovation and experimentation, including the use of new technology.[99] Many businesses have increased the use of alarms, target hardening, and video surveillance systems to counter commercial burglary.[100] Loss prevention professionals can better identify problem employees with video surveillance systems. Such systems can also improve performance of honest employees and have a dramatic effect on the profitability of an organization.[101]

Organizations should evaluate their need to increase technology use based on a number of considerations, such as the potential to

- Deter theft.
- Avoid loss of property.
- Record or prevent safety issues.
- Satisfy employee concerns.[102]

The Loss Prevention Research Council (LPRC) and the University of Florida Innovation Lab are working to enhance and connect multiple sensors for detecting and thwarting criminal activity at many levels, including reviews of offender databases and social and traditional media combined with coordination with local law enforcement and other sources in the community. Indicators gleaned from person-to-person communication, as well as actively selling items online or at the flea market, pawnshop, or another fencing opportunities, can assist in this endeavor.[103]

Spotlight
LERPnet2.0 - The Law Enforcement Retail Partnership Network

LERPnet2.0 provides a secure and confidential platform for retailers to report, share, and analyze their data, regarding both retail theft and critical incident, with each other and with law enforcement. Additionally, retailers have access to tools such as automated alerts and recent activity notifications; intelligent link-analysis; investigation collaboration tools; full text search capability; and advanced system reporting. This should help retailers and law enforcement to combat a variety of illegal activities, including organized retail crime, burglaries, robberies, counterfeiting, and online auction fraud.

LERPnet2.0, "The Law Enforcement Retail Partnership Network," 2015, http://www.lerpnet2.com

Automatic license plate readers assist parking lot patrols, while facial recognition, metal detection, RFID and EAS tag sensors, and smartphone signatures, can alert security professionals of a potential shoplifting. Video analytics, special CCTV applications, digital beacons, and human sources help security professionals track problematic people and shoppers in high-risk locations and hot products display and storage areas, hidden spots, stockrooms, restrooms, and cash offices. Each of these individual strategies can help security professionals gather intelligence. Combining them provides a viable storewide loss prevention strategy.

Technology is multipurpose and provides many unforeseen benefits. By helping document injuries, for example, it can help invalidate fraudulent workers' compensation claims, which may cover the cost of the technology alone. Additionally, as fewer companies authorize the apprehension of a violator outside of the retail establishment, recording movement for later identification is increasingly important. Moreover, the peace of mind brought about by satisfying employee concerns like deterring workplace violence and harassment is invaluable. Now we will discuss some of the most useful technological methods available today.

Video Surveillance

Following a basic risk analysis, many retail organizations are likely to install some form of video surveillance system. The effectiveness of such a device usually depends on its quality, which is often reflected in the unit's cost. An employee must view recordings to determine what evidence it contains. This process is simplified with a product such as BriefCam, which Longmore-Etheridge related provides software that allows users to pull recorded footage by specific dates and times; it then uses video-analytic software to compress the footage into a radically shortened synopsis.[104] An hour of footage can be viewed in an average of one minute. Hence, the return on investment can be realized in as little as six months.[105]

Radio-frequency identification (RFID) tags are used to enhance security and surveillance for retail organizations. RFID tags are wireless, no-contact tracking labels attached to objects. The tags use radio-frequency electromagnetic fields to transfer data and contain electronically stored information.[106] Figure 9–5 depicts the RFID process.

The two basic types of RFID tags according to Piazza are passive and active. Passive RFID tags have no power source. They are activated by energy that emanates from a reader, and once activated can transmit a small amount of data to the reader. The distance from which a reader can read passive tags is about 18 inches. These tags are used on pallets and cases of products, and occasionally on items themselves, particularly high-value and frequently shoplifted goods. They are also used in commuter passes and access-control badges. Passive tags are inexpensive, costing less than a quarter and are likely to drop to about a nickel per tag.[107]

radio-frequency identification (RFID) tags
Wireless, no-contact tracking labels attached to objects. The tags use radio-frequency electromagnetic fields to transfer data and contain electronically stored information.

Spotlight
Facial Recognition is a Game-Changer for Retailers

Retailers with facial-recognition systems can easily identify known shoplifters. Within seconds of a person walking in the store, the surveillance system determines their status and alerts a security professional or designated employee. The data provided by such a solution showed one retailer that 26 percent of the people they detained returned to the store within less than two weeks. The system works by capturing a person's image from the store security cameras, then comparing it against photos in the store's offender database.

Once alerted, the security professional can approach the offender and advise them that they are barred from the premises and ask them to leave. The original photo of the shoplifter is used to verify that the person who walked in the store is the same person as the one in the database. This technology promises to significantly limit the time spent watching suspected shoplifters: Thereafter, instead of an estimated 20 minutes of surveillance, it will now take 5 minutes or less to identify and warn a repeat offender.

C. Trlica, "Security Cameras with Facial Recognition: A Game-Changing Technology for Retailers," November 13, 2015, http://losspreventionmedia.com/insider/retail-security/facial-recognition-a-game-changing-technology-for-retailers/

According to Piazza, active tags use a small battery or similar power source to transmit a continuous signal that can be picked up by a reader. They are more expensive ($20 or more each) and much more powerful than passive tags, and they can be read from hundreds of feet away. These tags are used in applications such as EZ Pass automated toll collection cards or cargo transit systems that require long-range read capability.[108]

FIGURE 9–5
How RFID Tag Technology Works

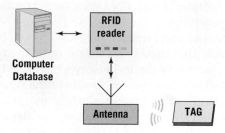

Emerging Forms of Theft

The cyber age presents new problems for security personnel and creates the need for innovative methods to achieve loss prevention in the cyber world. Although organizations using the online business model may experience fewer incidents of shoplifting, they may still suffer from employee theft. If their distribution centers or warehouses are burglarized or their shipments are intercepted, they may find their stolen merchandise being fenced on Internet sites such as Amazon, eBay, and Craigslist.[109] The move of retail to the online realm has brought additional technological challenges. The Retail Fraud Survey suggests that credit cards, used universally by retailers online, account for 83% of all online fraud.[110]

Another dilemma is produced by the replacement of cash money with e-money. The National Association of Convenience Stores reported that credit card skimming has become epidemic.[111] Skimming devices are card readers installed on ATMs, gas pumps, and other credit and debit card readers to steal (or skim) the card information. Another device is a small video camera placed above ATM card readers that records people entering their PIN numbers. They are often difficult to spot by an unassuming person who briefly stops at an ATM or a gas pump. The data can be transmitted to someone nearby via a Bluetooth wireless connection, but most of the time, the thieves return to the site to retrieve the information from the device. Purvis advised if a retail security professional finds a skimmer, they shouldn't remove it and should immediately contact law enforcement.[112]

Payments with debit and credit cards have recently become more secure. Beginning October 1, 2015, credit and debit cards in the United States issued by banks or credit unions were equipped with a chip to replace their existing cards that used outdated magnetic-stripe cards, using technology from the 1960s that was a source of most U.S. data breaches. The new chip cards generate a unique transaction code every time the card is used and help protect data.

Combined with a PIN number, the chipped cards have significantly reduced incidents of fraud in Canada and Europe.[113] But banks in the United States are only issuing chip and signature cards, a less secure standard, as signatures can easily be forged. The Federal Reserve reported that using a PIN makes a transaction up to 700% more secure. A senior executive at MasterCard explained that many consumers find it difficult to remember a four-digit PIN number.[114]

In addition to preventing theft, both in the physical and cyber world, loss prevention and retail security professionals must also prepare for other problems and issues that threaten retail establishments. Some of the most important are discussed below.

THINK ABOUT IT

In addition to those identified in this chapter, what kind of technology advancements could prevent the crimes that are discussed in this chapter? What advancements can you imagine?

Accident Prevention

An effective accident prevention program in retail organizations requires proper job performance from everyone in the workplace.[115] Nobody wants accidents to happen in their organization. A workplace fire, injury, or death can cause not only the loss of profit, but also a permanent blemish on a company's reputation. Good business sense and recognized prevention principles will help.[116]

An accident always has a cause, and if you can determine why it happened, it is possible to prevent future accidents, according to the U.S. Occupational Safety and Health Administration (OSHA).[117] It is important to develop a plan to enhance workplace safety.[118] The safety plan should address the types of workplace accidents and health hazard exposures that could happen. Because each workplace is different, the program should also address the organization's specific needs and requirements.[119] Each employee needs to know that

- No employee is expected to undertake a job until he or she has received job instructions on how to do it properly and is authorized to perform that job.

- No employee should undertake a job that appears unsafe.

You may be able to combine safety and health training with other training, depending on the types of hazards in your workplace.[120] Here are some actions to consider according to OSHA:

- Ask your state OSHA consultant to recommend training for your worksite. The consultant may be able to conduct training while he or she is there.

- Make sure employees are trained on every potential hazard and how to protect themselves. Then verify that they really understand what you taught them.

- Pay particular attention to new employees and to employees who are moving to new jobs. Because they are learning new operations, they are more likely to get hurt.

- Train supervisors to understand all the hazards faced by employees and how to reinforce training with quick reminders and refreshers, or with disciplinary action if needed.

- Make sure that top management staff understands their responsibilities and how to hold subordinate supervisory employees accountable for theirs. All employees should be given frequent accident prevention instructions.[121]

Vandalism, Burglary, and Robbery

In addition to thefts, retail organizations are frequently victimized by vandalism, burglary, and robbery. To be responsive to the organization's needs, security professionals must be aware of and prepared to respond to these threats.

Vandalism

Vandalism is any deliberate act that damages or defaces property. Common vandalism targets for retailers include store lights, signs or windows, and placing graffiti on walls or other surfaces.[122] Repairing vandalism in New South Wales costs businesses millions of dollars each year and most end up passing on such costs to their customers through higher prices.[123] Vandalism can be reduced in the following ways:

vandalism
Any deliberate act that damages or defaces property. Common vandalism targets for retailers include store lights, signs or windows, and placing graffiti on walls or other surfaces.

- Make sure the store and the surrounding area are well lit. This may increase the likelihood of detection, deterring vandals if located in a well-traveled area.

- Use toughened glass, open-style grilles or shutters on the windows to prove protection from breakage to the store windows.

- Repair or restore vandalized items and remove graffiti as soon as possible. Coordinate with law enforcement before doing so, as they may request the vandalism or graffiti be photographed to help determine the identity of the vandals. Property that is not maintained can invite further vandalism.

- Reduce access to the property. Use high open-style fences and lock gates to deter vandals. Ensure the fences are not easy to climb on or over.

- Report all illegal acts to the police.[124]

POLICE SERVICE of NORTHERN IRELAND
MOUNTPOTTINGER

▲ Graffiti artist paints CCTV camera. Graffiti "artists" who paint on the property of others without permission are vandals, no matter the quality of their "art." Many vandals attempt to thwart detection by disabling security cameras or otherwise concealing their activity. How can such vandalism be reduced?

Source: FotoSearch http://www .fotosearch.com/UNS044/u17256483/

Graffiti

Graffiti is the most common form of vandalism on business properties. The presence of *graffiti* indicates the absence of both formal and informal social control and symbolizes the dangers of urban life.[125] It is important to document its presence and the circumstance thereof, as it is used for more than just vandalism prosecution. Researchers use the presence of gang graffiti to determine the extent of an individual's fear of crime.[126]   Law enforcement officials may also use graffiti to gather intelligence on local criminal organizations. Padilla found that gang graffiti may contain the monikers of individual gang members, the symbols of the responsible or rival gang, or other alphanumeric communication.[127]   Security professionals can implement these strategies to reduce its impact:

- Improve the lighting throughout the area both during and after business hours.
- Install fencing that won't attract graffiti.
- Plant vegetation in front of walls/fences to obstruct the view of any graffiti painted there.
- Paint walls/fences with dark colors and consider paint that repels graffiti in high-risk areas.
- Paint over graffiti using the same color as the paint on the wall.[128]

Burglary

Burglary is generally defined as entering a property without permission in order to steal something. Various jurisdictions add specific requirements or additions, such as:

- Forcible entry
- Forcing a locking device without damaging it (lock picking)
- Entering through an open door or window
- Using trickery to enter with permission[129]

Burglaries are the most common and most costly crimes affecting businesses, according to Mawby.[130] Businesses are targeted for commercial burglaries based on three criteria:

- Attractiveness
- Accessibility
- Surveillance

The attractiveness of the target is considered based on what is available for stealing and how easy it can be resold.[131] The more difficulty the burglar would have in stealing the property, the higher the discount they would need to offer for resale. Accessibility relates to the level of difficulty to access the property.[132] If a level of target hardening has been emplaced, the burglar may be deterred. Alarms with identifying signage, floor-deposit safes, and bulletproof glass are examples of this strategy. Surveillance addresses the likelihood of the burglar being seen during the act.[133] Formal or natural surveillance measures limit the potential for anonymity and are likely to thwart the plans of most burglars.

Business Watch

In some areas, businesses collaborate to form a crime prevention venture intended to protect themselves and neighboring businesses from commercial burglary and related crimes.[134] The program known as Business Watch involves businesses and community groups taking steps to reduce opportunities for crimes in and around business locations. According to the U.S. National Crime Prevention Council, the strategy includes crime prevention police officers and business leaders who assist business owners, operators, and employees in reporting crime; observing activities that could lead to crime; implementing operation identification (marking equipment with traceable identification numbers); robbery and burglary prevention; and self-protection.[135] One or more police officers are usually assigned to be the liaison with the Business Watch group. Sometimes the businesses arc linked to each other and to the police through email, phone, or radio message trees.[136]

Robbery

Robbery is the act of stealing or taking anything of value by force, violence, or threat of force or violence. Although the incidence of robberies is relatively low, the victims of robberies may often suffer actual physical harm or psychological distress.[137] Retail stores that handle or keep large amounts of cash and locations that are open twenty-four hours per day are likely to be vulnerable to robberies. Some stores are more at risk than others; this may be dependent upon whether the business:

robbery
The act of using force, violence, or threat of force or violence to steal. Victims of robberies may suffer actual physical harm or psychological distress; they are put in fear.

- Is open during nighttime hours.
- Is in a high-risk or remote area.
- Keeps cash on the premises.[138]

Strategies to reduce losses from robbery in retail stores include the following:

- Form a neighborhood business watch system with nearby retailers, alerting each other of suspicious activity.
- Limit the amount of cash in the store and regularly clear out registers.
- Improve the lighting within your store.
- Design the flow of the store to make it harder for robbers.
- Install deadlocks on doors and fit alarm systems.
- Reduce opportunities for physical contact with staff, for example, by installing security screens.
- Install coded locks to restrict public access to staff areas.
- Fit electronic sensors that emit a sound when customers enter or leave.[139]

In addition to financial losses, organizations have additional incentives to protect their location and employees from robberies. Retailers owe a general duty of care or legal obligation to their employees to ensure the health, safety, and welfare at work of all employees and others who come into the store.[140] OSHA frequently considers the employer responsible for employee deaths and injuries during robberies of the establishment.[141] OSHA's *general duty* clause requires employers to provide a workplace free from recognized hazards likely to cause serious injury or death. The agency's decision is often based on the premise that "handling money, working alone and standing behind open counters leaves employees vulnerable to violent crimes. According to OSHA, a serious violation occurs when there is substantial probability that death or serious physical harm could result from a hazard about which the employer knew or should have known."[142]

Name: Ami Toben

Position: Director of Consulting and Training

Year hired: 2004

City, State where you are based: Oakland, California

College(s) attended (degree): UC Berkeley

Majors: Japanese language and culture

Please give a brief description of your job: Directing both internal and external consulting and training activities, in addition to being an acting account manager for various clients.

What qualities/characteristics are most helpful for this job? Customer service, problem-solving abilities, understanding of security programs and how to convey them properly to nonsecurity personnel.

What is a typical starting salary? No such thing.

What is the salary potential as you move up into higher-level jobs? There's no standard, but it ranges into six-figure territory.

What advice would you give someone in college beginning studies in security? Get in on the ground level—get some experience in everything from security shift work, to special event security, to security systems. Try to get as much training as you can, and work on increasing your network. Stay open-minded and flexible, and most importantly, learn how to give excellent customer service.

What appealed to you most about the position when you applied for it? Flexibility, the ability to work in different environments, the ability to experience all aspects of security—from client relations to vendor operations.

How would you suggest interested applicants gain experience? Get as much experience in as many different security fields, get some solid training, and expand your network.

Would you recommend military experience? Absolutely.

Does holding a full-time job during college help applicants get hired afterwards? I think so.

Summary

- **Define and distinguish retail security and loss prevention.**
  - Retail security generally describes the process of reducing theft and shrinkage in a retail organization, or the process by which goods are sold to the public in a secure fashion for both the consumer and store proprietor, preventing theft or harm.
  - Loss prevention is any method used by individuals or organizations to increase the likelihood of preventing and controlling loss from adverse occurrences. The various methods include security officers, safety measures, and audits. Loss refers to loss of people, money, productivity, or materials. The adverse occurrences might be crime, fire, accident, natural disaster, error, bad investment, or poor managerial decision.

Identify indicators of shoplifting.
  - Retail security professionals should be leery of shoppers who:
    - Spend more time watching the cashier or salesperson than shopping.
    - Wear bulky, heavy clothing during warm weather or coats when unnecessary.
    - Walk with unnatural steps, which may indicate that they are concealing stolen items.
    - Take several items into a dressing room and leave with only one (or no) item visible.
    - Look for staff instead of examining merchandise.
    - Seem nervous and may pick up random items with no interest.
    - Frequently enter the store and never make a purchase.

Define organized retail crime.
  - Organized retail crime is the activity of theft or fraud conducted with the intent to convert illegally obtained merchandise, cargo, cash, or a cash equivalent into financial gain (not personal use) where or when the theft/fraud is multiples of items, over multiple occurrences, and/or in multiple stores, and/or in multiple jurisdictions, by two or more persons, or an individual acting in dual roles.

- **Identify ways an organization's leadership can discourage employee theft.**
  - ○ Organizational leadership can take steps toward preventing employee theft, including:
    - *Create a positive work environment*: This encourages employees to follow established policies and procedures, and act in the best interests of the business.
    - *Implement internal controls*: These measures are designed to ensure the effectiveness and efficiencies of operations, compliance with laws and regulations, safeguarding of assets, and accurate financial reporting. These controls require policies and procedures addressing separation of duties, access controls, and authorization controls.
    - *Restrict personal belongings*: Petty theft and misunderstandings can be significantly reduced if your store employment policy restricts staff from taking personal items, such as bags, wallets, and money onto the shop selling floor.
    - *Recruitment checks*: Dishonest employees will search for ways to defeat internal controls. Preemployment background checks may help limit the hiring of dishonest employees.
    - *Educate your employees*: Inform employees about your policies and procedures and provide training on what behavior is considered fraudulent and criminal.
    - *Aim at the target*: Monitoring and prevention measures should be centered on items that are the most expensive and easiest to steal. The most important item a company should direct its focus on is cash, its most liquid asset.
    - *Implement an anonymous reporting system*: Provide a confidential reporting system for employees, vendors, and customers to report any violations of policies and procedures.
    - *Perform audits*: Every retailer should conduct regular audits and also conduct random, unannounced financial audits and fraud assessments.
    - *Keep a watchful eye*: No prevention step can be truly effective if it is not frequently checked and observed for flaws.
    - *Investigate every incident*: A thorough and prompt investigation of policy and procedure violations, allegations of fraud, or warning signs of fraud will provide the facts you need to make informed decisions and reduce losses.
    - *Staff sign-in*: Ensure all employees sign in and out when they start and finish work to help identify who is in the building and the hours they worked.
    - *Lead by example*: Senior management and business owners set the example for the business's employees. A relaxed approach to rules and regulations will be reflected in the attitude of employees.

KEY TERMS

asset protection   **182**

building a bank (in the register)   **194**

criminal flash mobs   **192**

fraudulent disbursements   **193**

larceny   **193**

loss prevention   **181**

offender profiling   **187**

organized retail crime   **189**

radio-frequency identification (RFID) tags   **197**

refund fraud   **194**

retail security   **181**

retail shrinkage   **182**

robbery   **201**

self-checkout fraud   **193**

shoplifting   **184**

skimming   **193**

sweet-hearting   **193**

vandalism   **199**

REVIEW QUESTIONS

1. What are some of the issues surrounding the use of the term *loss prevention*?
2. How much merchandise is the average shoplifter caught with?
3. What percentage of retailers report that they have been the victim of organized retail crime?
4. What can be done to prevent employee theft?

PRACTICAL APPLICATION

1. Using the Internet search engine of your choice, identify three retail organizations in the Fortune 500. Locate and examine their websites and identify any references to their policy and practice of retail security. Compare and contrast your findings.
2. Visit three retail businesses in your area. One should be a small business, one a medium business, and one large (according to your personal estimation). Identify indicators of the retail security environment, drawing conclusions without making contact with employees.
3. Visit a retail security and loss prevention employment-assistance website such as LPJobs .com. Search for loss prevention security positions in your geographic area, and analyze the job descriptions to find separate tasks. Identify those tasks that come naturally to people you know and those that require special training.
4. Search a social media site like LinkedIn.com, Twitter.com, or Facebook.com using keywords related to the topics in this chapter. Evaluate the prevalence of several keyword combinations and identify usage patterns.

Homeland Security and the Terrorism Threat

Learning Objectives

After reading this chapter, you should be able to:

1. Identify the five core homeland security concepts. **209**

2. Examine the roles of private security professionals regarding homeland security. **211**

3. Determine the best definition for terrorism, international terrorism, and domestic terrorism. **215**

4. Distinguish homegrown violent extremists from domestic terrorists. **216**

5. Demonstrate understanding of the four major activities of terrorist groups. **224**

Introduction

Though there have been numerous terror attacks on American soil, five stand out:

- On February 26, 1993, a bomb was planted in the underground parking garage of the North Tower of the World Trade Center in the heart of New York City. The plan was for the bomb to collapse the North Tower or topple it into the South Tower, knocking it down, as well. Although the plan did not succeed, the explosion resulted in the deaths of six people and injuries to 1,042.

- On April 19, 1995, a vehicle bomb set off in front of the Alfred P. Murrah Federal Building in Oklahoma City, Oklahoma, killed 168 people and injured 674 more. Although most citizens were appalled by the act, it did not have a lasting impact on American perceptions of safety or on the political landscape, because it was viewed as an anomaly or common crime committed by Americans. Timothy McVeigh was captured shortly after the attack, and his accomplice, Terry Nichols, was arrested shortly thereafter. No indications of widespread or recurring threat were detected.

- On September 11, 2001 (9/11), terrorists directed by Osama Bin Laden commandeered four commercial passenger jets and flew two of them into the North and South towers of the World Trade Center in New York City. The third hit the Pentagon, the headquarters of the U.S. Department of Defense in Arlington, Virginia. The fourth jet, thought to be headed for the U.S. Capitol Building in Washington, D.C., crashed into a field near Shanksville, Pennsylvania, after passengers physically confronted the hijackers. Nearly 3,000 people died in the coordinated attacks, including all nineteen hijackers aboard the four jets.

- On April 15, 2013, at 2:49 p.m., an improvised explosive device (IED) detonated nearby as runners crossed the finish line of the Boston Marathon, a challenging and well-known 26.2 mile course. A second explosion twelve seconds later also sprayed nails, ball bearings, and metal shards into the nearby crowds.[1] Because the explosions occurred near the finish line, where a few thousand spectators were tightly packed, the effects of the blast were devastating: three people died and more than 260 others needed hospital care, having suffered horrific wounds.[2] Using surveillance tapes, the FBI released photographs to the media of the suspects three days later. Fearing they would be identified, the bombers, brothers Dzhokhar and Tamerlan Tsarnaev, then drove to the nearby campus of the Massachusetts Institute of Technology (MIT), where they shot and killed police officer Sean Collier and attempted to steal his gun. They then carjacked a vehicle and drove to Watertown, Massachusetts, where a shootout occurred when city police officers identified the pair. Tamerlan was killed while his brother escaped and was later apprehended hiding in a dry-docked boat in a Watertown backyard. Dzhokhar and Tamerlan Tsarnaev were identified as lone-wolf terrorists, not connected with a specific terrorist group.

- On December 2, 2015, Syed Rizwan Farook and Tashfeen Malik, a married couple, killed fourteen people and injured twenty-two in an attack at the Inland Regional Center in San Bernardino, California. Farook and Malik, who lived in Redlands, CA targeted Farooks' employer, San Bernardino County, CA, during a training event and Christmas holiday party that Farook had attended prior to the shootings. Farook was an American-born U.S. citizen of Pakistani descent, and Malik was a Pakistani-born legal resident of the U.S. Farook and Malik pledged allegiance to the leader of the Islamic State of Iraq and the Levant (ISIL). President Barack Obama called the shooting an act of terrorism, and FBI Director James Comey said that the perpetrators were home-grown violent extremists, but they were not part of a terrorist cell or network.[3]

Each of these attacks had an unprecedented influence on the American public, and in so doing illustrate the varied extent of terrorism. Two attacks were clearly the product of foreign terror groups, while so-called lone wolves who were apparently not part of any group or organization carried the others out. Tim McVeigh and Terry Nichols were native born, while the Tsarnaev brothers and Farook and Malik had immigrated to the U.S. from abroad. The attacks in Boston and San Bernadino although horrific in their own right, were neither as devastating in terms of lives lost and property destroyed as the attacks of 9/11, nor were they as unprecedented as the attack in Oklahoma City. Nonetheless, both caused many Americans to reevaluate how they defined and responded to acts of terrorism. Even the classification of the attacks were a challenge. Whereas some experts called them acts of domestic terrorism, others identified to them as an act of international terrorism: the confusion was owing to the fact that these two independent yet interrelated concepts often share some of the same indicators and characteristics. By the time of the Boston bombing, media coverage had made even the most complacent American aware of the threat of terrorism on the homeland and abroad. Even today, we are bombarded with daily stories of people hiding explosives in their shoes, underwear, and cell phones. Stories from abroad have made the terrorist groups Boko Haram and Islamic State household terms. Many people feel that no place is totally safe, and we no longer believe that terrorist attacks can't happen here. These attacks became a heated issue in the 2016 presidential campaign when candidates such as Donald Trump suggested that Muslims be banned from entering into the United States or that they be listed on a national data base, forgetting that one of the most devastating attacks on American soil was carried out by Timothy McVeigh an ex-GI, born in New York State.

This chapter is focused on the general topic of homeland security, with a special focus on the terrorist threat. Other topics in this text, namely critical infrastructure, information security, and emergency practices and crisis-disaster management, are directly related to homeland security. A working knowledge of terror and homeland security is essential for those involved in the security industry. Recent surveys show that counterterrorism is one of the eighteen core elements of security identified by security professionals.[4] The threat of terrorism, specifically regarding crisis management and response, along with bombings and bomb threats were among the top twenty greatest security concerns facing Fortune 1000 companies in 2012.[5] This chapter delves into the foundational issues of homeland security and the threat of terrorism applicable to security professionals. Given the diversity and fluidity of the terrorism landscape, the chapter is intentionally limited to those topics deemed to have relevance to the contemporary security industry.

Defining Homeland Security

Eleven days after the 9/11 terrorist attacks, the Office of Homeland Security was formed in the White House. The office, initially headed by former Pennsylvania governor Tom Ridge, oversaw and coordinated a comprehensive national strategy to safeguard the country against terrorism and respond to any future attacks. Congress formally created the Department of Homeland Security with the passage of the Homeland Security Act in November 2002, and the newly formed department formally launched on March 1, 2003.

On October 26, 2001, President G. W. Bush signed into law the *Uniting and Strengthening America by Providing Appropriate Tools Required to Intercept and Obstruct Terrorism (USA PATRIOT) Act*, commonly known as the Patriot Act. The act was intended to significantly reduce restrictions on the way law enforcement agencies gathered intelligence within the United States. The act also expanded the U.S. Secretary of the Treasury's authority to regulate financial transactions involving foreign individuals and entities. It significantly broadened the ability that law enforcement has to exercise discretion when detaining and deporting noncitizens suspected of terrorism-related acts. The definitions of *terrorism* and *domestic terrorism* were also expanded. On May 26, 2011, President Barack Obama signed a four-year extension of three key provisions of the Patriot Act: roving wiretaps, searches of business records, and conducting surveillance of individuals suspected of terrorist-related activities that were not linked to terrorist groups.

Although the Patriot Act provides a legal context for homeland security, there are additional viewpoints on homeland security that need to be considered. For example, the U.S. Department of Homeland Security, defines **homeland security** as "a concerted national effort

homeland security
A concerted national effort to protect the nation and ensure that it is safe, secure, and resilient against terrorism and other hazards.

to ensure a homeland that is safe, secure, and resilient against terrorism and other hazards where American interests, aspirations, and ways of life can thrive."[6]

While this definition is quite broad, Bellavita found there are a number of subcategories within this encompassing definition that should also be considered as an important part of the equation:

- *Terrorism*: Homeland security is a concerted countrywide effort by federal, state, and local governments, the private sector, and individuals to prevent terrorist attacks within the nation, to reduce America's vulnerability to terrorism, and to minimize the damage and recover from attacks that do occur.

- *All hazards*: Homeland security is a concerted national effort to prevent and disrupt terrorist attacks, protect against human-created and natural dangers, and respond to and recover from incidents that do occur.

- *Terrorism and catastrophes*: Homeland security is what the U.S. Department of Homeland Security, supported by other federal agencies, does to prevent, respond to, and recover from terrorist and catastrophic events that affect the security of the United States.

- *Jurisdictional hazards*: Homeland security means something different in each jurisdiction. It is a locally directed effort to prevent and prepare for incidents most likely to threaten the safety and security of its citizens.

- *Meta hazards*: Homeland security is a countrywide effort to prevent or lessen any social trend or threat that can disrupt the long-term stability of the American way of life.

- *National security*: Homeland security is an element of national security that works with the other instruments of national power to protect the sovereignty, territory, domestic population, and critical infrastructure of the nation against threats and aggression.[7]

Considering this broad mandate, Homeland Security practitioners typically place their focus on what are seen as the activities with the most destructive consequences should they be ignored or unattended. Consequently, activities that take priority include preventing terrorism; managing critical infrastructure risks; securing and managing the borders; enforcing and administering immigration laws; safeguarding and securing cyberspace; and ensuring resilience to disasters.[8] When Bellavita asked what homeland security means to them (see Figure 10–1), more (40%) security professionals gave a definition that either blended elements of other definitions, or did not define the term.[9]

THINK ABOUT IT

What do you think of when you hear the term *homeland security*? At what level of government is the primary responsibility?

FIGURE 10–1
What Does Homeland Security Mean to You? Definitions From Fifty Practitioners.
Source: C. Bellavita, "Changing Homeland Security: What is Homeland Security?" *Homeland Security Affairs*, Vol. 4, No. 2, (2008). pp. 1–30.

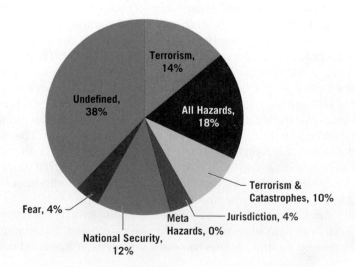

The Goals of Homeland Security

According to the Quadrennial Homeland Security Reviewers, a group of department leaders including the secretaries of Homeland Security, the Attorney General, the Secretary of State, the Secretary of Defense, the Secretary of Health and Human Services, the Secretary of the Treasury, the Secretary of Agriculture, and the Director of National Intelligence, several assumptions are made concerning the security environment in the United States and the challenges it faces in the future. They are as follows:

- Violent extremist groups, including potential homegrown extremists, will continue to use terrorism to attack U.S. targets.
- Technologies associated with weapons of mass destruction (WMD), often dual-use, will circulate easily in a globalized economy, challenging traditional WMD nonproliferation and counter-proliferation efforts, especially in the nuclear and biological areas.
- Terrorists, proliferators, and other criminal elements will seek to take advantage of the increasingly globalized financial system and its legitimate and beneficial functions to move money in support of their dangerous conduct.
- Economic crises and disparities will continue to induce social and/or political instability, in some cases increasing migrant and refugee flows—legal and illegal—into the United States.
- Globalization will continue to make it increasingly difficult to prevent health threats to the United States, whether from emerging disease or deliberate attacks, or via imports.
- Technological change and cyber threats from state and nonstate actors will continue to alter social, economic, and political forces, allow for the rapid dissemination of information, and provide new means for adversaries to challenge the United States.
- Climate change will increase the severity and frequency of weather-related hazards such as extreme storms, high rainfalls, floods, droughts, and heat waves.
- The security environment will continue to pose the potential for multiple simultaneous crises.
- There is a danger of complacency as memory of major crises recede.[10]

Considering these challenges, the mission of homeland security professionals ranges from preventing terrorist attacks to controlling immigration and managing cyberspace.

Who has jurisdiction over carrying out this mission? While the Department of Homeland Security takes the lead, other agencies of local, state, federal, tribal, and territorial governments, the private sector, and other nongovernmental organizations are involved in carrying out the mission of homeland security. The professionals involved must have a clear sense of what it takes to achieve the overall vision and know that strengthening the homeland security enterprise is critical for the security of all Americans and for the growth of the U.S. economy.

Practicing Homeland Security

Although the term *homeland security* often evokes thoughts of terrorism, the *practice* of homeland security is much broader, controlled and shaped by three main concepts: security, resilience, and customs and exchange.[11] Security entails protecting the country and its people, vital interests, and way of life. Resilience is the concept that fosters individual, community, and system robustness; adaptability; and capacity for rapid recovery. Customs and exchange are the components that expedite and enforce lawful trade, travel, and immigration.[12] These key concepts control areas of activity that define the homeland security mission:

1 Identify the five core homeland security concepts.

1. Prevent
2. Protect
3. Respond

4. Recover

5. Ensure resilience

6. Facilitate customs and exchange[13]

Said another way, all activities related to homeland security must be built upon a foundation of ensuring both security and resilience, as well as facilitating the normal, daily activities of society and interchange of a community, country, or similar entity with the rest of the world.[14] Within this framework, homeland security spans the authorities and responsibilities of federal departments and agencies, most of which are set out in Figure 10–2.

FIGURE 10–2
Federal (U.S.) Agencies Engaged in Homeland Security
Source: Adapted from Quadrennial Homeland Security Review Report, "A Strategic Framework for a Secure Homeland," 2010, http://www.dhs.gov/xlibrary/assets/qhsr_report.pdf

Federal agencies and organizations in the United States that engage in some aspect of the homeland security mission include:

- *The Executive Branch*. The president, through the National Security and Homeland Security councils and the National Security staff, provides overall homeland security policy direction and coordination.
- *The Department of Homeland Security*. DHS prevents terrorism and manages risks to critical infrastructure; secures and manages the border; enforces and administers immigration laws; safeguards and secures cyberspace; and ensures resilience to disasters.
- *The Department of Justice*. DOJ conducts criminal investigations of terrorist acts or threats inside the country, or directed at U.S. citizens or institutions abroad, and related intelligence collection activities within the United States.
- *The Department of State*. The State Department coordinates activities with foreign governments and international organizations related to the prevention, preparation, response, and recovery from a domestic incident, and for the protection of U.S. citizens and U.S. interests overseas.
- *The Department of Defense*. The DoD defends the country from direct attack; deters potential adversaries; fosters regional stability; secures and assures access to sea, air, space, and cyberspace; builds the security capacity of key partners; and supports civil authorities when the capabilities of state and local authorities to respond effectively to an event are overwhelmed.
- *The Department of Health and Human Services*. This agency coordinates functions relevant to Public Health Emergency Preparedness and Disaster Medical Response, incorporating steady-state and incident-specific activities as described in the National Health Security Strategy.
- *The Department of the Treasury*. The Treasury Department safeguards the U.S. financial system, combats financial crimes, and cuts off financial support to terrorists, WMD proliferators, drug traffickers, and other national security threats.
- *The Department of Agriculture*. This federal agency provides leadership on food, agriculture, natural resources, rural development, and related issues based on sound public policy, the best available science, and efficient management.
- *The Director of National Intelligence*. The DNI, as the head of the U.S. intelligence community, composed of sixteen elements across the U.S. government, is the principal advisor to the president and National Security Council for intelligence matters relating to national security. It assesses threats to the homeland and informs planning, capability development, and operational activities of homeland security enterprise partners and stakeholders. The DNI oversees the National Counterterrorism Center (NCTC), National Counterproliferation Center, and National Counterintelligence Executive. NCTC serves as the primary U.S. government organization for analyzing and integrating all intelligence pertaining to terrorism and counterterrorism, and conducts strategic operational planning for integrated counterterrorism activities.
- *The Department of Commerce*. This agency promulgates federal information technology and cybersecurity standards; regulates export of security technologies; represents U.S. industry on international trade policy and commercial dataflow matters, security and privacy policies that apply to the Internet's domain name system; protects intellectual property; conducts cybersecurity research and development; and assures timely availability of industrial products, materials, and services to meet homeland security requirements.

- *The Department of Education*. This agency oversees federal discretionary grants and technical assistance to help schools plan for and respond to emergencies that disrupt teaching and learning.
- *The Department of Energy*. The DOE maintains stewardship of vital national security capabilities, from nuclear weapons to leading-edge research and development programs. The DOE provides a unifying structure for the integration of federal critical infrastructure and key resources protection efforts specifically for the energy sector.
- *The Environmental Protection Agency*. The EPA is charged with protecting human health and the environment. For certain incidents, the EPA is the coordinator and primary agency in response to an actual or potential discharge and/or uncontrolled release of oil or hazardous materials.
- *The Department of Housing and Urban Development*. HUD is the coordinator and primary agency for Long-Term Community Recovery, which provides a mechanism for coordinating federal support to state, tribal, regional, and local governments, nongovernmental organizations, and the private sector to enable community recovery from the long-term consequences of extraordinary disasters.
- *The Department of the Interior*. This federal agency develops policies and procedures for all types of hazards and emergencies that impact Federal lands, facilities, infrastructure, and resources; tribal lands; and insular areas.
- *The Department of Transportation*. The DOT collaborates with DHS on all matters relating to transportation security and transportation infrastructure protection and in regulating the transportation of hazardous materials by all modes (including pipelines).

Since most critical infrastructure is maintained by the private sector, private security professionals are expected to interface with homeland security professionals at all government levels. Documents such as the National Infrastructure Protection Plan (NIPP) and National Response Framework (NRF), as well as documents produced by the National Counterterrorism Center (NCTC), guide these interactions and spell out roles and responsibilities for various aspects of homeland security.[15] For example, the NRF defines the key principles that enable first responders, decision makers, and supporting entities to provide a unified national response to domestic incidents. In addition, the NCTC works with the private sector to integrate all elements of national power to counter and prevent violent extremism and address domestic radicalization. Where appropriate, the NCTC also supports and coordinates engagement with American communities where terrorists are recruiting.

Private Homeland Security

The private sector is heavily engaged in homeland security activities, so effective homeland security must include a plan for private security personnel to work directly with law enforcement, state and local leaders, community-based organizations, private sector and international partners. Since 9/11, the DHS has prioritized the preparedness of the private sector through programs such as the Private Sector Preparedness Accreditation and Certification Program (PS-Prep), Ready Business, the development and deployment of new technologies, and by incorporating the input of private-sector partners when developing new homeland security policies, programs, and initiatives.[16]

2 Examine the roles of private security professionals regarding homeland security.

Among the most important areas to which the private sector can contribute in supporting the homeland security mission are:

- Critical infrastructure and key resource (CIKR) owners and operators create protective programs and measures to ensure their systems and assets are secure from and resilient to cascading, disruptive impacts. This protection includes taking actions to mitigate the overall risk to CIKR assets, systems, networks, functions, or their interconnecting links.
- Major and multinational corporations operate in all sectors of trade and commerce and support the operation, security, and resilience of global logistics systems. These corporations support prudent business planning and operations, and contribute to developing

the ideas, science, and technology that underlie innovation in homeland security. During disasters, they often provide resources through public–private emergency plans/partnerships or mutual aid and assistance agreements, often in response to requests from government and nongovernmental-volunteer initiatives.

- Small businesses contribute to all aspects of homeland security and employ more than half of all private-sector workers. Small businesses also develop contingency plans and work with local planners to ensure that their plans are consistent with pertinent response procedures. Additionally, they conduct research and development, inspire new thinking, and serve as engines of innovation for development of new solutions to key challenges related to homeland security.[17]

Private/Public Cooperation

Because there is an overlap between the private and public sector in achieving the mission goals of homeland security, cooperation between the two sectors has become routine. Here are a few examples. Because there is a near-term response and recovery activities, Federal Emergency Management Agency (FEMA) has widely embraced public–private partnerships.[18] The response to Hurricane Katrina and the BP Deepwater Horizon oil spill show why FEMA has embraced these partnerships. Hurricane Katrina was a valuable (albeit expensive) lesson in what not to do. While FEMA received the majority of public blame for an inadequate response, systemic failures at all levels of government were responsible. With little hesitation, Walmart deployed trucks full of relief supplies to the area as volunteers arrived to help distribute them. When the BP oil spill happened, the public sector lacked the necessary equipment and technical expertise to stop the flow of oil from the Gulf floor. It became necessary, then, to work with the company regarded as responsible for the spill to respond to it, according to Busch and Givens.[19]

FEMA has made public–private partnerships a high priority. The agency leads a major national initiative to forge closer ties with the business community. FEMA's regional offices, in all fifty states and U.S. territories, each house a private-sector liaison officer.[20] The private sector has demonstrated its commitment to work with various local, state, federal, and nonprofit entities to respond to community needs. Busch and Givens have observed that FEMA's leadership team and its personnel in regional offices have cooperated in public–private sector partnerships that carry tremendous importance and have real-world impact in disaster response.[21]

Private security professionals also partner with the public sector in Port Security and Emergency Management.[22] The Customs Trade Partnership Against Terrorism (C-TPAT) is a government–business sector initiative that was created to enhance worldwide supply chain security.[23] As part of the C-TPAT program, firms are certified and enjoy a close working relationship with the U.S. Customs and Border Protection (CBP). In that capacity, they are able to obtain government risk assessments of their supply chain and can attend special government-sponsored supply chain security training sessions.[24] Busch and Givens observed that programs such as the C-TPAT are useful to homeland security and they provide a broad administrative framework for regular public–private sector coordination.[25]

The private sector also helps the public sector fill hiring needs. Although government agencies conduct individual background checks for security clearances, the process is quite slow, sometimes taking years to complete.[26] Because of the significant time lag effect between when an applicant is offered a position in a sensitive area and when that applicant is actually cleared for the position, Boyne found that private companies working in the homeland security realm are often able to clear and bring in their new employees faster and more efficiently than

▼ A TSA inspector looks out at the view during a vulnerability assessment done by the Army Corps of Engineers on the Mackinac Bridge in Michigan. Why might terrorists target a bridge?

Source: Wally Schroder/Department of Homeland Security.

the public sector.[27] These private-sector employees perform a number of traditional government functions, such as intelligence analysis, emergency planning, and critical infrastructure protection. Private companies can augment the total homeland security workforce faster than government acting alone, providing a solution to the need for more personnel in homeland security positions.[28]

International Homeland Security

The goals and objectives of providing homeland security cannot be effectively accomplished without international cooperation.[29] Kahan noted that in the United States, the DHS works closely with international partners, including major organizations and global businesses, to strengthen the security of the networks of global trade and travel. DHS has personnel stationed in more than seventy-five countries, the third-largest civilian footprint of any U.S. agency working overseas. These personnel work with their international counterparts to identify known or suspected terrorists and cyber threats, take down organized crime rings, and stop the proliferation of dangerous weapons. They interdict drugs and human smugglers. In addition to cooperating with U.S. authorities and allowing professionals to be stationed in their country, a number of nations have instituted homeland security efforts. Some of the most significant are described in the following sections.[30]

United Kingdom

The United Kingdom uses a more legalistic approach to homeland security. The Terrorism Act of 2000 was the watershed U.K. legislation, criminalizing a range of activities such as financing terrorism and belonging to or supporting a terrorist organization. The Anti-Terrorism, Crime and Security Act of 2001 (ATCSA) authorized indefinite detention of terrorism suspects. Similar to the U.S. government, the British government retains the undisputed power to maintain lists of designated terrorist groups, both those seen as foreign threats and those considered only domestic. O'Connor observed that to carry out its homeland security mission, the British government deployed numerous closed circuit television (CCTV) surveillance cameras, and the police and courts regularly rely on and use video evidence.

Authorities use biometrics (facial recognition software) to identify suspects in crowds. They also rely on informants, although they do not provide as many rewards and/or witness protection services as the United States does.[31] Among the government agencies deployed to fight terrorism around the world, the MI5 (Security Service) and MI6 (Secret Intelligence Service) are arguably among the most well known.

France

France relies heavily on human intelligence to uproot terrorist networks within the context of wide criminal dragnets. France has extensive experience with counterinsurgency, counter-resistance movements, assassination prevention, and using attractive men and women to lure suspects into revealing secrets (honey traps), according to O'Connor.[32]

The most highly intrusive powers for ensuring homeland security are granted to the Direction de la Surveillance du Territoire (DST), the country's primary internal security service, and its counterterrorist investigative magistrates. The military (part of the Ministry of Defense) and the Interior Ministry provide most of the country's homeland security efforts. The International Police collaboration Interpol, located in St. Cloud, France, has long been active with crime threat assessments and a fusion intelligence function since 9/11. Interpol services are used more by foreign countries than by France itself.[33]

Israel

Israel has tied together the police, fire, EMS, the health system, and the military for its homeland security.[34] O'Connor noted there were many terrorism-related laws in Israel which outlaw unlawful associations, impose curfews on citizens, and regulate the media.[35] The most controversial of these may be the Defense Emergency Regulations of 1945, which says that Israel always operates in a state of emergency and therefore can do what is necessary to reduce risk in homeland security.

There are no less than three well-staffed and funded intelligence agencies: Shin Bet, Mossad, and Aman, supplemented by rather large police and military forces.[36] Each entity functions in its own operational sphere and according to its own operational doctrine.[37] Shin Bet is primarily responsible for intelligence and counter-espionage activities affecting internal security, and security of critical infrastructure. Mossad is responsible for addressing national security overseas. Aman's focus is on military intelligence and security.

Most of the homeland security efforts in Israel fall under the Ministry of Public Security. The ministry has strong policy-making authority and oversees the Israel National Police and the Israeli Civil Guard, an all-volunteer force created in 1974, consisting of networks of neighborhood command centers, armed patrol units, and rapid emergency response teams according to O'Connor.[38] Morag noted that during periods in which Israel is facing an active wartime scenario (or potentially, a WMD terrorist attack or other mass casualty event), the Cabinet can declare a limited state of emergency whereupon the Homefront Command (HFC) is given command and control over the other response agencies.[39]

In the post 9/11 world, airline security is critical, and Israeli security professionals sometimes identify people based on racial and behavioral profiling for further screening by conducting extensive searches and lengthy questioning. Screeners pay attention to tone of voice and body language and the like. Israeli profiling has been remarkably successful, making Israel's national airline and busiest airport the safest in the world.[40]

Russia

The Russian Federation approach to homeland security focuses on the protection of vital national interests. Russia is particularly sensitive to international threats, not just from international terrorism but from transnational criminal groups and threats such as asymmetric cyberattacks. According to Phillips, cyberattacks occur rapidly, and although the buildup to a confrontation may be undetectable, once it has occurred, it could be impossible to determine its origin.[41]

In Russia, several security agencies exist across many ministries, and they are all coordinated centrally via a strong presidential office which delegates regional authority to federal security service. Military leaders are frequently fired when a terrorist incident embarrasses the government. Citizens regularly participate in preparedness exercises but are denied most access to media coverage of terrorism.

Russia (like the United States, Poland, India, Slovakia, and the Ukraine) provides shootdown authority of civilian aircraft for any information considered "reliable" regarding a threat to a power plant, transportation hub, government building, or sensitive urban landmark. Although periodically there are allegations of such conduct, no undisputed incidents are officially recorded.[42] Apparently, the closest any country ever came to this action was on the morning of 9/11, when hurried discussions about the threat of Flight 93 led to Vice President Cheney's order for the military to engage it. Air Force fighter pilots, however, never received the order and passengers crashed the plane into a field after overwhelming the terrorists who had hijacked it.[43]

Another aspect of Russian antiterrorism law allows opening fire on terrorists who are holding hostages.[44] This occurred at the end of the Moscow theater hostage crisis, in which forty to fifty armed Chechen rebels seized the Dubrovka Theater on October 23, 2002. After two-and-a-half days, Russian forces raided the building after pumping a chemical agent into the ventilation system. According to Krechetnikov, all forty of the attackers were killed by Russian forces during the ensuing raid, and about 130 hostages died due to adverse reactions to the gas. The incident was also known as the 2002 Nord-Ost siege, because the popular musical *Nord-Ost* was showing.[45]

Canada

Canada is heavily influenced by its proximity to and historic relationship with the United States, and has moved closer to the U.S. model of a homeland security enterprise. Canada's national security policy incorporates law enforcement, intelligence, emergency management, public health, transportation, and border security. It includes many aspects of international security that take it outside the sphere of the homeland security enterprise.[46] Organizationally, while Canada does not incorporate security and emergency management under the same framework, Morag noted that it does view these disciplines as part of the overall public safety mission. The premier federal security department in the country is Public Safety Canada, which is responsible for federal law enforcement (via the Royal Canadian Mounted Police, RCMP) and intelligence (via the Canadian Security Intelligence Service, CSIS). Public Safety Canada coordinates with federal ministries responsible for health and critical infrastructures, as well as with provincial and municipal authorities and the private sector, although it does not have direct organizational responsibility for emergency management.[47]

The Threat of Terrorism

Terrorist organizations can be placed into two major groups. One, which we will examine first, is homegrown violent extremists (those mostly influenced by foreign groups or individuals). The second are domestic terrorists, which are formed and influenced by groups or individuals within the country. The latter will include the other ten extremist groups the DHS has identified. These two primary categories were chosen as they represent the current policy of the U.S. DHS.

3 Determine the best definition for terrorism, international terrorism, and domestic terrorism.

The most significant aspect of homeland security is the threat of terrorism, a concept defined in a number of ways by various groups. Here are a few contemporary definitions:

Department of Homeland Security

Any criminal activity that involves an act that is dangerous to human life or potentially destructive to critical infrastructure or key resources and appears to be intended to intimidate or coerce a civilian population to influence the policy of a government by intimidation or coercion, or to affect the conduct of a government by mass destruction, assassination, or kidnapping.[48]

U.S. Department of State

Premeditated, politically motivated violence perpetrated against noncombatant targets by subnational groups or clandestine agents, usually intended to influence an audience.[49]

The Federal Bureau of Investigation (FBI), Department of Justice

(According to the Code of Federal Regulation (C.F.R.) and the U.S. Code):

The unlawful use of force and violence against persons or property to intimidate or coerce a government, the civilian population, or any segment thereof, in furtherance of political or social objectives.[50]

United States Criminal Code, Title 18 U.S.C. § 2331

Acts dangerous to human life that violate federal or state law that appear intended (i) to intimidate or coerce a civilian population; (ii) to influence the policy of a government by intimidation or coercion; or (iii) to affect the conduct of a government by mass destruction, assassination, or kidnapping; and that occur primarily within the territorial jurisdiction of the U.S.

In addition, Title 18 of the U.S. Code (U.S.C.), § 2331 provides a definition of international terrorism as activities that:

Involve violent acts or acts dangerous to human life that violate federal or state law; appear to be intended (i) to intimidate or coerce a civilian population; (ii) to influence the policy of a government by intimidation or coercion; or (iii) to affect the conduct of a government by mass destruction, assassination, or kidnapping; and occur primarily outside the territorial jurisdiction of the United States, or transcend national boundaries in terms of the means by which they are accomplished, the persons they appear intended to intimidate or coerce, or the locale in which their perpetrators operate or seek asylum.

FIGURE 10–3
Terrorism Defined
There are several definitions of terrorism. Three U.S. Government departments each use their own, quite different, definitions.

international terrorism
Violent acts or acts dangerous to human life that are intended (i) to intimidate or coerce a civilian population; (ii) to influence the policy of a government by intimidation or coercion; or (iii) to affect the conduct of a government by mass destruction, assassination, or kidnapping. International terrorism occurs primarily outside the territorial jurisdiction of a specific country, the persons they appear intended to intimidate or coerce, or the locale in which their perpetrators operate or seek asylum.

Homegrown Violent Extremists

4 Distinguish homegrown violent extremists from domestic terrorists.

homegrown violent extremist
A person of any citizenship who has lived and/or operated primarily in a specific country or its territories who advocates, is engaged in, or is preparing to engage in ideologically motivated terrorist activities (including providing support to terrorism) in furtherance of political or social objectives promoted by a foreign terrorist organization, but is acting independently of direction by a foreign terrorist organization.

The U.S. DHS considers a **homegrown violent extremist** (HVE) as any person of any citizenship who has lived and/or operated primarily in the United States or its territories who advocates, is engaged in, or is preparing to engage in ideologically motivated terrorist activities (including providing support to terrorism) in furtherance of political or social objectives promoted by a foreign terrorist organization, but is acting independently of direction by a foreign terrorist organization. HVEs are distinct from traditional domestic terrorists who engage in unlawful acts of violence to intimidate civilian populations or attempt to influence domestic policy without direction from or influence from a foreign actor, according to the DHS.[51]

The National Counterterrorism Center reported that some HVEs have targeted law enforcement, mainly because a core element of their subculture perceives that persecution by law enforcement reflects the West's inherent aggression toward Islam. That perception reinforces the violent opposition by some HVEs to law enforcement. Some HVEs claim entrapment in the use of undercover informants. These critical investigations often involve plot developments, weapons access for HVEs, and tactics.[52] Successful informant and undercover operations have been crucial to disrupting a number of high-profile plots.[53]

Southers identified six characteristics that are manifested in violent extremists:

- *Intolerance and superiority*: Extremists make racial, religious, or ethnic claims of superiority, believe that they hold the moral high ground, and that outsiders are not fit to live in the same world.

- *Otherism*: Extremists presume that a segment of the population should not be considered part of the mainstream. These folks use derogatory names to refer to outcast groups, often doing so to divert attention from their extremist ideology.

- *Absolutism*: Extremists typically embrace a worldview of moral absolutes: They are right and just; their opponents are corrupt and evil. There are not grays, just blacks and whites.

- *Generalizations lacking foundation*: This characteristic requires dismissing or ignoring facts that contradict their position. Without facts to support their conclusions, they reach false conclusions, which support their ideological agenda.

- *Doomsday scenarios and conspiracy theories*: Apocalyptic outcome in response to failure brings these believers motivation. Their concerns range from the government being overthrown or villainized, and they attribute acts of terror to government conspirators.

- *Code speak*: Many extremists learn specific code words to denigrate their opponents. They learn clichéd phrases from others in the group and use them to build their self-confidence.[54]

Extremism

When identifying terrorist groups as extremists, the DHS officially incorporated terminology previously used interchangeably. It now appears there is a need for distinguishing between terrorists and extremists. Extremism has been defined as a radical expression of one's political values. It is a precursor to terrorism, used by terrorists to justify their violent behavior.[55] Violent extremism occurs when individuals or groups openly express their ideological beliefs through violence or a call for violence.[56] The content and the style of one's beliefs are basic elements for defining extremism, which is characterized not only by what one believes, but also in how they express their beliefs. Beliefs alone do not make one an extremist.[57]

Extremism may, in fact, be inevitable. When observed from the political point of view, Sotlar found that extremism displays at least two troubling dimensions.[58] First is the diverse political environment in which a particular phenomenon or action is detected, perceived, defined and observed; and second, in such a political environment, there is always a significant number of political movements and parties that operate on the margins (extremes) of the prevailing political culture, and these groups offer a haven to different forms of extremism and extremists.[59]

The FBI's public formulation of extremism suggests two components. First, extremism involves following particular ideologies. Second, it also includes using criminal activity to advance these ideologies.[60] According to Bjelopera, using the term *extremist* allows prosecutors, policymakers, and investigators to discuss terroristlike activity without having to actually label the activity as terrorism.[61]

Spotlight
Nidal Hasan

On November 5, 2009, Major Nidal Hasan attacked his fellow soldiers at Fort Hood, Texas. Hasan shouted, "Allahu-akbar!" ("God is great!") before shooting several soldiers with a handgun fitted with laser sights.

Hasan was an American-born Muslim and a psychiatrist for the Army. He had exchanged e-mails with a leading al-Qaeda imam, the late Anwar al-Awlaki, asking al-Awlaki whether those who attacked their fellow soldiers would be considered martyrs. Hasan reportedly told others that Muslims should be allowed to leave the U.S. armed forces as conscientious objectors to avoid what he identified as "adverse events."

He was shot while being arrested and as a result he was paralyzed from the waist down. Hasan was charged and convicted of thirteen counts of premeditated murder and thirty-two counts of attempted premeditated murder in the worst mass murder at a military installation in U.S. history. He was sentenced to death.

Source: B. Kenber, "Nidal Hasan Sentenced to Death for Fort Hood Shooting Rampage," August 28, 2013, http://www.washingtonpost.com/world/national-security/nidal-hasan-sentenced-to-death-for-fort-hood-shooting-rampage/2013/08/28/aad28de2-0ffa-11e3-bdf6-e4fc677d94a1_story.html

---

Religious Extremism

Religious extremists are willing to kill because they embrace specific theologies that sanction violence in the service of their god. Iannaccone and Berman suggested that they have no sympathy for their victims, because they view those victims as enemies of their god.[62] Although some may limit those they view as practicing violent extremism to Islamic radicals, that view is ill-informed.[63] Many religions have been represented by individuals and groups with extreme and violent interpretations of their doctrine.

- *Christian Identity groups*: Although nominally considered Christian, the Christian Identity movement shares few similarities to even the most conservative American Catholic or Protestant groups.[64] According to the Southern Poverty Law Center, the relationship of the Christian Identity movement with evangelicals and fundamentalists has generally been hostile due to the latter's belief that the return of Jews to Israel is essential to the fulfillment of end-time prophecy. Christian Identity group members professed a unique anti-Semitic and racist theology, and rose to a position of influence on the racist right in the 1980s. Only a prolonged period of aggressive efforts by law enforcement, together with the demise of influential leaders who were not replaced, brought about its decline.[65] Members of the Christian Identity movement are not inherently violent, but some followers have been involved in violent incidents and some have advocated violence. In many of these cases, followers of the movement employed, recommended, or prepared for violence because they thought their religion required it.[66]

  Examples of Christian Identity groups include (none of which have much of a contemporary presence):

  - Aryan Nations[67]
  - Covenant, Sword and Arm of the Lord (CSA)
  - The Order
  - Phineas Priesthood

- *Jewish Defense League*: The Jewish Defense League (JDL) preaches a violent form of anti-Arab, Jewish nationalism. The JDL's position with regard to Israel is denial of any Palestinian claims to land and calling for the removal of all Arabs from the "Jewish-inherited soil." According to the Southern Poverty Law Center, the JDL has orchestrated countless terrorist attacks in the United States and abroad, and has engaged in intense harassment

THINK ABOUT IT

Is there something about religion that makes extremism more likely? Are members of one religion more likely to consider members of another extremists?

of foreign diplomats, Muslims, Jewish scholars and community leaders, and officials.[68] In 1971, JDL's founder, Rabbi Meir David Kahane, pled guilty to charges that he had conspired to manufacture explosives. The JDL today has chapters in Eastern Europe, Canada, Australia, South Africa, Russia, and the United Kingdom, in addition to those in the United States.[69] Kahane was assassinated in New York City by an Arab gunman in 1990, following a speech that he had given in a midtown Manhattan Marriott hotel.

- *Muslim Identity:* While the overwhelming majority of global Muslim communities denounce violence, some see a predatory relationship between the United States and the West and the Islamic world (nations with a Muslim majority).[70] This perceived predatory relationship serves as the principal worldview behind Muslim Identity. The perception is that the U.S. and other Western countries seek to gain control of natural resources in Muslim-majority nations and destroy Islam as a religious or political force.[71] While those who adhere to Muslim Identity do not have the cohesion found in the other extremist groups, they do ascribe to the notion of Jihadism.

Spotlight
Best Terminology for Describing the Terrorist Threat

In 2007, DHS Secretary Chertoff met with a group of influential Muslim Americans to discuss ways the DHS could work with their communities to protect the country, promote civic engagement, and prevent violent radicalization from taking root in the United States. Part of the discussion involved the terminology used to describe terrorists who invoke Islamic theology in planning, carrying out, and justifying their attacks. While there was a broad consensus that the terminology used impacted both national security and the ability to win hearts and minds, some of the leading U.S.-based scholars and commentators on Islam subsequently proposed the best terminology to use when describing the terrorist threat:

- Respond to ideologies that exploit Islam without labeling all terrorist groups as a single enemy.
- Do not give terrorists the legitimacy that they seek.
- Proceed carefully before using Arabic and religious terminology.

- Reference the cultlike aspects of terrorists, while still conveying the magnitude of the threat we face.
- Use terms such as *mainstream*, *ordinary*, and *traditional* instead of *moderate* when describing broader Muslim populations.
- Pay attention to the discourse on *takfirism* (Islamic Messianistic ideology that permits or encourages the killing of non-Muslims).[72]
- Emphasize the positive.
- Emphasize the success of integration.
- Emphasize the U.S. government's openness to religious and ethnic communities.

Source: DHS, "Terminology to Define the Terrorists: Recommendations from American Muslims." Office for Civil Rights and Civil Liberties, 2008.

Becoming an Extremist

No matter one's religious or political background, Borum observed that part of becoming an extremist involves accepting four positions that define this ideology. Consequently, violent extremists are generally characterized as being:

- *Polarized*: Having an "us versus them" mind-set.
- *Absolutist*: They regard their beliefs as truth in the absolute sense, sometimes supported by sacred authority. This notion allows them to reject questioning, critical thinking, and dissent and adds moral authority to framing the "us versus them" as a battle between good and bad (or evil).
- *Threat-oriented*: External threat causes group members to grow closer. When leaders persistently remind adherents that the "us" is at risk from "them," this works not only to promote internal cohesion but also opposition to all nonbelievers.
- *Hateful*: Hate energizes violent action. It allows principled opposition to impel direct action and allows moral disengagement, or dehumanization, of the adversarial them. The process erodes the normal social and psychological barriers to engaging in violence. It is the active support for violence that distinguishes the simple extremist from the terrorist.[73]

In addition to accepting the extremist mind-set, the extremist recruit goes through the process of radicalization found in many religious, ethnic, and cultural populations.[74] In the radicalization process, individuals begin to identify, embrace, and engage in furthering their growing extremist ideology and goals.[75] According to the European Commission's Expert Group on Violent Radicalization, a fostering environment for radicalization is characterized by widespread feelings of inequity and injustice, where a very acute sense of marginalization and humiliation exists.[76] The European Commission also believes that nothing creates so fertile a breeding ground for political radicalization than the feeling of belonging to those left behind in the progress of mankind while resenting injustice in an "us versus them" paradigm.[77] Unfortunately, the radicalization process is not a fixed trajectory that can be acknowledged or identified by using a checklist.[78]

Radicalization and recruitment of prisoners is an ongoing concern in the United States. Radicalization primarily occurs through anti-U.S. sermons calling on inmates to embrace the Salafi form of Sunni Islam (including versions commonly known as Prislam, for "prison Islam") and an extremist view of Shia Islam.[79] Prison radicalization and recruitment is conducted by two distinct groups.

- Converts to Islam.
- Contract, volunteer, and staff personnel, the majority of which are imams, who enter correctional facilities with the intent to radicalize and recruit.[80]

The danger of prison recruitment is that converts may get involved in terror activities upon their release and/or recruit friends and family who are on the outside.[81] Prisoner radicalization occurs primarily with one-on-one proselytizing by charismatic leaders who target the most vulnerable of inmates—those incarcerated under maximum security. Those inmates often have antiauthoritarian attitudes and are easily swayed. Nonetheless, moving from radicalization to actual terrorism is a rare event. Only a small percentage of prisoners actually join radical groups upon their release.[82]

It is, however, important to recognize that ideology is an important and constant factor in the radicalization process, as it plays a crucial role in turning a small but significant minority of people into militants.[83] Ideology is often used to teach acceptance of violence as a method to bring about political change and is used to reduce moral inhibitors.[84]

Spotlight
Sovereign Citizens

A man pulled a loaded gun on a law enforcement officer, believing the law did not apply to him. In a homemade video, a man police identified as Anthony Williams was in possession of a badge and handcuffs. Officers say he made a fake law enforcement vehicle tag with a state seal. "Today is officially my first day of being a sovereign police officer out in Nashville," Williams said in the video.

Eric Stanberry Jr. was asked to leave a Nashville strip club in late June after he allegedly urinated on the property. He then pulled a loaded gun on an unarmed security guard. Metro police used a stun gun on him. He had a 9-mm pistol, two ammunition magazines, a box of bullets, and a badge with a special police logo.

FBI officials say sovereign citizens commit bank fraud, mail fraud, wire fraud, and mortgage fraud, and have been known to confront authority figures by putting false liens on their homes and businesses.

Source: C. Gordon, "FBI Warns Police of Growing Sovereign Citizen Movement," July 8, 2013, WSMV, http://www.wsmv.com/story/22788061/fbi-warns-police-of-growing-sovereign-citizen-movement

Domestic Terrorists

Domestic terrorism according to the DHS is any act of violence that is dangerous to human life or potentially destructive of critical infrastructure or key resources committed by a group or individual based and operating entirely within the United States or its territories without direction or inspiration from a foreign terrorist group.[85] Domestic terrorism defines those actions that appear to be intended to intimidate or coerce a civilian population, to influence the policy of a government by intimidation or coercion, or to affect the conduct of a government by mass destruction, assassination, or kidnapping. A domestic terrorist differs from a homegrown violent extremist in that the former is not inspired by and does not take direction from a foreign terrorist group or other foreign power.[86]

domestic terrorism
Those actions that appear to be intended to intimidate or coerce a civilian population, to influence the policy of a government by intimidation or coercion, or to affect the conduct of a government by mass destruction, assassination, or kidnapping. A domestic terrorist differs from a homegrown violent extremist in that the former is not inspired by and does not take direction from a foreign terrorist group or other foreign power.

animal rights extremists
Individuals or groups that oppose any individual and/or institutional entity (e.g., corporations, government agencies) perceived to be exploiting or abusing animals.

environmental rights extremists
Oppose people, businesses, or government entities destroying, degrading, or exploiting the natural environment.

anti-abortion extremists
Believe that the practice of abortion should end and therefore oppose abortion providers and their related services.

lone offenders
Terrorists motivated by one or more extremist ideologies and, operating alone, support or engage in acts of violence in furtherance of that ideology or ideologies.

anarchist extremists
Believe that (a) all forms of institutional globalization designed to maximize business profits should be opposed and (b) government institutions are unnecessary and harmful to society.

militia extremists
who profess belief that the government deliberately is stripping Americans of their freedoms and is attempting to establish a totalitarian regime.

Domestic terrorist groups that are operating or which operated in the past include the following:

- **Animal rights extremists**, who are against people, businesses, or government entities perceived to be exploiting or abusing animals.

- **Environmental rights extremists**, who are against people, businesses, or government entities perceived to be destroying, degrading, or exploiting the natural environment.

- **Anti-abortion extremists**, who are against the providers of abortion-related services, their employees, and their facilities in support of the belief that the practice of abortion should end.

- **Lone offenders**, individuals who appear to be motivated by one or more extremist ideologies and, operating alone, support or engage in acts of violence in furtherance of that ideology or ideologies.

- **Anarchist extremists**, who say they believe that all forms of capitalism and corporate globalization should be opposed and that governing institutions are unnecessary and harmful to society.

- **Militia extremists**, who profess belief that the government deliberately is stripping Americans of their freedoms and is attempting to establish a totalitarian regime.

- **Sovereign citizen extremists**, who claim belief that the legitimacy of U.S. citizenship should be rejected; almost all forms of established government, authority, and institutions are illegitimate; and that they are immune from federal, state, and local laws.

- **Black supremacist extremists**, who claim they oppose racial integration and/or efforts to eliminate nonblack people and Jewish people.

- **Racist skinhead extremists** and **white supremacist extremists**, who both claim to believe that Caucasians are intellectually and morally superior to other races and that the government is controlled by Jewish persons.[87]

Domestic terrorism has also been divided into left-wing, right-wing, and single-issue terrorism.[88]

Spotlight
Wolf Packs

Perlmutter, Director of the Symbol Intelligence Group, proposed the examination of such individuals in the context of group behavior, rather than solely as individuals. She posited the notion that the lone wolf (or lone offender) profile works well with active shooters like the Columbine, Sandy Hook, and Virginia Tech school shooters. Perlmutter noted there was a new breed of terrorists emerging that were better characterized as 'Wolf Packs.' While lone wolves have often been shunned by society or have withdrawn into their own world, members of wolf packs are part of a community of true believers. Most lone wolves kill out of a sense of alienation, while wolf pack members kill out of a sense of belonging and honor.

Examples of wolf pack attacks include the Boston marathon bombings by the Tsarnaev brothers, the Charlie Hebdo shooting in Paris by the Kouachi brothers, and the San Bernardino shooting by Syed Rizwan Farook and his wife Tashfeen Malik. The Islamic

State's social media campaign includes videos of sadistic violence appeals to the humiliated disaffected loner who fantasizes about making others suffer their pain.

The Islamic State recruits everyone from the misfits to the true believers and advises them through social media how to blend into society and hide in plain sight. The misfit becomes a virtuous mass murderer whose humiliation is replaced with honor and respect by killing in the name of Allah. Jihadist mass murder functions to restore honor, serve vengeance, attain purity, save face and achieve everlasting life in paradise. And now they are hunting in packs.

D. Perlmutter, "The Wolf Pack Profile: The disturbing pattern of terrorism in America becoming a family affair," December 15, 2015, http://www.frontpagemag.com/fpm/261107/wolf-pack-profile-dawn-perlmutter

sovereign citizen extremists
who claim belief that the legitimacy of US citizenship should be rejected; almost all forms of established government, authority, and institutions are illegitimate; and that they are immune from federal, state, and local laws.

Terrorist Activity in the United States

Terrorist activity has been seen across the United States from New York City to Los Angeles, but also in well-known (and smaller) cities such as Phoenix, Arizona, and Miami, Florida. LaFree and Bersani reported that terrorism hot spots are located predominantly in large, metropolitan areas.[89] Terrorism and ordinary crime occur in many of the same areas. Some traditional predictors of ordinary crime also predict terrorist attacks, but many do not.[90]

While some areas seem to remain prime targets of terrorist attacks from the 1970s through today (i.e., Los Angeles, Manhattan), for the most part those identified as hot spots change. San Francisco County, California, was a prime target in the 1970s whereas Maricopa County, Arizona, has recently moved toward the top of the list. These shifts are likely due to changes in ideological motivation of the areas over the same time period.[91]

racist skinhead extremists and white supremacist extremists, who both claim to believe that Caucasians are intellectually and morally superior to other races and that the government is controlled by Jewish persons.

Spotlight
Terrorism in Texas

On May 3, 2015, Elton Simpson and Nadir Soofi of Phoenix, Arizona opened fire on police at the Curtis Culwell Center in Garland, Texas. Simpson and Soofi were apparently heading to a cartoon exhibit and contest depicting the prophet Muhammad, and the police were blocking the entrance. Muslims consider artistic portrayals of the prophet offensive. The two were fatally shot by a police officer when they opened fire with assault rifles. An unarmed security guard was wounded in the attack.

Simpson had been under federal surveillance since 2006 and was convicted in 2011 of lying to FBI agents about his desire to join violent jihad in Somalia. Just before the attack, one of the gunmen posted "May Allah accept us as mujahideen," on the social media site Twitter and pledged allegiance to the Islamic State, which later claimed responsibility for the attack, the first time the terrorist organization took credit for an attack in the United States. The American Freedom Defense Initiative, a free-speech organization that the Southern Poverty Law Center has described as a hate group, organized the event.

Source: M.K. Hosenball and I. Simpson, "U.S. probing Islamic State claims it was behind Texas cartoon attack," May 6, 2015, http://www.reuters.com/article/us-usa-shooting-texas-idUSKBN0NP01G20150506

Terrorists and Crime

Most terrorist groups are now or have been engaging in traditional criminal activities. Consequently, the potential for collaboration between terrorists and traditional criminals must not be overlooked. Private security professionals should remain alert for all types of adversaries, which are likely to include members of groups like gangs, crime organizations, or terrorist groups. A U.S. Department of Justice report identified several similarities between terrorists and individuals engaged in gang activity and organized crime. Members of each type of organization commit fraud, theft, forgery, and violent street crime.[92] They also engage in trafficking drugs and human beings, extortion, intimidation, and bribing of government representatives.[93] Some street gangs are highly sophisticated, with goals of political power or financial acquisition.[94]

Such advanced gangs that have recently operated in North America are the Gangster Disciples, Vice Lords, Mara Salvatrucha, and 18 Street.[95] Their actions may traverse the continuum along which street gangs and terrorism reside. Terror groups partnering with these gangs would likely be looking for a full and equal partner, one that would serve as a force multiplier. The actions of these groups, whether criminal in nature or not, should be evaluated for potential terrorism connections. The U.S. DHS identified a sampling of terrorist criminal activity, as depicted in Figure 10–4.

- *Breach/attempted intrusion*: Unauthorized personnel attempting to or actually entering a restricted area or protected site. Impersonation of authorized personnel (e.g., police/security, janitor).
- *Misrepresentation*: Presenting false or misusing insignia, documents, and/or identification, to misrepresent one's affiliation to cover possible illicit activity.
- *Theft/loss/diversion*: Stealing or diverting something associated with a facility/infrastructure (e.g., badges, uniforms, identification, emergency vehicles, technology or documents—classified or unclassified—which are proprietary to the facility).
- *Sabotage/tampering/vandalism*: Damaging, manipulating, or defacing part of a facility/infrastructure or protected site.
- *Cyberattack*: Compromising or attempting to compromise or disrupt an organization's information technology infrastructure.
- *Expressed or implied threat*: Communicating a spoken or written threat to damage or compromise a facility/infrastructure.
- *Aviation activity*: Operation of an aircraft in a manner that reasonably may be interpreted as suspicious or as posing a threat to people or property. Such operation may or may not be a violation of federal aviation regulations.

FIGURE 10–4
Criminal Activity That May Be Considered Terrorism
Source: Department of Homeland Security, "Information Sharing Environment (ISE)," Suspicious Activity Reporting (SAR) Version 1.5, Functional Standard (FS) 200. Author, 2009. Retrieved from http://www.dhs.gov/xlibrary/assets/privacy/privacy-pia-dhswide-sar-ise-appendix.pdf

(Continued)

FIGURE 10-4
Continued

Activity that may not be criminal or may further acts of terrorism:

- *Eliciting information*: Questioning individuals at a level beyond mere curiosity about particular facets of a facility's or building's purpose, operations, security procedures, etc., that would arouse suspicion in a reasonable person.
- *Testing or probing of security*: Deliberate interactions with, or challenges to, installations, personnel, or systems that reveal physical, personnel, or cybersecurity capabilities.
- *Recruiting*: Building of operations teams and contacts, personnel data, banking data, or travel data.
- *Photography*: Taking pictures or video of facilities, buildings, or infrastructure in a manner that would arouse suspicion in a reasonable person. Examples include taking pictures or video of infrequently used access points, personnel performing security functions (patrols, badge/vehicle checking), security-related equipment (perimeter fencing, security cameras), etc.

Terrorism outside the United States

Terrorism is not unique to the United States, nor is it limited only to countries with a significant Western influence. A number of terror groups operating abroad have the goal of subverting the government and replacing it with one that reflects their religious or moral beliefs. Two highly destructive groups are described in the sections that follow.

The Islamic State (IS)

Formed as Al Qaeda in Iraq, the group has rebranded itself as the Islamic State of Iraq and Syria (ISIS) and then the Islamic State of Iraq and Levant (ISIL) before turning to its current designation as the Islamic State (IS). The group's popularity grew in part from opposition to the continued presence in the Middle East of U.S. forces, then swelled as the split between the Sunni sect of former Iraqi president Saddam Hussein clashed with the Shi'ite administration led by then-Prime Minister Nuri al-Maliki. Abu Bakr al Baghdadi became the organization's leader in 2010 after founder Abu Omar al Baghdadi was killed in a joint U.S.–Iraqi operation.[96]

To sustain operations, IS looted the Iraqi central bank in Mosul of $429 million when they overran the city and emptied the vaults of cash and gold. The group also seized several U.S.-made and provided tanks, Blackhawk helicopters, cargo planes, and an unknown quantity of guns, all part of a $14 billion arsenal the United States sold or donated to the beleaguered Iraqi security forces.[97]

The money and weapons are helping ISIS in its bid to carve out a nation governed by strict and merciless Sharia law in northern Iraq and northwestern Syria. The group already saw itself as an independent state in control of large sections of the two battle-scarred nations, areas it now controls and is bent on expanding.[98] By some estimates, looting the national bank made ISIS the wealthiest terrorist organization in the world. The Taliban has closer to $70 to $400 million, while groups such as Hezbollah, Hamas, and Al Qaeda operate on far less.[99] Its beheading of captured Western journalists and innocent others in 2014 prompted the United States and its allies to begin a bombing campaign in an attempt to neutralize or destroy the Islamic State.

Boko Haram

Boko Haram promotes a version of Islam that forbids Muslims to take part in any political or social activity associated with society in the West. The forbidden activity includes voting in elections, wearing shirts and trousers, or receiving a secular education. Its followers claim strict adherence to the Koranic phrase, which says: "Anyone who is not governed by what Allah has revealed is among the transgressors."[100]

The group's official name is Jama'atu Ahlis Sunna Lidda'awati wal-Jihad, which in Arabic means "People Committed to the Propagation of the Prophet's Teachings and Jihad" according to Chothia, but residents dubbed it Boko Haram. Loosely translated from the region's Hausa language, this means "Western education is forbidden."[101] Muslim cleric Mohammed

Spotlight
Islamic State in Europe

Paris and the surrounding area was the site of a coordinated attack on the Bataclan concert hall, restaurants, and a soccer stadium just north of Paris, making 2015 the deadliest year for terrorism in Western Europe since 2004. At the Stade de France, the national stadium of France, a suicide bomber attacked, killing one. Shortly thereafter, two gunmen started shooting as they stepped out of a car in front of a cafe-bar in the city center. They then fired at the Cambodian restaurant across the street. Not far from there, gunmen with assault weapons exited the same black car and began shooting at an Italian restaurant, a nearby cafe, and a laundromat.

Moments later, a second explosion was heard at the stadium. The black car then pulled up at a popular eatery and gunmen fired several rounds before returning to the car. A third explosion occurred when a suicide bomber blew himself up outside a McDonald's restaurant, but no one else was hurt. A black Volkswagen then pulled up in front of the Bataclan concert hall, and three gunmen entered and started shooting, then held hostages for the next two hours.

As police entered the concert hall, the attackers blew themselves up. A total of 89 people were killed, and more than 200 were injured. The Islamic State claimed responsibility for the attacks. Abdelhamid Abaaoud, a 28 year old Belgian of Moroccan descent was the suspected mastermind behind the Paris attacks, and French authorities suspected he was planning a new attack near Paris when he was killed while police were attempting his arrest. Abaaoud was one of Europe's most wanted men before the attacks.

The theater is less than a mile from the site of the January 7, 2015 shooting at the Charlie Hebdo Paris headquarters offices, where two gunmen forced their way into the building and opened fire. Twelve were killed in the attack, including two police officers, and eleven were wounded. During the attack, the gunmen shouted "Allahu akbar" ("God is great" in Arabic) and also "the Prophet is avenged".

After those attacks, the phrase "Je suis Charlie," French for "I am Charlie", was adopted by many people around the world to show support for those killed and wounded in the attack. The Islamic State claimed responsibility for the Charlie Hebdo attacks, as well.

Source: The Washington Post. "What we know about the Paris attacks and the hunt for the attackers," Dec. 9, 2015, https://www.washingtonpost.com/graphics/world/paris-attacks/

Yusuf formed Boko Haram in Maiduguri in 2002. He set up a religious complex, which included a mosque and an Islamic school. Many poor Muslim families from all across Nigeria and neighboring countries enrolled their children at the school. But Boko Haram was not only interested in education. Its goal was to create an Islamic state, and the school became a recruiting ground for jihadists.[102]

In 2010, the United States designated Boko Haram a terrorist organization, after much political pressure and fears that it had developed links with other terrorist groups to wage a global jihad. Boko Haram's original strategy included using gunmen on motorbikes, killing police, politicians, and anyone who criticizes the organization, including clerics from other Muslim traditions and Christian preachers. The group has also staged attacks in northern and central Nigeria, including bombing churches, bus ranks, bars, military barracks, and even police and UN headquarters.[103]

In 2014, Boko Haram escalated its campaign against Western education, which it believes corrupts the moral values of Muslims, by attacking two boarding schools: in Yobe in March and in Chibok in April. The group abducted more than 200 schoolgirls from the schools during the Chibok raid, saying it would treat them as slaves and marry them off—a reference to an ancient Islamic belief that women captured in conflict are part of the "war booty."[104] Boko Haram pledges allegiance to the Islamic State.

Al-Shabaab

The Harakat al-Shabaab al-Mujahidin known as *al-Shabaab* was the clan-based insurgent and terrorist group that served as the militant wing of the Somali Council of Islamic Courts. The group has exerted temporary control over strategic locations in parts of Somalia by recruiting, sometimes forcibly, regional subclans and their militias.[105] Al-Shabaab's members come from disparate clans, and the group is susceptible to clan politics, internal divisions, and shifting alliances. Al-Shabaab is associated with Al Qaeda, and some of its leaders were believed to have trained and fought in Afghanistan. Since 2013 al-Shabaab has launched high-profile attacks, such as the September 2013 Westgate Mall attack in Nairobi and the May 2014 attack against a restaurant in Djibouti.[106] In April 2015, al-Shabaab gunmen killed 148 people when they stormed the Garissa University College campus in Kenya. In response, the Kenyan air force destroyed two al-Shabaab camps in Somalia to stop fighters from those camps from conducting further attacks in Kenya.[107]

Terrorist Planning and Preparation

<table>
<tr><td>5</td><td>Demonstrate understanding of the four major activities of terrorist groups.</td></tr>
</table>

Throughout the planning process of a terrorism incident or act, meetings take place, phone calls are made, and crimes are committed. These acts occur in locations such as the terrorists' residence, a relative or friend's residence, a home base or safe house, or even during surveillance of the intended target, according to research by Smith, Damphousse, and Roberts. These behaviors occur in measurable dimensions of time and space. This terrorist activity occurs along a continuum with four major activities: (1) recruitment, (2) preliminary organization and planning, (3) preparatory conduct, and (4) terrorist acts.[108] These general principles and examples of each type of behavior are presented in Figure 10–5.

Terrorist groups engaged in an average of two known preparatory, planning, and ancillary behaviors per incident. With the exception of the right-wing groups studied, about two-thirds (70.6%) of the behaviors recorded by these groups were noncriminal.[109] Each of these behaviors could serve as pre-incident indicators to analysts monitoring such activities. However, many of these behaviors, such as buying legally obtainable bomb-making components or conducting surveillance on a target, are not illegal.[110] That may preclude the monitoring of such conduct in the absence of ongoing intelligence investigations. Furthermore, terrorist groups engage in much conduct that is merely ancillary behaviors that may or may not be criminal, but they were conducted for purposes not directly related to the planning and preparation for the terrorist incident. These behaviors, however, may attract the attention of police and could be used as pre-incident indicators of terrorist group activity.[111] Such behavior might only make a typical law enforcement officer suspicious of the individual, without any information amounting to probable cause. Hopefully the officer would document and retain such documentation of the activity if it was later discovered to be connected to terrorist activity. Security professionals should document each time behavior such as this is detected and by whom it was detected to protect their organizations from loss or liability.

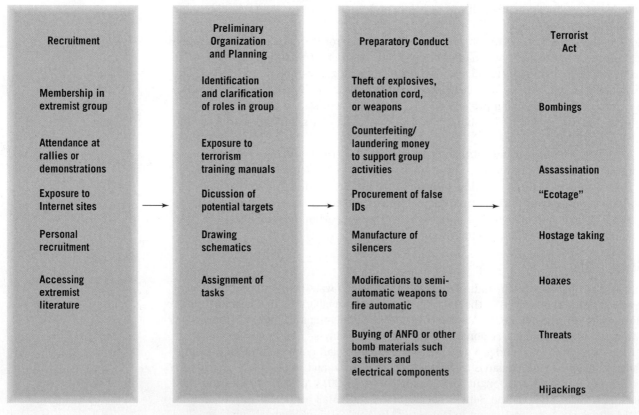

FIGURE 10–5
Flowchart of Terrorist Group Activity
Source: B. L. Smith, K. R. Damphousse, and P. Roberts, *Pre-Incident Indicators of Terrorist Incidents: The Identification of Behavioral, Geographic, and Temporal Patterns of Preparatory Conduct.* Terrorism Research Center in Fulbright College, University of Arkansas, 2006.

The most common of these crimes involved acquiring, manufacturing, or testing bombs (16.6%). Conspiracies do not frequently become known to law enforcement agencies until after the completion of the act or other arrests are made so nonovert acts such as meetings and phone calls may not come to the attention of local law enforcement agencies either. However, three-fourths of these crimes involved observable offenses which might lead the police to suspicion of more sinister activities. Robbery (14%), murder (6%), and training (6%) constituted the remaining most common preparatory and ancillary offenses committed.[112]

The DHS defined suspicious activity as observed behavior that appears indicative of preoperational planning related to terrorism or other criminal activity.[113] The DHS found that some examples of such behavior include:

- New or increased advocacy of violence including providing material support or recruiting others to commit criminal acts.

- Adoption of new lifestyles and segregation from normal peer and family groups in association with advocating criminal or terrorist activity.

- The adoption of a new name.

- Behavior that could indicate participation in surveillance of potential targets.

- Acquisition of excessive quantities of weapons or materials that could be used to produce explosives such as ammonium nitrate-based fertilizers or hydrogen peroxide.

- Travel to or interest in traveling overseas to attend violent extremist institutions or paramilitary training camps.

- New or increased interest in websites and reading materials that advocate violence and then initiating action in support of this activity.

- New or increased interest in critical infrastructure locations and landmarks, including obtaining aerial views of these locations.[114]

The wide array of indicators in case studies, coupled with best practices from a variety of U.S. organizations best placed to detect specific signs, cautions against adopting a checklist-like mentality, according to the NCTC.[115] Simplistically interpreting any single indicator as confirmation of mobilization probably will lead to ineffective and counterproductive efforts.

Terrorist Motivation

Continued focus is placed on jihadist (radical Islamic) terrorists as the primary terrorist threat known to the United States. There are many terrorist groups, and many ways to classify them. Unlike the DHS or FBI, the National Consortium for the Study of Terrorism and Responses to Terrorism (START) categorizes terrorists by their ideological motivation. These classifications can be found in the Profiles of Perpetrators of Terrorism-U.S. report compiled by START:

Extreme right-wing: Groups that are fiercely nationalistic (as opposed to universal and international in orientation), antiglobal, suspicious of centralized federal authority, reverent of individual liberty (especially their right to own guns, be free of taxes), believe in conspiracy theories that involve grave threat to national sovereignty and/or personal liberty. These folks believe that their personal and/or national "way of life" is under attack and is either already lost or that the threat is imminent (sometimes such beliefs are amorphous and vague, but for some the threat is from a specific ethnic, racial, or religious group), and that they need to be prepared for an attack either by participating in paramilitary preparations and training or survivalism.[116]

Extreme left-wing: Groups that want to bring about change through violent revolution rather than through established political processes. This category also includes secular left-wing groups that rely heavily on terrorism to overthrow the capitalist system and either establish "a dictatorship of the proletariat" (Marxist-Leninists) or, much more rarely, a decentralized, nonhierarchical political system (anarchists).[117]

Religious terrorist: Groups that seek to engage in battle with the purported enemies of God and other evildoers, impose strict religious tenets or laws on society (fundamentalists), and forcibly insert religion into the political sphere.[118]

extreme right-wing terrorists
Fiercely nationalistic, antiglobal, suspicious of centralized federal authority, reverent of individual liberty (especially their right to own guns, be free of taxes), believe in conspiracy theories that involve grave threat to national sovereignty, and/or personal liberty. They believe that their personal and/or national "way of life" is under attack and is either already lost or that the threat is imminent and that they need to be prepared for an attack either by participating in paramilitary preparations and training or survivalism.

extreme left-wing terrorists
Want to bring about change through violent revolution rather than through established political processes.

religious terrorist
Seek to engage in battle with the purported enemies of God and other evildoers, impose strict religious tenets or laws on society (fundamentalists), forcibly insert religion into the political sphere.

ethno-nationalist/separatist terrorists

Regionally concentrated minority groups, whose goal is political autonomy. The Basques in Spain, IRA in Ireland, and Tamils in Sri Lanka at one time engaged in terrorist activity to secure a homeland.

single-issue terrorist

Obsessively focus on very specific or narrowly defined causes on all sides of the political spectrum (e.g., antiabortion, anti-Catholic, antinuclear, anti-Castro).

Ethno-nationalist/separatist: Regionally concentrated groups with a history of organized political autonomy with their own state, traditional ruler, or regional government, who have supported political movements for autonomy.

Single-issue terrorist: Groups or individuals that obsessively focus on very specific or narrowly defined causes (e.g., antiabortion, anti-Catholic, antinuclear, anti-Castro). This category includes groups from all sides of the political spectrum.[119]

Figure 10–6 shows the dominant ideology of 125 terrorist groups that attacked the United States between 1970 and 2010. Most (32%) were formed around an ethnonationalist/separatist agenda. About one-fourth (28%) of the groups were committed to some single cause. Only 6% of groups that have attacked the United States were focused on a religious ideology. Those organizations, though, include the group that has inflicted the greatest amount of damage on the United States: Al-Qaeda.

FIGURE 10–6

Dominant Ideology of Groups

Source: E. E. Miller, K. Smarick, and J. Simone, Jr., Profiles of Perpetrators of Terrorism in the United States (PPTUS): Data Collection and Descriptive Analysis, Interim Report to Human Factors/Behavioral Sciences Division, Science and Technology Directorate, U.S. Department of Homeland Security (College Park MD: START, September 2011), http://www.start.umd.edu/pubs/START_PPTUS_DataCollectionDescriptiveAnalysis_Sept2011.pdf.

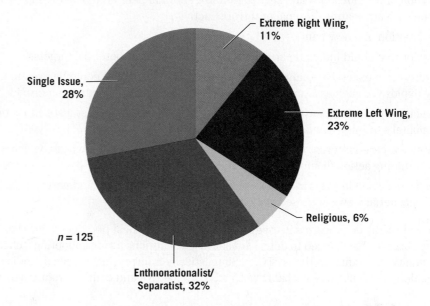

Domestic Terrorism and Law Enforcement

In the United States and in many other countries, domestic terrorism is the primary focus when it comes to law enforcement and private security. According to Bjelopera, there are five potential reasons domestic terrorism should be a priority for policymakers:

- *Level of activity*: Domestic terrorists have been responsible for more than two dozen terrorist incidents since 9/11, and there appears to be a growth in antigovernment activity.

- *Use of nontraditional tactics*: A large number of domestic terrorists do not necessarily use tactics such as suicide bombings or airplane hijackings.

- *Exploitation of the Internet*: Domestic terrorists are often Internet savvy and use it as a resource.

- *Decentralized nature of the threat*: Many domestic terrorists rely on the concept of leaderless resistance. This involves two apparently separate levels of activity. On an operational level, militant, underground, ideologically motivated cells or individuals engage in illegal activity without any participation in or direction from an organization that maintains traditional leadership positions and membership rosters. The second level is represented by the public face of the domestic terrorist movement, focused on propaganda and the dissemination of ideology—usually seen as protected speech.

- *Prison radicalization*: Prison has been highlighted as an arena in which terrorist radicalization can occur. Some prison gangs delve into radical or extremist ideologies similar to those that motivate domestic terrorists. In many instances, these ideologies are integral to fashioning cohesive group identities within prison walls, although criminal enterprises largely drive their activities.[120]

Terrorism is not random violence for its own sake. It is violence guided by an ideology that provides the rules for one's behavior. Borum found that ideology is often defined as rules an individual will follow, and that help to regulate and determine behavior.[121]

Bombings and Bomb Threats

The Global Terrorism Database lists more than 52,500 terrorist bombings in the world since it began tracking such events in 1970.[122] Many of the identified terror groups have used bombs or other explosives when delivering their message. In addition to the Boston attack in the United States, over the two previous years, extremists attempted to detonate IEDs or bombs at such targets as the Federal Reserve Bank in New York, the U.S. Capitol, and commercial establishments in Chicago, Tampa, and Oakland.[123]

Security professionals who identify a bomb or reported bomb should immediately notify local law enforcement. All persons in the area should then be accounted for and moved to a safe location in line with organizational procedures. Bomb threats should be treated as legitimate warnings every time, until there is sufficient evidence to the contrary. The calculations in Figure 10–7 are offered for general emergency planning.

Observing the specified distances does not guarantee safety. They are only estimates provided by the DHS based on test data. The area around the evacuation distances is still potentially dangerous, and a building's vulnerability to explosions depends on its construction and composition, and many other variables. The data in these tables may not accurately reflect these variables. The minimum evacuation distance is the range at which a life-threatening injury is unlikely; however, non-life-threatening injury from blast or fragmentation hazards or temporary hearing loss may occur.

terrorism
Activities that involve violent acts or acts dangerous to human life that are intended (i) to intimidate or coerce a civilian population; (ii) to influence the policy of a government by intimidation or coercion; or (iii) to affect the conduct of a government by mass destruction, assassination, or kidnapping.

Threat Description Improvised Explosive Device (IED)		Explosives Capacity[1] (TNT Equivalent)	Building Evacuation Distance[2]	Outdoor Evacuation Distance[3]
	Pipe Bomb	5 LBS	70 FT	1200 FT
	Suicide Bomber	20 LBS	110 FT	1700 FT
	Briefcase/ Suitcase	50 LBS	150 FT	1850 FT
	Car	500 LBS	320 FT	1500 FT
	SUV/Van	1,000 LBS	400 FT	2400 FT
	Small Moving Van/Delivery Truck	4,000 LBS	640 FT	3800 FT
	Moving Van/ Water Truck	10,000 LBS	860 FT	5100 FT

FIGURE10–7
Bomb Standoff Chart
Source: Department of Homeland Security (DHS), "Lessons Learned Information Sharing," 2009, https://www.llis.dhs.gov/sites/default/files/DHS-BombThreatChart-6-5-09.pdf

1. These capacities are based on the maximum weight of explosive material (TNT equivalent) that could reasonably fit in a container of similar size.

2. Personnel in buildings are provided a high degree of protection from death or serious injury; however, glass breakage and building debris may still cause some injuries. Unstrengthened buildings can be expected to sustain damage that approximates 5 percent of their replacement cost.

3. If personnel cannot enter a building to seek shelter they must evacuate to the minimum distance recommended by Outdoor Evacuation Distance. The distance is governed by the greater hazard of fragmentation distance, glass breakage, or threshold for eardrum rupture.

Fires, Bombs, and Explosive Devices

Fires affecting retail establishments may be caused by natural events (lightning strikes), accidents, or arson. It is not just the fires that endanger lives but also the smoke, heat, poisonous gas (carbon dioxide), and the panic associated with them. Fire safety is everyone's job, and each organization should have a fire plan. All employees, especially security professionals, should know where fire extinguishers and alarm devices are located. The U.S. Department of Labor advises that the organization's fire safety plan should outline the assignments of key personnel in the event of a fire and provide an evacuation plan for workers on the site.[124]

Although they are not new to some areas, the use of bombs and explosive devices has become more prevalent since the creation of the IED. These devices are essentially homemade bombs constructed from conventional military explosives such as artillery rounds, or unconventional explosives like agricultural fertilizer and Semtex, a plastic explosive used in commercial blasting and demolition. Once the IED is fitted into containers ranging in size from a lunchbox to a large delivery truck, a timer or remote device linked to a cell phone or other form of electronic communication is used to set it off. For example, the IEDs constructed by the Boston Marathon bombers were made from ball bearings, nails, gun powder, and other components placed in pressure cookers and were set off by remote-control devices from model cars triggered by mobile telephones.[125]

The toughest challenge of detecting IEDs is the identification of trace chemicals that are easily masked by compounds like perfumes or diesel exhaust. Bomb-sniffing dogs and laboratory-grade equipment are the best tools for trace chemical detection. However, both of these options are expensive and require a trained professional to handle effectively. Because these devices have become more prevalent, safety and security professionals have been looking for ways to detect them in an efficient manner. Scientists at the U.S. Naval Research Laboratory (NRL) have developed sensor technology that may revolutionize the way trace chemical detection is conducted. The sensor is called Silicon Nanowires in a Vertical Array with a Porous Electrode 9SiN-VAPOR). It is a small, portable, lightweight, low power, low overhead sensor that NRL researchers hope can be used by soldiers in the field and airport security personnel across the globe.[126]

Spotlight
INTERCON Bomb Threat Plan

The Center for Problem-Oriented Policing offered the INTERCON Bomb Threat Plan for security professionals. The plan includes a five-step process for effectively dealing with bomb threats. The five steps are:

1. Receiving the call and notifying the control point.
2. Evaluation of the call by the control point, and determining which of the following steps is required:
   - A search
   - No search
   - An evacuation
3. A search of the premises.
4. If necessary, evacuation of the premises in an orderly manner.
5. All clear.

The plan also includes a sample "threatening call form" that can be used to assist anyone receiving a threatening call. As communication of a bomb threat may come in other forms, like posts on social media, emails, or text messages, the form can be adapted or used to the extent relevant to the threat.

Source: Center for Problem-Oriented Policing, 2014, http://www.popcenter.org/problems/bomb_threats/PDFs/planCanada.pdf

---

Countering Terrorism with Private Security

The private sector is engaged in countering the terrorism threat in many ways. If they are supplementing military forces in the battlefield, they provide a key service, of course. The threat is not limited to the traditional battlefield, however, and the private sector engages this enemy in other locations. Brian Jenkins, a long-time terrorist scholar, suggested that the contribution of the private security industry was necessary to counter a terrorist threat.[127] Creating close relationships between the private sector, local police departments, and private security to ensure that there are mechanisms to share information are necessary. This is being done in several large metropolitan cities. In London, for example, Straw noted that companies access a private security network with the police to regularly share information so they can be informed and can rapidly respond to a large-scale event.[128]

The DHS has also recognized the need to connect with the private sector and the community. To increase public awareness and reporting of signs of criminal activity and violent extremism, DHS implemented and expanded its national "If You See Something, Say Something" campaign in collaboration with law enforcement, organizations in the private sector, and local community groups. The DHS is partnering with a variety of entities including: transportation systems, universities, states, cities, sports leagues, and local law enforcement. The core message of the campaign is self-defining: If you see something suspicious taking place then report that behavior or activity to local law enforcement or, in the case of emergency, call 9-1-1.[129]

The DHS reminds citizens that factors that identify a person such as race, ethnicity, national origin, or religious affiliation alone are not reason to be suspicious. Consequently, the public should report only actual suspicious behavior and situations (e.g., an unattended backpack in a public place or someone trying to break into a restricted area) rather than another person's beliefs, thoughts, ideas, or speech that are unrelated to terrorism or other criminal activity. Only reports that document behavior reasonably indicative of criminal activity related to terrorism will be shared.[130]

Executive and Protection Services

Business and government leaders, as well as sports and entertainment celebrities are among those who seek personal protection (often called bodyguard) services to protect them from harm. Business leaders may be (and have been) assaulted, murdered, and kidnapped, and the use of a security professional skilled in providing personal protection can limit the chances of those occurrences. Leaders may encounter adversaries wishing to do them harm.[131] The attackers may be motivated by their perceived mistreatment during layoffs or terminations, or because of dangerous or unstable environments. Personal protection services include a combination of advance travel preparations, timely intelligence and information, liaison with local authorities, and the use of highly trained protection professionals. Planning can be enhanced by security surveys and liaison with local law enforcement and security.[132]

There are numerous ways for an attacker to get to an executive, including through family members. Duffy observed that protecting an individual is a very different discipline from securing a facility, and offered the following tips.

1. Ask questions early (and often). Identify critical individuals in the organization, assess the impact to the corporation if they were lost and examine the risks that each of those people faces. Conduct a thorough risk analysis on each of them, including any past threats they received, the frequency of their travel to dangerous destinations, or vulnerable situations they may experience.

2. Ditch the bouncer profile for security professionals. The profile of personal protection services has evolved. The tall and wide profile has ben replaced by the security professional who conducts research and preparation to keep the principal safe.

3. Make protection a perk. The job can seem dull and uneventful. Good organizational and research skills will prevent the majority of problems, and the principal may not realize how needed his or her security detail really is. Security professionals excel at helping an executive eliminate many of the usual annoyances of travel, making protection more of a perk than a pain for the principal.

4. Stand against resistance. Security professionals need to educate the executive about security recommendations. Executives may argue against their need for protection, and it can be helpful to use terms that the business executive feels comfortable with, like cost-benefit and return on investment when making the case for security.

5. Build a big Rolodex. The security professional must work closely with executive assistants, hotel personnel, and event organizers, in addition to law enforcement and other security professionals. When executives network for an event, it is also a good opportunity for security personnel to network. These connections can be helpful in the future, assuming the contact is pleasant and willing to collaborate for mutual benefit.

6. Don't forget the family. The most vulnerable people may not be the executives who have protection, but their spouses and children. Family members are far more accessible and are often left out of security planning. The security professional should identify possible risks to the executive, as well as providing solutions within the scope of his or her employment.[133]

Assessing the Threat of Terrorism

Private security professionals can serve the community by providing insight to local police for their Terrorism Threat Assessment, conducting Terrorism Threat Assessments for their own organization, and encouraging and offering to assist organizations adjacent to them in doing the same. The U.S. Bureau of Justice Assistance defines a *Terrorism Threat Assessment* as a systematic effort conducted to identify and evaluate existing or potential terrorist threats to a jurisdiction and its assets.[134] These assessments consider the full spectrum of threats, like natural disasters, criminal activity, and major accidents, as well as terrorist activity. As it is difficult to assess terrorist capabilities, intentions, and tactics, threat assessments may provide only general information. Law enforcement cannot function alone in these assessments. Threat assessments should incorporate the knowledge, assessments, and understanding of government and private organizations and agencies with the potential threats being assessed.[135] The threat assessment should include both relevant, open-source, and nonproprietary threat assessments, as well as intelligence information. Assessments should provide a high level of awareness and understanding regarding the changing threat and threat environment.

Essential data to collect for analysis prior to conducting a threat assessment includes:

- *Type of adversary*: Terrorist, activist, employee, other.
- *Category of adversary*: Foreign or domestic, terrorist or criminal, insider and/or outsider of the organization.
- *Objective of each type of adversary*: Theft, sabotage, mass destruction (maximum casualties), sociopolitical statement, other.
- *Number of adversaries expected for each category*: Individual suicide bomber, grouping or "cells" of operatives/terrorists, gangs, other.
- *Target selected by adversaries*: Critical infrastructure, governmental buildings, national monuments, other.
- *Type of planning activities required to accomplish the objective*: Long-term "casing," photography, monitoring police and security patrol patterns, other.
- *Most likely or "worst case" time an adversary could attack*: When facility/location is fully staffed, at rush hour, at night, other.
- *Range of adversary tactics*: Stealth, force, deceit, combination, other.
- *Capabilities of adversary*: Knowledge, motivation, skills, weapons and tools.[136]

To further convey the likelihood of the threat, threat levels may be assigned based on the degree to which combinations of these factors are present:

- *Existence*: A terrorist group is present or is able to gain access to a given locality.
- *Capability*: The capability of a terrorist group to carry out an attack has been assessed or demonstrated.
- *Intent*: Evidence of terrorist group activity, including stated or assessed intent to conduct terrorist activity.
- *History*: Demonstrated terrorist activity in the past.
- *Targeting*: Current credible information or activity exists that indicates preparations for specific terrorist operations—intelligence collection by a suspect group, preparation of destructive devices, other actions.
- *Security environment*: Indicates if and how the political and security posture of the threatened jurisdiction affects the capability of terrorist elements to carry out their intentions and addresses whether the jurisdiction is concerned with terrorism and whether it has taken strong proactive countermeasures to deal with such a threat.[137]

Contrary to concerns of many citizens, law enforcement, and terrorism experts, Islamist or jihadist terrorism has been no more deadly in the United States than domestic terrorism since 9/11. The United States has yet to see an Islamist terrorist incident involving chemical, biological, radiological, or nuclear weapons, and no Islamist militant has made a documented attempt to even acquire such devices in the United States. If a chemical, biological, or radiological attack were to take place in the United States, it is more likely that it would come from a right-wing extremist or anarchist than an Islamist terrorist. In fact, there were five instances of successful or attempted development or purchase of biological, chemical, or radiological weapons by violent non-jihadists identified in the NAF-MSPP study:

- William Krar, a right-wing militia activist, and his wife, Judith Bruey, had stored enough chemicals to produce a quantity of hydrogen cyanide gas that could kill thousands, along with more than a hundred weapons, nearly 100,000 rounds of ammunition and more than one hundred pounds of explosives. They were arrested in 2003. Krar was sentenced to more than eleven years in prison, while Bruey received nearly five years.

- Joseph Konopka, an anarchist, was stockpiling dangerous chemicals, including sodium cyanide. He was arrested by Chicago police in 2002 and was sentenced to thirteen years.

- Bruce Ivins, a microbiologist, killed five people when he sent letters filled with anthrax to politicians and journalists during fall 2001. Ivins committed suicide in 2008.

- Demetrius van Crocker, a white supremacist, was arrested in 2004 after trying to purchase sarin nerve gas and C-4 explosive from an undercover agent. He was sentenced to thirty years in prison.

- James Cummings, another white supremacist, acquired a supply of radiological materials from scientific research companies and was planning to build a "dirty" radiological bomb when his wife killed him after years of domestic abuse in 2008.

Careers in Security

Name: Michael Knight

Position: Special Agent/Public Information Officer

Year hired: 1990

City, State where you are based: Nashville, Tennessee

College(s) attended (degree): DePaul University, BA Accounting

Major(s): Accounting

Did you attend graduate school? Yes

College(s) attended (degree): Georgetown University post grad studies

Please give a brief description of your job. Enforce the federal firearms and explosive laws. Promote ATF through the media and respond to congressional inquiries.

What qualities/characteristics are most helpful for this job? Ability to communicate in all forms, think outside the box, be aggressive, leadership.

What is a typical starting salary? $60,000

What is the salary potential as you move up into higher-level jobs? $150,000

What advice would you give someone in college beginning studies in security? Besides school become involved with extracurricular groups, internships.

What appealed to you most about the position when you applied for it? The ability to be creative in position unlike most other agencies where tasks are delegated.

How would you describe the interview process? Have to be able to communicate orally and in written form. Need the confidence to answer a variety of questions and dress appropriately.

What is a typical day like? Combination of intelligence gathering on individuals in violation of the federal firearms and explosive laws, court appearances, and documentation of all activities. Conduct post blast investigations. In the public information role, meet with media outlets on a daily basis to either respond to their questions on incidents or pitching stories that will benefit the public. Also, meet with congressional staff to respond to inquiries from their constituents.

In a typical day, what do you like best/least about it? Best—I like to be creative in accomplishing the tasks, and my job allows me that opportunity.

Least—I don't want to leave work for outside activities due to the enjoyment I find in my job.

How would you suggest interested applicants gain experience? Internships, participate in explorer program, civic clubs, and organizations

Would you recommend military experience? Military experience will only add to your experience but is not a prerequisite.

Does holding a full-time job during college help applicants get hired afterwards? Any job will provide experience but doesn't necessary help in getting hired.

Summary

- **Identify the five core homeland security missions.**

  The five homeland security missions are:

  ○ Prevent terrorism and enhancing security.

  ○ Secure and manage our borders.

  ○ Enforce and administer our immigration laws.

  ○ Safeguard and secure cyberspace.

  ○ Ensure resilience to disasters.

- **Examine the roles of private security professionals regarding homeland security.**

  The roles of private security professionals regarding Homeland Security include:

  ○ Critical infrastructure and key resource (CIKR) owners and operators develop protective programs and measures to ensure that systems and assets, whether physical or virtual, are secure from and resilient to cascading, disruptive impacts.

  ○ Major and multinational corporations operate in all sectors of trade and commerce that foster the American way of life and support the operation, security, and resilience of global movement systems.

  ○ Small businesses contribute to all aspects of homeland security and support response efforts by developing contingency plans and working with local planners to ensure that their plans are consistent with pertinent response procedures.

- **Determine the best definition for terrorism, international terrorism, and domestic terrorism.**

  The FBI is the primary agency for investigating terrorism, international terrorism, and domestic terrorism, and the agency uses the definitions from the U.S. Code of Federal Regulation and Title 18 of the U.S. Code.

  ○ The U.S. Code of Federal Regulation defines terrorism as the unlawful use of force and violence against persons or property to intimidate or coerce a government, the civilian population, or any segment thereof, in furtherance of political or social objectives (28 C.F.R. Section 0.85).

  ○ Title 18 of the U.S. Code (U.S.C.), § 2331 defines international terrorism as activities that:

    ■ Involve violent acts or acts dangerous to human life that violate federal or state law.

    ■ Appear to be intended (i) to intimidate or coerce a civilian population; (ii) to influence the policy of a government by intimidation or coercion; or (iii) to affect the conduct of a government by mass destruction, assassination, or kidnapping.

    ■ Occur primarily outside the territorial jurisdiction of the United States, or transcend national boundaries in terms of the means by which they are accomplished, the persons they appear intended to intimidate or coerce, or the locale in which their perpetrators operate or seek asylum.

  ○ 18 U.S.C. § 2331 defines domestic terrorism as activities that:

    ■ Involve acts dangerous to human life that violate federal or state law.

    ■ Appear intended (i) to intimidate or coerce a civilian population; (ii) to influence the policy of a government by intimidation or coercion; or (iii) to affect the conduct of a government by mass destruction, assassination. or kidnapping.

    ■ Occur primarily within the territorial jurisdiction of the U.S.

- **Distinguish homegrown violent extremists from domestic terrorists.**

  ○ A homegrown violent extremist (HVE) is a person of any citizenship who has lived and/or operated primarily in the United States or its territories who advocates, is engaged in, or is preparing to engage in ideologically motivated terrorist activities (including providing support to terrorism) in furtherance of political or social objectives promoted by a foreign terrorist organization, but is acting independently of direction by a foreign terrorist organization. HVEs are distinguished from domestic terrorists who engage in unlawful acts of violence to intimidate civilian populations or attempt to influence domestic policy without direction from or influence from a foreign actor.

○ A domestic terrorist is one who commits any act of violence that is dangerous to human life or potentially destructive of critical infrastructure or key resources committed by a group or individual based and operating entirely within the United States or its territories without direction or inspiration from a foreign terrorist group. The act is a violation of the criminal laws of the United States or of any state or other subdivision of the United States and appears to be intended to intimidate or coerce a civilian population, to influence the policy of a government by intimidation or coercion, or to affect the conduct of a government by mass destruction, assassination, or kidnapping. A domestic terrorist differs from a homegrown violent extremist in that the former is not inspired by and does not take direction from a foreign terrorist group or other foreign power.

● Demonstrate understanding of the four major activities of terrorist groups.

The four major activities of terrorist groups are:

○ Recruitment, preliminary organization and planning, preparatory conduct, and the terrorist act. Each of these behaviors could serve as "pre-incident indicators" to analysts monitoring such activities.

KEY TERMS

anarchist
   extremists   **220**
animal rights
   extremists   **220**
anti-abortion
   extremists   **220**
domestic terrorism   **219**
environmental rights
   extremists   **220**
ethno-nationalist/
   separatist
   terrorists   **226**

extreme left-wing
   terrorists   **225**
extreme right-wing
   terrorists   **225**
homegrown violent
   extremist   **216**
homeland security   **207**
international
   terrorism   **215**
lone offenders   **220**

militia extremists   **220**
racist skinhead
   extremists   **221**
religious terrorists   **225**
single-issue
   terrorists   **226**
sovereign citizen
   extremists   **220**
terrorism   **227**

REVIEW QUESTIONS

1. Which of the core homeland security concepts do you best understand? Which could be removed?

2. How do private security professionals contribute to the nation's homeland security posture?

3. If you were tasked with providing a concise, legal, definition of homeland security, what steps would you take to determine the best response?

4. Other than the differences stated, what distinguishes homegrown violent extremists from domestic terrorists?

5. Describe a situation, real or fictitious, in which at least three of the four major terrorist activities occurred.

PRACTICAL APPLICATION

- You are the new State Homeland Security Director. What percentage of your organization's resources will be dedicated to understanding and tracking local, regional, and national terrorist threats versus international terrorist threats?
- Describe a scenario in which a security professional is likely to detect some of the indicators of terrorism covered in this chapter.
- You are a security manager in a large manufacturing corporation that has recently experienced protests aimed at the hazardous materials used in the manufacturing press. You want to explain to local media outlet that the materials are safely secured and do not endanger citizens or the environment. Who in your company should you coordinate with before the meeting?

Emergency Practices and Crisis/Disaster Management

Learning Objectives

After reading this chapter, you should be able to:

1. Identify the basic styles or approaches for incident management and response. **237**

2. Distinguish some differences between a crisis, a disaster, and an emergency. **238**

3. Explain what the National Incident Management System was designed to accomplish. **249**

4. Describe the incident command system. **250**

5. Identify and distinguish a business impact analysis, business continuity management, and continuity of operations. **252**

Introduction

Consider these events in the context of security challenges:

- The Fukushima Daiichi nuclear disaster followed an earthquake and tsunami in Japan on March 11, 2011. A state of nuclear emergency was declared and thousands of residents were evacuated from their homes. Generators failed at the nuclear plant when a tsunami followed an earthquake, cutting power to the pumps needed to continuously circulate coolant water through the nuclear reactor to keep it from melting down. The reactors overheated, and several hydrogen-air chemical explosions occurred. As of August 2013, there were no deaths caused by radiation exposure, while approximately 18,500 people died due to the earthquake and tsunami.[1]

- From October 22 to 29, 2012, Hurricane Sandy became the deadliest and second-costliest tropical cyclone on record, after Hurricane Katrina of 2005. It was the largest Atlantic hurricane measured by diameter, with winds spanning 1,100 miles. Estimates assessed damage to have been over $68 billion, and at least 286 people in seven countries were killed. Damage in the United States amounted to $65 billion in 24 states.[2]

- On April 27, 2011, tornadoes in Alabama, Mississippi, and four other states in the South caused billions of dollars in damage and represented the nation's deadliest tornadoes in thirty-seven years. Although residents received warning that tornadoes were on their way, the storms were too wide and strong for people to escape.[3]

- The *Deepwater Horizon* oil spill (the BP oil spill) began in April 2010 in the Gulf of Mexico on the Macondo Prospect (operated by BP) with the explosion and sinking of the *Deepwater Horizon* oil rig. Following the explosion, oil flowed for eighty-seven days, with a total of 4.9 million barrels (210 million U.S. gallons) discharged into the Gulf, the largest accidental oil spill in history. According to the U.S. Environmental Protection Agency, due to the spill and subsequent response and cleanup activities, extensive damage to marine and wildlife habitats, fishing and tourism industries, as well as human health problems have occurred. In November 2012, BP and the U.S. Department of Justice settled federal criminal charges with BP pleading guilty to several counts of manslaughter and a felony count of lying to Congress.[4]

What do these events all have in common? They are examples of incidents that create new challenges for security professionals and that add to their more traditional responsibilities. The emergency management realm is an added challenge to security professionals. It is not surprising then that one of the most significant contemporary security challenges has been the increased focus on emergency, crisis, and disaster management—a task that includes preparation for and response to catastrophic events, including droughts, famines, floods, fires, explosions, pandemics, volcanic eruptions, earthquakes, tsunamis, winter storms, and other disasters.[5] Such events can be the result of either natural or technological (human-made) activity. These cataclysmic events require an immediate response that is not only thoughtful and effective, but also flexible and evolving.

Preparation and planning for catastrophe is the responsibility of the security professional, a fact that is now recognized by both governmental and business leaders alike.[6] For example, in a recent study of planning, organization, training, and exercises identified in the 2013 National Preparedness Report (NPR), on-scene security and protection received the highest national assessment average.[7]

Emergency management practices are increasingly the responsibility of security professionals. The terrorist attacks of 9/11 redirected the emergency response focus on national preparedness and homeland security. Although the impact of weather-related emergencies has grown in severity, preparedness and security are still the primary focus. Emergency management has evolved from a focus on ensuring safety in the wake of a disaster to a full-fledged program of before, during, and after analysis of the threat posed by an emergency situation.

Public and private security professionals have paid more attention to collaboration, information sharing, and partnership. As of 2006, there were more than 450 established private security–law enforcement partnerships. The United States recently realigned their preparedness posture, identifying five preparedness mission areas—prevention, protection, mitigation, response, and recovery—to ensure and enhance national preparedness.

In the following sections we will explore this important topic in some detail. First, however, we will examine the history of emergency, crisis, and disaster management.

History of Emergency, Crisis, and Disaster Management

Emergency crisis management is a relatively new concept. Until the early 1900s, the U.S. government rarely got involved in assisting local governments that were affected by natural or human-created disasters. President Franklin D. Roosevelt (1933–1945) initiated the use of government funding for emergency management concerns to stimulate local economies.[8] In 1932, the Reconstruction Finance Corporation was authorized to make disaster loans for repair and reconstruction of public facilities, and in 1934 the Bureau of Public Roads was authorized to provide funding for damaged highways and bridges.[9] The United States was not alone in making provisions for disaster relief: Canada began emergency planning after World War II.[10]

In the 1950s, the primary activity of emergency planners shifted to preparation for a nuclear attack. The Cold War between the United States and Soviet Union caused much paranoia and U.S. citizens were routinely warned to be prepared for a nuclear attack; some were encouraged to build fallout shelters.[11] During the 1960s increased legislation in the United States helped people deal with damage caused by natural disasters. For example, in 1968, the National Flood Insurance Act offered flood protection to homeowners for the first time, and in 1974, the Disaster Relief Act established the process for disaster declarations by the U.S. president.[12]

In the most serious accident in American nuclear power plant history, a nuclear reactor at Three Mile Island, near Middletown, Pennsylvania, partially melted down on March 28, 1979. Although there were no detectable health effects on plant workers or the public due to the limited radioactive release, its aftermath brought about many changes involving nuclear power plant operations and regulatory oversight.[13]

Supporting Emergency Management Legislation

The advent of emergency practices in the United States was aided by accompanying laws and legislation that enabled relief agencies to operate freely when dealing with emergencies and also provided funding to make those operations possible. One of the first such pieces of legislation, the Flood Control Act of 1936 illustrated Congress's determination that floods would be considered a national menace.[14] The stated intent of the act was for *the benefit of navigation and the control of destructive floodwaters and other purposes.*[15] The solution, it was decided, was some form of nationwide flood control administered by the federal government, and at least partially financed by federal funds. The Flood Control Act of 1936 shifted the emphasis of the U.S. Army Corps of Engineers from building dikes and levees to contain rivers to a focus on building multiple-purpose dams to improve flood control and navigation and generate hydropower, according to the Northwest Power and Conservation Council.[16] Later, The National Flood Insurance Act of 1968 created the Federal Insurance Administration and made flood insurance available for the first time. The legislative evolution continued when the Flood Disaster Protection Act of 1973 made the purchase of flood insurance mandatory for the protection of property located in special flood hazard areas.[17]

The National Governor's Association (NGA) developed the first model framework for government-run emergency management in 1979 during its study of emergency preparedness. The NGA identified the four phases of emergency management: mitigation, preparedness, response, and recovery.[18] In 1979, by executive order President Jimmy Carter consolidated many of the dozens of federal agencies involved in handling disasters and emergencies into the Federal Emergency Management Agency (FEMA). Another key piece of legislation, the Disaster Relief Act of 1974 established the process of presidential disaster declarations to better handle disasters throughout the United States.[19] The act also helped to provide more

1 Identify the basic styles or approaches for incident management and response.

THINK ABOUT IT

What is it about an "all hazards" approach that can make things more simple for government and private enterprise to respond to events? What makes such an approach potentially more difficult to apply?

all-hazards approach
An approach used by emergency management to respond to incidents or events, natural or human caused, that require an organized response by a public, private, and/or governmental entity in order to protect life, public health and safety, values to be protected, and to minimize any disruption of governmental, social, and economic services.

functions-based approach
Used when a jurisdiction focuses its planned response on the potential effects of generalized emergencies and hazards, to avoid duplication of the planning effort for every hazard and every task for the organizations that use the approach. A functions-based approach builds plan performance around "generic" functions, and permits an emphasis on hazards that pose the greatest risk.

2 Distinguish some differences between a crisis, a disaster, and an emergency.

emergency
An extraordinary situation in which people are unable to meet their basic survival needs, or there are serious and immediate threats to human life and well-being. Conditions may become chaotic during emergencies, producing confusion and an interruption of communications.

fixed relief to disaster victims. In November 1988, the U.S. Congress amended the Disaster Relief Act of 1974 and renamed it the Robert T. Stafford Disaster Relief and Emergency Assistance Act (named after Robert Stafford, who served as the seventy-first governor of Vermont, a U.S. Representative, a U.S. Senator, and an ardent environmentalist who died in 2006). That act created the Federal Response Plan (FRP), outlined the statutory authority for federal disaster response activities, and embodied the principles and mechanisms needed to assist state and local communities in times of disasters.

The FRP established both an all-hazards and functions-based approach to emergency management that aimed for a coordinated and efficient use of resources during disasters. As defined, the **all-hazards approach** to emergency management is used to respond to "any incident or event, natural or human caused, that requires an organized response by a public, private, and/or governmental entity in order to protect life, public health and safety, protect values, and to minimize any disruption of governmental, social, and economic services."[20] A disaster response plan that uses the all-hazards approach can be very detailed because it often addresses every possible incident of potential concern. In contrast, a **functions-based approach** is used when a community or jurisdiction focuses their planned response on the potential effects of emergencies in general and covers a variety of hazards, rather than requiring the development of separate plans for each hazard. This approach avoids duplication of the planning effort for every hazard and every task for the organizations that use the approach. According to FEMA, a functions-based approach builds plan performance around "generic" functions, and permits an emphasis on hazards that pose the greatest risk.[21]

The FRP identified twelve emergency support functions (ESFs), designed to group organizations based on their responsibilities, capabilities, capacity, and expertise. That approach established not only the framework for coordination but also collaboration among agencies representing different sectors and levels of government.[22] The Disaster Mitigation Act of 2000 further amended the Stafford Disaster Relief and Emergency Assistance Act. The FRP was replaced by the National Response Plan (NRP) in 2004, which was then replaced by the National Response Framework (NRF) in 2008. The NRF became the first of the National Planning Frameworks (NPF), which was designed to identify coordinated roles and responsibilities for the whole community. Each framework covers one mission preparedness area: prevention, protection, mitigation, response, or recovery. Each framework addresses the roles of individuals, nonprofit entities and nongovernmental organizations (NGOs), the private sector, communities, critical infrastructure, governments, and the United States as a whole. The areas covered represent a spectrum of activity that is highly interdependent and requires regular coordination to prevent, protect against, mitigate, respond to, and recover from all threats and hazards.

Emergency, Crisis, or Disaster Management?

The terms used to describe incidents or events are critical to the understanding of the severity of the event. In contemporary language, the terms *emergency*, *disaster*, and *crisis* are often used to describe similar events. Although these terms may sometimes be treated the same, it is important to ensure that they are distinguishable so varying degrees of emergency events can be identified and classified to ensure proper response.

Emergencies

According to the Simeon Institute, an **emergency** is an extraordinary situation in which people are unable to meet their basic survival needs, or there are serious and immediate threats to human life and well-being.[23] The definition of *emergency*, as distinguished from a disaster or crisis, is dependent on the level of assistance needed to save lives and protect property and public health and safety. During an emergency, ASIS International suggests that we expect confusion and an interruption of communication links, as conditions may become chaotic.[24]

To deal with such urgent situations, the practice of emergency management has evolved. It is the process of organization and management of resources and responsibilities for all aspects of emergencies, especially preparedness, response, and the initial recovery steps.[25] An emergency situation may arise as a result of neglect or environmental degradation, or when emergency measures have to be taken to prevent or limit the effects of some natural or human-created tragedy.[26] According to strategy developed by the United Nations, emergency management involves plans to engage and guide the efforts of government, non-government, voluntary, and private agencies in comprehensive and coordinated ways to respond to the entire spectrum of emergency needs.[27]

ASIS International observed that emergency management has three primary objectives:

- Minimize the probability of a threat or emergency (possible with human or accidental threats, not with natural threats).
- Mitigate the impact if the event occurs.
- Recover from the emergency and resume normal operations.[28]

Crisis

A **crisis** is an incident or situation involving a threat to a specific country, its territories, citizens, military forces, possessions, or national security interests that develops rapidly and creates a condition of such diplomatic, economic, political, or military importance that commitment of military forces and resources is contemplated to achieve national objectives.[29]

An emergency situation becomes a crisis when it has reached a critical phase. Elliot found that crises often have a symbolic importance, beyond the physical properties, that lead security personnel and others to question existing procedures, core values, and assumptions.[30] The existence of a crisis is indicated when normal operational procedures are severely impacted, traumatic events or situations occur, or the lives and the well-being of employees are directly impacted.[31]

Crisis management can occur before, during, and after an emergency takes on a critical form.[32] Three phases typify crisis management:

- Crisis of management, which occurs before the incident. This precrisis stage is where the potential for failure is incubated. It is an historical phase in which decisions are made that cause the organization to be more or less vulnerable to crises. Critical decisions made at this stage might include: (1) adjustments to staffing levels; (2) management response to safety reviews or security assessments; (3) responses to information or intelligence regarding a potential threat.[33] A crisis management approach examines how the potential for crisis may come from the organizational culture and structure.
- Operational crisis, which reflects the manner in which the organization handles the incident.
- Crisis of legitimation, which happens after the incident when an organization looks toward consolidation and repositioning itself. This phase may feed back into phase one if organizations do not learn from their experiences, especially regarding corrections to the culture and changes in leadership.[34]

Disaster

The term **disaster** defines dangerous events that are concentrated in time and space that disrupt the social structure and prevent certain societal functions.[35] Disasters often seriously disrupt functioning of a community and involve widespread human, material, economic or environmental losses and impacts. Disasters usually exceed the ability that the affected community has to cope using its own resources.[36]

The potential impact of disasters includes loss of life, injury, and disease, damage to property, loss of services, economic disruption and environmental degradation.[37] Elliott noted that natural events such as floods and tsunamis are disasters that cannot be stopped or prevented, but may be predicted in advanced so that life-saving preparations can occur.[38] He found that disaster management studies focus on the human element rather than the event, examining the impact of disasters on members of the community and how organized responses can minimize the negative shock of these events.[39]

crisis
An incident or situation involving a threat to a specific country, its territories, citizens, military forces, possessions, or national security interests that develops rapidly and creates a condition of such diplomatic, economic, political, or military importance that commitment of military forces and resources is contemplated to achieve national objectives. An emergency situation becomes a crisis when it has reached a critical phase.

disaster
Defines dangerous events that are concentrated in time and space that disrupt the social structure and prevent certain societal functions. Disasters often seriously disrupt functioning of a community and involve widespread human, material, economic, or environmental losses and impacts.

The Effect of Emergency, Crisis, or Disaster Management on Security

The terrorist attacks of 9/11, along with recent natural disasters like hurricanes Sandy and Katrina have further highlighted the need for security professionals to coordinate more effectively across the private and public sectors. This is especially important because the private sector controls and protects most of the nation's critical infrastructure.[40] Public law enforcement has made a lot of progress in obtaining terror-related information, but they have been reluctant to share this information with private industry because some government officials fear that information they give to private-sector security agencies may end up being disseminated to the public.[41] While these fears persist, the Department of Homeland Security (DHS) has recommended that public law enforcement and private security establish and maintain cooperative agreements to address homeland security needs.[42]

Maintaining Partnerships

In recent years, both police departments and private security have paid more attention to collaboration, information sharing, and partnerships. The legal powers and training of law enforcement officers combined with the size, resources, and technical expertise of private security can create successful partnerships.[43] In 2000, the Department of Justice reported that more than sixty private security and policing partnership programs were in operation; today there are more than 450 established private security–law enforcement partnerships. The success of these partnerships hinges on several key factors, including:[44]

- A compelling mission.
- External support of models for formation.
- Strong, active founders, leaders, and facilitators.
- Regular communication.
- Established methods to sustain structure and sufficient resources.

▲ FEMA responds to recent flooding. Flooding can happen without much warning. What sort of security concerns are caused by flooding?
Source: U.S. Federal Emergency Management Agency (FEMA), https://www.fema.gov/media-library/assets/images/83609

A compelling mission is important to keep members interested and attract new members. Regular communication includes activities such as meetings, training sessions, newsletters, email, and websites. To succeed long term, these partnerships must be nurtured. They cannot simply be started and expected to continue and grow under their own power.[45]

Emergency Management and National Preparedness

Disasters can happen at any time and in any place, but their human and financial consequences are hard to predict.[46] In 2012, Hurricane Isaac tested the enhanced levee systems protecting New Orleans. The size of the storm and its slow movement resulted in storm surges in certain areas that rivaled those of Hurricane Katrina, but the enhanced levee systems recently built around New Orleans post-Katrina withstood the storm's surge, lessening its overall effects.[47] Local, state, and federal governments mounted the response, but security professionals in affected organizations needed to fill similar roles and employ similar efforts.

Although there were many actions seen as successes, the response to Sandy, the second-largest Atlantic storm on record, revealed notable challenges in how FEMA coordinates with federal, state, and local partners.[48] Difficulties with issuing timely assignments, the implementation of incident management structures, and meeting the needs of survivors early in the response phase were examples of the challenges experienced. Ultimately, the experience confirmed that larger-scale incidents stress the agency's capacity for effective response and recovery.

In response to these and similar events, the U.S. government has issued a number of directives defining needs for emergency management and creating a framework for national preparedness. For example, Presidential Policy Directive (PPD) 8, released in March 2011, was designed to develop policy and planning guides to prepare for natural and human-made disasters.[49] To reach that goal, it defined the five preparedness mission areas—prevention, protection, mitigation, response, and recovery.[50] The directive identified: "A secure and resilient nation with the capabilities required across the whole community to prevent, protect against, mitigate, respond to, and recover from the threats and hazards that pose the greatest risk."[51] The goal is to share the responsibility of promoting national preparedness through integrated planning, training, and exercising. According to the U.S. Department of Homeland Security, protection should involve the following features:

- A unified approach to protection.

- Synchronization and interoperability within and across all the mission areas (prevention, protection, mitigation, response, and recovery).

- Collaboration and engagement to achieve the objectives of the National Preparedness Goal.[52]

Synchronization occurs when various activities are arranged in a determined and sequenced time or speed, coordinated across all aspects of the mission area. *Interoperability* refers to the ability of a system to work with or use the components of another system. Public–private collaboration and information sharing between all relevant stakeholders in the public and private sector are essential to meeting protection mission objectives. The various federal departments and agencies that are assigned coordinating roles, providing the basis for ongoing coordination, management, and maintenance of the protection framework, accomplish collaboration.

Prevention

Prevention includes those capabilities necessary to avoid, prevent, or stop a threatened or actual act of terrorism. It involves the whole community, from local residents to senior leaders in government.[53] The Department of Homeland Security's publication *National Protection Framework* (NPF) provides guidance to government leaders and practitioners at all levels; private and nonprofit sector partners; and other individuals to help prevent, avoid, or stop a threatened or actual act of terrorism. The NPF describes the core capabilities needed to prevent an imminent act of terrorism and aligns key roles and responsibilities to deliver prevention capabilities in time-sensitive situations. Prevention also requires providing a foundation for further operational coordination and planning that will synchronize efforts within the whole community.[54] According to DHS, prevention includes the core capabilities of:

prevention
Includes those capabilities necessary to avoid, prevent, or stop a threatened or actual act of terrorism. It involves the whole community, from local residents to senior leaders in government.

- Planning
- Public information and warning
- Operational coordination
- Forensics and attribution
- Intelligence and information sharing
- Interdiction and disruption
- Screening, search, and detection[55]

Each capability is an important aspect of prevention. Intelligence, and information sharing requires timely, accurate, and actionable information resulting from the acquisition and processing of information concerning national threats. Interdiction and disruption involves delaying or intercepting threats or hazards. The process of screening, search, and detection includes locating threats or hazards through active and passive surveillance and other procedures.

Protection

protection

Involves actions used to deter threats, mitigate vulnerabilities, or minimize the consequences associated with an emergency or crisis incident. Protection can include a wide range of activities, such as improving physical security, building redundancy, incorporating resistance to hazards in facility design, initiating active or passive threat countermeasures, installing security systems, promoting workforce security, training and exercising, and implementing cybersecurity measures to delay or deter unauthorized access.

Protection involves actions used to deter threats, mitigate vulnerabilities, or minimize the consequences associated with an emergency or crisis incident. Protection can include a wide range of activities, such as improving physical security; building redundancy; incorporating resistance to hazards in facility design; initiating active or passive threat countermeasures; installing security systems; promoting workforce security training, and exercising; and implementing cybersecurity measures. The ability to provide effective protection depends on the close coordination and alignment of protection practices across the whole community as well as coordination with international partners and organizations.[56]

In the United States, federal departments and agencies typically take the lead in protection services, but overall success is dependent on close and continuous coordination between government organizations and the private sector. The National Preparedness Goal, released by FEMA in September 2011, is to create: "A secure and resilient nation with the capabilities required across the whole community to prevent, protect against, mitigate, respond to, and recover from the threats and hazards that pose the greatest risk."[57] As outlined in the National Preparedness Goal, these risks include events such as natural disasters, disease pandemics, chemical spills and other human-created hazards, terrorist attacks, and cyberattacks.

Mitigation

mitigation

Describes efforts to reduce the loss of life and property by lessening the impact of disasters in an effort to mitigate harm and reduce human and financial consequences. Mitigation strategies are aimed at improving safety, financial security, and self-reliance in the future.

Mitigation describes efforts to reduce the loss of life and property by lessening the impact of disasters in an effort to mitigate harm, and reduce human and financial consequences. Mitigation strategies are aimed at improving safety, financial security, and self-reliance in the future. It is critical to consider the implications in the context of the economy, housing, health and social services, infrastructure, and natural and cultural resources when preparing for mitigation plans and activities. The DHS lists four guiding principles for mitigation, which include:

- Resilience and sustainability
- Leadership and locally focused implementation
- Engaged partnerships and inclusiveness
- Risk-conscious culture[58]

Resilience involves preparing people, property, critical infrastructure resources, and the economy to absorb the impact of an incident and recover in a way that sustains their way of life in the aftermath that makes their communities more resilient. Sustainability uses a longer-term approach through plans, policies, and actions that reflect a comprehensive understanding of the economic, social, and environmental systems within a community.[59]

The focus on leadership and locally focused implementation empowers formal and informal local leaders to embrace their ownership of building resilient and sustainable communities. The local community is responsible for ongoing mitigation, working together to identify, plan for, and reduce vulnerabilities and promote long-term personal and community resilience and sustainability. Leaders at the state and national levels support local leadership by facilitating effective ongoing mitigation.[60]

Engaged partnerships and inclusiveness may include government leaders at all levels joining forces with faith-based organizations, nonprofit organizations, private and corporate entities, academia, and other groups. According to the DHS, the most effective partnerships within a community capitalize on all available resources—identifying, developing, fostering, and strengthening new and existing coordinating structures to create a unity of effort. Many of the community organizations and partners in one mission area have active roles in other mission areas as well.[61]

A mature, risk-conscious culture is measured by the reduction in loss of life and whether there is sufficient capacity to continue promoting the vitality of the community when adapting to changing conditions or recovering from an adverse incident.[62]

In the United States, *mitigation* includes:

- Planning
- Public information and warning
- Operational coordination
- Community resilience
- Long-term vulnerability reduction
- Risk and disaster resilience assessment
- Threats and hazard identification[63]

The coordinating structures for mitigation focus on creating a shift in culture that effectively embeds risk management and mitigation in all planning, decision making, and development. As the owners and operators of the majority of the nation's infrastructure, private-sector entities are essential to improving community resilience through planning and long-term vulnerability reduction efforts. A more resilient private sector strengthens community resilience by helping to sustain economic vitality and ensuring the continued delivery of goods and services after a disaster. Considering risk management and mitigation will reduce the nation's risk and associated consequences.

Among numerous activities that promote and implement the mitigation core capabilities, business professionals analyze and manage their organization's risks, volunteer time and services, operate business emergency operations centers, help protect the nation's infrastructure, and promote the return on investment realized by all from increased resilience and reduced vulnerability.[64]

Response

The *response* mission area objectives define the capabilities necessary to save lives, protect property and the environment, and meet basic human needs. Additionally, they are intended to stabilize the incident, restore basic services and community functionality, and establish a safe and secure environment when transitioning to recovery.[65] The response mission area includes fourteen core capabilities:

1. Planning
2. Public information and warning
3. Operational coordination
4. Critical transportation
5. Environmental response/health and safety
6. Fatality management services
7. Infrastructure systems
8. Mass care services
9. Mass search and rescue operations
10. On-scene security and protection
11. Operational communications
12. Public and private services and resources
13. Public health and medical services
14. Situational assessment[66]

Some of the most important elements of this list include *operational communications*, which ensures the capacity for timely communications in support of security, situational awareness, and operations. *Critical transportation* includes evacuating both people and animals, and the delivery of vital response personnel, equipment, and services into affected areas. *Fatality management services* provide body recovery and victim identification, providing temporary mortuary solutions, and reunifying family members and caregivers with missing persons/remains. *Mass search and rescue operations* provide both a traditional and atypical search and rescue capabilities with the goal of saving the greatest number of endangered lives in the shortest time possible.

According to the National Response Framework, the best response measures are tiered, and not those with a one-size-fits-all construct, emphasizing that response to incidents should be handled at the lowest jurisdictional level. Private-sector organizations contribute to response efforts through partnerships with each level of government.[67] They play key roles before, during, and after incidents. Private-sector entities include large, medium, and small businesses; commerce, private cultural and educational institutions; and industry, as well as public/private partnerships that have been established specifically for emergency management purposes.[68] Private-sector organizations may play multiple roles simultaneously. During an incident, key private-sector partners should have a direct link to emergency managers and, in some cases, be involved in the decision-making process. Strong integration into response efforts can offer many benefits to both the public and private sectors.

A fundamental responsibility of private-sector organizations is to provide for the welfare of their employees in the workplace. In addition, some businesses play an essential role in protecting critical infrastructure systems and implementing plans for the rapid reestablishment of normal commercial activities and critical infrastructure operations following a disruption. In many cases, private-sector organizations have immediate access to commodities and services that can support incident response, making them key potential contributors of resources necessary to deliver the core capabilities.[69] How the private sector participates in response activities varies based on the type of organization and the nature of the incident. Examples of key private-sector activities include:

- Addressing the response needs of employees, infrastructure, and facilities.
- Protecting information and maintaining the continuity of business operations.
- Planning for, responding to, and recovering from incidents that impact their own infrastructure and facilities.
- Collaborating with emergency management personnel to determine what assistance may be required and how they can provide needed support.
- Contributing to communication and information-sharing efforts during incidents.
- Planning, training, and exercising their response capabilities.
- Providing assistance specified under mutual aid and assistance agreements.
- Contributing resources, personnel, and expertise; helping to shape objectives; and receiving information about the status of the community.[70]

These activities are necessary to support the community and are contained in many areas of the emergency management mission for security professionals.

Recovery

Citizen participation is critical in the *recovery* stage for its successful implementation.[71] To speed recovery from Hurricane Sandy and the 2012 drought, citizens in the community partnered to help implement recovery procedures. In addition, following the impact of a catastrophic 2011 tornado, the community of Joplin, Missouri, repaired or rebuilt nearly 80% of its damaged structures and began an ambitious $800 million development effort. On the Gulf Coast, community partners continued to implement a comprehensive recovery agenda to restore livelihoods and the environment following the 2010 BP *Deepwater Horizon* oil spill.[72] Recovery procedures guide effective recovery, especially for large-scale or catastrophic incidents, and enable effective recovery support to disaster-impacted communities. They also help responders focus on how best to restore, redevelop, and revitalize the health, social, economic, natural, and environmental fabric of the community.

The recovery process allows communities to capitalize on opportunities to rebuild stronger, smarter, and safer. The eight core capabilities for recovery, according to DHS, are

1. Planning
2. Public information and warning
3. Operational coordination
4. Economic recovery
5. Health and social services
6. Housing
7. Infrastructure systems
8. Natural and cultural resources.

The private sector plays a critical role in economic recovery, establishing public confidence immediately following a disaster. When the private sector is working and operational, the community recovers more quickly by retaining and providing jobs and a stable tax base. If local business and community leadership work together before the disaster and develop a recovery plan, the public is more likely to believe in the community's ability to recover after the disaster. Some requirements include stabilizing critical infrastructure functions, minimizing health and safety threats, and efficiently restoring and revitalizing systems and services to support a viable, resilient community. The partnership between government and business leaders is critical, because the private-sector owns and operates the vast majority of the nation's critical infrastructure, such as electric power, financial and telecommunications systems. These areas play a major role in the recovery of a community.

Planning

Planning is one of only three core capabilities that are identified in each of the five areas of the National Preparedness Goal. Recently, 85% of U.S. states rated their emergency operations plans as adequate to accomplish their missions. This rating was consistent with the overall improvements identified in the 2006 and 2010 *Nationwide Plan Reviews* by the Department of Homeland Security.[73] In addition, 61% of states reported they involved the whole community in developing those plans, including nongovernmental organizations, the private sector, and groups representing individuals with access and functional needs.

Security professionals and private-sector organization leaders have many areas that interface with these state and federal organizations. Response plans often contain several sections, with each section focused on a specific topic, and the topics are designed to provide specific guidance to be followed in the event of an emergency. Miehl found that guidance can be presented in a checklist.[74] Several models are available online, and one of the simplest plan templates is found at Ready.Gov.[75]

Plans may also include the following:

- A critical operations section that identifies the staff responsible during an emergency.
- An evacuation plan that details how occupants will be notified and moved to a safe location, as well as shelter-in-place procedures.
- A communications plan that designates public information officers for internal and external communications.[76]

Some view the traditional method of planning for emergencies, including the stages of preparedness, response, recovery, and mitigation as being outdated in today's highly vulnerable environment.[77] The format used for planning directly affects the updating process.[78] If the all-hazards approach is used, it is relatively simple to update and disseminate information common to multiple emergencies, such as emergency contact information. If an organization has chosen to publish stand-alone plans, it will have to update every plan each time common points of contact or emergency numbers change.[79] Although this may be easier if the plans are maintained in digital format, the process may still be more tedious than expected.

The specific emergency planning format used in a given organization depends on the nature of the organization and the organization's policy. The all-hazards approach has been adopted in the United States and can be used in business and organizational plans as well as community plans.[80] The approach provides for a basic emergency plan, or emergency operations plan (EOP), with functional annexes (such as emergency call lists) that apply to multiple emergency situations, and threat-specific annexes (such as procedures for bomb incidents). This approach recognizes that many planning requirements are similar regardless of whether an incident is a natural threat, a human threat, or an accident.[81] For example, an evacuation plan is necessary for fires, bomb incidents, and HAZMAT (hazardous materials) spills.

An alternative planning approach involves developing stand-alone plans for each relevant emergency or contingency.[82] Some scholars have called for a more comprehensive approach, rather than the all-hazards model, which they call comprehensive vulnerability management. The process involves the identification of vulnerabilities for communities and efforts are made to reduce risks.[83] This approach is more proactive, rather than reactive, as seen through the different phases of emergency management because it considers the most likely risks for a community.[84] Regardless of the format, plans should be developed in the simplest way possible, including outlines of the specific responsibilities for those assigned to emergency response.[85]

Emergency Response Plans

Security officers may be part of an organization with an established emergency response plan, or they may inherit a complete or partial plan. Good plans are best reviewed regularly and kept updated. The review should include an in-depth examination of the procedures in light of any events that would warrant reexamination. The emergencies or contingencies for which plans may be developed can be grouped into three major categories: natural, human (clients, customers, or outsiders), and accidental.[86] Emergencies for which planning is appropriate include:

- Fire
- Explosion
- Water outage
- Power outage
- Computer system failure
- Telecommunications failure
- Fuel leak
- Hazmat (hazardous materials) incident
- Bomb incident
- Civil disorder
- Armed attack
- Barricade/hostage incident
- Severe weather
- Tornado
- Hurricane
- Thunderstorm
- Flood
- Other natural occurrences
- Earthquake
- Volcano[87]

Each emergency plan requires coordination with local, state, and possibly federal law enforcement, as well as the liaison coordinators for fire, hospitals, utility companies, and service providers you will need. Not every organization needs to plan for all of the emergencies listed here; it depends on the nature of the organization's activities, the organization's criticality, its attractiveness as a target, location, and the types of facilities it occupies, among other considerations.

When constructing an emergency plan, consider the relative importance of different types of activities. Each organization must set its own priorities, including:

- Protecting human life.
- Preventing or minimizing personal injury.
- Reducing the exposure of assets.
- Optimizing loss control for assets when exposure cannot be reduced.
- Restoring normal operations as quickly as possible.[88]

In setting priorities, certain time-tested principles should be applied to the protection of life. Those principles include evacuation and shelter, personal protection, and rescue and relief.[89]

There is a strong need for the management of the plan to be successfully implemented. The emergency plan should provide for an orderly release of information, preferably through a single source.[90] The public relations department may perform this function, so plans should ensure that the director and alternates are regularly updated by the emergency coordinator.[91] Educating the public about emergency management plans can be potentially very beneficial for the community.[92]

Security professionals should consider the complex networks of professionals involved when creating or revising an organizational plan. These networks include both key players in the organization and the local responders expected to assist. As with many public–private initiatives, there are likely to be differences of opinion, policy, and procedure that must be addressed and reconciled—hopefully before an event makes such activity critical. Such differences must be addressed if there is to be a successful outcome. Pre-incident coordination is essential, and likely will take some time to achieve.[93]

Public Information and Warning

Public information and warning is one of the three core capabilities included in all five mission areas. Public information is also one of the three key organizational systems on which the National Incident Management System (NIMS) standard incident command structures are based. Good communication is essential for disseminating information during emergency situations. The process of providing public information and warning identified by the Centers for Disease Control (CDC) and Prevention includes the ability to develop, coordinate, and disseminate information, alerts, warnings, and notifications to the public and incident management responders.[94] This capability consists of the ability to perform the following functions:

- *Function 1*: Activate the emergency public information system.
- *Function 2*: Determine the need for a joint public information system.
- *Function 3*: Establish and participate in information system operations.
- *Function 4*: Establish avenues for public interaction and information exchange.
- *Function 5*: Issue public information, alerts, warnings, and notifications.[95]

Although many of these functions will be performed by public-sector personnel, private security professionals in larger organizations will have similar requirements, and all private security professionals should be familiar with the functions, as they may be called on to assist with operations, depending on the event's impact.

Function 1: Activate the emergency public information system. This includes notifying and assembling key public information personnel and potential spokespersons, who were identified prior to an incident to provide information to the public during an incident.[96] For security professionals, this would include actions to centralize public information dissemination.

Function 2: Determine the need for a joint public information system. This function requires a determination of the need for, and scale of, a joint public information system, including if appropriate, activation of a Joint Information Center within the public health agency.[97] This function could apply to security professionals in a multilocation or multiorganization area such as a business or industrial park.

Function 3: Establish and participate in information system operations. Function 3 includes monitoring jurisdictional media, conducting press briefings, and providing rumor control for media outlets, using a National Incident Management System (NIMS) compliant framework for coordinating incident-related communications.[98] Applications for security professionals mirror these actions.

Function 4: Establish avenues for public interaction and information exchange. Providing methods for the public to contact the health department through call centers, help desks, hotlines, social media, web chat, or other communication platforms is the primary focus, according to the CDC.[99] Establishing avenues for public interaction and information exchange is especially necessary for security professionals to be aware of in keeping with the business continuity needs of the organization.

▲ FEMA Public Information Officer Susan Solomon walks by state transportation vehicles involved in debris removal and military personnel providing security in this area affected by a deadly May 20, 2013, tornado. How can security professionals prepare employees for challenges caused by tornados?

Source: FEMA https://www.fema.gov/media-library/assets/images/70985

Function 5: Issue public information, alerts, warnings, and notifications. This includes using crisis and emergency risk communication principles, disseminating critical health and safety information to alert people to potential health risks and reducing the risk of exposure to ongoing and potential hazards.[100] Coordination with and contribution to the public-sector professionals for these updates is critical for security professionals.

The public and private sector have quite different perspectives about how emergencies should be reported and handled; and those perspectives are often based on political considerations. The public sector would prefer to be notified of the emergency situation at the earliest possible time, with detailed information about the situation to provide an accurate picture of the situation. Standard policy indicates that a knowledgeable person would meet the incident commander (IC) at the scene to provide necessary information and start working in a unified command mode.[101] Alternatively, security professionals in the private sector prefer to delay (or eliminate) notification to municipal responders because of potential negative publicity and possible regulatory activity, and would prefer to provide minimal information to minimize the apparent significance of the event and help ensure a minimal response.[102] Private-sector sites may not have a knowledgeable individual available to meet incoming responders, often because all knowledgeable resources are working to mitigate the incident. Many in the private sector believe their personnel must be in charge because public-sector responders do not have the facility's best interests at heart.[103]

Media and Public Relations

The media plays a critical role in informing the public about emergency and disaster events.[104] Security professionals will find it beneficial to determine who will be leading the media relations efforts to ensure the organization is able to make contributions as a source of accurate information. The local public authorities will accentuate their position as the main sources of information. More joint media-related training will enhance this activity.[105] News representatives should be told what has occurred through prepared press releases and oral briefings. Any organization-arranged and approved interviews should avoid answering questions with "no comment."[106] If media representatives feel that the organization is not releasing adequate information, they may contact individuals further removed from the actual situation who have little or no information. As rumors, conjecture, and speculation grow, public impression that the organization is hiding something could produce a lasting, unfavorable view of the organization.[107]

News representatives will usually be cooperative if the organizational representative explains why they must limit the release of information.[108] It is necessary to protect responders and victims from media pressure whenever possible.[109] Safety considerations might make it necessary for the organization to limit access to the area.[110] In those instances, the problem should be explained, and individuals who have been in the area should be available for interviews. The strategy for handling sensitive information should be included in the organization's emergency plan and familiar to those charged with media coordination.[111]

In the past, the traditional way was to use the mass media such as television or radio to simply inform citizens in the region of the disaster. Communicating with the public is important, as they represent the community in which business is conducted and the neighborhood in which the business or organization is located. Oftentimes, citizens will hear about the organization's activities from a neighbor or friend who is employed by the organization or by the media. They may hear about events from their personal friends and network via social media such as Facebook, Twitter, YouTube, or other methods. It is important for companies to identify and adhere to a policy of community outreach and communication that represents the intentions of company leadership. All employees should be aware of the contributions they make to the company's reputation in the eyes of community members. Security professionals are likely to encounter elderly persons who have lived in the area their whole life and youth who are members of an ethnic group that only recently established their presence in that location. Both populations need to leave the encounter with a positive impression of the organization.

There have been increased demands for an innovative, independent system to provide citizens with relevant information where there have been difficulties listening or watching radio or television broadcasting. Between 2000 and 2002, the South Korean government invested $11.2 million to establish a system to send either voice or text messages to citizens in an emergency.[112] Similar systems exist in other countries, such as the service provided by Nixle, a community information service dedicated to helping citizens stay connected to emergency services and urgent information, depending on their physical location. Nixle was built exclusively for secure and reliable communications.[113] Nixle messages can be received by mobile phone text message, by email, and over the web. Social media sites such as Twitter.com and Facebook.com have also been used for both government and citizen emergency reporting and communication.

THINK ABOUT IT

What are some of the critical components to include when informing the public about a crisis or disaster? What should be included? What should be left out? Who should decide in which category specific information goes?

National Incident Management System

As we have seen with the alignment of the frameworks, there is a benefit to standardizing certain functions to improve strategic communication during an emergency. Although these efforts may be challenging to introduce and implement, the aligned results warrant such challenges. The **National Incident Management System** (NIMS) enables responders at all jurisdictional levels and across all disciplines to work together with effective and efficient deployment of resources.

NIMS was developed by the Department of Homeland Security and issued in March 2004. NIMS was created in response to the determination that first-responders on various scenes were using different terms to describe the same actions and events. The NIMS provided a universal emergency management system and provided a common technical language. Beginning in 2006, federal funding for state, local, and tribal preparedness grants were tied to compliance with the NIMS.[114] The NIMS identifies concepts and principles that are used to manage emergencies from preparedness to recovery. NIMS provides a

3 Explain what the National Incident Management System was designed to accomplish.

National Incident Management System
Enables responders at all jurisdictional levels and across all disciplines to work together with effective and efficient deployment of resources. It was developed to identify concepts and principles that are used to manage emergencies from preparedness to recovery and provide a consistent, nationwide approach and common vocabulary so that multiple agencies or jurisdictions can communicate as they work together to respond to emergency situations.

consistent, nationwide approach and common vocabulary. This allows multiple agencies or jurisdictions to communicate as they work together to build, sustain, and deliver the core capabilities needed to achieve a secure and resilient nation.

A solid comprehensive and consistent implementation of NIMS by all organizations provides a solid foundation across jurisdictions and disciplines to ensure effective and integrated preparedness, planning, and response. Security professionals should be familiar with NIMS, so management of incidents in the private sector can be conducted in tandem with incident management in the public sector. NIMS empowers the National Preparedness System and describes the planning, organizing, equipping, training, and exercising needed to build and sustain the core capabilities in support of the National Preparedness Goal. To achieve the goal, existing preparedness networks and activities such as NIMS are used to improve training and exercise programs, promote innovation and ensure that the administrative, finance, and logistics systems are in place to support these capabilities.[115]

NIMS standard incident command structures are based on three key systems:

- *Incident Command System* (ICS) is a standardized, on-scene, all-hazards incident management approach that allows for the integration of facilities, equipment, personnel, procedures, and communications. ICS enables a coordinated response among various jurisdictions and functional agencies, both public and private; with common processes for planning and managing resources.[116]

- *Multiagency Coordination System* (MACS) occurs across different disciplines and can occur on a regular basis, whenever personnel from different agencies interact, and it allows them to work together more effectively.[117]

- *Public Information Systems* are made up of processes, procedures, and systems for communicating timely, accurate, and accessible information related to an incident; its functions must be coordinated and integrated across jurisdictions and across functional agencies.[118]

Private security professionals and others interested in proficiency can access and attend interactive online courses on subjects such as NIMS and ICS at FEMA's Emergency Management Institute. The courses are free, and successful completion will result in certification of the student. Many of the courses are incorporated into traditional college and university curriculums.[119]

Individual states may also standardize their emergency procedures. In California, for example, the Standardized Emergency Management System (SEMS) is the fundamental structure for the response phase of emergency management. SEMS unifies all elements of California's emergency management community by incorporating the Incident Command System (ICS) with the California Disaster and Civil Defense Master Mutual Aid Agreement (MMAA) and other multiagency coordination. State and local governments in California must use SEMS to be eligible for reimbursement of response-related costs under the state's disaster assistance programs.[120]

Incident Command System

4 Describe the incident command system.

incident command system
A standardized, on-scene, all-hazards approach to incident management. It integrates facilities, equipment, personnel, procedures, and communications enabling a coordinated response among jurisdictions, while establishing common processes for planning and managing resources.

The **Incident Command System** (ICS) is a standardized, on-scene, all-hazards approach to incident management. ICS integrates facilities, equipment, personnel, procedures, and communications (see Figure 11–1). It enables a coordinated response among jurisdictions, and establishes common processes for planning and managing resources.[121] The ICS approach is designed to be flexible and can be used for incidents of any type, scope, or complexity. ICS provides an integrated organizational structure to meet the demands of single or multiple incidents. This helps the incident commander safely and effectively manage and employ resources, and ensures responder safety through a coordinated planning and response effort.

Without use of an ICS, responses typically:

- Lack accountability.
- Have poor coordination.

- Use an uncoordinated and nonsystematic planning process.
- Order and use most resources inefficiently and ineffectively.
- Fail to efficiently and effectively integrate on-scene responders.
- Tend to have safety issues.[122]

ICS uses a combination of facilities, equipment, personnel, procedures, and communications to aid in the management of resources during incident response. ICS is based on eight core concepts:

1. *Common terminology*: Use of similar terms and definitions.
2. *Integrated communications*: Ability to transmit information within an organization and externally.
3. *Modular organization*: Resources organized according to their responsibilities.
4. *Unified command structure*: Multiple disciplines establish common objectives to prevent conflict or duplication of effort.
5. *Manageable span of control*: Each supervisory level oversees a limited number of assets so it can maintain effective supervision.
6. *Consolidated action plans*: A single, formal documentation of incident goals, objectives, and strategies.
7. *Comprehensive resource management*: Systems to describe, maintain, identify, request, and track resources.
8. *Predesignated incident facilities*: Assignment of locations where expected functions will occur.[123]

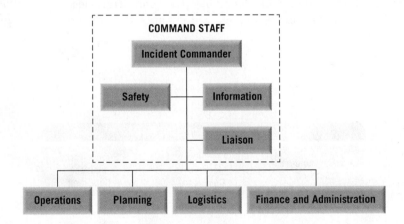

FIGURE 11–1
Incident Command System Structure
Source: OSHA.gov. *What is an Incident Command System?* U.S. Department of Labor, Occupational Safety and Health Administration.

ICS is used by all levels of government as well as by many nongovernmental and private-sector organizations. Security professionals should be familiar with the ICS approach to facilitate interagency communications before and during an incident. ICS is structured to facilitate activities in five major functional areas: command, operations, planning, logistics, and finance/administration. Intelligence and investigations is an optional sixth functional area that is activated on a case-by-case basis.[124]

Location and industry-specific adaptations of ICS are also beneficial. For example, in the United States, the Hospital Incident Command System (HICS) is used by hospitals in both emergency and nonemergency situations. HICS provides hospitals of all sizes with the tools needed to improve their emergency preparedness and response capability, both individually and as members of the broader response community. HICS was developed from the Hospital Emergency Incident Command System (HEICS) used for disaster management since the 1980s.[125] Roles and responsibilities of all relevant personnel are delineated in the HICS, and an emergency operation center coordinates all activities both within and outside the institution.[126]

▲ High Park Fire Incident Commander Bill Hahnenberg leads an Incident Command Post fire briefing for Gov. John Hickenlooper (second row, far right), Sen. Mark Udall (second row, center), Sen. Michael Bennet (second row, left) and FEMA Region VIII Administrator Robin Finegan (third row, left) on Saturday, June 16, 2012.

Source: FEMA https://www.fema.gov/media-library/assets/images/64642

Friction may arise when public-sector crews respond to an incident at a private-sector facility. This may be because of a perception of conflicted missions. At the core, the primary mission of public-sector responders is to protect the community while the primary mission of private-sector responders is to protect the company's assets.[127] Conflict arises not because of intentional malice or dislike; rather, it is related to differing or competing priorities and often internal politics. To overcome this, both parties must take the time to coordinate efforts and plans, and practice them in joint exercises. By discussing and implementing organizational priorities, each side can gain a better understanding of the other's position and identify a solution that addresses the needs of both organizations.[128]

Although a single IC normally handles the command function, an ICS organization may need to be expanded into a Unified Command (UC). The UC process brings together all major organizations involved in the incident and allows for coordination of an effective response while carrying out their own jurisdictional responsibilities (see Figure 11–2).[129] The UC is responsible for overall management of the incident. According to the U.S. Occupational Safety and Health Administration, members of the UC work together to develop a common set of incident objectives and strategies, share information, maximize the use of available resources, and enhance the efficiency of the individual response organizations.[130]

FIGURE 11–2
Unified Command

Unified Command Organization		
HazMat Incident Command	Law Enforcement Incident Command	Public Works Incident Command

---

5 Identify and distinguish a business impact analysis, business continuity management, and continuity of operations.

business continuity management
Involves counteracting threats to an organization's continuing operation. The primary objective is to resume critical functions as quickly as possible and to restore the business to its pre-emergency condition and location or, if that is not possible, to a new location or level of operations.

Business and Operations Continuity

Business continuity management examines an organization's exposure to various threats to prioritize certain processes, identify threats to operation, and plan mitigation strategies.[131] Business continuity (BC) is to the private sector what **continuity of operations** (COOP) is to the public sector. With COOP, individual government executive departments and agencies need to ensure that critical organizational functions continue to be performed during emergencies.[132] These include events from localized acts of nature, accidents, and technological or attack-related emergencies. Any event that makes it impossible for employees to work in their regular facility (from a fire, to a natural disaster, to a terrorist attack) could result in the activation of the BC plan.[133]

FEMA's Continuity Guidance Circular 1 (CGC 1) addresses Continuity Guidance for Non-Federal Governments and outlines COOP guidance for all government agencies and private-sector organizations, delineated into ten elements of continuity:

1. *Essential functions*: The identification and prioritization of essential functions establishes the planning parameters that drive an organization's efforts in all other planning and preparedness areas.

2. *Orders of succession*: Organizations are responsible for maintaining orders of succession for key positions to ensure that the organization has clearly established and identified leadership and key personnel, if these leaders are incapacitated or otherwise unavailable.

3. *Delegations of authority*: Delegation of authorities for making policy determinations and taking necessary actions at all levels of an organization ensures a rapid and effective response to any emergency requiring the activation of a continuity plan.

4. *Continuity facilities*: The use of continuity facilities refers to both alternate and devolution sites where essential functions are continued or resumed during a continuity event. These sites refer to not only other facilities and locations, but also work arrangements such as telework and mobile work concepts.

5. *Continuity communications*: The ability of an organization to execute its essential functions at its continuity facilities depends on the identification, availability, reliability, and redundancy of critical secure and nonsecure communications and information technology (IT) systems.

6. *Essential records management*: Identification, protection, and ready availability of electronic and hard-copy documents, references, records, information systems, and data management software and equipment (including classified and other sensitive data) is vital during a continuity activation.

7. *Human resources*: Organizations should activate continuity personnel and expect them to perform their assigned duties following their organization's particular plans and procedures. Organizations should also incorporate telework into their continuity of operations plans.

8. *Test, training, and exercise (TT&E) program*: An effective TT&E program facilitates the validation of an organization's continuity capabilities and its ability to perform essential functions during any emergency. Deficiencies, actions to correct them, and a timeline for remedy are documented in an organization's corrective action program (CAP).

9. *Devolution of control and direction*: Devolution requires the transition of roles and responsibilities for performance of essential functions through preauthorized delegations of authority and responsibility. Devolution planning supports overall continuity planning (see Figure 11–3) and addresses the full spectrum of threats and all-hazards emergency.

10. *Reconstitution operations*: Reconstitution is the process of resuming normal operations from the original or replacement primary operating facility. Reconstitution embodies the ability of an organization to recover from an event that disrupts normal operations and consolidates the necessary resources so that the organization can resume its operations as a fully functional entity.[134]

continuity of operations
A strategy in which individual government executive departments and agencies ensure that functions continue to be performed during emergencies such as acts of nature, accidents, and technological or attack-related emergencies that make it impossible for employees to work in their regular facility.

Depending on the nature and needs of the organization, BC may include resumption and recovery in place, contracting out selected functions, or relocating critical functions and personnel to one or more alternative sites. The primary objective is to resume critical functions as quickly as possible and to restore the business to its pre-emergency condition and location or, if that is not possible, to a new location or level of operations.[135]

Business disruptions can mean lost revenues and profits, as well as the permanent loss of some finicky customers, a cost not covered by insurance.[136] Having a plan to continue business is essential to ensure that business activities carry on in the aftermath of disaster.[137]

Development of a BC plan includes four steps:

1. Conduct a business impact analysis (BIA) and identify time-sensitive or critical business functions and the processes and resources that support them.

2. Identify, document, and implement each of the various steps necessary to recover critical business functions and processes.

3. Organize a BC team to manage business disruption.

4. Conduct training for the BC team as well as testing and exercises to evaluate recovery strategies and the plan.[138]

Business Impact Analysis	Recovery Strategies	Plan Development	Testing & Exercises
• Develop questionnaire • Conduct workshop to instruct business function and process managers how to complete the BIA • Receive completed BIA questionnaire forms • Review BIA questionnaires • Conduct follow-up interviews to validate information and fill any information gaps	• Identify and document resource requirements based on BIAs • Conduct gap analysis to determine gaps between recovery requirements and current capabilities • Explore recovery strategy options • Select recovery strategies with management approval • Implement strategies	• Develop plan framework • Organize recovery teams • Develop relocation plans • Write business continuity and IT disaster recovery procedures • Document manual workarounds • Assemble plan; validate; gain management approval	• Develop testing, exercise, and maintenance requirements • Conduct training for business continuity team • Conduct orientation exercises • Conduct testing and document test results • Update BCP to incorporate lessons learned from testing and exercises

FIGURE 11–3
Business Continuity Planning Process Diagram
Source: Ready.gov http://www.ready.gov/business/implementation/continuity

business impact analysis
Predicts the potential consequences of disruption of a business function or process and the information needed to develop effective recovery strategies. Potential loss scenarios are identified, and risk assessments conducted. The BIA can be used to identify the operational and financial impacts resulting from disruption of business functions and processes.

A **business impact analysis** (BIA) predicts the potential consequences of disruption of a business function or process and is used to gather the information needed to develop effective recovery strategies.[139] Potential loss scenarios should be identified, and risk assessments should be conducted. The BIA can be used to identify the variety of operational and financial impacts resulting from disruption of business functions and processes. Some of the impacts to be considered are:

- Lost sales and income.
- Delayed sales or income.
- Increased expenses (e.g., overtime labor, outsourcing, expediting costs, etc.).
- Regulatory fines.
- Contractual penalties or loss of contractual bonuses.
- Customer dissatisfaction or defection.
- Delay of new business plans.
- Timing and duration of disruption.[140]

According to Ready.gov, the timing of a disruption can have a significant bearing on the degree or type of loss sustained. A power outage lasting a few minutes would be a minor inconvenience for most businesses but one lasting for hours could result in significant business losses. A short disruption of production may be overcome by shipping finished goods from a warehouse but disruption of a product that is in high demand could have a significant impact.[141]

ASIS International advises that a realistic test of the BC Plan is just as important as testing other critical plans and therefore testing and review of the BC plan should be conducted at least annually.[142] There are many benefits to testing and exercises, including training personnel to clarify roles and responsibilities, evaluating policies, plans, and procedures, and gaining recognition for the emergency management and the BC program.[143]

Additionally, the BC plan should be evaluated and modified as required after training drills, emergencies, or changes in personnel, their responsibilities, the facility's physical design, or in policies or procedures.[144]

FEMA provides a continuity plan template for nonfederal governments, as shown in Figure 11–4.

Continuity Plan Template for Non-Federal Governments September 2013

TABLE OF CONTENTS

FIGURE 11–4
Continuity Plan Template for Nonfederal Governments
Source: FEMA, *Continuity of Operations, Planning and Templates*, https://www.fema.gov/planning-templates#

The template follows the traditional functional Emergency Operations Plan format detailed in the FEMA's National Preparedness Directorate's Comprehensive Preparedness Guide 101, *Developing and Maintaining Emergency Operations Plans*, dated November 2010. By using this planning template, organizations can address each of the planning elements and requirements. The guidance applies to all levels of state, territorial, tribal, and local government jurisdictions. The private sector and other nongovernment organizations may also benefit from the use of this template.[145]

Challenges and Future Considerations for Security Professionals

Security professionals will be affected by government policy and the political decisions attached to reductions in government spending in support of disasters. In the current model, the federal governments bear much of the costs for recovery and rebuilding in the wake of a disaster. Given the growing costs of disasters, a struggling economy, and shrinking budgets, this model is likely to change.[146] An example of a more functional and sustainable model was seen in the *Deepwater Horizon* oil spill. British Petroleum (BP) was able to shoulder the cost for much of the recovery effort itself, paying over $10 billion in claims, advances, and settlements from a trust BP established. Rising costs of disasters may necessitate a significant reevaluation of government priorities.[147] Changes of this nature would require changes in emergency management policy.

Risk-oriented management is considered to be superior to politics-oriented management in resolving emergencies in the long run. Because politics often causes bureaucratic corruption as a result of managing emergencies, people's satisfaction with risk-oriented management will be much higher in the long run.[148] Emergency response resources and leadership are less effective and efficient under a politics-oriented management than under risk-oriented management.[149] Complacency is often what gets in the way of preparation for a large-scale event. Public complacency happens when people become less alert if they perceive their risk from a disaster is not great. Public complacency can be reduced when the government develops effective communication strategies to reduce complacency.[150] It is important to find ways to ensure that organization members do not grow complacent. Sometimes fear and emotion about the potential threat to a community can lead to costly expenditures, which would not normally be the most efficient use of resources.[151]

Security professionals will increasingly need to look internationally for guidance when working with or for global organizations. We previously described both an all-hazards and functional approach to disaster and emergency planning. Cronstedt identified other approaches, including the comprehensive approach (prevention, preparation, response, and recovery—PPRR), the all-agencies approach, and the prepared community approach, as shown in Table 11.1.[152] In many countries, the process of **disaster risk reduction** (DRR) guides the approach chosen. DRR is a systematic attempt to identify, assess, and reduce the risks of disaster. It aims to reduce socioeconomic vulnerabilities to disaster and assist citizens in dealing with the environmental and other hazards that trigger such vulnerabilities.

DRR programs can be found in several practice areas, including geohazards, information management and coordination, protection, public health, nutrition, livelihoods, and agriculture and food security. Generally, the United Nations reports that these programs aim to increase community resilience and work to reduce risk to future problems.[153]

disaster risk reduction
A systematic attempt to identify, assess, and reduce the risks of disaster. It aims to reduce socioeconomic vulnerabilities to disaster and assist citizens in dealing with the environmental and other hazards that trigger such vulnerabilities.

TABLE 11-1
Types of Approaches to Disaster and Emergency Planning

Type of Approach	Focus
All-hazards approach	A planned effort to respond to any incident or event, natural or human caused, that requires an organized response by a public, private, and/or governmental entity to protect life, public health, and safety, values to be protected, and to minimize any disruption of governmental, social, and economic services.
Functions-based approach	A planned effort to respond to the potential effects of emergencies in general. This approach avoids duplication of the planning effort for every hazard and for every task.
All-agencies approach (aka Unified Command approach)	A planned effort to define the incident management structure of agencies with different legal, geographic, and functional responsibilities to have them coordinate, plan, and interact effectively. Each participating agency maintains its own authority, responsibility, and accountability.
Comprehensive approach	An integrated approach to the management of emergency programs and activities for all emergency phases, for all types of emergencies and disasters, and for all levels of government and the private sector.
Prepared community approach	An incident management strategy that develops, maintains, and uses a realistic preparedness plan that is integrated with routine practices of the community.

Sources: B. W. Blanchard, *Guide to Emergency Management and Related Terms, Definitions, Concepts, Acronyms, Organizations, Programs, Guidance, Executive Orders and Legislation: A Tutorial on Emergency Management, Broadly Defined, Past and Present, 2008,* http://training.fema.gov/EMIWeb/edu/docs/terms%20and%20definitions/Terms%20and%20Definitions.pdf; U.S. Coast Guard, *Incident Management Handbook,* Incident Command System, U.S. Coast Guard, Department of Homeland Security, https://etesting.uscg.mil/mstrefs/Incident_Management_Handbook.pdf

all-agencies approach
A planned effort to define the incident management structure of agencies with different legal, geographic, and functional responsibilities to have them coordinate, plan, and interact effectively. Each participating agency maintains its own authority, responsibility, and accountability.

comprehensive approach
Includes an emphasis on prevention, preparation, response, and recovery. It is an integrated approach to the management of emergency programs and activities for all emergency phases, for all types of emergencies and disasters, and for all levels of government and the private sector.

Careers in Security

Name: Charles (Chuck) Robinson

Position: Association Safety Director of the YMCA of Middle Tennessee

Year hired: 2014

City, State where you are based: Nashville, Tennessee

College(s) attended (degree): Middle Tennessee State University

Majors: Aerospace and Business Administration

Minors: Homeland Security

Did you attend graduate school? Yes

College(s) attended (degree): American Military University, MA Homeland Security with a concentration in Emergency Management

Please give a brief description of your job: I oversee the Risk Management and Safety processes for the YMCA of Middle Tennessee

and ensure all of our buildings and programs are current with local/state/federal guidelines regarding their concentration.

What qualities/characteristics are most helpful for this job? One has to be a self-starter and work with a proactive approach. An individual in this field must also be willing to continue their education on a regular basis either by attending seminars and conferences or taking classes online or at a local college.

What is a typical starting salary? $45,000–$55,000 per year

What is the salary potential as you move up into higher-level jobs? As one moves up the career ladder in the Safety field they could find themselves making upwards of $85,000 if they find the right company. However, I would suggest culture over salary when looking to progress up the career ladder.

What advice would you give someone in college beginning studies in security? Learn as much as you can about the entire field. The field is

(Continued)

expanding at a rapid rate and now includes Safety, IT, as well as traditional law enforcement or justice system roles.

What appealed to you most about the position when you applied for it? The fact that my current position was new and I would be in the driver's seat so to speak on what the position would look like in five or even ten years.

How would you describe the interview process? Lengthy with several rounds of panel interviews.

What is a typical day like? I start my day as a traditional office job with answering emails and attending meetings. However, it is not unusual to find myself at one of our centers performing audits or working with our insurance company regarding any plethora of issues.

In a typical day, what do you like best/least about it? I love the fact that no matter what I expect going into work it is never the same two days in a row. The thing I would say I like the least about the position is you are never off the clock and if the phone rings sometime after 9pm you can almost guarantee it's not for something good.

How would you suggest interested applicants gain experience? Volunteer or work with programs around your school or community. Also do not be afraid to take an entry-level hourly job while attending college. This actually is something I look for whenever I hire a new employee.

Would you recommend military experience? Military experience is an invaluable asset. Veterans come into the workforce with a drive and ability to lead almost immediately. The one thing I would suggest to veterans, however, is to make sure you understand the culture of the company where you are applying for the job. Not every company's culture will match with a veteran's personality.

Does holding a full-time job during college help applicants get hired afterwards? In my opinion, yes. As I stated earlier I look for it when I interview applicants and have found that applicants with work experience while they attended college have a better understanding of what the workplace is actually like.

Summary

- **Identify the basic styles or approaches for incident management and response.**
  - The all-hazards approach (to emergency management) is a planned effort to respond to any incident or event, natural or human caused, that requires an organized response by a public, private, and/or governmental entity in order to protect life, public health and safety, values to be protected, and to minimize any disruption of governmental, social, and economic services.
  - The functions-based approach (to emergency management) is a planned effort to respond to the potential effects of emergencies in general. This approach avoids duplication of the planning effort for every hazard and for every task.
  - The comprehensive approach is an integrated approach to the management of emergency programs and activities for all emergency phases, for all types of emergencies and disasters, and for all levels of government and the private sector.

- **Distinguish some differences between a crisis, a disaster, and an emergency.**
  - A crisis is an incident or situation involving a threat to a specific country, its territories, citizens, military forces, possessions, or national security interests that develops rapidly and creates a condition of such diplomatic, economic, political, or military importance that commitment of military forces and resources is contemplated to achieve national objectives.
  - A disaster is a serious disruption of the functioning of a community or a society involving widespread human, material, economic, or environmental losses and impacts, which exceeds the ability of the affected community or society to cope using its own resources.
  - An emergency is an extraordinary situation in which people are unable to meet their basic survival needs, or there are serious and immediate threats to human life and well-being.

- **Explain what the National Incident Management System was designed to accomplish.**
  - The National Incident Management System (NIMS) identifies concepts and principles that answer how to manage emergencies from preparedness to recovery regardless of their

cause, size, location, or complexity. NIMS provides a consistent, nationwide approach and vocabulary for multiple agencies or jurisdictions to work together to build, sustain, and deliver the core capabilities needed to achieve a secure and resilient nation.

- **Describe the incident command system.**
  - The Incident Command System (ICS) a standardized, on-scene, all-hazards incident management approach that allows for the integration of facilities, equipment, personnel, procedures, and communications operating within a common organizational structure; enables a coordinated response among various jurisdictions and functional agencies; and establishes common processes for planning and managing resources.
- **Identify and distinguish a business impact analysis, business continuity management, and continuity of operations.**
  - A business impact analysis (BIA) predicts the potential consequences of disruption of a business function or process and gathers the information needed to develop effective recovery strategies.
  - Business continuity management examines an organization's exposure to various threats to prioritize certain processes, identify threats to operation, and plan mitigation strategies.
  - Continuity of operations (COOP) is readiness examination by individual government executive departments and agencies to ensure that functions continue to be performed during emergencies from accidents to attacks.

KEY TERMS

all-agencies
  approach **257**
all-hazards
  approach **238**
business continuity
  management **252**
business impact
  analysis **254**
comprehensive
  approach to disaster

and emergency
  planning **257**
continuity of
  operations **253**
crisis **239**
disaster **239**
disaster risk reduction **257**
emergency **238**
functions-based
  approach **238**

incident command
  system **250**
mitigation **242**
National Incident
  Management
  System **249**
prevention **241**
protection **242**

REVIEW QUESTIONS

1. What were the original four phases of emergency management and how has the focus changed since then?
2. Is there a better term or usage than what is used to describe events as crises, disasters, and emergencies?
3. Describe two emergency response scenarios based on actual events - one with the National Incident Management System (NIMS) in place, and one without it.
4. Apply the principles of the incident command system (ICS) to a typical family get-together. Distinguish the conversations before and after.
5. How could applying business continuity management techniques help someone you know make it through an otherwise life-changing event?

PRACTICAL APPLICATION

1. Sixteen Caribbean states are currently represented within the Caribbean Disaster Emergency Management Agency (CDEMA). Member agencies apply the principles and practice of comprehensive disaster management (CDM), an integrated and proactive approach to disaster management to reduce the risk and loss associated with natural and technological hazards to enhance regional sustainable development.[154] What other regional emergency response organizations do you think could be formed? See how many you can locate.

2. The International Emergency Management Society (TIEMS) was founded in 1993. TIEMS stimulates the exchange of information on the use of innovative methods and technologies within emergency and disaster management to improve society's ability to avoid, mitigate, respond to, and recover from natural and technological disasters.[155] What other roles could such an organization fill?

3. Campus security may be responsible for emergency management activities such as securing buildings, restricting access to campus, and responding to students in distress either due to illness or injury or illness/injury of others or requesting transport for medical care.[156] Locate and examine your institution's emergency plan and see what types of activities are identified.

4. We have all heard about the reported widespread looting by Louisiana residents affected by Hurricane Katrina, and looting occurs quite often with such events, though not necessarily to such an extent. Select a few of the events discussed in this chapter and determine to what extent looting could have occurred compared to how much it actually did.

5. There are 48 million deaf, deaf-blind, and hard-of-hearing (HH) people living in the United States, and they do not see themselves as disabled but rather as members of a linguistic minority group centered on the use of sign language.[157] Does your community have an effective plan in place that includes this population?

Critical Infrastructure Security

Learning Objectives

After reading this chapter, you should be able to:

1. Explain the activities of the Homeland Infrastructure Threat and Risk Analysis Center. **264**

2. Identify the sixteen critical infrastructure sectors. **265**

3. Explain the function of the National Infrastructure Protection Plan. **267**

4. Contrast a sampling of public–private partnerships for infrastructure security. **277**

5. Analyze and identify the basic steps of a vulnerability assessment. **279**

Introduction

In 2011–2012, a loosely associated hacktivist group, self-identified as Anonymous, conducted cyberattacks on critical infrastructure agencies including the Pentagon, the Federal Bureau of Investigation, the U.S. Department of Justice, the U.S. Copyright Office, and government sites in Tunisia, Anguilla, Brazil, Zimbabwe, Turkey, and Australia. They also attacked the websites of private companies including News Corporation.[1] Hacktivism, a term coined in 1995 by techno-culture writer Jason Sack, describes the use of computer networks to promote a social or political agenda.[2] The group also publicly threatened the Mexican drug cartel known as Los Zetas after one of their members was kidnapped; it attacked Visa and MasterCard websites; and claimed responsibility for taking down websites for genetically modified crops.[3] In mid-September 2012, Anonymous threatened the National Education Centre of Hong Kong and launched a series of attacks on Israeli government websites. They also shut down websites of the Syrian government in response to a government-imposed Internet blackout in that country.[4]

The Anonymous attacks were not unique. Another group of cyberattacks targeted a different area of the nation's infrastructure—major energy firms—around the globe with troubling frequency. In 2012, three alerts were issued by the U.S. Department of Homeland Security (DHS) about potential attacks against U.S. and Canadian natural gas pipelines. In September of that year, Telvent Canada Ltd., a company that the *Financial Post* learned helps manage 60% of all oil and gas pipelines in the Western hemisphere, experienced a cyberattack that compromised its security systems and penetrated its internal firewall.[5]

These cyberattacks clearly show that terror is no longer a local phenomenon: attacks can occur across the globe, and on every continent acts of terrorism have destroyed property, disrupted activities, and taken lives. Rather than being directed toward people, some of the most damaging attacks target critical infrastructure and key resources (CIKR). What are these institutions, how they are defined, and how they can be defended are some of the topics we examine in this chapter. We will examine the cyberattacks and the perpetrators more in the following chapter.

This chapter describes security measures relative to critical infrastructure and key resources. The focus on CIKR may not be foremost in the minds of security students, but perhaps it should be. Like the many important things in our personal lives that we often take for granted, the time when we notice issues with CIKR is when they are not available. These areas require a great deal of collaborative and coordinated security by both public- and private-sector players. The various areas and topics examined in this chapter provide a general overview. Use them to increase your awareness of CIKR and to help find other areas where your personal and professional interests and expertise can be challenged.

Critical Infrastructure Defined

critical infrastructure
Includes the assets, systems, and networks, whether physical or virtual, considered so vital that their incapacitation or destruction would weaken a country's physical and economic security, public health and/or safety, or any combination of these.

Critical infrastructure includes the assets, systems, and networks, whether physical or virtual, considered so vital to the United States that their incapacitation or destruction would weaken physical and economic security, public health and/or safety, or any combination of these elements according to the U.S. Department of Homeland Security (DHS).[6] The term describes a variety of assets, ranging from the physical infrastructure—highways, dams, the electrical grid, and oil pipelines—to those in cyberspace including both local and wide area computer networks. Because the private sector owns the vast majority of the nation's infrastructure, including banking and financial institutions, commercial facilities, telecommunications networks, and energy production and transmission facilities, it is vital that private security professionals are able to understand the interrelationships of the public and private sectors so they can assist their companies in protecting these assets and systems.[7]

Governmental institutions are not the only targets: attacks against critical infrastructure may involve a variety of industries, businesses, and activities that are of great importance to a country's economy and safety. These may include public transit; the Internet; banking networks, criminal justice agencies; private businesses; and public gatherings such as the Super Bowl; college basketball games, and high school baseball games. Though it wasn't well known outside of the U.S. government, the World Trade Center complex was regarded as a part of our critical infrastructure, not just a landmark, prior to 9/11. The qualification was partly based on its contribution to the business community as a headquarters for many

◀ Contractors and local water company employees are repairing water and sewer lines damaged by Hurricane Sandy. Extensive damage here resulted from storm flooding. Why should security professionals ensure they are aware about flood damage?

Source: FEMA, https://www.fema .gov/media-library/assets/ images/67344

influential companies. The complex's function as a communications hub for many Internet and telecommunications companies also contributed to the classification.

Key Resources

The second half of CIKR, **key resources**, is composed of those publicly or privately controlled resources essential to the operation of the economy and government. Examples include oil processing plants, banks, telecommunications and power grids. These may include **key assets**, individual targets whose destruction would not damage vital systems but could create a local disaster or significantly damage the nation's morale or confidence. They also include symbolic and historical attractions, such as prominent national, state, or local monuments and icons. Examples of key resources and assets are government buildings and monuments such as the Smithsonian Museum and Capitol building or icons such as the Golden Gate Bridge, the Washington Monument, or Mount Rushmore.

Key assets also include facilities that deserve special protection because of their potential for destruction or their value to the local community. Their damage or destruction might have a psychological impact on local citizens and harm the local economy. Such smaller events, for example, may impact the transportation of goods and people in part of a city or geographic area, but may not be substantial enough to have a severe adverse impact on society at large.[8]

key resources
Publicly or privately controlled resources essential to the operation of the economy and government. Example includes oil processing plants, banks, telecommunications and power grids.

key assets
Include critical resources whose destruction could create a local disaster or significantly damage the nation's morale or confidence. They include symbolic and historical attractions, like prominent national, state, or local monuments and icons.

Spotlight
The New World Trade Center

The new World Trade Center (WTC) Port Authority Trans-Hudson (PATH) Transportation Hub promises not only to bring architectural beauty to downtown Manhattan but also to significantly improve mass-transit connections throughout the region. Designed by Santiago Calatrava, the transportation hub features pedestrian concourses to existing and future transportation services. Construction on the project began in 2007.

Located close to the northeast corner of the WTC site at Church and Fulton streets (between Towers 2 and 3), the transportation hub is designed to accommodate 250,000 pedestrians per day, which corresponds to projected ridership numbers for 2025. (The temporary station can accommodate up to 50,000 daily pedestrians.) The transportation hub's innovative design features retractable 150-foot-high, glass-and-steel "wings" that allow natural light to pass through to the rail platforms sixty feet below street level.

The new WTC Transportation Hub includes a multistory central transit hall designed in the style of Grand Central Terminal, incorporating a lower concourse, an upper (balcony) concourse, a public waiting area, and first-class retail amenities. An integrated network of underground pedestrian connections from the lower and upper concourses leads to the adjoining subway stations and Transit Center. Pedestrians also can access locations on and around the WTC site, including the five WTC office towers, the Memorial and Museum, Hudson River ferry terminals, the World Financial Center, PATH trains, thirteen subway lines, and the rail link. Retail facilities within the transit hub and the pedestrian concourses accommodate a wide variety of restaurants and stores.

Source: World Trade Center: Transportation Hub, http://www.wtc.com/about/ transportation-hub

Threat Analysis

1 Explain the activities of the Homeland Infrastructure Threat and Risk Analysis Center.

threat analysis
The continual process of compiling and examining all available information concerning activities, which could target and threaten an organization's facility. A threat analysis reviews the factors of the threat's existence, capability, intentions, history, and targeting, as well as the security environment within which the organization operates and is an essential step in identifying the probability of an attack.

Threat analysis is the continual process of compiling and examining all available information concerning activities, which could target an organization's facility or resources. A threat analysis reviews the factors of the threat's existence, capability, intentions, history, and targeting, as well as the security environment within which the organization operates and is an essential step in identifying the probability of an attack.

Who conducts the nation's threat analysis? The DHS Office of Infrastructure Protection oversees the national program to protect the nation's CIKR, and provides leadership for infrastructure modeling, simulation, and analysis.[9] The Infrastructure Analysis and Strategy Division (IASD) provides analytic systems and tools to support DHS decision makers and other stakeholders. The IASD is also the risk analysis component of the Homeland Infrastructure Threat and Risk Analysis Center (HITRAC).[10] The HITRAC provides risk, threat, and consequence analyses to give the DHS and its security partner's information on threats, infrastructure vulnerabilities, and potential consequences of attacks or natural disasters.[11] HITRAC experts analyze the effects of risk mitigation actions for strategic threat and risk analysis; modeling and simulation; and analytic support during incidents. Additionally, HITRAC produces intelligence-based reports that support threat-mitigation strategies and investment decisions, identify physical and cyber threats against critical infrastructure, and provide education on adversary tactics and use of weapons and explosives.[12] HITRAC threat analysis focuses mainly on regional, critical infrastructure, cyber, and explosives threats. The office provides a variety of contributions to the CIKR community, including:

- *Regional threat analysis*: With cross-sector and cross-state threat analysis, tailored threat assessments, and analytic outreach.
- *Weekly threat teleconferences*: With threat briefings prepared by the DHS and state representatives.
- *Regional threat conferences*: Which include identifying topics of interest to the specific region and general interest information to facilitate coordination among federal, state, and local analysts.
- *Threat briefing support*: To state, local, and private-sector officials.
- *Critical infrastructure threat analysis*: Of threats to specific critical infrastructure sectors, such as transportation, energy, and commercial facilities.
- *Cyber threat analysis*: For critical infrastructure, tailored cyber threat assessments, cyber-analytic outreach, and cyber-related requirements.[13]

  These analyses include:
  - Cyber-related homeland intelligence reports
  - Cyber monitor
  - Homeland security cyber threat report
  - Drafting or contributing to intelligence community bulletins
  - Cyber-threat briefing
  - Explosives threat analysis[14]

In addition to the DHS, several other government organizations contribute to national security by providing some variation of infrastructure threat analysis. Those organizations include:

- Office of Infrastructure Protection
- National Counterterrorism Center
- National Intelligence Program
- National Criminal Intelligence Resource Center
- National Infrastructure Advisory Council
- Federal Bureau of Investigation
- Central Intelligence Agency

- Defense Intelligence Agency
- U.S. Coast Guard
- U.S. Secret Service
- Local and state law enforcement[15]

Protecting CIKR

Protecting critical infrastructure is essential to a nation's security, public health and safety, economic vitality, and way of life. Though the terrorist attacks of 9/11 sparked an increased awareness of CIKR in the United States and many other countries, they were by no means the first to be aimed at disrupting critical infrastructure. Take, for instance, the attack by right-wing terrorists Timothy McVeigh and Terry Nichols on the Murrah Federal Building in Oklahoma City, Oklahoma, in 1995 that caused much national concern and an unprecedented level of response by federal, state, and local government investigators, and which resulted in increased security in most government buildings.

2 Identify the sixteen critical infrastructure sectors.

Due to these attacks, protection of CIKR is a national concern and triggered a variety of actions designed to mitigate and minimize risk. The DHS views critical infrastructure protection as important to a nation for three key reasons:

1. Attacks on critical infrastructure could significantly disrupt government and business functions and produce cascading effects far beyond the targeted sector and physical location of the incident.

2. Direct terrorist attacks and natural, human-created, or technological hazards could produce catastrophic losses of human casualties, property destruction, economic effects, and profound damage to public morale and confidence.

3. Attacks using components of the nation's critical infrastructure as weapons of mass destruction could have even more devastating physical and psychological consequences.[16]

On December 17, 2003, Homeland Security Presidential Directive 7 established U.S. policy for critical infrastructure protection by providing a framework to identify, prioritize, and protect critical infrastructure based on the USA PATRIOT Act of 2001 and the Homeland Security Act of 2002. The directive initially identified seventeen critical infrastructure sectors. An eighteenth sector, the Critical Manufacturing Sector, was added in March 2008. Two (Postal and Shipping and National Monuments and Icons) were removed in the implementation of Presidential Policy Directive 21 (PPD-21), which superseded Directive 7 in February 2013. The sixteen critical infrastructure sectors are:

Critical Infrastructure Sectors

- Chemical
- Commercial Facilities
- Communications
- Critical Manufacturing
- Dams
- Defense Industrial Base
- Emergency Services
- Energy
- Financial Services
- Food and Agriculture
- Government Facilities
- Healthcare and Public Health
- Information Technology

- Nuclear Reactors, Materials and Waste
- Transportation Systems
- Water and Wastewater

Identifying these sectors as critical helps government leaders to enumerate security priorities.

Most nations are susceptible to threats from cyberattacks that could disrupt power, water, communication, and other critical systems. Government leaders should implement policies that reinforce the need for holistic thinking about security and risk management, or thinking that encompasses all of the areas identified here. Doing so will enhance the efficiency and effectiveness of the government's work to secure CIKR and make it more resilient. These actions include determining the threat, mitigating vulnerabilities, and minimizing the consequences of a terrorist attack or natural disaster. To contribute to the potential for success in those endeavors, the following goals have been established:

- Assess and analyze threats, vulnerability, and effects of CIKR activities.
- Secure CIKR against human, physical, and cyber threats.
- Enhance CIKR resilience by minimizing the effect of adverse consequences.
- Share actionable and relevant information across the CIKR community.
- Promote learning and adaptation during and after exercises and incidents.

It is the responsibility of the CIKR community to set specific national priorities to drive action. Performance measures should be based on goals and priorities. These interrelated considerations are depicted in Figure 12–1.

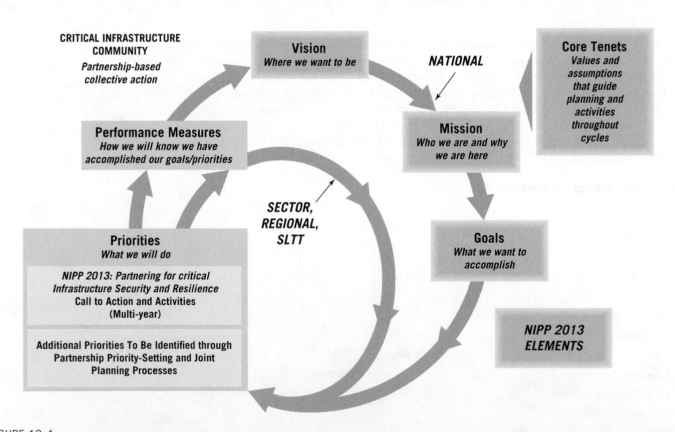

FIGURE 12–1

The National Plan's Approach to Building and Sustaining Unity of Effort

Source: U.S. Department of Homeland Security, National Infrastructure Protection Plan, http://www.dhs.gov/national-infrastructure-protection-plan

National Infrastructure Protection Plan

The **National Infrastructure Protection Plan (NIPP)** was developed in 2009 to provide guidance for protecting our infrastructure and key assets. The NIPP integrates and guides a range of efforts designed to enhance the safety of the nation's critical infrastructure. According to the DHS, the primary goal of the NIPP is to build a safer, more secure, and more resilient America by preventing, deterring, neutralizing, or mitigating the effects of a terrorist attack or natural disaster.[17] Strengthening national preparedness, response, and recovery in the event of an emergency is another core part of the goal for the plan. The NIPP was developed with collaboration by critical infrastructure partners including federal departments and agencies, state and local government agencies, and private-sector entities.[18] NIPP provides a risk analysis and management framework for conducting risk assessments and encouraging the continuous improvement of CIKR protection. See Figure 12–2 for a pictorial view of the process used.

The Department of Homeland Security oversees NIPP management and implementation in the United States. Recognizing that implementation of the CIKR protection mission requires the cooperation of, and coordination between, federal departments and agencies, the DHS has worked to engage state, local, tribal, and territorial governments; regional coalitions; private-sector owners and operators; and many international partners.[19] The NIPP provides part of the foundation for the country's CIKR preparedness, protection, response, and recovery efforts in an all-hazards context.

Regular and frequent communication and coordination between representatives of the public and private sectors enable coordination and support using information-sharing networks and risk management frameworks for CIKR protection and restoration for incident-management activities. Each of the CIKR sectors rely on information-sharing programs such as **Information Sharing and Analysis Centers (ISACs)**, which provide operational and tactical capabilities for information sharing and support for incident response activities. Originally recommended by Presidential Decision Directive 63 in 1998, these ISACs are examples of the sector-specific entities that advance physical and cyber CIKR protection efforts by establishing and maintaining frameworks for operational interaction between and among members and external security partners.[20]

Coordinating and implementing strategies for prevention, protection, preparedness, response, and recovery requires significant cooperation and collaboration between and among CIKR partners. A primary objective of this collaboration is to ensure that resources are applied where they offer the most benefit for mitigating risk, deterring threats, and minimizing the consequences of incidents.[21] The DHS manages risks to critical infrastructure by collaborating with government and private sector partners and the public to:

- Share information.
- Develop and implement protective actions.
- Enhance resilience.
- Ensure rapid recovery from natural disasters or terrorist actions.[22]

3   Explain the function of the National Infrastructure Protection Plan.

National Infrastructure Protection Plan (NIPP)

Provides guidance on protecting infrastructure and key assets. The NIPP integrates and guides a range of efforts designed to enhance the safety of the nation's critical infrastructure, by preventing, deterring, neutralizing, or mitigating the effects of a terrorist attack or natural disaster. NIPP provides a risk analysis and management framework for conducting risk assessments and encouraging the continuous improvement of CIKR protection.

Information Sharing and Analysis Centers (ISACs)

Provide operational and tactical capabilities for information sharing and support for incident response activities. ISACs are sector-specific entities that advance physical and cyber CIKR protection efforts by establishing and maintaining frameworks for operational interaction between and among members and external security partners.

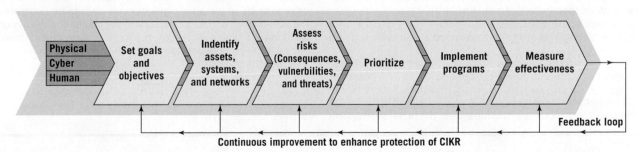

FIGURE 12–2
NIPP Risk Management Framework
Source: U.S. Department of Homeland Security, National Infrastructure Protection Plan, http://www.dhs.gov/xlibrary/assets/NIPP_Plan.pdf

The National Response Framework

National Response Framework (NRF)

A collection of guidelines and policies that responders use to ensure a unified response to natural disasters, terrorist attacks, and other emergencies. The document in the framework are based on best practices and lessons learned from similar events. NRF provides guiding principles so all participating agencies can prepare for and provide a unified national response to disasters and emergencies.

The **National Response Framework (NRF)** is a collection of guidelines and policies that responders at all levels of government use to ensure a unified response to natural disasters, terrorist attacks, and other emergencies. The DHS updates the documents in the framework based on best-practices and lessons learned from similar events. NRF provides guiding principles so all participating agencies can prepare for and provide a unified national response to disasters and emergencies.[23] The NRF establishes a comprehensive, national, all-hazards approach to domestic incident response. In it key principles, roles, and structures are defined. These provide the foundation on which to base the preferred response and enable first responders, decision makers, and others to provide a unified national response.

The organizational structures described in the NRF and NIPP provide for formal and informal public- and private-sector coordination, situational awareness, impact assessments, and information sharing. The NIPP is well synchronized with the guidelines of the NRF. This coordination allows for broader engagement in the affected sectors, and allows partners to plan for and quickly react to far-reaching effects from an incident. They are then able to alert individual critical infrastructure owners and operators of the need to take specific actions to minimize the negative effects.[24]

Information Sharing

The key to any collaboration effort is communication. With so many agencies and organizations, you can imagine that the process of information sharing can be quite challenging. The DHS identified several methods for information sharing within and among the critical infrastructure sectors. These include the following:

- Homeland Security Information Network (HSIN) Critical Sectors is a secure Web-based platform used for sharing sensitive information among federal, state, local, tribal, private sector, and international partners.
- Protected Critical Infrastructure Information (PCII) program works with government organizations and the private sector to protect critical infrastructure information needed for incident management, steady-state operations, and preparedness.

Spotlight
Critical Infrastructure in Occupied Territory

The military describes infrastructure elements to include basic facilities, services, and installations needed for a community or society to function. The state of the infrastructure determines the resources required for reconstruction. Typical key infrastructure includes sewers, water, electrical, academic, trash, medical facilities, safety, and other considerations. The degradation or destruction of infrastructure will negatively affect both the host nation and its population. Thus, the degradation or destruction of infrastructure often helps the insurgency, especially with respect to propaganda and the population's perception of the host nation.

Existing structures can play many significant roles. Bridges, communications towers, power plants, and dams are important infrastructure. Others, such as churches, mosques, national libraries, and hospitals are cultural sites, play important roles in the community. Still others are facilities with practical applications

such as jails, warehouses, television/radio stations, and print plants. Some aspects of the civilian infrastructure, such as the location of toxic industrial materials, may influence operations. Analyzing a structure involves determining how its location, functions, and capabilities support an operation. Commanders also consider the consequences of using a certain structure. Commanders must carefully weigh the expected military benefits against costs to the community that will have to be addressed in the future. The long-term success of any counterinsurgency often relies on the ability of the security force to protect and maintain critical infrastructure until the host nation government can resume that responsibility.

Source: FM 3-24.2 (FM 90-8, FM 7-98), Field Manual No. 3-24.2, Headquarters Department of the Army, Washington DC, April 21, 2009, Tactics in Counterinsurgency,' www.train.army.mil

- Homeland Infrastructure Threat and Risk Analysis Center (HITRAC) is the joint fusion center of Infrastructure Protection and the Office of Intelligence and Analysis for national integration, analysis, and sharing of information.

- National Infrastructure Coordinating Center (NICC) is a twenty-four-hour watch center that maintains situational and operational awareness, communication, and coordination among the CIKR public and private stakeholders.

- DHS Daily Open Source Infrastructure Report is a summary of open-source published information about significant critical infrastructure issues.[25]

The information-sharing strategy described in the NIPP includes connections between many government and private organizations. Figure 12–3 illustrates the exchange of information among the diverse interests represented by the DHS, the federal intelligence community, and other federal, state, local, and tribal agencies and private-sector partners.

CIKR Protection at the Federal Level

The DHS partners with many organizations to provide additional information-sharing support to its security partners.[26] Some of the DHS security partners, namely those considered sector-specific agencies (SSAs) maintain ongoing relationships with partners in each critical infrastructure sector and work together to identify vulnerabilities and all-hazard risks and develop protective programs.[27] For example, the office of the Director of National Intelligence manages the Federal Information Sharing Environment (ISE). The ISE is a combination of physical and digital environments that support information and intelligence sharing by law enforcement, homeland security, intelligence, defense, and foreign affairs personnel in their endeavors to protect national security and related activities. Investigators share information in the environment with allies in both the public and private sector.

Many states and large cities have also established fusion centers to share information and intelligence (see below).[28] DHS is also responsible for leading, integrating, and coordinating the national effort to enhance CIKR protection, including developing and implementing risk management programs; developing cross-sector and cross-jurisdictional protection guidance and protocols; and recommending risk management and performance criteria and metrics within and across sectors.

The DHS responsibilities for support of CIKR during incident responses include:

- Protect critical assets, systems, and networks, particularly those that might cause catastrophic health effects or mass casualties if controlled by outsiders.

- Provide an information-sharing network to provide threat information, assessments, and warnings to public- and private-sector security partners.

- Manage risk-assessment programs for high-risk CIKR, identifying priorities across sectors, and integrating programs with the all-hazards approach.

- Maintain plans for threat-based increases in protective measures that align to all-hazards warnings, specific threat vectors, and each level of the Homeland Security Advisory System.

- Develop modeling and simulations to analyze sector, cross-sector, and regional dependencies and interdependencies, and sharing the results with security partners.

- Support efforts to protect and recover CIKR, including analysis, warning, information sharing, vulnerability reduction, and mitigation activities and programs.

- Share lessons learned from exercises, actual incidents, and predisaster mitigation efforts.

- Working with the Department of State, SSAs, and other security partners, to ensure CIKR protection efforts are fully coordinated with international partners.[29]

FIGURE 12 8
NIPP Networked Information-Sharing Approach
Source: U.S. Department of Homeland Security, National Infrastructure Protection Plan, http://www.dhs.gov/xlibrary/assets/NIPP_Plan.pdf

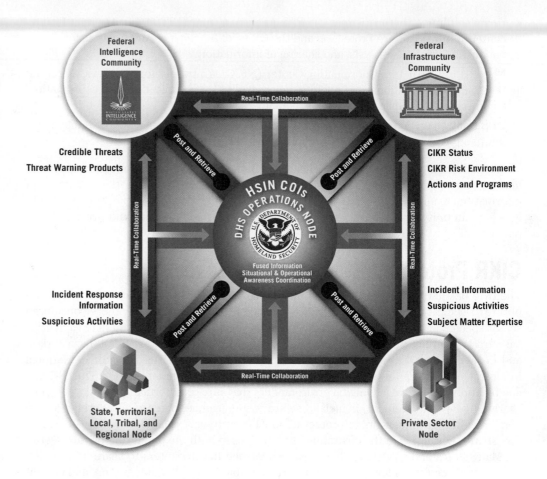

Interagency Cooperation

CIKR support at the national level involves coordination with and between many organizations, including:

- The National Security Operations Center (NSOC)
- The National Response Coordination Center (NRCC)
- The National Infrastructure Coordinating Center (NICC)
- The Department of Justice (DOJ)/Federal Bureau of Investigation (FBI) Strategic Information and Operations Center (SIOC)
- The National Coordinating Center for Telecommunications (NCC)
- The United States Computer Emergency Readiness Team (US-CERT)
- Other Federal Department and Agency Emergency Operations Centers (EOCs)[30]

These agencies work together during the incident management activities required for natural disasters, industrial accidents, and terrorist events. The CIKR support activities align to the specific requirements of the incident and function in conjunction with the processes described in the NRF.[31] Their flexibility allows responders to communicate in a familiar technical language about many different issues. As a result, agencies are more able respond to previously unimagined situations.

Security Exercise

Examine the descriptions of CIKR provided in this text. Think of some of the CIKR in your area. What makes them most vulnerable? How could that be limited?

State, Local, and Tribal CIKR Concerns and Responsibilities

State, tribal, and local government leaders have responsibilities in protecting CIKR. These governmental entities partner, facilitate information sharing, and enable planning and preparedness within their jurisdictions. States, regions, and communities have unique concerns with interdependencies of CIKR in their areas, and each agency has different responsibilities.

State governments are specifically responsible for the following:

- Implementing statewide or regional CIKR protection programs integrated into homeland security and incident management programs.

- Coordination, bringing prevention, preparedness, protection, response, and recovery authorities, capacities, and resources together.

- Providing conduits for federal assistance when the threat or incident situation exceeds the capabilities of public- and private-sector security partners.

- Coordinating with others to ensure full integration with national and regional-level CIKR support efforts.[32]

Local governments are responsible for emergency services and first-level responses. In some sectors, local and tribal governments own and operate the CIKR instrumentalities that they are entrusted with protecting, such as water, wastewater, and storm water systems and electric utilities. As a result, they are responsible for initial prevention, response, recovery, and emergency services provision, and are responsible for public health, welfare, safety, CIKR protection, and continuity of essential services within their jurisdictions.[33] One of the most significant approaches is the development of fusion centers, a concept described in detail in the following section.

◀ Shawnee Tribal Police Captain Anthony Johnson and Officer Shawn Crowley speak with a May 19–20, 2013, tornado survivor. State and local officials are partners with FEMA in helping eligible storm survivors receive recovery information and assistance. What types of events would warrant involvement from local, state, and federal agencies?

Source: FEMA, https://www.fema.gov/media-library/assets/images/71175

Fusion Centers

Fusion centers provide operational capabilities that focus on securing CIKR and advancing federal, state, local, and private-sector CIKR protection efforts. The capability of these centers includes the development of analytical products, such as risk and trend analysis, and the dissemination of those products to appropriate CIKR partners. Fusion centers are designed to provide a comprehensive understanding of the threat, local CIKR vulnerabilities, the potential for and consequences of attacks, and the effects of risk-mitigation actions. According to the

fusion centers
Provide operational capabilities that blend the activities and intelligence sharing efforts of enforcement agencies at various levels and focus on securing critical infrastructure and key resources, and advancing federal, state, local, and private-sector CIKR protection efforts. Fusion centers are designed to provide a comprehensive understanding of the threat, local CIKR vulnerabilities, the potential for and consequences of attacks, and the effects of risk-mitigation actions.

DHS, CIKR protection capabilities in fusion centers assist state, regional, and local CIKR partners in the mitigation and response to terrorist threats as well as human-made or natural hazards.[34] Fusion centers assist with both information sharing and broad-based data collection.

As CIKR partners, each state, region, or locality is encouraged to work with their state and local fusion centers to ensure they understand the information-sharing requirements, so that they can develop a coordinated plan for collecting and producing the necessary information. The collection process for CIKR information should draw on various mechanisms and sources, such as existing state fusion center records or databases, open-source searches, site-assistance visits, technical systems, federal and state resources, subject matter experts, utilization of associations (including Sector Coordinating Councils), and information shared by owners and operators.

Information that is exchanged between fusion centers and CIKR partners include:

- Site-specific risk information.
- Interdependency information.
- Suspicious activity reports.
- Communications capability information.
- Adversary tactics, techniques, and procedures.
- Best practices.
- Standard operating procedures for incident response.
- Emergency contact/alert information.[35]

The CIKR capability must become an integral component in the information and intelligence cycle of the fusion center. The information and intelligence cycle is a process for collecting, evaluating, and disseminating information and intelligence obtained by the fusion center. The CIKR capability must be integrated throughout all aspects of this process. The steps in the information and intelligence cycle identified by the DHS are as follows:

Step 1. *Planning and requirements development*: Ascertain the current capabilities and CIKR requirements of stakeholders and then develop a coordinated plan that assigns responsibilities for collecting and/or producing CIKR intelligence that meets the requirements of those stakeholders.

Step 2. *Information gathering/collection*: Purposeful acquisition of raw CIKR-related information from which an intelligence product will be produced. Collection activity begins with the identification and assessment of strategies and methods that will yield the information necessary to meet the intelligence requirements to enable the fusion center to develop and organize collection systems and commence actual collection of CIKR data.

Step 3. *Intelligence analysis and production*: Intelligence analysis and production refer to the process of evaluating and transforming the CIKR information into descriptions, explanations, and conclusions for the consumers. The activities associated with this step involve the arrangement by subject matter and data reduction. The analysis involves formulating hypotheses, testing them with data, and integrating the results into explanations, assessments, and forecasts or early warning. The analysis of information is necessary to produce intelligence.

Step 4. *Intelligence/information dissemination*: The finished CIP intelligence product is disseminated to the consumers to prepare, protect, mitigate, or respond to threats targeting their CIKR asset using different reports as appropriate.

Step 5. *Reevaluation*: CIKR analysts lead the evaluation of both the efficacy of the process and the value of the intelligence derived from the process. This evaluation and feedback informs the improvement of the cycle for future actions.[36]

Although many fusion centers are making significant contributions to the intelligence operations of homeland security and CIKR operations, many improvements are possible. Examples of these areas are found in Table 12.1.

TABLE 12-1
Fusion Center–Private-Sector Interconnectivity

Critical Operational Capabilities (COCs)	Ideal/Optimal Role	Actual Role
Receive	• Fully developed, tailored HSIN portals • Private-sector access to secret and unclassified portals • Receipt of classified and unclassified information from the private sector • Appropriate handling and safeguarding of information or private-sector information	• General email/phone capabilities to receive inquiries/tips • Ad hoc reporting of threats from the private sector to its respective fusion center • Diverse set of state "Sunshine Laws" varying in degrees of protection for critical infrastructure information
Analyze	• Full-time critical infrastructure analyst(s) or a Critical Infrastructure Protection unit or desk with focus on critical infrastructure protection and resilience • Geographic, jurisdictional, and/or sector inventories • Site assistance visits/comprehensive reviews • Sector-specific assessment tools • Periodic data calls • Integrated critical infrastructure analysis with other agencies • Overlay international or national intelligence with State, local, and regional information to develop timely and actionable intelligence products for their respective critical infrastructure partners • Frame the Intelligence in the context of their geographic area of responsibility • Sponsoring of critical infrastructure analytical training	• Law enforcement staff performing "all-hazard" analysis • Critical infrastructure threats and risks analyzed by fusion center; information not used to inform critical infrastructure protection threat landscape • "80% of fusion centers have procedures for information sharing and two-way communication with the private sector and CIKR owners and operators." • Forward open-source information that may or may not pertain to critical infrastructure partners • Procedures in place to share information with the private sector
Disseminate	• Fusion center analytic products provided to affected industry sectors • Feedback loop acknowledging receipt of critical infrastructure intelligence • Feedback loop also incorporates customer feedback (critical infrastructure owners and operators) regarding the quality, timeliness, and relevance of the fusion center's products into an informed production process • Routinely coordinating or modifying information requirements • Relevant analysis reported to appropriate federal agencies • Technology-assisted methods to distribute critical infrastructure intelligence and information • Available and protected space for vetted critical infrastructure partners to share and receive sensitive information from their State and local fusion center	• Open-source threat information directed to sectors of importance for situational awareness • Fusion center receipt of critical infrastructure intelligence—no follow-up after original information sharing—one-way information sharing • "The BCA results indicate that 63% of fusion centers do not have a feedback mechanism in place." • No change to private sector information requirements despite lapse in time and evolving threat environment • Electronic alert blast to inform businesses about breaking news, alerts, possible threats, and suspicious activity
Gather	• Tracking and monitoring of Suspicious Activity Reports (SARs) from the private sector • Fully engaged in the implementation of the Nationwide Suspicious Activity Reporting (SAR) Initiative (NSI) • Site assistance visits • Utilization of associations • Information-sharing working groups designed to gather intelligence and sector intelligence needs (SINs) of private sector	• SAR mechanism for general public to report suspicious activity • General terrorism tip line • Privacy policy in place to protect shared information • Ad hoc calls with critical infrastructure partners

Source: National Infrastructure Advisory Council, *Intelligence Information Sharing Final Report and Recommendations*, January 10, 2012, http://www.dhs.gov/xlibrary/assets/niac/niac-intelligence-information-sharing-final-report-01102012.pdf, p.J-8-9 [183-4]

Protecting CIKR and the Private Sector

It is not just the public-sector organizations that have significant CIKR support roles. Private-sector CIKR owners and operators are responsible for risk and incident management planning, security, and preparedness investments. Other activities that are considered part of business and continuity of operations plans include:

- Developing plans to address the direct effects of incidents and critical dependencies and interdependencies.
- Building increased resiliency, backup capabilities, and redundancy into business processes and systems.
- Maintaining coordination with incident management, information-sharing, and CIKR protection programs.
- Reporting CIKR status for inclusion in the national common operating picture.
- Developing and coordinating CIKR protective and emergency-response actions, plans, and programs.
- Guarding against insider threats.
- Providing technical expertise to federal, state, tribal, and local government entities.
- Identifying CIKR and prioritizing related protection and restoration activities.[37]

Industry Concerns

ASIS International has voiced concerns related specifically to CIKR protection and utilities. These include what is seen as unnecessary regulation, CIKR protection standards, smart grid advancement, privacy, aging infrastructure, and the future of a skilled workforce and professional qualifications.[38] One option for ensuring these concerns are addressed in the security industry is to implement government regulation. As regulation comes with increased work and cost, it is rarely expedient and bears no likeness to the streamlined management processes that many industry experts advocate.

There is a general concern with the need for regulated standards related to critical infrastructure protection, and part of the concern is due to disagreement on what constitutes critical infrastructure and critical cyber assets, and the risk associated with these assets in a fully redundant operation such as the power grid. This appears to be a situation where there may be a good argument for the application of government resources to national security in sufficient scope to make regulation of critical infrastructure security less of a requirement.

To meet these concerns, private CIKR protection plans and resiliency strategies are just now being developed. In the future to align with the NIPP, DHS advised that private CIKR plans should address:

- CIKR protection roles and responsibilities.
- Partnerships and information sharing.
- The NIPP Risk Framework.
- Procedures for data use and protection.
- Leveraging of ongoing sector-based activities for CIKR protection and resiliency.
- Integrating federal and sector CIKR protection activities.[39]

Public-Private Partnerships for Infrastructure Security

Because both public and private organizations are affected by any threat to CIKR, a partnership of public law enforcement and private security organizations is critical to protect the nation's infrastructure. The strength of a united private-sector business and security community working with public-sector law enforcement and other government organizations produces a unified team to detect and attempt to prevent attacks of all kinds.

Law enforcement agencies can bring to the table their special legal powers and extensive relevant and current training.[40] Private security brings a large body of employee/agents (employment in private security is nearly three times that in law enforcement, and spending on private security is more than double law spending on enforcement). Additionally, law enforcement's employment and spending are fairly constant, while those of private security can scale according to the perceived need. Private security organizations are often more advanced than the public sector in the use of technology to prevent and detect crime, investigation of high-tech and economic crime, and crime and loss prevention. Further, in-house security organizations have unique relationships that situate them especially well to address certain crimes, such as computer crime.

Benefits of Cooperation

What are the actual benefits of law enforcement–private security cooperation? The benefits are many and mutual, including:

- Networking and the opportunity to develop ongoing relationships professionals in related fields.

- Collaboration on specific projects both at present and in the future.

- Increased crime prevention and public safety.

- Cross-fertilization of community policing initiatives and the use of technology to enhance security.

- Information and intelligence sharing (police can share some crime data; private security can supply business information and can share research and resources).

- Leveraging of resources to shift to the private sector some work that law enforcement handles, including various noncrime, nonemergency tasks; likewise, security organizations may be able to get police to help in reducing a variety of crimes.[41]

New crimes are constantly arising and only a combined effort between the public sector and private sector can lead to a solution. The U.S. Bureau of Justice Assistance advised that public–private collaboration is the needed approach for problems in the twenty-first century.[42] Powell and Starkey noted that the Internet has been seen as a place for both constructive and destructive purposes.[43] The advancement and maturity of the various models used to respond to catastrophic events controls how one infrastructure relates to and depends on another. This guides the need of backup systems, business continuity plans, and disaster recovery models for critical infrastructure, often limiting the strategies for those looking to protect it. While critical infrastructure is necessary for all aspects of society, not all components are critical to the infrastructure, so the commitment and ability to protect assets without such collaboration will vary.[44]

The process of sharing information and intelligence is a process of balancing diverse interests. That is especially true when sharing between government agencies competing for a decreasing amount of funding and between CIKR partners in both the public and private sectors. The common "language" is the risk management process identified elsewhere in this chapter, in which all of the stakeholders examine both the threat and the need to share. Figure 12–4 shows how the various steps in the process are achieved.

Today's threats often asymmetrically blend national and homeland security threats and require a response by a public–private partnership.[45] Previously established lines of communication between public and private entities facilitate the exchange of intelligence and need to be developed, evaluated, and improved on regularly. The private sector is a critical element, as it owns and operates the vast majority of the nation's critical infrastructure. The sources of the intelligence are also changing. The widespread availability of open-source

THINK ABOUT IT

If private security professionals have a cooperative agreement with law enforcement, how would they determine financial responsibility? In other words, if the private company acted on behalf of government interests, could they recoup some of the expenses for providing security to the government? What if public law enforcement provided security for private interests?

FIGURE 12-4
Intelligence Information as a Component of Risk Management
Source: National Infrastructure Advisory Council, *Intelligence Information Sharing Final Report and Recommendations,* January 10, 2012, http://www.dhs.gov/xlibrary/assets/niac/niac-intelligence-information-sharing-final-report-01102012.pdf, p.2.

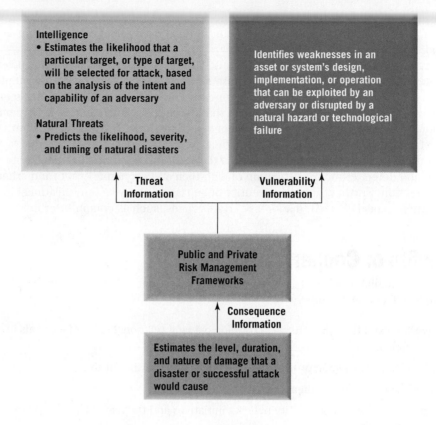

FIGURE 12-5
Bidirectional Exchange of Intelligence Information between the Public and Private Sector
Source: National Infrastructure Advisory Council, *Intelligence Information Sharing Final Report and Recommendations,* January 10, 2012, http://www.dhs.gov/xlibrary/assets/niac/niac-intelligence-information-sharing-final-report-01102012.pdf.

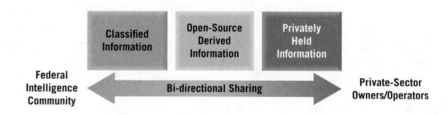

information along with new information collection and analysis tools are making the private sector much more of a producer of intelligence information in concert with the public sector.[46]

The public sector has begun to leverage sector-specific private-sector capabilities and information to enhance its own intelligence posture. This practice is expected to increase, and the private sector has demonstrated its ability to scale such activity much more effectively and efficiently than the public sector. The federal government generates classified information, while the private sector provides information concerning suspicious activities and privately held information. Both entities examine open-source information, and share the results using a bidirectional intelligence-sharing model, such as the one portrayed as Figure 12-5.

The DHS is one of a few federal organizations able to share information with members of the private sector. Table 12.2 provides a summary of laws, policies, and strategies assigning the DHS such authority.

TABLE 12–2
Major Authorities for Public–Private Intelligence and Information Sharing

Law	Homeland Security Act of 2002	Created Department of Homeland Security. Required president to implement procedures for federal agencies to share classified and unclassified homeland security information with appropriate state and local personnel (i.e., private-sector entities).
	Intelligence Reform and Terrorism Prevention Act of 2004	Established Office of the Director of National Intelligence (ODNI) to coordinate intelligence and information sharing within the federal government. Directed president to establish Information Sharing Environment (ISE) with policies and procedures for sharing terrorism information with the private sector.
	Implementing Recommendations of the 9/11 Commission Act of 2007	Required DHS Secretary to establish departmentwide procedures to receive and analyze intelligence from state, local, and tribal authorities, and the private sector. Specified authorities for DHS Under Secretary for Intelligence and Analysis to integrate and standardize Department intelligence components.
		Required DHS Secretary to establish a fusion center initiative and provide intelligence advice and analysis to fusion centers. Created Interagency Threat Assessment and Coordination Group (ITACG) to set processes to share intelligence information with state and local governments and the private sector within ISE.
Policy	Homeland Security Presidential Directive - 7 (HSPD-7) (2003)	Defined critical infrastructure protection (CIP) responsibilities for DHS and SSAs.
		Directed DHS to establish uniform policies for integrating Federal CIP and risk management activities across all 17 (now 18) Critical Infrastructure and Key Resources (CIKR) sectors.
	Executive Order 13311 (2003)	Delegated the functions of the president under Section 892 of the Homeland Security Act to the Secretary of Homeland Security.
	Executive Order 13388 (2005)	Directed agencies to give highest priority to developing information systems and disseminating intelligence-related information to fellow agencies, state and local governments, and private-sector entities.
Strategy and Implementing Structure	National Infrastructure Protection Plan (NIPP) (2006, 2009)	Established risk management framework across government and CIKR sectors.
		Defined sector partnership model and delineated roles and responsibilities.
	Program Manager (PM)-ISE Information Sharing Environment Implementation Plan (2006)	ISE Plan established specific objectives for the sharing of terrorism-related information with the private sector.
	National Strategy for Information Sharing (2007)	Integrated ISE-related initiatives.

Source: National Infrastructure Advisory Council, *Intelligence Information Sharing Final Report and Recommendations,* January 10, 2012, http://www.dhs.gov/xlibrary/assets/niac/niac-intelligence-information-sharing-final-report-01102012.pdf.

Cooperation in Practice

4 Contrast a sampling of public–private partnerships for infrastructure security.

Many examples of interagency cooperation to promote CIKR security are available. Some of the most prominent efforts are described in some detail in what follows.

New York Police Department SHIELD

The **New York Police Department (NYPD) SHIELD** is an umbrella program that coordinates efforts of both public and private security activities with the goal of protecting New York City from terrorist attacks, whether foreign or homegrown, based on providing best practices, lessons learned, counterterrorism training, and information sharing.[47] The SHIELD website displays weekly threat reports and analysis of global and domestic terrorist incidents that include implications for the city. Counterterrorism training, as well as risk assessment and

New York Police Department (NYPD) SHIELD
An umbrella program that coordinates efforts of both public and private security activities with the goal of protecting New York City from terrorist attacks, whether foreign or homegrown, based on providing best practices, lessons learned, counterterrorism training, and information sharing.

mitigation for manager's classes, and training on operational security measures for frontline personnel, are available.[48] Private-sector partners are uniquely qualified to assist NYPD personnel during counterterrorism deployments. Information that applies to a particular sector or neighborhood is transmitted directly to affected residents by one of several methods:[49]

- In-person intelligence and threat briefings conducted by Counterterrorism Bureau and Intelligence Division personnel
- Informal conferrals with patrol borough counterterrorism coordinators
- NYPD website postings
- SHIELD alert e-mail messages

The Law Enforcement and Private Security Organization El Paso

Law Enforcement and Private Security Organization (LEAPS)
Promotes the concept of crime prevention; to enhance communication; and to encourage joint cooperation between law enforcement agencies, corporate security, and private security organizations to reduce the opportunity of crime primarily in the area in and around El Paso, Texas.

The **Law Enforcement and Private Security Organization (LEAPS)** acts as a catalyst for change and an advocate for new ideas, in restating the fundamental purposes of policing, and in ensuring that an important link remains intact between the police and the public they serve.[50] The mission of LEAPS, which primarily serves the area in and around El Paso, Texas, is to promote the concept of crime prevention; to enhance communication; and to encourage joint cooperation between law enforcement agencies, corporate security, and private security organizations to reduce the opportunity of crime.[51]

Target & BLUE

Target & BLUE
A partnership between the Target Corporation and law enforcement and public safety organizations to build stronger, safer communities across the nation. The effort supports local communities through law enforcement grants, national night out, Safe City, forensic services and technical support, training, investigative tools and resources.

The Target Corporation is committed to partnering with law enforcement and public safety organizations to build stronger, safer communities across the nation.[52] The effort is called **Target & BLUE**, and supports law enforcement and public safety agencies through Law Enforcement Grants, National Night Out, Safe City, forensic services and technical support, training, investigative tools and resources.[53] Target supports disaster preparedness, too, assisting relief and recovery efforts through partnerships with national emergency management organizations, city and state emergency managers, and relief organizations.[54] Additionally, Target offers the Public Safety Grant Program to provide funding to law enforcement agencies and emergency management organizations across the country to support crime prevention, community preparedness, and training.[55] Target also supports training in areas of executive leadership, forensics, investigations, crime prevention, and best practices in policing, cutting-edge technology, organized crime, terrorism, integrity, ethics, and accountability.[56]

Operation Cooperation

Operation Cooperation
A major nationwide initiative to encourage partnerships between law enforcement and private security professionals. It serves to increase the efforts of the public and private sectors across the country, pooling their strengths to prevent and solve crimes and work toward the protection of life and property.

Operation Cooperation represents a major nationwide initiative to encourage partnerships between law enforcement and private security professionals. Operation Cooperation serves to increase the efforts of the public and private sectors across the country, pooling their strengths to prevent and solve crimes. The efforts vary, but they all work toward the protection of life and property.[57] Operation Cooperation is funded by the Bureau of Justice Assistance (BJA), U.S. Department of Justice, and supported by ASIS International. The International Association of Chiefs of Police (IACP) and National Sheriffs' Association (NSA) also support the program. Operation Cooperation attempts to persuade police, sheriffs, and security professionals to talk, walk, and work together, and it identifies some of the best ways to make their collaboration successful, based on years of national research and ideas from groundbreakers in public–private cooperation.[58]

InfraGard

InfraGard
An information sharing and analysis effort, with members in businesses, academic institutions, state and local law enforcement agencies, and other participants dedicated to sharing information and intelligence to prevent hostile acts against the United States.

One of the many ways that critical infrastructure partners share information is through active membership in a public–private partnership known as InfraGard. **InfraGard** is an information sharing and analysis effort, with members in both the public and private sectors.[59] It is an association of businesses, academic institutions, state and local law enforcement agencies, and other participants dedicated to sharing information and intelligence to prevent hostile acts against the United States.[60] InfraGard chapters are geographically linked with FBI field offices, and each InfraGard chapter has an FBI special agent coordinator assigned to it.[61]

InfraGard has a number of Special Interest Groups (SIGs) in which members collaborate and discuss mutual efforts to protect CIKR through multilevel engagement using information-sharing networks and a private secure portal of communication. The SIGs include:

- The electromagnetic pulse (EMP) SIG focuses on threats that could cause nationwide long-term critical infrastructure collapse, such as extreme space weather, coordinated physical attack, cyberattack, and pandemics.[62]

- The research and technology SIG provides actionable and relevant information to defense contractors with proper security clearance, private industry, and academia so that they are better able to protect their research, technology, and information. The main concern is the protection of classified information, but the same principles can be applied to the protection of trade secrets and other intellectual property.[63]

- The food-agriculture SIG is dedicated to safeguarding the food and agriculture sectors. This SIG enhances sharing of information among private-sector stakeholders who assist the FBI in detecting, deterring, assessing, and preventing threats and attacks.[64]

- The chemical SIG is directed to safeguarding the chemical industry including both the public and private sectors.[65]

The Process of CIKR Protection

How do these agencies and systems actually carry out CIKR protection? There are a number of steps in the process, beginning with a vulnerability assessment.[66] A **vulnerability analysis** is an assessment performed on a variety of systems, including information technology, energy supply, water supply, transportation, and communication systems. Such assessments may be conducted on behalf of a range of different organizations, from small businesses to large regional infrastructures. A key component of disaster management includes conducting vulnerability assessments of the hazards to the population and to infrastructure in political, social, economic, or environmental fields. Vulnerability assessment tends to be performed according to the following steps, according to the U.S. Department of Energy:

- Cataloging assets and capabilities (resources) in a system.
- Assigning quantifiable value (or rank order) and importance to those resources.
- Identifying vulnerabilities or potential threats to each resource.
- Mitigating or eliminating the most serious vulnerabilities for the most valuable resources.[67]

Vulnerability Assessment Guidelines

Guides for completing a vulnerability assessment are available from numerous U.S. Federal agencies including the Department of Energy (DOE), the Environmental Protection Agency, and the Department of Transportation.[68] Additionally, the risk management framework in the NIPP is a foundation for state, regional, and community CIKR protection plans and resiliency strategies. Following the framework helps ensure that all the plans are compatible and that CIKR partners can communicate clearly about the different plans. Guidance is available from the DOE regarding the intent and suggested content, including:

- Setting goals, objectives, and criteria
- Identifying assets, systems, and networks
- Assessing risks
- Prioritizing infrastructure
- Developing and implementing protective programs and resiliency strategies
- Measuring progress[69]

5 Analyze and identify the basic steps of a vulnerability assessment.

vulnerability analysis
An assessment conducted on a range of different organizations, from small businesses to large regional infrastructures that is performed on a variety of systems, including information technology, energy supply, water supply, transportation and communication systems. Vulnerability assessment tends to include cataloging assets and capabilities, assigning quantifiable value and importance to those resources, identifying vulnerabilities or potential threats, and mitigating or eliminating the most serious vulnerabilities for the most valuable resources.

The NIPP provides guidelines for consequence, vulnerability, and threat assessments. The objectives and expected outcomes of the DHS's Vulnerability Assessment (VA) program include the identification, prioritization, and protection of CIKR by assessing vulnerabilities, providing recommended protective measures, and by coordinating and partnering with public- and private-sector CIKR partners. The DHS provides CIKR partners with the tools, processes, and methodologies to streamline security investment decisions and reduce vulnerabilities. The VA program is DHS's focal point for strategic planning, coordination, and information sharing in the planning and execution of vulnerability assessments of the nation's CIKR.[70]

Vulnerability Assessment Tools

Some of the core programs and tools the DHS uses to conduct vulnerability assessments include:

- Comprehensive Review, a cooperative analysis of CIKR facilities and systems that incorporates potential terrorist attack scenarios, consequences of an attack, and preparedness and response capabilities of the organizations.[71]

- Site Assistance Visit (SAV) using dynamic and static vulnerabilities. During SAVs, DHS informs CIKR owners and operators of ways to increase their ability to detect and prevent terrorist attacks, and provides options for reducing vulnerabilities. SAVs assemble consequence and vulnerability information to support the collection of data for risk analyses for the stakeholder.[72]

- Buffer Zone Protection Program, a grant program designed to assist local law enforcement and owners and operators of CIKR with increased security in the area outside of a facility that can be used by an adversary to conduct surveillance or launch an attack.[73] Local law enforcement, facility owners and operators, federal, state, local, territorial, and tribal stakeholders work together to identify specific threats and vulnerabilities associated with a facility and its assets.[74]

Careers in Security

Name: Anthony Troeger

Position: President/CEO, Private Investigator
AARDWOLF INTERNATIONAL: Investigations & Consulting

Year hired: 2013

City, State where you are based: Greensboro, North Carolina

College(s) attended (degree): Western Illinois University (B.S.); Parkland Community College (A.S.), Criminal Justice

Major: Law Enforcement Administration

Minor: Public Administration

Did you attend graduate school? No, but having an MBA would be nice at this stage.

Please give a brief description of your job. I am a Certified Financial Crime Specialist and formerly conducted criminal investigations for more than twenty-five years as a Special Agent for the United States Government (1988–2014). I now own my own company, providing private investigative, protective, and consulting services.

In 2013, I began my own private investigation, executive protection, and consulting firm. In May 2014, I retired from government service to pursue this endeavor full time. I spend my days networking with attorneys, private investigators, and other business people who may be interested, or may have clients who are interested, in my company's services. I also have found that volunteering is an excellent way to network and build relationships that will eventually lead to opportunities for my business.

What qualities/characteristics are most helpful for this job? Integrity, innovation, a desire to be the best at what you do, inquisitiveness, a desire to solve puzzles, solid deductive reasoning, and logical thought process. Play chess (and get good at it).

What is a typical starting salary? For a federal special agent today, about $50,000+/yr. It was about $23,000/year when I started in 1988. As my own boss, there isn't one. Fortunately, I have a pension that allows me to survive even though I have no earned income while I build my business.

What is the salary potential as you move up into higher-level jobs? When I retired, I was making over $130,000 a year, working fifty-plus hours a week. Special agents who start today may retire making over $200,000/year when taking into account promotions and cost-of-living increases (inflation) over the next twenty-five years. With my business, as a Certified Fraud Examiner (which I will soon be), I should be able to demand up to $150/hour, the equivalent of about $300,000 a year, less business expenses. Ordinary private investigators with my level of experience, but without the certifications, can demand about $75/hour.

What advice would you give someone in college beginning studies in security? Stay in college until you have your MBA. Get straight As (or at least a 3.5+/4.0 GPA) if you want to get into the job of your choice right out of college. Otherwise, you'll have to prove your-self through several years of work experience. Intern everywhere you can. Volunteer. Join ASIS International as a student and be active in your local chapter and attend the annual conferences.

What appealed to you most about the position when you applied for it? With the government, while it was partly the prestige, the pay, and the benefits, especially the twenty-five-year retirement, it was also my belief that I would be the best at what I did, and that working for the federal government would ensure that. As for working for myself, it's largely the freedom I have to make the choices I want, to work when, where, and with whom I want.

How would you describe the interview process? The nice thing about working for yourself is that there are no interviews required in order for you to say you are employed. However, every customer is another job interview.

What is a typical day like? There is no such thing as a typical day. With my business, I have spent most of my time networking with potential lead generators while dealing with all of the administrative tasks, like obtaining my P.I. license or ordering my badge and credentials, that are required for my business to be operational.

In a typical day, what do you like best/least about it? BEST: Talking with people. I have the freedom to do as I choose . . . every day! LEAST: I work out of my home and miss having co-workers, but

that encourages me to get out of the house and generate business leads.

How would you suggest interested applicants gain experience? Internships. Take jobs in retail loss prevention or as a uniformed security officer. If you are not tech-savvy, do what you need to do to get there. Teach yourself or associate yourself with others who will help you learn. I volunteered as a student security officer during concerts at my college as well as at the Tenth Pan American Games in Indianapolis. Being a Resident Assistant also provided me with some excellent leadership training early in my life.

Would you recommend military experience? Yes. Some of the best managers for whom I have worked had a military background. I especially encourage people to consider the Coast Guard's Office of Investigations, Army-CID, Air Force OSI, or NCIS.

Does holding a full-time job during college help applicants get hired afterwards? That depends on if having that job hurts their grades. If they can maintain a high GPA and work full-time in an area related to their career interest (retail loss prevention, for example), it may certainly give them a leg up against other applicants who do not have that experience. But, bagging groceries for forty hours a week at the grocery store is not going to be much help. That said, if you have *no* employment experience during college, I would consider that a negative.

Summary

- **Explain the activities of the Homeland Infrastructure Threat and Risk Analysis Center.**
  - The HITRAC provides risk, threat, and consequence analyses to give the DHS and its security partner's information on threats, infrastructure vulnerabilities, and potential consequences of attacks or natural disasters. HITRAC experts analyze the effects of risk mitigation actions for strategic threat and risk analysis; modeling and simulation; and analytic support during incidents. HITRAC analysts produce intelligence-based reports that support threat-mitigation strategies and investment decisions, identify physical and cyber threats against critical infrastructure, and provide education on adversary tactics and use of weapons and explosives.

- **Identify the sixteen critical infrastructure sectors.**
  - The sixteen critical infrastructure sectors are Chemical; Commercial Facilities; Communications; Critical Manufacturing; Dams; Defense Industrial Base; Emergency Services; Energy; Financial Services; Food and Agriculture; Government Facilities; Healthcare and Public Health; Information Technology; Nuclear Reactors, Materials and Waste; Transportation Systems; and Water and Wastewater.

- **Explain the function of the National Infrastructure Protection Plan.**
  - The primary goal or function of the NIPP is to build a safer, more secure, and more resilient America by preventing, deterring, neutralizing, or mitigating the effects of a terrorist attack or natural disaster. Strengthening national preparedness, response, and recovery in the event of an emergency is another core part of the goal for the plan. The NIPP was developed with collaboration by critical infrastructure partners including federal departments and agencies, state and local government agencies, and private-sector entities. NIPP provides a risk analysis and management framework for conducting risk assessments and encouraging the continuous improvement of CIKR protection.

- **Contrast a sampling of public-private partnerships for infrastructure security.**
  - An example includes LEAPS El Paso, which gives adults the time and opportunity to develop an understanding of college and the skills needed for a successful transition. The goal of NYPD Shield, in contrast, is protecting New York City from terrorist attacks. Target & BLUE is a partnership between the Target Corporation and law enforcement and public safety organizations to build stronger, safer communities across the nation.
- **Analyze and identify the basic steps of a vulnerability assessment.**
  - Vulnerability assessment tends to be performed according to the following steps:
    - Cataloging assets and capabilities (resources) in a system
    - Assigning quantifiable value (or rank order) and importance to those resources
    - Identifying vulnerabilities or potential threats to each resource
    - Mitigating or eliminating the most serious vulnerabilities for the most valuable resources

KEY TERMS

critical infrastructure **262**
fusion centers **271**
Information Sharing
   and Analysis Centers
   (ISACs) **267**
InfraGard **278**
key assets **263**
key resources **263**
Law Enforcement and
   Private Security

Organization
   (LEAPS) **278**
National Infrastructure
   Protection Plan
   (NIPP) **267**
National Response
   Framework (NRF) **268**
New York Police
   Department (NYPD)
   SHIELD **277**

Operation
   Cooperation **278**
Target & BLUE **278**
threat analysis **264**
vulnerability
   analysis **279**

REVIEW QUESTIONS

1. What essential mission(s) does the HITRAC provide to private security interests?
2. What defines a critical infrastructure sector?
3. What does the National Infrastructure Protection Plan provide?
4. How do ASIS International and InfraGard differ? In what ways are they similar?
5. How does a vulnerability assessment differ from a risk assessment?

PRACTICAL APPLICATION

1. Your team has been chosen to restructure the sixteen critical infrastructure sectors and reduce the number to a list of ten that includes all of the previous elements. What process would you use to make these decisions? What would be your results?
2. Use the Web to examine the federal agencies identified in the chapter and to identify the membership of your local Chamber of Commerce or another association of business owners. Can you find at least five potential partnerships related to critical infrastructure and key resources?
3. Visit the "Stop. Think. Connect." initiative at DHS on the Web at http://www.dhs.gov/stopthinkconnect. What is the purpose of the initiative? What can you do to help secure cyberspace?

4. Study Appendix 1B of the NIPP (International CIKR Protection), available from the Department of Homeland Security at http://www.dhs.gov/xlibrary/assets/NIPP_Plan.pdf, with specific focus on the responsibilities of each department for international cooperation. Review the description for contributions by academia. Consider an applicable scenario, real or imagined, and list up to ten specific actions that would fit in this category.

5. Research what would be considered critical infrastructure and key resources in a country of your choice (other than the U.S.). Based on a variety of criteria you determine (such as the political, economic, and military posture of the country), choose several areas that should be considered critical infrastructure and several that should be considered key resources. Identify how you would suggest your choices should be defended in a memo to the new president or leader of that country.

Information, Cyber, and Computer Security

Learning Objectives

After reading this chapter, you should be able to:

Introduction

Citigroup, Bank of America, J. P. Morgan Chase, and many other financial institutions recently experienced widespread online issues consistent with a cyberattack. During the spring of 2012, several hackers commandeered unprotected servers around the world and directed an overwhelming amount of Internet traffic toward the banks' websites. The assaults, believed to have been launched by the Iranian government, brought the sites down and disrupted customer business. The event was the first digital assault of significant proportions against American computers by a foreign adversary. It produced at least three times the volume of traffic that the banks' websites were built to handle.[1] Most of the problem came from distributed denial-of-service (DDoS) style attacks that are hard to defend against, and which can slow or even shut off online access to the website for customers.[2] Hackers, especially those trying to send an anti-American or anti-capitalistic message, have repeatedly targeted the customer-access websites of U.S. banks.[3] Radware, a security firm, found that the cost of downtime for financial-services companies was an estimated $32,560 for each minute of lost online connectivity.[4]

Wary of provoking even more intense cyberattacks, U.S. leadership chose not to hack into the adversary's network in Iran to defeat the problem at its source. Instead, the *Washington Post* reported U.S. officials appealed to more than 100 countries to limit the debilitating computer traffic at Internet traffic nodes around the world. Even though this kind of joint action had never been attempted on such a scale, the attacks subsided. This was not the first time a counterattack worked. A similar maneuver had been used in 2008 in Operation Buckshot Yankee, to counter an intrusion into classified military networks by foreign hackers.[5] In that operation, action was taken against the disseminators of malware, which had infiltrated a secure military network. The malware, named Agent.btz, was neutralized when government intelligence experts created a counterattack strategy to give false directions that caused the malware to shut itself down. That action by the U.S. Department of Defense and National Security Agency was taken in defense of their controlled government networks (not the public Internet).

Denial-of-service attacks are not the only threat faced by security professionals employed to guard the nation's cyberspace. In 2014, a fatal flaw in a key safety feature for Internet browsing made headlines. The "heartbeat read overrun vulnerability," popularly known as *Heartbleed*, is a flaw in part of the most widely used encryption system on the Internet and, when exploited, it exposed practically everyone's data to both hackers and spies for at least two years.[6] CNN Money explained that the Heartbleed bug was a hole in the software that the vast majority of websites on the Internet use to encode personal information (like credit card numbers). The software displayed a padlock image in the address bar, although network administrators didn't realize that their systems were not fully secure.[7] For years, exploits of the Heartbleed flaw allowed outsiders to access personal information that was supposed to be protected. Most major websites were vulnerable, including Amazon, Google, and Yahoo. After the software was patched on the affected sites, users were advised to log out of all websites and to change their passwords.[8]

In addition to the Heartbleed flaw, hackers have accessed a variety of websites containing sensitive information. In the summer of 2014, a cyberattack on JPMorgan Chase compromised the accounts of 83 million households and small businesses. Hackers accessed at least ninety servers, and gained access to the names, addresses, phone numbers, and emails of account holders. Investigators were unable to determine how the hackers gained access and found no evidence that the attackers looted any money from customer accounts.[9] In similar fashion, hackers accessed the information of at least 40 million cardholders and 70 million others by accessing servers used by the Target Corporation in the Christmas holiday season of 2013. In an attack on Home Depot's servers, hackers stole an estimated 56 million debit and credit card numbers between April and September 2014. The hackers used custom-built malware installed mostly on Home Depot's self-checkout systems.[10] And in 2014, the Sony Pictures website was hacked, an incident described in the accompanying Security in Practice feature.

Security in Practice
Securing Client Networks

One of the most rapidly growing areas in security today concerns proprietary information stored in electronic media. In 2014, for example, Sony Pictures fell victim to a cyberattack in which many of the company's movies were pilfered and made available through illegitimate black market sites to anyone who wanted to download them. Even more seriously, the company's internal documents—including email communications—were stolen and laid bare for all to see. The release of those messages proved highly embarrassing to company executives and created a negative atmosphere among actors, directors, and motion picture writers. The monetary loss to the company was hard to estimate, but the damage done to its reputation was beyond measure.

The attack on Sony demonstrates the importance of safeguarding digital information. In a follow-up investigation, the FBI laid the blame for the Sony attack on North Korean hackers, who it said were likely backed by government agencies. Some claimed that the impending release of Sony's movie *The Interview* provided motivation for the incident. *The Interview*, a comedy about the assassination of North Korean leader Kim Jong-un, was apparently offensive to the North Korean government, and the FBI discovered that the software used in the attack was similar to that previously deployed by North Korea.

Not long after the Sony debacle, the FBI issued warnings to private companies throughout the United States, telling them to be on the lookout for similar attacks. The Bureau noted that energy and defense companies should be especially vigilant.

Warnings by the FBI were reinforced by press releases issued by security firm Cylance, which said it had learned that an Iranian group referred to as "Cleaver" was working to penetrate computers at U.S. hospitals, energy firms, military institutions, and transporta-

tion companies. Cylance warned that critical infrastructure components were especially likely to be targeted by Cleaver operatives. Mark Weatherford, former Deputy Under Secretary for Cybersecurity at the U.S. Department of Homeland Security agreed. "Global critical infrastructure organizations need to take this threat seriously," he said. "The Iranian adversary is real and they're coming, if not already here."

The Web publication *Digital Trends* told its readers that all of this was "a reminder that large-scale cyber warfare is being waged in the background while we idly click around our favorite news and social media sites."

QUESTIONS

1. *How important is cybersecurity to the average American company?*

2. *How much effort do you think the average company makes to secure its proprietary data and communications?*

3. *Other than hardening networks with the installation of effective firewalls, virus protection software, and the like, what else can be done to increase cybersecurity?*

References: David Nield, "FBI Warns U.S. Energy and Defense Firms Over Hacking Threat," *Digital Trends*, December 13, 2014, http://www.digitaltrends.com/computing/fbi-warns-u-s-energy-defense-firms-hacking-threat/ (accessed January 2, 2015); FBI, "Update on Sony Investigation," press release, December 19, 2014, http://www.fbi.gov/news/pressrel/press-releases/update-on-sony-investigation (accessed January 5, 2015); Cylance, Inc., *Operation Cleaver*, http://cylance.com/assets/Cleaver/Cylance_Operation_Cleaver_Report.pdf December, 2014 (accessed January 5, 2015).

These examples are but a small segment of the threats cybercriminals pose to government and business enterprise. It is ironic that at a time in which the official rate of crime has dropped significantly, the cybercrime rate has exploded. One reason is the rapid expansion of Internet commerce and communication. Worldwide enterprise information technology (IT) spending was estimated at $2.5 trillion in 2015.[11] Worldwide, more than 2 billion people are using email, sending 90 trillion messages per year. Social media sites such as Facebook and Twitter are expanding exponentially and are approaching 1 billion users.[12] Though it is difficult to calculate exact numbers, it is possible that the amount of money lost to cybercrime exceeds the costs exacted by traditional property crimes.

Another reason for the explosion of cybercrime is globalization. Many corporations are now international enterprises operating in a variety of global economic spheres. Business is done via the Internet, and transactions conducted in India can influence the price of raw materials in Germany. Cybercriminals therefore have the luxury of carrying out their attacks across borders, time zones, and jurisdictions. They have the luxury of being anonymous, not risking a personal appearance at the site of their criminal activities. Countering this new array of crimes presents a vexing task for security professionals because (a) such crimes are rapidly evolving, with new schemes being created daily, (b) they are difficult to detect and counter through traditional security, and (c) their control demands that security professionals develop technical skills that match those of the perpetrators.

This chapter is intended to provide an overview of what many in private security refer to as information and cyber/computer security, an area of the security profession that is undergoing organic growth and evolving so rapidly that information and cyber/computer security is now considered one of the thirteen identified security knowledge categories in the academic security realm.[13]

Information Security and Cyber/Computer Security

While these terms seem similar and are often used interchangeably, there are subtle differences between the terms *information security* and *cyber/computer security*:[14]

- **Information security** describes the various processes and methodologies used to protect print, electronic, and, according to the SANS Institute, other data from unauthorized access, use, misuse, disclosure, destruction, modification, or disruption.[15] Information security is a broader term and is usually used to describe the protection of information stored in computer systems and films, recordings, spoken language (conversational), and even the memory of people.[16] Consequently, the protection of data (information security) is often identified as the most important mission of organizations.[17] Government security experts chose the term *information security* to describe the problem of securing both information and digital systems.

- **Cyber/computer security** is the process of protecting data, networks, and computing power that make up computer systems.[18] The word *cyber* has evolved from the Greek word meaning one who guides a boat, such as a pilot. It was adapted to mean governance, taking on connotations of central government control. The term *cybernetics* was first used in the twentieth century to describe the process of controlling robotic mechanisms. **Cyberspace** became a euphemism for online interactions and went on to become the standard term to describe the Internet universe and its various computer networks.[19]

- Protection of networks is important to security professionals because it can prevent the loss of an organization's computer resources as well as to protect the computer network from being accessed for unauthorized or illegal purposes. The protection of computing power is especially significant when talking about large supercomputers.[20]

- Cyber/computer security involves the use of various technologies to protect networks, computers, programs, and data from attack or unauthorized access.[21] The main goal of cyber/computer security is to ensure the protection of the properties and assets of the organization and user against security risks in the cyber environment.[22] Both of these terms are closely related and overlap in some areas. Cyber/computer security is focused on the application of the policies and procedures that protect digital information shared on computer systems. It involves the actions, tactics, and strategies that secure the larger Internet network. Information security describes the security of the digital data protected by both cyber/computer security, as well as the protection of information stored, shared, and transmitted by other means.[23] Both areas are complementary and interact constantly so that security professionals must be aware of their aims and procedures. In the following sections we will set out these two significant security issues of the new millennium.[24]

In our always-on, always-connected world, we already experience a significant degree of increased technology involvement and engagement in our daily routines. We have begun accepting privacy intrusions from merchants, and we have likely had our privacy intruded upon by our government. State-sponsored hackers, organized cyber syndicates, hackers for hire, and terrorists, have been involved in making cyber threats and appropriating state and trade secrets. They are able to strike our critical infrastructure and our economy. The threat of cybersecurity has topped the list of global threats for the second consecutive year, surpassing both terrorism and espionage.[25]

In the United States, the FBI is one of the organizations targeting high-level intrusions—from botnets, state-sponsored hackers, and global cyber syndicates, to predict and prevent attacks before they happen. If a company is hacked, they can send a sample of the malware used to the FBI and receive a report within hours detailing how the malware works, what it might be targeting, and whether others have suffered a similar attack. The FBI is also working on a real-time electronic means for reporting intrusions, sharing information so that cyber threats can be prevented.[26]

1 Explain the differences between the terms *information*, *cyber*, and *computer security*.

Information security
The various processes and methodologies used to protect print, electronic, and other data from unauthorized access, use, misuse, disclosure, destruction, modification, or disruption.

Cyber/computer security
The process of protecting data, networks, and computing power that make up computer systems.

cyberspace
A euphemism for online interactions, and describes the Internet universe and its various computer networks.

Information Security (INFOSEC)

Information security, also known as Information Systems Security (ISS), describes the process of defending information from unauthorized access, use, disclosure, disruption, modification, perusal, inspection, recording or destruction, regardless of the form of the information.[27] Information security is a very broad area and involves the protection of information stored in computer systems and films, digital and other recordings, and even the memory of people, according to Security Intelligence.[28] Information security is comprised of two major categories:

- Information assurance, which is the ability to ensure data is not lost to a breakdown in system security, due to theft, natural disasters, or technological malfunction.

- Information technology security, which is the security applied to computer networks.

Governments, the military, health and financial institutions, and private businesses and corporations are all interested in implementing and preserving information security. There is a need to protect proprietary and confidential information specifically related to business and organizational practices and operations. Private citizens are also concerned with information security, and depend on the organizations with whom they interact to keep their personal information secure.

The information security field has expanded significantly since the 1990s due to rapid advances in computer technology. These advances have fostered improved methods of IT security and information assurance, but they have also led to more ways to infiltrate protected systems. Information security in the twenty-first century is primarily concerned with protecting computer networks, but protecting paper files and other sources remains a priority.

Most information security professionals agree that the biggest vulnerability to security is the human user, or insider threat. This became evident in the case of Bradley Manning, a U.S. Army soldier who was convicted in July 2013 on seventeen charges of passing classified material to the organization WikiLeaks related to the wars in Iraq and Afghanistan. Information security specialists work to mitigate these types of vulnerabilities through increased monitoring of all systems and proper training of all personnel with access to critical information.[29]

Information security can be viewed as including three important functions:

1. Access control
2. Secure communications
3. Protection of private data

Access control includes the initial entrance to an area by an individual or computerized entity, and also any reentry of that participant (individual or computer process) or the access of additional participants. Access control determines who can rightfully access a computer system or data and is aimed at the operating system level with a required login.[30]

Secure communication includes the encrypted transfer of information, coding or scrambling the information so that it can only be decoded and read by someone who has the right

THINK ABOUT IT

What should be done about individuals who divulge classified government documents and information and make it accessible via the Internet?

Spotlight
Wikileaks

Wikileaks is a not-for-profit media organization with the goal of bringing important news and information to the public. It claims to provide an innovative, secure, and anonymous way for sources to leak information to journalists (by serving as an electronic drop box). The people who operate Wikileaks stated that one of their most important activities was to publish original source material alongside other news stories so that readers and historians alike can see the truth of what is happening around them. Wikileaks, and its founder, Julian Assange, have been accused of facilitating the release of classified government documents that demonstrate events ranging from those claimed to be war crimes to international human rights violations.

Sources: Wikileaks.org, About » What Is Wikileaks? 2014, https://wikileaks .org/About.html; and The Guardian, Wikileaks News Portal, 2014, http:// www.theguardian.com/media/wikileaks

key. The encryption process is used by secure websites, for electronic mail (email), and for other mediums of data transfer. If a third party intercepted information sent using an encrypted connection, they would not be able to read the document.[31]

The protection of data includes securing storage devices, processing units, and even cache memory.[32] Data is secured by using passwords and digital certificates.[33] Frequently, the more information there is that is required to ensure proper access, the more private information that can be exposed.

Information Security Threats and Concerns

The level of security required is not the same for all organizations. Even within the same organizations some areas may require only low security operations, while others need to have high security activities associated with them. The highest security is used for data, such as corporate product designs or nuclear weapon applications.[34]

Classification of Information

The methods and labels applied to data are different, but some patterns do emerge. Paquet identified some common ways that governments classify or identify data, which include:

- *Unclassified*: Data that has little or no confidentiality, integrity, or availability requirements.
- *Restricted*: Data that if leaked could have undesirable effects on the organization.[35]
- *Confidential*: Data that must be protected with basic confidentiality requirements. This is the lowest level of classified data.
- *Secret*: Data for which a significant effort must be made to keep secure because its disclosure could lead to serious damage. This classification is considerably more restrictive than confidential data.
- *Top secret*: Data for which a great effort is necessary to guarantee its secrecy since its disclosure could lead to exceptionally grave damage. A particular individual's need to know also controls their access to top-secret data.
- *Sensitive But Unclassified (SBU)*: A popular classification by government that designates data that could be embarrassing if revealed, but constitutes no great security breach should it be released.

SBU is a broad category that also includes the "For Official Use Only" designation.[36]

There is no actual standard for private-sector classification. Paquet observed that different countries tend to have different approaches and labels.[37] A common, private-sector classification scheme includes:

- *Public*: Data contained in marketing literature or on publicly accessible websites.
- *Sensitive*: Data similar to the SBU classification in the government model, that might result in embarrassment if revealed, but no serious security breach would be involved.
- *Private*: Private data is considered important to an organization. An effort is made to maintain its secrecy and accuracy.
- *Confidential*: Companies make the greatest effort to secure confidential data, which includes trade secrets and employee personnel files.[38]

Competitive Intelligence

Competitive intelligence helps businesses face competitive environments more effectively. Competitive intelligence is both a process and a product. It is the set of legal and ethical methods for collecting, developing, analyzing, and disseminating actionable information pertaining to competitors, suppliers, customers, the organization itself, and a business environment that can affect a company's plans, decisions, and operations. Yap, Rashid, and Sapuan found that as a product, it is information about the present and future behavior of competitors, suppliers, customers, technologies, government, market and general business environment. The ultimate goal of competitive intelligence practices is to facilitate effective decision making that leads to actions.[39]

competitive intelligence
The set of legal and ethical methods for collecting, developing, analyzing, and disseminating actionable information pertaining to competitors, suppliers, customers, the organization itself, and the business environment that can affect a company's plans, decisions, and operations.

Copyrights

copyright

A form of protection provided by law to the authors of original works of literary, dramatic, musical, artistic, and certain other intellectual efforts. This protection is available to both published and unpublished works. Innovations with original shape and design are automatically regarded as copyrighted works on a worldwide basis.

Copyright is a form of protection provided by law (e.g., title 17, U. S. Code) to the authors of original works of authorship, including literary, dramatic, musical, artistic, and certain other intellectual works. According to the U.S. Copyright Office, this protection is available to both published and unpublished works.[40] Innovations with original shape and design are automatically regarded as copyrighted works on a worldwide basis. The assignment of copyright is subject to complex legal rules.[41]

Social Media

social media

Internet-based communities in which users interact with each other online on websites such as Facebook, Twitter, LinkedIn, Instagram, YouTube, and Pinterest.

Social media refers to Internet-based communities in which users interact with each other online. This includes a number of websites, but the term is most often used to describe popular social networking websites including Facebook, Twitter, LinkedIn, Instagram, YouTube, and Pinterest. Social media became popular as websites became more dynamic and enabled greater user interaction. Its growth was further fueled by the growing use of mobile devices, such as tablets and smartphones.[42] It is anticipated that the popularity of social media and social collaboration services will continue to increase. Security professionals should be aware of the many security threats connected to social media, and ensure that all organizational employees are aware of these threats and of ways to limit exposure. According to the ASIS Utilities Security Council, a variety of tools, attack vectors, vulnerabilities, and exploits exist in this environment, and policies should be very clear regarding allowed and prohibited behavior.[43]

Spotlight
Facebook

Facebook, as the world's largest social network, has more than 1 billion active users. The Facebook site is available to users across multiple platforms—both mobile and computer. A Facebook account contains a significant amount of personal data, including both a user's background information and updates they post periodically, some posting several times per day. Facebook users post text updates, photos, and videos to stay in touch with friends and relatives regardless of their geographic location or availability.

The Facebook Corporation also owns Instagram, a popular social media site known more for sharing of photos and videos. The Facebook business model provides free site access to the majority of its users in return for accessing user data. Facebook has business agreements with advertisers and software application (app) developers and allows them to access the data of its users. Those business relationships could make Facebook the most powerful data broker in the world.

Sources: Facebook Corporation, Company Info. » Newsroom, 2015, http://newsroom.fb.com/company-info/; P. Olson, "Facebook Moves to Become the World's Most Powerful Data Broker," *Forbes*, April 30, 2014, http://www.forbes.com/sites/parmyolson/2014/04/30/facebook-moves-to-become-the-worlds-most-powerful-data-broker/

Industrial Espionage

industrial espionage

The theft of information by legal or illegal means. It entails obtaining confidential information from other companies such as strategic plans or pricing policies, with the intent to use the information to gain a competitive edge in the marketplace.

Industrial espionage is the theft of information by legal or illegal means. It entails obtaining confidential information from other companies like strategic plans or pricing policies, with the intent to use the information to gain a competitive edge in the marketplace. The *Financial Times* reported there has been a rise in industrial espionage due to a more competitive environment, with increased pressure to gain such information driven by advances in technology.[44] The release of information by industrial espionage is more dangerous than inadvertent disclosure by employees because highly valuable information is stolen for release to others who plan to exploit it.[45] Industrial espionage techniques include:

- Offering employment to another organization's employees.
- Examination of another organization's trash.
- Electronic intrusion.
- Wiretaps, microphones, and other listening devises.
- Unauthorized access—frequently using a ruse.
- Romantic involvement with employees.[46]

◄ Digging through trash can provide valuable information. Criminals who conduct industrial espionage and social engineering activities can find out a lot by examining trash. Such a low-tech start can be enhanced by hi-tech searches for additional information. How can the kinds of security "holes" illustrated here be eliminated?

Source: Fotolia

Social Engineering

Social engineering refers to the use of social skills or relationships to manipulate people who have access to a network to get them to provide the information needed to access that network.[47] Social engineering entails gaining access to sensitive information or access privileges by building inappropriate trust relationships with insiders. The goal of a social engineer is to deceive someone and fool him or her into providing valuable information or access to that information, often unwittingly. These social engineers depend on the people they contact not being aware of the value of the information they possess and being careless about protecting it. Onwudebelu and Akpojaro observed that social engineers take advantage of natural human behavior, such as the desire to be helpful, the attitude to trust people, and the fear of getting into trouble.[48] One of the fundamental tactics of social engineering is gaining access to information treated as innocuous, when in fact it is not. Apart from passwords, other types of critical information include security codes, health records, customer lists, account usernames, employee numbers, birth dates, and other personal identifying information.[49]

Social engineering is often used on social networking websites to get victims to click on malicious links. Social engineering is also used with phishing schemes that tell users they have to verify their account information or else their account will be closed. Social engineering is not just limited to digital information. Attackers can also call a victim over the phone or contact them by text or email to try and glean sensitive information. According to Paquet, social engineering can also be done by searching through an organization's dumpsters or trash cans to look for information, such as phone books, organization charts, manuals, memos, charts, and other documentation that can provide a valuable source of information for hackers.[50] Bowles noted that some social engineers have pretended to be maintenance personnel to gain access to a computer or phone network room.[51]

In years past, social engineers might have called a receptionist and asked to be transferred to a targeted employee so that the call appeared to be coming from within the enterprise if caller ID was being used.[52] Such tactics are no longer needed if the cybercriminal is looking for details that are posted on social networks. Social networks are about connecting people, and a convincing-looking profile purporting to be representing a legitimate company or person followed by a friend or connection request can be enough to start a social engineering endeavor.[53]

Trade Secrets

A **trade secret** is a process, device, or something else that is used continuously in the operation of the business. Efforts to keep them secret are the responsibility of all employees. Trade

THINK ABOUT IT

Consider your presence on Internet sites, including social media. How hard would it be for someone to build a profile about you? How much information would that expose? How could that be dangerous to you?

Spotlight
Edward Snowden

Edward Joseph Snowden is a former contractor (through subcontractor Booz Allen) for the National Security Agency (NSA). While working for the NSA, Snowden began collecting top-secret documents regarding the NSA's domestic surveillance practices, including spying on American citizens under the umbrella of programs such as PRISM, an NSA program that allows real-time information collection, in this case, solely information on American citizens. On May 20, 2013, after telling his NSA supervisor he needed a medical leave of absence, Snowden flew to Hong Kong, China. The following month, on June 5, the *Guardian* and *Washington Times*

newspapers began releasing the classified documents obtained from Snowden. When the United States charged Snowden under the Espionage Act, Snowden fled to Russia, while the U.S. government attempted extradition. Many groups consider Snowden a hero for exposing the practices of the NSA. Snowden's actions may have caused so much damage to NSA security that the cost to repair it may run in the billions. Snowden remains in exile in Russia.

Source: Edward Snowden, Biography.com, 2014, http://www.biography.com/people/edward-snowden-21262897

secrets include processes, lists of customers, and discount codes. Salary information, profitability margins, unit costs, and personnel changes are not trade secrets. Trade secrets have actual or potential economic value, and the courts have said that the degree of legal protection of the information depends on the amount of labor and money used to develop the information.

Trade secrets are entitled to more protection than other proprietary information, and a company can file a civil action to keep it from being disclosed. According to ASIS International, the most serious threat to a trade secret is the organization's employees.[54]

To be afforded legal protections, a trade secret must meet these conditions:

- Be identifiable by group or type.
- Be not available through public sources.
- Be disclosed only to persons with a duty to protect it.
- Persons must know it is a secret.
- Organization must prove efforts to protect it.

Cyber/Computer Security

Cyber/computer security is the process of protecting data, networks, and computing power that make up computer systems.[55] The professional journal *Security Intelligence* advises that the protection of computer networks is critically important to prevent loss of server resources and to protect the network from being used for illegal purposes.[56] The need to protect computing power applies to all types of devices on the network, from laptops to expensive machines such as large supercomputers.[57]

Security in computers systems and network environments includes limiting access and protecting assets from threats. Security policy determines who is permitted to access a system's resources, and how such access is to occur. Problems arise when events violate security policy. Security aims at preventing, detecting, and recovering from attacks, as well as implementing strategies for preventing attacks. Security also necessitates backup and recovery when a system fails.[58] Recent surveys showed that the threat of cybersecurity and communications security was the greatest security concern facing Fortune 1000 company leaders in 2012.[59] The International Telecommunications Union defines *cybersecurity* as the term used to describe a collection of tools, policies, security concepts, security safeguards, guidelines, risk management approaches, actions, training, best practices, assurance, and technologies that can be used to protect the cyber environment and organization and user's assets.[60]

According to Gartner's IT glossary, cyber/computer security encompasses a broad range of practices, tools, and concepts related closely to those of information and operational technology security. The practice of cybersecurity includes the offensive use of information technology to attack adversaries.[61] Gartner advised that security leaders should use the term *cybersecurity* to designate only those security practices related to combined offensive and defensive actions related to information technology and/or operational technology environments and systems.[62]

Cybercrimes

The term **cybercrime** is used to describe cyber fraud and identity theft, downloading illegal music files, and stealing millions of dollars from online bank accounts. Cybercrime also includes many nonmonetary offenses, such as creating and distributing viruses on other computers or posting confidential business information on the Internet.[63] According to the FBI's Internet Crime Complaint Center (IC3) report, cybercriminals have started focusing their efforts more and more on targeting the networks of financial institutions. According to the agency, they rely on spam, keyloggers, remote access Trojans (RATs), phishing, and other malicious elements to steal employee login credentials. This is especially concerning when coupled with the fact that 87 billion spam emails are sent out each day, 1.9 billion of them containing malware according to Commtouch's October 2012 "Internet Threats Trend Report."[64] ASIS International advised that cybercrime that manipulates the supply chain could pose a threat to national security interests and U.S. consumers.[65]

Cybercrimes can be distinguished by how computers are used in their commission. The three primary areas of cybercrime are computer integrity crimes, computer-related crimes, and computer content crimes:

- *Computer integrity crimes* are attacks against the integrity of network access mechanisms, according to Wall. These attacks include hacking and cracking, vandalism, spying, denial of service, and use of viruses and Trojans. Computer integrity cybercrimes also pave the way for further offending. For example, identity theft from computers becomes serious when the information is subsequently used against the owner. Similarly, crackers may use Trojans to install "back doors," which are later used to facilitate other crimes.[66] Computer integrity crimes deal with the use of the computer network to commit a crime. They require an interconnected network, and the criminal has an active role in the crime.

- *Computer-related crimes* are committed using networked computers. They engage with victims to dishonestly acquire cash, goods, or services. Crimes such as "phishing," advanced fee frauds, and the manipulation of online sales environments like auction sites are examples.[67] Computer-related crimes are typically fraudulent and require a confidence game of sorts. Although such crimes are often inspired by offline criminal activity, they necessarily use a computer network to commit crimes.

- *Computer content crimes* relate to the content of computers—materials held on networked computer systems. They include the trade and distribution of pornographic materials, the dissemination of hate crime materials, and the publication of video of murders. Most jurisdictions have variants of the obscenity laws and laws that prohibit incitement, although laws protecting free speech may allow certain behavior.[68] Computer content crimes are those for which the computer and network have the lesser role. These crimes occur without computers or computer networks, and are simply facilitated by the existence of both. People who commit computer content crimes initially have an active role, which can shift to a passive role as distribution of the product continues.

What is considered a cybercrime is usually limited to those crimes that are only possible with the Internet and which can only be perpetrated within cyberspace (for example, online intellectual property thefts, spamming).[69]

cybercrime
Involves criminal activity carried out via the internet. Within this basket of crimes are cyber fraud and identity theft, downloading illegal music files, and online bank theft. Cybercrime also includes many nonmonetary offenses, ranging from cyberterrorism to distributing destructive worms and viruses.

Spotlight
Nigerian Scams

The African country of Nigeria enjoys a unique position in the realm of cybercrime. The instances of crime based in Nigeria range from unsolicited emails announcing the recipient is the winner of a fake lottery to the biggest Internet scams such as requesting the recipient's assistance with an international money transfer. The perpetrators are between 18 and 25 years old and mostly reside in urban centers. The Internet has helped to modernize fraudulent practices, and online fraud is an accepted means of economic sustenance by those involved. The corruption of the political leadership in Nigeria appears to have enhanced the growth of the cybercrime subculture.

Source: F. Ibikunle and O. Eweniyi, "Approach to Cyber Security Issues in Nigeria: Challenges and Solution," *International Journal of Cognitive Research in Science, Engineering and Education* (IJCRSEE), Vol. 1, No. 1 (2013).

identity theft
The theft of someone else's personal information—name, credit card number, or other identifying information—to obtain money, credit, or other things of value.

THINK ABOUT IT

What can be done to thwart identity theft? Are most people willing to take steps to protect their identity? Should they be held liable if they don't take the most basic precautions?

hacking
Secretly getting access to another person or organization's computer network in order to steal information, cause damage, or disrupt communication.

Identity theft

Identity theft is the illegal use of someone else's personal information to obtain money, credit, or other things of value.[70] Identity theft is a crime in which a criminal obtains personal information like their name, credit card number, or other identifying information, for personal gain. Saleh observed that identity theft techniques can range from being unsophisticated, such as mail theft, to sophisticated measures, in which a thief adopts somebody else's identity to gain access to his or her assets.[71] Recent surveys showed that the threat of identity theft was in the top ten of security concerns facing Fortune 1000 companies.[72] Identity theft is not new, and there have always been criminals who would use someone else's personal information to carry out fraudulent activities. Advances in technology facilitate more schemes that may result in major financial losses. In some cases, identity theft victims may have difficulty obtaining credit or restoring credit.[73]

Aggravated identity theft, under U.S. federal law, occurs when someone *knowingly transfers, possesses, or uses without lawful authority, a means of identification of another person* in the commission of certain felony violations.[74] Identity theft did not become a federal crime in the United States until 1998, when Congress passed the Identity Theft Assumption Deterrence Act to deal with the rapid increase in identity theft and the expansion of the use of the Internet and technology as a method to defraud innocent victims.[75]

Consumers do not have a great deal of trust that the organizations and businesses holding their personal information are protecting them against identity theft. Many consumers believe that it is the merchant's responsibility to prevent identity theft during and after any online transaction. That suggests if any security issues occur while on the site or in the future, not only will the blame fall on the merchant, but also, it will impact future transactions. Trust is central to customer–merchant relationships, and it is even more crucial when it involves risk and uncertainty.[76]

Identity theft can happen to anyone in any location in any country. All of us can take simple steps to protect our online identity by:

- Locking and password protecting computers and cell phones.
- Not sharing specific personal information online, such as full name or birthday.
- Setting proper privacy settings on social networking sites.[77]

Cybercriminals

Who commits these cybercrimes? As a group, they are referred to as **hackers** and are generally subdivided into the following categories:

- White hat (antihacker)
- Gray hat (ethically questionable hacker)
- Black hat (unethical hacker)

Security professionals should be familiar with the black hat hackers, who are often identifiable by their level of expertise or motivation:

- *Crackers* (criminal hackers) are hackers who have a criminal intent to harm information systems. Crackers generally are after financial gain. They are sometimes called black hat hackers.
- *Phreakers* (phone breakers) pride themselves on compromising telephone systems. They reroute and disconnect telephone lines, sell wiretaps, and steal long-distance services.[78]
- *Script kiddies* consider themselves hackers, but they have very low skill levels. They run scripts written by other, more skilled attackers, and do not write their own code.
- *Hacktivists* are individuals with a political agenda and motivation. When government websites are defaced, it is usually the work of a hacktivist.

Bowles observed that hacking was born in the 1970s and 1980s and concentrated on compromising phone companies in order to make free long distance calls and to otherwise disrupt services (i.e., "phreaking"). With the technology boom at the end of the twentieth century, the hacker community divided into three groups—the black hat hacker group and the white hat hacker group, with a gray hat group that fits somewhere with the two.[79] The black hat hacker group includes people, groups, criminal organizations, governments, and military with malicious intent. The white hat hacker group includes members of groups, organizations, and governments who are employed to protect their employers and counteract or neutralize malicious hackers. In between are gray hat hackers, who typically "bend" without breaking the law. Paquet noted that gray hats generally mean no harm to the system and do not expect financial gain. Unfortunately, however, they may pass valuable information on to people who do intend to harm the system unintentionally.[80] The gray and black hat groups are often distinguished by security professionals as those who operate within legal limits, and those having no regard for what laws they break or who is hurt by their actions, respectively.

How Do They Do It?

Powell, Wick, and Fergus explained that gray and black hat hackers use "exploit kits," complete with instructions and help desk support and have access to hacker-friendly sites that list thousands of scripts, tips, and tutorials.[81] The most common tools used by private and state-sponsored hackers are Distributed Denial of Service (DDoS), Structured Query Language (SQL) code injection, and worms. While the use of each tool alone does not result in damage, their combined use can quickly facilitate an attack. On their own, these tools of the hacker trade may look like espionage activities, but used in conjunction and with the right intent, may bring about effects similar or equivalent to those of an armed attack. Recognizing that cyber tools can rise to the level of armed attacks, the issue facing security professionals, the white hats, in the international community is how to regulate and limit the use of this technology in cyberspace, according to Kirsch.[82] It is the job of the white hats employed by security companies, government agencies, and business enterprise to counter these tools and foil malicious hackers. There are a number of strategies used by malicious hackers that must be understood and neutralized by security professionals. These are discussed in the sections below.

Denial-of-Service Attacks

A **denial-of-service** (DoS) attack is an effort to flood computer systems with emails, logons, requests, or other types of intrusions. These attacks are typically targeted at web servers, but they can also be used on other systems such as mail servers and name servers.[83] Bowles observed that denial-of-service attacks were one of the most frequent attacks seen on the Internet.[84] According to the U.S. Computer Emergency Readiness Team (CERT), the most

denial of service
One of the most frequent attacks seen on the Internet is an effort to flood computer systems with emails, logons, requests, or other types of intrusions. These attacks are typically targeted at web servers, but they can also be used on other systems, such as mail servers and name servers. Denial-of-service (DoS) attacks may be initiated from a single machine, but they typically use many computers to carry out an attack.

Spotlight
U.S. Computer Emergency Readiness Team

The U.S. Computer Emergency Readiness Team (US-CERT) was formed in 2003 as a partnership between the Department of Homeland Security and the public and private sectors to protect the nation's Internet infrastructure. US-CERT coordinates defense against and responses to cyberattacks, and is responsible for analyzing and reducing cyber threats and vulnerabilities, disseminating cyber threat warning information, and coordinating incident response activities. US-CERT engages with federal departments and agencies, industry, the research community, state and local governments, and others to disseminate reasoned and actionable cybersecurity information to the public. US-CERT provides state and local government personnel with cyber alerts, tips, and other public information on how to better protect cyber networks, access tools, and training. According to the Office of Management and Budget's report on implementation of the Federal Information Security Management Act (FISMA), about 40,000 cyber incidents of malicious intent occur each year, a number that has risen more than 40% in the past five years.

Sources: "A Guide to Critical Infrastructure and Key Resources Protection at the State, Regional, Local, Tribal, and Territorial Level," September 2008; and Office of Management and Budget, "Report to Congress on the Implementation of the Federal Information Security Management Act of 2002, Fiscal Year 2010, http://www.whitehouse.gov/sites/default/files/omb/assets/egov_docs/FY10_FISMA.pdf

common DoS attack occurs when an attacker "floods" a network with information, such as requests for Internet Web pages. When you type a website address into your browser, for example, the site's server responds by providing the page. The server can only process a certain number of requests at once, so if an attacker overloads the server with requests, it is unable to process your request. These attacks may be initiated from a single machine, but attackers typically use many computers to carry out an attack.[85] New DoS attacks can be discovered if security professionals know what to look for.[86]

DoS attacks are among the most difficult to eliminate.[87] Some system administrators install software fixes to limit the damage, but hackers continually develop new DoS attack techniques.[88] Because most servers have firewalls (that protect computers and networks from malicious or unnecessary Internet traffic)[89] and other security software installed, it is easy to lock out individual systems. As a result, distributed denial-of-service (DDoS) attacks are often used to coordinate multiple computer systems in a simultaneous attack, making it much more difficult to defend against.[90] Paquet noted that a DDoS attack generates much higher levels of traffic to flood the system by using the combined power of many machines to target a single machine or network.[91]

The computers in a DDoS attack will send as many requests as possible to a victim server in an effort to overwhelm it and deny legitimate users access to the resource. The victim server could be made unavailable by any number of actions, whether the excessive network traffic, exhausting available computer resources (like memory, a hard drive, or a processor), or the resulting lack of power. If the server is unable to respond to the large number of simultaneous requests, incoming requests will eventually become queued. Bowles observed that this backlog of requests may result in a slow response time or no response at all.[92]

Possibly one of the biggest reasons why DoS attacks are seen so often on the Internet is the simplicity and effectiveness of the DoS attack. When the server is unable to respond to legitimate requests, the denial-of-service attack has succeeded.[93] DDoS attacks are the "next generation" of DoS attacks on the Internet.[94] McDowell identified the following symptoms that could indicate a DoS or DDoS attack:

- Unusually slow network performance (opening files or accessing websites).
- Unavailability of a particular website.
- Inability to access any website.
- Dramatic increase in the amount of spam you receive in your account.[95]

SQL Code Injection

SQL is an international programming language designed for managing data in relational database management systems. Programmers with malicious intent can use the technique of code injection to introduce (inject) code into a computer program to cause the processing of invalid data by changing the course of code execution. Code-injection attacks manipulate specific system variables, giving hackers the opportunity to access that information. Beaver related that hackers can use this information to learn about the Web application, which can lead to a system compromise.[96] Ediger and Mior suggested this for those who cannot quite grasp the process of code-injection:

> Imagine you are writing a check. You write the dollar amount numerically in one field, then you'd write the same thing in words. If you didn't use the entire long second field, you might draw a line to the end. If you left some space in the second (numerical) field, someone could modify the field, and then use the extra space in the longer field to reflect that. The modifier could obtain more money than you intended when you wrote the check.

SQL code injection

The technique of malicious code injection to introduce (inject) code into a computer program, SQL is an international programming language designed for managing data in relational database management systems.

SQL code injection is like that: it creates an error that allows unscrupulous people to modify an entry field so that more information comes back to them than the original programmer intended.[97] Kirsch reported that hackers using SQL injection techniques may gain legitimate username and password information to sensitive databases and aid in intelligence gathering or espionage activities.[98]

Worms

A **worm** describes a type of computer virus or malware. Computer viruses are small programs or scripts that can negatively affect the health of the host computer. Worms consume a computer's memory and cause it to not function correctly. Just as regular worms tunnel through dirt and soil, computer worms tunnel through a computer's memory and hard drive. Computer worm's replicate, but do not alter any files on the host computer. Worms can still cause havoc by taking up all of the computer's available memory or hard disk space. Worms do this by self-replicating, using a computer network to send copies of themselves to computers on a network, sometimes without any user intervention.[99] Kirsch advised that the presence of a worm almost always results in damage to the computer network.[100] Worms are hard to detect because they are typically invisible files. Worms often go unnoticed until the computers they infect begin to slow down or start having other problems.[101]

Over the last half decade, worms have become major tools for knocking out entire computer networks. A self-replicating worm called Stuxnet worked its way into computers throughout the world in 2010. Stuxnet's goal was to physically, not figuratively, destroy its military target. Stuxnet particularly targeted the Siemens Company's industrial software and equipment, specifically the computer systems that ran Iran's main nuclear enrichment facilities. Stuxnet was programmed to activate when it detected the presence of a specific configuration of controller that appeared to exist only in a nuclear centrifuge plant.

worm
A type of computer virus or malware. Worms consume a computer's memory; and cause it to not function correctly. Computer worm's replicate, and cause havoc by taking up all of the computer's available memory or hard disk space.

Malware

Malware (short for malicious software) refers to software programs that are designed to damage or do other unwanted actions to a computer system.[102] Examples of malware include viruses, worms, Trojan horses, and spyware. Viruses, for example, can delete files or directory information on a computer's hard drive. Spyware can gather data from a computer system without the user knowing it and send that information to a predesignated Web address. The data can include anything from the Web pages a user visits to personal information, such as credit card numbers.[103]

malware
Stands for malicious software—software programs that are designed to damage or do other unwanted actions to a computer system. Examples of malware include viruses, worms, Trojan horses, and spyware.

Trojan Horses

As in the legendary tale about the hollow wooden horse that the Greeks used to smuggle their soldiers into Troy, a **Trojan horse** is a destructive program that masquerades as a legitimate file or application to gain entry to a computer (or, more recently, mobile phone or gaming device). Hughes and DeLone advised that once in the system, a Trojan horse may perform any number of undesirable actions, like deleting or damaging files, launching a DoS attack, playing beeping sounds, starting and stopping processes, stealing passwords, and opening a back door into the operating system that allows an attacker to control the compromised computer remotely.[104]

Trojan horse
A destructive program that masquerades as a legitimate file or application to gain entry to a computer (or, more recently, mobile phone, personal digital assistant, or gaming device). Once in the system, a Trojan horse may perform any number of undesirable actions, like deleting or damaging files, launching a DoS attack, playing beeping sounds, starting and stopping processes, stealing passwords, and opening a back door into the operating system that allows an attacker to control the compromised computer remotely.

Adware and Spyware

Adware includes programs that "facilitate delivery of advertising content to the user through their own window, or by utilizing another program's interface, in some cases also gathering usage information from the infected computer and sending it to a remote location," according to Hughes and DeLone.[105] By definition, they advised that Spyware has "the ability to scan systems or monitor activity and relay information to other computers or locations in cyber-space." Adware and spyware are spread in the same way, by being placed onto a computer when the user downloads a seemingly legitimate program or visits a website in which either or both types of threats are hidden.[106]

Ransomware

Ransomware is a kind of malware (malicious software) that criminals install or trick computer users into installing on computers so they can lock it from a remote location. Ransomware often generates a pop-up window, Web page, or email warning that looks official, and advises that your computer has been locked because of possible illegal activities on it. The message demands payment before you can access your files and programs again.

ransomware
A type of malware that once installed on a victim's computer via the Internet both locks the device and also generates a pop-up window, Web page, or email warning and demands payment be made in order for the system to be unlocked.

Ransomware is usually installed when you open a malicious email attachment or when you click a malicious link in an email message or instant message or on a social networking site or other website. According to Microsoft, ransomware can even be installed when you visit a malicious website.[107]

Hackers have been spreading ransomware, anonymously shaking down users of unprotected computers, from lawyers and police officers to government offices and businesses. Leger notes that once a ransomware virus invades an unprotected computer, it encrypts existing files so the owner cannot access data without a key or password.[108] Then, an ominous warning message pops up on the victim's screen with detailed instructions about how to pay the ransom and obtain the code to unlock the computer. The warning typically threatens to destroy all the data on the computer if payment is not made within hours.[109]

Spotlight
Ransomware

Ransomware creators intend to instill fear and panic into their victims. They want them to click on a link or pay a ransom, infecting their computer with malware, and seeing messages similar to these:

1. "Your computer has been infected with a virus. Click here to resolve the issue."
2. "Your computer was used to visit websites with illegal content. To unlock your computer, you must pay a $100 fine."

"All files on your computer have been encrypted. You must pay this ransom within 72 hours to regain access to your data."

Paying the ransom does not guarantee the encrypted files will be released. US-CERT recommends users and administrators take the following preventive measures:

- Perform regular backups of all critical information to limit the impact of data or system loss and to help expedite the recovery process.
- Maintain up-to-date anti-virus software.
- Keep the computer's operating system and software up-to-date.
- Do not follow unsolicited web links in email.
- Use caution when opening email attachments.
- Follow safe practices when browsing the web.

Source: US-CERT. Alert (TA14-295A): Crypto Ransomware. October 22, 2014. https://www.us-cert.gov/ncas/alerts/TA14-295A

The culprit is CryptoLocker, computer malware that freezes access to all the files on an infected computer, including photos, documents, and programs and allows access only with a passkey known only to the hacker. In a three-month period, 771 ransom payments worth $1.1 million were made in bitcoin (a nonbank payment system using digital money).[110] Those payments were transferred to a central online wallet that contained bitcoins worth $6 million.[111] That amount doesn't reflect the total in ransoms, as it does not include ransoms paid through anonymous credit cards, an option also offered by the hackers. Ransomware has been infecting computers since 2006 and appears to have originated in Russia.[112]

Rootkits

rootkits
Collections of software tools that enable administrators to access a computer or computer network. Malicious rootkits can be installed by nonauthorized users attempting to take over a computer or network. Malicious rootkits are designed to hide unauthorized programs from view and make it difficult to see them running.

A **rootkit** is a collection of software tools that enables administrators to access a computer or computer network. Malicious rootkits can be installed by nonauthorized users attempting to take over a computer or network. Malicious rootkits are designed to hide unauthorized programs from view and make it difficult to see them running. Bowles advised that the only way to be sure of removing malicious rootkits was to wipe the hard drive, reinstall the operating system, install patches, and then start moving forward with configuration of the machine.[113] Rootkits are very difficult to detect and even harder to remove without completely rebuilding the system on a computer.

Phishing

phishing
The criminal acquisition of sensitive information, such as usernames and passwords, by acting like trustworthy entities. Phishing occurs when a victim is contacted via email and tricked into revealing personal or confidential information that the scammer can use illicitly or fraudulently.

Phishing is attempting to criminally acquire sensitive information, such as usernames and passwords, by acting like trustworthy entities.[114] Paquet noted that phishing occurs when an email user is tricked into revealing personal or confidential information that the scammer can use illicitly or fraudulently. Phishing attacks may take the form of an authentic-looking website or a personalized email. According to the U.S. Department of Homeland Security, you can secure yourself from phishing attacks by:

- Turning off the option to automatically download attachments.
- Saving and scanning any attachments before opening them.
- Before providing any kind of information, call and verify with the source that they are indeed the ones who sent the email.[115]

Mobile Security

Mobility is an important asset in today's workforce and marketplace. With mobility comes an increase in security concerns for an organization's security professionals. The ability to work from anywhere at any time raises the level of concern about who can access what and the number of technology assets on the organization's network.

2 Identify steps to evaluate the effectiveness of an organization's mobile security plan.

We are an increasingly mobile society, accessing mobile computing devices throughout the day. As of January 2014:

- 90% of American adults had a cell phone.
- 58% of American adults had a smartphone.
- 32% of American adults owned an e-reader.
- 42% of American adults owned a tablet computer.[116]

As a result, many of the security challenges experienced by organizations are likely to be connected to mobile technology in some way. Security professionals should be aware of the general threat of mobile applications (apps) such as those that generate maps of buildings, identify the location of a mobile device user, allow payments between individuals, delete messages, pictures, and videos after viewing, and provide for anonymous communications.

The ASIS Utilities Security Council advised that higher incidence of asset loss, including the loss of information contained on the asset, can be expected to occur when the workforce is mobile.[117] *Bring your own device* (BYOD) policies allow employees to use any personal device over the enterprise network. Each added device presents security challenges that would not otherwise appear. The addition of personal devices to organizational networks creates several security problems, including registration, tracking, data flow and control, and audit and compliance issues.[118]

To improve the security of mobile devices on their network, the U.S. National Institute of Standards and Technology (NIST) advised that organizations should:

- Develop a mobile device security policy that identifies which resources can be accessed via mobile devices, the mobile devices permitted, degrees or levels of access, and how provisioning should be handled.
- Develop system threat models for mobile devices and the resources accessed through such devices. This helps organizations to identify security requirements and to design effective solutions.
- Consider the merits of each provided security service, determine the needed services, and design and acquire solutions that provide the services. Categories of services to be considered include general policy, data communication and storage, user and device authentication, and applications.
- Implement and test a pilot of the mobile device solution before putting the solution into production. Consider connectivity, protection, authentication, application functionality, solution management, logging, and performance of the mobile device solution.

cloud computing
Providing IT services, applications, and data using dynamically scalable storage locations possibly residing remotely, so users do not need to consider the physical location of the storage that supports their needs. Cloud computing is a model for enabling convenient, on-demand network access to a shared pool of configurable computing resources that can be rapidly provisioned and released with minimal management effort or service provider interaction.

smart grid
An interoperable utility environment that includes the energy markets and consumer services. It adds a market dimension to the power grid, allowing customers who periodically generate more energy than they need to be suppliers, among other benefits. The smart grid is a digital information network and modernized power generation, transmission, distribution, and consumption network system, which enables more competition between providers, better use of energy, and the use of market forces to drive conservationism.

- Fully secure each organization-issued mobile device before allowing access. This ensures a basic level of trust in the device before it is exposed to threats.
- Maintain mobile device security on a regular basis. Organizations should periodically assess mobile device policies and procedures to ensure that users are properly following them.[119]

Mobile Payments

Mobile payments (using mobile phones) have become commonplace in many countries. Payment options include attaching a device to the phone (such as the option provided by Square); paying with an app like Starbucks; paying by text message (supported by PayPal); barcode or QR Code scanners like LevelUp or PayNearMe; and paying with other secure methods, such as Mobile wallets using near-field communication (NFC) chips inside the mobile phone provided by Android Pay, Apple Pay, Isis Wallet (named for the Egyptian goddess of motherhood, magic and fertility and not the terrorist group), and Wal-Mart Pay. Mobile payments have been used to replace some payments with debit and credit cards.

Cloud Computing

Many small business and individual users experience their own variation of cloud computing with storage and software options such as Dropbox.com, Box.net, and Google Drive. **Cloud computing** refers to providing IT services, applications, and data using dynamically scalable storage locations possibly residing remotely, so users do not need to consider the physical location of the storage that supports their needs. According to the NIST the current definition of cloud computing is "a model for enabling convenient, on-demand network access to a shared pool of configurable computing resources (e.g., networks, servers, storage, applications, and services) that can be rapidly provisioned and released with minimal management effort or service provider interaction."[120]

The cloud can include what is referred to as Infrastructure as a Service (IaaS) and Platform as a Service (PaaS) provisions. An example of these services is one of the many Internet-based email providers, where the contact and content data for each user resides in the cloud and the primary interface is via a browser. A user with an account who may be traveling can access email from any location in the world from any computing device by typing in a web address along with a username and password to access the email account.[121]

Security in cloud computing requires a strategy that addressed shared resources in the same environment with a variety of security levels. Security solutions must also consider the trade-offs of security versus performance.[122] Cloud computing requires holistic security solutions based on multiple aspects of a large and loosely integrated system. Securing a system is dependent on the success of each of the system functions and the interactivity between them.[123] Going outside the firewall to access the cloud requires added layers of security.[124]

The Smart Grid

Smart grid is an interoperable utility environment that includes the energy markets and consumer services. It adds a market dimension to the power grid, allowing customers who periodically generate more energy than they need to be suppliers, among other benefits. The smart grid is a digital information network and modernized power generation, transmission, distribution, and consumption network system, according to the ASIS Utilities Security Council. The grid enables more competition between providers, better use of energy, and the use of market forces to drive conservationism.

Proponents envision a future where energy is bought and sold through the distribution grid rather than through generation and transmission systems. Conceivably, any home could produce its own energy and sell surplus. The ASIS Utilities Security Council advised that the smart grid provides an information flow related to energy market demands, power generation peaks, power demand peaks, and a variety of data that utilities will use to manage power supply and efficiencies. Devices that require electricity, from mobile communications to plug-in electric vehicles, could be recharged anywhere and be billed to an individual account.[125] The council reported that wireless technology advancements were fueling utility modernization like the smart grid, and were causing an increase in mobile devices used to install smart grid devices and manage the utility. The resulting mix of mobile devices for personal and job use, combined with the uptake in social media, social collaboration, and cloud services, creates cybersecurity problems that utilities must factor into their risk management cycle.[126] New "smart grid" and "smart home" products, generally designed to provide remote communication and control of devices in our homes and businesses must include protection from unauthorized use. Otherwise, each new device could become a doorway into our computer systems for adversaries to use for their own purposes, according to Snow.[127]

Coordinated attacks on other nation's electric systems could cause the entire electric power network to collapse. Smith reported that the Federal Energy Regulatory Commission used software to model the electric system's performance under the stress of losing important substations, and found the United States could suffer a blackout if just nine of the country's 55,000 electric-transmission substations were knocked out at peak use times. This was possible because the substations use large power transformers to boost the voltage of electricity so it can move long distances and then reduce the voltage to a usable level as the electricity nears homes and businesses.[128]

Mesh Networks

A **mesh network** is an ad hoc network that wirelessly connects computers and devices directly to each other without passing through any central authority or organization (like an Internet Service Provider, or ISP). They are designed to be resistant to disaster and other interference and are more robust than typical networks. De Filippi advised the only way to shut down a mesh network is to shut down every single node in the network.[129]

Mesh networks are a bit different than what most people think of when they imagine a network. Most small networks (office, home, etc.) use a star topology, with a central node (a device such as a switch or router) that transfers information and is connected to a bunch of clients (laptop, smartphone, gaming device, etc.) The star topology requires data to go through the central point (the router) if two devices want to communicate. A mesh topology is one in which each node/device in the network is connected to every other node around it. If an office or home network used the mesh topology, the smartphone, laptop, and gaming device could talk directly to each other without a router.[130]

Many mesh networks have been installed as part of humanitarian programs, and provide the basic infrastructure for connectivity for people who can't afford to pay for or don't have access to a proper Internet connection. Most mesh networks are operated by a specific community, for the community. Instead of relying on the network infrastructure provided by third-party ISPs, De Filippi advised that mesh networks rely on the infrastructure provided by a network of peer computers that self-organize according to a defined bottom-up system of governance. Mesh networking therefore provides an alternative perspective to traditional models based on top-down regulation and centralized control.[131] Depending on the expertise of the users, they will also be likely to provide a security challenge.

mesh network
An ad hoc network that wirelessly connects computers and devices directly to each other without passing through any central authority or organization (like an Internet Service Provider, or ISP). They are designed to be resistant to disaster and other interference and are more robust than typical networks.

Internet of Things

Much discussion on predicting the future of information and communication technology has focused on the **Internet of Things (IoT)**. The IoT refers to a development in the Internet's function: it enables communication among "intelligent" physical objects.[132] According to Ferber, this global system of interconnected computer networks, sensors, actuators, and devices all using the Internet protocol holds much potential to change our lives.

Not long ago we were told to imagine a time in the future when the problems were large, complex, and required unprecedented scientific, mathematical, and technology skills for their solution. That time is upon us. As predicted, there is a fast, reliable, inexpensive e-infrastructure providing all communication services. People are connected to this e-infrastructure via computing devices that are continuously online.[133] The networking components of this e-infrastructure invisibly and seamlessly provide optimal connectivity

Internet of Things (IoT)
A global system of interconnected computer networks, sensors, actuators, and devices all using the Internet protocol that enables communication among "intelligent" physical objects.

in terms of performance, reliability, cost, and security. Jeffery observed that the e-infra-structure physically senses, detects, records, and curates everything, using all the interconnected computers, storage devices, networks, and sensors.[134]

The physical world has effectively merged with the virtual world and potentially every physical object can be made both intelligent and networked. Organizations and web-based business models have been created that have turned these ideas into reality. In the same way Apple provides devices to access music in their iTunes Store, consumers and industrial product buyers alike are seeing their relationship to equipment manufacturers changed by smart, connected things. According to Ferber, workplaces will have machines of all shapes and sizes that are fitted with sensors that advise what condition they are in and initiate maintenance, replenishment, or replacement.[135]

▶ The physical world has effectively merged with the virtual world and potentially every physical object can be made both intelligent and networked. What types of devices can you imagine being connected to the Internet?

Source: Fotolia

Subject to various security, privacy, ownership and commercial rights, all types of computational, storage, detector, and communication facilities are accessible to everyone. Jeffery suggested that detectors and subsystems would occur in all environments, across all industries and social services, and especially in our homes.[136] In 2013, there were 13 billion Internet-connected devices, and that number was expected to reach 50 billion by 2020.[137] Many of the earlier predictions have already come true, and we are being told of advances much more frequently than before. The evolution of wearable devices (not just watches) will likely increase this growth exponentially. Many of these can impact the way security professionals do their jobs. The challenge to security professionals will be to continuously adapt to changes in technology and ensure employees are aware of their responsibilities.

Human Enhancements

Human enhancement defines attempts to overcome the current limitations of the human body through natural or artificial means. Artificial intelligence and facial recognition, delivered with augmented reality to identify the threat and assess the risk immediately, will provide security professionals with additional tools, and challenges, in the not-so-distant future. Google Glass and other wearable technology demonstrate the power of the information we have collected and stored about people, places, and things. Google Glass allows the wearer to access data on the go from an advanced mobile computer and monitor combination built into a device resembling a set of eyeglasses.[138] When paired with augmented reality, this technology provides access to data about the various things and locations the wearer is viewing. When facial recognition is added, the wearer can instantly access databases with identification, residence, credit history, and criminal records of individuals in real time. This ability may sound like a revolutionary development for law enforcement officers and security professionals, but adversaries can also benefit from these enhancements. Security professionals will need to evolve their technology strategies as advancements in technology and acceptance of that technology by their adversaries create applications that allow information to be examined in real time about targets and their guardians.

Driverless Vehicles

In another major initiative, Google and other companies are working on driverless automobiles. Suggesting that most accidents are caused by human error, Google asks, "What if we can make this go away?"[139] The project is likely to face big issues such as liability for accidents, the technology's sensitivity to hackers, and serious weather.[140] This "revolution" may bring good things for security professionals. There are significant opportunities in the concept of a driverless vehicle that will increase the ability of security professionals to perform tasks they are unable to do when driving a car manually, such as surveilling multiple targets and sites. The risk of distraction or poor judgment leading to an accident would be substantially reduced. In addition, the near silent operation of the electric vehicles makes observing adversaries while remaining undetected a lot easier.

The use of unmanned aircraft (UA) has been publicized for its use in wartime, border patrol, and retail package delivery. UAs are a very advanced version of what was previously referred to as radio-controlled aircraft, which are smaller than the typical aircraft because they don't have room for a human pilot or passenger. Communications devices, cameras, and weapons can be mounted on them, and they are able to move undetected due either to their silence or to the height at which they can operate, or both. Typically, UAs for security purposes are used for detection, but they can also be used for communication and apprehension. As these technologies advance, opportunities in the security profession are likely to expand.

Here Come the White Hats: Security's Role in Countering Cyberattacks

A good information security system is designed around confidentiality, possession, integrity, authenticity, availability, and utility. Security professionals who are interested in this area can obtain Certified Information Systems Security Professional (CISSP) certification. CISSP certification is a globally recognized standard of achievement that confirms an individual's knowledge in the field of information security. Security professionals designated as CISSPs define the architecture, design, management, and/or controls that assure the security of business environments. CISSP was the first certification in the field of information security to meet the stringent requirements of ISO/IEC Standard 17024.[141]

Elicit Management Commitment

An organization's trusted insiders can be primary threats to cybersecurity, and it is that type of threat that is the most difficult to mitigate, because these individuals have authorized access to systems, according to Powell and colleagues.[142] Senior managers have been found to be the worst offenders of information security, often because they regularly face a combination of job pressures, busy schedules, and an attitude that they are above the rules. Gonsalves found that most senior managers regularly upload work files to a personal email or cloud account, and more than half have accidentally sent sensitive information to the wrong person and also have taken files with them after leaving a job.[143]

Additionally, 34 percent of cybersecurity teams surveyed by the Ponemon Institute in 2014 reported they never spoke with the organization's executive team about cybersecurity. Seventy-nine percent of respondents said their organization's leaders did not equate losing confidential data with a potential loss of revenue. Most executives considered their systems inadequately protected, and 46 percent of them had experienced one or more substantial cyberattacks in the past year.[144]

Securing Passwords

Passwords are often misunderstood. When it comes to passwords, longer is better. Short complex passwords can be cracked much faster than a longer, less complex password. Users should change passwords often and not use the same password for multiple logins or reuse them. Bowles suggested a minimum of fifteen characters in a password should be used on a typical computer system.[145]

Require Firewalls

A firewall helps protect computers from hackers. Most operating systems come with prein-stalled firewalls, antivirus, and spyware protection. Firewalls can be made from a separate piece of equipment that is visible outside the computer or server, or software installed on the device itself. Beyond firewall protection, which is designed to fend off unwanted attacks, Lance suggested turning the computer off, which effectively and immediately severs an attacker's connection.[146]

Encourage a Computer User Baseline

By knowing what normal operation of a computer looks like, users should then be able to determine when something is out of the ordinary. Create a baseline of what the computer does during normal operation. Document items such as services, installed programs, disk and memory usage statistics, open ports, sample network traffic, and usernames. This will provide a baseline of how the system should be operating normally. Any deviation from that could indicate a potential issue and warrant investigation.[147]

The next big problem to be faced by utilities security professionals has not been born yet. There is always something new emerging. As technology changes, so will the efforts used by adversaries to compromise the efforts of security professionals.[148]

Countering Cyberthreats

Cyberthreats against an organization can result in significant economic losses, but not just for financial institutions. Threats to critical infrastructure, theft of intellectual property, and supply chain issues are also of serious concern. For some organizations, Bowles noted that not being online means a loss of sales, and that directly affects the bottom line.[149] Researchers with the Ponemon Institute found 63 percent of IT executives felt their organization did not have security that can stop cybercriminals from stealing corporate information.[150]

Spotlight
Cyber Storm

Security professionals should consider participating in the DHS-sponsored biannual national cyber exercise known as Cyber Storm, a multiday exercise that allows federal agencies, states, the private sector, and international partners to exercise their cybersecurity response capabilities and builds awareness about the importance of cybersecurity in CIKR protection.

DHS, specifically NCSD, is available to work with state and local governments as they develop new or enhance existing CIKR protection plans to ensure they address cybersecurity issues and fully leverage available federal and CIKR sector resources.

Source: "A Guide to Critical Infrastructure and Key Resources Protection at the State, Regional, Local, Tribal, and Territorial Level," September 2008, http://www.dhs.gov/xlibrary/assets/nipp_srtltt_guide.pdf

---

Cyberthreats from Within

Insiders cause most of the cyber incidents affecting public-sector sites. According to Sternstein, only 1 percent of reported public-sector incidents were the result of attackers exploiting security vulnerabilities in websites.[151] Ninety-one percent of respondents to the Ponemon Institute survey reported they knew another security professional whose company had sensitive or confidential data stolen as a result of an insider threat.[152] That contrasted with private-sector industries in which cyberespionage accounted for over 30 percent of incidents. Those differences were more reflective of a difference in reporting standards than the actual frequency of specific types of incidents. Sternstein observed that many public-sector organizations were required by law to report even minor data leaks that private-sector companies usually do not bother recording.[153] Responsibility for cybersecurity was shared across public- and private-sector entities, including state and local governments and individual citizens. DHS's National Cybersecurity Division (NCSD), the nation's focal point for cybersecurity, works with entities at various jurisdictional levels to enhance national cybersecurity posture.[154]

Cyberwarfare and Cyberterrorism

In the United States, the FBI investigates high-tech crimes, including cyberterrorism, espionage, computer intrusions, and major cyber fraud. Also, to stay in front of current and emerging trends, they gather and share information and intelligence with public- and private-sector partners worldwide.[155]

3 Distinguish between cyberwarfare and cyberterrorism.

Cyberwarfare covers the doctrine regarding the tactics, techniques, and procedures involving attacks, defense, and exploitation, and often social engineering. It is important to be able to distinguish annoyance or criminal activity from what is considered warfare. Passive cyber activities that merely observe or gather data are not considered weapons or acts of war. SQL injection, as an example, enters the realm of cyberwarfare by operating as a stepping-stone for further cyberattacks. As noted by Kirsch, once a computer network has been infiltrated, a hacker can execute a variety of attacks, including planting logic bombs or other malicious coding to damage the computer network.[156] Cyber threats to U.S. national security affect more than just the military targets and affect all aspects of society. Hackers and foreign governments are increasingly able to launch sophisticated intrusions into the networks and systems that control critical civilian infrastructure. The U.S. Department of Defense advises that given the integrated nature of cyberspace, computer-induced failures of power grids, transportation networks, or financial systems could cause massive physical damage and economic disruption.[157]

cyberwarfare
Uses the Internet to infiltrate or attack an enemy's computer network. Once a computer network has been infiltrated, a hacker can execute a variety of attacks, including planting logic bombs or other malicious coding to damage the computer network.

While the threat to intellectual property is often less visible than the threat to critical infrastructure, the threat to intellectual property may be the most pervasive current cyber threat. Every year, an amount of intellectual property larger than that contained in the Library of Congress is stolen from networks maintained by businesses, universities, and government departments and agencies in the United States.[158] According to the Ponemon Institute, the most common targets of cyberattacks after intellectual property is customer data.[159]

Just as a nation's military strength ultimately depends on a nation's economic vitality, sustained intellectual property losses can erode both a nation's military effectiveness and its national competitiveness in the global economy. The defense of a nation's security interests in cyberspace depends on the talent and ingenuity of the citizens. Technological innovation is at the forefront of national security, and government leaders can foster rapid innovation to ensure effective cyberspace operations by investing in people, technology, and research and development to create and sustain the cyberspace capabilities that are vital to national security.[160]

Governments are largely unprepared to respond to an act of cyberwarfare. As such warfare evolves with new technologies, our understanding of how to interpret them changes as well. Countries and nongovernmental groups are engaging in cyberwarfare. The capabilities of cyberattacks are innumerable.[161] Though the act of causing another an inconvenience and delay in communications is not normally considered an act of war, these scenarios are analogous to a missile being used to take out a government's communication center: such a DDoS attack would constitute an act of war.[162] Gervais observed that the effects of a cyberattack can range from a simple inconvenience (such as a DDoS), to physical destruction (such as changing commands to an electrical power generator causing it to explode), and even to death (disrupting the emergency lines to first responders so calls cannot be made to police or ambulance services).[163]

Cyberterrorism

cyberterrorism
Use of the Internet for terrorist activities, including large-scale acts of deliberate disruption of computer networks. Terrorist organizations are capable of launching cyberattacks against the networks of both government and critical infrastructure, and electric grids.

Closely aligned with cyberwar is **cyberterrorism**, the use of the Internet for terrorist activities, including large-scale acts of deliberate disruption of computer networks. Although some observe that there have been few, if any, verifiable cases of cyberterrorism, terrorist organizations such as al-Qaeda, Hamas, Hezbollah, Palestinian Al Aqsa, Martyrs Brigade, Aleph, and various Chechen groups are capable of launching such cyberattacks against the networks of both government and critical infrastructure, and electric grids. According to Powell, Wick, and Fergus, if terrorist organizations acquire highly sophisticated malware, a global Internet blackout and crippling attacks against key infrastructure are possible.[164]

STRATFOR Analysts have observed that the Islamic State is more technologically advanced than many other terror organizations. The Internet has been a significant part of the organization's growth and attack strategies. The analysts observed that the group will likely continue to pursue increased technology leveraging and offensive attacks in addition to their developed channels for online communications, though not to the point of committing catastrophic cyberattacks.[165] Further, the wide availability of cybercrime tools and mercenary hackers on underground criminal markets will allow the Islamic State to increase its existing capabilities. Analysts observed that the Islamic State is probably not capable of targeting critical infrastructure, though they would welcome such capabilities.[166]

Terrorist organizations typically want to see loss of life and to spread terror through horrific and violent acts, so cyberattacks against chemical, nuclear, and other industries relating to dangerous materials are always possible. As bright as many young hackers are, resources and time are important elements in a successful large-scale hack. The ASIS Utilities Security Council advised that significant coordination is needed for hackers to create havoc at the same level as a well-funded nation state or criminal organization.[167]

Dangers from state-sponsored criminal hackers come from economic espionage, where foreign governments, companies, and citizens illegally acquire intellectual property and confidential business information. Arquilla and Ronfeldt observed that if cybersecurity is compromised, then potentially huge amounts of capital invested or spent on research and development can end up aiding others to compromise national defense and security.[168]

Spotlight
Anonymous

Anonymous is a loosely associated international network of hacktivists and activists. A website nominally associated with the group describes it as "an internet gathering" with "a very loose and decentralized command structure that operates on ideas rather than directives." Among the activities credited to the group are the targeting of government, religious, and corporate websites such as MasterCard, Visa, and PayPal by DDoS attack. Anonymous originated in 2003 on the imageboard known as 4chan. Anonymous members (known as "Anons") can be distinguished in public by the wearing of a mask depicting Guy (or Guido) Fawkes, the best-known member of the Gunpowder Plot, an attempt to blow up the House of Lords in London in 1605. The group was the subject of the *We Are Legion: The Story of the Hacktivists* documentary.

Source: Luminant Films, LLC, *We Are Legion: The Story of Hacktivists*, 2014, http://wearelegionthedocumentary.com/hacktivist-timeline/

Cyber Vigilantism

Internet vigilantism is the phenomenon of taking the law into your own hands through the Internet (the communication network or its service providers) or through the use of applications (World Wide Web, email) that depend on the Internet. The term encompasses vigilantism against scams, crimes, and non-Internet related behavior. It was termed digilantism by Internet news and trends site TechCrunch in the wake of the Boston Marathon Bombing.

The Hacktivist group Anonymous has claimed to engage in such activity against a variety of adversaries, ranging from the Ku Klux Klan (KKK) to the Islamic State (ISIS). In January 10, 2015, Anonymous declared war on the attackers of Charlie Hebdo headquarters, in which 12 people were murdered. Their announcement stated, "We, Anonymous around the world, have decided to declare war on you, the terrorists." They promised to avenge the killings by "shut[ting] down your accounts on all social networks."[169] On January 12, they brought down one of the Jihadists' websites.

On October 28, 2015, they launched Operation KKK, after a chapter of the KKK reportedly threatened people protesting the killing of teenager Michael Brown by a Ferguson, Missouri, police officer.[170] An Anonymous representative vowed to wage a "cyber war" saying: "You are more than a hate group. You operate much more like terrorists and you should be recognized as such. You are terrorists that hide your identities beneath sheets and infiltrate society on every level."[171] Anonymous announced that it would reveal the names of members of the Ku Klux Klan and other affiliated groups.

Within days of launching the campaign, Anonymous members claimed to have taken over the KKK's main Twitter account and other associated websites.[172] In the past, Anonymous has claimed credit for cyber attacks on government, religious, and corporate websites by distributed denial-of-service (DDoS) attacks.[173]

Fighting the Cyberwar

The hacking of a U.S. surveillance drone by Russian forces was just one of many indications that the global battlefield includes cyberspace. The United States protects cyberspace as part of national defense, and initially took a defensive approach. In an intriguing analysis, Feif noted that the posture shifted to one that is more offensive beginning in 2011, when the Pentagon reported that cyber weapons were a viable part of military action in a theater of active conflict.[174]

As both military and civilian organizations increased their use of and dependence on digital technology, the military started defending national interests online. Military strategy naturally follows conventional warfare, with reconnaissance, maneuver over terrain, and use of weapons where necessary. This mind-set considers security the defense of terrain, meaning the terrain of cyberspace. If you are defending cyberspace, what you are doing is called cybersecurity.[175]

▲ The Guy Fawkes mask is a well-known symbol used by Anonymous, an international loosely associated network of hacktivists and activists. What dangers do hackers represent to an organization or business?

Source: N. Thompson, "Guy Fawkes Mask Inspires Occupy Protests around the World," CNN, November 5, 2011, http://www.cnn.com/2011/11/04/world/europe/guy-fawkes-mask/

Cyber Caliphate

A Caliph is a spiritual/political leader in Islam and a Caliphate is a jurisdiction controlled by a Caliph under Muslim law. The original Caliphate was established in the year 632, and Abu Bakr as-Siddiq was the first Caliph (Successor), after the death of the Prophet Muhammad. Ottoman Turkish sultans held the last Caliphate until Kemal Atatürk abolished it in 1924. Until now, that is. Recently, the Islamic State declared that it is restoring the Islamic Caliphate, naming leader Abu Bakr al-Baghdadi as Caliph.

Unlike the earlier Caliphates, ISIS has adapted to contemporary society, relying heavily on the Internet to spread its dogma. ISIS had declared a "cyber caliphate." In a video released in 2015, a digitized, hooded and faceless figure, akin to the symbol of Anonymous is shown reading a prepared speech in Arabic with English subtitles. A group calling itself the "Islamic State's Defenders in the Internet," claimed responsibility for the video. Anonymous posted a video response of their own detailing how they would stop the Islamic State's online activities.[176]

Spotlight
What Can We Do with Cyberspace?

Cyberspace describes the virtual world of computers. It is a popular term and is often overused. Paul Rosenzweig offered ten truths about cyberspace:

1. *Cyberattacks Are Indirect.* Cyber domains function across geographic boundaries. Through cyberspace, nation-states can perpetrate espionage, industrial spies can steal trade secrets, criminals can steal money, and militaries can disrupt command-and-control communications. These are real and powerful dangers, but these real-world effects are collateral to cyber effects rather than their immediate product.

2. *Cyberspace Is Everywhere.* The Department of Homeland Security has identified critical infrastructure sectors, covering everything from transportation to the defense industrial base. Virtually all of the sectors substantially depend on cyber systems.

3. *The Internet Has No Boundaries.* The Internet spans the globe and it does so near-instantaneously. This creates a profound challenge for policymakers because the reality is that cybersecurity is an international issue.

4. *Anonymity Is a Feature, Not a Bug.* The predilection for anonymity is inherent in the structure of the Internet. As originally conceived, the cyber domain serves simply as a giant switching system, routing data around the globe using general "Internet" protocols. The simplicity of this system is, to a large degree, the cause of its pervasiveness. Regardless of whether anonymity is good (it protects political speech) or bad (it allows hackers to hide), it is here to stay.

5. *Maginot Lines* (a reference to French defenses during World War I) *Never Work in the Long Run.* In many ways, cybersecurity is in the midst of its Maginot Line period. Governments, companies, and other users hunker down behind firewalls and deploy virus protections and intrusion-detection systems in a principally passive defensive effort. Like the Maginot Line, America's current system of firewalls is rather ineffective. Billions of dollars in theft occur each year. Counteracting that vulnerability will require the development of active defenses that look beyond those gateways to assess systems patterns and anomalies. Cybersecurity could then transition from detecting intrusions after they occur to preventing intrusions before they occur.

6. *85 percent to 90 percent of U.S. Government Electronic Traffic Travels over Nongovernment Networks.* The best defenses (whether government or private) must operate in the private-sector domain. This concept is highly controversial, and rightly so. The need for active defenses operating in the private sector cannot really be denied. There must be an effective means of protecting the privacy and personal liberties of innocent users of the cyber domain.

7. *There Is a Legitimate Role for Government.* Just as there is a role for government law enforcement to protect tangible private property, there is a role in protecting cyberspace properties. In part, this is because the security failure of one network can affect others outside of that network.

8. *NSA Does It Better Than DHS.* The strong preference should be for a civilian response for what is, after all, a predominantly civilian network. But the hard truth is that the civilian side of the government lacks the expertise and power to effectively do the job—which is why DHS has announced its plan to hire 1,000 new cyber experts. But until these new experts are on board (and finding and hiring that many will be a long process), civilian defenses will have to rely on existing expertise that lies predominantly with the NSA.

9. *No Defense Will Ever Be 100 Percent Perfect.* A critical component of any strategy is to plan for the inevitable instances in which the country's defenses fail. This means the creation of incentives and structures that encourage the development of a resilient cyber network that can contain any intrusion and rapidly repair any damage. Some computers will inevitably become infected. To deal with this possibility, the United States should have policies that call for widely distributing known vaccines, quarantining infected computers, and swarming resources to the site of the cyber infection to eliminate them.

10. *Hardware Attacks Are Even Harder to Prevent Than Software Attacks.* One little noticed and poorly understood aspect of cybersecurity is the degree to which American cyber hardware is manufactured overseas. Virtually all of the chips in computers are constructed elsewhere. This is a significant vulnerability. Both private-sector and public-sector strategies to eliminate risks are nonexistent. The steps that the U.S. government is currently taking to enhance supply chain security cannot eliminate the risks to cyber assurance posed by the use of commercial systems.

Source: P. Rosenzweig, "10 Conservative Principles for Cybersecurity Policy," Backgrounder #2513 on Homeland Security, The Heritage Foundation, January 31, 2011, http://www.heritage.org/research/reports/2011/01/10-conservative-principles-for-cybersecurity-policy

Careers in Security

Name: Alexander Berta

Position: Security Specialist/Forensics Examiner

Year hired: 2013

City, State where you are based: Nashville, Tennessee

College(s) attended (degree): Fire Service & Code Enforcement Academy—Fire Science/Homeland Security; Smart Certify Direct—General Computer Classes; AccessData—Digital Forensics; University of Arkansas—Comprehensive Cyber Terrorism Defense

Majors: Fire Science/Homeland Security

Please give a brief description of your job. As a security specialist for NSG my job is to come up with solutions to current threats. By staying current with threats this gives us an edge on how cyber criminals are working. I often spend many hours researching and reverse-engineering software to come up with a practical solution to fix the problem.

What qualities/characteristics are most helpful for this job? As a teenager I spent my time hacking with select hacking collectives around the world. This gives me an insight on how hacking collectives and cyber organizations operate. That being said you will need an understanding of how the underground hacking culture works and operates. The culture has its own set of rules that are closely followed by participants. By understanding these rules, it will give you an understanding of the culture.

What is a typical starting salary? $40,000–$50,000

What is the salary potential as you move up into higher-level jobs? $75–$100,000 a year. Also free schooling.

What advice would you give someone in college beginning studies in security? Hacking is not about causing the most damage when gaining access to a system, it's about understanding how the system can be compromised. Any person can gain access to a system at any time, but to understand how the code works will put you ahead of everyone else.

What appealed to you most about the position when you applied for it? I was able to build a security department from the ground up. This would allow us to stay ahead of the game. My bosses allow me to go out and research what the bad guys are doing and download and use the tools so I can help prevent breaches for our clients.

How would you describe the interview process? Our interview process was a lot of fun. It was more like a panel interview. Everyone around the table got to ask me questions and I got to ask questions back. They made me feel very at home.

What is a typical day like? This is a tough question. A typical day around here is different all the time. All I can really say is, I could be cleaning up a mess from Cryptolocker, or I could be writing policies.

In a typical day, what do you like best/least about it? I love everything about my job. I have no real complaints about it. We all work hard and play hard here.

How would you suggest interested applicants gain experience? Don't be afraid to break something. It's a computer, it can be fixed. To fully break something and then put it back together is all the experience that you need. Also never be afraid to ask questions. If you are unsure or don't think something is right, then challenge it and ask questions.

Would you recommend military experience? Depends on where you want to work. I have DOD experience and that does not come into play where I am working. It's a different environment and a different kind of people.

Does holding a full-time job during college help applicants get hired afterwards? Not sure.

Summary

- **Explain the differences between the terms *information*, *cyber*, and *computer security*.**
  - Computer security is protecting data, networks, and computing power that make up computer systems. Protection of networks is important to prevent loss of server resources as well as to protect the network from being used for illegal purposes. The protection of computing power applies to expensive machines such as large supercomputers. Computer security is focused on the application of the policies and procedures that protect digital information shared on computer systems.
  - Cybersecurity is the use of various technologies and processes to protect networks, computers, programs, and data from attack, damage, or unauthorized access. Cybersecurity strives to ensure the attainment and maintenance of the security properties of the organization and user's assets against relevant security risks in the cyber environment. Cybersecurity describes the actions, tactics, and strategies that secure the larger Internet network.
  - Information security includes the processes and methodologies designed and implemented to protect print, electronic, or any other form of confidential, private and sensitive information or data from unauthorized access, use, misuse, disclosure, destruction, modification, or disruption. Information security is a broader term than the others. It involves the protection of information stored in computer systems and films, recordings, using the spoken language and the memory of people. Information security describes the security of the digital data protected by both computer security and cybersecurity, as well as the protection of information stored, shared, and transmitted by other means.

- **Identify steps to evaluate the effectiveness of an organization's mobile security plan.**
  - An organization's mobile security plan should be designed to improve the security of mobile devices on their network. In order to accomplish this, organizations should:
    - Develop a mobile device security policy that defines what types of resources can be accessed via mobile devices, what types of mobile devices are permitted, degrees of access, and how provisioning should be handled.
    - Develop system threat models for mobile devices and the resources accessed through such devices. This helps organizations to identify security requirements and to design effective solutions.
    - Consider the merits of each provided security service, determine the needed services, and design and acquire solutions that provide the services. Categories of services to be considered include general policy, data communication and storage, user and device authentication, and applications.
    - Implement and test a pilot of the mobile device solution before putting the solution into production. Consider connectivity, protection, authentication, application functionality, solution management, logging, and performance of the mobile device solution.
    - Fully secure each organization-issued mobile device before allowing access. This ensures a basic level of trust in the device before it is exposed to threats.
    - Maintain mobile device security on a regular basis. Organizations should periodically assess mobile device policies and procedures to ensure that users are properly following them.
- **Distinguish between cyberwarfare and cyberterrorism.**
  - Cyberwarfare covers the doctrine regarding the tactics, techniques, and procedures involving attacks, defense, and exploitation, and often social engineering.
  - Cyberterrorism is the use of the Internet in terrorist activities, including acts of deliberate, large-scale disruption of computer networks. Terrorist organizations want to see loss of life and to spread terror through horrific and violent acts.

KEY TERMS

cloud computing 300	denial of service 295	ransomware 298
competitive intelligence 289	hacking 294	rootkits 299
	identity theft 294	smart grid 301
copyright 290	industrial espionage 290	social engineering 291
cybercrime 293	information security 287	social media 290
cyber/computer security 287	Internet of Things (IoT) 302	SQL code injection 297
cyberspace 287	malware 297	trade secrets 291
cyberterrorism 306	mesh network 301	Trojan horse 297
cyberwarfare 305	phishing 299	worm 297

REVIEW QUESTIONS

1. What key elements are found in a good information security system?
2. Describe the effect that a BYOD policy can have on an organization's mobile security plan.
3. Distinguish cybercrime and cyberterrorism.

PRACTICAL APPLICATION

1. You are being considered for a position in which access to Top Secret access is required. Conduct a self-assessment of your own cyber habits. How much of an asset would you appear to be in the eyes of those doing the hiring.

2. You are responsible for implementing a security program for your new employer. In order to see what you might do, assess the practices of a group or organization with which you are acquainted. How are members of the organization vulnerable to the many types of hackers?

3. Evaluate your mobile security posture, both personally and professionally. Which is least likely to be successfully targeted? How could that change?

Chapter 1: Origins and Foundations of Security

1. G4S, "Careers," http://www.g4s.us/en-us/Careers/ (accessed January 4, 2014).

2. "London Olympic Security Contractor Called 'Incompetent' by Panel," *Los Angeles Times*, July 17, 2012, http://latimesblogs.latimes.com/world_now/2012/07/british-olympics-security-contractor-faces-grilling-from-lawmakers-.html (accessed January 6, 2014).

3. Officially known as the Games of the XXX Olympiad, but commonly known as London 2012.

4. The company fell short of its goal of providing 10,000 personnel, being able to hire and train only about 7,000 by the time of the games. See Laura Smith-Spark, "London's Olympic Security Headache," *CNN International,* July 26, 2012, http://edition.cnn.com/2012/07/26/sport/olympic-security-overview/index.html (accessed January 5, 2014).

5. Martin Beckford, "London 2012 Olympics: Met Police Spend 6 Million Pounds on Officer's Accommodation," *The Telegraph*, May 9, 2012, http://www.telegraph.co.uk/sport/olympics/news/9252868/London-2012-Olympics-Met-Police-spend-6m-on-officers-accommodation.html (accessed January 5, 2014).

6. Learn more about G4S's operations in the United States at http://www.g4s.us.

7. Bureau of Labor Statistics, *Occupational Employment Projections to 2020*, January 2012, http://www.bls.gov/opub/mlr/2012/01/art5full.pdf (accessed November 9, 2013).

8. In most instances, unless referring to an organization or function, the term *law enforcement* is used to identify both *law enforcement* and *police* functions. The term *law enforcement* tends to be used to identify the function of ensuring obedience to the laws, whereas *police* is used either to describe an organization with those responsibilities or members of the organization who have a duty to maintain law and order in the community. The two terms are most often interchangeable.

9. R. S. Post and A. A. Kingsbury, *Security Administration: An Introduction*, 2nd ed. (Springfield, IL: Charles C. Thomas, 1973).

10. It was a common practice in those times to use eunuchs in security positions, to ensure they would be wholly devoted to their king. Enduring Word Media Resources (n.d.), Online Commentary, http://www.enduringword.com/commentaries/0139.htm

11. Post and Kingsbury, *Security Administration*.

12. Anson County (NC) Sheriff's Office, "History—The Middle Ages," http://www.ansonsheriff.com/history.php (accessed 2013).

13. Post and Kingsbury, *Security Administration*.

14. Henry County Sheriff's Office, "A Brief History of the Office of the Sheriff," http://www.henrycountysheriff.net/SheriffsofHenryCounty/HistoryoftheOfficeoftheSheriff/tabid/208/Default.aspx (accessed 2013).

15. Post and Kingsbury, *Security Administration*.

16. U.S. Department of Justice, *Private Security Report of the Task Force on Private Security* (Washington, DC: National Advisory Committee on Criminal Justice Standards and Goals. Law Enforcement Assistance Administration, 1976), https://www.ncjrs.gov/pdffiles1/Digitization/40543NCJRS.pdf

17. Ibid.

18. Ibid.

19. Library of Congress (n.d.). *The Industrial Revolution in the United States—Library of Congress Primary Source Sets,* http://www.loc.gov/teachers/classroommaterials/primarysourcesets/industrial-revolution/

20. Ibid.

21. Ibid.

22. M. Lipson, "Private Security: A Retrospective," *The Annals of the American Academy of Political and Social Science, The Private Security Industry: Issues and Trends,* Vol. 498 (1988), pp. 11–22.

23. U.S. Department of Justice, *Private Security Report.*

24. Pinkerton website, "About Us," http://www.pinkerton.com/history (accessed 2013); and Central Intelligence Agency website, "Intelligence in the Civil War," https://www.cia.gov/library/publications/additional-publications/civil-war/SML.htm (accessed 2013).

25. U.S. Department of Justice, *Private Security Report.*

26. Lipson, "Private Security."

27. Post and Kingsbury, *Security Administration*.

28. Usmarshals.gov website, "U.S. Department of Justice Historical Timeline," http://www.usmarshals.gov/history/timeline.html (accessed 2014).

29. Post and Kingsbury, *Security Administration*.

30. California Department of Consumer Affairs, "Bureau of Security and Investigative Services," http://www.bsis.ca.gov/about_us/history.shtml (accessed 2013).

31. Ibid.

32. Ibid.

33. U.S. Department of Justice, *Private Security Report.*

34. Lipson, "Private Security."

35. U.S. Department of Justice, *Private Security Report.*

36. Lipson, "Private Security."

37. U.S. Department of Justice, *Private Security Report.*

38. Ibid.

39. Ibid.

40. Ibid.

41. D. H. Bayley and C. D. Shearing, "The Future of Policing," *Law & Society Review*, Vol. 3, No. 3, (1996), pp. 585–606.

42. Lipson, "Private Security."

43. U.S. Department of Justice, *Private Security Report.*

44. E. J. Criscuoli Jr., "The Time Has Come to Acknowledge Security as a Profession," *The Annals of the American Academy of Political and Social Science, The Private Security Industry: Issues and Trends*, Vol. 498, (July 1988), pp. 98–107.

45. Ibid.

46. J. S. Kakalisk and S. Wildhorn, "Private Police in the United States: Findings and Recommendations," U.S. Department of Justice, Law Enforcement Assistance Administration, National Institute of Law Enforcement and Criminal Justice (Santa Monica, CA: The Rand Corporation, 1972).

47. Ibid.

48. Ibid.

49. Ibid.

50. Ibid.

51. Ibid.

52. U.S. Department of Justice, *Private Security Report.*

53. C. D. Shearing and P. C. Stenning, "Modern Private Security: Its Growth and Implications," *Crime and Justice*, Vol. 3 (1981), pp. 193–245.

54. N. South, "Privatizing Policing in the European Market: Some Issues for Theory, Policy, and Research," *European Sociological Review*, Vol. 10, No. 3 (1994), pp. 219–233.

55. Ibid.

56. M. Lansu, "Security Guard Shoots Robber at Oakbrook Center Mall Jewelry Store," *Chicago Sun-Times,* June 23, 2013, http://www.suntimes.com/news/20925062-418/security-guard-shoots-robber-at-oakbrook-center-mall-jewelry-store.html

57. FoxNews.com/Associated Press. "Pirates Reportedly Hijack Fuel Tanker, Kidnap Crew Off Nigeria's Coast," May 28, 2013, http://www.foxnews.com/world/2013/05/28/fuel-tanker-reportedly-hijacked-off-nigeria-coast/

58. A. Gale and I. Nam, "Hackers Target South Korea," *Wall Street Journal,* June 25, 2013, http://online.wsj.com/article/SB10001424127887324637504578566484152780530.html

59. Fox News, "FBI Points Digital Finger at North Korea for Sony Hacking Attack," December 18, 2014, http://www.foxnews.com/politics/2014/12/18/fbi-points-digital-finger-at-north-korea-for-sony-hacking-attack-formal/

60. Bureau of Labor Statistics (BLS), "Occupational Employment Statistics," 2012, http://www.bls.gov/oes/current/oes339032.htm

61. D. L. Ray and C. A. Hertig, "The Future of Security," in S. J. Davies and C. A. Hertig, eds., *Security Supervision and Management: Theory and Practice of Asset Protection*, 3rd ed. (Burlington, MA: Butterworth-Heinemann, 2007).

62. Bayley and Shearing, "The Future of Policing."

63. S. H. Belshaw, "Private Investigation Programs as an Emerging Trend in Criminal Justice Education? A Case Study of Texas," *Journal of Criminal Justice Education*, Vol. 23, No. 4 (2012), pp. 462–480, doi:10.1080/10511253.2012.683876.

64. Ibid.

65. Federal Emergency Management Agency, "National Disaster Recovery Framework," (n.d.), http://www.fema.gov/national-disaster-recovery-framework

66. U.S. Coast Guard, "Missions: Maritime Security," (n.d.), http://www.uscg.mil/top/missions/MaritimeSecurity.asp

67. D. Adolf, "Security Studies and Higher Education," *Journal of Applied Security Research,* Vol. 6, No. 1 (2011), pp. 124–134.

68. C. F. Smith, and T. Choo, "Revisiting Security Administration in the Classroom: A Decade Later," *Security Journal*, March 25, 2013, doi: 10.1057/sj.2013.7.

69. Post and Kingsbury, *Security Administration.*

70. The definition of "security" is from *The American Heritage Dictionary of the English Language*, 4th ed., 2003, http://www.thefreedictionary.com/security

71. Post and Kingsbury, *Security Administration.*

72. U.S. Department of Justice, *Private Security Report.*

73. G. Manunta and R. Manunta, "Theorizing About Security," in M. Gill, ed., *The Handbook of Security* (New York: Palgrave Macmillan, 2005).

74. U.S. Department of Justice, *Private Security Report.*

75. Ibid.

76. ASIS International, "Security glossary," 2013, http://www.asisonline.org/library/glossary/index.xml

77. Post and Kingsbury, *Security Administration.*

78. P. J. Ortmeier, *Introduction to Security: Operations and Management,* 4th ed. (Upper Saddle River, NJ: Pearson, 2013); K. M. Hess, *Introduction to Private Security,* 5th ed. (Belmont, CA: Wadsworth/Cengage, 2009); J. J. Fay, *Contemporary Security Management,* 3rd ed. (New York: Elsevier, 2011).

79. A. H. Maslow, *Motivation and Personality,* R. Cox and R. Frager, eds. (New York: Addison Wesley Longman, 1987). The basic needs are Physiological, Safety and Security, Love, Affection and Belongingness, Esteem, and Self-Actualization. In the hierarchy of needs, we do not feel the second need until the demands of the first are satisfied, nor do we feel the third until the second has been satisfied, and so on.

80. M. E. Koltko-Rivera, "Rediscovering the Later Version of Maslow's Hierarchy of Needs: Self-Transcendence and Opportunities for Theory, Research, and Unification," *Review of General Psychology,* Vol. 10, No. 4 (2006), pp. 302–317, doi: 10.1037/1089-2680.10.4.302.

81. Post and Kingsbury, *Security Administration.*

82. E. E. Joh, "The Paradox of Private Policing," *The Journal of Criminal Law and Criminology,* Vol. 95, No. 1, (2004), pp. 49–132.

83. ASIS Foundation, *Compendium of the ASIS Academic/Practitioner Symposium, 1997–2008,* 2009.

84. Post and Kingsbury, *Security Administration.*

85. D. A. Axt, "Is Private Security a Profession?" *Security Management*, Vol. 46, No. 8 (August 2002), p. 142.

86. Ibid.

87. Ibid.

88. T. M. Scott and M. McPherson, "The Development of the Private Sector of the Criminal Justice System," *Law & Society Review*, Special Police Issue Vol. 6, No. 2 (1971), pp. 267–288.

89. Ibid.

90. M. K. Nalla, "Designing an Introductory Survey Course in Private Security," *Journal of Criminal Justice Education,* Vol. 12, No. 1 (2001), pp. 35–52.

91. B. Kooi and S. Hinduja, "Teaching Security Courses Experientially," *Journal of Criminal Justice Education,* Vol. 19, No. 2 (2008), pp. 290–307.

92. Ibid.

93. C. L. Buckley Jr., Chief, Security Office, National Aeronautics and Space Administration, 1970, in Post and Kingsbury, *Security Administration.*

94. IACP et al., Building Private Security/Public Policing Partnerships (Washington, DC: COPS, 2004), p. 2, as cited by U.S. Department of Justice, *Engaging the Private Sector to Promote Homeland Security: Law Enforcement-Private Security Partnerships* (Washington D.C.: Office of Justice Programs, Bureau of Justice Assistance, 2005), https://www.ncjrs.gov/pdffiles1/bja/210678.pdf

95. U.S. Department of Justice, *Engaging the Private Sector.*

96. U.S. Department of Justice, *Private Security Report.*

97. K. Strom, M. Berzofsky, B. Shook-Sa, K. Barrick, C. Daye, N. Horstmann, and S. Kinsey, "The Private Security Industry: A Review of the Definitions, Available Data Sources, and Paths Moving Forward," *Literature Review and Secondary Data Analysis*, Bureau of Justice Statistics, 2010.

98. Shearing and Stenning, "Modern Private Security."

99. D. Walker, L. Glovka, B. Greenawalt, and J. McNulty, eds., "Top Security Threats and Management Issues Facing Corporate America: 2012 Survey of Fortune 1000 Companies," Securitas Security Services USA, Inc., 2013.

100. U.S. Department of Justice, *Engaging the Private Sector.*

101. Strom et al., "The Private Security Industry."

102. Post and Kingsbury, *Security Administration.*

103. Bureau of Labor Statistics (BLS), "Occupational Employment Statistics: May 2009 National Occupational Employment and Wage Estimates United States," 2010, http://www.bls.gov/oes/current/oes_nat.htm

104. Strom et al., "The Private Security Industry."

105. D. Walker et al., "Top Security Threats and Management Issues."

106. Shearing and Stenning, "Modern Private Security."

107. Ibid.

108. Ibid.

109. P. C. Stenning and C. D. Shearing, "The Quiet Revolution: The Nature, Development, General Legal Implications of Private Security in Canada," *Criminal Law Quarterly,* Vol. 22 (1980), pp. 220–248.

110. Bayley and Shearing, "The Future of Policing."

111. R. Abrahamsen and M. C. Williams, "The Politics of Private Security in Kenya: Oiling the Wheels of Imperialism," *Review of African Political Economy,* Vol. 32, Nos. 104/105 (2005), pp. 425–431.

112. Ibid.

113. Bayley and Shearing, "The Future of Policing."

114. Ibid.

115. B. Olin, "About Interagency Cooperation," 2010, http://thesimonscenter.org/about-interagency-cooperation/thesimonscenter.org/about-interagency-cooperation/

116. R. C. Davis, C. Ortiz, R. Rowe, J. Broz, G. Rigakos, and P. Collins, "An Assessment of the Preparedness of Large Retail Malls to Prevent and Respond to Terrorist Attack," U.S. Department of Justice, 2006.

117. Bayley and Shearing, "The Future of Policing."

118. Scott and McPherson, "The Development of the Private Sector."

119. E. J. Criscuoli Jr., "The Time Has Come."

120. S. Wildhorn, *Issues in Private Security,* RAND Corporation, 1975, http://www.rand.org/pubs/papers/P5422.html

121. E. J. Criscuoli Jr., "The Time Has Come."

122. Scott and McPherson, "The Development of the Private Sector."

123. S. Wildhorn, *Issues in Private Security.*

124. E. J. Criscuoli Jr., "The Time Has Come."

125. U.S. Government Accountability Office, *Critical Infrastructure Protection: Progress Coordinating Government and Private Sector Efforts Varies by Sectors' Characteristics,* 2006, retrieved from http://www.gao.gov/new.items/d0739.pdf, as cited by Strom et al., "The Private Security Industry."

126. AFCEA International, "The Need to Share: The U.S. Intelligence Community and Law Enforcement," AFCEA Intelligence Committee, 2007, http://www.afcea.org/mission/intel/documents/SpringIntel07whitepaper_000.pdf

127. A. Morabito and S. Greenberg, *Engaging the Private Sector to Promote Homeland Security: Law Enforcement–Private Security Partnerships* (NCJ 210678) (Washington, DC: U.S. Department of Justice, Office of Justice Programs, Bureau of Justice Assistance, 2005), retrieved from http://www.ncjrs.gov/pdffiles1/bja/210678.pdf, as cited by Strom et al., "The Private Security Industry."

128. Strom et al., "The Private Security Industry."

129. E. Connors, W. Cunningham, P. Ohlhausen, L. Oliver, and C. Van Meter, *Operation Cooperation: Guidelines* (Washington, DC: Bureau of Justice Assistance, 2000), http://www.ilj.org/publications/docs/Operation_Cooperation.pdf

130. Strom et al., "The Private Security Industry."

131. Connors et al. *Operation Cooperation.*

132. Bayley and Shearing, "The Future of Policing."

133. Ibid.

134. USAonWatch.org website, "About Neighborhood Watch," http://www.usaonwatch.org/ (accessed 2013).

135. Ibid.

136. Post and Kingsbury, *Security Administration.*

137. S. Sullivan, "Everything You Need to Know about 'Stand Your Ground' Laws," *The Washington Post,* Politics section, July 15, 2013, http://www.washingtonpost.com/blogs/the-fix/wp/2013/07/15/everything-you-need-to-know-about-stand-your-ground-laws/

138. M. Clark, "Zimmerman Verdict Renews Focus on 'Stand Your Ground' Laws, *USA Today,* July 15, 2013, http://www.usatoday.com/story/news/nation/2013/07/15/stateline-zimmerman-stand-your-ground/2517507/

139. Bayley and Shearing, "The Future of Policing."

140. Ibid.

141. ASIS International, "Protection of Assets (POA)" Online [Crisis Management], 2013.

142. D. Walker et al., "Top Security Threats and Management Issues."

143. Ibid.

144. Ibid.

145. Department of Homeland Security, "National Strategy for Global Supply Chain Security," 2013, http://www.dhs.gov/national-strategy-global-supply-chain-security

146. ASIS Foundation, *Compendium of the ASIS.*

147. E. J. Criscuoli Jr., "The Time Has Come."

148. ASIS International website, https://www.asisonline.org/About-ASIS/Pages/default.aspx

149. Association of Certified Background Investigators website. "About Us," http://www.acbi.net/ (accessed 2014).

150. ACFS website, "ACFS Overview," http://acfsnet.org/about-us (accessed 2013).

151. ALOA website, "About Us," http://www.aloa.org/about/ (accessed 2008).

152. ESA website, "What Is ESA?" http://www.esaweb.org/?page=ESAOverview (accessed 2013).

153. IPCA website, "Certification and Accreditation Explained,"http://ipca-cert.org (accessed 2015).

154. IACC website, "About the IACC," http://www.iacc.org/about-the-iacc/ (accessed 2013).

155. IAHSS website, "About IAHSS," www.iahss.org/IAHSS (accessed 2013).

156. IAPSC website, "About the IAPSC," http://iapsc.org/about-us/ (accessed 2013).

157. IFPO website, http://www.ifpo.org/ (accessed 2013).

158. International Professional Security Association website, "About IPSA," http://www.ipsa.org.uk/ (accessed 2013).

159. LPF website, "About LPF," http://www.losspreventionfoundation.org/retail-loss-prevention.html (accessed 2015).

160. NASSLEO website, "Welcome to NASSLEO," http://www.nassleo.org/ (accessed 2013).

161. NASCO website, "Mission," http://www.nasco.org/ (accessed 2013).

162. OSPA website, http://www.opsecprofessionals.org/ (accessed 2013).

163. SIA website, "About SIA," http://www.siaonline.org/Pages/AboutSIA/Mission.aspx (accessed 2013).

164. USAPI website, "About," http://www.usapi.org/about.asp (accessed 2013).

Chapter 2: Theoretical Foundations of Security

1. M. Dalton, "Gem Heists Dull Antwerp's Sparkle: Series of Diamond Robberies Clouds Outlook of World Trading Hub, Amid Worries of Insider Operation," April 11, 2013, http://www.wsj.com/articles/SB10001424127887324096404578354283117138840

2. "Celebrity Shoplifters," *The Daily Beast,* 2011, http://www.thedailybeast.com/galleries/2011/02/08/celebrity-shoplifters.html

3. J. Healy, "Video Shows Florida State QB Jameis Winston Shoplift Crab Legs from Publix," *New York Daily News,* May 15, 2014, http://www.nydailynews.com/sports/college/security-cam-shows-winston-shoplifting-crab-legs-publix-article-1.1794189

4. "Center for Problem-Oriented Policing," *Crime Analysis for Problem Solvers,* 2013 http://www.popcenter.org/learning/60steps/index.cfm?stepnum=8

5. P. Palin, S. Hall, T. Lewis, and C. Baldwin, *Deterrence and the United States Coast Guard: Enhancing Current Practice with Performance Measures.* Acquisition Directorate. Research and Development Center, 2012.

6. G. Farrell and K. Pease, "Criminology and Security," in M. Gill, ed., *The Handbook of Security* (New York: Palgrave Macmillan, 2005).

7. R. V. Clarke and D. Weisburd, "Diffusion of Crime Control Benefits: Observations on the Reverse of Displacement," in R. V. Clarke, ed., *Crime Prevention Studies,* Vol. 2 (1994), pp. 165–183, http://www.popcenter.org/library/crimeprevention/volume_02/08clarke.pdf

8. Palin et al., *Deterrence and the United States Coast Guard.*

9. T. O'Connor, "Psychobiology and Crime," *MegaLinks in Criminal Justice,* 2008, http://www.drtomoconnor.com/1060/1060lect03b.htm

10. A. Piquero and S. Tibbetts, "Specifying the Direct and Indirect Effects of Low Self-Control and Situational Factors in Offenders' Decision Making: Toward a More Complete Model of Rational Offending," *Justice Quarterly,* Vol. 13 (1996), pp. 481–508.

11. D. Forde and L. Kennedy, "Risky Lifestyles, Routine Activities, and the General Theory of Crime," *Justice Quarterly,* Vol. 14 (1997), pp. 265–294.

12. C. R. Tittle and R. F. Meier, "Specifying the SES/Delinquency Relationship," *Criminology,* Vol. 28, No. 2 (1990), pp. Z271–299.

13. C. R. Shaw and H. D. McKay, *Juvenile Delinquency and Urban Areas* (Chicago, IL: University Press, 1942).

14. S. G. Tibbetts and C. Hemmens, *Criminological Theory: A Text/Reader* (Los Angeles, CA: SAGE Publications, 2010).

15. J. M. Miller, C. J. Schreck, and R. Tewksbury, *Criminological Theory: A Brief Introduction* (Upper Saddle River, NJ: Prentice Hall, 2011).

16. E. H. Sutherland, "White-Collar Criminality," *American Sociological Review,* Vol. 5, No, 1 (1940), p. 1, doi:10.2307/2083937

17. Tibbetts and Hemmens, *Criminological Theory.*

18. T. Hirschi, *Causes of Delinquency* (Berkeley, CA: University of California Press, 1967).

19. R. V. Clarke, "Introduction," in R.V. Clarke, ed., *Situational Crime Prevention: Successful Case Studies,* 2nd ed. (Albany: Harrow and Heston, 1997), pp. 1–43, http://www.criminology.fsu.edu/crimtheory/clarke.htm

20. Farrell and Pease, "Criminology and Security."

21. Center for Problem-Oriented Policing, "Crime Analysis for Problem Solvers," http://www.popcenter.org/learning/60steps/index.cfm?stepnum=8, (accessed 2013).

22. Ibid.

23. C. Beccaria, *On Crimes and Punishments and Other Writings,* R. Bellamy, ed. (New York: Cambridge University Press, 1995).

24. Ibid.

25. Law Courts Education Society, *Community Crime Prevention Guide* (n.d.), http://www.pssg.gov.bc.ca/crimeprevention/shareddocs/pubs/crime_prevention.pdf

26. Ibid.

27. S. Geason and P. Wilson, *Designing Out Crime* (Canberra, Australia: Australian Institute of Criminology, 1989), http://www.aic.gov.au/documents/9/E/8/%7B9E810185-7D54-4480-8EEC-D92D84C3FB36%7Dcpted.pdf

28. Ibid.

29. Ibid.

30. Ibid.

31. ASIS International, *Protection of Assets (POA) Online* [Physical Security]. ASIS International, 2013.

32. Ibid.

33. Oakland, California Police Department, *Crime Prevention through Environmental Design (CPTED) Security Handbook* (n.d.), http://rockridgencpc.com/documents/fliers/CPTED%20Security%20Handbook-rev%20simlin.pdf

34. Farrell and Pease, "Criminology and Security."

35. Ibid.

36. Ibid.

37. T. Bennett, "Situational Crime Prevention from the Offender's Perspective" in K. Heal and G. Laycock, eds., *Situational Crime Prevention: From Theory into Practice* (London: Her Majesty's Stationery Office, 1986), as cited in S. Geason and P. R. Wilson, *Crime Prevention: Theory and Practice* (Canberra, Australia: Australian Institute of Criminology, 1988).

38. Farrell and Pease, "Criminology and Security."

39. R. V. Clarke and D. Weisburd, "Diffusion of Crime Control Benefits."

40. Farrell and Pease, "Criminology and Security."

41. J. Q. Wilson and G. L. Kelling, "Broken Windows: The Police and Neighborhood Safety," *The Atlantic Monthly,* March 1982, http://www.theatlantic.com/magazine/archive/1982/03/broken-windows/304465/

42. Wilson and Kelling, "Broken Windows."

43. Ibid.

44. R. V. Clarke and D. Weisburd, "Diffusion of Crime Control Benefits."

45. M. Tambe and B. An, *Game Theory for Security: An Important Challenge for Multiagent Systems,* (Teamcore Group, Department of Computer Science, University of Southern California, 2012), http://teamcore.usc.edu/papers/2012/eumas.pdf More on the application of game theory to real-world security challenges can be found at www.aamas-conference.org, www.aaai.org/, and ijcai.org/

46. P. Viotti and M. Kauppi, eds., *International Relations Theory* (New York: Macmillan Publishing Company, 1987), as cited by M. Beavis, "IR Theory Knowledge Base," http://www.irtheory.com/know.htm (accessed 2013).

47. Ibid.

48. Ibid.

49. Tambe and An, *Game Theory for Security.*

50. Ibid.

Chapter 3: Security Administration and Management

1. J. Harper, "Unprecedented Security: Even Super Bowl Officials Took 'Active Shooter Preparedness' Training," *The Washington Times,* January 30, 2015, http://www.washingtontimes.com/news/2015/jan/30/unprecedented-security-even-super-bowl-officials-t/\#ixzz3U6Lqi795

2. ASIS International, "Protection of Assets (POA) Online" [Administrative Management Principles], 2013.

3. Ibid.

4. L. Chapa, "Security on the Edge," Case Study, Security Management, January 2014.

5. Ibid.

6. Ibid.

7. Ibid.

8. 8. C. A. Hertig and R. G. Watson, "Outsourcing in Security," in S. J. Davies and C. A. Hertig, eds., *Security Supervision and Management: Theory and Practice of Asset Protection,* 3rd ed. (Burlington, MA: Butterworth-Heinemann, 2008).

9. Ibid.

10. Ibid.

11. ASIS International, "ASIS Online/Foundation/Security Management/Business Principles and Practices," https://www.asisonline.org/Certification/Board-Certifications/CPP/Pages/Business-Principles-and-Practices.aspx, 2014.

12. Goldman Sachs, "Business Principles and Standards," *Goldman Sachs Business Principles,* 2014, http://www.goldmansachs.com/who-we-are/business-standards/business-principles/index.html

13. Philips company website, "General Business Principles," 2003, http://www.philips.com/shared/assets/Investor_relations/pdf/businessprinciples/GeneralBusinessPrinciples.pdf

14. JP Morgan Chase website, "Our Business Principles," 1933, http://www.jpmorganchase.com/corporate/About-JPMC/document/business_principles.pdf

15. Shell website, "Shell General Business Principles," 2010, http://www.shell.com/global/aboutshell/who-we-are/our-values/sgbp.html

16. C. E. Johnson, *Meeting the Ethical Challenges of Leadership*, 4th ed. (Los Angeles, CA: Sage, 2012).

17. Ibid.

18. D. Collins, *Essentials of Business Ethics: Creating an Organization of High Integrity and Superior Performance* (Hoboken, NJ: John Wiley, 2009).

19. S. S. Souryal, *Ethics in Criminal Justice: In Search of the Truth*, 5th ed. (Burlington, MA: Anderson Publishing, 2011).

20. C. Rainbow, "Descriptions of Ethical Theories and Principles," 2002, http://www.bio.davidson.edu/people/kabernd/indep/carainbow/theories.htm

21. Souryal, *Ethics in Criminal Justice.*

22. Ibid.

23. Ibid.

24. Ibid.

25. M. Moussa, "What Security Executives Should Know about Ethics," *Security Info Watch*, Cygnus Business Media, January 8, 2007, http://www.securityinfowatch.com/article/10546226/what-security-executives-should-know-about-ethics

26. Souryal, *Ethics in Criminal Justice.*

27. Ibid.

28. D. Hopen, "Guiding Corporate Behavior: A Leadership Obligation, Not a Choice," *The Journal for Quality & Participation*, Vol. 25, No. 4 (2002), pp. 15–19.

29. Souryal, *Ethics in Criminal Justice.*

30. Ibid.

31. J. M. Pollock, *Ethical Dilemmas and Decisions in Criminal Justice*, 5th ed. (Belmont, CA: Thomson-Wadsworth, 2007).

32. Moussa, "What Security Executives Should Know about Ethics."

33. Ibid.

34. Pollock, *Ethical Dilemmas and Decisions in Criminal Justice.*

35. Ibid.

36. Moussa, "What Security Executives Should Know about Ethics."

37. Ibid.

38. Ibid.

39. Occupational Safety & Health Administration (OSHA), "Safety and Health Topics," 2014, https://www.osha.gov/SLTC/workplaceviolence/

40. Moussa, "What Security Executives Should Know about Ethics."

41. A. Murray, "Developing a Leadership Style: What Do Managers Do?" *A How-To Guide*. Adapted from "The Wall Street Journal Guide to Management," *The Wall Street Journal*, April 7, 2009, http://guides.wsj.com/management/developing-a-leadership-style/what-do-managers-do/tab/print/

42. Peter Drucker, "The British Library Board," *Business and Management History—Management Thinkers*, 2015, http://www.mbsportal.bl.uk/taster/subjareas/busmanhist/mgmtthinkers/drucker.aspx

43. Collins, *Essentials of Business Ethics.*

44. Moussa, "What Security Executives Should Know about Ethics."

45. Pollock, *Ethical Dilemmas and Decisions in Criminal Justice.*

46. Ibid.

47. Collins, *Essentials of Business Ethics.*

48. C. C. Verschoor, "New Survey of Workplace Ethics Shows Surprising Results," *Strategic Finance*, April 2012, pp. 13–15.

49. Ibid.

50. Moussa, "What Security Executives Should Know about Ethics." The Ethics and Compliance Officer Association is the largest association exclusively for ethics and compliance executives with more than 1,300 members across six continents.

51. Verschoor, "New Survey of Workplace Ethics Shows Surprising Results."

52. Johnson, *Meeting the Ethical Challenges of Leadership.*

53. Ibid.

54. Collins, *Essentials of Business Ethics.*

55. T. J. Burns, "A Force to Reckon With," *Security Management Magazine*, 2014, http://securitymanagement.com/print/8664

56. ArcelorMittal, "Security Personnel Policy on the Use of Force, Arms and Firearms," 2011, http://corporate.arcelormittal.com/~/media/Files/A/ArcelorMittal/corporate-responsibility/security-personnel.pdf

57. R. S. Post and A. A. Kingsbury, *Security Administration: An Introduction*, 2nd ed. (Springfield, IL: Charles C. Thomas, 1073).

58. ASIS International has a Code of Ethics. See https://www.asisonline.org/About-ASIS/Pages/Code-of-Ethics.aspx

59. L. Stelter, "The Business of Security: Why Current (and Future) Security Leaders Need Business and Management Education," September 13, 2013, http://amusecurityinfo.com/the-business-of-security-why-current-and-future-security-leaders-need-business-and-management-education/

60. D. A. Axt, "Is Private Security a Profession?" *Security Management*, Vol. 46, No. 8 (August 2002), p. 142.

61. G. V. Hulme, "The 7 Best Habits of Effective Security Pros," *CSO Online*. CXO Media Inc., January 8, 2014, http://www.csoonline.com/article/print/745655

62. Securitas Security Services USA, Inc. "Top Security Threats and Management Issues Facing Corporate America 2012 Survey of Fortune 1000 Companies," 2013.

63. Mobile Satellite Ventures, "Confidentiality, Non-competition and Non-solicitation Agreement," Securities and Exchange Commission, 2005, http://www.sec.gov/Archives/edgar/data/756502/000119312507057198/dex1065.htm

64. M. Moran, "Who's Winning the Wage Wars?" *Security Management Magazine*, December 2013.

65. U.S. Department of Justice, "Engaging the Private Sector to Promote Homeland Security: Law Enforcement-Private Security Partnerships," Office of Justice Programs, Bureau of Justice Assistance, 2005, https://www.ncjrs.gov/pdffiles1/bja/210678.pdf

66. K. Strom, M. Berzofsky, B. Shook-Sa, K. Barrick, C. Daye, N. Horstmann, and S. Kinsey, "The Private Security Industry: A Review of the Definitions, Available Data Sources, and Paths Moving Forward," *Literature Review and Secondary Data Analysis*, Bureau of Justice Statistics, 2010.

67. R. S. Post and A. A. Kingsbury, *Security Administration: An Introduction*, 2nd ed. (Springfield, IL: Charles C. Thomas, 1973).

68. D. Walker, L. Glovka, B. Greenawalt, and J. McNulty, eds. "Top Security Threats and Management Issues Facing Corporate America: 2012 Survey of Fortune 1000 Companies," Securitas Security Services USA, Inc., 2013.

69. Bureau of Labor Statistics (BLS), "Occupational Employment Statistics: May 2012 National Occupational Employment and Wage Estimates in the United States," 2013, http://www.bls.gov/oes/current/oes_nat.htm

70. Strom et al. "The Private Security Industry."

71. F. W. Taylor, *Principles of Scientific Management* (New York: Harper, 1947).

72. Ibid.

73. Ibid.

74. M. Weber, "Bureaucracy" in H. Gerth and C. W. Mills, *Max Weber* (New York, Oxford University Press, 1946).

75. H. Fayol, *General and Industrial Management*, trans. Constance Storrs (London: Pitman, 1949).

76. L. Von Bertalanffy, "General Systems Theory: A New Approach to the Unit of Science," *Human Biology*, December 1951, Johns Hopkins Press.

77. J. H. Ehrenreich, "Personality Theory: A Case of Intellectual and Social Isolation?" *The Journal of Psychology*, Vol. 131, No. 1 (1997), p. 33.

78. American Society for Quality, "Total Quality Management (TQM)," Knowledge Center/Learn About Quality/TQM Overview, 2014, http://asq.org/learn-about-quality/total-quality-management/overview/overview.html

79. Douglas McGregor, *The Human Side of Enterprise* (New York: McGraw-Hill, 2005).

80. Ibid.

81. "Theory X and Theory Y," *The Economist*, October 6, 2008. Adapted from *The Economist Guide to Management Ideas and Gurus*, by Tim Hindle, Profile Books, http://www.economist.com/node/12370445

82. W. Ouchi, *Theory Z: How American Management Can Meet the Japanese Challenge* (Reading, MA: Addison-Wesley, 1981).

83. W. G. Ouchi, *Theory Z: How American Business Can Meet the Japanese Challenge* (New York: Avon Books, 1982).

84. D. C. McClelland and D. H. Burnham, "Power Is the Great Motivator," *Harvard Business Review,* Vol. 54, No. 2 (1976), pp. 100–110.

85. N. Burton, "Our Hierarchy of Needs: Why True Freedom Is a Luxury of the Mind," *Hide and Seek*, May 23, 2012, http://www.psychologytoday.com/blog/hide-and-seek/201205/our-hierarchy-needs

86. Ibid.

87. A. H. Maslow, "A Theory of Human Motivation," *Psychological Review*, Vol. 50 (1943), pp. 370–396. Cited by C. D. Green, Classics in the History of Psychology, http://psychclassics.yorku.ca/Maslow/motivation.htm

88. A. H. Maslow, *Motivation and Personality*, R. Cox and R. Frager, eds. (New York: Addison Wesley Longman, 1987).

89. Boundless.com, Management /Organizational Behavior/ Employee Needs and Motivation, 2014, https://www.boundless.com/management/organizational-behavior/employee-needs-and-motivation/two-factor-theory-herzberg/

90. B. Drake, "Number of Older Americans in the Workforce Is on the Rise," Pew Research Center, January 7, 2014, http://pewrsr.ch/1adnWGq

91. Ibid.

92. Pew Research Center, "The Rising Cost of Not Going to College," February 11, 2014, http://www.pewsocialtrends.org/2014/02/11/the-rising-cost-of-not-going-to-college/

93. M. Holt, Demand Media, "Culture Awareness in the Workplace," *Houston Chronicle*, http://smallbusiness.chron.com/culture-awareness-workplace-737.html (accessed 2014).

94. Ibid.

95. Ibid.

96. ASIS International, "Certifications," 2014, https://www.asisonline.org/Certification/Board-Certifications/Pages/Benefits-to-Public-Sector-Security-Professionals.aspx

Chapter 4: Legal Aspects, Liability, and Regulation

1. South African guards shoot dead five miners outside Amplats mine. Staff writer, February 18, 2013, http://www.presstv.ir/detail/2013/02/18/289610/s-african-guards-shoot-5-miners-dead/

2. Polish employers can be liable for work-related violence. Squire Sanders, Malgorzata P. Grzelak, Poland, February 18, 2013, http://www.lexology.com/library/detail.aspx?g=2db9fbc9-1797-48c7-81d6-36d5f87d6d45

3. U.S. Department of Justice, "Private Security Report of the Task Force on Private Security," National Advisory Committee on Criminal Justice Standards and Goals, Law Enforcement Assistance Administration, 1976, https://www.ncjrs.gov/pdffiles1/Digitization/40543NCJRS.pdf

4. Ibid.

5. K. Strom, M. Berzofsky, B. Shook-Sa, K. Barrick, C. Daye, N. Horstmann, and S. Kinsey, "The Private Security Industry: A Review of the Definitions, Available Data Sources, and Paths Moving Forward," *Literature Review and Secondary Data Analysis* (Bureau of Justice Statistics, 2010).

6. Ibid.

7. ASIS International, Protection of Assets (POA) Online [Legal Sources], 2013.

8. Ibid.

9. U.S. National Archives, "The Charters of Freedom: A New World Is at Hand," 2013, http://www.archives.gov/exhibits/charters/bill_of_rights_transcript.html

10. *J.D.B.* v. *North Carolina*, 564 U.S. 113 S. Ct. 2394, 2011.

11. *Miranda* v. *Arizona*, 384 U.S. 436, 1966. More on the decision at the Legal Information Institute. http://www.law.cornell.edu/supct/html/historics/USSC_CR_0384_0436_ZS.html

12. Bureau of Business Practice, *The Legal Side of Security* (Waterford, CT: Prentice Hall, 1992).

13. Ibid.

14. Ibid.

15. L. Pinson and J. Jinnett, *How to Write a Business Plan*, 1993, http://www.sba.gov/content/how-write-business-plan

16. ASIS International, POA Online.

17. Ibid.

18. Ibid.

19. U.S. Department of Labor, Wage and Hour Division, 2013, http://www.dol.gov/whd/regs/compliance/web/SCA_FAQ.htm

20. Legal Information Institute, 29 USC § 142—Definitions, 2013, http://www.law.cornell.edu/uscode/text/29/142

21. ASIS International, POA Online.

22. U.S. Department of Labor, Workers' Compensation, 2013, http://www.dol.gov/dol/topic/workcomp/

23. ASIS International, POA Online.

24. Ibid.

25. Ibid.

26. Ibid.

27. Bureau of Business Practice, *The Legal Side of Security*.

28. Washington State Legislature, RCW 18.170.080. c 334 § 8, 1991, http://apps.leg.wa.gov/rcw/default.aspx?cite=18.170.080

29. Central Insurance Agency website, "About," 2015, http://www.ciainsures.com

30. U.S. Equal Employment Opportunity Commission, "Enforcement Guidance on Vicarious Employer Liability for Unlawful Harassment by Supervisors," 1999, www.eeoc.gov/policy/docs/harassment.html

31. U.S. Equal Employment Opportunity Commission, "Religious Discrimination," 1999, http://www.eeoc.gov/policy/docs/religion.html

32. This is increasingly seen in litigation, where expert witnesses are used. See: E. M. Schneider, "The Dangers of Summary Judgment: Gender and Federal Civil Litigation," in *Trial by Jury or Trial by Motion? Summary Judgment*," IQBAL, and Employment Discrimination, the Interplay of Pleading Standards & Summary Judgment, 2012, http://www.nylslawreview.com/wordpress/wp-content/uploads/2011/10/Employment-Law.CLE-materials.panel-34.pdf

33. ASIS International, POA Online.

34. U.S. Department of Labor, The Fair Labor Standards Act of 1938, as Amended, 2011, www.dol.gov/whd/regs/statutes/FairLaborStandAct.pdf

35. The National Labor Relations Board, National Labor Relations Act, 2013, http://www.nlrb.gov/national-labor-relations-act

36. Pub. L. 80–101, 61 Stat. 136, enacted June 23, 1947.

37. ASIS International, POA Online.

38. U.S. Department of Labor, http://www.dol.gov/compliance/laws/comp-lmrda.htm

39. U.S. Equal Employment Opportunity Commission (EEOC), "The Equal Pay Act of 1963," 2013, http://www.eeoc.gov/laws/statutes/epa.cfm

40. Congress Link, "Major Features of the Civil Rights Act of 1964" (Public Law 88-352), 2013, http://www.congresslink.org/print_basics_histmats_civilrights64text.htm

41. U.S. Equal Employment Opportunity Commission (EEOC), "The Age Discrimination in Employment Act of 1967," 2013, http://www.eeoc.gov/laws/statutes/adea.cfm

42. 29 USC 651-678, signed into law in December 1970 and became effective on April 28, 1971. The primary responsibility for administration of this act falls on the Department of Labor.

43. Department of Justice, The American with Disabilities Act of 1990, http://www.ada.gov/pubs/ada.htm

44. ASIS International, POA Online.

45. Federal Trade Commission, Fair Credit Reporting Act, 15 U.S.C. § 1681 et seq., 2013, http://www.ftc.gov/os/statutes/031224fcra.pdf

46. U.S. Department of Labor, Family and Medical Leave Act, 2013, http://www.dol.gov/whd/fmla/

47. U.S. Department of Labor, Affordable Care Act, 2013, http://www.dol.gov/ebsa/healthreform/

48. Standard Deviants, "Public Broadcasting Station," *Business Law Resources: All about Business Law*, n.d., http://www.pbs.org/standarddeviantstv/transcript_business.html

49. National Institute of Justice, "The Use-of-Force Continuum," 2009, www.nij.gov/topics/law-enforcement/officer-safety/use-of-force/continuum.htm.

50. R. Phillips, "Legal Update for Law Enforcement," 2008, http://www.legalupdateonline.com/4th/140

51. T. J. Burns, "A Force to Reckon With. Law Enforcement: Legal Issues," *Security Management Magazine*, 2013, http://www.securitymanagement.com/print/8664

52. C. Butler, "The Use of Force Model and Its Application to Operational Law Enforcement – Where Have We Been and Where Are We Going?" Calgary Police Service, (n.d.), http://www.cacole.ca/resource%20library/conferences/2009%20Conference/Chris%20Butler.pdf

53. *Tennessee v. Garner,* 471 U.S. 1, 1985, which directed that deadly force cannot be used to prevent the escape of a fleeing felon, unless it is necessary to prevent the escape and the officer has probable cause to believe that the suspect poses a significant threat of death or serious physical injury to the officer or others.

54. *Black's Law Dictionary*, 2nd ed., 2014, http://thelawdictionary.org

Chapter 5: Understanding, Analyzing, and Managing Risk

1. C. Caldwell, "Report: Mayor Kasim Reed Adds Officers at Airport after Delta Security Breach," *American City Business Journal*, December 26, 2014, http://www.bizjournals.com/atlanta/morning_call/2014/12/report-mayor-kasim-reed-adds-officers-at-airport.html

2. M. P. Johnson and J. M. Spivey, "ERM and the Security Profession," *Risk Management* (00355593), Vol. 55, No. 1 (2008), pp. 30–35.

3. M. L. Garcia, "Risk Management," in M. Gill, ed., *The Handbook of Security* (New York: Palgrave Macmillan, 2006).

4. Department of Homeland Security (DHS), DHS Risk Lexicon, 2010.

5. Federal Emergency Management Agency (FEMA), *Primer for Design Professionals: Communicating with Owners and Managers of New Buildings on Earthquake Risk*, Risk Management Series (FEMA 389), 2004.

6. Ibid.

7. Ready.gov website, "Business – Planning – Risk Assessment," 2014, http://www.ready.gov/tl/risk-assessment

8. Ibid.

9. Ibid.

10. Garcia, "Risk Management."

11. Ibid.

12. PricewaterhouseCoopers LLP (PWC), *A Practical Guide to Risk Assessment: How Principles-Based Risk Assessment Enables Organizations to Take the Right Risks*, 2008.

13. Ibid.

14. Ibid.

15. C. Rogers, "A Security Risk Management Approach to the Measurement of Crime in a Private Security Context," Acta Criminologica: CRIMSA Conference, Special Edition 3, 2008, pp. 150–166.

16. Ibid.

17. Federal Emergency Management Agency (FEMA), "Threat and Hazard Identification and Risk Assessment," 2014, http://www.fema.gov/threat-and-hazard-identification-and-risk-assessment

18. Ibid.

19. Ibid.

20. Ibid.

21. U.S. Army, *Army Field Manual 3.19-30* (Washington, DC: Department of the Army, January 8, 2001).

22. Ibid.

23. Ibid.

24. Department of Education, "Security Survey and Risk Assessment," (Bangor, United Kingdom: Department of Education, 2014), http://www.deni.gov.uk/security_risk_assessment-3.pdf

25. Rogers, "A Security Risk Management Approach."

26. J. J. Phillips, *Return on Investment in Training and Performance Improvement Programs*, 2nd ed. (Woburn, MA: Butterworth-Heinemann, 2003); and Rogers, "A Security Risk Management Approach."

27. M. G. Stewart and J. Mueller, "Cost-Benefit Analysis of Australian Federal Police Counter-Terrorism Operations at Australian Airports," Australian Research Council (ARC) Centre of Excellence in Policing and Security, 2013.

28. Department of the Army, *U.S. Army Cost Benefit Analysis Guide*, 3rd ed., Office of the Deputy Assistant Secretary of the Army (Cost and Economics), 2013, http://asafm.army.mil/Documents/OfficeDocuments/CostEconomics/guidances/cba-gd.pdf

29. Ibid.

30. Garcia, "Risk Management."

31. Ibid.

32. Department of Homeland Security (DHS), "Homeland Security Risk Management Doctrine," *Risk Management Fundamentals*, 2011.

33. Rogers, "A Security Risk Management Approach."

34. Ibid.

35. Johnson and Spivey, "ERM and the Security Profession."

36. DHS, "Homeland Security Risk Management Doctrine."

37. M. Lee, "Security Risk Management: Where Companies Fail and Succeed," *ZD Net,* December 2, 2013, http://www.zdnet.com/security-risk-management-where-companies-fail-and-succeed-7000023747/

38. E. Kutsch, T. Browning, and M. Hall, "Bridging the Risk Gap," *Research Technology Management*, Vol. 57, No. 2 (2014), pp. 26–32.

39. Kutsch, Browning, and Hall, "Bridging the Risk Gap."
40. Ibid.
41. Ibid.
42. Department of Homeland Security (DHS), "National Infrastructure Protection Plan," *NIPP 2013: Partnering for Critical Infrastructure Security and Resilience*, 2013.
43. Ibid.
44. DHS, "Homeland Security Risk Management Doctrine."
45. Ibid.
46. Ibid.
47. Ibid.
48. M. Bruch and R. Kreutzer, "The Inside Job, Which Risks Will Be More Dangerous in the Future: Internal or External Risks?" *Strategic RISK*, 10th anniversary issue, 2009, pp. 41–43.
49. DHS, "Homeland Security Risk Management Doctrine."
50. Ibid.
51. DHS, "National Infrastructure Protection Plan."
52. FEMA, *Primer for Design Professionals*.
53. DHS, "National Infrastructure Protection Plan."

Chapter 6: Physical Security

1. I. Rodriguez, "Thieves Snatch $100K in TVs from Lauderdale Warehouse," *Sun Sentinel*, July 31, 2012, http://articles.sun-sentinel.com/2012-07-31/news/fl-audio-video-distributor-theft-20120730_1_televisions-vans-warehouse
2. C. Clarridge, "One Suspect Caught in Two-Day $648K Wine Warehouse Heist," *Seattle Times*, December 4, 2013, http://seattletimes.com/html/localnews/2022396486_wine-theftxml.html
3. Department of Defense, 2009, Physical Security Program, DoD 5200.08-R (April 9, 2007, Incorporating Change 1, May 27, 2009), referencing Joint Publication 1-02, "Department of Defense Dictionary of Military and Associated Terms," as amended through April 15, 2013.
4. It should be noted that many of the references in this chapter and elsewhere in the textbook come from the U.S. military. This organization, because of its size and mission, has what many consider the most expansive and complete body of literature and reference on security, generally, and physical security, specifically.
5. Bureau of Business Practice, *The Legal Side of Security, Bureau of Business Practice* (Waterford, CT: Prentice Hall, 1992).
6. K. Wan, CISSP Exam Notes: Physical Security, KP Lab Ltd, 2003, http://home.pacific.net.hk/~kplab/CISSP_Exam_Notes_Physical_Security_v1.1.pdf
7. Ibid.
8. Royal Canadian Mounted Police (RCMP), "Guide to the Application of Physical Security Zones," *RCMP Guide G1-026*, 2005, http://www.rcmp-grc.gc.ca/physec-secmat/pubs/g1-026-eng.htm
9. B. J. Steele, "Security Systems Engineering Overview," U.S. Department of Energy/Sandia National Laboratories, 1997, http://www.osti.gov/bridge/servlets/purl/432939-mj5qql/webviewable/432939.pdf
10. Ibid.
11. Ibid.
12. Ibid.
13. Ibid.
14. Ibid.
15. ASIS International, *Protection of Assets (POA) Online* [Physical Security], 2013.
16. Steele, "Security Systems Engineering Overview."
17. Ibid.
18. Ibid.
19. ASIS International, *POA Online*, 2013.
20. Steele, "Security Systems Engineering Overview."
21. Ibid.
22. ASIS International, *POA Online*, 2013.
23. U.S. Army, *Army Field Manual 3.19-30* (Washington, DC: Department of the Army, 2001), January 8, 2001.
24. Ibid.
25. ASIS International, *POA Online*, 2013.
26. P. K. Huth, "Deterrence and International Conflict: Empirical Findings and Theoretical Debate," *Annual Review of Political Science,* Vol. 2 (1999), pp. 25–48, doi 10.1146/annurev.polisci.2.1.25
27. U.S. Army, *Army Field Manual 3.19-30.*
28. Ibid.
29. Ibid.
30. Ibid.
31. ASIS International, *POA Online*, 2013.
32. Ibid.
33. Ibid.
34. U.S. Army, *Army Field Manual 3.19-30.*
35. ASIS International, *POA Online*, 2013.
36. Security Management Office, U.S. Geological Survey, *Physical Security Handbook* 440-2-H, U.S. Department of the Interior, 2005, http://www.usgs.gov/usgs-manual/handbook/hb/440-2-h/440-2-h-ch4.html
37. Ibid.
38. Ibid.
39. Ibid.
40. Ibid.
41. ASIS International, *POA Online*, 2013.
42. U.S. Army, *Army Field Manual 3.19-30.*
43. Ibid.
44. Security Management Office, *Physical Security Handbook 440-2-H.*
45. ASIS International, *POA Online*, 2013.
46. Security Management Office, *Physical Security Handbook 440-2-H.*
47. Ibid.
48. Ibid.
49. U.S. Army, *Army Field Manual 3.19-30.*
50. Security Management Office, *Physical Security Handbook 440-2-H.*
51. U.S. Army, *Army Field Manual 3.19-30.*
52. Ibid.
53. ASIS International, *POA Online*, 2013.
54. National Crime Prevention Council, "Bumping a Trend in Home Burglary," *NewsUSA*, (n.d.), http://www.ncpc.org/resources/files/pdf/neighborhood-safety/Bumping%20-%20A%20Trend%20in%20Home%20Burglary.pdf
55. ASIS International, *POA Online*, 2013.
56. National Crime Prevention Council, "Safety Tips," 2002, http://www.ncpc.org/resources/files/pdf/workplace-safety/safewrk.pdf
57. U.S. Army, *Army Field Manual 3.19-30.*
58. ASIS International, *POA Online*, 2013.
59. Ibid.
60. Ibid.
61. E. Elkins and M. Farrar, "User's Guide on Controlling Locks, Keys, and Access Cards," DoD Lock Program, Naval Facilities Engineering Service Center, 2000, https://portal.navfac.navy.mil/portal/page/portal/NAVFAC/ NAVFAC_WW_PP/NAVFAC_NFESC_PP/LOCKS/PDF_FILES/UG-2040-SHR.pdf
62. Ibid.
63. U.S. Army, *Army Field Manual 3.19-30.*
64. ASIS International, *POA Online*, 2013.
65. Ibid.
66. Ibid.
67. Ibid.
68. Elkins and Farrar, "User's Guide on Controlling Locks, Keys, and Access Cards."

69. ASIS International, *POA Online*, 2013.
70. Ibid.
71. J. Goudlock, "New Technologies Help Meet the Demand to Ward Off Strangers," *Security Today* [online], First Line of Defense, April 1, 2013, http://security-today.com/Articles/2013/04/01/First-Line-of-Defense.aspx
72. ASIS International, *POA Online*, 2013.
73. U.S. Army, *Army Field Manual 3.19-30*.
74. ASIS International, *POA Online*, 2013.
75. Ibid.
76. Ibid.
77. Ibid.
78. Ibid.
79. Ibid.
80. Ibid.
81. Ibid.
82. Ibid.
83. U.S. Army, *Army Field Manual 3.19-30*.
84. Ibid.
85. Ibid.
86. ASIS International, *POA Online*, 2013.
87. Ibid.
88. Ibid.
89. Elkins and Farrar, "User's Guide on Controlling Locks, Keys, and Access Cards."
90. Ibid.
91. Editor, *Biometric Technology in the Future*, March 19, 2014, http://bd24live.net/biometric-technology-future
92. P. Bhatia, "Biometric Identification That Goes beyond Fingerprints," *USA Today*, April 19, 2014, Ozy.com http://www.usatoday.com/story/news/world/2014/04/19/ozy-biometric-identification/7904685/
93. Bhatia, "Biometric Identification That Goes beyond Fingerprints."
94. Ibid.
95. G. Hill, "Trick Surveillance Cameras by Wearing Artist's Face Mask," *Security Today*, May 14, 2014, http://security-today.com/articles/2014/05/14/trick-surveillance-cameras-by-wearing-artists-face-mask.aspx
96. Security Management Office, *Physical Security Handbook 440-2-H*.
97. ASIS International, *POA Online*, 2013.
98. U.S. Army, *Army Field Manual 3.19-30*.
99. Ibid.
100. Ibid.
101. Ibid.
102. Ibid.
103. ASIS International, *POA Online*, 2013.
104. National Crime Prevention Council, "Safety Tips."
105. M. Rabkin et al., "Transit Security Design Considerations," U.S. Department of Transportation, Office of Program Management, 2004, http://transit-safety.volpe.dot.gov/security/securityinitiatives/designconsiderations/ CD/front.htm
106. Security Management Office, *Physical Security Handbook 440-2-H*.
107. ASIS International, *POA Online*, 2013.
108. Rabkin et al., "Transit Security Design Considerations."
109. Ibid.
110. Security Management Office, *Physical Security Handbook 440-2-H*.
111. Ibid.
112. Ibid.
113. Ibid.
114. U.S. Army, Army Regulation 190-12, "Military Police – Military Working Dogs," 2013, http://www.apd.army.mil/jw2/xmldemo/r190_12/main.asp
115. ASIS International, *POA Online*, 2013.
116. "The Police Dogs of Ghent, How They Are Trained to the Duties of Town Constables," *New York Times* [archive], November 9, 1902.
117. Ibid.
118. D. Brown, *With Courage and Trust: 20 Years with Police Dogs* (Cromford, UK: Scarthin Books, 1994).
119. ASIS International, *POA Online*, 2013.
120. U.S. Army, Army Regulation 190-12.
121. ASIS International, *POA Online*, 2013.
122. U.S. Army, Army Regulation 190-12.
123. ASIS International, *POA Online*, 2013.
124. U.S. Army, Army Regulation 190-12.
125. Ibid.
126. ASIS International, *POA Online*, 2013.
127. U.S. Army, Army Regulation 190-12.
128. ASIS International, *POA Online*, 2013.
129. U.S. Army, Army Regulation 190-12.
130. Ibid.
131. Ibid.
132. Ibid.
133. ASIS International, *POA Online*, 2013.
134. Ibid.
135. "Area of Law Outlines/Torts Capsule Summary: The Common Law Status Approach," *LexisNexis*, 2007, http://www.lexis-nexis.com/lawschool/study/outlines/html/torts/torts09.htm
136. ASIS International, *POA Online*, 2013.
137. *Person of Interest*, CBS, 2011–, http://www.imdb.com/title/tt1839578/
138. P. Dominiczak, "CCTV: New Controls on Private Security Cameras to Stop Homeowners Snooping on Neighbours," *The Telegraph*, June 9, 2013, http://www.telegraph.co.uk/news/uknews/law-and-order/10109384/CCTV-new-controls-on-private-security-cameras-to-stop-homeowners-snooping-on-neighbours.html
139. Rabkin et al., "Transit Security Design Considerations."
140. Ibid.
141. Ibid.
142. Security Management Office, *Physical Security Handbook 440-2-H*.
143. ASIS International, *POA Online*, 2013.
144. Ibid.
145. Ibid.
146. Ibid.
147. Ibid.
148. Rabkin et al., "Transit Security Design Considerations."
149. National Security Agency, "Defense in Depth: A Practical Strategy for Achieving Information Assurance in Today's Highly Networked Environments," (n.d.). http://www.nsa.gov/ia/_files/support/defenseindepth.pdf
150. *RCMP Guide G1-026*.
151. Ibid.
152. Ibid.
153. Rabkin et al., "Transit Security Design Considerations."
154. Ibid.
155. ASIS International, *POA Online*, 2013.
156. O. Newman, "Creating Defensible Space," U.S. Department of Housing and Urban Development, Office of Policy Development and Research, April 1996, http://www.huduser.org/publications/pdf/def.pdf
157. Ibid.
158. R. A. Gardner, "Crime Prevention through Environmental Design," revision of *Security Management Magazine* article, http://www.crimewise.com/library/cpted.html
159. U.S. Army, *Army Field Manual 3.19-30*.
160. Gardner, *Crime Prevention through Environmental Design*.
161. Ibid.
162. ASIS International, *POA Online*, 2013.
163. Ibid.

164. U.S. Army, *Army Field Manual 3.19-30.*

165. D. Zahm, "Using Crime Prevention through Environmental Design in Problem Solving," U.S. Department of Justice – Office of Community Oriented Policing Services, 2007, http://www.cops.usdoj.gov/Publications/e0807391.pdf

166. U.S. Army, *Army Field Manual 3.19-30.*

167. Gardner, *Crime Prevention through Environmental Design.*

168. ASIS International, *POA Online,* 2013.

169. Rabkin et al., "Transit Security Design Considerations."

170. ASIS International, *POA Online,* 2013.

171. Gardner, *Crime Prevention through Environmental Design.*

172. U.S. Army, *Army Field Manual 3.19-30.*

173. ASIS International, *POA Online,* 2013.

174. U.S. Department of Labor, National Census of Fatal Occupational Injuries in 2013 (preliminary results), 2013, http://www.bls.gov/news.release/pdf/cfoi.pdf

175. U.S. Fire Administration, "Overall Fire Death Rates and Relative Risk (2001–2010)," 2013, http://www.usfa.fema.gov/statistics/estimates/trend_overall.shtm

176. J. Rudy, "Fire Protection: A Complete Approach," 2012 http://ohsonline.com/Articles/2012/12/01/Fire-Protection-A-Complete-Approach.aspx

177. U.S. Department of Labor, "Fire Safety," Occupational Safety and Health Administration, 2013, http://www.osha.gov/SLTC/firesafety/index.html

178. Ibid.

179. Rudy, "Fire Protection."

180. U.S. Fire Administration, "Facts about NFIRS," 2013, http://www.usfa.fema.gov/fireservice/nfirs/

181. U.S. Department of Labor, "Fire Detection Systems," Occupational Safety and Health Administration, 2013, http://www.osha.gov/SLTC/etools/evacuation/fire_detection.html

182. FEMA Fire Alarm Systems, (n.d.), http://www.usfa.fema.gov/downloads/pyfff/alarmsys.html

183. U.S. Department of Labor, "Fire Detection Systems."

184. U.S. Fire Administration, "Nonresidential Building Fires," Federal Emergency Management Agency, 2010, http://www.usfa.fema.gov/downloads/pdf/statistics/nonresidential_building_fires.pdf

185. U.S. Department of Labor, "Fire Detection Systems."

186. Ibid.

187. Ibid.

188. U.S. Department of Labor, "Classification of Portable Fire Extinguishers," Occupational Safety and Health Administration, 2013, http://www.osha.gov/doc/outreachtraining/html-files/extmark.html

189. U.S. Fire Administration, "Nonresidential Building Fires."

Chapter 7: Institutional and Workplace Security

1. M. Snider, "Apple to Hire Own Security and Put Them on Payroll," *USA Today* (online), March 3, 2015, http://www.usatoday.com/story/tech/2015/03/03/apple-security-guards/24314285/

2. K. Strom, M. Berzofsky, B. Shook-Sa, K. Barrick, C. Daye, N. Horstmann, and S. Kinsey, "The Private Security Industry: A Review of the Definitions, Available Data Sources, and Paths Moving Forward," *Literature Review and Secondary Data Analysis* (Bureau of Justice Statistics, 2010).

3. Federal Bureau of Investigation, "Preliminary 2012 Crime Statistics: Violent Crime Up, Property Crime Down," June 3, 2013, http://www.fbi.gov/news/stories/2013/june/preliminary-2012-crime-statistics

4. S. J. Romano, M. E. Levi-Minzi, E. A. Rugala, and V. B. Van Hasselt, "Workplace Violence Prevention Readiness and Response," *FBI Law Enforcement Bulletin*, Vol. 80, No. 1 (December 2011), pp. 1–10, http://www.fbi.gov/stats-services/publications/law-enforcement-bulletin/january2011/workplace_violence_prevention

5. Ibid.

6. P. Williams and T. Connor, "LAX Suspect's Family 'Shocked and Numbed' by Shooting," *NBC News,* November 4, 2013, http://usnews.nbcnews.com/_news/2013/11/04/21306689-lax-suspects-family-shocked-and-numbed-by-shooting

7. Transportation Security Administration (TSA), "About TSA," 2013, http://www.tsa.gov/about-tsa

8. A. Ubaka, "Security Boosted at Fun Spot Amusement Park in Orlando: Shooting Last Weekend at Park Left Two People Injured," *Click Orlando*, February 27, 2015, http://www.click-orlando.com/news/security-boosted-at-fun-spot-amusement-park-in-orlando/31532228

9. IndyChannel.com, "Four Charged in Alleged ID Theft Ring," November 1, 2013, http://www.theindychannel.com/news/local-news/four-charged-in-alleged-id-theft-ring

10. J. Michaels, "Plan to Ship Chemicals from Syrian Port Is Approved," *USA Today*, November 15, 2013, http://www.usatoday.com/story/news/world/2013/11/15/syria-chemicals-opcw/3594591/

11. Newszap, "Convenience Store Security Guard Shooting in Glendale," *Independent News Media*, October 17, 2013, http://arizona.newszap.com/westvalley/126545-114/convenience-store-security-guard-shooting-in-glendale

12. Associated Press, "Prison Riot Inmate Sentenced to Ten Years," *The Sun-Herald/Natchez Democrat*, November 20 2013, http://www.sunherald.com/2013/11/20/5130847/prison-riot-inmate-sentenced-to.html\#storylink=cpy

13. "Thieves Steal Tonne of Steak from Unit," *Daventry Express*, November 11, 2013, http://www.daventryexpress.co.uk/news/local/thieves-steal-tonne-of-steak-from-unit-1-5670658

14. N. Rayman, "Navy Yard Gunman's Security Clearance Had Been Temporarily Revoked Weeks Earlier," *TIME.com*, November 22, 2013, http://nation.time.com/2013/11/22/navy-yard-gunmans-security-clearance-had-been-temporarily-revoked-weeks-earlier/\#ixzz2lg3FlaE9

15. P. L. McGuire, "Rumford Man Charged with Theft of Hospital Supplies," *Sun Journal*, November 18, 2013, http://www.sunjournal.com/news/oxford-hills-river-valley/2013/11/19/rumford-man-charged-theft-hospital-supplies/1454063

16. A. Kelley, "Myrtle Beach Hotel Changes Policy after Burglary," *Myrtle Beach Online/Sun News*, September 13, 2013, http://www.myrtlebeachonline.com/2013/09/13/3707597/myrtle-beach-hotel-changes-policy.html\#storylink=cpy

17. E. Gismatullin, "Pirates Looting Cargoes with AK-47s Threaten African Oil: Energy," *Bloomberg.com*, November 21, 2013, http://www.bloomberg.com/news/2013-11-21/pirates-looting-cargoes-with-ak-47s-threaten-african-oil-energy.html

18. D. Ferrara, "Securing Cash and Drug: The Other Side of Nevada's Pot Business," *Las Vegas Review-Journal* (online), May 9, 2014, http://www.reviewjournal.com/business/securing-cash-and-drug-other-side-nevada-s-pot-business

19. Ibid.

20. CNN Library, "Colorado Theater Shooting Fast Facts," November 22, 2013, http://www.cnn.com/2013/07/19/us/colorado-theater-shooting-fast-facts

21. B. Twist, "Pair Charged after Break-in at Portland Head Light Museum in Cape Elizabeth," *The Forecaster*, November 11, 2013, http://www.theforecaster.net/node/179207\#.UoJDCFSG

22. B. Ravid, "Israeli-Owned Kenya Mall Targeted as Bloody Nairobi Terror Attack Kills Fifty-nine," *Reuters*, September 21, 2013, http://forward.com/articles/184318/israeli-owned-kenya-mall-targeted-as-bloody-nairob/

23. Associated Press, "Newtown Report Fails to Determine Shooting Motive: Full Evidence File into Last Year's Shooting in Newtown, Conn., Will Not Be Released," *CBC News*, November 25, 2013, http://www.cbc.ca/news/world/newtown-report-fails-to-determine-shooting-motive-1.2438976

24. CNN Library, "Boston Marathon Terror Attack Fast Facts," October 24, 2013, http://www.cnn.com/2013/06/03/us/boston-marathon-terror-attack-fast-facts/

25. Romano, Levi-Minzi, Rugala, and Van Hasselt, "Workplace Violence Prevention."

26. U.S. Department of Labor (DOL), Workplace Violence Program, 2013, http://www.dol.gov/oasam/hrc/policies/dol-workplace-violence program.htm

27. Ibid.

28. E. Licu and B. S. Fisher, "The Extent, Nature and Responses to Workplace Violence Globally: Issues and Findings," in M. Gill, ed., *The Handbook of Security* (New York: Palgrave Macmillan, 2006).

29. C. M. Wilson, K. S. Douglas, and D. R. Lyon, "Violence Against Teachers: Prevalence and Consequences," *Journal of Interpersonal Violence,* Vol. 26, No. 12 (2011), pp. 2353–2371. doi: 10.1177/0886260510383027.

30. Wilson, Douglas, and Lyon, "Violence Against Teachers."

31. Ibid.

32. Ibid.

33. Romano, Levi-Minzi, Rugala, and Van Hasselt, "Workplace Violence Prevention."

34. Federal Bureau of Investigation (FBI), *Workplace Violence: Issues in Response*, E. A. Rugala and A. R. Isaacs, eds., Critical Incident Response Group, National Center for the Analysis of Violent Crime, FBI Academy, Quantico, Virginia, U.S. Department of Justice, 2002.

35. Ibid.

36. Ibid

37. M. L. Ta, S. W. Marshall, J. S. Kaufman, D. Loomis, C. Casteel, and K. C. Land, "Area-Based Socioeconomic Characteristics of Industries at High Risk for Violence in the Workplace," *American Journal of Community Psychology*, Vol. 44 (2009), pp. 249–260, doi 10.1007/s10464-009-9263-7

38. FBI, "Workplace Violence."

39. Licu and Fisher, "The Extent, Nature and Responses to Workplace Violence Globally."

40. Ibid.

41. Ibid.

42. DOL, Workplace Violence Program.

43. Romano, Levi-Minzi, Rugala, and Van Hasselt, "Workplace Violence Prevention."

44. Ibid.

45. DOL, Workplace Violence Program.

46. T. Anderson, "Developing a Prevention Policy," *Security Management,* May 2013.

47. Ibid.

48. Ibid.

49. Federal Bureau of Investigation, "Active Shooter/Mass Casualty Incidents," Critical Incident Response Group, http://www.fbi.gov/about-us/cirg/active-shooter-and-mass-casualty-incidents (accessed October 6, 2014).

50. M. Greenblatt, "FBI: Active Shooting Incidents Triple in Recent Years – I-Team Story," WCPO Cincinnati, 2013, http://www.wcpo.com/news/local-news/i-team/fbi-active-shooting-incidents-triple-in-recent-years

51. Ibid.

52. Ibid.

53. H. Hayes, "Businesses Need Plan in Place to Combat 'Active Shooter' Situation," *Kingsport Times-News,* June 21, 2014, http://www.timesnews.net/article/9078365/businesses-need-plan-in-place-to-combat-active-shooter-situation

54. Greenblatt, "FBI: Active Shooting Incidents Triple in Recent Years."

55. Romano, Levi-Minzi, Rugala, and Van Hasselt, "Workplace Violence Prevention."

56. Ibid.

57. Ibid.

58. DOL, Workplace Violence Program.

59. Romano, Levi-Minzi, Rugala, and Van Hasselt, "Workplace Violence Prevention."

60. DOL, Workplace Violence Program.

61. Romano, Levi-Minzi, Rugala, and Van Hasselt, "Workplace Violence Prevention."

62. DOL, Workplace Violence Program.

63. Romano, Levi-Minzi, Rugala, and Van Hasselt, "Workplace Violence Prevention."

64. U.S. Department of Labor, "Workplace Violence," Occupational Safety and Health Administration, 2013, http://www.osha.gov/SLTC/workplaceviolence/

65. Romano, Levi-Minzi, Rugala, and Van Hasselt, "Workplace Violence Prevention."

66. Ibid.

67. National Crime Prevention Council, "Safety Tips," 2002, http://www.ncpc.org/resources/files/pdf/workplace-safety/safewrk.pdf

68. Ibid.

69. Ibid.

70. FBI, *Workplace Violence: Issues in Response.*

71. DOL, Workplace Violence Program.

72. American National Standards Institute (ANSI), "ASIS International and SHRM Release American National Standard on Workplace Violence Prevention and Intervention," October 20, 2011, http://www.ansi.org/news_publications/news_story.aspx?menuid=7&articleid=3042

73. Ibid.

74. FBI, *Workplace Violence: Issues in Response.*

75. Ibid.

76. DOL, Workplace Violence Program.

77. U.S. Department of Labor, Occupational Safety and Health Administration (OSHA), "Workplace Violence," OSHA FactSheet, 2002, https://www.osha.gov/OshDoc/data_General_Facts/factsheet-workplace-violence.pdf

78. U.S. Department of Labor (DOL), "Safety and Health Topics: Workplace Violence," 2013, https://www.osha.gov/SLTC/workplaceviolence/

79. Ibid.

80. FBI, *Workplace Violence: Issues in Response.*

81. DOL, Workplace Violence Program.

82. Ibid.

83. Ibid.

84. O. Emmanuel, "Nigeria: How Crude Oil Is Stolen, Refined, Sold in Niger Delta," *Premium Times*, November 22, 2013, http://allafrica.com/stories/201311220913.html

85. International Criminal Police Organization (INTERPOL), "Pharmaceutical Crime: A Major Threat to Public Health," http://www.interpol.int/Crime-areas/Pharmaceutical-crime/Pharmaceutical-crime

86. Ibid.

87. "Database: Incidents Involving Cruise Ships," *Orlando Sun-Sentinel*, 2013, http://databases.sun-sentinel.com/news/broward/ftlaudcruise/ftlaudcruise_list.php

88. Federal Maritime Commission (FMC). "Notice to Cruise Passengers," 2014, http://www.fmc.gov/about/notice_to_cruise_passengers.aspx

89. Attackers Ramp Up Threats to the Energy Sector," *Info Security*, October 30, 2013, http://www.infosecurity-magazine .com/view/35306/attackers-ramp-up-threats-to-the-energy-sector-/
90. Bureau of Labor Statistics (BLS), "Injuries, Illnesses, and Fatalities," 2013, http://www.bls.gov/iif/oshstate.htm

Chapter 8: Security Investigations and Prosecution

1. M. Douglas, "Tampa Investigator Warns of Dangers of Cyberspace Dating," WFLA-News Channel 8, August 5, 2014, http://wfla.membercenter.worldnow.com/story/26201793/ plenty-of-fish-on-cyberspace-dating-site-but-not-all-of-them-are-the-real-deal
2. Private Investigator, "Job Duties," *Vocationary*, 2014, http:// www.vocationary.com/career-profile/private-investigator
3. Bureau of Security and Investigative Services, "Private Investigator Fact Sheet," Department of Consumer Affairs, 2013, http://www.bsis.ca.gov/forms_pubs/pi_fact.shtml
4. Private Investigator, "Job Duties."
5. Ibid.
6. Ibid.
7. ASIS International, Protection of Assets (POA), Kindle Version [Investigation], 2013.
8. S. H. Belshaw, "Private Investigation Programs as an Emerging Trend in Criminal Justice Education? A Case Study of Texas," *Journal of Criminal Justice Education*, Vol. 23, No.4, (2012), pp. 462–480, doi:10.1080/10511253.2012.6838 76.
9. Ibid.
10. D. Walker, L. Glovka, B. Greenawalt, and J. McNulty, eds., "Top Security Threats and Management Issues Facing Corporate America: 2012 Survey of Fortune 1000 Companies," Securitas Security Services USA, Inc., 2013.
11. Bureau of Labor Statistics (BLS), Protective Service » Private Detectives and Investigators, *Occupational Outlook Handbook*, 2014, http://www.bls.gov/ooh/protective-service/private-detectives-and-investigators.htm
12. The median annual wage for private detectives and investigators was $45,740 in May 2012.
13. Bureau of Labor Statistics, "Private Detectives and Investigators," *Occupational Outlook Handbook*, U.S. Department of Labor, 2014, http://www.bls.gov/ooh/protective-service/ private-detectives-and-investigators.htm
14. ASIS International, POA.
15. Ibid.
16. "Investigate," *Dictionary.com Unabridged*, based on the *Random House Dictionary*, 2014 http://dictionary.reference.com/ browse/investigate
17. Association of Chief Police Officers, "Practice Advice on Core Investigative Doctrine," National Centre for Policing Excellence, 2005, http://www.caerphilly.gov.uk/pdf/Health_Social-Care/POVA/Core_Investigation_Doctrine_Interactive.pdf
18. Association of Chief Police Officers, "Practice Advice on Core Investigative Doctrine."
19. Ibid.
20. ASIS International, POA.
21. Ibid.
22. Ibid.
23. White-collar crime, Legal Information Institute, 2014, http:// www.law.cornell.edu/wex/white-collar_crime
24. Federal Bureau of Investigation (FBI), "What We Investigate: White-Collar Crime," 2014, http://www.fbi.gov/about-us/ investigate/white_collar/whitecollarcrime
25. Department of the Army, "Law Enforcement Investigations," *Field Manual (FM) 3-19.13*, Department of the (U.S.) Army, 2005.
26. Utah Insurance Department, "What is Insurance Fraud?" Fraud Division, 2014, https://insurance.utah.gov/agent/ fraud/what.php
27. Ibid.
28. Legal Information Institute, "Healthcare Fraud: An Overview," Cornell Law, 2014, http://www.law.cornell.edu/wex/ healthcare_fraud
29. Ibid.
30. S. K. Jones, "Workers' Compensation Fraud and the Insurance Producer," *Insurance Journal*, March 24, 2014, http://www.insurancejournal.com/news/southcentral/2014/03/24/324275.htm
31. Ibid.
32. Ibid.
33. International Trademark Association, "Fact Sheets Protecting a Trademark," Global Trademark Resources, 2014, http:// www.inta.org/TrademarkBasics/FactSheets/Pages/ Counterfeiting.aspx
34. ASIS International, POA.
35. Ibid.
36. Ibid.
37. Canadian Centre for Occupational Health and Safety, "Accident Investigation," OSH Answers » Health & Safety Programs, 2014, http://www.ccohs.ca/oshanswers/hsprograms/investig.html
38. "Ibid.
39. Occupational Safety and Health Administration, "Accident Investigation," U.S. Department of Labor, 2014, https://www .osha.gov/SLTC/accidentinvestigation/
40. Ibid.
41. Health and Safety Executive, "Investigating Accidents and Incidents," 2014, http://www.hse.gov.uk/managing/delivering/ check/investigating-accidents-incidents.htm
42. Ibid.
43. Ibid.
44. Canadian Centre for Occupational Health and Safety, "Accident Investigation."
45. Ibid.
46. R. C. Coleman, "Combating Economic Espionage and Trade Secret Theft," Statement Before the Senate Judiciary Committee, Subcommittee on Crime and Terrorism, Federal Bureau of Investigation, May 13, 2014, FBI.gov, http://www.fbi.gov/news/testimony/ combating-economic-espionage-and-trade-secret-theft?utm_ campaign=email-Immediate&utm_medium=email&utm_ source=congressional-testimony&utm_content=321581
47. Ibid.
48. Ibid.
49. Ibid.
50. Department of the Army, "Law Enforcement Investigations."
51. J. Hunt, Work » Careers » Legal Jobs » "What Are the Duties of a Private Investigator?" Demand Media, 2014, *Houston Chronicle* [online edition]. http://work.chron.com/duties-private-investigator-13439.html
52. Department of the Army, "Law Enforcement Investigations."
53. ASIS International, POA.
54. Department of the Army, "Law Enforcement Investigations."
55. E. Inbau, J. E. Reid, J. P. Buckley, and B. P. Jayne, *Criminal Interrogations and Confessions* (Gaithersburg, MD: Aspen, 2001), as cited by J. P. Blair, "Interview or Interrogation?: A Comment on Kassin et al.," 2003, http://www.reid.com/ pdfs/Blair2003Interview.pdf
56. Department of the Army, "Law Enforcement Investigations."
57. Inbau, et al., *Criminal Interrogations and Confessions*.

58. Department of the Army, "Law Enforcement Investigations."
59. ASIS International, POA.
60. Department of the Army, "Law Enforcement Investigations."
61. Ibid.
62. Ibid.
63. Ibid.
64. Ibid.
65. Skills You Need, "Non-Verbal Communication," 2014, http://www.skillsyouneed.com/ips/nonverbal-communication.html\#ixzz31bwmuteF
66. Skills You Need, "Listening Skills," 2014, http://www.skillsyouneed.com/ips/listening-skills.html\#ixzz31X9FXta6
67. D. Schilling, "10 Steps To Effective Listening," November 9, 2012, http://www.forbes.com/sites/womensmedia/2012/11/09/10-steps-to-effective-listening/
68. John E. Reid & Associates, "Note-Taking during an Interview," *Interview and Interrogation Tips and Case Studies,* June 4, 2008, http://www.policeone.com/investigations/articles/1697350-Note-taking-during-an-interview/
69. Ibid.
70. Ibid.
71. Department of the Army, "Law Enforcement Investigations."
72. Hunt, "What Are the Duties of a Private Investigator?"
73. ASIS International, POA.
74. Department of the Army, "Law Enforcement Investigations."
75. Ibid.
76. Ibid.
77. Ibid.
78. Ibid.
79. Ibid.
80. Ibid.
81. ASIS International, POA.
82. Ibid.
83. Ibid.
84. Department of the Army, "Law Enforcement Investigations."
85. Ibid.
86. Ibid.
87. ASIS International, POA.
88. United Nations Office on Drugs and Crime (UNODC). *Criminal Intelligence Manual for Analysts* (Vienna: UNODC, 2011), https://www.unodc.org/documents/organized-crime/Law-Enforcement/Criminal_Intelligence_for_Analysts.pdf
89. Ibid.
90. G. Moore, "Intelligence and Counterintelligence," *Salem Press Encyclopedia*, January 2013.
91. Ibid.
92. L. Guerin, "Legal Topics: Employment Law," Nolo.com, 2014, http://www.nolo.com/legal-encyclopedia/state-laws-polygraphs-lie-detector-tests.html
93. ASIS International, POA.
94. Guerin, "Legal Topics: Employment Law."
95. ASIS International, POA.
96. Ibid.
97. Ibid.
98. Ibid.
99. Department of the Army, "Law Enforcement Investigations."
100. Ibid.
101. ASIS International, POA.
102. Ibid.
103. Ibid.
104. Ibid.
105. Ibid.
106. FindLaw, "Civil Cases vs. Criminal Cases: Key Differences," FindLaw.com, 2014, http://litigation.findlaw.com/filing-a-lawsuit/civil-cases-vs-criminal-cases-key-differences.html\#sthash.eM5zYXh9.dpuf
107. Ibid.
108. Ibid.
109. Ibid.
110. Deposition, "Legal Information Institute," 2014, http://www.law.cornell.edu/wex/deposition
111. Ibid.
112. Ibid.
113. J. Murphey, "Going to Court," securityofficerhq.com, 2012 http://securityofficerhq.com/blog/2012/09/26/Going-To-Court
114. "Preparing for a Deposition: A Guide to Understanding the Process and Avoiding the Pitfalls," *WORLDLawDirect*, 2011 http://www.worldlawdirect.com/article/1020/preparing-deposition.html
115. Ibid.
116. Ibid.
117. Ibid.
118. Department of Justice, Justice 101 » Steps in the Federal Criminal Process » Discovery. Office of the United States Attorneys, 2014, http://www.justice.gov/usao/justice101/steps/discovery.html
119. Department of the Army, "Law Enforcement Investigations."
120. Ibid.
121. Ibid.
122. Ibid.
123. Ibid.
124. Ibid.
125. Ibid.
126. Ibid.
127. Ibid.
128. Hunt, "What Are the Duties of a Private Investigator?"
129. Association of Certified Fraud Examiners, Certified Fraud Examiner Credential, 2014, http://www.acfe.com/cfe-credential.aspx
130. California Association of Licensed Investigators, Certification: Certified Professional Investigator, 2014, http://www.cali-pi.org/group/cpi
131. Criminal Justice Networking and Information Exchange, Group Description, LinkedIn.com, 2014, https://www.linkedin.com/groups/Criminal-Justice-Networking-Information-Exchange-6671155
132. W. Gunter, and J. Kidwell, "Law Enforcement and Private Security Liaison: Partnerships for Cooperation," International Foundation for Protection Officers, 2004, http://www.ifpo.org/resources/articles-and-reports/security-management-and-supervision/law-enforcement-and-private-security-liaison-partnerships-for-cooperation/
133. ASIS International, POA.
134. Ibid.
135. Ibid.
136. Ibid.
137. Ibid.
138. Ibid.
139. Ibid.
140. Ibid.

Chapter 9: Retail Security and Loss Prevention

1. FBI, "'Booster' Behind Bars: Professional Shoplifter Gets Prison Term," April 17, 2012, http://www.fbi.gov/news/stories/2012/april/shoplifter_041712
2. M. Pettus, "DC Police Search for Men from Flash Mob Robbery," retrieved from WUSA – 9NewsNow, April 29, 2011, http://wusa9.com/news/article/148817/77/DC-Police-Search-For-Men-From-Flash-Mob-Robbery

3. S. Phillips, "When Flash Mobs Attack, It's Plain Anti-Social," National Public Radio [online], April 3, 2010.

4. K. Sheehan, N. Velez, and N. O'Neill, "Hundreds of Teens Trash Mall in Wild Flash Mob," *New York Post*, December 27, 2013, http://nypost.com/2013/12/27/hundreds-of-teens-trash-mall-in-wild-flash-mob/

5. V. Frost, "The Definitions of Loss Prevention, Retail Security, and Electronic Article Surveillance," 2006, http://EzineArticles.com/145894

6. P. P. Purpura, *Security and Loss Prevention: An Introduction*, 6th ed. (Waltham, MA: Butterworth-Heinemann, 2013).

7. V. Frost, *The Definitions of Loss Prevention, Retail Security, and Electronic Article Surveillance*, 2006, http://EzineArticles.com/145894

8. R. Hayes, "Store Detectives and Loss Prevention," in M. Gill, ed., *The Handbook of Security* (New York: Palgrave Macmillan, 2005).

9. ASIS International, "Protection of Assets (POA) Online" [Introduction to Assets Protection], 2013.

10. Ibid.

11. C. A. Sennewald and J. H. Christman, *Retail Crime, Security and Loss Prevention: An Encyclopedic Reference* (Oxford, England: Butterworth-Heinemann, 2008), p. 302.

12. Ibid.

13. W. Jared, "Tackling Theft: Increasing Profitability in an Ever-Changing Retail Environment," *Security Products Magazine. Security Today,* December 1, 2012, http://security-today.com/articles/2012/12/01/tackling-theft.aspx?admgarea=mag

14. A. Beck, "Shrinkage and Radio Frequency Identification (RFID): Prospects, Problems, and Practicalities," in M. Gill, ed., *The Handbook of Security* (New York: Palgrave Macmillan, 2005).

15. P. J. Ortmeier, *Introduction to Security: Operations and Management,* 4th ed. (Upper Saddle River, NJ: Pearson, 2013).

16. Beck, "Shrinkage and RFID."

17. Ibid.

18. "Survey Reveals U.S. Retail Industry Lost Billions to Theft in 2011," *Security Products Magazine. Security Today,* November 27, 2012, http://security-today.com/articles/2012/11/27/security-survey-reveals-us-retail-industry-lost-billions-to-theft-in-2011.aspx?admgarea=mag

19. "American Retail," *Professional Security Magazine Online,* October 7, 2013, http://www.professionalsecurity.co.uk/news/retail/american-retail/

20. "Survey Reveals U.S. Retail Industry Lost Billions," *Security Products Magazine.*

21. Center for Retail Research, *The Global Retail Theft Barometer,* 2011. http://www.retailresearch.org/grtb_currentsurvey.php

22. Ibid.

23. "Eight in 10 Retailers Agree Organized Retail Crime Activity Has Increased in Past Three Years," *Security Products Magazine. Security Today,* June 6, 2013, http://security-today.com/articles/2013/06/06/eight-in-10-retailers-agree-organized-retail-crime-activity-has-increased-in-past-three-years.aspx?admgarea=mag

24. R. Cameron, *Department Store Shoplifting,* unpublished dissertation, Indiana University, 1955, as cited by Arboleda-Florez, H. Durie, and J. Costello, "Shoplifting: An Ordinary Crime?" *International Journal of Offender Therapy and Comparative Criminology,* Vol. 21, No. 201 (1977), doi: 10.1177/0306624X7702100301.

25. Hayes, "Store Detectives and Loss Prevention."

26. Ibid.

27. Jared, "Tackling Theft."

28. Hayes, "Store Detectives and Loss Prevention."

29. Jared, "Tackling Theft."

30. Hayes, "Store Detectives and Loss Prevention."

31. D. A. Dabney, R. C. Hollinger, and L. Dugan, "Who Actually Steals? A Study of Covertly Observed Shoplifters, *Justice Quarterly,* Vol. 21, No. 4 (2004), pp. 693–728, http://dx.doi.org/10.1080/07418820400095961

32. M. D. White and C. M. Katz, "Policing Convenience Store Crime: Lessons from the Glendale, Arizona Smart Policing Initiative," *Police Quarterly,* Vol. 16, No. 3 (2013), pp. 305–322, doi: 10.1177/1098611113497045.

33. Dabney, Hollinger, and Dugan, "Who Actually Steals?"

34. New South Wales Police Force, "Retail Security Resource," State of New South Wales, Australia, Department of Attorney General and Justice, 2012, http://www.crimeprevention.nsw.gov.au/agdbasev7wr/_assets/cpd/m660001l2/retail_security_resource_web_160212.pdf

35. Ibid.

36. Ibid.

37. Dabney, Hollinger, and Dugan, "Who Actually Steals?"

38. New South Wales Police Force, "Retail Security Resource."

39. Ibid.

40. Ibid.

41. R. Hayes and C. Cardone, "Stoptheft," in M. Gill, ed., *The Handbook of Security* (New York: Palgrave Macmillan, 2005).

42. Hayes, "Store Detectives and Loss Prevention."

43. Sennewald and Christman, *Retail Crime, Security and Loss Prevention.*

44. New South Wales Police Force, "Retail Security Resource."

45. Ibid.

46. D. A. Dabney, L. Dugan, V. Topalli, and R. C. Hollinger, "The Impact of Implicit Stereotyping on Offender Profiling: Unexpected Results from an Observational Study of Shoplifting," *Criminal Justice and Behavior,* Vol. 33, No. 5 (2006), pp. 646–674, doi: 10.1177/0093854806288942.

47. Ibid.

48. New South Wales Police Force, "Retail Security Resource."

49. Dabney, Hollinger, and Dugan, "Who Actually Steals?"

50. Ibid.

51. Ibid.

52. K. Burke, G. O. Adams, and D. Gregorian, "Rob Brown, Star of 'Treme,' Says He Was Arrested at Macy's After Buying Mom Watch," *New York Daily News,* October 25, 2013, http://www.nydailynews.com/new-york/black-man-sues-macy-cuffed-making-legit-purchase-article-1.1496735

53. Dabney, Hollinger, and Dugan, "Who Actually Steals?"

54. Dabney, Dugan, Topalli, and Hollinger, "The Impact of Implicit Stereotyping on Offender Profiling."

55. Ibid.

56. Ibid.

57. Ibid.

58. Associated Press, "Some Major Retailers to List Shoppers' Rights," *The Wall Street Journal,* December 9, 2013, http://online.wsj.com/article/APdb68bc8196c84c04ba-5b65ea53439fa4.html?KEYWORDS=security

59. R. Hayes, *Shoplifting Control* (Orlando, FL: Prevention Press, 1993); R. W. Helena, Steal Me Blind: *The Complete Guide to Shoplifting and Retail Theft* (Charleston, SC: Bluelight Publishing, 2000), as cited in D. A. Dabney, R. C. Hollinger, and L. Dugan, "Who Actually Steals? A Study of Covertly Observed Shoplifters," *Justice Quarterly*, Vol. 21, No. 4 (2004), pp. 693–728, http://dx.doi.org/10.1080/07418820400095961

60. "Organized Retail Crime Background," National Retail Federation, 2013, http://www.nrf.com/modules.php?name=Pages&sp_id=1464

61. S. Brown and K. Grannis, "Eight in 10 Retailers Agree Organized Retail Crime Activity Has Increased in Past Three Years," June 6, 2013, http://www.nrf.com/modules.php?name=News&op=viewlive&sp_id=1592

62. Ibid.

63. Federal Bureau of Investigation (FBI), "Organized Retail Crime Report," *FBI Law Enforcement Bulletin*, Vol. 78, No. 10 (October 2009), p. 8.

64. Ibid.

65. Ibid.

66. Ibid.

67. Hayes and Cardone, "Stoptheft."

68. J. Goodchild, "Four Steps Retailers Can Take to Combat Flash Robs," Data Protection » Social Networking Security, CSO Online, November 29, 2011, http://www.csoonline.com/article/695361/4-steps-retailers-can-take-to-combat-flash-robs

69. B. Gregg, "Fighting Organized Retail Crime: Forget the Hype!" CSO Online, March 24, 2011, http://www.csoonline.com/article/print/678103

70. M. Fitzgerald, "Organized Crime and Retail Theft: Facts and Myths," Physical Security » Loss Prevention, CSO Online, September 28, 2009, http://www.csoonline.com/article/503306/organized-crime-and-retail-theft-facts-and-myths?page=4

71. A. Duran, "Flash Mobs: Social Influence in the 21st Century," *Social Influence*, Vol. 1, No. 4 (2006), pp. 301–315.

72. Goodchild, "Four Steps Retailers Can Take."

73. C. F. Smith, J. P. Rush, D. Robinson, and M. Karmiller, "Flashgangs and Flashgangbanging: How Can Local Police Prepare?" *Journal of Gang Research*, Vol. 20, No. 1 (Fall 2012), pp. 33–50. Flash mob instructions are usually distributed via digital communication networks, such as Internet postings, e-mail, or mobile phones, see Duran.

74. C. F. Smith, "Flash Mobs and Street Gangs Morphing Into . . . ?" The Gangfighters Network Blog, 2011, http://gangfighters.blogspot.com/2011/06/flash-mobs-and-street-gangs-morphing.html

75. J. Custer, "To Stop or not to Stop: Is this still a question?" March-April 2012, http://www.losspreventionfoundation.org/___pdfs/lpfpublished/20120330_StopOrNotStop.pdf

76. "American Retail," *Professional Security Magazine Online*."

77. "Preventing Employee Theft," National Federation of Independent Business (NFIB), 2013, http://www.nfib.com/business-resources/business-resources-item?cmsid=29624

78. Ibid.

79. Jared, "Tackling Theft."

80. "Preventing Employee Theft," NFIB.

81. Ibid.

82. "American Retail," *Professional Security Magazine Online.*

83. B. Aronhalt and K. Grannis, "Retailers Estimate Holiday Return Fraud Will Cost Them $3.4 Billion, According to NRF Survey," 2013, http://www.nrf.com/modules.php?name=News&op=viewlive&sp_id=1712

84. ASIS International, POA Online.

85. J. Bologna, *Corporate Fraud: The Basics of Prevention and Detection* (Oxford, England: Butterworth-Heinemann, 1984), pp. 98–99, as cited by C. P. Nemeth, *Private Security and the Investigative Process*, 3rd ed. (Boca Raton, FL: Auerbach Publications/CRC Press, 2010).

86. J. Goodchild, "Physical Security: Five Top Tactics in Retail Theft Today: Technologies That Offer Convenience to Shoppers Also Assist Criminals (Including Employees) with Retail Theft," CSO Online, April 30, 2010, http://www.csoonline.com/article/592374/5-top-tactics-in-retail-theft-today

87. "American Retail," *Professional Security Magazine Online*."

88. R. C. Hollinger and J. L. Davis, "Employee Theft and Staff Dishonesty," in M. Gill, ed., *The Handbook of Security* (New York: Palgrave Macmillan, 2005).

89. "Preventing Employee Theft," NFIB.

90. E. F. Ferraro, *Investigations in the Workplace* (New York: Auerbach Publications, 2006), as cited by ASIS International, POA Online.

91. New South Wales Police Force, "Retail Security Resource."

92. A. Beck and C. Peacock, "Breaking the Retail Shrinkage Life Cycle," December 9, 2015, http://losspreventionmedia.com/insider/inventory-shrinkage/breaking-the-retail-shrinkage-life-cycle/

93. Ibid.

94. Ibid.

95. Ibid.

96. Ibid.

97. Ibid.

98. Ibid.

99. A. Beck, "Effective Retail Loss Prevention: 10 Ways to Keep Shrinkage Low," 2007 http://www2.le.ac.uk/departments/criminology/people/bna/10WaystoKeepShrinkageLowpdf

100. R. I. Mawby, "Commercial Burglary," in M. Gill, ed., *The Handbook of Security* (New York: Palgrave Macmillan, 2005).

101. Jared, "Tackling Theft."

102. S. Greenwald, "Putting an Extra 'Eye/I' on CCTV: Managing Risk in Retail," in L. J. Fennelly, ed., *Handbook of Loss Prevention and Crime Prevention*, 4th ed. (Waltham, MA: Butterworth-Heinemann, 2004).

103. R. Hayes, "Evidence-Based LP: Good Sensors Lead to Good Data." December 3, 2015, http://losspreventionmedia.com/insider/retail-security/evidence-based-lp-good-sensors-lead-to-good-data/

104. A. Longmore-Etheridge, "Case Study: A Wrinkle in Time. Security Management," August 23, 2012, http://securitymanagement.com/print/10139

105. Ibid.

106. P. Piazza, "A Chip Off the Privacy Block?" *Security Management* (n.d.), http://www.securitymanagement.com/print/1476

107. Ibid.

108. Ibid.

109. A. Longmore-Etheridge, "Finding the Fencers of Stolen Retail Goods," *Security Management*, July 9, 2013, http://www.securitymanagement.com/news/finding-fencers-stolen-retail-goods-0012566

110. "American Retail," *Professional Security Magazine Online*."

111. C. Purvis, "Convenience Store Group Raises Awareness about Credit Card Skimming," *Security Management,* August 15, 2011, http://www.securitymanagement.com/print/8898

112. Ibid.

113. B. Dodge, "A big problem with your new credit cards," August 20, 2015, http://www.cnn.com/2015/08/20/opinions/dodge-credit-cards-chip-and-pin/

114. Ibid.

115. Occupational Safety & Health Administration (OSHA), *Small Business Handbook*, Small Business Safety and Health Management Series, 2005, https://www.osha.gov/Publications/smallbusiness/small-business.html

116. Ibid.

117. Ibid.

118. Ibid.

119. Ibid.

120. Ibid.

121. Ibid.

122. New South Wales Police Force, "Retail Security Resource."

123. Ibid.

124. Ibid.

125. A. Piquero, "The Validity of Incivility Measures in Public Housing," *Justice Quarterly*, Vol. 16, No. 4 (1999), pp. 793–818.

126. J. Lane and J. W. Meeker, "Women's and Men's Fear of Gang Crimes: Sexual and Nonsexual Assault as Perceptually Contemporaneous Offenses," *Justice Quarterly,* Vol. 20, No. 2 (2003), pp. 337–371.

127. For more on the hidden messages in gang graffiti, see S. H. Decker and B. Van Winkle, *Life in the Gang* (New York:

Cambridge University Press, 1996); M. W. Klein, *The American Street Gang: Its Nature, Prevalence, and Control* (New York: Oxford University Press, 1995); F. M. Padilla, *The Gang as an American Enterprise*, 3rd ed. (New Brunswick, NJ: Rutgers University Press, 1996); and C. R. Wilson, "What's in a Name? Gang Monikers," *FBI Law Enforcement Bulletin*, Vol. 66, No. 5 (1997). p. 14.

128. New South Wales Police Force, "Retail Security Resource."
129. Mawby, "Commercial Burglary."
130. Ibid.
131. Ibid.
132. Ibid.
133. Ibid.
134. Ibid.
135. National Crime Prevention Council, Strategy: Business Watch. From 350 Tested Strategies to Prevent Crime: A Resource for Municipal Agencies and Community Groups, 1995, http://www.ncpc.org/topics/home-and-neighborhood-safety/strategies/strategy-business-watch
136. Ibid.
137. New South Wales Police Force, "Retail Security Resource."
138. Ibid.
139. Ibid.
140. Ibid.
141. E. Todd, and J. Rodriguez, U.S. Department of Labor's OSHA Cites TMT in Dallas, Texas, following Robbery, Death of Worker at Garland Whip in Store, November 19, 2012, https://www.osha.gov/pls/oshaweb/owadisp.show_document?p_table=NEWS_RELEASES&p_id=23283
142. Ibid.

Chapter 10: Homeland Security and the Terrorism Threat

1. H. B. Leonard, C. M. Cole, A. M. Howitt, and P. B. Heymann, "Why Was Boston Strong? Lessons from the Boston Marathon Bombing," Harvard University, 2014.
2. Ibid.
3. Botelho and R. Ellis "San Bernardino shooting investigated as 'act of terrorism,'" 2015, December 4, http://www.cnn.com/2015/12/04/us/san-bernardino-shooting/index.html
4. ASIS Foundation, Compendium of the ASIS Academic/Practitioner Symposium, 1997–2008.
5. D. Walker, L. Glovka, B. Greenawalt, and J. McNulty, eds., "Top Security Threats and Management Issues Facing Corporate America: 2012 Survey of Fortune 1000 Companies," Securitas Security Services USA, 2013.
6. *Quadrennial Homeland Security Review Report,* A Strategic Framework for a Secure Homeland, Department of Homeland Security, 2010, http://www.dhs.gov/xlibrary/assets/qhsr_report.pdf
7. C. Bellavita, "Changing Homeland Security: What Is Homeland Security?" *Homeland Security Affairs*, Vol. 4, No, 2 (2008), pp. 1–30.
8. *Quadrennial Homeland Security Review Report,* 2010.
9. Bellavita, "Changing Homeland Security."
10. *Quadrennial Homeland Security Review Report,* 2010.
11. Ibid.
12. Ibid.
13. Ibid.
14. Ibid.
15. Ibid.
16. Department of Homeland Security (DHS), "Strengthening the Homeland Security Enterprise: Implementing 9/11 Commission Recommendations," *Progress Report 2011*, http://www.dhs.gov/strengthening-homeland-security-enterprise
17. *Quadrennial Homeland Security Review Report,* 2010.

18. E. Pittman, "What Big-Box Retailers Can Teach Government about Disaster Recovery," *Government Technology*, November 28, 2011, http://www.govtech.com/policy-management/Big-Box-Retailers-Teach-Disaster-Recovery.html.
19. N. E. Busch and A. D. Givens, "Public-Private Partnerships in Homeland Security: Opportunities and Challenges," *Homeland Security Affairs* 8, Article 18 (October 2012), http://www.hsaj.org/?article=8.1.18
20. Federal Emergency Management Agency (FEMA), "About Industry Liaison Program," 2010, http://www.fema.gov/privatesector/industry/about.shtm.
21. Busch and Givens, "Public-Private Partnerships."
22. Ibid.
23. C-TPAT Overview, U.S. Customs and Border Protection, December 13, 2007, http://www.cbp.gov/xp/cgov/trade/cargo_security/ctpat/what_ctpat/ctpat_overview.xml
24. A. Diop and D. Hartman, "Customs-Trade Partnership Against Terrorism Cost-Benefit Survey," U.S. Customs and Border Protection, *C-TPAT Overview*, August 2007, http://www.cbp.gov/border-security/ports-entry/cargo-security/c-tpat-customs-trade-partnership-against-terrorism
25. Busch and Givens, "Public-Private Partnerships."
26. Ibid.
27. G. Boyne, "Public and Private Management: What's the Difference?" *Journal of Management Studies*, Vol. 39, No. 1 (2002), pp. 97–122; M. K. Feeney and H. G. Rainey, "Personnel Flexibility and Red Tape in Public and Nonprofit Organizations: Distinctions Due to Institutional and Political Accountability," *Journal of Public Administration Research & Theory*, Vol. 20 (2010), pp. 801–826, as cited by Busch and Givens, "Public-Private Partnerships."
28. Busch and Givens, "Public-Private Partnerships."
29. J. H. Kahan, "Looking Outward: U.S. Homeland Security Beyond the Borders," *Journal of Homeland Security Education*, Vol. 3 (2014), pp. 1–13, http://www.journalhse.org/v3-kahan.html
30. N. Morag, "Does Homeland Security Exist Outside the United States?" *10 Years After: The 9/11 Essays*, Vol. 7, 2011. Homeland Security Affairs, Naval Postgraduate School Center for Homeland Defense and Security
31. T. O'Connor, *Comparative Homeland Security*, MegaLinks in Criminal Justice, 2014, retrieved from http://www.drtomoconnor.com/3430/3430lect08b.htm.
32. Ibid.
33. Ibid.
34. Morag, "Does Homeland Security Exist Outside the United States?"
35. O'Connor, *Comparative Homeland Security.*
36. Ibid.
37. Morag, "Does Homeland Security Exist Outside the United States?"
38. O'Connor, *Comparative Homeland Security.*
39. Morag, "Does Homeland Security Exist Outside the United States?"
40. O'Connor, *Comparative Homeland Security.*
41. A. Phillips, "The Asymmetric Nature of Cyber Warfare," *U.S. Naval Institute News*, October 14, 2012, http://news.usni.org/2012/10/14/asymmetric-nature-cyber-warfare
42. P. Sonne and A. Troianovski, "Ukraine Says Plane Downed by Missile Probably Fired from Russia: Tension Climbs in Border Area as Rebels Dig In: NATO Says Russian Troops Back," *The Wall Street Journal*, July 14, 2014, http://online.wsj.com/articles/ukraine-reports-progress-against-pro-russia-separatists-1405340926. See also Reuters, "Ukraine Says Malaysian Airliner Shot Down, 295 Dead," Interfax-Ukraine News Agency, July 17, 2014, http://www.reuters.com/article/2014/07/17/us-ukraine-crash-airplane-idUSKBN0FM1TU20140717

43. E. Schrader, "Cheney Gave Order to Shoot Down Jets: 9/11 Commission Staff Seems to Question Whether Bush OKd the Command," *Los Angeles Times,* June 18, 2004, http://articles.latimes.com/2004/jun/18/nation/na-cheney18

44. O'Connor, *Comparative Homeland Security.*

45. A. Krechetnikov, "Moscow Theatre Siege: Questions Remain Unanswered," British Broadcasting Corporation (BBC), October 24, 2012, http://www.bbc.com/news/world-europe-20067384

46. Morag, "Does Homeland Security Exist Outside the United States?"

47. Ibid.

48. Department of Homeland Security (DHS), "Domestic Terrorism and Homegrown Violent Extremism Lexicon," Office of Intelligence and Analysis, Homeland Counterterrorism Division, Homegrown Violent Extremism Branch, (2011).

49. U.S. Department of State, "Legislative Requirements and Key Terms," U.S. Department of State, 2004, http://www.state.gov/documents/organization/65464.pdf, contained in Title 22 of the United States Code, Section 2656f(d).

50. 28 C.F.R. Section 0.85

51. DHS, "Domestic Terrorism and Homegrown Violent Extremism Lexicon."

52. National Counterterrorism Center (NCTC), Advisory: Homegrown Violent Extremists Targeting Law-Enforcement Officers, September 12, 2012.

53. Ibid.

54. E. Southers, *Homegrown Violent Extremism* (Waltham, MA: Anderson Publishing, 2013).

55. G. Martin, *Understanding Terrorism*, 94th ed. (Thousand Oaks, CA: Sage Publications, 2013).

56. Southers, *Homegrown Violent Extremism.*

57. Martin, *Understanding Terrorism.*

58. A. Sotlar, "Some Problems with a Definition and Perception of Extremism within a Society," in G. Mesko, M. Pagon, and B. Dobovsek, eds., *Policing in Central and Eastern Europe: Dilemmas of Contemporary Criminal Justice* (Slovenia: University of Maribor, 2004), https://www.ncjrs.gov/pdffiles1/nij/Mesko/208033.pdf

59. Sotlar, "Some Problems with a Definition."

60. Federal Bureau of Investigation, "Domestic Terrorism: Anarchist Extremism, A Primer," December 16, 2010, http://www.fbi.gov/news/stories/2010/november/anarchist_111610/anarchist_111610

61. J. P. Bjelopera, "The Domestic Terrorist Threat: Background and Issues for Congress," 7-5700 www.crs.gov R42536, Congressional Research Service, May 15, 2012.

62. L. R. Iannaccone and E. Berman, "Religious Extremism: The Good, the Bad, and the Deadly," in C. Rowley, ed., *Public Choice on the Political Economy of Terrorism*, n.d., http://econweb.ucsd.edu/~elib/rex.pdf

63. Southers, *Homegrown Violent Extremism.*

64. Southern Poverty Law Center (SPLC), "Christian Identity," 2014, Get Informed » Intelligence Files » Ideology, www.splcenter.org/get-informed/intelligence-files/ideology/christian-identity

65. Ibid.

66. M. Barkun, "Essay: The Christian Identity Movement," Southern Poverty Law Center, n.d., Get Informed » Intelligence Files » Ideology » Christian Identity, http://www.splcenter.org/get-informed/intelligence-files/ideology/christian-identity/the-christian-identity-movement

67. Southers, *Homegrown Violent Extremism.* Aryan Nations is one of the country's best-known anti-Semitic groups professing white nationalism. While founded as a Christian Identity group, the organization also incorporates neo-Nazi themes.

68. Southern Poverty Law Center (SPLC), Jewish Defense League, 2014, Home » Get Informed » Intelligence Files » Groups, http://www.splcenter.org/get-informed/intelligence-files/groups/jewish-defense-league

69. Ibid.

70. Southers, *Homegrown Violent Extremism.*

71. Ibid.

72. "Takfirism," refers to the practice of declaring a Muslim a kafir or nonbeliever, and then proclaiming that their lives can be forfeited.

73. R. Borum, "Understanding Terrorist Psychology," in A. Silke, ed., *The Psychology of Counter-Terrorism* (Oxon, UK: Routledge, 2010).

74. Southers, *Homegrown Violent Extremism.*

75. Ibid.

76. F. Reinares et al., "Radicalisation Processes Leading to Acts of Terrorism: A Concise Report Prepared by the European Commission's Expert Group on Violent Radicalisation," 2008, http://www.clingendael.nl/sites/default/files/20080500_cscp_report_vries.pdf

77. Ibid.

78. Southers, *Homegrown Violent Extremism.*

79. D. Van Duyn, "Testimony—Prison Radicalization: The Environment, the Threat, and the Response," Senate Committee on Homeland Security and Governmental Affairs and Related Agencies, September 16, 2006, http://www.fbi.gov/news/testimony/prison-radicalization-the-environment-the-threat-and-the-response

80. Ibid.

81. Ibid.

82. M. S. Hamm, "Prisoner Radicalization: Assessing the Threat in U.S. Correctional Institutions," *National Institute of Justice (NIJ) Journal*, Vol. 261, 2008, pp. 14–19, http://www.nij.gov/journals/261/pages/prisoner-radicalization.aspx

83. Reinares, "Radicalisation Processes Leading to Acts of Terrorism."

84. Ibid.

85. DHS, "Domestic Terrorism and Homegrown Violent Extremism Lexicon."

86. Ibid.

87. Ibid.

88. B. L. Smith, K. R. Damphousse, and P. Roberts, "Pre-Incident Indicators of Terrorist Incidents: The Identification of Behavioral, Geographic, and Temporal Patterns of Preparatory Conduct," Terrorism Research Center in Fulbright College, University of Arkansas, 2006.

89. G. LaFree and B. Bersani, "Hot Spots of Terrorism and Other Crimes in the United States, 1970 to 2008," *Final Report to Human Factors/Behavioral Sciences Division, Science and Technology Directorate*, U.S. Department of Homeland Security (College Park, MD: START, 2012), http://www.start.umd.edu/sites/default/files/files/publications/research_briefs/LaFree_Bersani_HotSpotsOfUSTerrorism.pdf

90. Ibid.

91. Ibid.

92. L. I. Shelley, J. T. Picarelli, A. Irby, D. M. Hart, P. A. Craig-Hart, P. Williams, S. Simon, N. Abdullaev, B. Stanislawski, and L. Covill, "Methods and Motives: Exploring Links between Transnational Organized Crime and International Terrorism," U.S. Department of Justice, 2005, Retrieved from http://www.ncjrs.gov/pdffiles1/nij/grants/211207.pdf

93. Ibid.

94. J. P. Sullivan and R. J. Bunker, "Third Generation Gang Studies: An Introduction," *Journal of Gang Research*, Vol. 14, No. 4, pp. 1–10 (Chicago, IL: National Gang Crime Research Center, 2007).

95. J. P. Sullivan, "Transnational Gangs: The Impact of Third Generation Gangs in Central America," *Air & Space Power*

Journal, 2008, http://www.airpower.maxwell.af.mil/apjinterna-tional/apj-s/2008/2tri08/sullivaneng.htm

96. "Extortion, Bank Robbery Fuel ISIS Bloody Drive to Establish Sharia Caliphate," Fox News (online), June 14, 2014, http://www.foxnews.com/world/2014/06/14/extortion-bank-rob-bery-fuel-isis-bloody-drive-to-establish-sharia-caliphate.

97. Ibid.

98. Ibid.

99. Ibid.

100. F. Chothia, "Who Are Nigeria's Boko Haram Islamists?" BBC Africa, May 20, 2014, http://www.bbc.com/news/world-africa-13809501

101. Ibid.

102. Ibid.

103. Ibid.

104. Ibid.

105. National Counterterrorism Center (NCTC), "Terrorist Groups: Al-Shabaab," 2015, retrieved from http://www.nctc.gov/site/groups/al_shabaab.html

106. Ibid.

107. D. Georgic and E. Honan, "Kenya Says It Destroys Two al-Shabaab Camps in Somalia," April 6, 2015. Retrieved from http://www.reuters.com/article/2015/04/06/us-kenya-security-military-idUSKBN0MX0EA20150406

108. Smith, Damphousse, and Roberts, "Pre-Incident Indicators of Terrorist Incidents.

109. Ibid.

110. Ibid.

111. Ibid.

112. Ibid.

113. Department of Homeland Security, Information Sharing Environment (ISE), Suspicious Activity Reporting (SAR) Version 1.5, Functional Standard (FS) 200. Author, 2009. Retrieved from http://www.dhs.gov/xlibrary/assets/privacy/privacy-pia-dhswide-sar-ise-appendix.pdf

114. Department of Homeland Security, "Identifying Homegrown Violent Extremists Before They Strike: An Information Needs Review," Author, 2010. Retrieved from http://www.scribd.com/doc/37873835/DHSHomegrownThreats

115. National Counterterrorism Center, "Behavioral Indicators Offer Insights for Spotting Extremists Mobilizing for Violence," Author, 2011. Retrieved from http://publicintelligence.net/ufouo-national-counterterrorism-center-mobilizing-homegrown-violent-extremists-hves-behavioral-indicators

116. E. E. Miller, K. Smarick, and J. Simone, Jr., "Profiles of Perpetra-tors of Terrorism in the United States (PPTUS): Data Collection and Descriptive Analysis," *Interim Report to Human Factors/Behavioral Sciences Division*, Science and Technology Directo-rate, U.S. Department of Homeland Security, College Park, MD: START, September 2011, http://www.start.umd.edu/pubs/START_PPTUS_DataCollectionDescriptiveAnalysis_Sept2011.pdf

117. Ibid.

118. Ibid.

119. Ibid.

120. Bjelopera, "The Domestic Terrorist Threat."

121. Borum, "Understanding Terrorist Psychology."

122. Global Terrorism Database, National Consortium for the Study of Terrorism and Responses to Terrorism (START): A Center of Excellence of the U.S. Department of Homeland Security, 2014, http://www.start.umd.edu/gtd/

123. J. B. Comey, "Homeland Threats and the FBI's Response," Statement Before the Senate Committee on Homeland Security and Governmental Affairs, Federal Bureau of Investigation, November 14, 2013, http://www.fbi.gov/news/testimony/homeland-threats-and-the-fbis-response

124. U.S. Department of Labor, "Fire Safety," Occupational Safety and Health Administration, 2013, http://www.osha.gov/SLTC/firesafety/index.html

125. S. Wingfield, "Boston Marathon Bombers Used 'Sophis-ticated' Bombs Made of Parts from Christmas Lights, Model Cars: Prosecutors," *New York Daily News*, May 22, 2014, http://www.nydailynews.com/news/crime/boston-marathon-bombers-sophisticated-bombs-prosecutors-article-1.1801484

126. D. McKinney, "NRL SiN-VAPOR Technology Improves IED Detection," August 14, 2013, http://www.nrl.navy.mil/media/news-releases/2013/nrl-sin-vapor-technology-improves-ied-detection\#sthash.Ple3moRO.dpuf

127. J. Straw, "What's Wrong with the War on Terrorism," *Secu-rity Management Magazine*, September 2007.

128. Ibid.

129. Department of Homeland Security (DHS), "Get Involved: If You See Something, Say Something," 2014, http://www.dhs.gov/if-you-see-something-say-something

130. Ibid.

131. Pinkerton, "Executive Protection," 2015, http://www.pinkerton.com/executive-protection\#sthash.XJMCeYD9.dpuf

132. Ibid.

133. D. Duffy, "The Six Things You Need to Know About Executive Protection"

134. Executive protection requires risk assessment, cost-benefit analysis and old-fashioned legwork." CSO \| April 1, 2005, http://www.csoonline.com/article/2112401/infosec-staffing/the-six-things-you-need-to-know-about-executive-protection.html

135. Bureau of Justice Assistance, "Assessing and Managing the Terrorism Threat," U.S. Department of Justice, Office of Jus-tice Programs, September 2005.

136. Ibid.

137. Ibid.

138. Ibid.

Chapter 11: Emergency Practices and Crisis/Disaster Management

1. *The Guardian*, "Fukushima," 2011, http://www.theguardian.com/environment/fukushima?page=1

2. CNN, "Hurricane Sandy Fast Facts," CNN Library, 2013 http://www.cnn.com/2013/07/13/world/americas/hurricane-sandy-fast-facts

3. IBTimes Staff Reporter, "Alabama Tornadoes 2011: Death Toll Nears 300 as Survivors Search Continues," *International Business Times,* April 28, 2011, http://www.ibtimes.com/alabama-tornadoes-2011-death-toll-nears-300-survivors-search-continues-281631

4. Environmental Protection Agency (EPA), "EPA Response to BP Spill in the Gulf of Mexico," 2013, http://www.epa.gov/bpspill/

5. ASIS International, Protection of Assets (POA) Online [Cri-sis Management], 2013.

6. D. Walker, L. Glovka, B. Greenawalt, and J. McNulty, eds., "Top Security Threats and Management Issues Facing Cor-porate America: 2012 Survey of Fortune 1000 Companies," Securitas Security Services USA, 2013.

7. Department of Homeland Security, *National Prepared-ness Report*, 2013, http://www.fema.gov/media-library-data/20130726-1916-25045-0015/npr2013_final.pdf

8. Haddow, Bullock, and Coppola, *Introduction to Emergency Management,* 4th ed., (Oxford, England: Butterworth-Heinemann, 2010).

9. Federal Emergency Management Agency (FEMA), "About the Agency," http://www.fema.gov/about-agency

10. David McConnell, *Plan for Tomorrow, Today! The Story of Emer-gency Preparedness Canada, 1948–98* (Ottawa: Canadian Gov-ernment Publishing, 1998), p. 19.

11. Immediately after seeing a flash, people were told to stop what they were doing, get prone on the ground, face-down, covering exposed skin. See also ASIS International, Protection of Assets (POA) Online [Crisis Management], 2013.

12. ASIS International, POA Online.

13. U.S. Nuclear Regulatory Commission (NRC), "Backgrounder on the Three Mile Island Accident," NRC Library, 2013, http://www.nrc.gov/reading-rm/doc-collections/fact-sheets/3mile-isle.html

14. Many texts and FEMA publications have referenced the Flood Control Act of 1934. Although there are countless references to it (including on the FEMA training pages), the act was actually in 1936, as can be seen in the text maintained by the Library of Congress, http://www.usbr.gov/power/legislation/fldcntra.pdf (which references the 1936 Act, not 1934).

15. Library of Congress, Flood Control Act of 1936, Committee Reports, 112th Congress (2011–2012), House Report 112–118, n.d., http://thomas.loc.gov/

16. J. Harrison, U.S. Army Corps of Engineers, Northwest Power and Conservation Council, 2008, http://www.nwcouncil.org/history/USArmyCorps

17. Federal Emergency Management Agency (FEMA) National Flood Insurance Act of 1968 and Flood Disaster Protection Act of 1973, n.d., http://www.fema.gov/media-library/assets/documents/7277?id=2216

18. C. Reddick, "Information Technology and Emergency Management: Preparedness and Planning in U.S. States," *Disasters*, Vol. 35, No. 1 (2011), pp. 45–61, doi:10.1111/j.1467-7717.2010.01192.x

19. Public Law 93-288.

20. U.S. Coast Guard, *Incident Management Handbook*, Incident Command System, Department of Homeland Security, 2006, https://etesting.uscg.mil/mstrefs/Incident_Management_Handbook.pdf.

21. FEMA, *Guide for All-Hazard Planning*, 1996, http://www.fema.gov/pdf/plan/slg101.pdf

22. N. Kapucu and V. Garayev, "Designing, Managing, and Sustaining Functionally Collaborative Emergency Management Networks," *The American Review of Public Administration*, Vol. 43, No. 3 (2012), pp. 312–330, doi: 10.1177/0275074012444719

23. Simeon Institute 1998, as cited by B. W. Blanchard, *Guide to Emergency Management and Related Terms, Definitions, Concepts, Acronyms, Organizations, Programs, Guidance, Executive Orders & Legislation: A Tutorial on Emergency Management, Broadly Defined, Past and Present*, 2008, http://training.fema.gov/EMIWeb/edu/docs/terms%20and%20definitions/Terms%20and%20Definitions.pdf

24. ASIS International, POA Online.

25. United Nations (UN) International Strategy for Disaster Reduction, "Terminology," 2007, http://www.unisdr.org/we/inform/terminology

26. Simeon Institute 1998.

27. UN International Strategy for Disaster Reduction, "Terminology."

28. ASIS International, POA Online.

29. *The Joint Staff Officer's Guide* (JSOG), PUB 1, Appendix G – Glossary, 2000, http://www.au.af.mil/au/awc/awcgate/pub1/index2000.htm. There was no identifiable UN definition of crisis.

30. D. Elliott, "Disaster and Crisis Management," in M. Gill, ed., *The Handbook of Security* (New York: Palgrave Macmillan, 2005).

31. Department of Justice (DOJ), *Crisis Management Plan* (Washington, DC: USDOJ, December 12, 2002) 25 pp., www.usdoj.gov/jmd/ps/epm/tab10.pdf, as cited by B. W. Blanchard, *Guide to Emergency Management and Related Terms*.

32. Elliott, "Disaster and Crisis Management."

33. Ibid.

34. Ibid.

35. L. Bonkiewicz and R. B. Ruback, "The Role of the Police in Evacuations: Responding to the Social Impact of a Disaster," *Police Quarterly*, Vol. 15, No, 2 (2012), pp. 137–156, doi: 10.1177/1098611112442808

36. UN International Strategy for Disaster Reduction, "Terminology."

37. Ibid.

38. Elliott, "Disaster and Crisis Management."

39. Ibid.

40. U.S. Government Accountability Office, "Critical Infrastructure Protection: Progress Coordinating Government and Private Sector Efforts Varies by Sectors' Characteristics," 2006, Retrieved from http://www.gao.gov/new.items/d0739.pdf, as cited by Strom, et al.

41. A. Morabito and S. Greenberg, "Engaging the Private Sector to Promote Homeland Security: Law Enforcement–Private Security Partnerships" (NCJ 210678), Washington, DC: U.S. Department of Justice, Office of Justice Programs, Bureau of Justice Assistance, September 2005, http://www.ncjrs.gov/pdffiles1/bja/210678.pdf, as cited by Strom, et al. "The Private Security Industry: A Review of the Definitions, Available Data Sources, and Paths Moving Forward," *Literature Review and Secondary Data Analysis*, Bureau of Justice Statistics, 2010.

42. K. Strom, M. Berzofsky, B. Shook-Sa, K. Barrick, C. Daye, N. Horstmann, and S. Kinsey, "The Private Security Industry: A Review of the Definitions, Available Data Sources, and Paths Moving Forward," *Literature Review and Secondary Data Analysis*, Bureau of Justice Statistics, 2010.

43. E. Connors, W. Cunningham, P. Ohlhausen, L. Oliver, and C. Van Meter, *Operation Cooperation: Guidelines* (Washington, DC: Bureau of Justice Assistance, 2000). http://www.ilj.org/publications/docs/Operation_Cooperation.pdf

44. Strom, et al., "The Private Security Industry."

45. Connors, et al., *Operation Cooperation*.

46. Federal Emergency Management Agency (FEMA), "What Is Mitigation?" n.d., http://www.fema.gov/what-mitigation

47. Department of Homeland Security, *National Preparedness Report*, 2013, http://www.fema.gov/media-library-data/20130726-1916-25045-0015/npr2013_final.pdf

48. Federal Emergency Management Agency (FEMA), "Hurricane Sandy FEMA After-Action Report," 2013, http://www.fema.gov/media-library-data/20130726-1923-25045-8218/sandy_fema_aar.pdf

49. Department of Homeland Security, "Overview of the National Planning Frameworks," 2013 http://www.fema.gov/media-library-data/20130726-1914-25045-2057/final_overview_of_national_planning_frameworks_20130501.pdf

50. Ibid.

51. Ibid.

52. Department of Homeland Security, "National Protection Framework" (working draft), 2012, http://ne-cipa.org/html/pdf/peo_nationalprotectionframeworkdraft_20120501[1].pdf

53. Department of Homeland Security, "Overview of the National Planning Frameworks."

54. Ibid.

55. Ibid.

56. Department of Homeland Security, "National Protection Framework."

57. FEMA, National Preparedness Goal, http://www.fema.gov/national-preparedness-goal.

58. Department of Homeland Security, "National Mitigation Framework," 2013, http://www.fema.gov/media-library-data/20130726-1914-25045-9956/final_national_mitigation_framework_20130501.pdf

59. Ibid.

60. Ibid.
61. Ibid.
62. Ibid.
63. Ibid.
64. Ibid.
65. Department of Homeland Security, "Overview of the National Planning Frameworks."
66. Ibid.
67. Department of Homeland Security, "National Response Framework," 2013 http://www.fema.gov/media-library-data/20130726-1914-25045-1246/final_national_response_framework_20130501.pdf
68. Ibid.
69. Ibid.
70. Ibid.
71. M. G. Kweit and R. W. Kweit, "Citizen Participation and Citizen Evaluation in Disaster Recovery," *American Review of Public Administration*, Vol. 34, No. 4 (2004), pp. 354–373.
72. Department of Homeland Security, "National Preparedness Report," 2013, http://www.fema.gov/media-library-data/20130726-1916-25045-0015/npr2013_final.pdf
73. Department of Homeland Security, *Nationwide Plan Review*: Phase 1 Report, February 10, 2006, http://training.fema.gov/EMIWeb/edu/docs/Nationwide%20Plan%20Review%20-%20Phase%201%20Report.pdf
74. G. F. Miehl, "Community Emergency Response," *Professional Safety*, Vol. 56, No. 12 (2011), pp. 35–41.
75. www.ready.gov/business/downloads/sampleplan.pdf
76. Miehl, "Community Emergency Response."
77. D. A. McEntire, C. Fuller, C. W. Johnston, and R. Weber, "A Comparison of Disaster Paradigms: The Search for a Holistic Policy Guide," *Public Administration Review*, Vol. 62, No. 3 (2002), pp. 267–281.
78. ASIS International, POA Online.
79. J. F. Broder, *Risk Analysis and the Security Survey*, 3rd ed. (Burlington, MA: Elsevier/Butterworth-Heinemann, 2006).
80. ASIS International, POA Online.
81. Ibid.
82. J. Walsh, ed. *Asset Protection and Security Management Handbook* (Boca Raton, FL: Auerbach Publications, CRC Press, 2002).
83. D. Rahm and C. G. Reddick, "U.S. City Managers' Perceptions of Disaster Risks: Consequences for Urban Emergency Management," *Journal of Contingencies & Crisis Management*, Vol. 19, No. 3 (2011), pp. 136–146, doi:10.1111/j.1468-5973.2011.00647.x
84. Ibid.
85. ASIS International, POA Online.
86. Ibid.
87. Walsh, ed. *Asset Protection and Security Management Handbook.*
88. Ibid.
89. ASIS International, POA Online.
90. Ibid.
91. Ibid.
92. McEntire and Myers, "Preparing Communities for Disaster."
93. B. Bennett, "Effective Emergency Management: A Closer Look at the Incident Command System," *Professional Safety*, Vol. 56, No. 11 (2011), pp. 28–37.
94. Centers for Disease Control and Prevention, "Public Health Preparedness Capabilities: National Standards for State and Local Planning, Capability 4: Emergency Public Information and Warning," Office of Public Health Preparedness and Response, 2012, http://www.cdc.gov/phpr/capabilities/capability4.pdf
95. Ibid.
96. Ibid.
97. Ibid.
98. Ibid.
99. Ibid.
100. Ibid.
101. Bennett, "Effective Emergency Management."
102. Ibid.
103. Ibid.
104. J. L. Garnett and A. Kouzmin, "Communicating throughout Katrina: Competing and Complementary Conceptual Lenses on Crisis Communication," *Public Administration Review*, Vol. 67, No. s1 (2007), pp. 171–188.
105. P. Palttala, C. Boano, R. Lund, and M. Vos, "Communication Gaps in Disaster Management: Perceptions by Experts from Governmental and Non-Governmental Organizations," *Journal of Contingencies & Crisis Management*, Vol. 20, No. 1 (2012), pp. 2–12, doi:10.1111/j.1468-5973.2011.00656.x
106. ASIS International, POA Online.
107. Ibid.
108. Ibid.
109. Garnett and Kouzmin, "Communicating throughout Katrina."
110. ASIS International, POA Online.
111. Ibid.
112. J-H.J. Yun, S. Park, and M. V. Avvari, "Development and Social Diffusion of Technological Innovation: Cases Based on Mobile Telecommunications in National Emergency Management. Science," *Technology & Society*, Vol. 16, No. 2 (2011), pp. 215–234, doi: 10.1177/097172181001600205
113. Nixle.com, "FAQs," 2013, http://www.nixle.com/faqs.html
114. Federal Emergency Management Agency (FEMA), "NIMS and the Incident Command System," 2013, http://www.fema.gov/txt/nims/nims_ics_position_paper.txt
115. FEMA, "National Incident Management System (NIMS)," *NIMS and National Preparedness*, 2013, http://www.fema.gov/national-incident-management-system
116. FEMA, "Introduction to the Incident Command System (ICS)," *Student Manual*, 2010, http://training.fema.gov/EMIWeb/IS/IS100b/SM/02ICS100b_SM_Aug2010.pdf
117. FEMA, "National Incident Management System Components," 2013, http://www.fema.gov/vi/node/34958
118. FEMA, "NIMS Public Information," n.d., http://emilms.fema.gov/IS702A/PIOsummary.htm
119. FEMA, "Independent Study Program," Emergency Management Institute, 2013, http://training.fema.gov/IS/NIMS.aspx
120. State of California, "Planning and Preparedness," Standardized Emergency Management System, 2001, http://www.calema.ca.gov/planningandpreparedness/pages/standardized-emergency-management-system.aspx
121. FEMA, "Plan, Prepare and Mitigate, National Preparedness, National Incident Management System Components: Incident Command System," 2013, http://www.fema.gov/incident-command-system
122. Bennett, "Effective Emergency Management."
123. U.S. Department of Health and Human Services, *Medical Surge Capacity Handbook: Emergency Management and the Incident Command System*, Assistant Secretary for Preparedness and Response (ASPR), 2012, http://www.phe.gov/Preparedness/planning/mscc/handbook/chapter1/Pages/emergencymanagement.aspx
124. FEMA, "Plan, Prepare and Mitigate."
125. C. Mbewe and M. Jones, "Hurricane Sandy: Competencies Needed to Contend with Natural Disasters," *MEDSURG Nursing*, Vol. 22, No. 4 (2013), pp. 1–5.

126. Ibid.
127. Bennett, "Effective Emergency Management."
128. Ibid.
129. Occupational Safety and Health Administration (OSHA), "What Is a Unified Command?" U.S. Department of Labor, 2013, https://www.osha.gov/SLTC/etools/ics/what_is_uc.html
130. Ibid.
131. Elliott, "Disaster and Crisis Management."
132. FEMA, "Continuity of Operations: An Overview," FEMA brochure, n.d., http://www.fema.gov/pdf/about/org/ncp/coop_brochure.pdf
133. Ibid.
134. FEMA, "Continuity Guidance Circular 1" (CGC 1), Continuity Guidance for Non-Federal Governments (States, Territories, Tribes, and Local Government Jurisdictions), July 2013, http://www.fema.gov/media-library-data/1386609058803-b0040723006374 9ab1d6da4b6472e691/CGC-1-Signed-July-2013.pdf
135. ASIS International, POA Online.
136. Ready.gov, "Business Continuity Planning," Business » Implementation » Business Continuity Plan, 2012, http://www.ready.gov/business/implementation/continuity
137. ASIS International, POA Online.
138. Ready.gov, "Business Continuity Planning."
139. Ibid.
140. Ibid.
141. Ibid.
142. ASIS International, POA Online.
143. Ready.gov, "Business Continuity Planning."
144. ASIS International, POA Online.
145. FEMA, Continuity Plan Template and Instructions for Non-Federal Governments, 2013, http://www.fema.gov/media-library-data/1389194640607-1a5f9a6d-6557846f6e5924eea089f798/Non%20Federal%20Continuity%20Plan%20Template%20and%20Instructions.pdf
146. S. S. Kostro, A. Nichols, and A. Temoshchuk, "U.S. Disaster Preparedness and Resilience: Recommendations for Reform" (Series on Community Resilience), Center for Strategic and International Studies-Pennington Family Foundation, 2013.
147. Ibid.
148. K. Ha, "The Choice between Politics-Oriented and Risk-Oriented Management in Korea: Transition to Manage All Kinds of Risks," African and Asian Studies, Vol. 10, No. 4 (2011), pp. 347–365, doi:10.1163/156921011X60559
149. Ibid.
150. X. Wang and N. Kapucu, "Public Complacency Under Repeated Emergency Threats: Some Empirical Evidence," Journal of Public Administration Research and Theory, Vol. 18, No. 1 (2007), pp. 57–78.
151. D. M. West and M. Orr, "Managing Citizen Fears: Public Attitudes Toward Urban Terrorism," Urban Affairs Review, Vol. 41, No. 1 (2005), pp. 93–105.
152. M. Crondstedt, "Prevention, Preparedness, Response, Recovery—An Outdated Concept?" n.d., http://cidbimena.desastres.hn/pdf/eng/doc14849/doc14849-contenido.pdf
153. For more on DRR, see United Nations Office for Disaster Risk Reduction, "What Is Disaster Risk Reduction?" 2013, http://www.unisdr.org/who-we-are/what-is-drr or USAID; and "Disaster Risk Reduction," 2013, http://www.usaid.gov/what-we-do/working-crises-and-conflict/disaster-risk-reduction
154. Caribbean Disaster Emergency Management Agency, "What is CDEMA?" 2013 http://www.cdema.org/
155. The International Emergency Management Society (TIEMS), "Welcome to TIEMS," 2013, http://tiems.info/
156. "Emergency Planning Guidelines for Campus Health Services: An All-Hazards Approach," Journal of American College Health, Vol. 59, No. 5 (2011), pp. 438–449, doi:10.1080/07448481.2011.569693
157. A. Engelman, S. L. Ivey, W. Tseng, D. Dahrouge, J. Brune, and L. Neuhauser, "Responding to the Deaf in Disasters: Establishing the Need for Systematic Training for State-Level Emergency Management Agencies and Community Organizations," BMC Health Services Research, Vol. 13, No. 1 (2013), pp. 1–10, doi:10.1186/1472-6963-13-84

Chapter 12: Critical Infrastructure Security

1. Maija Palmer, "Anonymous Attacks UK Government Websites," Financial Times, August 12, 2012, http://www.ft.com/intl/cms/s/0/a25154b6-eb87-11e1-b8b7-00144feab49a.html\#axzz2KotVhzsT
2. Hacktivism, in Wikipedia, The Free Encyclopedia, March 9, 2015, http://en.wikipedia.org/w/index.php?title=Hacktivism&oldid=650676548
3. Dara Kerr, "Anonymous: 'Expect Us 2013,'"'CNET News, January 1, 2013, http://news.cnet.com/8301-1009_3-57561530-83/anonymous-expect-us-2013/. See also YouTube and other online videos with the same message.
4. "Anonymous Downs Government, Music Industry Sites in Largest Attack Ever," RT News, January 20, 2012, http://rt.com/usa/news/anonymous-doj-universal-sopa-235/
5. Stephen Starr, "Cyberattack Threat in Canada's Oil Patch Raises Risk of Disruptions, Stolen Data," Financial Post, January 3, 2013, http://business.financialpost.com/2013/01/03/cyberattack-threat-in-canadas-oil-patch-raises-risk-of-disruptions-stolen-data/
6. Department of Homeland Security (DHS), "Critical Infrastructure Protection and Resilience," 2012, http://www.dhs.gov/files/programs/gc_1189168948944.shtm
7. United States Government Accountability Office (USGAO), "Critical Infrastructure Protection: DHS Could Better Manage Security Surveys and Vulnerability Assessments," Report to Congressional Requesters, May 2012.
8. D. Powell and S. Starkey, Utilities Critical Infrastructure Protection: Security Dependencies and Trends, ASIS Utilities Security Council (Prepublication edition), April 17, 2012.
9. Department of Homeland Security (DHS), Infrastructure Analysis and Strategy Division, http://www.dhs.gov/infrastructure-analysis-and-strategy
10. Ibid. A Buffer Zone Plan is developed with department support by local jurisdictions in coordination with CIKR facility owners and operators. The DHS sponsors workshops, videoconferences, and technical assistance to help program participants become familiar with the methods and assistance available.
11. Ibid.
12. Ibid.
13. Department of Homeland Security (DHS), "About the Homeland Infrastructure Threat and Risk Analysis Center," http://www.dhs.gov/about-hitrac
14. Ibid.
15. Department of Homeland Security (DHS), "A Guide to Critical Infrastructure and Key Resources Protection at the State, Regional, Local, Tribal, and Territorial Level," September 2008, http://www.dhs.gov/xlibrary/assets/nipp_srtltt_guide.pdf
16. DHS, "Critical Infrastructure Protection and Resilience," 2012.
17. Department of Homeland Security (DHS), "National Infrastructure Protection Plan," http://www.dhs.gov/national-infrastructure-protection-plan

18. Ibid. It is important for state, regional, local, tribal, and territorial governments to help implement the NIPP and to support more specific, localized concerns so the plan can be functional at all levels.

19. Ibid.

20. Federal Emergency Management Agency (FEMA), "Critical Infrastructure and Key Resources Support Annex," January 2008, http://www.fema.gov/pdf/emergency/nrf/nrf-support-cikr.pdf. The Critical Infrastructure and Key Resources (CIKR) Support Annex describes policies, roles and responsibilities, and the concept of operations for assessing, prioritizing, protecting, and restoring critical infrastructure and key resources of the United States and its territories and possessions during actual or potential domestic incidents. See http://www.dhs.gov/critical-infrastructure-and-key-resources-support-annex

21. DHS, "A Guide to Critical Infrastructure and Key Resources Protection."

22. FEMA. "Critical Infrastructure and Key Resources Support Annex."

23. Federal Emergency Management Agency (FEMA), "National Response Framework," February 2008, http://www.fema.gov/national-response-framework

24. DHS, "A Guide to Critical Infrastructure and Key Resources Protection."

25. Department of Homeland Security (DHS), "Information Sharing: A Vital Resource for a Shared National Mission to Protect Critical Infrastructure," 2014, http://www.dhs.gov/information-sharing-vital-resource-shared-national-mission-protect-critical-infrastructure

26. DHS, "Information Sharing."

27. Ibid.

28. Ibid.

29. DHS, "A Guide to Critical Infrastructure and Key Resources Protection."

30. Ibid.

31. Ibid.

32. Ibid.

33. Ibid.

34. Ibid.

35. Ibid.

36. Ibid.

37. Ibid.

38. Powell and Starkey, *Utilities Critical Infrastructure Protection.*

39. DHS, "A Guide to Critical Infrastructure and Key Resources Protection."

40. Bureau of Justice Assistance, "Operation Cooperation: Guidelines for Partnerships between Law Enforcement and Private Security Organizations," 2000, http://www.ilj.org/publications/docs/Operation_Cooperation.pdf

41. Ibid.

42. Ibid.

43. Powell and Starkey, *Utilities Critical Infrastructure Protection.*

44. Ibid.

45. National Infrastructure Advisory Council, *Intelligence Information Sharing Final Report and Recommendations*, January 10, 2012, http://www.dhs.gov/xlibrary/assets/niac/niac-intelligence-information-sharing-final-report-01102012.pdf

46. Ibid.

47. NYPD SHIELD, "Countering Terrorism through Information Sharing," http://www.nypdshield.org/

48. Ibid.

49. Ibid.

50. LEAPS El Paso, "United We Move Forward toward a Better Future," http://www.leapselpaso.com/

51. Ibid.

52. Target and BLUE, April 14, 2009, http://pressroom.target.com/backgrounders/target-and-blue

53. Ibid.

54. Ibid.

55. Target, "Social Responsibility," http://sites.target.com/images/corporate/about/responsibility_report/responsibility_report_social.pdf

56. Ibid.

57. Bureau of Justice Assistance, "Operation Cooperation: Guidelines for Partnerships between Law Enforcement & Private Security organizations," http://www.ilj.org/publications/docs/Operation_Cooperation.pdf

58. Ibid.

59. InfraGard, "A Collaboration for Infrastructure Protection," http://www.infragard.net/

60. Ibid.

61. Ibid.

62. Ibid.

63. Ibid.

64. Ibid.

65. Ibid.

66. Ibid.

67. Department of Energy, "Vulnerability Assessment Methodology, Electric Power Infrastructure," September 30, 2002, DRAFT.

68. Ibid.

69. Ibid.

70. FEMA, "Critical Infrastructure and Key Resources Support Annex."

71. FEMA, "Critical Infrastructure and Key Resources Support Annex." The results are used to enhance the overall security posture of the facilities or systems, the surrounding communities, and the geographic region using short-term enhancements and long-term risk-based investments in training, processes, procedures, equipment, and resources for state and local stakeholders.

72. I FEMA. "Critical Infrastructure and Key Resources Support Annex. SAVs can be conducted if the facility is considered nationally significant CIKR, the loss of which would have significant national or regional economic and/or public health effects; of such complexity or unique design that a SAV would be beneficial to infrastructure protection activities; the owner or operator of a significant and highly consequential facility requests the SAV, or the facility supports or is in close proximity to a National Special Security Event.

73. DHS, "A Guide to Critical Infrastructure and Key Resources Protection."

74. Ibid.

Chapter 13: Information, Cyber, and Computer Security

1. E. Nakashima, "U.S. Rallied 120 Nations in Response to 2012 Cyberattack on American Banks." *The Washington Post*, April 11, 2014, http://www.washingtonpost.com/world/national-security/us-rallied-multi-nation-response-to-2012-cyberattack-on-american-banks/2014/04/11/7c1fbb12-b45c-11e3-8cb6-284052554d74_story.html

2. A DDoS attack tells all coordinated systems to send a stream of requests to a specific server at the same time, often overwhelming the server and preventing others from accessing it. See also M. Egan, "PNC Warns Customers about Ongoing Cyber Attack," Fox Business, January 4, 2013, http://www

.foxbusiness.com/industries/2013/01/04/pnc-warns-customers-on-likely-ongoing-cyber-attack/\#ixzz2H28Ne1Gv

3. Ibid.

4. Ibid.

5. Nakashima, "U.S. Rallied 120 Nations."

6. T. Fernholz, "The Heartbleed Bug Shows How Fragile the Volunteer-Run Internet Can Be," NextGov Government Executive Media Group, April 10, 2014, http://www.nextgov.com/cybersecurity/2014/04/heartbleed-bug-shows-how-fragile-volunteer-run-internet-can-be/82285/print/

7. J. Pagliery, "Heartbleed Bug: What You Need to Know," CNN Money, April 11, 2014.

8. Ibid.

9. J. Silver-Greenberg, M. Goldstein, and N. Perlroth, "JPMorgan Chase Hacking Affects 76 Million Households," October 2, 2014, http://dealbook.nytimes.com/2014/10/02/jpmorgan-discovers-further-cyber-security-issues/?_r=0

10. B. Krebs, "Home Depot: 56M Cards Impacted, Malware Contained," September 18, 2014, http://krebsonsecurity.com/2014/09/home-depot-56m-cards-impacted-malware-contained/

11. Gartner, Inc. "Forecast Alert: IT Spending, Worldwide, 2008–2015, 4Q11 Update," www.gartner.com/id=1886414 (accessed January 2013).

12. Internet World Stats, www.internetworldstats.com/stats.htm (accessed January 2013).

13. D. Adolf, "Security Studies and Higher Education," Journal of Applied Security Research, Vol. 6, No. 1 (2011), pp. 124–134.

14. There are various ways to write this term, but the Associated Press (@APStylebook) says it is one word: Cybersecurity.

15. SANS Institute, "Information Security Resources," SANS Institute, http://www.sans.org/information-security; Florida Tech University Online, Online Degree Resources » Cybersecurity vs. Information Security, 2014, http://www.floridatechonline.com/online-degree-resources/cybersecurity-vs-information-security/

16. SecurityIntelligence, "Computer Security or Information Security? What Are We Talking About?" SecurityIntelligence, a division of MalwareIntelligence that focuses on aspects related to Information Security, June 10, 2010, http://securityint.blogspot.com/2010/06/computer-security-or-information.html

17. Ibid.

18. Ibid.

19. E. Felten, "What's the Cyber in Cyber-Security? Freedom to Tinker," July 24, 2008, https://freedom-to-tinker.com/blog/felten/whats-cyber-cyber-security

20. Computer Security, "Definition of Computer Security," Ziff Davis, LLC, PCMag Digital Group, 2014, http://www.pcmag.com/encyclopedia/term/40169/computer-security

21. Florida Tech University Online, Online Degree Resources Cybersecurity vs. Information Security, http://www.floridatechonline.com/online-degree-resources/cybersecurity-vs-information-security/

22. International Telecommunication Union (ITU), "Definition of Cybersecurity," 2014, http://www.itu.int/en/ITU-T/study-groups/com17/Pages/cybersecurity.aspx

23. IT Glossary » Advanced Research Projects Agency Network (ARPANET), https://www.gartner.com/doc/2510116?pcp=itg

24. SecurityIntelligence, "Computer Security or Information Security?"

25. J. B. Comey, Director, Federal Bureau of Investigation, "Speech—The FBI and the Private Sector: Closing the Gap in Cyber Security," RSA Cyber Security Conference, San Francisco, California, February 26, 2014, http://www.fbi.gov/news/speeches/the-fbi-and-the-private-sector-closing-the-gap-in-cyber-security

26. Ibid. More information on the FBI program can be found at http://www.fbi.gov/stats-services/iguardian

27. 44 U.S.C. § 3542(b)(1).

28. SecurityIntelligence, "Computer Security or Information Security?"

29. Laura L. Lundin, "Information Security," Salem Press Encyclopedia, September 2013.

30. N. K. Sehgal, S. Sohoni, X. Ying, D. Fritz, W. Mulia, and J. M. Acken, "A Cross Section of the Issues and Research Activities Related to Both Information Security and Cloud Computing," IETE Technical Review, Vol. 28, No. 4 (2011), pp. 279–291.

31. "Encryption," TechTerms, 2014, http://www.techterms.com/definition/encryption

32. Sehgal, et al., "A Cross Section of the Issues and Research Activities."

33. Computer Security, "Definition of Information Security." Ziff Davis.

34. Sehgal, et al., "A Cross Section of the Issues and Research Activities."

35. This classification is common among NATO (North Atlantic Treaty Organization) countries but is not used by all nations.

36. C. Paquet, Network Security Concepts and Policies. Implementing Cisco IOS Network Security Foundation Learning Guide, 2nd ed. (Indianapolis, IN: Pearson Education, Cisco Press, 2013).

37. Ibid.

38. Ibid.

39. C. S. Yap, M. Z. A. Rashid, and D. A. Sapuan, "Perceived Environmental Uncertainty and Competitive Intelligence Practices," VINE, Vol. 43, No. 4 (2013), pp. 462–481, doi: 10.1108/VINE-11-2011-0058

40. U.S. Copyright Office, "Copyright Basics: What Is Copyright?" 2014 http://www.copyright.gov/circs/circ01.pdf

41. A. Bensoussan, L. Tellier-Loniewski, and C. Salomon, "Intellectual Property Rights. Regulation and Competition: Challenged by Open Innovation," Digiworld Economic Journal, No. 89, First quarter (2013), p. 119.

42. "Social Media," TechTerms, 2014, http://www.techterms.com/definition/social_media

43. ASIS Utilities Security Council, Utilities Critical Infrastructure Protection: Security Dependencies and Trends. Prepublication Edition, 2012.

44. Industrial Espionage, FT Lexicon, Financial Times, 2014, http://lexicon.ft.com/Term?term=industrial-espionage

45. ASIS International, CPP Study Guide, ASIS International Houston, 2008.

46. Ibid.

47. Paquet, Network Security Concepts and Policies.

48. U. Onwudebelu and J. Akpojaro, "Electronic Security Issues: Protecting Our Electronic Life from Social Engineering Attacks," International Journal of Advanced Research in Computer Science, Vol. 3, No. 4 (July–August 2012).

49. Ibid.

50. Paquet, Network Security Concepts and Policies.

51. M. Bowles, "The Business of Hacking and Birth of an Industry," Bell Labs Technical Journal, Vol. 17, No. 3 (2012), pp. 5–16, doi: 10.1002/bltj.21555.

52. T. Teller, "Looking to the Future: Security Predictions for 2013," Check Point, December 17, 2012, http://www.net-security.org/article.php?id=1788

53. Ibid.

54. ASIS International, CPP Study Guide.

55. SecurityIntelligence, "Computer Security or Information Security?"

56. Ibid,

57. Definition of Computer Security, Ziff Davis, LLC, *PCMag Digital Group*, 2014, http://www.pcmag.com/encyclopedia/term/40169/computer-security

58. S. V. Margariti, G. Meletiou, E. Stergiou, D. C. Vasiliadis, G. E. Rizos, "Security Systems Consideration: A Total Security Approach. Computation in Modern Science and Engineering: Proceedings of the International Conference on Computational Methods in Science and Engineering 2007" (ICCMSE 2007): 2, A & B. AIP Conference Proceedings, 963, 2007, pp. 954–958, doi: 10.1063/1.2836250.

59. D. Walker, L. Glovka, B. Greenawalt, and J. McNulty, eds., "Top Security Threats and Management Issues Facing Corporate America: 2012 Survey of Fortune 1000 Companies," Securitas Security Services USA, Inc., 2013.

60. International Telecommunications Union, Definition of Cybersecurity, referring to ITU-T X.1205, Overview of Cybersecurity, 2014, http://www.itu.int/en/ITU-T/studygroups/com17/Pages/cybersecurity.aspx

61. IT Glossary » Advanced Research Projects Agency Network (ARPANET), https://www.gartner.com/doc/2510116?pcp=itg

62. Ibid.

63. F. Ibikunle and O. Eweniyi, "Approach to Cyber Security Issues in Nigeria: Challenges and Solution," *International Journal of Cognitive Research in Science, Engineering and Education* (IJCRSEE), Vol. 1, No. 1 (2013).

64. Commtouch is an Internet security technology firm that provides security companies cyber protection.

65. ASIS International, *CPP Study Guide.*

66. D. S. Wall, "Policing Cybercrimes: Situating the Public Police in Networks of Security within Cyberspace," *Police Practice and Research*, Vol. 8, No. 2 (2007), pp. 183–205, doi: 10.1080/15614260701377729

67. Ibid.

68. Ibid.

69. Ibid.

70. Department of Homeland Security (DHS), "Stop Think Connect: Securing One Citizen, One Family, One Nation Against Cyber Threats," www.dhs.gov/stopthinkconnect

71. Z. Saleh, "The Impact of Identity Theft on Perceived Security and Trusting E-Commerce," *Journal of Internet Banking and Commerce*, Vol. 18, No. 2 (August 2013), pp. 1–11.

72. Walker, et al., eds., "Top Security Threats and Management Issues."

73. Saleh, "The Impact of Identity Theft."

74. 18 U.S. Code §1028A(a)(l).

75. Office for Victims of Crime, Identity Theft and Financial Fraud » Federal Identity Theft Laws, Office for Victims of Crime, 2010, http://www.ovc.gov/pubs/ID_theft/idtheftlaws.html

76. Saleh, "The Impact of Identity Theft."

77. DHS, "Stop Think Connect."

78. Paquet, *Network Security Concepts and Policies.*

79. Bowles, "The Business of Hacking and Birth of an Industry."

80. Paquet, *Network Security Concepts and Policies.*

81. D. Powell, A. Wick, and D. Fergus, "Protecting Against Cyberthreats," *Security Management Magazine*, 2013, http://securitymanagement.com/article/protecting-against-cyberthreats-0011335

82. C. M. Kirsch, "Science Fiction No More: Cyber Warfare and the United States," *Denver Journal of International Law & Policy*, Vol. 40, No. 4 (2012), pp. 620–647.

83. "Denial of Service Attack," *TechTerms*, 2014, http://www.techterms.com/definition/denial_of_service

84. Bowles, "The Business of Hacking and Birth of an Industry."

85. "Denial of Service Attack," *TechTerms.*

86. The Hack FAQ: How Can I Discover New DoS Attacks? Denial of Service Basics, Nomad Mobile Research Center, 2014, http://www.nmrc.org/pub/faq/hackfaq/hackfaq-05.html

87. Paquet, *Network Security Concepts and Policies.*

88. Ibid.

89. M. McDowell and A. Householder, Security Tip (ST04-004), Understanding Firewalls, 2013, https://www.us-cert.gov/ncas/tips/ST04-004. Firewalls can be configured to block data from certain locations while allowing the relevant and necessary data through. Firewalls are offered in two forms: hardware (external) and software (internal). While both have their advantages and disadvantages, the decision to use a firewall is far more important than deciding which type you use.

90. "Denial of Service Attack," *TechTerms.*

91. Paquet, *Network Security Concepts and Policies.*

92. Bowles, "The Business of Hacking and Birth of an Industry."

93. "Denial of Service Attack," *TechTerms.*

94. Paquet, *Network Security Concepts and Policies.*

95. M. McDowell, Security Tip (ST04-015), Understanding Denial-of-Service Attacks, US-CERT., Department of Homeland Security, 2013.

96. K. Beaver, *Code Injection and SQL Injection Hacks in Web Applications for Dummies*, 2014, http://www.dummies.com/how-to/content/code-injection-and-sql-injection-hacks-in-web-appl.html

97. B. Ediger and M. Mior, "In Response to: How Can I Explain SQL Injection without Technical Jargon?" *Information Security Stack Exchange*, 2012, http://security.stackexchange.com/questions/25684/how-can-i-explain-sql-injection-without-technical-jargon

98. Kirsch, "Science Fiction No More."

99. Ibid.

100. Ibid.

101. "Worm," *TechTerms*, 2014, http://www.techterms.com/definition/worm

102. "Malware," *TechTerms*, 2014, http://www.techterms.com/definition/malware

103. Ibid.

104. L. A. Hughes and G. J. DeLone, "Viruses, Worms, and Trojan Horses: Serious Crimes, Nuisance, or Both?" *Social Science Computer Review*, Vol. 25, No. 1 (2007). pp. 78–98 doi: 10.1177/0894439306292346.

105. Ibid.

106. Ibid.

107. Microsoft, Resources » What is Ransomware? Safety and Security Center, 2014, http://www.microsoft.com/security/resources/ransomware-whatis.aspx

108. D. L. Leger, "Hackers Ramp Up Computer Attacks That Demand 'Ransom:' Some Victims Get Lost in the Details of the Payment Process and Run Out of Time," *USA TODAY* [online], http://www.usatoday.com/story/news/nation/2014/05/14/ransom-ware-computer-dark-web-criminal/8843633

109. Ibid.

110. Bitcoin is a consensus network with a new payment system and completely digital money. From a user perspective, Bitcoin is like cash for the Internet. "Bitcoin," 2014, https://bitcoin.org/en/faq\#what-is-bitcoin

111. Leger, "Hackers Ramp Up Computer Attacks That Demand 'Ransom:' Some victims get lost in the details of the payment process and run out of time. USA TODAY [online]. http://www.usatoday.com/story/news/nation/2014/05/14/ransom-ware-computer-dark-web-criminal/8843633/

112. Ibid.

113. Bowles, "The Business of Hacking and Birth of an Industry."
114. Paquet, *Network Security Concepts and Policies*.
115. DHS, "Stop Think Connect."
116. Pew Research Center, "Mobile Technology Fact Sheet," Pew Research Internet Project, 2014, http://www.pewinternet.org/fact-sheets/mobile-technology-fact-sheet/
117. ASIS Utilities Security Council, *Utilities Critical Infrastructure Protection.*
118. Ibid.
119. E. Lennon, "Information Technology Laboratory Bulletin," National Institute of Standards and Technology, July 2013, http://csrc.nist.gov/publications/nistbul/itlbul2013_07.pdf
120. Sehgal, et al., "A Cross Section of the Issues and Research Activities."
121. Ibid.
122. Ibid.
123. Ibid.
124. ASIS Utilities Security Council, *Utilities Critical Infrastructure Protection*.
125. Ibid.
126. Ibid.
127. G. M. Snow, Statement Before the Senate Judiciary Committee, Subcommittee on Crime and Terrorism, Federal Bureau of Investigation, Washington, DC, April 12, 2011, http://www.fbi.gov/news/testimony/cybersecurity-responding-to-the-threat-of-cyber-crime-and-terrorism
128. R. Smith, "U.S. Risks National Blackout from Small-Scale Attack," WSJ.com, March 12, 2014, http://online.wsj.com/news/articles/SB10001424052702304020
129. P. De Filippi, "It's Time to Take Mesh Networks Seriously (And Not Just for the Reasons You Think)," *Wired*, January 2, 2014, http://www.wired.com/2014/01/its-time-to-take-mesh-networks-seriously-and-not-just-for-the-reasons-you-think/
130. S. Anthony, "What Is Mesh Networking, and Why Apple's Adoption in iOS 7 Could Change the World," *ExtremeTech*, March 24, 2014, http://www.extremetech.com/computing/179066-what-is-mesh-networking-and-why-apples-adoption-in-ios-7-could-change-the-world
131. De Filippi, "It's Time to Take Mesh Networks Seriously."
132. S. Ferber, "How the Internet of Things Changes Everything," HBR Blog Network, *Harvard Business Review*, May 7, 2013,), http://blogs.hbr.org/2013/05/how-the-internet-of-things-cha/
133. K. G. Jeffery, "The Internet of Things: The Death of a Traditional Database?" *IETE Technical Review*, Vol. 26, No, 5 (September-October 2009).
134. Ibid.
135. Ferber, "How the Internet of Things Changes Everything,"
136. Jeffery, "The Internet of Things."
137. M. della Cava, "Internet of Things Will Mushroom by 2025, Report Says," *USA TODAY* (online), May 14, 2014, http://www.usatoday.com/story/tech/2014/05/14/internet-of-things-pew-report/9095941/
138. Google.com, The Glass Explorer Program, 2014, http://www.google.com/glass/
139. della Cava, "Internet of Things Will Mushroom."
140. M. della Cava, "Google's Self-Driving Car Makes Strides," USA TODAY, May 19, 2014, http://www.usatoday.com/story/tech/2014/05/13/google-self-driving-car-demo-mountain-view/9046385/
141. (ISC)², Certification Programs, CISSP—Certified Information Systems Security Professional, 2014, https://www.isc2.org/CISSP/Default.aspx
142. Powell, et al., "Protecting Against Cyberthreats."
143. A. Gonsalves, "Senior Managers Fumble Security Much More Often Than Rank and File," *CSO* January 8, 2014, http://www.csoonline.com/category/security-leadership/
144. "Exposing the Cybersecurity Cracks: United States," Ponemon Institute, Research Report, 2014.
145. Bowles, "The Business of Hacking and Birth of an Industry."
146. P. Lance, "How to Protect Your Computer from Viruses and Hackers," FoxNews.com, May 2, 2014, http://www.foxnews.com/tech/2014/05/02/how-to-protect-your-computer-from-viruses-and-hackers/
147. Bowles, "The Business of Hacking and Birth of an Industry."
148. ASIS Utilities Security Council, *Utilities Critical Infrastructure Protection*.
149. Bowles, "The Business of Hacking and Birth of an Industry."
150. "Exposing the Cybersecurity Cracks: United States," Ponemon Institute.
151. A. Sternstein, "Government Employees Cause Nearly 60 Percent of Public Sector Cyber Incidents," NextGov.com, April 22, 2014, http://www.nextgov.com/cybersecurity/2014/04/government-employees-cause-nearly-60-public-sector-cyber-incidents/82933/
152. "Exposing the Cybersecurity Cracks: United States," Ponemon Institute.
153. Sternstein, "Government Employees Cause Nearly 60 Percent of Public Sector Cyber Incidents."
154. Department of Homeland Security (DHS), "A Guide to Critical Infrastructure and Key Resources Protection at the State, Regional, Local, Tribal, and Territorial Level," September 2008. http://www.dhs.gov/xlibrary/assets/nipp_srtltt_guide.pdf
155. Federal Bureau of Investigation (FBI), About Us, 2014, http://www.fbi.gov/about-us/investigate/cyber
156. Kirsch, "Science Fiction No More."
157. Department of Defense (DOD), "DoD Strategy for Operating in Cyberspace," 2011, http://www.defense.gov/news/d20110714cyber.pdf
158. Ibid.
159. "Exposing the Cybersecurity Cracks: United States," Ponemon Institute.
160. DOD, "DoD Strategy for Operating in Cyberspace."
161. M. Gervais, "Cyber Attacks and the Laws of War," *Berkeley Journal of International Law*, Vol. 30, No. 2 (2012), pp. 525–579.
162. Kirsch, "Science Fiction No More."
163. Gervais, "Cyber Attacks and the Laws of War."
164. Powell, et al., "Protecting Against Cyberthreats."
165. STRATFOR Analysts, "This is how the Islamic State will exploit cyberterrorism," December 2, 2015, http://www.marketwatch.com/story/this-is-how-the-islamic-state-will-exploit-cyberterrorism-2015-12-02
166. Ibid.
167. ASIS Utilities Security Council, *Utilities Critical Infrastructure Protection*.
168. J. Arquilla and D. Ronfeldt, *Networks and Net-wars* (Santa Monica, CA: RAND, 2001).
169. K. Lockhart, 'Hacktivist' group Anonymous says it will avenge Charlie Hebdo attacks by shutting down jihadist websites, Video source YouTube/anonymous belgique, 10 Jan 2015, http://www.telegraph.co.uk/news/worldnews/europe/france/11335676/Hacktivists-Anonymous-says-it-will-avenge-Charlie-Hebdo-attacks-by-shutting-down-jihadist-websites.html
170. D. Mosbergen, Anonymous Vows To Unhood 1,000 Ku Klux Klan Members." October 28, 2015, http://www

.huffingtonpost.com/entry/anonymous-kkk-identities_56308b
60e4b0631799101e7f

171. Ibid.
172. W. Robinson, Four US Senators and five mayors deny
     they are part of the Ku Klux Klan after list of 'members' is
     released online, November 2, http://www.dailymail.co.uk/
     news/article-3300936/US-Senator-Kentucky-mayor-
     forced-deny-Ku-Klux-Klan-list-members-released-online
     .html
173. Ibid.
174. J. A. Feif, "Cyberwar and Unmanned Aerial Vehicles: Using
     New Technologies, From Espionage to Action," *Case Western
     Reserve Journal of International Law*, 45, 2012.
175. E. Felten, "What's the Cyber in Cyber-Security? Freedom to
     Tinker," July 24, 2008, https://freedom-to-tinker.com/blog/
     felten/whats-cyber-cyber-security/
176. D. Lohmann, Cyber Terrorism: How Dangerous is the ISIS
     Cyber Caliphate Threat?, May 18, 2015, http://www.govtech
     .com/blogs/lohrmann-on-cybersecurity/Cyber-Terrorism-How-
     Dangerous-is-the-ISIS-Cyber-Caliphate-Threat.html

access control Prescribes who or what is to have access to a specific system or resource, and the level of access that is permitted.

active shooter An individual actively engaged in killing or attempting to kill people in a confined and populated area. Active shooters arrive on the scene with the specific intent to commit mass murder. Unlike other mass killings or mass shootings, active shooter situations do not include incidents such as bank robberies or drug deals that may turn lethal.

administrative law The application of statutory civil law to the activities of government agencies. Administrative law addresses the functions, powers, and procedures of the administrative agencies and departments of federal, state, and local government, and is relevant to the ways in which government agencies carry out the tasks assigned under statutes.

administrative theory Devoted to find an effective means to design, manage, and comprehend an organization as a whole.

administrators Oversee the performance of an organization's operations and guide and direct the activities of employees and other resources toward organizational goals and objectives.

admission A statement in which a person admits a fact or facts that would tend to prove the person guilty of a crime, but which does not constitute a full acknowledgement of guilt.

adversary A person, group, or force that opposes, attacks, or plans to attack a target. Security professionals typically separate human adversaries into classes, identified as insiders and outsiders.

agency A fiduciary relationship created by express or implied contract or by law, in which one party acts for another party and their words or actions bind or commit the other party.

all-agencies approach A planned effort to define the incident management structure of agencies with different legal, geographic, and functional responsibilities to have them coordinate, plan, and interact effectively. Each participating agency maintains its own authority, responsibility, and accountability.

all-hazards approach An approach used by emergency management to respond to incidents or events, natural or human caused, that require an organized response by a public, private, and/or governmental entity in order to protect life, public health and safety, values to be protected, and to minimize any disruption of governmental, social, and economic services.

anarchist extremists Believe that (a) all forms of institutional globalization designed to maximize business profits should be opposed and (b) government institutions are unnecessary and harmful to society.

animal rights extremists Individuals or groups that oppose any individual and/or institutional entity (e.g., corporations, government agencies) perceived to be exploiting or abusing animals.

anti-abortion extremists Believe that the practice of abortion should end and therefore oppose abortion providers and their related services.

asset protection An aspect of retail security that involves managing and protecting both physical property and information storage capacity. Asset protection involves providing a safe and healthy environment and maintaining smooth business operations.

Bill of Rights The first ten amendments to the U.S. Constitution, which guarantee such rights as the freedom of religion and press, freedom from search and seizure, confrontation of witnesses and counsel at trial. They are the cornerstone of procedural law in the United States.

Bow Street Runners A group formed by magistrate Sir Henry Fielding in London in the mid-1700s who traveled around England to serve court-ordered writs and arrest offenders on the authority of magistrates.

broken windows theory Suggests that (a) maintaining urban environments in a well-ordered condition and (b) controlling incivilities and nuisance behavior will prevent the emergence of serious crime patterns.

building a bank (in the register) The unauthorized practice by a cashier of taking the money paid for an item(s) and voiding the order after the customer leaves. The cashier puts money in the drawer, keeps track of how much he or she is banking, and embezzles the money as the shift ends.

bureaucratic approach Considers the security organization as a part of broader society and sees organizations based on the principles of structure, specialization, predictability and stability, rationality, and democracy.

business continuity management Involves counteracting threats to an organization's continuing operation. The primary objective is to resume critical functions as quickly as possible and to restore the business to its pre-emergency condition and location or, if that is not possible, to a new location or level of operations.

business impact analysis Predicts the potential consequences of disruption of a business function or process and the information needed to develop effective recovery strategies. Potential loss scenarios are identified, and risk assessments conducted. The BIA can be used to identify the operational and financial impacts resulting from disruption of business functions and processes.

case law Comprised of decisions made by the Supreme Court that are considered precedent, or *stare decisis*, meaning they guide future lower court decisions. Precedent means that appellate case law should be considered as binding upon lower courts.

civil law Controls disputes between individuals and with the duties private parties owe to one another, to be settled with appropriate remedies like monetary damages or injunctive relief.

closed-circuit television (CCTV) A type of video surveillance system that is used to transmit a signal from cameras set up in a specific place to a limited set of monitors, so that areas that may need surveillance such as banks and convenience stores can be monitored.

cloud computing Providing IT services, applications, and data using dynamically scalable storage locations possibly residing remotely, so users do not need to consider the physical location of the storage that supports their needs. Cloud computing is a model for enabling convenient, on-demand network access to a shared pool of configurable computing resources that can be rapidly provisioned and released with minimal management effort or service provider interaction.

competitive intelligence The set of legal and ethical methods for collecting, developing, analyzing, and disseminating actionable information pertaining to competitors, suppliers, customers, the organization itself, and the business environment that can affect a company's plans, decisions, and operations.

comprehensive approach to disaster and emergency planning Includes an emphasis on prevention, preparation, response, and recovery. It is an integrated approach to the management of emergency programs and activities for all emergency phases, for all types of emergencies and disasters, and for all levels of government and the private sector.

confession A statement in which a person acknowledges guilt and may include a description of the details of a crime.

constitutional law Developed through court decisions, or precedent, as opposed to legislation or regulations.

continuity of operations   A strategy in which individual government executive departments and agencies ensure that functions continue to be performed during emergencies such as acts of nature, accidents, and technological or attack-related emergencies that make it impossible for employees to work in their regular facility.

contract law   Used to enforce agreements between two or more parties to perform an agreed-upon activity. Parties to the contract must be competent and must have the legal capacity to enter into a contract. The subject matter of the contract must be legal, meaning two parties can agree to illegal acts but the agreement cannot be considered a contract for enforcement or other legal purposes.

contract security firms   Sell their services to the public, including businesses, homeowners, and banks.

control view   Suggests that deviant, criminal, and illegal behavior can be fun, profitable, and beneficial and therefore adolescents must develop the ability to control their behavior lest they get involved in a delinquent way of life. Those who are attached to others, committed to their future, involved in conventional behaviors, and hold positive values and beliefs are the ones most likely to be able to maintain control.

copyright   A form of protection provided by law to the authors of original works of literary, dramatic, musical, artistic, and certain other intellectual efforts. This protection is available to both published and unpublished works. Innovations with original shape and design are automatically regarded as copyrighted works on a worldwide basis.

corporate security   The subdivision that exists within many organizations whose goal is to protect both physical and cyber elements of the corporate structure.

crime prevention through environmental design   (CPTED, pronounced "sep-ted") Describes the concept of design and use of the environment to reduce opportunities of fear and incidence of predatory crime, and improve the quality of life.

criminal flash mobs   When a group of people coordinate the arrival of a crowd to overwhelm a retail outlet and steal merchandise.

criminal law   Designed to regulate social behavior. Contemporary criminal law is concerned with actions that are regarded as harmful to society, or an omission to act when required by status or occupation, and provides for punishment of people who threaten, harm, or otherwise endanger the health, safety, and moral welfare of other people.

criminals   In the context of physical security, people whose goal is theft from the site and financial gain from selling the stolen items.

crisis   An incident or situation involving a threat to a specific country, its territories, citizens, military forces, possessions, or national security interests that develops rapidly and creates a condition of such diplomatic, economic, political, or military importance that commitment of military forces and resources is contemplated to achieve national objectives. An emergency situation becomes a crisis when it has reached a critical phase.

critical infrastructure   Includes the assets, systems, and networks, whether physical or virtual, considered so vital that their incapacitation or destruction would weaken a country's physical and economic security, public health and/or safety, or any combination of these.

Cyber/computer security   The process of protecting data, networks, and computing power that make up computer systems.

cybercrime   Involves criminal activity carried out via the internet. Within this basket of crimes are cyber fraud and identity theft, downloading illegal music files, and online bank theft. Cybercrime also includes many nonmonetary offenses, ranging from cyberterrorism to distributing destructive worms and viruses.

cyberspace   A euphemism for online interactions, and describes the Internet universe and its various computer networks.

cyberterrorism   Use of the Internet for terrorist activities, including large-scale acts of deliberate disruption of computer networks. Terrorist organizations are capable of launching cyberattacks against the networks of both government and critical infrastructure, and electric grids.

cyberwarfare   Uses the Internet to infiltrate or attack an enemy's computer network. Once a computer network has been infiltrated, a hacker can execute a variety of attacks, including planting logic bombs or other malicious coding to damage the computer network.

defeat   To thwart or prevent something from happening, to beat or overcome in a contest, or to prevail over.

defense in depth   A practice adopted from military strategy that involves multiple layers of defense that resist rapid penetration by an attacker.

defense   The act of making or keeping something or someone safe from danger, attack, or harm; warding off an attack from another; or guarding against assault, theft, damage or injury. In the context of physical security, defense is provided by a response force located either on-site or off-site.

defensible space   A residential environment whose physical characteristics allow inhabitants to be part of ensuring their own security. Four primary factors create defensible space territoriality, natural surveillance, image, and surroundings. The theory of defensible space explains that a person's demonstrated claim to a defined and shared residential territory diminishes with an increase in the number of people who share that claim.

denial of service   One of the most frequent attacks seen on the Internet is an effort to flood computer systems with emails, logons, requests, or other types of intrusions. These attacks are typically targeted at web servers, but they can also be used on other systems, such as mail servers and name servers. Denial-of-service (DoS) attacks may be initiated from a single machine, but they typically use many computers to carry out an attack.

deposition   A witness's sworn out-of-court testimony, used by prosecutors, plaintiffs, and defense attorneys to gather information during the discovery process.

detection   The process of discovering, discerning, or ascertaining something, usually something not previously known or of which you are unaware. Detection involves the use of appropriate devices, systems, and procedures to signal that an attempted or actual unauthorized access has occurred.

detention   The process in which a government or citizen lawfully holds a person by removing their freedom of liberty, often due to pending criminal charges. A detention does not always result in being escorted to a particular area, either for interrogation or as punishment for a crime, but takes place when a suspect is placed in custody.

deterrence   The practice of using threats to convince another to refrain from some course of action. A potential adversary who perceives a risk of being caught may be deterred from attacking.

diffusion of benefits   Refers to the spread of beneficial crime reduction strategies beyond the places, which were directly targeted, the individuals who were the subject of control, the crimes that were the focus of intervention, and the time periods in which an intervention was brought.

digital imaging systems   A current type of video surveillance system, which will eventually replace CCTV.

disaster risk reduction   A systematic attempt to identify, assess, and reduce the risks of disaster. It aims to reduce socioeconomic vulnerabilities to disaster and assist citizens in dealing with environmental and other hazards that trigger such vulnerabilities.

disaster   Defines dangerous events that are concentrated in time and space that disrupt the social structure and prevent certain societal functions. Disasters often seriously disrupt functioning of a community and involve widespread human, material, economic, or environmental losses and impacts.

discovery   The process in which prosecutors in criminal court must provide the defendant with copies of all the materials and evidence that the prosecution intends to use at trial. This process extends from the time the case begins to the time of trial. If the prosecutor does not provide the defendant with documents and other information, the prosecutor can be fined or sanctioned by the court.

disgruntled employees   Usually individuals, but could be a small group, who used to or currently work at a site and intend to attack a person or cause damage to property at the site. These threats are highly motivated and the people perpetrating them do not expect to be caught due to their authorized access.

displacement (or deflection)   A principle of crime prevention that maintains that, if crime is stopped in one area, law violators may simply move to other areas with less-protected targets.

domestic terrorism   Those actions that appear to be intended to intimidate or coerce a civilian population, to influence the policy of a government by intimidation or coercion, or to affect the conduct of a government by mass destruction, assassination, or kidnapping. A domestic terrorist differs from a homegrown violent extremist in that the former is not inspired by and does not take direction from a foreign terrorist group or other foreign power.

domestic violence   A pattern of physical, sexual, emotional, economic, or psychological abusive behavior used to gain or maintain power and control over another in a relationship.

due diligence   Reasonable steps and investigations taken by a person in an investigation of a business or person prior to signing a contract, purchasing property, or engaging in a business venture. It is seen as the level of activity expected from a reasonably prudent person, given the circumstances of a particular case, the goals of the investigation, and the available information.

emergency   An extraordinary situation in which people are unable to meet their basic survival needs, or there are serious and immediate threats to human life and well-being. Conditions may become chaotic during emergencies, producing confusion and an interruption of communications.

employment law   The laws, administrative rulings, and precedents, which cover the legal rights of, and restrictions on, working people and their organizations. Employment law guides the interactive relationship between trade unions, employers, and employees. Employment law is used to set the minimum socially acceptable conditions under which employees or contractors will work.

entry control   Allows movement of authorized personnel and material into and out of facilities, while detecting and possibly delaying movement of unauthorized personnel and contraband.

environmental rights extremists   Oppose people, businesses, or government entities destroying, degrading, or exploiting the natural environment.

ethics   The general principles a person uses to decide whether an action is good or bad, and involves the critical and structured examination of how we should behave in a given situation.

ethno-nationalist/separatist terrorists   Regionally concentrated minority groups, whose goal is political autonomy. The Basques in Spain, IRA in Ireland, and Tamils in Sri Lanka at one time engaged in terrorist activity to secure a homeland.

expert testimony   A form of testimony provided by an expert witness, a person who can provide insight as to the significance of the evidence collected in criminal and civil trials. Expert witnesses are generally qualified based on their qualifications or expertise, the acceptance of their theories or opinions, and the relevance of their theories or opinions to the case.

external risk   Risk to an organization that is based on factors external to the organization. External organizational risks include trends on a global, political, or societal scale, the effects of extreme weather, acts of terrorism, cyberthreats, pandemics, and human-made accidents or technical failures.

extreme left-wing terrorists   Want to bring about change through violent revolution rather than through established political processes.

extreme right-wing terrorists   Fiercely nationalistic, antiglobal, suspicious of centralized federal authority, reverent of individual liberty (especially their right to own guns, be free of taxes), believe in conspiracy theories that involve grave threat to national sovereignty, and/or personal liberty. They believe that their personal and/or national "way of life" is under attack and is either already lost or that the threat is imminent and that they need to be prepared for an attack by participating in paramilitary preparations and training.

extremists   People and groups with an ideological motivation, whose goal is to bring attention to a practice at the targeted site with which they disagree. Extremists range from religious fanatics to animal rights activists.

family law   Concerned with matters of marriage, divorce, child custody, and children's rights. Family law also spells out requirements as far as who can enter into marriage, what sort of testing (e.g., blood testing) is necessary, what license and fee requirements exist, what waiting periods are necessary, and so on.

fire detectors   Automatic fire detection systems designed to reduce property damage, personal injuries, and loss of life from fire in the workplace. Their main function is to quickly identify a developing fire and alert building occupants and emergency response personnel before extensive damage occurs through the use of sensors to detect the smoke, heat, or flames from a fire.

flame detectors   Devices that look for specific types of light (infrared, visible, ultraviolet) emitted by flames. When the detector recognizes light from a fire, it signals an alarm.

fraud   The intentional use of deception and deceit to obtain goods illegally. Fraud involves many individual acts, ranging from identity theft to forgery.

fraudulent disbursements   Include billing schemes, payroll schemes, register disbursement schemes, expense reimbursement schemes, and check tampering. Salespersons can charge a customer one amount, ring up a receipt for less and pocket the difference.

functions-based approach   Used when a jurisdiction focuses its planned response on the potential effects of generalized emergencies and hazards, to avoid duplication of the planning effort for every hazard and every task for the organizations that use the approach. A functions-based approach builds plan performance around "generic" functions, and permits an emphasis on hazards that pose the greatest risk.

fusion centers   Provide operational capabilities that blend the activities and intelligence sharing efforts of enforcement agencies at various levels and focus on securing critical infrastructure and key resources, and advancing federal, state, local, and private-sector CIKR protection efforts. Fusion centers are designed to provide a comprehensive understanding of the threat, local CIKR vulnerabilities, the potential for and consequences of attacks, and the effects of risk-mitigation actions.

game theory   The study of strategic decision making in the context of conflict and cooperation, provides a trusted mathematical approach to consider when deploying limited security resources for maximum effectiveness.

general deterrence theory   States that it is possible to create an environment in which criminal acts are absent because of the fear of punishment. If human beings are rational enough to consider the consequences of their actions and to be influenced by those consequences, then the threat or application of punishment should convince them that crime does not pay and that it would be foolish to attempt a criminal act.

goals   The general guidelines that explain expected achievements. They are usually long-term and often broad in scope.

hacking   Secretly getting access to another person or organization's computer network in order to steal information, cause damage, or disrupt communication.

heat detectors   Normally used in dirty environments or where dense smoke is produced. The most common heat detectors either react to a broad temperature change or a predetermined fixed temperature, using resistors that decrease in resistance with an increase in temperature.

hierarchy of needs   Proposes that human beings have certain needs, and that these needs are arranged in a hierarchy, with some needs (like safety) seen as more essential or basic than others (like social needs). The hierarchy is often presented as a five-level pyramid, with higher needs such as esteem and self-actualization coming into focus only once lower, more basic physiological, safety, love, affection, and belongingness needs are met.

homegrown violent extremist A person of any citizenship who has lived and/or operated primarily in a specific country or its territories who advocates, is engaged in, or is preparing to engage in ideologically motivated terrorist activities (including providing support to terrorism) in furtherance of political or social objectives promoted by a foreign terrorist organization, but is acting independently of direction by a foreign terrorist organization.

homeland security A concerted national effort to protect the nation and ensure that it is safe, secure, and resilient against terrorism and other hazards.

identity theft The theft of someone else's personal information—name, credit card number, or other identifying information—to obtain money, credit, or other things of value.

incident command system A standardized, on-scene, all-hazards approach to incident management. It integrates facilities, equipment, personnel, procedures, and communications enabling a coordinated response among jurisdictions, while establishing common processes for planning and managing resources. incident.

industrial espionage The theft of information by legal or illegal means. It entails obtaining confidential information from other companies such as strategic plans or pricing policies, with the intent to use the information to gain a competitive edge in the marketplace.

Industrial Revolution A time from 1760 to about 1870 in which manufacturing moved from hand production methods to machines. The transition began in England, and within a few decades it had spread to the rest of Western Europe and the United States. The Industrial Revolution transformed many areas in Europe and the United States from rural to urban societies centered in metropolitan areas.

information security The various processes and methodologies used to protect print, electronic, and other data from unauthorized access, use, misuse, disclosure, destruction, modification, or disruption.

Information Sharing and Analysis Centers (ISACs) Provide operational and tactical capabilities for information sharing and support for incident response activities. ISACs are sector-specific entities that advance physical and cyber CIKR protection efforts by establishing and maintaining frameworks for operational interaction between and among members and external security partners.

information Knowledge in raw form or raw data of any type. Security professionals will likely encounter many sources of information in their daily routine. Information can be provided by and gathered from other employees, law enforcement personnel, anonymous sources, and other means.

InfraGard An information sharing and analysis effort, with members in businesses, academic institutions, state and local law enforcement agencies, and other participants dedicated to sharing information and intelligence to prevent hostile acts against the United States.

injunctive relief A civil court remedy in which the court orders one party to perform certain acts or refrain from certain actions.

insiders Those who have regular, authorized access to a company's location, its physical components, and its intellectual property. They potentially include all employees, subcontractors, and vendors—although each may have limited access to only certain company components.

institutional security The unique security requirements of specific organizations, foundations, and associations.

intelligence Information that has been processed, evaluated, analyzed, or interpreted to give it meaning within a particular context. The term also describes information that is acquired, exploited, and protected by the activities of law enforcement and security organizations to decide upon and support their investigations.

internal risks Affect the individual and include egotism, ambition, resistance to change and pessimism, lack of checks and balances, tunnel vision, corporate crime, and lack of innovation or short-term thinking. Internal risks could also be seen as management failure or mismanagement.

international terrorism Violent acts or acts dangerous to human life that are intended (i) to intimidate or coerce a civilian population; (ii) to influence the policy of a government by intimidation or coercion; or (iii) to affect the conduct of a government by mass destruction, assassination, or kidnapping. International terrorism occurs primarily outside the territorial jurisdiction of a specific country, the persons they appear intended to intimidate or coerce, or the locale in which their perpetrators operate or seek asylum.

Internet of Things (IoT) A global system of interconnected computer networks, sensors, actuators, and devices all using the Internet protocol that enables communication among "intelligent" physical objects.

interrogation (Sometimes called questioning) is interviewing with the goal of extracting a confession or obtaining information of a criminal enterprise. Interrogation may involve an array of techniques, ranging from developing rapport with the subject to outright torture.

interrogations Conducted to learn the truth about the details of the crime from a suspect.

interviews Conducted to gather information that is relevant to the investigation, and include (a) finding who, what, when, where, how, and why things events unfolded; and (b) assessing the credibility of the source of the information.

investigating The process of examining, studying, or inquiring into the particulars of a specific subject in much detail.

key assets Include critical resources whose destruction could create a local disaster or significantly damage the nation's morale or confidence. They include symbolic and historical attractions, like prominent national, state, or local monuments and icons.

key resources Publicly or privately controlled resources essential to the operation of the economy and government. Examples includes oil processing plants, banks, telecommunications, and power grids.

larceny The unauthorized taking and carrying away of the personal property of another by an individual who intends to permanently deprive the owner of its possession.

Law Enforcement and Private Security Organization (LEAPS) Promotes the concept of crime prevention; to enhance communication; and to encourage joint cooperation between law enforcement agencies, corporate security, and private security organizations to reduce the opportunity of crime primarily in the area in and around El Paso, Texas.

layered security A strategy that provides security professionals with multiple opportunities for disrupting adversaries, whether criminal or terrorist. Layered security is a key aspect of an effective access management strategy, and combines multiple security controls to protect resources and data.

liaison Communicating with other professionals for the purpose of establishing, maintaining, and improving mutual understanding and cooperation.

listening The ability to accurately receive and interpret messages.

locks Devices for securing a door, file cabinet, access, and also used to secure the movable portions of barriers and gates, typically consisting of a bolt or system of bolts propelled and withdrawn by a mechanism operated by a key or dial.

lone wolves Terrorists motivated by one or more extremist ideologies and, operating alone, support or engage in acts of violence in furtherance of that ideology or ideologies.

loss prevention Any method used by individuals or organizations to increase the likelihood of preventing and controlling a loss of business or profits from an adverse event.

malware Stands for malicious software—software programs that are designed to damage or do other unwanted actions to a computer system. Examples of malware include viruses, worms, Trojan horses, and spyware.

management A set of planning, organizing, training, commanding, and coordinating functions.

managers Responsible for the smooth and effective operation of the specific system in which the administrator operates.

master keying   The practice of having several locks keyed alike, with one master key that will open them all, while each individual lock retains the ability to be opened by a separate subordinate key. In large organizations with security plans involving many individual locks, master keying is done for the convenience of persons with broad or variable access requirements to keep them from having to carry a separate key for each lock.

mesh network   An ad hoc network that wirelessly connects computers and devices directly to each other without passing through any central authority or organization (like an Internet Service Provider, or ISP). They are designed to be resistant to disaster and other interference and are more robust than typical networks.

militia extremists   who profess belief that the government deliberately is stripping Americans of their freedoms and is attempting to establish a totalitarian regime.

mitigation   Describes efforts to reduce the loss of life and property by lessening the impact of disasters in an effort to mitigate harm and reduce human and financial consequences. Mitigation strategies are aimed at improving safety, financial security, and self-reliance in the future.

monetary damages   Occur in civil cases when the party considered in the wrong is ordered to pay money to the other party.

National Incident Management System   Enables responders at all jurisdictional levels and across all disciplines to work together with effective and efficient deployment of resources. It was developed to identify concepts and principles that are used to manage emergencies from preparedness to recovery and provide a consistent, nationwide approach and common vocabulary so that multiple agencies or jurisdictions can communicate as they work together to respond to emergency situations.

National Infrastructure Protection Plan (NIPP)   Provides guidance on protecting infrastructure and key assets. The NIPP integrates and guides a range of efforts designed to enhance the safety of the nation's critical infrastructure, by preventing, deterring, neutralizing, or mitigating the effects of a terrorist attack or natural disaster. NIPP provides a risk analysis and management framework for conducting risk assessments and encouraging the continuous improvement of CIKR protection.

National Response Framework (NRF)   A collection of guidelines and policies that responders use to ensure a unified response to natural disasters, terrorist attacks, and other emergencies. The document in the framework are based on best practices and lessons learned from similar events. NRF provides guiding principles so all participating agencies can prepare for and provide a unified national response to disasters and emergencies.

natural surveillance   The ability of residents to be able to see what's going on in their neighborhood.

neighborhood watch   An effort by citizen volunteers to actively identify and report signs of criminal activity to make their neighborhoods safer and to improve their quality of life.

networking   Intentionally acquainting oneself with a diverse group of professionals and using those acquaintances to the benefit of all.

neutralization techniques   Allow people to justify their criminal behavior. Individuals who learn to neutralize the shame of committing crime feel free to engage in their criminal activities without damaging their conscience. Techniques associated with neutralization include a denial of responsibility, a denial of injury, a denial of the victim, condemnation of those condemning the perpetrator, and an appeal to higher loyalties.

New York Police Department (NYPD) SHIELD   An umbrella program that coordinates efforts of both public and private security activities with the goal of protecting New York City from terrorist attacks, whether foreign or homegrown, based on providing best practices, lessons learned, counterterrorism training, and information sharing.

nonverbal communication   Includes signals such as facial expressions, voice tone and pitch, body language, and the distance maintained between people who are communicating. Nonverbal messages allow people to modify what they said in words, convey information about their emotional state, provide feedback to the other person, and regulate the flow of communication.

objectives   The strategies or steps used to achieve identified goals. Objectives are specific, measurable, and have an expected completion date.

offender profiling   Focusing on those people believed to present the greatest risk of committing crime based on traits and characteristics of known criminals. The technique uses what is known about crime and criminals to more efficiently and accurately identify potential criminals.

Operation Cooperation   A major nationwide initiative to encourage partnerships between law enforcement and private security professionals. It serves to increase the efforts of the public and private sectors across the country, pooling their strengths to prevent and solve crimes and work toward the protection of life and property.

organized retail crime   The activity of theft or fraud conducted with the intent to convert illegally obtained merchandise, cargo, cash, or a cash equivalent into financial gain (not personal use). This includes theft or fraud and involves multiple items, over multiple occurrences, or in multiple stores, or in multiple jurisdictions, by two or more persons, or an individual acting in dual roles.

outsiders   Those who do not have authorized access to a site.

phishing   The criminal acquisition of sensitive information, such as usernames and passwords, by acting like trustworthy entities. Phishing occurs when a victim is contacted via email and tricked into revealing personal or confidential information that the scammer can use illicitly or fraudulently.

physical security   The physical protection of an organization's resources, including people, data, facilities, equipment, and systems. Physical security is primarily concerned with the safety of personnel.

polygraph machines   Measure the truthfulness of a person's statements by tracking bodily functions such as blood pressure, respiration, and perspiration.

prevention   Includes those capabilities necessary to avoid, prevent, or stop a threatened or actual act of terrorism. It involves the whole community, from local residents to senior leaders in government.

private security   The private-sector practice, by individuals and organizations, of providing security-related means or services, to protect and preserve persons, property, interests, information, and environments to allow for the continued conduct of needed activities within the organization or society, without disruption from varied adversaries or hazards, for compensation.

product counterfeiting   The practice of manufacturing goods, often with inferior quality, and selling them under a brand name without the authorization of the brand owner.

profession   A career field, vocation, or occupation requiring advanced training, and usually stressing mental or intellectual efforts rather than manual work. Teaching, engineering, writing, medicine, and law are examples of professions.

property law   Concerned with the acceptable uses of property, like those identified in zoning laws. Property law also governs property ownership, such as land but also personal property such as cash, conveyances, automobiles, and valuable items.

protection   Involves actions used to deter threats, mitigate vulnerabilities, or minimize the consequences associated with an emergency or crisis incident. Protection can include a wide range of activities, such as improving physical security, building redundancy, incorporating resistance to hazards in facility design, initiating active or passive threat countermeasures, installing security systems, promoting workforce security, training and exercising, and implementing cybersecurity measures to delay or deter unauthorized access.

psychodynamic (personality) theory   Provides explanations for development, human behavior, and psychopathology. It identifies methods to make predictions about treatment outcome. It emphasizes unconscious motives and desires, and highlights the importance of childhood experiences in shaping personality. Psychodynamic theory suggests that criminal tendencies are a function of disturbances in early human development that lead to mental instability and mood disorders, such as conduct, anxiety and bipolar (also known as manic-depression) disorder.

racist skinhead extremists and white supremacist extremists, who both claim to believe that Caucasians are intellectually and morally superior to other races and that the government is controlled by Jewish persons.

radio-frequency identification (RFID) tags Wireless, no-contact tracking labels attached to objects. The tags use radio-frequency electromagnetic fields to transfer data and contain electronically stored information.

ransomware A type of malware that once installed on a victim's computer via the Internet both locks the device and also generates a pop-up window, Web page, or email warning, demands payment be made in order for the system to be unlocked.

rational choice A view of crime causation based on the notion that law violators are reasoning people who make decisions by weighing the costs and the benefits of crime before they decide whether to violate the law. Potential criminals try to maximize the positive outcomes (gains) and minimize the negative outcomes (losses). People may choose to commit crime if they believe the risk of getting caught is low, the threat of being punished minimal, and that they can beat the legal system with a good lawyer.

recovery The restoration of full levels of service delivery following an incident.

refund fraud When a sales associate gets an item off the rack, processes the refund for the sale amount, and then puts the money on a gift card which is largely untraceable.

religious terrorist Seek to engage in battle with the purported enemies of God and other evildoers, impose strict religious tenets or laws on society (fundamentalists), forcibly insert religion into the political sphere.

response The implementation of measures to ensure that security incidents are reported to appropriate officials so that immediate and long-term corrective action can be taken.

retail security Retail loss prevention and/or asset protection, and generally describes the process of reducing theft and shrinkage in a retail organization. It involves the process in which goods are securely sold to the public for both the consumer and store proprietor, preventing theft or harm.

retail shrinkage The losses that occur during the merchandise production-distribution-sales process. It is a reduction in inventories not accounted for through sales or other legitimate activity, and represents the difference between the physical inventory that is actually available for sale and what the records say should be available for sale.

risk assessment Helps identify potential hazards and analyze possible outcomes if a hazard occurs. When conducting a risk assess-

ment, security professionals identify vulnerabilities or weaknesses that would make an asset more susceptible to damage, to determine the probability of security risks actually happening, determine the impact and consequences of such an occurrence, and prioritize the risk factors so they can be dealt with effectively.

risk management The process used to plan for continuing operations after a loss or other.

risk The measure of probability or potential and severity of adverse effects. Risk characterizes the likelihood of an unfavorable outcome or event occurring.

robbery The act of using force, violence, or threat of force or violence to steal. Victims of robberies may suffer actual physical harm or psychological distress; they are put in fear.

rootkits Collections of software tools that enable administrators to access a computer or computer network. Malicious rootkits can be installed by nonauthorized users attempting to take over a computer or network. Malicious rootkits are designed to hide from view unauthorized programs and make it difficult to see them running.

routine activity theory Suggests that crime has been part of the human experience for quite some time. Crimes are events that people will engage in for a variety of reasons: some people are impulsive, some are driven by need, others are psychologically disturbed while still others choose to victimize others because they are selfish and greedy.

Sarbanes-Oxley Act Federal legislation created to provide balance to the American financial system and help it recover from the criminal fraud scandals. The act requires top management in large, publicly traded corporations to individually certify the accuracy of financial information. Penalties for fraudulent activity are increased under the act, as is the independence of outside auditors who review financial statements.

scientific management approach Analyzes and synthesizes workflows to improve economic efficiency in the form of productivity. It is one of the earliest attempts to apply science to management and is based on planning work to achieve efficiency, standardization, specialization, and simplification.

search and seizure A process in which police or other authorities, who suspect that a crime has been committed, search a person or his or her property and confiscate (seize) evidence thought to be relevant to the crime.

security professional One who holds oneself and his or her role in security in high regard, and who is well qualified to perform the duties expected of someone in his or her position.

self-checkout fraud Occurs when customers use self-checkout systems as an opportunity to steal.

sexual harassment All forms of gender-based harassment, including same-sex, opposite-sex,

and harassment of transvestites and transgendered individuals. In the case of harassment by a supervisor of a subordinate where there is a tangible job action (like a demotion or undesirable reassignment), the employer's liability is absolute, and there is no defense.

shire reeve An appointed official that administered order in shires, and also administered justice in the county courts. The term morphed into the modern term *sheriff*, or chief law enforcement officer in a county.

shire A geopolitical division of a larger state or country. When King William I (William, the Conqueror) invaded and conquered England in 1066, he divided the country into shires, counties ruled and administered by a local nobleman, an earl, viscount, or baron.

shoplifting The theft of merchandise from commercial public display areas by a person posing as a legitimate customer.

single-issue terrorist Obsessively focus on very specific or narrowly defined causes on all sides of the political spectrum (e.g., antiabortion, anti-Catholic, antinuclear, anti-Castro).

situational crime prevention A method of crime control that relies on altering the circumstances in which people interact with one another and with the environment. By identifying risk factors for crime, and seeking solutions specific to those situations, the thought is that crime can be prevented, reduced, or displaced to other locations.

skimming The embezzlement of cash before it is recorded on the company's books, typically when the customer pays an employee in cash for goods or services.

smart grid An interoperable utility environment that includes the energy markets and consumer services. It adds a market dimension to the power grid, allowing customers who periodically generate more energy than they need to be suppliers, among other benefits. The smart grid is a digital information network and modernized power generation, transmission, distribution, and consumption network system, which enables more competition between providers, better use of energy, and the use of market forces to drive conservationism.

smoke detectors Detect the visible or invisible smoke particles from combustion. Smoke detectors warn occupants of the presence of fire, and are thought to play a significant role in the decrease in reported fires and fire deaths.

social engineering Entails gaining access to sensitive information or access privileges by building inappropriate trust relationships with insiders. The goal of a social engineer is to deceive someone and fool them into providing valuable information or access to that information, often unwittingly.

social media Internet-based communities in which users interact with each other online on websites such as Facebook, Twitter, LinkedIn, Instagram, YouTube, and Pinterest.

sources of information   Describe any person, document, or activity that provides information of an investigative nature is a source. Victims, witnesses, first responders, subject matter experts, and informants will provide some form of information that may assist in an investigation.

sovereign citizen extremists   Who claim belief that the legitimacy of US citizenship should be rejected; almost all forms of established government, authority, and institutions are illegitimate; and that they are immune from federal, state, and local laws.

specific deterrence   Assumes that once having experienced punishment, a person will not chance future criminal involvement. The more severe the punishment, the less likely an offender will be to recidivate.

SQL code injection   The technique of malicious code injection to introduce (inject) code into a computer program, SQL is an international programming language designed for managing data in relational database management systems.

stand your ground   Laws that grant people the right to defend themselves with reasonable or even deadly force if they are threatened, without making any attempt to flee or call for help. They are based on what is known as the castle doctrine, that is, every man's home is his castle—a principle of common law that allowed residents to defend themselves with deadly force if an intruder entered their home without invitation. Stand your ground laws typically extend the castle doctrine beyond the home or residence.

strikes or work stoppages   Any concerted stoppage, slowdown, or other interruption of work by employees. Economic strikes occur most frequently.

surroundings   In the context of CPTED, describes location relative to places that will help to prevent crime.

surveillance   The covert observation of individuals, places, or objects for the purpose of gathering information or intelligence. Surveillance techniques are used to identify criminal activity associated with terrorism, organized crime, drug and contraband trafficking, and serious crimes.

sweet-hearting   When a customer goes through the checkout line with an expensive item, and a confederate running the register runs through a bar code for a much less costly item they had obtained beforehand.

systems approach   Considers individual organizations as systems composed of sets of interrelated and mutually dependent subsystems. Modern theories like the systems approach are based on the concept that the organization is an adaptive system, which has to adjust to changes in its environment.

Target & BLUE   A partnership between the Target Corporation and law enforcement and public safety organizations to build stronger,

safer communities across the nation. The effort supports local communities through law enforcement grants, national night out, Safe City, forensic services and technical support, training, investigative tools and resources.

tens and hundreds   Groups of citizens in early English society that maintained the right of self-protection. Citizens lived in communities known as tuns, similar to contemporary towns divided into groups of ten families, called a tithing, that were pledged to defend one another from danger. Ten tithings were known as hundreds that elected their own chief to oversee their security.

terrorism   Activities that involve violent acts or acts dangerous to human life that are intended (i) to intimidate or coerce a civilian population; (ii) to influence the policy of a government by intimidation or coercion; or (iii) to affect the conduct of a government by mass destruction, assassination, or kidnapping.

theories   Designed to explain a significant association between an underlying cause and a predicted effect. Theories do not have to be absolute, but they must be significant.

Theory X and Theory Y   Encapsulate a fundamental distinction between management styles. Theory X is an authoritarian management style that emphasizes productivity, the concept of a fair day's work, and the practice of rewarding performance. Theory Y is a participative style of management, which assumes that people will achieve objectives to the degree that they are committed to those objectives.

Theory Z   A management approach that promotes stable employment, high productivity, and high employee morale and satisfaction.

thief takers   Private citizens who earned a living by capturing wanted criminals. They were paid first for every criminal arrested, and later for the successful conviction of criminals.

threat analysis   The continual process of compiling and examining all available information concerning activities, which could target and threaten an organization's facility. A threat analysis reviews the factors of the threat's existence, capability, intentions, history, and targeting, as well as the security environment within which the organization operates and is an essential step in identifying the probability of an attack.

total quality management   A system that involves all employees in continual improvement. Customer-focused, the approach uses strategy, data, and effective communications to instill a high level or quality and control into the culture and activities of the organization. All members of an organization are expected to participate in improving processes, products, services, and the culture in which they work.

trade secrets   Processes, devices, or something else that is used continuously in the operation of the business. Trade secrets include processes, lists of customers, and discount

codes. They may be forms and types of information, if the owner thereof has taken reasonable measures to keep such information secret and the information derives independent economic value, actual or potential, from not being generally known to, and not being readily ascertainable through proper means by the public. Salary information, profitability margins, unit costs, and personnel changes are not trade secrets.

Trojan horse   A destructive program that masquerades as a legitimate file or application to gain entry to a computer (or, more recently, mobile phone, personal digital assistant, or gaming device). Once in the system, a Trojan horse may perform any number of undesirable actions, like deleting or damaging files, launching a DoS attack, playing beeping sounds, starting and stopping processes, stealing passwords, and opening a back door into the operating system that allows an attacker to control the compromised computer remotely.

two-factor theory   States that some factors in the workplace cause job satisfaction, while others cause dissatisfaction. Satisfaction and dissatisfaction are not seen on a continuum with one increasing as the other diminishes, but are better considered independent phenomena.

undercover operations   Describe the process of taking on a covert role to gain needed information unavailable by other means. During an undercover operation the investigator conceals his or her true identity but not his or her presence, giving the impression they are ready to join in an illegal group or activity.

vandalism   Any deliberate act that damages or defaces property. Common vandalism targets for retailers include store lights, signs or windows, and placing graffiti on walls or other surfaces.

vandals   Individuals or groups who intend to cause relatively minor damage or disruption to an organizational system. They operate mostly at night, may be under the influence of drugs or alcohol, and may carry basic hand tools and cans of spray paint, paintball guns, or similar items.

vulnerability analysis   An assessment conducted on a range of different organizations, from small businesses to large regional infrastructures that is performed on a variety of systems, including information technology, energy supply, water supply, transportation and communication. Vulnerability assessment tends to include cataloging assets and capabilities, assigning quantifiable value and importance to those resources, identifying vulnerabilities or potential threats, and mitigating or eliminating the most serious vulnerabilities for the most valuable resources.

watch system   Authorized by legislation in the late 1200s in England, requiring ordinary citizens to provide community safety with a night patrol and guard force, in support of the local constable's efforts to provide security. Watchmen often encountered a variety of different security threats, including fires, wild animals, runaway slaves, thieves, and grave robbers. Some watchmen hired others to perform their duties and satisfy their community responsibilities. The system was adapted in the American colonies in the 17th century.

white-collar crimes Committed by a person of respectability and high social status in the course of the person's occupation. The term covers the full range of crimes committed by business and government professionals within the scope of their job or the jobs held by subordinates, including bribery, exploitation, fraud, chiseling, embezzlement, and other crimes involving business enterprise.

workplace security Encompasses many practices to secure the workplace, such as risk management, physical security, cybersecurity, and loss prevention practices.

workplace violence Any act or threat of physical violence, harassment, intimidation, or other disruptive behavior, ranging from threats and verbal abuse to physical assaults and homicide that occurs at the workplace. Acts of violence at the workplace can range in seriousness from simply raised voices and profanity to violent crimes like robbery or homicide.

worm A type of computer virus or malware. Worms consume a computer's memory; and cause it to not function correctly. Computer worms replicate, and cause havoc by taking up all of the computer's available memory or hard disk space.

Index

Note: Page numbers with "f" indicate figures; those with "t" indicate tables.